TEXAS

BAPTISTS

TEXAS
BAPTISTS

A Sesquicentennial History

By
Harry Leon McBeth

BAPTISTWAY PRESS ★ DALLAS, TEXAS

CONTENTS

AUTHOR'S PREFACE

"Our object has been to encourage the hearts of our brethren by showing that the Convention has an honorable history; that it is still full of vitality and strength. . . . In UNION there is strength; in DISUNION, weakness."

With these simple words, Corresponding Secretary Horace Clark closed his report on the Baptist State Convention for the year 1866. In addition to listing Texas Baptists' achievements for the year, Clark also summarized the highlights of the convention's eighteen-year history. He felt that a review of their past would strengthen the people to face the future. The Civil War had just closed and Texas was caught in the throes of postwar depression and dislocation. Yet even in these hard times, Clark believed that Texas Baptists had a vital future. Against the divisive forces among Baptists in his time, Clark urged cooperation, unity, and perseverance.

I offer this new account of Texas Baptist history in the same spirit that Horace Clark revealed in 1866. Today the Baptists of Texas have a much longer history than when Clark wrote, and it is still honorable. The past 150 years of convention history make a marvelous record of worthy achievements. I believe the Baptist General Convention of Texas is still full of vitality, that the future looks bright and promising and, like Clark, I believe that there is strength in cooperation and unity. I hope that these highlights of Texas Baptist heritage will bring encouragement to the readers, that readers will come to appreciate even more the Baptist heroes and heroines of early Texas who, despite great difficulties and challenges, bore faithful witness that has resulted in the great Baptist empire we see in the Lone Star State today. I sincerely hope that Baptists and others who read this book will learn more about their spiritual ancestors, and themselves, and that they will be strengthened in their faith and witness.

Researching Texas Baptist history has been a rewarding task for me, but writing the story has been difficult. The problem has been in deciding what to leave out, for the mass of data is at times almost overwhelming. Several concepts have guided me in writing this story. I have tried to tell the main story, to include as much biography as possible, and to include a few human interest anecdotes and details along with reports and statistics. In addition to setting out factual data, I have also tried to capture something of the epic drama and spirit of the Baptist people in this state over the past century and a half. The readers of course will judge to what extent these goals have been met.

By design I have sought to reconstruct the history of Texas Baptists from primary sources. Where secondary sources are available, I have consulted them but have not depended upon them, preferring to shell my own corn. I have intentionally given more space to the last half-century of Texas Baptist history, and for two reasons. First, this story had not yet been told in connected form. J. M. Carroll's massive *Texas Baptists* essentially ends with the close of the nineteenth century, including only a few pages on Baptist activity since 1900. My immediate predecessor in the task, Robert A. Baker in *The Blossoming Desert,* gives only one brief chapter to Baptist developments from 1946 to 1969, his cut-off date. A second reason I have given more space to the era since World War II is that so much has happened to Texas Baptists in that half-century, and there is simply more story to tell.

After working with Texas Baptists for a lifetime, Jimmy Landes said "We have two groups in our midst—or three." In my research I have met all of these diverse groups, but it has been difficult to name them. The more intense group prefers to be called *conservative,* but that word will not do because it fits all Texas Baptists and does not distinguish adequately between the groups. Another group often refers to its adherents as *mainline,* but all Texas Baptists claim that description. Some use the term *liberal* but that is simply not accurate when applied to Texas Baptists. I have sometimes used the words *moderate* and *fundamentalist* to distinguish the two main groups. I did not coin either term. Both have been standard descriptions in American religion for most of the twentieth century. While the adjective *fundamental* had long been applied to bedrock doctrines, in a 1920 editorial in the *Watchman-Examiner,* Curtis Lee Laws first used *fundamentalist* as a noun to designate those who, he said, were ready to "do battle royal" for certain doctrines, thus in one stroke naming the movement and documenting its militant spirit. Clearly some Texas Baptists are fundamentalists by any accurate use of the term. Others tend to blend between the groups, with shades of emphases from both. In addition to *fundamentalist,* I have at times used such terms as *ultraconservative, intensely conservative,* or *militant conservative.* I do not mean any of these terms in any pejorative sense. My preference would be for every group, and every person, to be called by the name they like best. However, I feel an obligation to designate as clearly as possible who I am talking about and, while I do not wish to be perceived as biased, I do want to be as precise and accurate as possible in telling the story of a diverse people, Texas Baptists.

A word about abbreviations. Like government agencies, denominational groups tend to have long names. Acronyms save space (as in FBI and IRS), and the same is true for agencies like Baptist General Convention of Texas (BGCT), Southern Baptist Convention (SBC), Christian Education Coordinating Board (CECB), and Christian Life Commission (CLC) to name just a few. Readers unfamiliar with these various agencies may find the acronyms confusing. With first usage I have generally spelled out the full name, and used acronyms thereafter. I have included a list of agencies and their acronyms for reference.

Many people helped with this project and I hereby thank every one of them in print as I have already done in person. However, some have played such an important role that their names should be mentioned. I thank William M. Pinson, Jr., executive director of the Executive Board of the BGCT, for inviting me to write this story. Roger Hall, chief financial officer and treasurer, was extremely helpful in making every arrangement to facilitate the project. Jerry F. Dawson, who was then head of the Christian Education Coordinating Board, served as liaison to work with me in completing this history. He read all the chapters in manuscript and made many helpful suggestions. He retired in 1997 but has continued to work with me as a consultant on this volume. Lawanna Bleakley, administrative assistant to the CECB, was immensely helpful, as was Doris Tinker, executive associate to the executive director. I thank all of the people in the Baptist Building, from department heads to part-time workers, who patiently answered my questions and added countless details about Baptist life in Texas.

Four other people read the manuscript and made constructive comments, including Jesse C. Fletcher, Chancellor of Hardin-Simmons University in Abilene; Alan Lefever, archivist of the Texas Baptist Collection at Southwestern Seminary (who recently accepted a similar position with the BGCT); Rosalie Beck, professor at Baylor University; and James H. Semple, head of the State Missions Commission of the BGCT. All of these hold doctorates in Baptist history and their comments were extremely helpful. Dr. Lefever was tireless in putting me in touch with relevant historical sources in the Texas Baptist Historical Collection. Several other people, whose identities are not known to me, also read parts of the manuscript and offered anonymous comments, some of which were helpful. However, the final wording and interpretations are my own, and any remaining defects in the text must be laid at my door.

I thank my efficient secretary at Southwestern Seminary, Sarah Ruth Boyles, for her "can do" spirit, for her super skills in putting all these words on the computer, and for her unfailing good spirit in assisting with this task over many months, all the while keeping up with the regular office routine. She also did some of the telephoning to collect and confirm historical facts and helped sort out the Executive Board Minutes on the new digitized CD Rom. Sarah also arranged the historical tables at the end of the book.

Finally, I dedicate this book to the many, many Texas Baptist men and women whose names do not appear in these pages. Some of them are known, but space limits did not allow their stories to be included. Countless others are not known to us; their names do not appear in the records. Thousands of them no doubt lived quiet lives, kept the faith, ministered in obscure places, and gathered no recognition or earthly fame. However, when the final Record on high is completed, their names and their deeds will not be forgotten.

HARRY LEON McBETH
Fort Worth, Texas

FOREWORD

by William M. Pinson, Jr.

Once the decision was made to commission the writing of the history of organized Baptist life in Texas as part of the Sesquicentennial Celebration of the first Baptist state convention in the state, the question was: Who should be the author? Although many capable historians could have carried out the task very well, Harry Leon McBeth, Distinguished Professor of Church History at the Southwestern Baptist Theological Seminary, received the invitation to author the history. As a distinguished professor of church history, a native Texan, a graduate of Wayland Baptist University —a university related to the Baptist General Convention of Texas—a devout Baptist, and a proven author of historical works he is exceptionally well qualified to tell the story of Baptist life in Texas. When approached about the assignment, he requested time to ponder and pray about the matter and then gave a positive reply.

From the beginning of the project all agreed that the author should have freedom to write the history without interference or censorship; this was to be his version of the drama of Baptists in Texas, not that of some committee or board. However, to his credit Professor McBeth sought input and suggestions from a wide variety of persons, following the Biblical admonition to seek wisdom from many counselors. Throughout the project Jerry F. Dawson, himself a former professor of history and director of the Christian Education Coordinating Board of the Baptist General Convention of Texas, provided excellent editorial coordination.

A request was made of the author to tell the story in a lively and interesting fashion, making it more than merely a collection of facts and bare bone accounts of events. Thus more so than is the case with many histories the volume contains a number of vignettes and almost incidental but nevertheless interesting stories. After all, the history of Baptists in Texas is colorful and so should the book that tells their story.

Writing a history that includes current events is much more difficult in many ways than authoring one of the long ago because the participants, still alive, have their own view of the events. Chronicling current events about controversy can thus itself become controversial. Such may be somewhat the case with this volume. For example, even the names chosen to identify certain current groups or movements in Baptist life can evoke deep emotions. But the intent of the author is not to stir controversy but to leave a story for the generations to come which will not only inform but also inspire.

And what an inspirational story it is! The first Baptists to arrive in

Texas were diverse and brought differences of opinion on certain issues. The Baptist ancestors of those who today are part of the Baptist General Convention of Texas came with convictions about the importance of cooperation and of organization for advancing the cause of the Kingdom of God. Not all early Baptists concurred with these convictions. In spite of resistance from some Baptists and difficulties afforded by the frontier the Baptist pioneer predecessors of the Baptist General Convention of Texas first established churches and then quickly formed associations of churches, organizations for education and missions, schools, and a state convention. Voluntary cooperation in support of institutions and organizations for missions, evangelism, education, and benevolence early became hallmarks of the kind of Baptists related to the Baptist General Convention of Texas. Through the years a veritable flood of such entities spread across the state. While the author touches on the story of other kinds of Baptists in Texas, the volume focuses on telling the story of those related to the current Baptist General Convention of Texas.

Therefore, this book is about those organizations, institutions, and structures formed through the past one hundred and fifty years. It tells a remarkable story of progress in the midst of a constantly changing society and in the face of obstacles, such as wars, depressions, and denominational controversies. Each Baptist association, convention, institution, or other organization in Texas deserves its own story told at length. Some have such a history; many do not. This volume by nature of its scope could tell only fragments of exciting, inspiring accounts of these entities. Hopefully in the years to come histories will be written of each to form a library that more completely tells the story of organization Baptist life in the Lone Star State.

As the reader peruses the pages of this volume he or she will find certain themes repeated over and over again, somewhat like the theme in a symphony: the Lordship of Christ, the Bible as the absolutely trustworthy authority for faith and practice, the vital importance of evangelism, missions, Christian education, ministry in Christ's name, voluntary cooperation, integrity, and Baptist emphasis such as salvation by grace through faith alone, believer's baptism, a regenerate church membership, local church autonomy, the priesthood of the believer, congregational church government, religious freedom and its corollary separation of church and state.

Although not perfect—for no group of persons is—trust in and love for God, a vision for the future, and courage and fortitude to fulfill the vision characterize their journey. The people called Baptists and their organizations in Texas have been anointed of God. Human ingenuity and effort alone do not explain their progress. God's hand is seen in their amazing growth and vitality through the past one hundred and fifty years.

The story told in these pages ends essentially with the year 1997, but the story of Baptists who are part of the Baptist General Convention of Texas goes on. The future is bright as they move into a new century—a new millennium. While they remain true to the convictions which have brought them thus far, the marvelous past will be but a prologue to the successes of the generations to come . . . to the glory of God.

Along with a host of others I am grateful to Professor McBeth for his careful research, diligent writing, and commitment to excellence which characterize this volume, each made all the more admirable because his work was done in a time of personal crisis due to the severe illness of his wife. Thus even in the writing he displayed qualities of those Baptists who have written well the story of ministry in Texas—trust in God, faith in the Lord Jesus Christ, and dependence upon the power and direction of the Holy Spirit.

WILLIAM M. PINSON, JR.
Executive Director of the Executive Board
Baptist General Convention of Texas

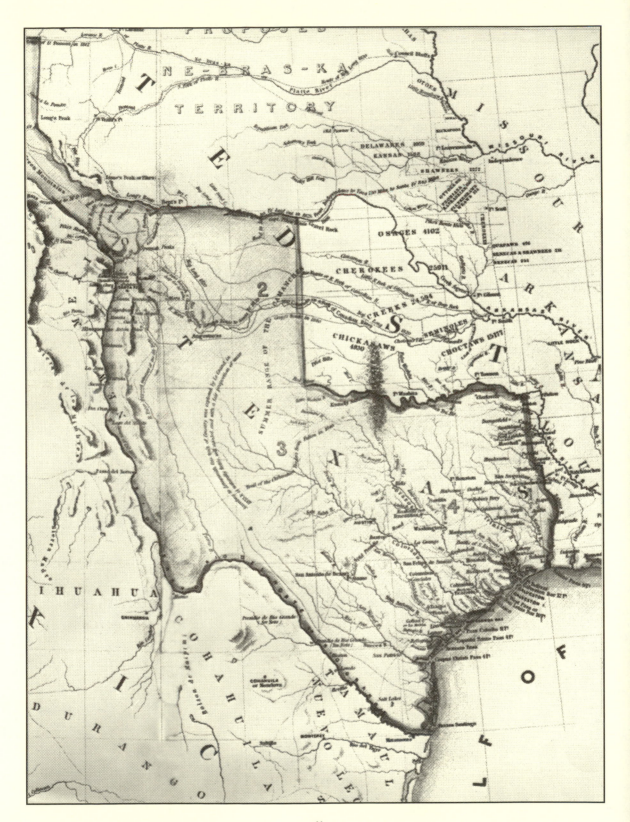

Editorial Introduction

by Jerry F. Dawson

The Historical Committee of the Executive Board of the Baptist General Convention of Texas is entrusted with the responsibility for preserving, promoting, and presenting the history of the Convention.

With the approach of the 150th anniversary of organized convention work in Texas in 1998, the Historical Committee sensed the need to present Texas Baptists with a complete and detailed account of their history.

The committee was unanimous in recommending to the Sesquicentennial Celebration Committee that Dr. Harry Leon McBeth, dean of Baptist historians, write the sesquicentennial history. McBeth was assisted by Dr. Jerry F. Dawson, Convention liaison for the Historical Committee, who served as editor for the project. The Historical Committee and the officers of the Texas Baptist Historical Society joined the advisory circle. Special recognition for technical assistance is due Tom Brannon, Office of Communications, and Clay Price III, Management Information Services, BGCT. Brannon's staff produced the pictorial galleries for the book and Clay Price served as chief resource for statistical data and tables used in the manuscript. This book, *Texas Baptists: A Sesquicentennial History,* is the result of their efforts and countless others too numerous to recount here.

The initial recommendation to commission the writing of a definitive history was almost immediately expanded to a broader goal. Texas Baptists should be able to read, see, and use their vast wealth of historical data. This expanded goal led to a monumental achievement hardly envisioned when the project began.

Texas Baptist archival materials have been scanned and reproduced in CD Rom format and will be available through the marvel of electronic technology to any church, Director of Missions, historian, student, or curious inquirer. The subsequent relocation of these resources to an archival center in Dallas, and the addition of countless new collections, will enhance dramatically any future study of the history of Texas Baptists.

Perhaps this comprehensive view of their past and the availability of resources to measure their current status will embolden Texas Baptists to fashion a greater history in the days ahead.

Jerry F. Dawson, Editor
Texas Baptist Historical Committee: Carr Sutter, Chair,
Ron Ellison, W. R. Estep, Robert Garcia,
JoAnn Means, Paul Stripling, Jerry L. Summers
Texas Baptist Historical Society: Alan Lefever
Sesquicentennial Celebration Committee: Mary Humphries, Chair

ABBREVIATIONS

AB	Annuity Board of SBC
BAH	Booz, Allen and Hamilton Study
BCLC	Baptist Church Loan Corporation
BDC	Baptist Distinctives Committee
BFT	Baptist Foundation of Texas
BGA	Baptist General Association
BGCT	Baptist General Convention of Texas
BSC	Baptist State Convention
BSU	Baptist Student Union
BTU	Baptist Training Union
BU	Baylor University
BYPU	Baptist Young People's Union
CEC	Christian Education Commission
CECB	Christian Education Coordinating Board
CFO	Chief Financial Officer
CJM	Criminal Justice Ministries
CLC	Christian Life Commission
CP	Cooperative Program
DBA	Dallas Baptist Association
DBU	Dallas Baptist University
DOM	Director of Missions
DSM	Department of Student Ministries
DVBS	Daily Vacation Bible School
E/EC	Efficiency/Effectiveness Committee
EB	Executive Board of the BGCT
EBM	Executive Board Minutes
ETBU	East Texas Baptist University
FBC	First Baptist Church
FMB	Foreign Mission Board of SBC
GA	Girls' Auxiliary
GNT	Good News Texas
HBU	Houston Baptist University
HMB	Home Mission Board of SBC
HSU	Hardin-Simmons University
HWC	Human Welfare Commission
HWCB	Human Welfare Coordinating Board
IMB	International Mission Board of SBC (the old FMB)
LMCO	Lottie Moon Christmas Offering
MHDO	Mary Hill Davis Offering for State Missions

MSC	Mission Service Corps
NAMB	North American Mission Board of SBC (the old HMB)
P&P	Plans and Policies Committee
PM	Partnership Missions
RA	Royal Ambassadors
RM	River Ministry
SBC	Southern Baptist Convention
SBT	Southern Baptists of Texas
SMC	State Missions Commission
SS	Sunday School
SWBTS	Southwestern Baptist Theological Seminary
TBA	Tarrant Baptist Association
TBC	Texas Baptists Committed
TBM	Texas Baptist Men
TEC	Theological Education Committee
WBU	Wayland Baptist University
WMU	Woman's Missionary Union
YWA	Young Women's Auxiliary

CHAPTER 1

CHANGING FLAGS OVER TEXAS

WHEN FRANCISCO VASQUEZ de Coronado and his *conquistadores* crossed over part of Texas in 1540-41 they were not scouting for farmland, and they did not intend to remain. Recently discovered evidence confirms that the Coronado party spent some time in Blanco Canyon east of Lubbock on an expedition which eventually took them as far as the Grand Canyon.[1] Motivated by the three G's, they sought gold, glory and service to God by the enforced "conversion" of Indians.[2] They intended to get the gold as quickly as possible and return to Spain to enjoy the glory.

For three centuries Spain's Texas policy differed little from that of Coronado. Spain could *conquer* but they could not *colonize*. They established military outposts but grew no towns; they assigned soldiers to Texas, but could not persuade families to settle there and, indeed, made little effort to do so. As Fehrenbach observes, in three centuries "Spain failed to put people in Texas."[3] The failure of the Coronado expedition to discover gold caused Spain to lose interest in a territory too vast, too harsh and too unpromising in terms of immediate value. They continued to claim Texas and established a string of missions and forts to keep others out, but did little to develop the area.

By contrast, when Stephen F. Austin settled three hundred families in Texas in 1822, they brought wives and children, with plows for farming, seeds for planting, and axes to fell timbers to build cabins. They came to stay, and in ten years they had cut more timber, built more cabins, raised more crops and birthed more babies than the Spanish in Texas had done in three centuries. In the long run, the future of Texas was determined more by the plow than the sword.

Our story concerns the Baptists of Texas, but Texas had a long and colorful history before the Baptists came. This brief chapter capsules the highlights of that history during which six different national flags flew over Texas.

1

EARLY EUROPEAN EXPLORERS

Coronado was neither the first Spaniard to explore the American Southwest, nor the last. Alonso Alvarez de Pineda explored the Gulf of Mexico in 1519 only six years after Ponce de Leon landed in Florida. Pineda stopped briefly in what is now Texas and made the first map of the Texas coast, but attempted no settlement. In 1528 a few half-dead Spaniards were driven ashore by storm in South Texas, perhaps on or near Galveston Island. Led by Cabeza de Vaca, a few later escaped from Indians, and eventually made their way to California and to Mexico. Cabeza de Vaca told stories of fabulous golden cities, none of which he had actually seen, but which he had been assured existed. Back in Spain, he published his *Relacion* in 1542, the first published description of the interior of Texas and the American Southwest.

The records show no fewer than ninety-two Spanish expeditions into "New Spain" from the time of Pineda to 1731.[4] Repeated efforts were made to find the "Seven Cities of Cibola" where even the houses were made of gold. This fable may have risen from the golden hue of Indian adobe houses gleaming in the sunset. To this day a mountain range in New Mexico is called "Sangre de Cristo" (Blood of Christ), from the golden-red tint of the landscape at sunrise and sunset.

Though disappointed in the quest for gold, the Spanish established a string of missions/forts in Texas, mostly from 1680 to 1735, though one or two (at San Saba, for example) came later. The French had explored Texas, but made no permanent settlement. However, partly to keep the French and English at bay, the King of Spain authorized a number of missions in Texas. These missions were coupled with a *presidio* (fort), and soldier and priest cooperated in the task of subjugating and converting the Indians. The plan was to reshape the Indian culture by imposing the Spanish language, religion, and economics. It never worked. A few Indians professed conversion, mostly under force or bribery, and while many of the priests gave heroic effort toward true conversion, the undisciplined behavior of the soldiers often undid the work of the priests. The Indians absorbed European diseases along with European religion and, when Spanish domination ended, the Indians sloughed off their thin veneer of Christianity with remarkable ease. They were converts in name, but slaves in reality. Padre Francisco Garces reported in 1775, "I see that for a century the faith has been planted in these provinces, and that nothing has prospered."[5] After three centuries, the religious legacy of Spain in Texas includes remnants of a few ruined missions, of which the famous Alamo in San Antonio is best known, an abundance of Spanish place names now hopelessly mispronounced, and traces of the brooding somberness of spirit that followed the black-robed priests.

However, while Spain's efforts to convert and colonize came to nought, in another way they changed the history of Texas: they brought the horse. Horses lost from Coronado's expedition, augmented by strays from later explorers, furnished Texas with herds of mustangs. The Indians, especially Apaches and Comanches, took to the mustang as if born on horse-back and became perhaps the world's greatest horsemen. The horse revolutionized Indian life at least as much as the Industrial Revolution changed European life. Indian migrations, war, hunting, and social structure changed completely. Spanish *conquistadores* who with Toledo steel had cut through vast Aztec and Mayan populations in Mexico with little resistance found themselves helpless against a few mounted Apaches and Comanches, who could strike lightning fast and then disappear in different directions to thwart pursuit.

The land now known as Texas has been called by many names, some of which no doubt could not be printed here. For reasons not entirely clear, the land was for a time known as "New Philippines," and some of the French called it "Paradise," whether or not with a straight face is not indicated. President Thomas Jefferson referred to the land as "Techas," and offered the judgment that "The province of Techas will be the richest state in our Union without any exception."[6] The most widely accepted explanation derives the word "Texas" from a Caddoan Indian term "Teychas," meaning "allies" or "friends."[7] The Spanish wrote this as "Tejas," hence ultimately "Texas." Early inhabitants were often known as "Texians" or "Texicans."

President Jefferson's remark in 1820 about "Techas" shows that the United States had an interest in annexing this territory long before the Mexican Revolution. For a time the United States tried to claim, unconvincingly, that Texas was part of the Louisiana Purchase of 1803. However, neither Spain nor, in their turn, Mexico was buying into this geographical theory. Even so, the powerful surge of "Manifest Destiny" never gave up the idea that someday, someway, Texas would be a part of the United States.

Some Texans today like to boast of the fact that the Republic of Texas existed for almost a decade as an independent nation, and of course that is true. There is less boasting, however, about conditions during that time. The economy never flourished, the Republic operated on the verge of bankruptcy, and any sustained military action would no doubt have toppled what Sam Houston once referred to as "a little two-by-four Republic." The Republic of Texas was never able to provide its citizens with roads, schools, or even basic police protection. The final vote to annex Texas to the United States was officially approved by the government in Austin, the government in Washington, and was overwhelmingly approved by a vote of Texas citizens who celebrated annexation as a great victory. To this day some Mexican nationalists dream of a time when Texas will again be a part of Mexico, while a few Texas nationalists dream of a day when Texas will be an independent nation again. Both dreams seem destined to disappointment.

ANGLO SETTLEMENTS

The waves of new settlers who followed the pilgrims who landed at Jamestown in 1607 and at Plymouth Rock a bit later did not long stay put. As the original thirteen colonies gained population, intrepid explorers pushed westward, ever westward, with a kind of restless seeking. The Louisiana Purchase of 1803 added vast western territories to the United States, and the Lewis and Clark expedition of 1804-06 opened the West and made Americans more conscious of the remainder of the continent. By the 1830s the political slogan "Manifest Destiny" documented the American conviction that the United States should and would occupy all the land from the Atlantic to the Pacific. Long before the discovery of gold at Sutter's Mill precipitated the great California gold rush of 1849, American interest in Texas was at fever pitch.

With only the Sabine River for an eastern boundary, some Americans had moved quietly into Spanish Texas by 1800 or before. Spain mostly turned a blind eye, and even encouraged Anglo settlement as a buffer against the Indian tribes and also to forestall incursions by the French. In the Mexican Revolution of 1819-1821, Mexico achieved independence from Spain. Officials of the new Mexican Republic at first allowed controlled immigration of Anglos into Texas, so long as they agreed to become Mexican citizens and adopt Mexican laws, language, and religion.

The Austin Colony. In 1820 a Missouri banker, Moses Austin, went to Mexico City and received permission to settle three hundred families in Texas. Before the settlement could take place, Moses Austin died and Mexico gained its independence from Spain. Moses' twenty-eight year old son, Stephen F. Austin, took up his father's venture and persuaded the new Mexican government to validate the Spanish grant. In 1822 Austin led about three hundred families from various parts of the United States and some foreign nations to settle amidst the rolling hills, open prairies and woodlands along the *Rio de los Brazos de Dios* (River of the Arms of God—the Brazos.) They established San Felipe de Austin as their main town. Each family was allotted a generous land grant, usually a league (4436 acres).

Austin was one of twenty-six *impresarios* commissioned to bring families in Texas. By 1829, there were contracts for seven thousand Anglo families to settle in Texas.[8] This did not count the numerous families who simply came on their own, not sponsored by any group. Mexico insisted that settlers be of good character, no drunks, thieves, idle loafers or profane swearers. Mexican officials were confident they could "Mexicanize" these settlers, but instead the Anglos "Americanized" Texas.

Religion in Mexican Texas. The Mexican constitution of 1824 specified that "The religion of the Mexican Nation is, and will be perpetually, the Roman Catholic Apostolic. The nation will protect it by wise and just laws, and prohibit the exercise of any other whatsoever."[9] This religious restriction, so reasonable to Catholic Spain and Mexico, was utterly foreign to Americans who had recently won complete religious liberty and whose constitution guaranteed separation of church and state. Even those Anglos who professed no religion of their own resented this effort to coerce them into Catholicism. This restriction upon religion provided one major cause of the Texas Revolution.

All settlers in Texas were expected either to be Catholic, or to become such upon arrival. Yet Protestants, and those of no religion, came by the thousands. How did they manage? No doubt many took the oath casually, calculating, somewhat like Henry IV, that a Texas ranch was worth a mass. Others promised that they would become Catholic when a priest came to receive them into the Church, but in many cases no priest ever came. In some cases, the priest arrived but became distracted by drink and the ceremony was never carried out. Not all priests and government officials favored these coerced conversions, and many connived to allow the new Texans to maintain a Protestant faith behind a Catholic facade. Often there was no one to baptize, bury, perform weddings or conduct worship, and such priests as were available were not always of the highest character. In 1832 it was reported to Colonel Piedras, Mexican commandant of Nacogdoches, that Methodist and Presbyterian preachers were conducting services in the area.

"Are they stealing horses?" the commandant inquired.

"No, Senor Commandant."

"Are they killing anybody?"

"No, Senor Commandant."

"Are they doing anything bad?"

"No, Senor Commandant."

"Then leave them alone."[10]

Apparently Austin regarded the religious restriction as temporary, though at first he tried diligently to enforce it in order to appear law-abiding to the Mexican officials. In October 1823 he wrote that "the Roman Catholic is the established religion to the absolute exclusion of all others and will so continue for a few years, but the natural operation of a republic will change that system." Austin urged the people to be patient and not make a public display of their Protestantism and in time "we shall succeed in getting a free toleration of all Religions."[11]

The Texas Revolution. In time Mexican officials realized that Texas was filling up with "lawless foreigners" who had not embraced Mexican religion or culture, and who showed no signs of accepting Mexican authority. Moreover, by 1830 Anglos outnumbered Mexicans in Texas by about five to one. In 1830 Mexico City forbad any further American immigration into Texas, but with hundreds of miles of open border the people then, as now, paid little attention to such laws. The Mexican government raised taxes, increased the number of Mexican troops in Texas, and took other steps to curtail the freedom of Texans. Texas was then part of the state of Coahuila with the capital far to the south in Saltillo. Not unlike the English colonies that rebelled against a distant and unresponsive government in London, the Texans felt they were justified in throwing off the rule of Mexico.

Even the irenic Stephen F. Austin, trying to maintain peace, was imprisoned for over a year in Mexico City. He came out of prison convinced that Texas must separate from Mexico, but his hope was to flood Texas with new immigrants who would peacefully transform Texas from a Mexican to an American regime. Other leaders, like Sam Houston and William Travis, preferred a military approach. A citizens' convention was called to meet at Washington-on-the-Brazos and there, on March 2, 1836, under the presiding of a Baptist layman, Richard Ellis, the delegates issued the Texas Declaration of Independence from Mexico. Sam Houston was elected commander of the army, and plans were made to enlist every able Texan with a rifle to defend their liberties.

Sam Houston was not yet widely known in Texas, but he became perhaps the most enduring hero of the Lone Star State. A prominent historian said, "Houston was the most remarkable figure, and most unusual agent of destiny, that ever appeared on the old frontier. He was a man of the times, . . . but something more."[12] Born in Virginia, Houston grew up in Tennessee. As a soldier in the War of 1812 under the command of Andrew Jackson, the 6 foot, 3 inch Houston was wounded in the battle of Horseshoe Bend. "Old Hickory," as Jackson was called, noticed the young frontiersman's bravery and the two men became lifelong friends and political allies. In Tennessee, Houston practiced law and served for a time as district attorney in Nashville. His political star rose rapidly. From 1823-1827 he served in the U.S. Congress, and in 1827 was elected governor of Tennessee. His first marriage ended in disaster in 1829, when his bride of three months informed him that she did not love him and never had, abruptly leaving him. If there was more to the story than that, no one ever knew, though Houston's political career was sorely damaged by gossip, not unlike that which plagued his friend and mentor Andrew Jackson. Houston then "abandoned the gubernatorial chair," as his friend Z. N. Morrell later put it, and lived for a time among the Cherokees in Arkansas and Oklahoma.[13] There he fell into a life of dissipation and heavy drinking.

However, Houston had had a taste of political power and he liked it. With astute insight, he saw the potential for Texas. He apparently came to Texas with the specific purpose of leading the American citizens to form a new Republic, of which he expected to become president. It was probably with this in mind that he sought and obtained the post of commander of the Texas army in 1836.

Exactly where in Washington the convention met has been debated. A widely accepted view says that for want of a more suitable building, the delegates met in a blacksmith shop owned by Noah T. Byars, a Baptist laymen who later became a preacher. The account of J. M. Carroll has been picked up and widely disseminated in both religious and secular histories of Texas. Carroll said that

> The largest and most convenient building for such a meeting was found
> to be a blacksmith shop, owned by N. T. Byars, one of the few Baptists at
> the time living in the town. All blacksmithing was stopped. Old plows,

wagons and other disabled vehicles, machinery, tools, etc., were cleared away, crude seats were provided and the shop voluntarily turned over to this first great Texas convention. And here, in this Baptist blacksmith shop, Texas declared its independence.[14]

However, the most careful research by D. D. Tidwell of Baylor, a later Texas Baptist historian, has called this account into question at two points.[15] Tidwell has shown rather convincingly that Byars established not a blacksmith but a gunsmith shop in Washington-on-the-Brazos in June 1835. At any rate, Tidwell believes the convention met, not at Byars' shop, but at a larger "public house" built by Byars and his partner Peter M. Mercer for commercial purposes. Byars and Peters had agreed to have "the house in complete order and repair for use of the members of the convention." No contemporary evidence refers to this building as a blacksmith shop. A Texas soldier who was present in the town in March 1836 said "There were only three good houses in it. All frames, and all in a row on the south side of Main Street; first, John Lott's hotel, the first from the river; second, one built for a commercial house in which the convention was sitting; and third, S. R. Roberts' hotel." Whatever the building, the conditions were primitive. Colonel William Fairfax Gray of Virginia said the thermometer stood at 33 degrees when the convention met "in an unfinished house, without doors or windows. In lieu of glass, cotton cloth was stretched across the windows, which partially excluded the cold winds."

Fall of the Alamo. The Texas Revolution was bloody, but of short duration. Just four days after the Declaration of Independence, the Alamo fell on Sunday, March 6, 1836. The Alamo Mission in San Antonio is to this day the emotional heart of Texas history. Established about 1722 as a mission, the Alamo was converted to a fort in 1793. When the Mexican general Santa Anna, who described himself as the "Napoleon of the West," launched his war of extermination against Anglos in Texas, about two hundred of the "Texians" took refuge in the Alamo. A disproportionate number of these men were from Tennessee. They were led by David Crockett and William Travis. With an overwhelming force variously estimated up to five thousand, Santa Anna besieged the Alamo from February 23 to March 6, 1836. The Texans fought bravely and their Tennessee long rifles inflicted great casualties upon the red-coated Mexican infantry. However, on Sunday morning of March 6, with orders to take no prisoners, the Mexicans finally overran the Alamo, killing the defenders to the last man. It was said that Travis, who had been wounded, was bayoneted on his cot. The fall of the Alamo increased the fear of Texas families and the brutality of the final slaughter made a deep emotional impact.

The Goliad Massacre. Three weeks after the fall of the Alamo, Col. James Fannin surrendered his troops to the Mexicans under promise that they would be treated as prisoners of war. Instead, they were marched to Goliad and on March 27, 1836, about three-hundred and thirty men, including Fannin, were shot down in cold blood upon the specific orders of Santa Anna. The Mexican general had not come just to capture the

Alamo, but to rid Texas once and for all of the rebellious Americans. To that end he swept through Texas on a mission of incredible destruction. In the confusion of the massacre a few escaped to bring the word to Houston. While the carnage proceeded, two Baptist preachers among them comforted the dying until they too were shot. J. M. Carroll draws upon the eye-witness testimony of survivors to describe the awful scene:

> In the last lot [of those to be shot] came two Baptist preachers [not identified] who went on exhorting their comrades. When they reached the place where they were to suffer, the eldest called upon his companions to join him in prayer. Not one refused. . . . Thy martyrs we are, but we lay it not to their charge. Let not our death be visited upon them. We, who bleed beneath their knives, beg it of thee! Here he was interrupted by the voice of the commander, who in a rage called out, in Spanish, Fire! Fire! Finish with them![16]

As news of the Alamo and Goliad spread, thousands in terror gathered what they could and fled toward the east, hoping to cross the Sabine before Santa Anna got that far. People who joined this "Runaway Scrape" met incoming settlers and urged them to turn back.

The Battle of San Jacinto. After receiving news of the Alamo and Goliad, Gen. Sam Houston retreated, much to the dissatisfaction of his troops. For over a month Houston fell back until he reached Buffalo Bayou, just below the city of Houston. There on April 21 near the mouth of the San Jacinto River, Houston made his stand. He sent a detachment under Deaf Smith to destroy the bridge which would cut off any retreat by either army. With over twice as many soldiers as Houston had, Santa Anna was supremely confident and took his time about launching the battle. At about 3:00 P.M. on April 21, while the Mexican general and troops alike took an afternoon *siesta,* Houston rallied his troops with an emotional speech. Who first made the cry "Remember the Alamo" is uncertain; some reports say it was Houston. With a fierce determination, and with "Remember the Alamo" and "Remember Goliad" ringing in their ears, the Texans took the Mexican troops completely by surprise. The battle lasted only about twenty minutes, and ended with a complete Texas victory. About half of Santa Anna's army was killed, the rest captured, and by nightfall Santa Anna was captured while trying to escape in the clothing of a private. The distraught Mexican general begged for opium, but was given just enough to settle him down lest he use it to commit suicide. Most of the Texans wanted to shoot Santa Anna at once, but the far-seeing Houston, with an eye on world opinion, refused to execute a prisoner of war.

The Battle of San Jacinto was brief, but it changed American history. With a huge section of mid-America controlled by Mexico, American expansion to the west was blocked. San Jacinto opened the way for America to expand to the Pacific and helped transform "Manifest Destiny" from a slogan to reality.

THE REPUBLIC OF TEXAS

What the Texans had declared on March 2 in Noah Byars' unfinished shop, the Battle of San Jacinto on April 21 confirmed: the Republic of Texas, an independent nation, was established. From independence in 1836 until annexation into the United States in 1845, the Republic existed under its own flag. Probably most Texans expected to become part of the United States; in fact, many held that hope even before they migrated to Texas. Whatever Sam Houston's personal preferences, he concluded that massive Anglo migration into Texas had in effect determined American affiliation of Texas before any votes were taken.

Successful battlefield generals are often elected to political office, and Houston was elected over Stephen F. Austin as the first president of Texas. He served from 1836 to the end of 1838, when he was succeeded by M. B. Lamar. Houston served a second term as president, 1841-1844, during which time he tried to reverse many of the disastrous policies of Lamar. After annexation Houston served as U.S. Senator from the Lone Star State from 1846-1859. In the Senate, he strongly opposed the growing movement for Southern secession. Failing in his bid for reelection to the Senate, Houston was again elected governor of Texas in 1859, but was deposed from office in 1861 because of his refusal to sign the oath of allegiance to the Confederacy.

Twice between 1836 and 1845 the Texas offer to join the Union was rejected. Z. N. Morrell attributed this to "the influence of chicken-hearted politicians [in the] east."[17] In the U.S. Congress, representatives from the North and East generally opposed annexation on three grounds: Texas would add a slave state, annexation would bring war with Mexico, and Texas was too remote to have any value to the United States. Leaders from the Southern states generally favored annexation.

Not all Texans favored annexation. M. B. Lamar, who served one term as president of Texas, favored the continued existence of the Republic. He pushed the claim that the Rio Grande formed the western as well as southern boundary, and thus Texas claimed the territory of New Mexico and Colorado. However, efforts to control that vast area failed and most Texans realized that their future was inevitably linked with the United States.

The politically astute Houston said that he intended "to turn coquette for awhile, and court England and France."[18] The recognition of the Republic of Texas by these nations and the prospects of extensive trade agreements, especially with England, turned the tide even among eastern politicians. Having so recently fought a war to evict England from America, the prospect of England gaining a new foothold in the middle of the continent was unacceptable.

After favorable votes in both Washington and Austin, annexation was completed in 1845. When the Texas flag was lowered for the last time,

President Anson Jones declared, "The Republic of Texas is no more." The Lone Star became the twenty-eighth state. In the Boundary Act of 1850, Texas sold to the United States all their claims to New Mexico and Colorado for $10 million and the boundaries of Texas assumed essentially their present shape.

THE LONE STAR STATE

With the threat of Mexican invasion removed, and with hostile Indians pushed westward, the Lone Star State attracted a floodtide of immigration, along with land speculation, social dislocation, and inadequate law and order. As governor and later as United States Senator, Houston tried to chart a course to peace and prosperity. However, the slavery conflict inevitably involved Texas. By the 1850s at least one fourth of the Texas population was composed of black slaves, and the majority of immigrants had come from the southern states. Probably 90% of Texans favored the Confederate cause in the Civil War.[19]

Fully one-fourth of the Texas troops died in the war, and the Texas economy was shattered.[20] The Union blockade of the Texas coast, especially Galveston, shut down the trade in cotton upon which the Texas economy depended. Though few battles were fought in Texas, by 1865 the Lone Star State was devastated. After several years of painful Reconstruction, Texas was readmitted to the Union. Since then, along with the Lone Star, the Stars and Stripes of the United States have flown over Texas. The sixth flag was permanently in place.

LIFE ON THE TEXAS FRONTIER

Life on the Texas frontier in the 1820s and 1830s was not for the faint of heart. Travel was by walking, riding horseback, or driving slow ox carts along trails and a few roads bogged with mud in the rainy seasons. The rivers had no bridges and few ferries: swimming them was hazardous and, in winter, downright uncomfortable. Communication was primarily by word of mouth. By the 1830s there were one or two small newspapers, but no way to distribute copies to the remote settlers.

As to housing, the fortunate lived in log cabins, the less fortunate in tents or "half dugouts." Most cabins had dirt floors, and often the wind whistled through cracks between the logs. Some reports tell of snow coming through cracks in the roof or walls to form a sifting of snow overnight on bed covers. Settlers always cleared away brush near the cabins to deprive Indians of hiding places, and the proper cabin always had a well-swept yard. There were of course no glass windows, but slits were cut in the logs large enough to point a rifle out but too small for an Indian to enter. The tents were supposed to be temporary, but often lasted for years. By 1837, Morrell reported, Houston was still largely a tent-city.

The half-dugout, still occasionally used into the twentieth century, consisted of a cellar dug a few feet deep into the earth with upright logs to form walls extending from two to four feet above ground. The result was a living room about half below ground and half above, almost always with a dirt floor. The better planned half-dugouts were so arranged that rain would drain away from the entrance, rather than into the room.

Store-bought clothing was not to be had on the frontier. People made do for years with such clothing as they brought from the States, or made their own. Some became sensitive about their shabby clothing. When the missionary William Tryon arrived in 1841 he had a handsome, well-tailored black suit, and thus attired he sometimes intimidated the ragged frontiersmen. However, after a few months Tryon's suit was travel-stained, ragged and torn and he was better accepted. The settlers usually made and/or repaired their own boots. Morrell tells of an encounter with a Methodist circuit rider whose shoes were worn out and who appealed to Morrell for help. Morrell said, "There were no shoes in the country to buy, and nothing scarcely but rawhide to reset. My old Tennessee shoe tools were still on hand, and a few small pieces of leather." Morrell mended the shoes, asking nothing in return but "a kind remembrance . . . at the throne of grace." Though disagreeing on doctrine, the two preachers agreed that "a boy was not fit to marry till he could stock a plough and mend a shoe."[21]

Most settlers grew and ground their own corn, but occasionally barrels of white flour could be bought in Houston or Galveston. Meat was abundant, including deer, antelope, buffalo, longhorn cattle and smaller game such as rabbits. Some foodstuff was grown and wild onions and other plants provided flavoring. Seasoning was mostly with bear fat and salt was plentiful in most places. On November 5, 1830, Julia Ray, recently arrived in Texas, wrote a letter to a friend back in Virginia describing life on the frontier.[22] "If the mail reaches us once a month, we consider ourselves fortunate," she wrote. "Never did I see true hospitality until I came here. At every house, be it ever so humble, you are a welcome guest." Describing her own house, she said "It was a log house with two large rooms and a broad hall between; it was considered the palace of the surrounding country. I never remember experiencing a greater thrill than when I stepped into my log-castle. Doors were unheard-of luxuries so I hung gay quilts across the openings where the doors ought to be." There was no place where food could be bought, so it was often obtained by barter. "About a week after our arrival," Mrs. Ray wrote, "our nearest neighbor, only thirty miles away, sent us some butter and eggs and chickens with the request for coffee in exchange. I was only too willing, as I was anxious for the poultry. This system of trade is rather common." As to religion, Mrs. Ray wrote:

> Don't be shocked when I tell you we heard our last sermon in Virginia. If we wanted to go to church, we could find in this part of Texas no church and no minister. I have heard that in other portions of the country a few

preachers, in spite of the laws, do live and hold services. We have not
even a Roman Catholic church anywhere near us. However, we observe
the Sabbath and try to live as though we were in Virginia.[23]

Schooling was scant on the Texas frontier. In retrospect, it appears
that failure of the Mexican government to provide schools to incorporate
the Anglo settlers into Mexican language and culture was a major factor
in their eventual loss of Texas. Families were occupied with daily survival
and too few parents saw the importance of schooling for their children.
However, some did, and some parents who could taught their children at
home, and sometimes grouped neighbor children for rudimentary schooling. Itinerant schoolmasters, like Thomas J. Pilgrim, started a few boarding schools in the more populous communities, with children "boarding
out" with local families for longer or shorter periods. Costs ran from $6 to
$10 a month for a full course of study, with "board and washing in respect-
able families." Most schoolmasters, like Pilgrim, taught not only reading
and writing but also gave attention to "the chastity of their [pupils'] sentiments and the purity of their morals."[24] Schools were few, centered in the
larger settlements, inaccessible to most children, and beyond the financial
means of most parents.

CONCLUSION

Whether the Texas landscape was more foreboding or more promising was in the eye of the beholder. Many commented on the vastness,
emptiness, and loneliness of the new land, and many who came with high
hopes found they were not able to endure. Others saw a more promising
prospect. They saw fertile lands, great forests and broad prairies. What
looked like a great emptiness to some, to others appeared as the site of
future empire. When the new land had gone through its various flags,
finalized the spelling of its name, achieved political independence, and
had taken its place as part of the United States of America, the door to the
future was open wide. Among those who made the trek to the new land
were many Baptists. The next chapter turns to their story.

Presidents of the

Baptist General Convention

of Texas

1886-1998

A. T. Spalding — 1886-1889

PHOTO NOT
AVAILABLE

L. L. Foster — 1890-1891

R. C. Burleson — 1892-1893

R. C. Buckner — 1894-1913

S. P. Brooks — 1914-1916

M. H. Wolfe — 1917-1919

J. D. Sandefer — 1920-1922

O. S. Lattimore — 1923-1925

Pat M. Neff — 1926-1928

Lee R. Scarborough — 1929-1931

J. C. Hardy — 1932-1934

J. B. Tidwell — 1935-1937

J. Howard. Williams — 1938-1939

A. D. Foreman, Sr. — 1940-1942

W. R. White — 1943

E. D. Head — 1944-1946

Wallace Bassett — 1947-1948

William Fleming — 1949-1950

Forrest C. Feezor — 1951-1952

James N. Morgan — 1953-1954

J. Ralph Grant — 1955-1956

E. Herman Westmoreland — 1957-1958

M. B. Carroll — 1959-1960

James H. Landes — 1961-1962

K. Owen White — 1963

Abner V. McCall — 1964-1965

J. Carroll Chadwick — 1966-1967

Gordon Clinard — 1968-1969

Jimmy R. Allen — 1970-1971

Landrum P. Leavell — 1972-1973

Ralph M. Smith 1974-1975

James G. Harris — 1976

Milton E Cunningham — 1977-1979

Carlos McLeod — 1980-1981

D. L. Lowrie — 1982-1983

Winfred Moore — 1984-1985

Paul Powell — 1986-1987

Joel Gregory — 1988-1989

Phil Lineberger — 1990-1991

James Richard Maples — 1992-1993

Jerold R. McBride — 1994-1995

Charles Wade — 1996-1997

Russel H. Dilday — 1998

CHAPTER 2

BAPTIST BEGINNINGS IN TEXAS, 1820-1840

W HEN Z. N. MORRELL first came to Texas in 1835 careful inquiry revealed only two other Baptist preachers in the entire state. They were Daniel Parker and Abner Smith, both "Hardshell"[1] Baptists from Illinois. In 1837 Morrell listed all the missionary Baptists known to be in Texas, and they numbered barely over twenty.[2] However, by 1841 Baptist prospects were looking up. In that year, James Huckins reported to the Home Mission Society in New York that with proper effort Baptists might eventually form as many as twenty churches in the Lone Star State.[3] At the time that seemed quite optimistic, but no one then could have imagined in their wildest dreams the progress Texas Baptists would make in the years to follow.

Baptists in Texas got off to a slow start. Methodists and Presbyterians had a strong presence in Texas before many Baptists arrived. Those denominations sent missionaries, formed schools, and planted churches quite early. Baptists often appealed to them as examples of the ministry that Baptists should pursue in Texas. The earliest Baptist preachers in Texas came on their own, not sponsored by any church or missionary society. Some Baptist families no doubt held family Bible reading and prayer, and may on occasion have joined with neighbors in such worship long before organized churches made their advent.

THE FIRST BAPTISTS IN TEXAS

Only God knows for sure when Baptists first set foot in Texas; the lesser authorities disagree among themselves. Some reports place Baptists in Texas by 1812. Those reports may very well may be true, but they are based on hearsay and vague memories and no firm evidence confirms them. The first Baptist preacher in Texas for whom we have proof was Joseph Bays who preached along the Sabine in 1820.[4]

Joseph L. Bays (1796-1854) grew up in Kentucky where he was a friend of Daniel Boone, from whom he picked up a sense of pioneer adventure. He later moved to Missouri where he came to know Moses Austin and decided to join the Austin colonists' trek to Texas. While Moses Austin was in Mexico City negotiating the charter, several families, including the Bays family, were so confident of his success that they left for Texas even before Austin returned. Bays had been preaching since he was sixteen, and while they waited on the Louisiana side of the Sabine he exercised his gifts. His sermons found ready acceptance. As news got around, he was invited to preach among settlers west of the Sabine, in Texas territory. His first sermon in Texas was preached in 1820 at the cabin of Joseph Hinds, about eighteen miles from the San Augustine mission.[5]

Bays was also a physician of sorts and when Moses Austin returned ill from Mexico, Bays treated him for a time in the camps along the Sabine. When Moses Austin died, his son Stephen F. Austin took up the project, and the Bays family became a part of the original three hundred settlers on the Brazos.

Bays continued to preach and in 1823 while holding services in San Felipe, he was arrested by Mexican authorities. On the way to San Antonio for trial, Bays clubbed his guard and escaped to Louisiana. He later returned to Texas where he became a close friend of Sam Houston. He preached for a time in San Antonio until "ordered away by the Mexican authorities."[6] Bays and his son Henry fought in the Battle of San Jacinto in 1836. He ended his days at Matagorda in 1854. Bays has the distinction of being the first *known* Baptist preacher in Texas, and preaching the first known Baptist sermon in the state.

Freeman Smalley (b.1791) was apparently the first Baptist preacher in North Texas. He came from Ohio in 1822 in search of his sister who had married and lost touch with the family. Smalley found his sister in what is now Lamar County in far Northeast Texas. There at Pecan Point on the Red River in the home of his sister and her husband William Newman, Smalley conducted worship and preached what was probably the first sermon in North Texas.[7] Smalley went back to Ohio, but returned to Texas about 1847. His abolition views prevented him from winning much of a following in Texas, but he did establish the first anti-slavery Baptist church in the state. His son moved to Texas, and in his home near Round Rock in 1847 R. H. Taliaferro preached the first Baptist sermon in Williamson County.[8]

In 1829 Thomas Hanks preached in the home of Moses Shipman, near San Felipe, and Lydia Allcorn was converted. This was the first recorded Baptist conversion in the state.[9] Lydia and her husband James later joined the Independence church. Hanks came from Tennessee where he and Morrell had labored together. This was probably the first Baptist sermon west of the Brazos.

There were eleven known Baptist families among Stephen F. Austin's original settlers in 1821-1822, and perhaps even more among those not identified as to religion.[10] William Kincheloe and his wife were among the

Baptist believers, but they had not had an opportunity to join a church. Kincheloe settled on "Old Caney," where the town of Wharton now stands, and reportedly had preaching in his cabin as early as 1822. The preacher's name was not recorded, but very likely was Joseph Bays. The Kincheloes formed a Sunday School in their home in late 1829, and Z. N. Morrell later baptized their daughter, Nancy. Mr. and Mrs. J. P. Cole, also among the original Austin three-hundred, settled Cole's Hill, later renamed Independence. Mrs. Cole remembered attending a Baptist worship service in 1822, but did not recall the preacher's name.[11]

As *impresario* (leader in charge of land settlement), Austin apparently tried to enforce the Mexican prohibition against Protestant worship, especially in the early days. He knew how precarious the entire settlement venture was and he needed the goodwill of Mexican authorities. Individual settlers, however, probably took the Mexican prohibition less seriously. No doubt religious families conducted their own Bible reading and prayer, and on occasion even combined with neighbors for that purpose. Despite the law they probably heard sermons on occasion if a Baptist preacher happened through the community. However, there is no record of an organized church during the first ten years of the Austin colony.

ZACHARIAS N. MORRELL (1803-1883)

No one guessed it at the time, but when Z. N. Morrell crossed the Sabine in 1835, the future of Texas Baptists was assured. Morrell was by all odds the greatest pioneer preacher in Texas, and one of the greatest in America. He was tireless in travel, deeply committed to the Baptist cause, and had a vision to see the greatness which would one day crown Baptist witness in Texas. Morrell was born in South Carolina, but grew up in Tennessee. In fourteen years as a pastor in Western Tennessee he struggled against the anti-mission Baptists and also resisted the tendency of many Baptists to accept the views of Alexander Campbell, father of the Church of Christ. This experience stood Morrell in good stead in Texas, where he faced the same challenges.

More than six feet tall, Morrell was a rugged individual. Because of his fiery temperament, impulsive nature, and great courage he was nicknamed "Wildcat," and sometimes as an adult was known as "Zet." While cleaning a deep well, Morrell fell in and sustained an injury which caused him to limp for the rest of his life. He also contracted "consumption of the lungs," probably tuberculosis, and his doctor advised him to move to a drier climate. Morrell had read reports on Texas in the *Tennessee Baptist* and was already interested in the new land. He had, by his description, "Texas on the brain." Selling his land, Morrell gathered his family and headed west in 1834. However, reports of the bloody struggle between Anglo Texans and the Mexicans, along with depredations of the hostile Indians, gave Morrell cold feet and he held over in Mississippi for a year.

Morrell could not get Texas off his mind, so in 1835 he determined to go on ahead to scout the land with a view to bring his family later. In April 1835 he crossed the Sabine, just as the bluebonnets came into full bloom. Morrell fell in love with the new land, a love which never left him. He thought of Isaiah 35:1, and applied that verse to Texas: "The desert shall rejoice and blossom as the rose." Riding a mule, Morrell crossed through Nacogdoches and East Texas, as far as the Falls of the Brazos, near the present town of Marlin. He was supposed to meet David Crockett, whom he had known in Tennessee, for a bear hunt. There Morrell found a small settlement, but Crockett was delayed. Their first supper, Morrell said, "consisted principally of bear bacon, turnip greens, and fresh buffalo beef."[12] Upon learning that Morrell was a preacher, the group asked him to conduct evening prayers which he did.

Proceeding on to Little River, Morrell found a settlement of about forty people from Tennessee, led by his friend Captain Goldsby Childers. Mrs. Childers was a Baptist and insisted that Morrell preach for them, and "accordingly I preached my first sermon in Texas, in camp, on the thirtieth of December, 1835."[13]

Morrell remained at Little River for some time, riding out daily to scout the land. He liked what he saw. "The country was all we could desire," he wrote, "lands very rich, range extraordinarily good, wood and water plenty, and the prospect for health very flattering." Morrell determined to make his home in Texas, and started back to Mississippi for his family. At Nacogdoches, he records, "My very soul burned within me to preach Jesus."[14] In the past weeks he had conducted a prayer meeting or two, and had preached once, but had often felt compelled to travel on the Lord's Day. A large crowd had gathered in Nacogdoches for an election, and Morrell determined to seize the opportunity to preach. He tied his mule and looked around for a suitable place. He stood on the foundation timbers of a building that had been begun, and then

> I held up my watch in my hand, and cried at the top of my voice, "O-yes! o-yes! everybody that wants to buy without money and without price, come this way," and commenced singing the old battle-song: "Am I a soldier of the cross?" Before I finished my song there was around me a large crowd of all sorts and sizes and colors. A brief prayer was offered, . . . Astonishment, rather than reverence, was stamped upon their features. . . . My text was announced from Isaiah xxxv.1: *"The wilderness and the solitary place shall be glad for them; and the desert shall rejoice and blossom as the rose."* Never did the cane-brake preacher receive better attention. God blessed me with great liberty for one hour, amid many tears shed all around me.[15]

At the conclusion of this stirring impromptu sermon, Morrell said, "My soul was full to overflowing, and at that moment I believed the text." This verse became the golden text of Morrell's life, and the persistent faith and expectation of his ministry in Texas. Over forty years later he wrote, "God has not disappointed me."

On April 1, 1836 the Morrell family boarded the steamer *Statesman* and landed a few days later at Nachitoches, Louisiana, where they outfitted with ox teams and wagons and provisions for several months. Morrell says that "every day till we reached the Sabine, we met families running away from Texas."[16] These frightened families who fled in the "Runaway Scrape" told fearful news: Santa Anna had captured the Alamo, Fannin and his troops had been massacred at Goliad, and now Santa Anna was sweeping through Texas in a bloodbath of extermination of Anglo settlers. "I was upbraided by everybody I met," Morrell wrote, "and by some cursed as a fool, declaring that my family would be slain either by Mexicans or by Indians before we would get much beyond the Sabine." However, Morrell had a deep conviction that God had called him to Texas. With watchful eye, keeping his powder dry, "and trusting in God, we traveled on." Within days Morrell heard the news of Houston's victory at San Jacinto and concluded that his faith was justified.

Morrell settled near the Falls of the Brazos with six or eight other families, none of them Baptist. In addition there were perhaps thirty or forty soldiers at the nearby fort. Morrell staked out land and planted a crop, took his turn at guard duty, and preached as he had opportunity. The immediate danger was Comanches. The crops had to be worked under armed guard, and the settlers learned to dread the full moons of summer. The Comanches might come at any time, but they always came during the full moons. When the fort ran short of ammunition, Morrell took his ox team at his own expense to Washington-on-the-Brazos to obtain powder and lead. He returned just in time to help the newly replenished soldiers repel a major attack.

Morrell traveled constantly, preaching wherever he found people. By his account he carried two weapons: his "Jerusalem blade" (Bible) in his saddle bag, and his "carnal weapon" (a Tennessee long rifle) in his hands across the saddle. Morrell knew how to use both weapons, and was not loath to do so. He had countless skirmishes with Indians, outrunning them when he could and fighting when he could not. At church services armed guards patrolled outside the building, and men inside kept their rifles across their laps even during worship.

On one occasion, Morrell and a companion encountered a group of Comanches in war dress. The two groups, equally surprised, shouted at each other awhile for intimidation purposes. Timberland a few miles away offered safety, and Morrell and his companion headed for the timber. The Comanches were closer to the timber, but Morrell's grain-fed horses distanced the Indian mustangs and at the edge of the timber Morrell swung down, his "carnal weapon" at the ready. After a brief standoff, Morrell thought of a ruse: he shouted in Spanish, which many Comanches understood, as if directing a group of reinforcements coming up through the timber. The Indians fell for the trick and withdrew.

This incident gave Morrell great moral and spiritual concern. There *were* no reinforcements; it was a trick, and Morrell had deceived the Comanches, in effect, *lied* to them. He agonized over this moral dilemma, wondering if he should forfeit his ministerial credentials. "My mind was not at ease," he wrote, for "I had made a deliberate misrepresentation to the Indians. . . . I was without question guilty of deliberate falsehood."[17] He could shoot the Indians with no qualms, but his conscience balked at deceiving them. It is no wonder that Morrell's nickname was "Wildcat," and his description was "cane-brake preacher and Indian fighter."[18]

Morrell traveled extensively in early Texas, preaching, baptizing converts, forming churches, and laying foundations for the future. At times he was discouraged, but on such occasions he said, "My heart is fixed. God gave me an inward token . . . that he would recognize my offerings in years to come. The wilderness would yet blossom as the rose."[19] In almost fifty years in Texas, Morrell laid solid Baptist foundations. When churches were formed, he was there. He helped form the first association, the first state convention, the first Baptist university. He guarded against the incursion of doctrinal error into Baptist life, and he never wavered in his vision of a great Baptist empire in Texas.

Like many persons of meager education, Morrell valued schools and was a major factor in the formation and early promotion of Baylor University. However, for all his strengths, Morrell was primarily a frontier missionary preacher. He never shirked hard duty, as his diary entry for 1846 shows. He was under appointment as a frontier missionary, riding a circuit in central Texas. His travel involved crossing swollen rivers, since there were no ferries or bridges then. He wrote,

During the spring of 1846 I encountered many difficulties in traversing the broad field assigned to me. The Little Brazos and Navasota Rivers both had to be crossed on every trip, and there was no ferry on either stream. . . . [in March] I found a creek swimming . . . It was very cold and I dreaded it. Finally, my horse was plunged into the swollen stream. He swam with me to the opposite bank without any difficulty; but as he struggled amid obstructions on the Springfield side, I was compelled to dismount in the water and give the animal my assistance.

My boots were full of water, and all my clothing thoroughly saturated. A blue Texas norther whistled around my ears, and appeared almost to penetrate my quivering limbs, as I mounted the horse, at four o'clock in the afternoon, with twenty-five miles lying stretched before me and Springfield . . . and not a single house on the way that I knew of. To my great surprise and gratification, after traveling about eight miles, my clothing now freezing, I came suddenly upon a camp by the roadside, made since my February trip. Here was a good fire, a little log cabin covered, no floors, cracks not lined and no chimney. The familiar voice of a brother in Christ was recognized; and brother Sanders, whom I had known in Washington County . . . invited me to share with him for the night . . . . It was by this time almost sunset, and as I drew off my boots and exposed my wet and almost frozen feet to the fire, the good sister Sanders gave me a cup of coffee. The wind, 'tis true, whistled through the open cracks in the new log cabin, but this was far better than shivering all night alone on the bank of some swollen creek ahead.[20]

FOUNDATION LAYERS

Texas Baptists were fortunate to gain several new leaders in the late 1830s, and they were mostly of high quality like R. E. B. Baylor and Noah T. Byars. After 1840 more immigrants came, including Baptists, and names like Huckins, Tryon, Burleson, and Graves show up in Baptist records. These Baptist immigrants, pastors and people alike, all came from elsewhere and brought with them the diversities of their backgrounds. They did not always agree on matters of faith and church practice, and most tended to think the way they did things back home was the way all Baptists should do. It is not always easy to distinguish preachers and laymen, for many who came to Texas as laymen later became preachers; one thinks of Richard Ellis, Noah T. Byars, and perhaps even Judge Baylor himself.

Robert Emmett Bledsoe Baylor (1793-1873). This man with many names made a great name for himself, and for Baptists, in Texas.[21] He was born in Kentucky, attended common schools of that state, and served in the War of 1812 against England. He read law in the office of his uncle, and served in the Kentucky legislature. Baylor later set up his own law practice in Alabama, where he also served in the state legislature in 1824 and in the United States Congress in 1832. He was converted and baptized in Talladega, Alabama, in July 1839, while attending a revival conducted by his cousin, Thomas Chilton. He was licensed to preach soon after. He came to Texas in 1839 at age 48 and settled at LaGrange where he taught school for a year. Baylor never married.

In Texas Baylor continued his law practice, and carved out a brilliant legal career. Tall and impressive in appearance, Baylor was an excellent speaker and had a quality that propelled him to leadership in any enterprise. He served as judge of the Third Judicial District of the Republic of Texas, and also served on the Supreme Court of the new Republic, thus his name of "Judge Baylor." He later settled at Independence. On his circuit Baylor held court by day and preached by night, winning numerous converts and helping form a number of churches. Though there is no specific record of it, he was probably ordained by the LaGrange church in 1840. In later years Baylor baptized converts, administered the Lord's Supper, and sat on ordaining councils, all of which would require that he be ordained himself.

Baylor's distinguished career in Texas gave added status to the struggling Baptist cause. He served as Corresponding Secretary of the Union Association and dictated the charter for the university that took his name. He gave generously to the university, served without pay as its first law professor, and later donated his considerable law library to the school. He took an active combat role in the Mexican and Indian wars of the time, and proved himself a leader of substance not only for Baptists but for the new Republic of Texas.

Thomas W. Cox. One of the most capable preachers in early Texas was T. W. Cox who came from the same Alabama church as Baylor. He formed and served as pastor of churches at LaGrange and Travis, both in 1839. He preached at each church only one Sunday a month, which left him time to serve as part-time pastor at Independence as well. Cox was known as an outstanding preacher, and he was strongly missionary. He was pastor of all three of the small churches which formed the Union Association in 1840, and was its first moderator.

Though strongly missionary, Cox absorbed the views of Alexander Campbell whose "reform" movement led to the Church of Christ or, as most Baptists of the time called them, the "Campbellites." This doctrinal deviation from Baptist views, plus convincing reports of dishonest business dealings in Alabama, led to Cox's ouster from Baptist life in 1841. His later life, some reported, was not marked by "Christian rectitude."[22]

Noah Turner Byars (1808-1888). Noah Byars was born in South Carolina, and came to Texas in 1835. He established a gunsmith shop at Washington-on-the-Brazos, and with his partner Peter M. Mercer owned the building where the Texas Declaration of Independence and Constitution were adopted on March 2, 1836. Byars was appointed "armorer" to Sam Houston's army and participated in the Battle of San Jacinto. However, he was later denied a military pension on the grounds that he was never officially enlisted. He lived for a time in Houston and Bastrop, serving as justice of the peace and sergeant-at-arms of the Texas senate.

Byars resisted the call to ministry, but was finally ordained in 1841 at the Macedonia church below Austin, in the presence of M. B. Lamar, President of the Republic, and several of his cabinet. This was probably the second ordination of a missionary Baptist preacher in Texas. The ordination of Byars is the first for which we have records, but almost certainly R. E. B. Baylor had been ordained in 1840.[23] Byars served for a time as pastor of churches, most of which he had formed, but preferred the work of frontier missionary. He was at times employed by the Baptist State Convention, the Home Mission Board of the Southern Baptist Convention, and various Baptist associations in Texas. He is said to have ridden horseback more than 100,000 miles, during which time he formed sixty churches, five associations and two Baptist schools (including the short-lived Byars Institute in Chambers County).[24] On Saturday, May 31, 1851 Byars formed the First Baptist Church of Waco with four members, and the next day he was called as pastor. He served there for two years, though he had to ride 75 miles for the monthly services. In 1876 Byars formed the First Baptist Church of Brownwood and later served fifteen months as its pastor. His last active ministry was as pastor of the Clear Creek Church in Brown County in 1884, after which Byars described himself as "like an old vessel laid up."[25] After a lifetime of faithful service to Baptists, Byars came to a destitute old age and the Baptist Convention of Texas voted him $8 a month for subsistence until his death in 1888.

Judge Richard Ellis (1781-1846). Ellis was born in Virginia, but moved to Alabama where he studied law and was elected judge of the fourth Alabama circuit. This outstanding Baptist layman moved to Pecan Point in Bowie County in 1825 and soon came to leadership in Texas. He presided over the convention at Washington on March 2, 1836, which declared independence from Mexico. Ellis was elected four times to the Texas congress between 1836 and 1840 and served as president *pro tem* of the Texas senate. Ellis County is named for him and his statue stands in Waxahachie, the county seat. As an active Baptist, Ellis was a member of the first Texas Baptist Education Society and served on its board of managers. Two cousins of Judge Ellis, J. L. Ellis and B. F. Ellis, came to Texas in 1836 and became active Baptist laymen.

Pastor Richard Ellis. Not to be confused with Judge Ellis, the young Richard Ellis who later became a pastor lived for a time at Washington on the Brazos, but may have moved south of Austin before the Washington church was formed. The Macedonia church called him as pastor and asked the Plum Grove church to ordain him, which was done in 1842, with Z. N. Morrell and R. E. B. Baylor as presbytery. Ellis succeeded Morrell as pastor of the Travis church. Baylor was a close friend of Ellis, and probably enlisted him in the ministry. Of their first meeting Baylor wrote,

> Brother Ellis was present. He sang beautifully and was wonderfully gifted in prayer. I called on him to pray at the close of the service. He did so with much feeling and pathos, and I immediately left the pulpit, went to him and taking him by the hand with tears in my eyes I said, "Why do you not preach?" He immediately commenced weeping and said, "I ran away from Virginia to keep from preaching." I replied, "You have been a runaway long enough from the Master: obey the divine impression you have, take up the cross and preach Jesus to a lost and ruined world.[26]

Ellis accepted this challenge and was ordained in 1842. He and Baylor often preached together and Baylor became a kind of mentor to help Ellis overcome his shyness and develop his preaching powers. Baylor must have been a good teacher and model, for Ellis became one of the better preachers among Texas Baptists. "He often wept whilst preaching," Baylor recalled, "and his sermons always had a telling effect on the congregation."[27] He was "tenaciously a Baptist" and ruined his voice, J. B. Link says, by "preaching too lengthily."[28]

Anderson Buffington. Buffington came to Texas from Tennessee in 1835. He served in the Texas Revolution, including the Battle of San Jacinto. He and his wife were charter members of the first missionary Baptist church in Texas, at Washington-on-the-Brazos in 1837, where he was ordained in 1841. Buffington, along with Z. N. Morrell and Noah T. Byars, served as a missionary for the Texas Baptist Missionary Society in 1841, largely at his own expense. He later spent much of his time preaching among the African-American population, especially in Grimes County.

Lay Leaders in Early Texas. The Baptist presence in early Texas was greatly strengthened by a number of lay persons, men and women alike. It is not always easy to distinguish laymen and ministers, for most ministers earned their bread by secular work and many laymen preached and exhorted. Such names appear as William Kincheloe and Eli Mercer, said to be a cousin of the famed Jesse Mercer of Georgia. H. R. Cartmell, who had been a deacon at First Baptist in Nashville, Tennessee, moved to Texas and helped form the first missionary Baptist church in the state at Washington-on-the-Brazos in 1837. He served on the committee of correspondence which eventually brought missionaries to Texas.

William Scallorn, also a deacon back in Tennessee, brought his large family to Texas and located in Fayette County. Scallorn was "a plain farmer of practical good sense, a devoted consistent Christian, a firm and earnest Baptist."[29] His house was open for worship and often as many as twenty would meet for worship, take dinner and spend the night. For many years Scallorn was a deacon in the Plum Grove church. A pioneer physician, Dr. Thomas Anderson, came to Texas with his wife in 1835, where they became active members of the Webberville Baptist Church. Their son, Washington, married a daughter of pioneer pastor R. H. Taliaferro, and they were charter members of the old Brushy Creek Church near Round Rock. Chester S. Gorbet, one of Austin's 300 settlers, was an active Baptist layman, and took part in forming the Baptist State Convention in 1848. A. C. Horton and his wife came to Texas in 1835. He was with Colonel Fannin at Goliad, but escaped the massacre. He was an active Baptist layman, and later became governor of Texas. The great bell at Baylor college was a gift from Horton. John and Mary Waglay were already Baptists when they settled in Red River County in 1833.[30]

Two Baptist women of note were Mrs. Goldsby Childers, in whose home Morrell preached his first sermon in Texas; and Mrs. Massie Millard of Nacogdoches, who started the first prayer meeting in East Texas which probably led to formation of the Union Church. Mrs. Eli Mercer, Penelope Mercer Borden, Lydia Allcorn, Annette Lea Bledsoe, and Mrs. R.B. Jarman also show up in the records.

EARLY BAPTIST CHURCHES

The earliest Baptist church to *exist* in Texas was the Pilgrim Predestinarian Regular Baptist Church, formed by Daniel Parker in Illinois in 1833. When Parker came to Texas in 1832 to apply for a land grant he met Stephen F. Austin and learned that no Baptist church could be legally formed in Texas. However, Parker interpreted this to mean that no Baptist church could be *formed* in Texas, but one might be formed somewhere else and imported into Texas. Some reports say, unconvincingly, that Austin suggested this interpretation. Parker returned to Lamote, Illinois, and there on July 26, 1833, formed a church with seven members. He and the other church members traveled by wagon train to Texas where they settled in Austin's colony. The first meeting of the church as such in Texas was in January 1834. Because of the threat of Mexican opposition, Parker's group soon moved to the Nacogdoches area where their church was still illegal but further removed from immediate Mexican threat.

The first Baptist church actually *formed* in Texas was the Providence Church, formed on March 29, 1834, on the Colorado River below the present town of Bastrop, with Abner Smith as the first pastor. This was an offshoot from the Parker "Hardshell" group. Sometimes known as "Primitive" Baptists, the Parker movement was anti-missionary and opposed all human organizations for Christian effort, such as mission societies, conventions, Sunday Schools, Bible societies, and all secret societies such as the Masonic Lodge. In East Texas Parker formed a number of such "anti" churches and some of them later grouped into "do nothing" associations. The associations met, recorded the fact that they had met, set the time and place for the next meeting, and adjourned. The movement grew slowly, but blanketed parts of East Texas with a persistent anti-mission, anti-effort, and anti-denominational flavor that persists to this day.

Washington-on-the-Brazos. The first missionary Baptist church formed in Texas was at Washington-on-the-Brazos, November 1837. Z. N. Morrell found a few Baptists there, but they had not formed a church. The Washington population was growing, augmented by a large group of idle soldiers who had been recently mustered out of the Texas army. Rowdiness, gambling, and an oversupply of intoxicating drink convinced the Baptists they needed to bring the gospel to Washington. They had conducted a weekly prayer meeting for some time, but by November determined to form a church. Morrell wrote,

> We determined, let come what might, to organize a church. The day was appointed, and eight Baptists assembled to keep house for God. Brother H. R. Cartmell was recognized as deacon, and Z. N. Morrell chosen as pastor. Thus sprung into existence the first church, according to my information, that was ever organized in Texas on strictly gospel principles, having the ordinances and officers of ancient order, and with no anti-missionary element in its body.[31]

In one of its first actions the church appointed a Committee on Correspondence, composed of J. R. Jenkins, Anderson Buffington, and H. R. Cartmell, to write to Baptist mission societies in the United States seeking help for Texas. The committee came up with a powerful letter describing spiritual needs and potential of the new land. Uncertain about whether work in Texas would come under foreign or home missions, they covered all bases by sending copies to both the Baptist Foreign Mission Society in Boston and the Home Mission Society in New York. Copies of this letter were also published in the *Christian Index* of Georgia, edited by Jesse Mercer.

People in the United States were becoming more aware of Texas, and this letter had a great impact. The Home Mission Society appointed James Huckins to travel in Georgia, raising funds for a Texas mission. News of San Jacinto had spread through the country and interest in Texas was growing. Huckins had no trouble raising money for a Texas mission. Jesse Mercer himself contributed $2,500 and offered to double that amount if necessary. Mercer's kinsman Eli Mercer was already in Texas, as was Eli's daughter Penelope, wife of Gail Borden, Jr. Not surprisingly, Huckins himself volunteered as a missionary to Texas, arriving in 1840.

He was followed in 1841 by William M. Tryon. Thus the first two missionaries to Texas were appointed as a result of the letter from the brethren of the Washington church.

When the capital of Texas did not locate at Washington-on-the-Brazos, as many had expected, the population there waned. By 1838 many of the Baptists had moved away, and the church lapsed. It was reconstituted later but never achieved the prominence many had expected.

Union Church. The second missionary Baptist church formed in Texas, and the first to survive, was the Union Church near Nacogdoches, often called the Old North church. Located so near the Sabine, Nacogdoches was one of the earliest Anglo settlements in Texas. Mrs. Massie Millard with her family located a few miles north of Nacogdoches in 1832 or 1833, about a mile from where the Old North church now stands. During Indian raids Mrs. Millard often fled with her children to hide in an oak thicket near her home. While hiding, she would gather her children and pray. Sometimes other families joined these hideout devotions, and when Indian raids no longer threatened the prayer meetings continued. This was probably the first Baptist prayer meeting in the state.

Isaac Reed, who had been a pastor in Tennessee, came to the Nacogdoches area in 1834. In the summer of 1836 he began preaching under a spread of oak trees not far from Massie Millard's prayer meeting. On the first Sunday of May 1838 Reed and a fellow-minister Robert E. Green formed the Union Church with seven white and two black slave members, with Reed as pastor. J. B. Link says that "although full of the missionary spirit, he [Reed] was opposed to Boards and Missionary Societies."[32] Reed formed other churches and later helped form the Sabine Baptist Association, second in the state. This association turned anti-missionary, and the Union Church split off to help form the East Texas Missionary Association.

Plum Grove. The Plum Grove community was located on the Colorado River, just below the present town of Bastrop. After he left Washington, Morrell located in that area where he began to preach in the home of William Scallorn. In April, 1839, Robert G. Green and Asael Dancer led in forming a church at Plum Grove, with Dancer as the first pastor. Dancer had been associated with the Primitive Baptists, and occasionally Abner Smith, the anti-missionary colleague of Daniel Parker, preached at Plum Grove and for a time the church included both missionary and anti-missionary members. Morrell also preached occasionally at Smith's Providence church, and baptized converts for them (including Mrs. Dancer) when the pastor was disabled. Several other converts presented themselves for baptism in the Plum Grove church. Morrell records that

> nine candidates came forward and gave the reasons of their hope. I was again greatly encouraged by the presence of brother R. E. B. Baylor from LaGrange. Sunday morning, at ten o'clock, we met at the water, and after a short discourse on the subjects and action of baptism, nine converts testified their belief in the burial and resurrection of Jesus, by allowing themselves to be buried in and raised out of the water of the Colorado

River. On retiring to a small house, with an arbor of brush built in front of it for the occasion, brother Baylor, in his usual happy manner, preached a most excellent sermon.[33]

However, troubles plagued the church as the strict Calvinists continued their agitation. In February, 1842, Morrell received an urgent letter from Deacon Scallorn:

Dear Brother Morrell: Our conference meeting comes on at Plum Grove next Saturday. We are in trouble. The anti-missionaries have been among us, sowing the seeds of discord. We are on the eve of a rent in the body. Come and help us. You may effect a reconciliation. Come if possible; and may the Lord come with you.[34]

Morrell received the letter late Friday. He borrowed a horse (his own was recently stolen) and just at sunset on Saturday set out on a dangerous night ride through Indian country, with his "Jerusalem blade" (Bible) in his saddlebags and his "carnal weapon" (Tennessee long rifle) across the saddle. Arriving after sunrise and with less than an hour's sleep, Morrell preached and led a discussion of missions. The group was reconciled for a time and took the Lord's Supper together, and Morrell again rode all night to reach home by early Monday morning. But soon the truce broke down and the anti-mission group was excluded by a vote of fourteen to eight, largely under the influence of Morrell, and Plum Grove continued actively in missionary Baptist life.

Travis. Apparently R. E. B. Baylor and T. W. Cox were responsible for forming a church near Brenham, probably in 1839. The church, which took the name of Travis, began with seven members, with Cox as the first pastor. The church did not long survive, but took an active role while it existed. The Union Baptist Association, first in Texas, was formed at this church in 1840. When Cox was excluded from the churches at LaGrange and Independence for embracing "Campbellite"[35] views, a majority at Travis sustained him. However, he and his followers later pulled out and formed a new congregation on nearby Kentucky Ridge more in line with his new views. The split marked the demise of the Travis church and the remaining members scattered.

Independence. One of the greatest Baptist churches in early Texas was formed at Independence in 1839. The community was first settled by J. P. Cole in the early 1820s, and was called Cole's Hill until patriotic fervor during the Texas Revolution gave it the name of Independence. In August 1839 Thomas Spraggins, a visiting preacher from Mississippi, gathered the few Baptists and formed the church, with T. W. Cox called as pastor. James Allcorn and his wife Lydia united with the church by baptism. Lydia had been converted years before by Thomas Hanks who preached in the cabin of Moses Shipman, but had had no chance to be baptized.[36] She was probably the first Baptist convert in Texas. A number of outstanding Baptist leaders located in the Independence area, including Judge Baylor and William Tryon. They often preached at Independence and strengthened the church. For a time it appeared that Independence might become the capital of Texas and population increased. A series of great revivals increased the church membership and, of course, the location of Baylor University there in 1845 added to the church and the town became known as "the Baptist Jerusalem of Texas." The church also had its trials. It was badly split when its pastor, T. W. Cox, was excluded for adopting the views of Alexander Campbell.

LaGrange. Whether this church was formed in 1839 or 1840 is not clear. Z. N. Morrell, writing years later from memory with no written records before him, sets the date at 1839. However, Judge Baylor, who lived in the area, in a letter to the *Christian Index* of Georgia names March 25, 1840, as the date. The founding presbytery consisted of James Huckins and T. W. Cox. Additional confusion arises about the exact name and location of the church. The church may have been formed at the adjacent community of Huntersville or Clear Creek but, because this was only five miles from LaGrange, the church took the latter name. Another possibility is that there was a church formed in LaGrange in 1839, but it split in 1840 with the pro-missionary group forming the new church described by Baylor.

FIRST SUNDAY SCHOOLS IN TEXAS

In the 1820s Sunday Schools were fairly new everywhere. A few such schools existed in the South by 1800, but when the Southern Baptist Convention was formed in 1845 probably fewer than five hundred Baptist Sunday Schools existed in all the South. In 1829 three Sunday Schools were formed in Texas, but they did not long endure. It would be another generation before such schools caught on in the Lone Star State.

Thomas J. Pilgrim started the first Sunday School in Texas in 1829 at San Felipe. Pilgrim was born in Connecticut, and entered Hamilton Institute in New York to prepare for ministry. However, health problems caused him to drop out and seek a milder climate. Young Pilgrim joined a wagon train of about sixty families headed for Texas in 1828. Upon arrival at San Felipe, Pilgrim started a day school to earn a living. He was listed in the Austin colony records as a schoolmaster, aged 24.[37] He became a friend of Stephen F. Austin, who later wrote, "Remember me to Mr. Pilgrim. I am greatly pleased with him as a teacher."[38]

Pilgrim picked up a working knowledge of Spanish on the trip to Texas, and he became an official interpreter for the colony. In the spring of 1829 Pilgrim opened a school named for his friend Stephen F. Austin, with the blessings of its namesake. The day school succeeded so well that Pilgrim came up with the idea to form a Sunday School as well. He publicized the plan through his school, and on the first Sunday thirty-two pupils showed up, some from as far as ten miles away. Pilgrim described the first school:

In a black-jack and post-oak grove near the center of the town is a rude log cabin about eighteen by twenty-two feet, the roof covered with boards held down by weight-poles, the logs unhewn, and the cracks neither chinked or battened, a dirt floor, and across it are placed several logs hewn on one side for seats. At one end stands the superintendent, a mere stripling, and before him are about a dozen gentlemen and ladies as teachers, and thirty-two children, without any of those appendages which are now considered necessary to a well conducted Sunday-school.[39]

Though Pilgrim taught on an ecumenical basis that even Roman Catholics could accept, the school was not suffered to continue. It was clearly against the law and enforcement was strict, at least in the early days. The usual report is that the irate Mexican authorities closed the school, but that may not be technically accurate. Perhaps in time they *would* have done so, but before they did the cautious Austin beat them to it. Pilgrim wrote later that "The *empresario* [Austin] deemed it prudent to discontinue the Sunday-school for a time, as these Mexicans could not be deceived in relation to the character of our exercises, and it was well known that we were acting in violation of the colonization laws, which strictly prohibited Austin from introducing any but Catholics as colonists."[40]

Pilgrim later lived in Gonzales where he led a successful Sunday School. For the rest of his life he was known as the "Sunday School Man of Texas," and served on committees of the Union Association and the Baptist State Convention to promote this work.

Two more Baptist Sunday Schools were formed in Texas before the end of 1829, one at Old Caney (near present Wharton) in the home of Mr. and Mrs. Kincheloe, and another at Matagorda. Neither continued for long and it was another decade before the Sunday School began to catch on among Texas Baptists, and even longer before suitable Bible study materials were readily available.

CONCLUSION

The twenty years from 1820-1840 was the era of beginnings for Baptists in Texas. During that time about a half-dozen Baptist preachers and several committed lay persons entered the state, and their combined efforts led to six small churches by 1840. This was a day of small beginnings, but by 1840 the prospects were promising. If Morrell's dream of the desert blossoming as a rose was not yet realized, the early buds were beginning to appear. The next period, 1840-1848, will trace some of the emerging structures of Baptist growth.

CHAPTER 3

EMERGING BAPTIST STRUCTURES, 1840–1848

"WE ARE MAKING some headway."[1] That was the hopeful report of missionary James Huckins as he surveyed the situation among Texas Baptists in 1841.

Huckins, the first appointed Baptist missionary to Texas, had good reason for optimism. In a letter to the American Baptist Home Missionary Society (HMS), which had appointed him to Texas, Huckins wrote, "We now have an association of nine churches. We have a Home Missionary Society, an Educational Society, one missionary in the field sustained wholly by our funds, and arrangements made to supply the denomination with books. Our churches are all established on good ground."[2]

After scattered beginnings, the Baptist witness in Texas began to take root. The 1840s proved to be an eventful decade for Texas, and for Texas Baptists. In 1845 the Republic of Texas was annexed to the United States and that annexation, with the successful conclusion of the Mexican War of 1848, increased the floodtide of immigration into the new land. Among these new immigrants were many Baptists and during the 1840s the number of churches grew to thirty-five. New preachers also came, on their own or by appointment from the Home Mission Society. In addition to such stalwart veterans as Z. N. Morrell and R. E. B. Baylor, who had arrived earlier, the 1840s brought dynamic leaders such as James Huckins, William M. Tryon, Rufus C. Burleson, Henry Lea Graves and others. Before that decade was completed, Texas Baptists had formed several associations, a Baptist university, and a state convention. This chapter will sketch some of those achievements.

THE FIRST MISSIONARIES

The previous chapter told the story of the committee from the Washington church that wrote to the Baptist missionary societies in the United

States in 1837, describing the spiritual needs in Texas and urging that missionaries be sent there. That letter bore abundant fruit. In addition to reaching the American Baptist Home Mission Society, located in New York City, the letter was published in several Baptist papers including the *Christian Index* of Georgia. The editor, Jesse Mercer, already had family members in Texas and a keen interest in the new land. Early reports say that Mercer at once gave $2,500 to the Texas mission and offered to give more as needed.[3]

James Huckins (1808-1863). The prospects for Texas Baptists brightened greatly when missionary James Huckins landed in Galveston on January 24, 1840. During nineteen years in Texas, Huckins planted numerous churches (including First Baptist churches of both Galveston and Houston), helped found Baylor University, and served on its first board of trustees. By the force of his convictions he helped keep Texas Baptists doctrinally sound, and helped organize and provide leadership for the Baptist State Convention.

Born in New Hampshire, Huckins was baptized at age fifteen. After preparatory studies at the New Hampton Academical and Theological Institution, he entered Brown University in 1828. In the eventful year of 1832, Huckins graduated from Brown, was ordained, and married. For a time he served as pastor in Calais, Maine, but offended influential church members when he refused use of the church building for a radical abolitionist rally. Though a northern man, Huckins sided with the South on the slavery issue.[4] When this conflict led to his resignation in 1838, Huckins accepted appointment from the Home Mission Society to travel in the South, raising money for home missions and especially for the proposed Texas mission. In Georgia, where the contagious "Texas fever" was running high, he became acquainted with Jesse Mercer and others who not only helped him raise funds to send missionaries to Texas but also stirred his own interest in the new land.

When no suitable prospect for appointment to Texas appeared Huckins, not surprisingly, volunteered. The HMS first appointed him for a four-month fact-finding tour, and later his tenure was extended. In November 1839 he set out from New Orleans, sailing on the *Neptune* for Galveston where he arrived on January 24, 1840. Galveston then had about three thousand inhabitants but no Baptist church. Huckins intended merely to pass through Galveston on his way inland to Houston but, to his surprise, on his first morning off the *Neptune* he met a family who had been members of his church in Maine. They told him of a few other Baptists in town and urged him to tarry and preach for them. The result was that Huckins remained in Galveston almost a month, during which time he preached, gathered the few Baptists, baptized new converts, and formed the First Baptist Church with nine members, four men and five women, on January 30, 1840.[5]

In Galveston Huckins met Gail Borden, Jr. and his wife Penelope. They were Baptist believers who had been in Texas since 1829, but had no opportunity to be baptized. Among the original nine members was Mrs. Louisa Borden, probably Gail's mother. Borden, who later became well-known for his development of condensed milk, became a leading citizen of Galveston and a friend of Stephen F. Austin. On the first Sunday after the church was formed, Gail and Penelope Borden, along with Penelope's sister, presented themselves for baptism. A few days later Huckins baptized these three in the Gulf of Mexico. In his diary, Huckins described the unique scene on that bright and beautiful winter day:

> On the one side as far as the eye could see lay the vast prairies, on the other the boundless expanse of ocean, lashing with its deep blue waters the ground on which we stood. The beach, too, presented a highway of unparalleled beauty, leading on through the whole length of the island, surpassing in hardness and smoothness any road which art has ever formed. There, too, was to be heard the sound of the ever-rolling billows, resembling the distant voice of God. These all conspired to make us feel the majesty and power of that God in whose name we had assembled.[6]

This was the first Baptist immersion of record in the Texas Gulf of Mexico. Afterwards the candidates, with the Gulf saltwater still saturating their clothing, embraced each other and other believers on the beach. Huckins was too emotional to speak, but later wrote "there was not an eye present, however unused to tears, but filled; not a heart, however hard, but began to melt." The service made a great impact upon the witnesses, believer and unbeliever alike, and the crowd "dispersed in too solemn a mood for conversation."[7] The Bordens proved stalwart members of the church. Gail started one of the first newspapers in Texas, and later was named Collector of the Port of Galveston. Jesse Mercer's ongoing interest in Texas was sustained, at least partly, by the experiences of his kinsman Eli at Wharton and his niece Penelope Borden and her family in Galveston.

The church soon increased to thirteen members, and Huckins wrote that "Next Lord's Day we expect to receive ten or twelve brethren of color, who are well recommended."[8] Huckins later served twice as pastor of this great church. He was overwhelmed by the spiritual challenges of the growing population, both white and black. He said, "Religion here is weak and timid," and every day gives "ocular demonstration" of how depraved people can become without the gospel.

Late in February 1840 Huckins moved up Buffalo Bayou to Houston, then with a population of about three thousand and little evidence of religion. On February 23 he gathered a few Baptists in the town and preached. After ten days in Houston, Huckins set out to tour the area between the Brazos and Colorado rivers, visiting cabins, camps, and the few churches he found. About eighteen miles west of Houston Huckins came upon a cabin and introduced himself to the husband and wife there as a minister. The ensuing conversation illustrates the depth of spiritual hunger on the Texas frontier.

"A minister, did you say, sir?"

"Yes, madam."

"Of what denomination?"

"The Baptist."

Huckins then describes the response:

> And with tears gushing forth, she reached out her hand and exclaimed, "Allow me to call you brother! I am a Baptist. . . Husband is a Baptist also." It was a happy meeting, and we sat upon a log and talked . . . or rather, the brother and myself were seated, but the lady was so happy she could not sit. . . . This good sister informed me that she would willingly travel eighteen miles to enjoy the preaching of the gospel.[9]

As he continued his tour, Huckins spied out the land to assess its suitability for settlement and future prospects for mission work. He was overwhelmed by what he found. "In a short ride," he reported, "I saw no less than 180 deer, [and] 1000 head of cattle" whose long horns amazed him. He also saw wild horses, hogs, mules and antelope. In a letter to R. E. B. Baylor, he wrote, "The people in the states have no idea of this country. It is the loveliest land the sun ever set upon, . . . Lands here are cheap and very fertile."[10] This was high praise from a newcomer so recently from New England.

Much as he praised the land, Huckins was shocked at the hardships he found in Texas. When he first met R. E. B. Baylor at LaGrange, Huckins was distressed at Baylor's shabby, wornout clothing and crude log cabin. He could not believe that a highly educated man, a former United States congressman, should live so meanly. Huckins sent word at once to Houston to have a new suit made for Baylor. Baylor's reaction to this is not recorded.[11]

After his tour was completed, Huckins returned to the East and made a favorable report to the HMS. Upon his recommendation, the Society increased their commitment to Texas and at once appointed Huckins to return. With his wife Rhoda and daughters Caroline and Sarah, Huckins returned to Texas, where he became pastor at Galveston. However, his pastorate did not prevent him from making missionary tours from time to time. As pastor Huckins also raised money to erect a church building in Galveston, by far the most beautiful Baptist building in the state at that time. He was too ill to attend the dedication in 1847, and soon after was pressured into resigning.

Some church members had made serious complaints against Huckins, the exact nature of which we do not know. He was a slave owner and, on at least one occasion, was known to treat a slave harshly. That may have been one reason for the complaint. For all his greatness, Huckins had weaknesses. He was decidedly not a handsome man, with long and unruly hair, and distracting mannerisms along with what one described as "incessant use of tobacco."[12] Huckins later served another term as pastor in Galveston, resigning in 1859 to move to South Carolina where he ended his days.

It would be hard to overstate the importance of Huckins to early Texas Baptist life. This first missionary brought energy, social standing, zeal for education and, above all, a vision for the future of Texas Baptists.

William Milton Tryon (1809-1847). Tryon was born in New York City where he was converted at age 17. Ill health caused him to seek a warmer climate, and as a young man he moved to Augusta, Georgia. He was later licensed to preach by the First Baptist Church in Augusta, the same church where the Southern Baptist Convention was formed a few years later. He attended Mercer University on a scholarship from the Georgia Baptist Convention, and served for a time as instructor at Mercer. In 1836 Tryon became General Agent for the Georgia Convention to canvas the state for funds to support Baptist education and mission causes. In 1837 he was called as the first pastor of a new church in Irwinton, Alabama. There he married a young Methodist widow who owned farms and several slaves.

Like so many others, Tryon picked up from Jesse Mercer an interest in Texas, and he also met James Huckins when Huckins was raising money for a Texas mission. After his first Texas tour, Huckins went back through Alabama. While we have no proof that Huckins and Tryon met on that trip, Tryon must have been aware of Huckins's glowing reports of the prospects for the new land. It is therefore not surprising that Tryon volunteered as a missionary to Texas. Like Huckins, Tryon was first appointed to a temporary term, which was later extended. He arrived in Galveston on January 18, 1841, almost exactly one year after Huckins. Tryon preached in Galveston, Houston and Matagorda, but settled between Washington and Independence.

On March 14, 1841, Tryon, assisted by R. E. B. Baylor and T. W. Cox, reconstituted the church at Washington-on-the-Brazos with ten white members and two slaves. A church there was first formed by Z. N. Morrell in 1837, but it lapsed the next year. Tryon also preached at Independence, where T. W. Cox was pastor. Because Cox lived at LaGrange about sixty miles away, it seemed good for Tryon to assume the Independence pastorate, which he did. His report to the HMS in July 1841 reveals a busy schedule. He preached one Saturday and Sunday a month at Independence, one weekend at a new church in the area (probably the Providence church at Chappell Hill), and one Saturday and Sunday at the Travis church in Austin County. He also preached occasionally at Brazos Ferry, about forty miles from Houston. This was fairly typical of the time, when a Baptist preacher might serve as pastor of a number of churches, dividing his time among them.

In addition, Tryon also itinerated. He describes one trip to Matagorda, where he preached the first Baptist sermon ever heard in the town of about six hundred; from there he rode back north to LaGrange where he assisted R. E. B. Baylor in administering the Lord's Supper.

Tryon's original appointment to Texas was for one year. At the end of that year, he was reappointed. He returned to Alabama to close out business affairs, and to arrange the transfer to Texas of the numerous slaves his wife owned. They settled on a large farm at Hidalgo Bluff, between Washington and Independence, where the slaves worked the farm.

During the summer of 1841 Tryon led a great revival at the Washington church, and administered the first Baptist baptism in the Brazos. His own wife Louisa, who for some time had considered becoming a Baptist, was among those immersed. Tryon and Baylor led another revival that summer in the area, with twenty-one converts, most of whom joined the Independence church. In August the two men conducted a revival at the Mount Gilead church, with thirty-nine baptized. The church had been formed the previous year with thirteen members, and within little over a year it had become the largest Baptist church in Texas with 130 members, most of whom had been received by baptism. In September Tryon, again with the help of Baylor, formed the Providence church in Milam County, with thirteen members. After a revival there, Tryon baptized forty converts and, within weeks, the church had grown to between sixty and seventy members.

Tryon was especially effective in evangelism. His preaching was direct, included many examples and anecdotes, and majored on leading people to faith in Christ. When "wrought up," Tryon often became quite emotional and his appeals for faith in Christ were almost irresistible. After only seven years, Tryon's ministry in Texas was cut short. He died of yellow fever in Houston in 1847. His time in Texas was brief, but his impact was great.

UNION BAPTIST ASSOCIATION

The earliest Baptists in Texas came from many states, and they were nothing if not ambitious. They set out to reduplicate as soon as possible the structures they had known back in the United States. As soon as they had enough churches, and sometimes before, they formed associations and a state convention.

In June 1840 a call brought four ministers and about twenty-five Baptists to Independence for the purpose of forming a Baptist association. The ministers were T. W. Cox, pastor of the host church, R. E. B. Baylor, Abner Smith, and Ariel Dancer. The last two named were Calvinists with anti-missionary views. Smith was pastor of a church which had formed off from the Daniel Parker predestinarian group which had come to the Austin colony in 1834, and Dancer had sown anti-mission views in the Plum Grove church. Smith and Dancer insisted that the proposed association be anti-missionary, or at least make missionary activity optional. Baylor was hesitant, but Cox flatly refused to go along with this plan. After several days of fruitless discussion, the meeting adjourned without action.

Cox then called a second meeting for October 8, 1840, to meet at Travis, about twelve miles south of Brenham, where he also was pastor. Eleven messengers came from three churches: Travis, Independence, and LaGrange, with a combined membership of forty-five. Z. N. Morrell, pastor of the Plum Grove church, though sympathetic, did not attend because of illness. Of the three churches represented, Cox had formed two of them and was pastor of all three. The messengers voted unanimously to form a missionary association; they elected Cox as moderator, Baylor as corresponding secretary, and J. W. Collins as clerk. This was the first Baptist organization of any kind in Texas beyond the few churches. No specific name for the association is mentioned in the minutes of 1840. However, they spoke much of "union" and appealed for "unity." Some called the association "Unity," but in time "Union" was the name that stuck.

The infant association in 1840 adopted a list of eleven brief articles of faith, fifteen rules of decorum ("Brother" was the only title of address permitted), and laid out ambitious plans for ministry. The articles of faith had been "previously ratified by the Churches" initially composing the association, and Baylor introduced a resolution asking "the various Baptist Churches throughout western Texas to examine with prayerful attention the Articles of Faith adopted by this Association, and that they suggest to this body from time to time, such amendments or alterations as they may deem proper and consistent with the Word of God."[13] The authorship of the articles is not indicated, but they bear the stamp of Baylor's hand and resemble somewhat the New Hampshire Baptist Confession adopted seven years earlier. Given the tensions of the time between the missionary party and the anti-missionary Calvinists, it is interesting that the confession says, "We believe in the doctrine of God's sovereignty, and man's free agency as an accountable being. . . . [and] that salvation on these terms [repentance and faith] is freely offered to all."[14] They invited the few churches in "Western Texas" to affiliate with the association, and urged the churches to form temperance societies to stem the "stream of liquid fire" already flowing into Texas.[15] Realizing the importance of a Baptist paper, they recommended the *Baptist Banner and Western Pioneer* of Louisville, and appointed James Huckins to write a monthly column for that paper to give news about Texas. Baylor was appointed "to manage a Book and Tract Depository," to canvas friends in the States to send books and tracts for use in Texas.

Baylor was also assigned to write the "Circular Letter," a custom of associations at the time. In a brief but eloquent style, Baylor wrote:

> BELOVED FRIENDS,—You will perceive by a Resolution in the foregoing minutes that I am required to say a few things to the brethren of the various Baptist Churches. First, then, to those in our Father Land, we would represent our forlorn and destitute condition, and the many trials, and difficulties under which we are laboring. My Christian brethren, we have been enabled to organize a few scattering of Churches in these solitary places. . . . This Association and these Churches will form a nucleus around which we may rally.[16]

Baylor urged Baptists in the "Father Land" to send missionaries. He assured them that, small as their beginnings were, they had made a permanent start and Baptists who sent aid need not fear that their efforts would be wasted. He said, "We also ask you to send us such religious books, tracts, newspapers, and other publications as will instruct, cheer, and comfort us in this land, so far away from those we once loved." He continued, "To the sister Churches and Brethren in western Texas, who have not joined with us in this bond of union, we can only say, come and unite with us, we will meet you with tearful eye, and melting hearts."[17]

In a most revealing comment, Baylor noted that since Baptists in Texas had been "thrown together" from many places, "it could not be expected. . . [that] we could at once harmonize upon all points of doctrine." But though they differed on some matters, Baylor said, "on the great articles of our faith and practice we do not differ as Baptists." In a word of concern and wisdom, he cautioned that "Should our little Churches therefore be tenacious about these non-essentials, they will remain disjoined, and thus broken in fragments they will perish away."[18]

Non-essential or not, the evidence suggests the association struggled for years to maintain doctrinal unity. Their articles of faith set out cardinal Baptist doctrines, along with a strong statement about the autonomy and freedom of each church. At almost every subsequent meeting for many years, some doctrinal issue arose and some change was proposed in the doctrinal statement. Anti-missionism, Campbellism, and Calvinism seem to have caused the most problems. In 1841 T. W. Cox, primary founder and first moderator of the association, was excluded from his church, and from Baptist life, because he had embraced the "Reform" doctrines of Alexander Campbell, founder of the Church of Christ movement. Other concerns which surfaced in the association meetings included: how to protect the churches from renegade ministers, the basis for accepting separated or divorced persons into membership, and how to deal with church members who never attended. Z. N. Morrell, R. E. B. Baylor, James Huckins, and William Tryon were the most influential voices in shaping Baptist theology in early Texas.

At the 1841 meeting six new churches affiliated. The brethren formed a Texas Baptist Mission Society, and for a time Z. N. Morrell, Noah T. Byars and Anderson Buffington served under its auspices. At the 1841 meeting a Texas Baptist Education Society was formed, probably at the suggestion of William Tryon.[19] As a graduate of Mercer University, and a former instructor there, Tryon had a keen appreciation of the value of education. He brought to Texas a dream to establish in the Lone Star Republic a great Baptist university to train both ministers and lay persons for greater usefulness in church and society. Probably the idea for the university preceded the Education Society, and one might have expected plans to develop immediately after 1840.

However, the invasion by the Mexican army under General Woll in 1842 disrupted life in Texas, including church life. The new association did not hold its regular meeting that year, though a called meeting convened at the Mount Gilead church on November 26, 1842, despite "invasion and war." Z. N. Morrell preached the opening sermon, and William Tryon was elected moderator in place of the deposed T. W. Cox. Judge Baylor was continued as corresponding secretary. At this meeting the churches at Gonzales and Plum Grove sent in brief accounts of their founding, and these were appended to the Minutes. A chart shows that in

1842 there were twelve Baptist churches in Texas, with a total membership of 433. That year the churches baptized forty-two new converts,
received thirty-six new members by letter, and excluded eight.[20] James
Huckins wrote the *Circular Letter* for 1842, in which he appealed for more
missionaries for Texas and urged Texas churches to encourage gifted
members to become ministers. In pointing out some of their problems
and appealing for prayer, Huckins wrote:

> A very great majority of our number have been but recently converted;
> they are babes in Christ, young and tender, peculiarly exposed to injury
> and danger, like young plants. . . . And besides, we were all but as yester-
> day strangers to each other, having come from different sections of the
> country, and having brought with us different opinions and prejudices.
> Our ministers too, are few in number; they are young and inexperi-
> enced.[21]

Huckins urged church members to engage in family prayer and Bible
reading. He also cautioned, "Let us be very careful in admitting members
into our churches." A sincere Christian, he said, will not be injured by having membership delayed for a few weeks, but a hypocrite may bring scandal and harm to the church.

From the first, Union Association laid out an aggressive program of
ministry. Unlike the "do nothing" associations of the anti-missionary
group led by Daniel Parker, the missionary Baptists laid plans to plant
churches throughout the area. The Home Mission Society, connected with
the association, at one time sponsored both Z. N. Morrell and Anderson
Buffington to itinerate in "Western Texas." Realizing their need to be
informed, and also to tell their story in the States, the Texas leaders did
what they could to encourage the circulation of Baptist papers in Texas,
primarily the *Baptist Banner* of Kentucky and the *Tennessee Baptist.* They
also sought to obtain tracts, books, and Bible lesson materials for Texas.
This effort was led mostly by Baylor and Huckins, but others assisted.
Plans for a colportage ministry were made early, but took time to come to
fruition. The association also monitored the condition of the churches,
offering counsel on doctrinal and moral issues, and serving as a clearing
house to credential newly arriving ministers. By 1848, the association
reported a total of eighteen churches, with 811 members.[22]

BAYLOR UNIVERSITY

By far the largest undertaking of Texas Baptists in this early period
was the founding of Baylor University. That school was founded by the
Texas Baptist Education Society, a group distinct from but allied with the
Union Baptist Association. This was the first major university in the new
land, founded under the Republic of Texas. It antedates any Baptist convention in the state. The major founder was William Tryon, though he was
ably assisted by Judge Baylor, James Huckins, and Z. N. Morrell.

Due to unsettled conditions the Education Society did not meet in 1842 or 1843. The officers at the 1844 meeting included Baylor as president, Tryon as vice-president, and J. G. Thomas as secretary. Huckins was also a member of the society. All four of these were educated men, Baylor and Thomas as lawyers, Huckins and Tryon as graduates of Baptist universities. At the 1844 meeting of the Education Society Tryon and Baylor proposed the founding of a "literary institution" in Texas, offering both preparatory and collegiate levels of study. The Society approved, voting to "found a Baptist University in Texas, upon a plan so broad that the requirements of existing conditions would be fully met, and that would be susceptible of enlargement and development to meet the demand of all ages to come."[23] The idea of a school was not new; it surfaced as early as 1841, and in 1842 Huckins had discussed the idea of a Baptist school in Montgomery County.

Baylor, Tryon and Thomas were named to a committee to seek a charter. Because of his legal training, Baylor was asked to phrase the charter. At Tryon's home at Hildago Bluff Baylor dictated the proposed charter and Tryon wrote it down. In the first draft Tryon left blank the space for the name. Baylor suggested the name of Tryon, but Tryon demurred for fear that since he had pushed so hard for the school people might think he did it for his own glory. Tryon suggested the name of Baylor, but Baylor objected that he had done nothing worthy of such honor. The charter was presented to the Congress of the Republic of Texas and went through two readings before a name was finalized. Among the names suggested were San Jacinto University and Milam University. However, Kenneth Anderson, vice-president of the Republic, joined in support of Tryon's suggestion and the name of Baylor was written in the final draft of the charter.

The original charter was more general than specific. Clearly Baylor was a Baptist university, founded by Baptists and for Baptists, but it was never narrowly sectarian. The first professor was an Episcopal layman, and the charter did not require that all trustees be Baptist. The ties between Baylor University and Texas Baptists were strong, but the official documents never gave legal ownership and control to any convention. This would have been impossible at the beginning, since the university founded in 1845 preceded the Baptist State Convention (formed 1848) and its successor the Baptist General Convention of Texas (1886). The charter provided that "when any vacancy shall occur, either by death, resignation or otherwise, in the Board of Trustees, such vacancy shall be filled by the Executive Committee of the Texas Baptist Education Society."[24] The new university was located in Independence, though Travis, Shannon Prairie, and Huntsville also bid for the school. With a total offer of $7925.08, Independence easily eclipsed the other bids. The Independence inducement package included one section of land, five head of cattle, one cow and calf, one bay mare, one bale of cotton, twenty days of hauling and $200 in cash.[25] An offer like that could scarcely be declined.

Several factors favored Independence. From its first settlement in the early 1820s as "Cole's Hill," this site had attracted leading citizens. Many thought the state capitol would be located there, or perhaps in nearby Washington-on-the-Brazos and, in fact, for a time this was the case. However, a more immediate factor was the precedent of Independence as the site of a Baptist school. In 1835 Miss Frances Trask of Massachusetts opened a school there which, unfortunately, did not long survive. Judge J. P. Cole, acting for the people of the town, applied to the Congress of the Texas Republic to charter a school in 1837. The charter was granted in June 1837 and Henry Gillette purchased the building which Miss Trask's school had used, and opened Independence Female Academy, a school which also failed to survive. When it appeared they might be out-bid for the proposed university, leaders in Independence sweetened their offer by acquiring the two-story building formerly used by the Academy. This substantial building, with some repairs, provided an immediately available site for classes and gave Independence an additional advantage over other towns.

The very first teacher employed at Baylor University was Henry F. Gillette, an Episcopal layman who had once studied for the priesthood. Gillette was well-known and respected, having taught in the area for several years and boarded with leading Baptist families. He opened classes at Baylor on May 18, 1846, with twenty-four students.

Henry Lea Graves (1813-1881) was elected the first president of Baylor and he arrived on February 4, 1847. At age thirty-four, Graves had excellent background and experience. He was a graduate of the University of North Carolina and the Hamilton Theological Seminary. He served for a time as professor of mathematics at Wake Forest University in North Carolina and was later president of a Baptist school in Georgia. During his presidency at Baylor, Graves also served as pastor of the Independence church. Graves took a leading role in Baptist life in Texas, serving several churches part-time as pastor. He also helped form the Baptist State Convention in 1848 and took a leading role in its work.

The trustees authorized Baylor to open with preparatory level work and add the collegiate level later. It was not until 1854 that Baylor granted its first collegiate degree, to Stephen D. Rowe. In its early years the school was coeducational, with young men and women taught in the same classes by the same teachers. One historian says that early Baylor students "were taught co-educationally, but gradually [the university] drifted, or developed, or evolved, or was rent into two."[26] They began with one name, one faculty, and one building. However, when Rufus C. Burleson succeeded Henry L. Lea as president in 1851, he insisted that the men and women be taught separately. In 1851 a stone building was completed for the Male Department about a mile removed from the older frame building which was designated the Female Department. No end of trouble resulted from this division, to be described later.

The Baylor founders had high hopes but little cash and in its early days the school faced constant financial pressures. Several pastors sought to raise funds for the school, and in 1850 William Tryon was appointed financial agent to raise money in Texas and beyond. In 1847 the trustees faced a debt of $1200 on the president's salary, and $800 for Professor Gillette. The trustees were strongly encouraged to contribute to pay these debts, and individuals like Eli Mercer, Sam Houston, and Judge Baylor gave generously. The first major financial campaign at Baylor was an effort to raise $10,000 as a trust fund to endow the president's salary.

In 1847 the trustees tried a new experiment; they put the entire university under the control of President Graves who would receive all tuition and fees from the students. Graves was to personally choose all the professors, set their salaries, and pay them out of his tuition receipts. Any money left over, after all expenses and teachers were paid, would go to the president as his salary. In effect, he ran the university on commission but, not surprisingly, this plan did not endure.

A Department of Law was added in 1849, with local attorneys R. E. B. Baylor and A. S. Lipscomb offering lectures. The first plan called for lectures in law twice a week, May to December. In 1851 the trustees "reported as inexpedient at present" a proposal to form a theological department.[27] However, they did ask the president to give lectures on theology, and asked G. W. Baines to lecture occasionally on pastoral practice. Though ministerial education was often cited as a major motive for the founding of Baylor, from 1845 to 1850 only two ministerial students entered. They were James H. Stribling and David B. Morrill, both of whom made outstanding contributions later.

NEW RECRUITS

When Z. N. Morrell made his first tour of Texas in 1835 he was not aware of another missionary Baptist preacher in the entire region. Only three preachers were present to form the Union Association in 1840 and for many years it was necessary for each preacher to serve at least three or four churches. However, by 1848 the situation had improved greatly. Annexation to the United States in 1845 increased the floodtide of immigration and brought Baptist preachers as well as lay people. From 1841 the American Baptist Home Mission in New York had sent missionaries to Texas. Increasing tensions caused Baptists North and South to split apart, and the Southern Baptist Convention was formed in 1845. The Home Mission Board of the new SBC took an early interest in Texas and soon sponsored missionaries there. Z. N. Morrell noted that

> In the fall of 1846 the old Union Association received into her bounds a valuable addition of ministers. No ship that ever ploughed the waves between New Orleans and Galveston, I suppose, ever brought at one time a more valuable cargo for Texas than the one that landed Elders J. W. D. Creath, P. B. Chandler, Henry L. Graves and Noah Hill. Elder Graves came, under a call from the Board of Trustees of Baylor University, to take

his position as president of the school. The others came under appoint-ment of the Board of the Southern Baptist Convention, as missionaries.[28]

Rufus C. Burleson was chairman of a committee in 1848 to gather sta-tistics on Texas Baptists. By the next year he listed a total of twenty-nine preachers in the state, of whom twenty were in regular pastorates.[29] Burle-son himself had been in Texas only since 1847. A report at the 1849 meet-ing of the new Baptist State Convention emphasized the need for more recruits. "We believe that at least one hundred Baptist ministers could now be profitably employed, if we had the men and means. There are from three to five, and ten counties in a body, in which there is not a minister of our denomination."[30]

While space does not allow tracing out all these new recruits, perhaps it will do to sketch a few of the newly arriving ministers and laymen.

Joseph Warner Dossey Creath (1803-1881). He of the many names, J. W. D. Creath, cut a big swath in Texas. Born in Virginia, educated at the Virginia Baptist Seminary (now University of Richmond), Creath volun-teered as a missionary to Texas during a session of the Southern Baptist Convention. He arrived in 1846 and served the remainder of his life in the Lone Star State. He preached throughout the state raising funds for Bap-tist projects and forming churches, including those at Beaumont and Cor-pus Christi. In 1851 he was named "general agent" of the Baptist State Convention, precursor of the later office of executive director. He served for almost thirty years, with some interruptions, and helped to define that position for himself and his successors. He traveled throughout Texas on his faithful bay horse, named John the Baptist, and it was said that after a long ride Creath, no matter how weary, would not take a bite of refresh-ment until John the Baptist had been cared for. The only criticism heard of Creath was that at Convention meetings, he often assigned himself to lodge in the more affluent homes, leaving others to much less commodi-ous quarters. This pioneer missionary planted churches and raised funds for church buildings, including the church and parsonage in San Antonio. Creath died on a mission tour while projecting plans for new churches in Abilene, San Angelo, Laredo and El Paso. He died, it was said, with the cry, "On to El Paso!"[31] His name is memorialized in the Creath-Brazos Baptist Association in Central Texas.

Oliver Hazard Perry Garrett (1816-1886). Garrett was a layman who rendered valuable service to Texas Baptists. Reared on a South Carolina farm, he received a good education for the times. As a youth he heard about the Battle of San Jacinto along with glowing reports of the new land. In 1838 at age twenty-two he set out on horseback for Texas, arriving at Independence in November of that year. After returning to South Caro-lina, he married his cousin Nancy, daughter of Reverend Hosea Garrett. Young "Perry" Garrett, with his new wife and father-in-law returned to Texas and bought land near Chappell Hill in Washington County. He surveyed and laid out the present town of Brenham, and held office as county surveyor for some years. He later served as county judge. He sided with Sam Houston against secession, but when secession came he busied himself in supplying the Confederate troops and caring for soldiers' families. He was among those deposed by Federal forces in 1868 as "an impediment to reconstruction."[32]

Garrett was converted at age seventeen and proved a faithful Baptist for the remainder of his life. He was a deacon in his church, served as church clerk, and was one of the laymen present at the formation of the Union Baptist Association in 1840. He was active in Sunday School work, and was a generous contributor to his church. In 1859 he was elected Recording Secretary of the Baptist State Convention, which post he held until consolidation. One who knew him well said, "He was not brilliant, nor specially gifted in any one thing, yet he was a man of good judgment. . . . He is a part of the history of his denomination in Texas."[33]

Robert H. Taliaferro (1824-1875) attended the Western Theological Seminary in Covington, Kentucky, and came to Texas in 1847 to be pastor at Galveston. He preached among the Choctaws for a year or two, then returned to Austin. He preached throughout central Texas, including Webberville, Austin, Bastrop, and Round Rock. He served as chaplain in the Texas Senate for three terms. He was perhaps influential in the conversion of Sam Houston, for at one of his services Houston came forward for prayer. Taliaferro worked with G. W. Baines for a time at the first Texas Baptist paper, where he developed a reputation as a good writer. He was also known as a good preacher. He wrote his sermons in full, but preached them without notes. Pastors often invited him to preach revivals, but some said it was not easy to follow him in the pulpit after the people had heard his excellent sermons.

BAPTIST STATE CONVENTION

Baptist churches in Texas were small in the 1840s but their plans were big. By the mid-1840s their one tiny association had appointed missionaries to western Texas. In 1843 the Sabine Association was formed in East Texas. This was the second such body in the state, but others followed in short order. The Colorado Association was formed in 1847, affiliating mostly churches west of the Colorado River in what was then called "Western Texas." When the Sabine Association turned anti-missionary in 1847, four of its missionary churches withdrew to form the Eastern Missionary Association. In 1848 three more associations were added: Trinity River, Soda Lake, and Red River.[34]

These associations tried to send missionaries to work in their regions, but their resources were small. As the churches and associations multiplied, there grew a desire for a more general organization that would combine their efforts. In 1847 the Union Association adopted the following statement: "Resolved, That the Corresponding Secretary be, and hereby is, instructed to correspond with the several Associations in this state, and with as many of the Churches as it is convenient, in order to ascertain their views and wishes in regard to the formation of a Baptist State Convention."[35]

State conventions were still quite new among Baptists at this time. South Carolina in 1821 formed the very first state convention, followed by Georgia in 1822. By the mid-1830s several other southern states had Baptist state conventions, but some languished because of rivalry between strong associations and the new state bodies. The main purposes of the state conventions were to promote church planting in their area and to strengthen Christian education. It is not surprising that Texas Baptists, gathered as they were from several states, should seek to reduplicate the structures they had known earlier.

The response to the Union Association enquiry was overwhelmingly favorable, and representatives from twenty-two churches met on September 8, 1848, at the Antioch church at Anderson, Grimes County, "for the purpose of organizing a Baptist State Convention."[36]

Judge Baylor presided at the organizational meeting, and J. G. Thomas was elected secretary. Henry L. Graves, president of Baylor University, was elected the first convention president, with J. W. D. Creath, Hosea Garrett, and James Huckins as vice-presidents. Rufus C. Burleson, then pastor of the First Baptist Church of Houston, was chosen corresponding secretary and J. W. Barnes was named treasurer.[37] The constitution of the new body said, "The objects of this convention shall be Missionary and Educational, the promotion of harmony of feeling and concert of action in our denomination, and the organization of a system of operative measures to promote the interest generally, of the Redeemer's Kingdom within this state."

The 1848 constitution says clearly that "The convention shall be composed, only of members of Baptist churches in good standing." There is no hint that the *churches* as such joined the convention, a point which became a bone of contention a generation later in the Hayden controversy. Any member in good standing in one of the affiliated churches could be a voting member of the convention upon payment of $5.00 a year, or a life member upon payment of $25.00 at one time. Messengers could come from churches, associations, or mission societies on the basis of one messenger for each $5.00 contributed. Churches that were affiliated with one of the associations could be represented in the new BSC even without contribution. Visiting brethren were invited to have voice but not vote in convention sessions.

The convention heard discussion about founding a Baptist paper in Texas, but the committee appointed to consider the matter reported that they felt it was "impractical to start a denominational paper in Texas at this time." Instead, they recommended that Texans continue to read Baptist papers coming in from neighboring states. The convention went on record in favor of foreign and home missions, and distribution of Bibles and religious literature in Texas. Noah T. Hill chaired a committee to bring a report on the "religious condition of the Black Population," and R. C. Burleson was asked to "use all diligence in ascertaining the number of Baptists and Baptist churches in this State."

Hill's report on the slave population noted that slavery had recently become a controversial subject, but concluded that "we religiously believe that slavery is amply sustained by the bible."[38] The report also affirms that the coming of slaves to America was part of God's providence to bring Africans into contact with the gospel, and called for efforts to send black missionaries back to Africa. Churches and pastors were urged to make every effort to evangelize the blacks, and that report suggested "sending among them suitable missionaries to break the bread of eternal life." The report also noted that the slaves were unusually responsive to the gospel and predicted that further witness among them would bear good fruit.

The first constitution specified that the convention should annually elect a Board of Directors, of not less than twenty members, to meet quarterly or more often as needed. This Board had power to act for the convention between sessions, and specifically "The board of directors shall have the exclusive power of appointing agents and missionaries, and ordering the disbursement of money in the recess of the convention."[39] Later this was modified to make the Board more amenable to the convention in their decisions.

Since Baptist state conventions were new, some churches apparently feared they might forfeit some local freedom by affiliation. The convention addressed this concern by including in the constitution the following strong statement: "The convention shall never possess a single attribute of power or authority over any church or association. It absolutely and forever disclaims any right of any kind, hereby avowing that cardinal principle that every church is sovereign and independent."[40] This reassurance probably addressed anxieties raised by both the Alexander Campbell and Daniel Parker movements in early Texas, both of which had their doubts about the value and risks of church connectionalism.

SUMMARY

The 1840s provided a time of emerging structures for Texas Baptists. They formed their first association in 1840, and by the end of the decade several others followed. They formed Baylor University in 1845, and the Baptist State Convention in 1848. Despite their small beginnings, Texas Baptists had big plans, and by mid-century they had organizational structures in place to put those plans into effect.

CHAPTER 4

PROGRESS AMIDST PROBLEMS, 1848–1868

"OF THE INCREASE of his government and peace there shall be no end." This optimistic verse from Isaiah 9:7 provided the upbeat theme for Z. N. Morrell's introductory sermon at the formation of the Baptist State Convention at Anderson on September 8, 1848. The committee had named Henry L. Graves, president of Baylor University, to preach the opening sermon, with Noah T. Hill as alternate. For some reason, both men refused to preach and at the last minute Morrell agreed to step in since, he said, he had no reputation to risk. Morrell, the "cane-brake preacher," was probably a better choice anyway. If any of the fifty-five men from twenty-two churches who had gathered at Anderson knew about increase, it was Morrell. A dozen years earlier he had been the only missionary Baptist preacher in the state, with no Baptist church within hundreds of miles.

As the tall Tennessee pioneer surveyed his impressive crowd, he could have reflected on the increase that had already taken place. From ground zero, in a dozen years they now had a total of thirty-five churches and four associations at work in the Lone Star State. The much respected R. E. B. Baylor was called to the chair to convene the meeting, and a committee was named to frame a constitution. Henry L. Graves, despite his reluctance to preach, was elected the first president, and J. W. D. Creath, Hosea Garrett, and James Huckins were elected vice-presidents. Rufus C. Burleson was elected the first Corresponding Secretary; J. G. Thomas, Recording Secretary; and J. W. Barnes, Treasurer. This may have been a day of small beginnings, but these were no small plans. The men who formed the Baptist State Convention (BSC) planned for more increase to come. Already they had formed a university, a Home Mission Society, an Educational Society, and they laid plans for a Baptist paper, a book depository to distribute Christian literature, and aggressive mission work among the

44

new settlers pouring in, and among the black population, the Germans in central Texas, and the Mexicans in San Antonio and along the border.

The twenty years between formation of the Baptist State Convention (1848) and formation of a rival convention in East Texas (1868) helped set the pattern for Texas Baptists for years to come. During these early years, the Baptists established a working denomination that laid the foundations for the Baptist empire that later developed in Texas. The Baptist State Convention (BSC) developed methods of cooperative missionary work with local associations and the Home Mission Board of the Southern Baptist Convention that still endure. The BSC revised its constitution, fine-tuned its relationships with associations, modified its financial basis of operation and learned, sometimes the hard way, what missionary methods would work or would not.

During these years the new state faced a deluge of immigration from the older states and from Europe which taxed the economic and social fabric. The Civil War (1861-1865) wrecked the Texas economy by cutting off the market for cotton, and after the war lack of workers for the labor-intensive crops hampered economic recovery. The war almost depopulated some areas, as most men were away in the army and, for Texas, the Reconstruction era brought more uncertainty, bitterness, and hardship than did the war itself.

The primary institution fostered by Texas Baptists, Baylor University at Independence, grew strong during the two decades covered by this chapter. The university faced its own internal crisis over the role of its president and the administrative relationship of the male and female departments of the school. This turf dispute ultimately led to a schism in which the president and most of the male faculty and students transferred to Waco University. Though decimated by this withdrawal, and pressed by the economic hardships of the times, Baylor University came through the war in surprisingly good condition.

Ambitious plans and heroic efforts marked the work of the BSC during these formative years. The Convention of 1848 was formed for missionary and educational purposes, and the brethren took a broad definition of these. Scores of new churches emerged and when there were enough of these, and sometimes before, they formed new associations. Among the flood of new immigrants were numerous Baptist families and not a few preachers, and these were quickly integrated into church life in the new area. The BSC sponsored ethnic missions, especially among Germans, Mexicans and Indians, and they labored intensively, if not always successfully, among the burgeoning slave population. After years of planning, Baptists launched their own newspaper the *Texas Baptist* in 1855, succeeded by the *Texas Baptist Herald* a decade later. They urged the formation of Sunday Schools in every church, and made arrangements to obtain suitable lesson study material for them. They established a fund to distribute religious books in Texas, and raised money to provide Baylor scholarships for ministerial students.

The infant state convention faced its own internal tensions during these years. With a dozen equally deserving locations for every missionary appointed, some areas were bound to feel neglected. Baptists east of the Trinity came to feel that the BSC favored the western areas in missionary work, and the Convention leaders' fascination with Baylor University prevented them from lending a helping hand, or even an encouraging word, to Baptist schools in East Texas. This led to tensions as early as 1851, to rival associations by 1855, and a rival state convention in 1868.

NEW STRUCTURE, NEW DIRECTIONS

Along with hope, perhaps the predominant emotion at Anderson in 1848 was *enthusiasm.* Though they had little enough to work with, the minutes of their initial meeting reflect what one called a "Caleb spirit," a "can-do" enthusiasm undaunted by the challenge ahead. In those days, convention messengers did not book into hotels; they stayed in homes of families in the area, families of all denominations and none. They usually convened on Friday or Saturday, and one of the first matters of business was to finalize plans for worship on the upcoming Sunday. Preachers would be appointed not only for the Baptist church, but also for other churches in town, especially Methodist and Presbyterian, who would also invite one or more of the Baptist delegates to fill their pulpits. The people of these other denominations not only helped provide lodging for the visitors, but frequently contributed to the Baptist offerings for home missions and the promotion of union Sunday Schools. In some cases where the host church had no building of its own, the BSC convened in a Methodist church or the local Masonic Lodge hall. Observance of the Lord's Supper was a regular feature of the annual convention gathering. Records for 1854, for example, note that "a very large number of Baptists from different parts of the State, met and communed together around the Sacramental Board."[1]

The Baptists raised money at the convention meetings by having some brother preach on an area of ministry, like missions, and then taking an offering on the spot. Some gave cash, while others gave in personal pledges, or gave pledges which they later asked their churches to honor. Pastors were urged to preach periodically on causes sponsored by the convention, take up offerings and forward them to the treasurer. The first offerings of record in the new convention were for missions; in 1849 R. H. Taliaferro preached a sermon on foreign missions and raised an offering of $11.90 for the China Missions, and a black church sent in $11.50 for missions in Africa.[2] A sermon by Huckins at the same meeting raised $15.15 for education.

The committees appointed at the convention sessions reveal the range of concerns. The first meeting in 1848 saw committees on Education, Printing of Minutes, Foreign Missions, Home Missions, Finance, Distribution of Bibles and Religious Books, and Religious Conditions among the Black Population. In later years were added committees on the State of Religion in Texas, Indian Missions, German Missions, Mexican

Missions, Sabbath School Promotion, Temperance, Baylor University, Ministerial Education, and, years later, Obituaries. Occasionally there would be ad hoc committees to deal with some specific concern. The pattern called for the committees to be appointed early, and to report a day or two later at the same session. These committees reveal a wide range of concerns, and while their reports were often more talk than action they at least kept these ministry concerns before the people.

The original BSC constitution provided for financial rather than representative membership. A person could become a voting Annual Member by the payment of $5, and a gift of $25 at one time conferred Life Membership.[3] Some pastors paid their own, and others were given memberships by appreciative laymen. This financial basis of membership later led to tensions with people who were offended by the perceived elitism of buying membership, and who objected that some worthy individuals and churches were shut out of participation for lack of money. For years the Convention listed its life members in three categories: Elders (pastors), Brethren, and Sisters. A surprisingly large number of sisters held Life Memberships, establishing a precedent for women's support of Baptist mission work in Texas which has never wavered. However, no women show up in BSC records; no woman served on a committee, led a prayer, or spoke before the body. A few times it was pointed out that the Sisters might be effective in Sunday School work, but even that suggestion seemed to elicit little enthusiasm.

In addition to its officers, the convention annually elected a Board of Directors, not less than twenty members in the early years but more later. For a people professing democracy, this Board had unprecedented powers. Without consent or even consultation, the Board could receive and disburse funds, buy and sell property, appoint missionaries and set their salaries, launch new ministry programs, and obligate the convention financially. The convention heard reports and offered resolutions, but the Board made decisions. In time, some felt the Board should be more amenable to the voice of the Convention and the constitution was revised accordingly. On one thing the original constitution was crystal clear, and that has not changed: the BSC had no control over the local churches, and desired none.

A CHALLENGING TASK

By far the most pressing priority for the new Convention was to evangelize the vast territory lying about them. At the first meeting in 1848 the BSC adopted a report which said, "Here is presented to us a field, the condition and claims of which are amply sufficient to engage our anxious solicitude, and our most efficient exertions. . . . a field of vast extent, which is attracting the admiration of the world, and is being rapidly peopled from every quarter of our Union, and various other countries."[4] The next year J. W. D. Creath, who got about the state and knew conditions, said "the destitution is very great within our new and constantly growing State. . . . We believe that at least one hundred Baptist ministers could now be profitably employed, if we had the men and means. There are from three to five, and ten counties in a body, in which there is not a minister of our denomination."[5] Almost every meeting heard some version of this description of the challenges of the Texas field. As floods of new settlers poured in, new towns and villages emerged overnight, most of them with no Baptist witness. From the Sabine in the East, to the Red in the North, and beyond the Brazos and Colorado, new challenges appeared daily. Most pastors served from two to as many as six different churches, which meant that practically no Baptist church had preaching every Sunday. The Convention was besieged by "Macedonian calls" for help, most of which they could not answer.

Instead of the hundred they needed, the BSC appointed three or four missionaries a year, and sometimes five or six. The Board of Directors considered the calls, tallied their resources, and appointed missionaries for a year, or often for only a few months. The missionaries were urged to raise at least part of their support among people with whom they worked. The life of a pioneer missionary was not easy. In 1856 Noah T. Byars described his work in western Texas among both whites and Indians, and concluded, "I am laboring on the extreme frontier, and among the heathen, where it is impossible to raise money, and my salary is entirely inadequate, and I have not received my pay, small as it is, for the last quarter. Pray for me."[6] In the 1850s hostile Indians still represented a danger in western outposts like Austin and Waco, but by the end of the Civil War most of the Comanches and Apaches were pushed further west and smaller tribes had been to some extent pacified.

New churches led to new associations. J. M. Carroll notes that between 1846 and 1860 Baptists in Texas formed over five hundred new churches and twenty-four new associations, not counting the Union and Sabine associations which were formed earlier.[7] Just to list some of these new church groupings will show not only the vast growth, but also the geographical distribution of Texas Baptists at that time. Though many of the names have since changed due to expansion or consolidation, Carroll lists the Colorado Association (1847); Eastern Missionary (1847, formed from the breakup of the Sabine); Trinity River (1848); Soda Lake (1848, from parts of the Eastern); Red River (1848); Elm Fork (1849); Eastern Texas (1849, later called Central); Cherokee (1851); Bethlehem (1852); Sister Grove (1853); Judson (1853); West Fork (1855); Little River (1855); Rehobeth (1856); Austin (1857); Mt. Zion (1857); Richland (1858); Tryon (1858); Leon River (1858); Saline (1858); Brazos River (1858); San Antonio River (1858); San Marcos (1858); New Bethlehem (1860); Waco (1860). Thus by 1860 Texas Baptists had churches and associations scattered throughout the state, except the far west. And that would come: the intrepid pioneer J. W. D. Creath died, crying "On to El Paso!"[8] In 1868, the Convention listed the names of 355 known Baptist preachers in Texas, but estimated there might be at least 200 more whose names were not on the list.[9] This compares with only twenty-four known Baptist preachers in Texas in 1849, of whom twenty were pastors.[10]

In its missionary work, the BSC established partnerships with the associations and also with the Home Mission Board (then located in Marion, Alabama). Missionaries might be appointed by the Convention, or by an association. Several missionaries were jointly supported by the Convention and an association, the Convention and the Home Mission Board, or two or more associations together. This early example of cooperative missions has continued in some form to the present. The BSC often expressed its gratitude to the HMB, which by the late 1850s had more home missionaries in Texas than in any other state. By the 1860s some associations were disappointed with the BSC, feeling they did not get their share of mission appointees. For a time, the state convention experimented with the idea of the associations appointing their own missionaries, but sending the money for their support through the convention. This plan reduced the convention largely to a clearing house for associational missions and did not long continue.

During the 1850s many of the Texas churches experienced great revivals. This was especially the case at Independence, where in 1854 Rufus C. Burleson, pastor of the church and president of Baylor University, preached in a revival that saw twenty-one new converts presented for baptism. One of these converts was U.S. Senator Sam Houston, former president and later governor of Texas. Probably Burleson never baptized a more famous convert. In 1840 Houston had married Margaret Moffette "Maggie" Lea of Alabama, a devout Baptist who is credited with helping Houston straighten out his life. Miss Lea was also a friend of R. E. B. Baylor, and Baylor escorted her on at least one social occasion in Alabama. He is also credited with saving her from drowning in the Alabama River.[11] In Washington, the Houstons regularly attended a Baptist church under the pastorate of G. W. Samson. Houston considered joining that church, but decided instead to make his public confession of faith back in Texas.[12] He came forward during the revival at the Independence church and affirmed his faith in Christ in response to a few simple questions. He was baptized on November 19, 1854, at age sixty-three.

The baptism of a United States Senator attracted attention, and some mischief. The usual place of baptism for the Independence church was Kountz Creek, north of town, where a secluded pool had been carved out for that purpose. However, as a prank neighborhood boys filled that pool with tree branches and other debris. Learning of this, Burleson said, "Very well. I will outgeneral these mischievous boys from the country and baptize the General in Little Rocky."[13] Before he entered the water, Houston was given opportunity to put away his fine leather wallet, but he declined, insisting that his wallet be baptized too. In this beautiful creek, with clear water running over limestone which gave Little Rocky its name, and with the banks lined by stately oak trees, one of the greatest religious leaders of early Texas baptized the greatest political leader of early Texas, wallet and all.

Houston proved a faithful church member. He attended church and prayer meetings, regularly led in public prayer, gave generously to the church and to Baylor University, and served on Baylor's Board of Advisors. He attended sessions of the Baptist State Convention, of which he was a life member by virtue of his contributions, and he served on the convention's Board of Directors. He also served on Convention committees, especially those dealing with missions to the Indians, and he who had once been known as "Big Drunk" became a notable temperance lecturer. Z. N. Morrell visited Houston at his Huntsville home a few days before the General's death, and the two old men who had done more than most to create the Lone Star State spoke feelingly of their abiding faith in Christ.

MINISTRY CONCERNS

By its own description, the Baptist State Convention was formed for *missionary* and *educational* purposes, but these were broadly defined. Over the years the body engaged in a number of ministries, and as Baptists multiplied in Texas the ministry projects tended to become more numerous and more complex. Hardly a spiritual need arose but that Texas Baptists attempted to address it. This section will briefly survey the highlights of some of their ministries in the period 1848-1868.

Foreign Missions. Every session of the BSC had a committee on foreign missions, with a lengthy report printed in the minutes. These reports described work being done by the American Baptist Missionary Union (North) and the Foreign Mission Board (South), advocated foreign missions, cited Scripture for foreign missions, often scolded Texas Baptists for their meager support, and urged every pastor to preach on foreign missions and every church to take offerings for that cause. Z. N. Morrell set the tone in his 1848 report that "we highly approve" of foreign missions, but right now cannot offer much more than best wishes. Among early Texas Baptists, *verbal* support for foreign missions was great; *financial* support was limited. In 1857 the BSC heard sermons on both foreign and home missions, and raised $22.30 for the former and over $1,000 for the latter.[14] A report presented by one of the pastors said, "Your committee observes that a report on Foreign Missions has been written every year, and yet no special pains has [sic] been taken to raise funds for this portion of the great missionary work."[15]

James B. Taylor, head of the Foreign Mission Board in Richmond, often wrote to Texas Baptists, and sometimes made personal visits to the state promoting foreign missions. His correspondence and visits were always received with great appreciation. Taylor urged the pastors to preach missionary sermons, raise missionary offerings, and perhaps to form a foreign missionary society auxiliary to the state convention. He wrote, "While they [Texas Baptists] prosecute their plans for the supply of destitution within their own limits, I am satisfied it will be both wise and right, to adopt a systematic policy, affecting the spiritual welfare of the heathen in

Pagan Lands . . . who are sinking unpitied into perdition."[16] Taylor also made the point, heard often in Baptist life, that generous support of *foreign* missions will inevitably lead to greater prosperity in *home* missions.

However, the overwhelming needs at home could not be ignored. Surrounded by multitudes who had not heard the gospel, by countless families with no Bible, with thousands of children who had scarcely heard of Jesus, with new towns and villages from Galveston to Dallas with no Baptist voice, and thousands of black slaves who were unevangelized, German immigrants, Mexicans who were nominal Catholics but were open to the evangelical gospel, and Indians who were beginning to show a glimmer of interest in Christianity, Texas Baptists could not stretch their limited resources much beyond their own borders. They felt they had a window of opportunity, which might not long remain open, and they must seize the moment to evangelize Texas. They also made the point, and not for the last time, that effective home missions will in the long run make possible more extensive foreign missions.

Sabbath Schools. When the Baptist State Convention was formed in 1848, Sunday Schools among Baptists were few. The Sunday School in America was new, and that alone was enough reason for some Baptists to oppose it. Only sixteen years before the BSC was formed, a group of Baptists in Maryland gave a blistering attack against the new-fangled "human invention" of Sunday School which, they said, was at best a waste of time and at worst was an interference with the work of the Holy Spirit.[17]

Even so, every year the BSC heard a report urging every church to form a Sunday School. There is no evidence they gave much attention to the subject between conventions. It appears the Sunday School committee was appointed at the convention, presented a report two days later largely copied from the year before, and that was it. As we saw in a previous chapter, Thomas J. Pilgrim formed the first Sunday School in Texas at San Felipe in 1829, but the movement was slow to catch on. In 1868 the two largest Sunday Schools in Texas were at Waco, with 190 pupils and nineteen teachers, and at Brenham, with 185 pupils and fifteen teachers. In 1873 there were reported in all of Texas only ninety-one Baptist Sunday Schools, with 5,707 pupils and 716 teachers.[18]

Conditions in Texas before the Civil War did not favor the Sunday School movement. Most Baptist churches had preaching only once or, at most, twice a month and on their "vacant" days (when no preacher was available) most churches did not meet at all. In 1868 only two Texas Baptist churches had "full-time" pastors, San Antonio and Jefferson. Even the First Baptist Church of Dallas began as a "quarter-time" church, with preaching one Sunday a month by a non-resident pastor who rode in one Sunday a month from McKinney.[19] Even so, after three years the Dallas church formed a Sunday School which soon grew to an enrollment of twenty. Many churches had no building, or a one-room structure that did not lend itself to Bible classes. The few Sunday Schools that did exist were mostly on the "Union" plan, which included children from all denominations. The Union literature, readily available from the American Sunday

School Union, glossed over such Baptist distinctives as baptism of believers by immersion in order to remain acceptable to the other churches. There were few available teachers, and one cannot escape the conclusion that most of the pastors, burdened as they were by other duties, simply did not see the importance of Sunday Schools. Forming a Sunday School would oblige the church to meet every Sunday, pastor or no. Facing a choice of attending church one Sunday a month or four, no doubt many chose the former. On the positive side, some pastors pointed out that teaching the young would prepare them for conversion, would spiritually revitalize churches, and would provide a reservoir of church leaders for the future. They also pointed out that a regular Sunday School might encourage churches to meet every Sunday and have full-time preaching.

By 1858 the BSC recommended that "every church take the subject of Sabbath School instruction directly under its own supervision," that is, drop the idea of inter-denominational Union schools in favor of distinctly Baptist schools.[20] The same report laments the lack of distinctly Baptist study materials. They overlooked, or perhaps did not know about, excellent Baptist materials from the American Baptist Publication Society in Philadelphia and the Southern Baptist Publication Society in Charleston. They did later recommend materials from the Southern Baptist Sunday School Union, formed by J. R. Graves in Memphis as a private business venture. They also mentioned the "Bible question books" issued by Baron Stowe of Boston and A. C. Dayton, a Landmark leader in Nashville.

Another handicap to early Sunday Schools was their plan to assemble an extensive church library as a basis for Sunday School study. However commendable that might be, most churches had neither resources nor inclination to acquire such a library, though a depository to supply such books operated for a time in Bryan.

Prospects for the Sunday Schools improved greatly in 1865, when leaders of the Union Association called a meeting which resulted in formation of a Texas Baptist Sunday School Convention. Their aggressive promotion, greater availability of literature, and later the enlistment of influential leaders like B. H. Carroll of Waco and Major W. E. Penn of Jefferson helped turn the tide.

Ministry with Ethnic Groups. From the first, Texas had a various population made up of many races and nationalities. True to its mission statement, the BSC attempted to share the gospel with all these groups, in their own language where possible. By 1853 Baylor University included studies in German and Spanish to facilitate witness among these groups.

Indians. Of course, Indians made up the original "ethnic group" of Texas. In the early days pioneers like "Wildcat" Morrell probably spent more time fighting Indians than converting them. However, as hostilities diminished, the BSC sent missionaries to preach among the tribes. In Texas, as elsewhere, missions to the Indians was largely a story of noble motivation, heroic effort, and meager results. The fact that several tribes came out in favor of the Confederacy during the Civil War seemed to stimulate the BSC to greater missionary effort among them, and they rejoiced that "the faithful Buckner is still at his post, laboring for them."[21]

African-Americans. While some send missionaries to Africa, Texas Baptist leaders point out that they have Africa in their midst. When Texas was admitted to the Federal Union, and the land was found suitable for cotton cultivation, plantation owners from the South migrated to Texas in numbers, and they brought their slaves with them. They were so numerous that some thought Texas would soon become the "Empire State" of American slavery. Already by 1856, it was reported that Texas had over 40,000 slaves, some brought directly from Africa.[22] One of the earliest recorded slave conversions occurred in 1846 at Leona where Z. N. Morrell had just formed a church. "A very remarkable negro boy" named Jerry [no last name given] professed conversion and asked for baptism. After getting his master's approval, as required, Jerry gave his testimony before the church and, Morrell says, convinced the people "that he not only had a soul, but that his spirit had been moved by the power of God. I baptized him with the others."[23] The Colorado Association offered the judgment that black churches should remain under the leadership of whites for, they said, the blacks "did not yet possess sufficient intelligence and education to keep the doctrines and ordinances of God's word pure and unmixed with human error, when unaided by whites." When the First Colored Baptist Church of Houston applied to affiliate with the Union Association they were first required to elect a moderator and clerk from the white First Baptist Church.[24]

Each year the Convention heard a report on "Conditions Among the Colored Population," and some of those reports seem shocking today. Amidst evidence of genuine spiritual concern, and efforts to evangelize the slaves, one finds also prejudice, racism, and what appears today as incredible misunderstanding. Many Texas Baptists interpreted slavery as God's blessings for the Africans in bringing them out of their native superstition and into contact with the gospel. Like Joseph who was sold into slavery in order to deliver his brethren, God intended slavery for the African's salvation. With a curious view of history, the 1856 report says the original motive for slavery was not economic but religious, to bring the slaves to conversion, that slavery was basically a missionary venture. J. A. Kimball, who edited the *Texas Baptist* briefly, probably expressed the views of many Texas Baptists when he wrote that "the black man is intended by God to be the servant of the white man."[25]

Arrangements for preaching to the slaves varied. Some pastors preached to slaves on Sunday afternoon, and many owners (even non-Christian owners) encouraged this. Some slaves met with the white congregation in segregated sections. Some black churches had white pastors, and a few had black pastors under white supervision. The BSC appointed one or two missionaries, notably Noah Hill and Anderson Buffington, to itinerate among the slave communities, preaching as they had opportunity. The Convention noted in 1856, however, that "We employ none but discreet, *pious* and tried men [as missionaries to the blacks]—one wrong step might impede our cause for half a century—men who will *instruct,* and *not* merely excite the passions of this excitable population."[26] That same report complains of "the fanatical, the blinded Abolitionist" who has, in their words, "become the tool of Satan to produce discord and disunion." While recommending evangelism and oral instruction, the BSC said, "We do not recommend the plan of teaching them [slaves] to read under existing circumstances."[27] Instead, it was recommended that they be taught that slavery is biblical, that masters are the slaves' natural protectors, and they are better off in slavery than in freedom. Of this last, the whites had apparently convinced themselves, for they said "their [the slaves'] physical condition in the state of servitude in our midst is fully equal, if not superior to that of any other mere operatives [the least skilled manual laborers] on the face of the earth."[28]

After the war, Baptists tried to adjust to the new conditions. They still recommended evangelism among the blacks, but were less confident of the results. "The religious condition of the African race in our country, is truly deplorable," they said, and "The prospects for their moral elevation are gloomy. They are not much inclined to hearken to white ministers; and there are but very few of their own color competent to instruct them in pure religion." They urged continued efforts to reach the freedmen with the gospel, but said "We can suggest no definite plan, as the negroes are in a transition state."[29] J. W. D. Creath summed it up best: What methods can we find to reach the Africans with the gospel? "On this subject we greatly desire light."

Germans. Conditions in Europe in the mid-nineteenth century encouraged emigration, and Texas provided an inviting field. Some Germans came with Austin's colony, and several ventures led by German nobles settled large numbers from the Rhine to the Brazos, though their grandiose plans to create a "New Germany" in Texas never panned out.[30] Baron Bastrop settled a group in the town that still bears his name. Other settlements emerged at Industry, New Braunfels, Castroville, Fredericksburg, and Brenham. Some of the German settlers were Lutheran or Catholic, but most were unchurched; records of the BSC persist in referring to them as the "infidel Germans." Whether coming to Texas individually or as part of one of the large settlement ventures, most Germans congregated in their own communities where they maintained their language, practiced their frugal agricultural methods, and remained impervious to assimilation into Anglo cultural or religious life. Most of the Germans did not support Texas in the Civil War, which further distanced them from the Baptists.

In 1855 the Colorado Association attempted to find a missionary "for our benighted German population." The BSC also in 1855, unable to find a German-speaking missionary, set aside $50 for literature to distribute among the Germans. The *Texas Baptist* reported that Martin Marx arrived from Germany in 1855, and immediately sought support to establish a Baptist mission among the 3,000 German inhabitants of New Braunfels. It was reported that Marx had been baptized by the great Johann Oncken, pioneer founder of Baptist work in Germany and much of Europe. Marx (or whatever his real name was) proved to be a fraud and the mission ended ingloriously. Among the German immigrants were a few Baptists, mostly from the Oncken tradition. In 1855 a Prussian pastor, T. Straube, wrote to the Baptist ministers of Goliad that eleven of his most faithful members had migrated to that area, earnestly requesting the Texas Baptists "to extend your spiritual care and brotherly love to these dear friends."[31] Pastor Straube later determined to join his flock in Texas, but his ship was lost at sea. By 1859 it was estimated that Texas had at least 50,000 German settlers.[32]

The conversion of Frank Kiefer was a turning point for witness among the Germans. As a youth, Kiefer came to Texas on his own and set up a confectionary shop in Independence. Of course, in this "Baptist Jerusalem," he could not avoid contact with the Baptists. A Baylor professor invited young Kiefer to Sunday School, and he was converted under the preaching of Rufus C. Burleson, who did so much to encourage early witness among the German population. Kiefer enrolled in Baylor University and became fluent in English as well as in his native German. After graduating from Baylor with honors, he attended the state medical school in Galveston and earned his medical degree. Kiefer earned his livelihood as a physician, but he also served as an evangelist. He was appointed by the BSC and preached widely among both Germans and Anglos, and greatly increased the awareness and interest in German missions. He was also appointed for a time by the Union Association. In later years Kiefer served as medical examiner at Roby, in Fisher County.

The first German Baptist church was Ebenezer, near Brenham, formed in 1861 with about thirty members. The Ebenezer church, led by Kiefer, affiliated with the BSC, but later churches formed their own conference and eventually affiliated with the North American Baptist Conference, German Baptists in the North. F. J. Gleiss arrived from Germany in 1854, and was converted in Methodist revival at Cuero. After some time as a Methodist preacher, Gleiss became a Baptist under the influence of Frank Kiefer. Gleiss formed a church in the German community at Cedar Hill and served as its pastor.

One of the laymen in the Cedar Hill church was William Schmeltekopf, head of a leading family among the German Baptists that would figure prominently in Texas Baptist history. William's son Henry later joined the German Baptist Church near Kyle, where he married Mary Heidenreich. Their son Emil married Ruth Shaub, a Baptist from Gatesville who had come to Kyle to care for a sick relative, and they were active in the Kyle German Baptist Church. Their sons, E. Edward and Robert, grew up and were converted in the Kyle German Baptist Church and both became Texas Baptist pastors. Ed Schmeltekopf served as pastor of FBC, Burleson for nineteen years, and since 1980 has been associate executive director of the Executive Board for Texas Baptists. A third son, Don, is an administrator at Baylor University.[33]

Baptists also sought to witness among the Swedes and Czechs, but since these groups were small, insular, and not overly inclined to evangelical religion these efforts came to little.

Mexicans. The Mexicans were in Texas before the Anglos, and after the hostilities of the wars with Mexico simmered down the Texas Baptists attempted to witness among this large population. In the early days, local associations did more work among the Mexicans than did the state convention. The Mexican population was estimated at 5,000 in 1848.[34]

Pioneer preachers among the Mexicans in Texas include James Hickey, J. W. D. Creath, John O. Westbrook, and W. D. Powell. Hickey, born in Ireland, migrated to America where he did mission work in various states. Exactly when he came to Texas is unknown, but he became interested in Mexican missions and learned Spanish in order to witness in Brownsville, where he won a number of converts. The First Baptist Church, San Antonio was formed in 1861 and included Mexican members, including Angela Maria de Jesus Navarro, daughter of Jose Antonio Navarro, the famous hero of the Alamo. In that same year Creath was appointed as a missionary to Mexican people in Texas. The work of Westbrook and Powell came later and will be recounted in a later chapter.

Temperance. Baptists in the nineteenth century abhorred drunkenness, but allowed a moderate use of alcoholic beverages. It was a Baptist preacher in Kentucky who developed the process of making bourbon, and on the frontier some preachers received their salary in the form of whiskey. As a youth, B. H. Carroll often took a swig of whiskey to start the day, a practice he later regretted and gave up. However, in time Baptists in America changed their stance on alcohol from *temperance* to *total abstinence.* This move was greatly influenced by J. Newton Brown's well-known Church Covenant, which begins "Having been led as we believe by the Holy Spirit. . . ." This covenant asks Baptists to promise not to make, use, or sell alcoholic beverages. Considered quite radical when it originated in the 1830s in New Hampshire, this covenant became a standard of Baptist conduct.

The BSC took its first official notice of temperance in 1854, with a resolution "That it is the sense of this body that it is incompatible with our principles, and inconsistent with our Christian character for a Baptist to visit a grocery for the purpose of dram drinking, and that it is in direct variance with the teachings of the word of God, for our members to be allowed to traffic in the poison."[35] Thereafter, almost every year saw a similar resolution adopted. However, it was not until the 1890s that the Prohibition crusade completely engulfed the Texas Baptists.

BAYLOR UNIVERSITY

Baylor University was three years old when the state convention was formed in 1848, having been formed by the Baptist Education Society in 1845 and chartered under the Republic of Texas. Described in 1853 as "our beloved Institution," Baylor was the first great achievement of Texas

Baptists, and they loved and supported the school with a zeal which would brook no rivals.[36] The announced purpose of the university was to produce for Baptists "a pious laity and a holy ministry."[37]

Henry L. Graves, first president, continued in office until 1851, with every year a struggle for survival. In 1851 the college launched a plan to endow the presidency with a fund of $10,000 which would guarantee the salary of the president. For a time, the president earned part of his livelihood by serving as pastor, and by taking in boarders. Few, if any, of the early faculty were "full-time." In a time honored tradition of Baptist educators, they had to supplement their salaries by outside income, much of it from "boarding" students.

Growth was slow at first. In 1850 the faculty consisted of the president, one professor, a tutor in English, plus "a gentleman and his lady who give lessons in music and other ornamental branches." Three years later they reported eight professors, and an enrollment of 160. The Law School opened in 1857, with the advantage of access to Judge Baylor's considerable library. During its first years, Baylor was one school, with one faculty and one student body. Classes were coeducational, with all students taught in one building by the same faculty. There was one curriculum, though more of the young women were found in the "ornamental" classes such as music. However, during the 1850s Baylor faced its most severe internal crisis when the Male Department and the Female Department were separated. They were separated not only administratively and by curriculum, but also spatially, with the Male and Female departments occupying separate buildings about a mile apart. In his account of Baylor's tensions, J. M. Carroll says, "Baylor University and Baylor College, now two schools, began originally as one, and for five years were taught co-educationally, but gradually drifted, or developed, or evolved, or was rent into two. . . . from 1851 it was divided into two entirely separate departments, which were taught by different faculties, in separate buildings, and those buildings one mile apart."[38] The origin of this division, however, was less mysterious than Carroll makes it appear. Many educators of the time opposed coeducation, and Rufus C. Burleson, who was elected to the Baylor presidency in 1851, rather militantly held that view. In fact, he made it a condition of his acceptance that Male and Female departments must be separated. After the trouble this caused him at Baylor in Independence, when Burleson became president of Waco University ten years later, he just as militantly demanded that the school be coed.

After separation of the two departments, Burleson acted as Principal of the Male Department, while the very capable Horace Clark was named Principal of the Female Department. At first Burleson had little occasion to intervene in Clark's department. It was said that Burleson seldom visited the women's building, and it was implied that he hardly knew, or cared, what went on there. Burleson was most concerned for the Male Department which he apparently regarded as the real university. However, he regarded himself as *President* over both departments, with final administrative control. Clark exercised forceful leadership over his department, and a clash was inevitable.

In retrospect, this looks like a turf battle, complicated by personality conflicts between two strong leaders. Tensions led to embarrassing public conflicts and even Sam Houston was drawn into the contest. The Board of Trustees was remarkably unhelpful in the whole sorry mess. They put Burleson in an impossible situation, responsible for the entire school but without effective control. The trustees counseled, cajoled, appointed committees to study, and finally threatened to fire the entire administration and faculty if they did not settle their ugly public fuss. What the trustees did not do was clearly define where the administrative power lay, and see that it was accepted. With all respect for Clark's remarkably effective leadership, one can hardly avoid the conclusion that the trustees did not stand behind their president.

A report in 1856 said "The Female Department [of Baylor] furnishes evidence of increasing prosperity."[39] This probably pinpoints the heart of the problem. The women's department had nicer buildings, their enrollment grew more rapidly, and Clark proved to be an effective fund-raiser for his department. When Clark appealed for funds, especially when accompanied by two or three of the charming young women, donors opened their purses. Mrs. Clark was an able assistant to her husband. Texas Baptists wanted education for their daughters as well as their sons, and clearly they were pleased with the academic excellence, the wholesome living conditions, and the "ornamental" accomplishments of Clark's department. Jealousy was clearly a factor in the controversy.

Burleson made his play to control both departments, and failed to make it stick. Clark ignored him and the trustees waffled. This left Burleson little choice, and in 1861 he left Baylor University in Independence to become president of the newly formed Waco University to the north. The Waco Association had formed a high school in 1856 and with Burleson's coming, elevated the school to college status, at least in name. All the faculty of the Male Department resigned and followed Burleson to Waco. The entire senior class also defected from Baylor and joined their old faculty at the new school. The seniors adopted a statement that "we prefer receiving our diplomas from you, when you shall have established yourselves at Waco University, and [we] do not wish to graduate . . . as students of Baylor University."[40] Not only the seniors, but practically all the male students defected from Baylor.

This proved the death knell for Baylor University at Independence, and indeed for the town of Independence itself. From the first, Independence had the great Baptist leaders, the best land, and it was the center of everything. This "Baptist Jerusalem" regarded itself as the spiritual center of Texas Baptist life, and perhaps came to presume somewhat upon their exalted status. But all was not well in the "Baptist Jerusalem." First, Independence once had the state capital but lost it to upstart Austin on the frontier. Then Independence lost the railroad, some said by their arrogance in trying to dictate terms to the railroad company. In losing the railroad, Independence lost the future. The money went elsewhere, and the population followed the money. For another twenty-five years, Baylor University continued at Independence but the tide was set. The worthy William Carey Crane was elected to succeed Burleson, and he struggled manfully to keep afloat a sinking ship. The Female Department was made a separate school in 1867, Baylor Female College, with its own charter and its own trustees. The school was later moved to Belton, where it remains under the name of the University of Mary Hardin-Baylor. The remnant of Baylor University at Independence was merged with Waco University in 1886, with the combined school taking the name of Baylor University at Waco. The ruins of the historic buildings at Independence stand empty today, stark reminders of the glory that departed.

Nor was the change confined to Baylor alone. More and more the center of gravity in Texas Baptist life shifted northward, first to Waco and then to Dallas. South Texas was the early cradle for Texas Baptist life. The pioneer Union Association began there, as did the Baptist State Convention. The first Texas Baptist papers were published there, and for years the nearest thing to a state Baptist headquarters was Independence. No doubt Carroll is correct, that "South Texas has never, even to this day, recovered from that long past trouble."[41]

A PASSION FOR PRINT

"Texas Baptists need their own newspaper." On this subject there was complete agreement among the Baptists, ministers and laymen alike, in early Texas. The problem was how to bring it about. There was a recommendation at the first session of the Union Association in 1840 that Texas Baptists should launch a paper. The state convention, formed in 1848, heard such recommendations annually, each more insistent, but nothing was done until 1855 when the *Texas Baptist* began.

Most Baptists who migrated into Texas came from states that had a Baptist paper, and they felt the lack in Texas. A report in 1852 noted that "Our denomination in Texas is composed of members of the older States, from Maine to Louisiana, and from Canada, England, and Germany. These good brethren bringing their various little peculiarities with them often introduce confusion into our newly organized ranks. These little non-essential peculiarities are kept alive and nourished by reading local papers of other States. Whereas, if the whole Baptist family in this State would read the same paper, very soon these little differences would pass away, and we would all think the same way, feel the same way, and act the same way. . . . We must have a paper."[42] We must have, they concluded, "a paper more fully devoted to the interests of Texas." Gail Borden who was, among other things, a newspaper man, was a strong advocate of a Baptist paper.

However, the Baptists did not have the money or personnel to launch a paper. Until they could, they recommended that Baptists subscribe to and read Baptist papers from adjoining states, particularly the *Tennessee Baptist* and the *Baptist Banner* and *Pioneer* of Kentucky. Between 1850 and 1855, every session of the BSC heard urgent recommendations to establish a paper. The Board of Directors agreed to do so, but when they got down to business found they simply did not have the money. The state convention, while favoring a paper, adamantly refused to offer any financial supplement. Finally Texas Baptists moved beyond talk to action on this subject, and launched the *Texas Baptist* in January 1855, published from Anderson in Grimes County. George W. Baines was editor, with J. B. Stiteler and J. H. Stribling as associates. The *Texas Baptist* eventually reached a circulation of about 2,600, not bad for the times, and it was well received. The paper got excellent reports for interest and quality, and it was claimed that it had "reconciled conflicting opinions, promoted unanimity of sentiments and action in our churches, set forth our peculiar doctrines in a clear and convincing manner, cheered our hearts with religious intelligence, and sowed broad-cast the seeds of Divine truth."[43]

Baines resigned as editor in 1861, succeeded by J. A. Kimball. His tenure was short; later in 1861 the paper folded. The war made it almost impossible to obtain paper, and it was estimated that about 1,500 subscribers had not paid.[44]

Texas Baptists had no paper during the war years, 1861-1865, though near the end of that period William Carey Crane launched the *Christian Herald*. That paper failed, but its books and newsprint, along with $60 in cash, were given to John Bodkin Link, who had newly arrived in Texas. Link was born in Virginia, and had served as a Confederate chaplain during the war. He brought to Texas an incredible energy, a commitment to Baptist journalism, and good business as well as editorial skill. The coming of Link transformed Baptist journalism in Texas. He formed a new paper, the *Texas Baptist Herald*, in 1865, in Houston. The paper was later moved to Austin and eventually to Dallas. Unlike the earlier *Texas Baptist*, Link tried to distance himself somewhat from the state convention. He wanted the paper to report Baptist news, encourage Baptist work, but to remain distinctly independent of denominational control. In the paper he reported perhaps less general news than had the earlier paper, and carried more advertising. The paper survived financial problems, but once had to close temporarily because of an outbreak of yellow fever, and at times published irregularly. Yet the paper survived, due to the energy and determination of Link, and by the end of the period covered by this chapter the *Texas Baptist Herald* remained a flourishing paper.

THE WAR YEARS

Despite the earnest efforts of Sam Houston to remain with the Union, Texas voted to join the Confederacy in 1861. This sent Houston home to Huntsville a disillusioned man, and plunged Texas into four years of war which destroyed the economy, depleted their male population, and later subjected the state to years of galling "reconstruction." When the state convention met in Huntsville in 1861, part of their opening exercises was to offer "special prayers to the God of Battles for our beloved Confederacy."[45] Most Baptists were among the estimated 90% of Texans who favored the Confederate cause. They never wavered in their support of the lost cause, even when by 1865 "the probability of an adverse . . . [outcome] grew into a terrible certainty."[46]

Texas, the home of mustangs and ox teams, also became the home of a considerable herd of camels during the war. The U.S. government purchased camels in Asia Minor, and landed fifty of the hump-back beasts at the Texas port of Indianola in 1857, complete with Greek and Arab attendants. The camels were intended for transporting goods across the Staked Plains, but in 1861 Confederate forces captured many of the camels and used them to carry Texas cotton to market in Mexico. It was said that a good camel could travel up to 90 miles in a day, but few regrets were expressed when the "camel experiment" in Texas was abandoned.[47]

Baptist ministries, like everything else in Texas, suffered during the war. Most of the men left for the armies; Baylor students put aside their books for rifles; money which might have gone to ministry efforts went instead to the war effort. The Baptist periodical suspended for lack of paper, and annual convention minutes were reduced to a few pages, with print too small to read. During the war travel in Texas became more hazardous, and remaining men feared to leave their families for any length of time. For example, in 1862 the Corresponding Secretary of the BSC did not dare travel from Independence to Waco to attend the Convention because of the "perilous times." One report said, "Many seats . . . will be vacant," and that proved only too accurate. The Corresponding Secretary sent a letter urging the Convention to act only on the most urgent matters and postpone other decisions until a better attendance could be had.

The Convention reported for 1862 that "as a period of missionary labor it has been almost a blank. . . . We have no official information of any missionary labor having been performed during the year." Money was short because Union forces prevented Southern cotton from reaching the market, and the Southern currency lost much of its value. For a while the Convention could not pay missionaries even if they could be found. Many of the missionaries, like the students, had entered the army. Interruption of mail service made it impossible to keep up with foreign missions, or even events within Texas. What mission work the BSC did during the war was almost entirely with the troops, plus some work among the Germans by Kiefer and some work among the Mexicans in San Antonio. Conditions were such that the BSC agreed in 1865 that "the convention should attempt but little in the way of Domestic Missions during the present Conventional year."[48] The work of the state convention came to a virtual halt during the war, but many of the churches experienced revivals.

INTERNAL TENSIONS

From its formation in 1848, the state convention gave every appearance of harmony. The people were few, everyone knew and trusted each other, and few problems surfaced. However, after a few years the convention grew larger, its programs multiplied, and it tried to stretch limited resources to cover a multitude of ministries. Tensions surfaced by the late 1850s, centering in three areas.

First, many objected to the unlimited authority of the Board of Directors. After years of complaint, they pushed through a revision in the constitution which gave ultimate authority back to the Convention, with the Board acting to carry out decisions and policies set by the Convention. Second, the financial basis of membership offended many. Perhaps from reading the *Tennessee Baptist,* edited by J. R. Graves, they pushed through a constitutional change in 1860, changing the fourth article to read, "this convention shall be composed of delegates of regular Baptist churches and associations, in proportion to their members, as follows: Each Association shall be entitled to five delegates, and one additional delegate for every five hundred members after the first five hundred; each church shall be entitled to one delegate, and one additional delegate for every twenty members."[49]

This represents an important change. Previously, the Convention had operated on the basis that those who gave the money should decide the programs. The change, favored by the Landmark group, meant that every church had representation whether they gave anything or not. However, tensions escalated over territory. With money short and a dozen equally worthy places for every available missionary, it is not surprising that those who got passed over would feel slighted. The Corresponding Secretary noted that while many people were acutely aware of their own area, the larger field was more vast and the needs far greater than most were aware. In 1866 the Corresponding Secretary reported that, "objections have been met and answered; misrepresentations have been corrected; unfounded prejudices have been allayed; and many churches and Associations have . . . become during the past year reconciled to the Convention. . . . It is believed that nine-tenths of all the churches and Associations within the bounds of the Convention now harmonize, and will cooperate with it [the state convention]."[50]

This report proved entirely too optimistic. Baptists east of the Trinity felt the Convention favored western areas in mission appointments and support of schools. No amount of statistical analysis could allay this feeling of neglect, and in retrospect it appears the East Texas brethren had a point. When G. G. Baggerly, pastor of First Baptist Church in Tyler, asked the BSC to help sponsor a Baptist school in Tyler, the Board replied, "Our educational efforts extending only to the aid of ministers of the Gospel; and as we have under our patronage the Baylor University designed especially for that purpose, we cannot . . . promise to aid any other institution."[51]

The Convention may have been wise to try to build one strong college rather than several weak ones, but their reasons do not stand scrutiny. Baylor was not restricted to ministerial education; in fact, of around 150 students at that time, only two or three of them were studying for ministry. Not only educational support, but most missionary appointees went to the western areas. As a result, Baptists in the East felt alienated and eventually decided to pull away and form their own structures. Relations were further strained by the fact that East Texas had a persistent strain of anti-mission and Landmark sentiment. Baggerly kept the eastern churches inflamed, constantly referring to the BSC as "the convention of the west." After an abortive attempt in 1853, the Baptist Convention of Eastern Texas was formed in 1855 at Tyler with messengers from twenty-four churches. The new body soon affiliated churches and associations in East Texas in rivalry with the "convention of the west." In a move repeated many times over the years, the disgruntled East Texas leaders accused the BSC of financial improprieties and sectional favoritism. The Eastern Convention sponsored the Texas Baptist College at Tyler, appointed a few missionaries, but never really caught on. The Tyler college never recovered from the war when, as one historian noted, "books were thrown aside, and eighty students, at the call of their State, enlisted at one time, and consequently the school went down."[52] Failure to enlist much cooperation led the Eastern Convention to change its name and operation again in 1868. The persistent anti-mission spirit of the east hampered its work, despite the best efforts of D.B. Morrell, their general agent. In 1868 the body met in Chatfield, and restructured as the Baptist General Association.

CONCLUSION

For the next eighteen years, 1868 to 1886, Texas had two strong rival state conventions (and sometimes as many as five). This created no end of tension, misunderstanding, and overlapping of effort. Even those who realized this situation was intolerable seemed powerless to change it. The story of those rival conventions belongs to the next chapter.

CHAPTER 5

DIVIDED WE STAND, 1868–1886

THE YEARS AFTER THE Civil War proved difficult for Texas. The economy lay in ruins and even when crops were good markets were in disarray and transportation disrupted. The loss of men in the war and the changed labor relations after emancipation adversely affected the labor-intensive agrarian society. In some ways Reconstruction was more disruptive in Texas than the war had been. A series of crop failures in the 1870s, augmented by the "monetary panic" of the times, put money in short supply. It was during these years that the great Texas cattle drives developed. Hard-riding cowboys pushed herds of longhorns up the trails named for ranchers Charlie Goodnight and Jesse Chisholm in an effort to reach the northern markets.

Baptists shared fully in the social and financial disruption of the times. Churches had difficulty maintaining pastors, even for part-time ministry, and practically all pastors labored at secular work to earn their bread. Many churches had preaching only once a month and sometimes less. The Baptist schools struggled, partly because many of the gifts they received were in the form of land for which there was no sale. Occasionally Mrs. Crane, matron of the Baylor University boarding house and wife of its president, had to turn away students at mealtime for lack of provisions.[1]

The Baptist associations and state conventions tried to keep missionaries in the field to establish churches in the growing communities, especially the railroad towns, but shortage of funds often meant that missionaries could not be appointed, or appointed only for a few weeks at a time. The Convention repeatedly had to report that they were several weeks or months behind in paying even the meager salaries promised to the missionaries. For a time, the Baptist State Convention could not afford to have its minutes printed without special help from two or three of the stronger churches. J. B. Link wrote that Convention leaders were "burdened men," who appealed for support for the mission causes and received the reply, "Hard times! Hard times!"[2] A common refrain runs through the Baptist records of this era: vast spiritual needs confront us but we have no means to address those needs. Because the entire South shared in this post-war devastation, the Home Mission Board of the SBC could offer little more than encouragement until later in the period.

Despite these hardships Baptists in Texas managed to grow during the period 1868-1886. The number of churches and associations multiplied rapidly, and total Baptist membership reached a level which could hardly have been imagined when the first state convention was formed in 1848. The War barely slowed immigration into Texas, and among the newcomers were many Baptist families and not a few preachers. During these years Texas Baptists formed a number of state-wide structures to promote Sunday Schools, foreign missions, education, and training for deacons, Sunday School teachers, and pastors. Texas Baptist women organized local and state mission societies and put wholesome emphasis upon missionary education and offerings.

DIVISION IN THE RANKS

Like a jigsaw puzzle with its pieces scattered, Baptist structures in Texas were badly fragmented during this period. Since 1848 the Baptist State Convention (BSC) had worked throughout the state, but in 1868 Baptists in East Texas formed a rival general body, the Baptist General Association (BGA). These two state conventions overlapped and competed for allegiance of churches and associations, and relations between them were not always cordial. Each state convention sponsored its own college, Baylor University at Independence for the BSC, and Waco University at Waco for the BGA. For a time both conventions supported the same paper, *The Texas Baptist Herald,* published in Houston by J. B. Link, who tried to promote impartially the projects of both conventions. Later *The Texas Baptist,*[3] published in Dallas by R. C. Buckner, promoted causes of the BGA. Both papers were independent, neither being owned by the state conventions. Toward the end of this period, and lasting into the present century, hostility between the editors of these papers escalated into a bitter rivalry. Each general body also sponsored its own organizations for Sunday School work, Women's Missionary Unions, Deacon's Conferences and the like.

As if this was not enough division, by the early 1880s three additional state bodies were formed in Texas, making a total of five overlapping, competing conventions in one state. The East Texas Baptist Convention (1877-1884) was formed on December 12 at Overton. They affirmed that there was as much reason to form a third convention as a second, namely neglect of their territory by the other two. They said, "Resolved, that as the result of painful experience in the past, we now regard it as an inevitable necessity for us to do our own work in the best way we can." The North Texas Baptist Missionary Convention (1879-1883) was organized at

Allen on October 19, 1879, because of intense dissatisfaction with the General Association. It merged with the State Convention in 1883. The Central Texas Baptist Convention (1880-1884) was formed in Dublin on November 12, 1880, where the brethren affirmed that "there is lying between the Brazos River on the east, Belton and Lampasas on the south, the frontier on the west, and the clear fork of the Brazos River on the north— an extensive territory, many churches and much destitution not enlisted or cultivated by any general organization." The BSC could have contested the statement that no Baptist organization was at work in that area. At Hico in 1885 the Central Convention voted to merge with the others.[4]

In 1883 at Cleburne B. H. Carroll summed up the situation in a speech before the Baptist General Association.

> To the east and along our northwest and western borders are respectively, the East Texas, North Texas, and Central Texas Baptist Conventions, having in a great measure undefined and undefinable boundaries. . . . Hence, on all sides the territory of the different bodies intermingles.[5]

To make matters worse, the "district associations have been divided in council; some rent asunder; churches have been torn by faction; brethren alienated and strife engendered." These divisions, Carroll noted, led to fractured fellowship, for "the saddest and most lamentable antagonism has been developed on our mission fields." This antagonism permeated Baptist life in Texas, as brethren competed for support of schools, newspapers, and mission work. B. H. Carroll was one of the first to recognize the problem, but it took some years for consolidation to mature from dream to reality.

Along with external division came internal fragmentation of Baptist work in Texas. The Baptist State Convention of 1848 described its work as encompassing "missions and education." Church planting in Texas, helping send missionaries abroad, promoting Sunday Schools, and sponsoring Baptist schools all seemed to fit within this purpose statement. However, by 1870 many Texas Baptist leaders felt that each separate ministry cause required its own organization. This led to separate "conventions" or "societies" for foreign missions, Sunday School work, and education. These satellite organizations clustered around the state conventions, but were not structurally related. Each had its own constitution, officers, budget and corps of "agents" to canvas among the churches to raise funds. J. M. Carroll said Texas Baptists "created organizations within organizations— wheels within wheels—until one wheel could not turn without interfering with another."[6] These organizations usually met at the same time and place as the state convention, had their minutes printed with those of the convention, and had a great deal of membership overlap. The same pattern prevailed both around the BSC and the BGA. This represented a brief lapse from the unified *convention* approach to Baptist work in which one cooperative convention sponsored many kinds of ministry, to the more independent *society* approach in which each ministry cause had its own separate organization.[7] Within a few years the Baptists abandoned this scatter gun approach, and concluded that "missions" was sufficiently inclusive to cover many facets of ministry.

Baptists who strongly supported these auxiliary causes may have felt forced to form separate structures for fund-raising and promotion. More than once the BSC, for example, bluntly defined its primary task as *missions,* by which it meant church planting in Texas, and relegated everything else to secondary status to be pursued or not as funds might allow. Further, the formation of these auxiliary bodies is a tacit admission that these causes had not succeeded under the state conventions. Many concluded that Sunday Schools and colleges would never prosper until they had their own structures. The result was internal fragmentation of the Baptist witness, with a bewildering array of organizations, each pursuing worthy goals no doubt, but confusing the churches by the plentitude of financial agents bumping into each other as each tried to get to the churches first to raise money for his particular cause. In addition to Texas causes, the SBC Foreign Mission Board of Richmond, Virginia, and the Home Mission Board of Marion, Alabama (in 1882 moved to Atlanta), usually kept agents at work in Texas, as did the Southern Baptist Theological Seminary at Greenville, South Carolina (in 1877 moved to Louisville, KY). This caused lay persons, as B. H. Carroll noted, to "draw their purse strings tighter" when an agent approached, no matter how worthy his cause, because other agents had been there yesterday and more would arrive tomorrow. The agent system, though often lauded, never really worked well. Agents were usually paid a percentage of what they raised, and one who could raise his own salary plus as much more for his cause was considered a success.

THE BAPTIST STATE CONVENTION

The first state convention in Texas was formed in 1848. While it had no specific "headquarters," its Board of Directors usually met in Independence. While the BSC declined a proposal to meet every second year in Independence, preferring to meet at various locations around the state, Independence was always its spiritual and usually its geographical center. From the first, the BSC understood its field to include the entire state, though realistically they could occupy only portions of that vast territory. They seemed to concentrate on the South and West, describing their field as reaching from the Gulf Coast to New Mexico. Officers of the Convention during these years included a president, several vice-presidents, and a corresponding secretary, but the real power was in the hands of the "general agent," or major traveling fund-raiser. Sometimes the corresponding secretary and general agent were the same person. The names of H. L. Graves, O. C. Pope, Hosea Garrett, Noah T. Byars, J. H. Stribling, and J. W. D. Creath are prominent in leadership. For almost thirty years, with one or two brief interruptions, Creath served as general agent and fixed his aggressive leadership upon the entire Convention. His report for

1872-1873 listed 3734 miles traveled, 119 sermons preached, 85 lectures given, 320 visits made, 24 Sunday Schools visited, seven prayer meetings conducted, and eight associational meetings attended.[8] Areas of special concern where no church yet existed included New Braunfels, San Antonio, Brownsville, Indianola, Lavaca, and Victoria. Nowhere did the Baptists struggle harder to establish a Baptist work than in San Antonio, and it took years to succeed.

Another area of special concern was the growing German population in Texas. The first Baptist missionary to the Germans was Frank Kiefer, later assisted by F. J. Gleiss. By 1885 the BSC had five missionaries to the Germans, and wished for a dozen for, they said, "We must Christianize the Germans or they will Germanize Texas."[9]

During these years the BSC (and the BGA as well) evolved a cooperative pattern of work, the basic outlines of which endure to this day. Sometimes the BSC would appoint and support its own missionaries. At other times, the Convention and an association might make joint appointments and share in the support. Sometimes two or more associations would appoint mission preachers for their areas, and at other times, a frontier missionary in Texas might be jointly supported by the BSC, one or more associations, and the Home Mission Board of the SBC. One might rejoice that the gospel was preached, but often the Convention right hand did not know what the associational left hand was doing, and missionaries on the field hardly knew to whom to send their reports. Unlike the pattern of indefinite appointment today, missionaries then were appointed for a limited period, often no more than a matter of weeks or months. Their quarterly reports listed such data as miles traveled, number of sermons preached, number of conversions and baptisms, new churches and Sunday Schools formed, and amount of money raised. Most of these pioneer church planters in frontier Texas were expected to raise a large portion of their salary on the field. In 1878 the BSC reported three ways of raising funds: "Pledges at our annual meetings, collections in each Church, and contributions through our General Financial Agent."[10]

In 1872 Creath suggested a "New Plan" for Texas missions, but it was really just the old plan with minor refinements. The main change was to ask each association to form its own Domestic Mission Society, with pastors leading church members to make a continuing pledge for a five year period, suggested amounts being from $5 to $20 per year for five years. This ongoing pledge, with the pastor as collection agent, would eliminate the time and cost of an outside agent visiting every church every year to collect short-term pledges. In this way, it was said, "One General Agent can accomplish at least five times as much work on this plan as by any heretofore adopted."[11] B. H. Carroll suggested a similar plan for the BGA, but the idea was in advance of its time and never caught on.

From the first, some of the stronger associations preferred to do their own local mission work with their own money, rather than sending money to the BSC and hoping, often in vain, to have a missionary sent to their area.They apparently liked the local control of the work, and avoided the frustration of having the BSC bypass their area in the appointment of missionaries. However, this localism almost supplanted the state body in its own territory. In 1875 the BSC reported that its work had declined, while "the Associations are, in a great measure, assuming the work in their bounds." They said, "We suggest that unless we assume the vigorous prosecution of the Missionary labor, that the propriety or necessity of our future existence [as a state convention] may be seriously doubted, since other bodies of ample scope and power are already in existence to care for the Educational and Sunday-school interests of the State."[12]

The plain fact is that by the late 1870s the BSC was, if not declining, certainly not advancing as they had hoped. Some causes were aggressive work by the associations, the financial crises following the war, and a territory where large population and financial centers developed more slowly than in North and East Texas. Perhaps this sense of spinning their wheels helped lead to the 1881 agreement with the American Baptist Home Mission Society (ABHMS). This Northern Baptist society, headquartered in New York City, was a major center for the divisive controversy which resulted in formation of the Southern Baptist Convention in 1845 but by 1881 hard feelings had diminished. O. C. Pope traveled to New York and convincingly presented the Texas case before the HMS board. There is reason to believe the Northern Society welcomed an opportunity to work in the South, not only for the sake of ministry but also to make the point that theirs was a national and not a regional society.

The 1881 agreement specified that church planters on the Texas frontier would be chosen by the BSC, but jointly appointed and supported by the state convention and the New York Society. The HMS from its deep pockets would contribute $1 for every $1 raised in Texas, up to a maximum of $3,000 for any one year. All such missionaries would make quarterly reports to both bodies, and would work under the supervision of a "general missionary or superintendent of missions," jointly chosen by both bodies. This plan proved successful, for in 1883 the BSC reported twenty-one missionaries at work, far more than they had before. For three years O. C. Pope served as general missionary to promote "the work of the Society and of the Convention." A further condition called for the Texas churches to funnel their out of state offerings through the Northern Society rather than through the Southern Convention. This agreement also made the Texas churches eligible for loans and sometimes outright gifts from the Church Edifice Fund of the HMS.[13] Under this program several churches got grants to build or improve their buildings, including Sweetwater, $250; Lockhart, $200; Mineral Wells, $150; Abilene, $300; Pearsall, $200; Henrietta, $250; Jewett, $150; Honey Grove, $200; Orange, $200; and Burnett, $200.[14] These sums take on perspective in light of the fact that the annual salary for a missionary then was about $400.

Relations between the New York Society and the Home Mission Board of the SBC had not been cordial, and many Baptists felt that in teaming up with Northern Baptists the BSC acted disloyally toward the Southern Baptist Convention. O. C. Pope was stung by this criticism. In a letter in 1885 he said if by loyalty you mean that "one must sit idle and see his State pass into the hands of other denominations, because the Southern Convention cannot supply the destitution, that one must despise and abuse every other organization but the [Southern] Convention, and refuse to be helped when in distress, except by a Southerner—then I am not loyal, and I pity the narrow, contracted man who is."[15]

Pope said, "I do not think I am disloyal to Texas, or to the South, or to Jesus Christ when I wish, as I sincerely do, that we were less divided into Southern Baptists and Northern Baptists with sectional prejudice and sectional hate, but that American Baptists might be all one in Christ." He concluded, "If this be treason, make the most of it."

One who felt that cooperation with the North bordered on treason was I. T. Tichenor, newly elected head of the Home Mission Board. For some years the HMB had paid scant attention to Texas, but after the agreement between Texas and the Northern Society, Tichenor visited Texas frequently and, in effect, outbid the Northern Baptists for Texas affiliation. In 1883 Tichenor offered to contribute $2 to Texas missions for every $1 raised in Texas.[16] The BSC accepted aid from both Northern and Southern bodies until 1885 when the Northern Society opted out.

The report for 1884 shows that in cooperation with the Northern Society, sixteen missionaries worked 732 weeks, baptized 180, and formed six new churches. For the same period, nineteen missionaries aided by the HMB gave 733 weeks of work, baptized 292, and formed four new churches.[17]

THE BAPTIST GENERAL ASSOCIATION

Many Baptists in East Texas had never cooperated fully with the Baptist State Convention. From the 1830s the Daniel Parker influence in East Texas had imprinted upon the region the doctrines of strict Calvinism, anti-missions, opposition to Sunday Schools and ministerial education, and a generally contentious and uncooperative spirit. Even those brethren in the East who wanted to support missions and education felt, and with some justification, that the BSC favored the west and shortchanged the east. When in 1852 the state convention bluntly refused to extend any measure of sponsorship or support for the Tyler Baptist College, and gave a patently inconsistent reason for their refusal, feelings ran high in the east. A "general association" for the East was formed in 1853 at Larissa, and changed in 1855 to the Baptist Convention of Eastern Texas. The leader of the new group was G. G. Baggerly, pastor at Tyler. The constitution adopted shows more Landmark influence than does the BSC. At their first session, messengers from twenty-four churches discussed the "matters of difficulty between Brother Baggerly and the State Convention," in which "trouble, bad feelings, and hard words" abounded.[18] The eastern convention formed their own school, Texas Baptist College at Tyler, which for awhile rivaled Baylor in enrollment. Representatives from the BSC met with the disaffected brethren from the East, answered all their objections, and showed at least to their own satisfaction that the problems had risen not from intentional neglect, but misunderstanding, faulty records, and inadequate resources. These efforts did not smooth the troubled waters and eastern leaders continued to fan regional rivalries by referring to the BSC as the "Convention of the West."

For all its protestations, both in name, outlook and work, the new convention was regional; it was the Baptist Convention of the East. By 1868 population growth in North Texas shifted the center of gravity, and the convention reorganized with a new name, The Baptist General Association of Texas (BGA). This was more than a change of name. It also involved a change of focus, moving beyond the anti-mission and uncooperative remnants of the East. The new center of gravity was more North Texas than East. New leaders arose, as unlike Baggerly as one could imagine. In R. C. Buckner of Paris, Abram Weaver and G. W. Rogers of Dallas, R. C. Burleson of Waco, and especially B. H. Carroll of Waco, the BGA gained leaders of vision and stature. In retrospect, it now appears that when B. H. Carroll and the First Baptist Church of Waco, then the leading Baptist church west of the Mississippi, came into the BGA orbit the tide turned toward the General Association and the State Convention began its slow decline. Laymen of wealth and influence in Waco, Dallas, and Paris augmented BGA witness and illustrated the shift of focus from East Texas to North Texas. After its founding in 1877, the immensely popular Buckner Orphans Home, at least loosely related to the General Association, brought added prestige to the new body.

At its formation in 1868, the new state convention adopted a constitution combining financial and church bases of membership. Any church could send two messengers without regard to contributions and any association could send four. Beyond that, more contributions entitled to more messengers. In 1876 B. H. Carroll led a move to allow each church three messengers and each association five without regard to contributions. A Committee on Proposed Plan of Reform in 1877 proposed to limit the General Association to only one messenger per church and two per association, primarily from practical concerns. "As it is," they said, "the body is too large, and there are too many messengers to be entertained from churches, doing nothing, and a needless burden is imposed upon communities where the body meets." These proposed reforms were not enacted.

The BGA formed three boards: a Sunday School Board at Marshall, a Missionary Board at Ladonia, and Bible and Colportage Board at Waco. They related, more or less, to several schools, including Waco University, Ladonia Institute, the Charwood Institute in Tyler, and a school for young women in Paris. The new body claimed a field extending about 300 miles East-West, and about 225 miles North-South. In that territory only two churches had preaching every Sunday, and scores of churches had perished in the war and had not been restored. The new body announced a three-fold program: "to reorganize disorganized churches, to act in concert with and assist weak churches in the support of their pastors, and [work with] District Associations in the appointment and support of missionaries." To launch this work, they called for "a monthly concert of prayer." While pressing the needs at home, the BGA did not neglect foreign missions, as they felt the BSC had done, but affirmed that those who do most for foreign missions generally also do most for work at home. "Our anti-missionary brethren," they warned, "began with opposing Foreign Missions, and then opposed all Home Missions, and ended with deadly opposition to Sabbath-schools, and even to the support of their ministry and all other enterprises."[19]

At their origin the General Association claimed about 25,000 members in 300 churches, grouped into twenty associations.[20] Many of the churches were pastorless, but the churches in Dallas, Jefferson, and Sherman had recently obtained pastors. Important towns still without any Baptist voice included Rusk, San Augustine, Nacogdoches, Crockett, Palestine, Sulphur Springs, Kaufman, and Greenville.[21] Later they also looked westward, reporting that "From the Brazos on the South, to Kansas on the North, and from Wichita county on the east to the line of New Mexico on the west, making a territory of two hundred miles square, without a single church house or organized church or Baptist preacher . . . there has never been a Baptist sermon preached in all this vast section."[22]

Under the aggressive leadership of R. C. Buckner, the BGA set out to address these needs, but with less success than they hoped. At the end of the first year, Buckner had traveled 2,551 miles, preached 132 sermons, written 150 letters, administered 34 baptisms, formed one new church, and collected a total of $851.65. They had nine missionaries at work for part of the year, and they reported 159 baptisms and a number of new churches and Sunday Schools formed. By 1871 Rufus C. Burleson, Corresponding Secretary, challenged the BGA to raise at least $10,000, of which $4,000 would be allotted to home missions, $3,000 for Sunday School work, and $3,000 for ministerial education. Of course, they raised nowhere near that amount, though Burleson said they *could* have done it because they had grown to 35,000 members in 440 churches and twenty-two associations. The 1872 report is typical, if a bit candid: Burleson "regrets to report another year of noble resolutions, wise plans, and sinful inactivity."[23] At a meeting in Paris frustration surfaced about "the apparent indifference on the part of the churches" and the blame was laid squarely at the feet of pastors "from a lack of instruction from the pulpit." Anti-missions, the old nemeses of the East, surfaced again. Some leaders complained they had been preparing for three years and had as yet done practically nothing. Reports speak of the "want of sufficient energy in the Board and cooperation on the part of some district associations and individuals." There were calls for election of a new board, "composed of brethren who are not only willing to act, but are zealous and experienced in the cause of missions." They found such aggressive leadership in Adoniram Judson Holt, who had been a missionary to the wild Indians[24] before his election as general agent.

BUCKNER ORPHANS HOME

An event of great importance for Texas Baptists was the formation of the Buckner Orphans Home in 1877. Beginning in 1876 R. C. Buckner ran a series of articles in the *Texas Baptist,* outlining the need for an orphanage in Texas. At a Deacons Convention formed in Paris on July 18, 1877, he challenged the deacons present to help form and support such a home. Under the general chairmanship of Deacon W. L. Williams of Dallas, a committee composed of J. R. Rogers, R. C. Buckner, and B. H. Carroll recommended "That we will make an effort to build an Orphans Home within the bounds of the General Association of Texas." They named Buckner general superintendent of the project, and set in motion plans to raise money. Two years later, however, brethren voted "That this convention [the Deacons Convention] disapproves of concerts, magic lantern shows and everything of like character, to raise funds for the Orphans Home."[25] The charter, written by Buckner, was adopted in 1879 in a meeting in First Baptist Church, McKinney.

The home opened with three children in a rented cottage in Dallas in 1879, but the next year Buckner purchased forty-four acres just east of Dallas from Josiah F. Pinson, whom he had known in Kentucky before both migrated to Texas. The land was appraised for $1,216, but Pinson sold it to his old friend Buckner for $500.[26] Neither of them could have known that Pinson's great great grandson, William Pinson, would almost one hundred years later be elected executive director to lead Texas Baptists. By April, 1880, Buckner had erected a frame house able to house twenty-five children. After paying $841.19 for building the house, the home had a balance of $59.45.[27] By 1883 the home was caring for forty-six children. It was this ministry that gave the founder his nickname of "Father Buckner."

Under Buckner's leadership, the home helped earn its own way. The larger boys worked in the fields, while the larger girls helped with the housekeeping. In fact, at times they did more than help. At one point Buckner appealed for funds to hire an additional matron so the larger girls could return to their schooling. Women of Dallas and beyond helped by sewing clothing, quilts, and putting up canned food for the home. The children had their own Home Baptist Church with Buckner as pastor. He regularly baptized converts, conducted a Sunday School, and made every effort to maintain a healthy and wholesome home for the children. Dr. Robert Duncan, a physician nearby, gave free medical care. Buckner admitted that they took in, from time to time, a number of "wicked children," addicted especially to "profane swearing, inveracity, and kleptomania," but they seldom persisted in these habits beyond a few weeks. In time the Buckner Orphans Home became the best known and most distinguished child care facility in the state.

Beyond sponsoring the orphanage, the Deacons Convention offered programs to raise the qualifications of deacons, teach stewardship in the churches, foster better methods of Sunday School enlistment and teaching, and even occasionally hinted, deacon-like, at how the pastors might improve their preaching.

In many ways the two state conventions were mirror images of each other. Both espoused the same causes, used similar structures and methods in their work, and confronted the same challenges and difficulties. Despite the rivalry, often intense, some pastors moved freely between the two conventions. Even the three additional state conventions formed in the 1880s did not differ from the two older conventions, or from each other, in any significant manner. How, then, does one explain the fragmentation of Texas Baptists into so many competing groups? At least four causes may have contributed. First, regional jealousy and rivalry played a role. The piney woods of East Texas and the prairie grasslands of West Texas are in the same state, but in different worlds. When Baptist resources were inadequate to address all needs, it was easy for some regions to feel neglected. Because they were first, the Union Association (1840), Baylor University (1845), and the Baptist State Convention (1848) developed a self-image of superiority which many Baptists in other regions found galling. Second, the General Association inherited a residue of Parker anti-mission sentiment, a Landmark suspicion of denominational structures and leaders, and an exaggerated caution for local church independence which made denominational cooperation more difficult. The ultra-conservative system known as Landmarkism, while not entirely absent from the BSC, showed up more pervasively in the BGA.[28] J. R. Graves, creator and chief spokesman for the Landmark system, often spoke at BGA sessions. Landmark teachings were a primary factor in the disastrous split in First Baptist Church of Dallas in 1879, a local church conflict which served as a microcosm of the statewide divisions.[29] Because Landmarkers held a more restrictive doctrine of the church, they also held different views of the nature and purpose of denominational bodies.

Third, many found clear economic advantages in supporting one state convention over the other. This was especially the case with the colleges, where a dollar for one often meant a dollar less for the other. The conflict was especially intense between newspaper editors, and the economic factor shows in the fierce competition for subscribers. Fourth, large egos were at stake. One is tempted to conclude that personality conflicts, such as that between J. B. Link and R. C. Buckner, explain much of the conflict. Such BGA leaders as B. H. Carroll and R. C. Burleson, and BSC leaders like J. W. D. Creath and O. C. Pope, were happiest when having their own way and they were happy most of the time.

A strange episode occurred in 1880 which left the General Association apologizing for years to come. J. B. Link, editor of the *Texas Baptist Herald,* moved to Dallas in 1878 and with his wife, affectionately known as "Sister Ada," joined First Baptist Church on a rainy Wednesday night with only a handful of members present. R. C. Buckner, editor of the *Texas Baptist,* was also a member, but was absent that night, an absence that did not surprise some who said that "his attendance was far from regular, either in good or bad nights." By that time the two rival editors had become bitter enemies. When Buckner and his friends learned that Link was their fellow church member, they objected vigorously and demanded that the church rescind the membership. When the church refused, a major church brawl developed in which factions contested control of the church building, scuffled for possession of the keys, and made loud accusations against each other that scandalized the entire city. The upshot was that the highly respected "Father Buckner" was excluded from the church and asked to surrender his ministerial credentials. Along with several charges against Buckner, church records conclude that "We have found him to be a cantankerous old fool."[30] However, this controversy soon subsided and Buckner remains one of the great heroes of Texas Baptist history.

This might have remained a local brawl but for one fact; Buckner was also Corresponding Secretary of the General Association, and that body required that its officers be in good standing in their church in order to serve. Buckner's friends rallied vigorously to his defense and, unwisely it later appeared, held a special called meeting of the BGA in February 1880 in the Dallas church. In a packed assembly (controversy does draw a crowd), the denominational body in effect reversed the action of the local church and declared Buckner still in good standing and therefore still eligible to serve as Corresponding Secretary. B. H. Carroll was especially vigorous in defending Buckner and effectively steamrolled church leaders who claimed the Association had no authority to overturn a decision of a local church. Carroll claimed that the faction which excluded Buckner did not constitute the true church, and thus their actions were null and void. He insisted that "Principles, not majorities, constitute a church. Therefore, where there are two or more claimants to the name and rights of a church, that party, whether large or small, which stands upon the principles and laws of its organization, is the church."[31]

Messengers appointed to the called meeting by FBC were not allowed to present their case. Link repeatedly sought to speak, but permission was withheld until after the decision was made, whereupon Link refused to present his case since it was then moot. L. B. Kimbrough, also a member of FBC, preached the opening sermon, in which he warned that if the Association interfered with a decision of the church it "will split North Texas Baptists wide open." That is essentially what happened. Within a short time, three additional state conventions were formed in Texas and FBC, Dallas, which had formerly cooperated with the General Association, switched to the new Baptist Convention of North Texas. Within a year the BGA expressed regret for its hasty action, though insisting lamely that they did nothing wrong.

SUNDAY SCHOOL AND COLPORTAGE MINISTRY

From early days Texas Baptists promoted Sunday School work, not always with success, along with the distribution of religious literature for homes and churches. *Colporteur*, a word not widely used today, denotes one who peddles or sells religious literature, hence *colportage* to describe that work. There were of course no Baptist Book Stores in those days, but many families felt a print hunger for tracts, books, and hymnals. Various efforts were made to supply this material. The oldest and strongest Baptist publishing house was the American Baptist Publication Society at Philadelphia, which supplied good material at favorable prices. However, the schism between Northern and Southern Baptists which led to the Southern Baptist Convention in 1845 caused many Southern churches to drop the Northern literature.

Southern Baptists made several efforts to fill the literature gap. The Southern Baptist Publication Society, a mirror image of its Northern counterpoint, was formed in 1847 in Greenville, South Carolina. However, its distribution was limited, and even by the 1860s many Texas Baptists seemed unaware of its existence. The Bible Board, formed in 1851, supplied some literature along with Bibles, but fell out of favor when it came under control of the Landmark faction. The first Sunday School Board of the SBC was formed in 1863, but perished in the undertow of the Civil War. After 1873 the Home Mission Board gave limited and unenthusiastic promotion to Sunday School work and continued publication of *Kind Words,* which it had inherited from the defunct Sunday School Board. In 1857 J. R. Graves led in forming the Southern Baptist Sunday School Union to form more Sunday Schools, and also formed his own private company, the Southwestern Publishing Company, to provide them with literature. This was a private business enterprise, with profits going to Graves and his business associates. The Graves publishing company did not win full acceptance in Texas because of its Landmark emphases. Several influential leaders presented a resolution at the General Association, generally friendly territory for Graves, that "We the undersigned hereby protest against the endorsement of the proposed Southwestern Publishing House, at Memphis by this body."[32] It was not until 1891 that the present Baptist Sunday School Board was formed, providing a steady stream of materials for Baptist Sunday Schools in the South. The upshot was that, in addition to other problems, Baptist Sunday Schools in Texas during this period had difficulty obtaining suitable study materials.

The two state conventions formed "book depositories" in their territories, the BSC at Brenham and Bryan, and the BGA at Dallas. They purchased or solicited gifts of materials from Eastern publishers to stock these depositories. Colporteurs loaded buggies or saddlebags with Bibles, books, tracts, leaflets and hymnals and peddled these out among the churches and homes. This book peddlar received a percentage of his sales. In 1881 R. C. Burleson introduced the "Nickel System," a plan asking Sunday School pupils to contribute five cents a week to defray the cost of literature. In the 1840s some Texas churches had "union" Sunday Schools and used a non-denominational literature which soft-pedaled baptism by immersion in order to sell the same literature to other denominations. However, by the 1870s Texas Baptists of all stripes were agreed on one thing: they refused to use the union literature. "Baptists cannot afford to use [non-Baptist] . . . literature in their Sunday-schools," they said, for "Union literature suppresses a part of the truth."[33]

Each convention formed its own auxiliary organization for Sunday School work. The "Texas Baptist Sabbath School and Colportage Union" was formed at Independence in 1865 and loosely related to the BSC.[34] At that meeting J. H. Stribling preached a sermon from Proverbs 23:6, *"Train up a child in the way he should go."* That sermon was printed and widely distributed, and went a long way toward convincing Texas Baptists of the importance of this work.

Partly as a result of observing the success of the Sabbath School Union, the BGA in 1875 formed its own organization, "The Sunday School Convention of the General Association of Texas," to be located in Longview, and to meet annually in connection with the General Association. The president, R. C. Buckner, urged every association to form its own Sunday School convention, auxiliary to the state body. The Sunday School organizations of both conventions appointed, from time to time, "Sunday School Evangelists," who traveled the state urging churches to form Sunday Schools and training teachers in the work. One of the greatest of these was Major W. E. Penn of Jefferson, a layman who, like the great D. L. Moody, entered the ministry by means of Sunday School work. Penn first got interested in Sunday School work and his extraordinary ability as a speaker later propelled him into general evangelistic work. He is reckoned as the first full-time Baptist evangelist in Texas. Interestingly, Baptist university leaders in Texas proved to be among the most ardent proponents of religious education for children and lay persons in the churches. W. C. Crane, R. C. Burleson, R. C. Buckner, Abram Weaver and, above all, B. H. Carroll would not allow obstacles to defeat the dream of a Baptist constituency taught from childhood the doctrines of Scripture and the grace of giving. These leaders would have endorsed the life motto of M. V. Smith, Sunday School evangelist, "The Children for Christ, and a Baptist Sunday School in every church in Texas."

The obstacles were plentiful. Despite insistent sermons by advocates, many pastors remained unconvinced of the value of Sunday Schools. "The importance of Sunday-schools is not understood and appreciated by the brethren generally," complained the BGA in 1868.[35] In another report, the BGA lamented that "we find a large vacancy" in religious literature, with many families in their territory without even a copy of the Bible. The *Texas Baptist Herald* reported in July 1869 that "Sunday School work in Texas is only beginning to be appreciated. Even ministers seem but feebly to realize the momentous importance of this work." The work was slow. During its first year, the Sunday School Convention of the BGA raised only $10.15 for its work. However, some improvement was shown the next year when Sunday School Evangelist J. T. S. Park traveled about 3,000 miles in five months, organized eight Sunday School conventions in associations, formed eight new schools in churches and revived others, visited hundreds of families, and taught children to sing.[36] By then Baptists were catching on to the importance of singing in Sunday School, and they also put more emphasis upon teacher enlistment and training, and a new focus upon the importance of the Sunday School superintendent. The American Baptist Year Book for 1876 reported 250 Baptist Sunday Schools in Texas, with 1,250 teachers and about 10,000 pupils, which represented only a tiny fraction of total Baptist membership.[37]

The blunt reality is that it is hard to operate a full-time Sunday School in a part-time church. Sunday Schools began to prosper when more churches were full-time, when church buildings were improved, when suitable literature became readily available, and when Baptist women became more involved as teachers and leaders. In a day when many Baptists were frightened of women exercising any leadership in church, Sunday School was one arena where their efforts were welcomed. Early on, the Union Association recognized that Baptists had sufficient leaders "among our noble and pious women, if not among the men, to carry on our Sunday Schools."[38]

TEXAS BAPTIST WOMEN

Baptist women came to Texas as early as the men, but they do not show up as much in the records. One historian, Mrs. W. J. J. Smith, is convinced that there were Baptist women in Texas before 1830: she wrote, "They were here. We are sure of it. We feel their presence, . . . even in the dark."[39] A woman, Lydia Allcorn, became the first Baptist convert in Texas, and another, Massie Millard, formed the first Baptist prayer meeting. Lucinda Williams was the primary founder of First Baptist Church in Dallas, and Myra E. Graves, widow of Baylor president H. L. Graves, served as a delegate to the Southern Baptist Convention and later became a missionary to Mexico. Anne Luther was appointed a missionary to Brazil and helped awaken Texas Baptists to the challenge of foreign missions.

Mrs. Annette Lea Bledsoe came to Texas from Alabama in 1835, and in 1839 with Massie Millard formed a Women's Society in the Old North Church of Nacogdoches. This society, with sixty-five members, was the first Baptist Women's Society in Texas. Mrs. Bledsoe had freedom and resources to travel, which she did by ox cart and horseback, promoting missions. She spoke Spanish, an asset in Texas then and now. Her sister Margaret married Sam Houston and Mrs. Bledsoe later moved to Independence with the Houstons. Mrs. Bledsoe was educated at Judson College, and was active in forming prayer meetings, women's societies, and Bible study groups for women.[40] Ladonia had a women's society by 1860, and the Dorcas Society was active in Independence by 1860 or perhaps earlier. By 1880 there were many such societies in Texas.

Not all Baptists favored the formation of women's societies. Their historian says that "Even the more enlightened of them [pastors] were shy of women's societies." However, Elizabeth Pyle of Ladonia pointed out that women were capable of church leadership for they had experience in "managing their homes, their children, and even their husbands, though the poor dears knew it not."[41] In 1869 three women showed up as messengers to the General Association meeting in Tyler. According to the constitution, membership was on a contribution basis with no mention of gender, so the women paid their money and took their seats. The constitution was promptly changed to restrict membership to men.[42] Perhaps in reaction to their sister convention, the BSC in 1870 also revised its membership basis to read "brethren" instead of "members" in order to prevent similar problems arising in the BSC.[43] The fear of women was not restricted to Texas, for in 1885 the same gender restriction was written into the constitution of the SBC. W. C. Crane, president of Baylor University, was an advocate of the women's societies, as was B. H. Carroll of Waco. In 1879 Carroll led in setting aside six women as deaconesses in the First Baptist Church of Waco, perhaps the first Baptist women to serve in this role in Texas.[44]

The first statewide organization of Texas Baptist women came in October 1880 with formation of the Woman's Missionary Union of Texas in affiliation with the Baptist State Convention. While this organization was being formed in a basement Sunday School room of First Baptist Church in Austin, Miss Anne (often written "Annie") Luther was being interviewed upstairs for appointment as a missionary to Brazil. Mrs. F. B. Davis of Independence was the first president, and the women raised $35.45 for foreign missions at that first meeting. Texas Baptist women undertook to support Anne Luther, and within a year there were 345 Anne Luther societies in Texas churches. Anne and her new husband, William Buck Bagby, sailed for Brazil in January 1881, thus beginning the great saga of the "Bagbys of Brazil," which saw five generations of this remarkable family serving in Brazil. Anne Luther Bagby captured the hearts of Texas Baptists, and perhaps no person did more to awaken them to the foreign mission challenge.[45] That makes it even more remarkable that she is so little known today. Other Texans felt the missionary call: Zachary C. Taylor and his wife joined the Bagbys in Brazil, along with Mr. and Mrs. C. D. Daniel, Mr. and Mrs. E. A. Puthuff, and Miss Mina Everett. One source of this great interest in Brazil was A. T. Hawthorne, a Confederate general who expatriated to Brazil to escape a changed South. On a subsequent trip to Texas, General Hawthorne was converted and turned his attention to trying to enlist missionaries as well as settlers for his Brazilian colony. His vivid descriptions of Brazil attracted widespread interest, beginning with Anne Luther.

Not to be outdone, women of the General Association formed the Ladies General Aid Society in Paris in 1884 with Mrs. C. E.W. Priest as first president. Their constitution announced three areas of ministry: missions, education, and orphans. They hoped to lead every church affiliated with the BGA to form a woman's society, and they promoted their work through the pages of *The Good Samaritan,* a small Baptist paper. The Deacons Convention pointed out that "Many noble women are laboring earnestly in many appropriate ways," and the Deacons wanted to affirm them, but cautiously, "without intending to encourage the multiplying of organizations or the endorsement of any indiscretions of fanatical women."[46]

Through the churches, local societies, and these statewide organizations, Texas Baptist women promoted missions, raised funds, taught missions. They were also active in teaching among the black population, where they taught the Bible along with domestic skills. While Baptist men made rousing speeches about ministry to blacks, Baptist women did actual ministry. Women were also active in Sunday School work and even in church planting. Perhaps the role of Texas Baptist women is nowhere better illustrated than in Lucinda Williams who, with her husband Will, moved to Dallas in 1867.

On the first Sunday of their residence in Dallas, Lou Williams asked their Methodist landlady where the Baptist church was located. She was told there was no Baptist church, and the landlady hoped there never would be. What the landlady did not say, and probably did not know, was that three Baptist churches had been formed in Dallas, but none had survived. At first the Williamses attended the Presbyterian church, but Lucinda canvassed the neighborhood and located a few Baptists. As a result of her witness, eleven Baptists, including Will and Lucinda, gathered on July 30, 1868, at the Masonic Hall on Lamar Street near Ross Avenue and formed the present First Baptist Church of Dallas. However, the church struggled and seemed likely to go the way of its predecessors. The second pastor, C. A. Stanton, resigned in discouragement in May 1872 and as Mrs. Williams later recorded it,

> When he told me good-bye, he remarked that he thought if our women did not organize and do something for our church it would yet fail. The thought of failure was very disturbing to me. I left my two children with an old colored woman living near by, went to a home where three of our church women lived, and told them what Brother Stanton had said. One of the women agreed to see every woman in the church and, upon going, she found every one of them of one mind for the organization. We went to work with a purpose to succeed. When the brethren heard what we were doing they bestirred themselves and employed a Brother Abram Weaver as pastor. . . . The women organized and went to work, and before the summer of 1872 had passed we had secured enough money to build the foundation for the first Baptist church house ever built in Dallas. Five hundred dollars was the amount.[47]

With that determined spirit, the Baptist women of Dallas saw their church set on a firm foundation. Never again was the survival of the church in doubt.

A few churches, like Dallas, employed a "Bible woman" on the church staff. The Bible woman was often the first paid staff member after pastor and janitor. The Bible woman was essentially a Sunday School visitor, whose job was to visit in the neighborhood to enlist Sunday School attendance. She also taught Sunday School, and helped enlist and train other teachers. The Bible woman for First Baptist, Dallas, in the 1880s was Miss

Holly Harper. She later married E. G. Townsend and they traveled throughout the state in a chapel car ministry. In response to a letter from Lottie Moon in China, the Dallas women have the distinction of raising an offering for Miss Moon's work long before the Lottie Moon Christmas Offering was launched. In 1883 the women of this church raised $220, of which they sent $100 "to our western mission work through the North Texas Convention" to assist in church planting in Wichita Falls and westward.

One major contribution of the Baptist women of Dallas was in making missions a churchwide emphasis, not just a matter for the WMU. With the approval of the pastor and deacons, the women suggested "That we have protracted missionary services for several successive Sabbaths, and that one Sunday each month be designated as "Missionary Day," with mission emphasis in the Sunday School classes and from the pulpit.

Baptist women of Texas also participated in the Southern Baptist Convention. Myra E. Graves, widow of the Baylor president, attended the Convention, registered simply as "M. E. Graves." Later when women attempted to register as SBC messengers they were challenged and in 1885 the SBC constitution was changed from "messengers" to "brethren" to exclude women. That exclusion remained in the SBC constitution until 1918, when over intense opposition the wording was changed back to "messenger."[48] Several Texas women participated in formation of Woman's Missionary Union, Auxiliary to the Southern Baptist Convention, in 1888. Among them were Mrs. F. B. Davis, Mrs. A. C. Audrey, Mrs. W. L. Williams, Miss Minnie Slaughter, and Miss Jessie Williams. When it appeared the women might falter, Mrs. Williams, who was described on the occasion as "resplendent in a black dress," spoke with strength and the women rallied to form the national WMU.

BAPTIST EDUCATION IN TEXAS

Next to state missions, Texas Baptists expended more ink, money, and energy on schools than any other cause. Texas Baptists entered this era, 1868-1886, with several schools of which Baylor University and Baylor Female College, both at Independence, and Waco University in Waco were the main ones. Public schools were almost unheard of in those days in Texas, and in many communities the Baptists formed schools, variously called institutes, academies, seminaries, and colleges, most of them designed for youth from about age ten to eighteen. Some of these schools which show up in the records include Ladonia Institute, Ladonia; the Charwood Institute, Tyler; the Female School, Paris; the Henderson Atheneum, Athens; the Cleburne Institute, Cleburne; the Mount Calvary Academy; the Pleasant Grove Academy, near Longview; and many others. Separate schools were conducted for boys and girls, for coeducation was frowned upon by Baptists at that time. Baylor and Waco aspired to university status, but both enrolled children as young as ten.

After the War, Baylor University suffered the dislocations common to the entire state. Enrollment was slow to recover, and financial crises prevented needed improvement of buildings, enlargement of the library, and the gathering of more adequate "apparatus" for the science classes. The scholarly president, W. C. Crane, gave solid leadership, though he faced an uphill struggle for enrollment and funding. Perhaps his greatest handicap was the persistent rumor that Baylor would be moved from Independence, which hampered his efforts to build a permanent university. The Baptist State Convention never wavered in its support for Baylor, both moral and financial. Like Baptist schools everywhere, Baylor claimed an inflated enrollment, but actual attendance was much less. The 1872 report, for example, listed 120 enrolled, with 70 the largest number in attendance at any one time. That year the school had three full-time professors, and seven ministerial students. By the late 1870s the BSC had in place scholarship assistance for ministerial students. In 1873, eight licentiates (student ministers) preached through the summer in a kind of "youth revival" of its time. One of these licentiates, James M. Carroll, preached 45 sermons and 18 exhortations that summer in Burleson and Milam counties. Another, H. M. Haggard, reported 64 conversions in Brazos, Leon, and Madison counties.[49]

While the General Association tended to hold loose ties with its schools, the State Convention held a tighter rein. A blunt report in 1870 suggested more militant action than the Convention actually took. It said,

> Two institutions of learning, Baylor College and Baylor Female College are organically connected with it [the State Convention]. You elect their Boards of Trustees and fill all vacancies in them. You therefore virtually control them . . . . If the Presidents and faculties of these institutions do not please you, command your Trustees to dismiss them. If they will not obey you, then dismiss your Trustees and appoint others.[50]

The women's department had become a separate school, Baylor Female College, under the leadership of Horace Clark. The school continued at Independence in buildings decidedly superior to those for the men. In 1870 a proposal was heard to switch the Female College from State Convention to Union Association sponsorship. The trustees reported

> That in view of the embarrassments in which the Baptist State Convention is involved, in having under its control and patronage two institutions of learning, while it has scarcely the means of providing for one, and in view of the extent to which our interests are necessarily compromised, that a separation between Baylor Female College and the Baptist State Convention is desirable and expedient, provided a union can be formed upon the same basis with Union Association.[51]

No such switch took place, however, though it had the support of both presidents, Clark of the Female College and Crane of the University. After Clark, other presidents included H. L. Graves, W. W. Fontaine,

William Royall, and John H. Luther. President Luther's charming and talented daughter, Anne, also taught at the college and served in a role that today might be called dean of women. The curriculum differed somewhat from the men's department, with less math and science, but more emphasis upon the "ornamental subjects" of music and art. The school also took pride in its high quality musical instruments used for teaching and for public performances. As in the "finishing schools" of the day, the Baylor women were also taught the social graces and adequate social occasions were sponsored to allow them to practice their skills. Clark was deeply committed to the education of women as well as men, and he believed that "the humblest female may be the equal of him who fills the sacred desk; and in her sphere may do as much, possibly more, in commending the gospel of Christ to the world."[52]

Commencements were exciting times of pomp and circumstance. Usually the president would give a report on the state of the college, and some member of the faculty or trustees would make a speech commending the parents for sending their daughters to college, and especially to Baylor. Several students would give declamations, "literary pieces" and, of course, there would be music. Perhaps the commencement of 1885, described in the *Texas Baptist Herald*, was typical. That year the college graduated "a bright intelligent bevy of girls." President Luther gave out the usual academic and literary awards, and concluded by presenting four young ladies gold medals for special merit. In those days hair styles were changing, and "bangs" were becoming popular among the girls but not among the college officials. At the commencement, the president solemnly announced that during the year "four young ladies had discarded bangs."[53] For that they received gold medals, as he had promised.

The General Association fully matched the State Convention in its commitment to education. In 1869 the BGA voted that "we cheerfully commend to the confidence and patronage of the Baptists of Texas 'The Waco University,' presided over by the Rev. R. C. Burleson."[54] Like Baylor, Waco also made provision for ministerial students. Those who passed the rigid examination as to spiritual and intellectual qualifications were offered scholarships to attend either Baylor or Waco, for they voted that "no discrimination be made between institutions of learning." In fact, B. H. Carroll of Waco, a major leader of the BGA, suggested that his younger brother, James, attend Baylor instead of Waco. Those who did not continue in ministry were expected to pay back their scholarships. Both state conventions also provided aid for students to attend the Southern Baptist Theological Seminary in Greenville (after 1877, in Louisville).

In their reports, the BGA always made the point that much as they favored the schools, none had any organic connection to the General Association or any financial claims upon that body. Most of the schools were linked to associations, as was Waco University with the Waco Association. However, in 1880 the BGA appointed a committee to confer with trustees from Waco University and the Waco Association "with reference to organic connection of this General Association with Waco University as her denominational school."[55] There was some thought given to moving the university, probably to Dallas, but citizens of Waco raised enough money to convince the BGA to leave the school on the Brazos.

CONSOLIDATION, 1886

With five state conventions, each with its satellite organizations, Texas Baptist life in the 1880s presented a confusing hodge-podge of structures and programs. Those who saw how ridiculous the situation had become seemed powerless to change it. But gradually, sentiment for consolidation surfaced and within a few years reached a crescendo. Most of the initiative for consolidation came from the General Association, led by B. H. Carroll and R. T. Hanks, pastors at Waco and Dallas respectively. At first the State Convention dragged its heels but by 1885 grudgingly acknowledged that consolidation was inevitable and probably would be beneficial.

The push for consolidation began with an effort to merge Baylor and Waco universities. It became clear that Texas Baptists could continue to divide their support between two mediocre colleges, or pool their resources to create one first-class university. At first both colleges strongly resisted efforts to draw them together. People who favored Baylor at Independence especially refused to acknowledge that history had passed them by. In 1869 the BSC voted "That after full and free discussion, we are satisfied that it is impractical now, or at any future time, to remove Baylor University or Baylor Female College." For added emphasis, they voted to "re-adopt" the same resolution in 1870.[56] That mild expression had replaced an earlier statement that "it is inexpedient to *consider* [emphasis added] the question of removal of Baylor University from its present location." Even by 1885 when merger was inevitable and Baptists were convinced that Baylor must move or die, a group of diehards said they would rather see the school die in Independence than live in Waco.

R. C. Burleson, president of Waco University, issued a proposal in 1870 that both schools move to a new location, and that Texas Baptists unite around one great university. A committee met in Navasota in 1875 where, during an all night session, they hammered out an agreement known as "the Navasota Compromise." By this improbable agreement, there would be *one* university and *both* Baylor and Waco would be integral parts in it. Baylor would get the first $25,000 of endowment and the theology department, while Waco would get the bulk of the endowment and the classical department. One is not surprised that this Navasota Compromise was later repudiated. However, reality eventually set in. Dr. W. C. Crane, president of Baylor, died in 1885 and in effect the school died with him. Later that year the convention session in Lampasas voted that "the time has fully come when these institutions [Baylor University and Baylor Female College] should be removed to some more eligible place in the state, and we therefore recommend that this be done." The Convention could recommend, but only the trustees could act, and they reluctantly voted to merge with Waco University. By the terms of this agreement, the buildings and grounds at Independence reverted to the Union Association. The merged school would bear the name of *Baylor University at Waco*. Most of the library and apparatus went to Waco. Some of the endowment went to Waco, some remained in Independence, and some reverted to donors. In an effort to retain something at Independence, leaders there formed the William Carey Crane College but it was short-lived. Dr. Burleson was named Chancellor For Life of the new Baylor. Observers at the time would have said the larger and wealthier Waco University won by absorbing the Independence school, but in the long run they would be mistaken. It was the Baylor name, charter, and traditions that continued. Baylor Female College was later moved to Belton where it still flourishes today as the University of Mary Hardin-Baylor.

While education led the move to consolidation, the several state conventions were not far behind. In 1883 B. H. Carroll made a strong appeal for unification, and led the BGA to send a proposal to the BSC seeking to negotiate a merger. The BSC made a cool response. As Dr. Crane put it, "The plums were too green then to be gathered."[57] The brethren voted that the BSC "will cordially . . . welcome to its membership all general Baptist organizations . . . who may desire it, upon the basis of membership prescribed in the Constitution of the Convention."[58] Their idea of consolidation was for all the other conventions to dissolve and join the State Convention. In fact, the North Texas Convention was in process of doing just that in 1883, and in 1884 the Central and East Texas conventions also joined the BSC. However, by 1885 the plums were ripe: as to division, the *Texas Baptist Herald* said, "The Baptists of Texas have had enough of it."

In 1885 the General Association adopted a resolution saying, "That it is the sense of the Association that . . . the interests of our denomination in the state would be best subserved by the existence of one general body, and that this Association is willing to co-operate with other general bodies for the accomplishment of this end, on terms honorable and equal to all."[59] At its annual meeting in Lampasas a few weeks later the State Convention voted that "The Baptist State Convention having considered the importance of consolidating our General Bodies, and believing that the interests of our educational and Missionary work, as well as the peace, harmony and prosperity of the denomination, in the entire state, will be promoted thereby, we announce our readiness to meet like committees from the General Association and the East Texas Convention for the purpose of securing organic union on terms of equity and fairness to all parties."[60] By that time most Texas Baptists would have agreed with A. J. Holt, who said "My heart is state-wide."

A large gathering of various committees, trustees, convention board members and other interested persons met in Temple on December 9, 1885, to discuss merger of the colleges and conventions. Upon motion of B. H. Carroll a subcommittee of five each was appointed from the BSC and BGA. This important committee was composed of C. R. Breedlove, J. B. Link, M. V. Smith, R. J. Sledge, and F. M. Law for the State Convention; and for the General Association, L. L. Foster, R. C. Burleson, J. L. Whittle, W. B. Denson, and B. H. Carroll.[61] This was the committee, with power to act, that worked out the final terms of consolidation. Their report concluded:

> We, your committee, believing that the consolidation of general bodies is desirable, recommend:
> 1. That the Baptist General Association of Texas be consolidated with the Baptist State Convention of Texas.
> 2. That the name of the consolidated body shall be 'The Baptist General Convention of Texas.'
> 3. That the basis of representation in the first meeting of the consolidated body shall be the same as heretofore. . . .
> 4. That the mission work be continued till the first meeting as heretofore under the direction of the two general bodies respectively, and be reported to that meeting.
> 5. That the first meeting of the consolidated body be held at Waco, beginning on Tuesday after the first Sunday in July, 1886.[62]

The provisional joint session approved these recommendations, and the merger was done. With the two main bodies merged, the various satellite organizations had little difficulty following suit; in fact, some had already united. A series of committees met, negotiated and reported, the details of which need not be recounted here. The Sunday School and Colportage Convention (BSC) and the Sunday School Convention (BGA) had never developed the bitter rivalry that their sponsoring conventions did. The two organizations merged with each other in 1885, but did not unite with the consolidated convention until 1900. The Woman's Missionary Union of Texas (BSC) and the Ladies General Aid Society (BGA) merged in 1886 to form the Baptist Women Mission Workers, with Mrs. F. B. Davis as first president. They retained that name until 1919.

By 1886 the five Texas Baptist conventions, two colleges, two organizations for women, and other related organizations had merged, but the task was not yet complete for two rival papers kept the controversy going, one from Austin and the other from Dallas. Both papers were privately owned and the convention had no control over them. Both editors agreed to submit the matter to a committee, which recommended that the papers be merged. The committee, however, could not agree on where the consolidated paper should be located. They submitted the matter to the first meeting of the consolidated Convention in 1886, asking that body by a non-binding straw vote to indicate the preference of the denomination, insofar as any convention could speak for the denomination. J. B. Link of *The Baptist Herald* held out for Waco, while S. A. Hayden of the *Texas Baptist* argued for Dallas. Link and Hayden were given fifteen minutes each to make their pitch and then the Convention voted.[63] At the last moment, B. H. Carroll, pastor in Waco, asked that no Waco delegates vote, expecting apparently that the Dallas delegates, who had equal vested interests, would also abstain. The Waco people abstained but the Dallas people voted, and the tally came out 168 for Waco and 169 for Dallas. Within hours Link sold the *Texas Baptist Herald* for $10,000 to Hayden, who promptly moved it to Dallas and merged it with his own paper to form the *Texas Baptist and Herald.* This left the contentious Hayden as sole editor of the only Baptist paper in Texas. Future events would confirm that this was a recipe for trouble.

THE BAPTIST GENERAL CONVENTION OF TEXAS

The newly formed Baptist General Convention of Texas (BGCT) elected A. T. Spalding, a BSC man, as its first president and named A. J. Holt, a BGA man, as its first corresponding secretary. Every effort was made to include representatives from both sides on the various boards, trustees, and committees of the consolidated convention. The new body located its offices at Waco. For the first time since 1868, Texas Baptists had organizational union. Spiritual *unity,* however, proved more elusive.

CHAPTER 6

SEARCH FOR UNITY, 1886–1900

"THE FIRST ANNUAL SESSION of the Baptist General Convention of Texas met in the Baptist church of Waco, on Tuesday, June 29, 1886, at 10 o'clock, A.M."

These simple words mark a momentous new beginning for Texas Baptists. For the first time since the 1850s the divided tribes of the Texas Baptist Israel sat down in one council. No longer were they divided into several state conventions. Union was *voted* at Waco in a few minutes, but it was *actually achieved,* to the extent it ever was, on the field and in the trenches over the next decade. The transition was not without its rough spots, and complete unity of mind and ministry always seemed to recede like a mirage in the distance. However, after a generation of runaway fragmentation, Texas Baptists at least tried to come together.

If the union of '86 be likened to a wedding, it was definitely a shotgun wedding. The State Convention came reluctantly to the altar, with no great fondness for the powerful and pervasive General Association. In the three major areas of consolidation, the colleges, conventions, and papers, Baptists of the State Convention came out with the short end of the stick in all three. In the short run, very little of Baylor University at Independence transferred to Waco, either students, faculty, or endowment. In the long run, however, it was the Baylor name, charter, and traditions which survived. The new General Convention was essentially the old General Association under a new name, though they dated the new Convention from 1848. The old State Convention brought to the union limited resources, abundant debt, and diminished enthusiasm. The major leaders of the new BGCT were brought over from the BGA. The State Convention had no leaders who could stand up to the likes of B. H. Carroll, Rufus C. Burleson, Robert C. Buckner, and A. J. Holt. The giants of the past who might have stood up were gone. Z. N. Morrell, R. E. B. Baylor, and J. W. D. Creath were dead, J. H. Stribling was aged, and O. C. Pope had become an agent for the Northern Baptist HMS. In 1886 J. B. Link moved his *Texas Baptist Herald* to Waco,[1] probably expecting it to become the voice of the consolidated Convention. However, as previously noted, in a strange vote Link's paper, which had so loyally supported State Convention causes, fell to S. A. Hayden's *Texas Baptist* of Dallas, a paper which supported the General Association and had shown a distinctly unfriendly attitude toward the BSC and its work. Turning Texas Baptist journalism from the cooperative Link to the divisive Hayden may have been the one greatest mistake at Waco in 1886. The center of gravity in Texas Baptist life shifted northward; almost overnight, Dallas became the hub of the Baptist wheel in Texas, though the Convention offices remained in Waco until 1896. The one exception to the total victory of the General Association in the merger was in the Sunday School work. The old Sunday School and Colportage Convention, related to the State Convention, declined to merge and continued until 1900 though with diminishing influence.

The committee to draw a new constitution, led by B. H. Carroll, reported in 1887.[2] Articles I through IV are taken almost word for word from the old BGA constitution. Membership was on a combined church/contribution basis. Any cooperating church could send two messengers (by then the term "delegate" had disappeared) without regard to contributions and an additional messenger for each $25 contributed up to a maximum of eight. Each association could send two, with one additional for each $100 expended in missions in its own territory or each $100 contributed to the convention. Any Baptist Missionary Society could send one messenger for each $25 given, up to a maximum of four.

Article V departs significantly from the BGA pattern and, in fact, picks up a feature from the older convention. It calls for a Board of Directors with thirty members, three of them nominated by the president but all elected by the Convention. This Board had authority to oversee all the work of the Convention, employ missionaries and set their compensation, and generally make decisions for the Convention between sessions. It anticipates the Executive Board of the BGCT formed in 1914, and also the Executive Committee formed by the SBC in 1917. Other provisions of Article V call for the Convention to elect trustees for Baylor University, Baylor Female College, and a Ministers Relief Board. The Board of Directors held property and funds of the Convention, and had authority to appoint missionaries and an assistant superintendent of missions when they felt it was necessary. However, the Convention reserved to itself the election of the corresponding secretary.

NEW STRUCTURES FOR OLD TASKS

The vote to consolidate did not change the fact that Texas had hundreds of towns and communities with no Baptist witness, and countless others where the Baptist presence was weak. Eighty-five Texas counties still had no Baptist church in 1887, and A. J. Holt reported that "The Rio

Grande touches 1500 miles of Texas frontier, and we have only two mission stations along its whole length."[3] By 1886 the worst of Reconstruction was over and the Texas economy showed signs of recovery despite periodic drouths. Travel by the missionaries was greatly improved by better roads, the extension of railway service, and relative safety since most of the hostile Indians had been pushed further to the west. The new Baptist General Convention of Texas (BGCT) began its work with ambition and energy, determined to practice the unity they had voted. In one of its first actions, the Convention agreed "to set our faces like flint against anything that would tend to a disruption of our fellowship or our faith."[4]

Between 1886 and 1900 five men served as Corresponding Secretary of the General Convention. All were committed and capable, but four of the five were pressured out of office after a brief tenure. Though the issues differed slightly with each man, S. A. Hayden, the extremist editor of the *Texas Baptist and Herald,* provoked most of the controversy. Space allows only a brief sketch of the ministry of these five leaders.

Adoniram Judson Holt. Texas Baptists were fortunate in their first corresponding secretary of the new Convention. Adoniram Judson Holt, named for the great Baptist missionary, served from 1886-1889. He was a man of good insight, high motivation, and incredible energy. As corresponding secretary his job was to raise money for all Convention tasks, oversee the appointment and direct the work of over 100 missionaries, and keep Texas Baptists motivated and active. He was imminently successful in all of these. He had held a similar post with the General Association, and before he directed missionaries, he had been one. One Baptist said of Holt, "He will be the eyes, the ears, the mouth of the Board."[5]

Born in Florida, Holt migrated to Texas in 1858 where he came under the influence of his uncle, R. C. Buckner. Encouraged by Buckner to secure an education, Holt attended McKenzie College in Paris and later was a student on two different occasions at the Southern Baptist Theological Seminary while it was still in Greenville, South Carolina.

Holt faced plenty of problems. Unification had been voted, but not yet achieved on the field. "It may take some time to adjust the machinery," he said, "but let no one become fretful or discouraged." He urged Baptists to accept the past and turn their attention to the future. "Brethren, the opportunity is ours. Quit discussing the dead issues as to whether consolidation was best. Let us deal with the living present." Holt, though he had been a strong General Association man, was probably as truly ecumenical as any of his peers in his willingness to work with State Convention people to make consolidation a success. He urged, "Let not one single expression escape lips or pens which would uncover or resurrect past unpleasantness."[6]

From the BSC Holt inherited very limited funds along with a sheaf of pledges which proved mostly uncollectible. Missionaries carried over from the BSC had for years followed their own procedures on how they reported their work, and many of them were slow to conform to the new report

forms which Holt brought over from the General Association. Hard feelings arose when Holt sometimes delayed salary payments until the missionaries made the proper reports. Another problem which both earlier
bodies had faced but which came into sharper focus under the new BGCT
was the tendency of mission stations to remain dependent for too long.
The plan called for the Convention to sponsor missionaries to begin the
work, form churches, and then lead those churches to become self-suffi-
cient as soon as possible. However, many of the new churches remained
dependent upon Convention aid year after year.

Baptists had often discussed this problem, but Holt attempted to do
something about it and thereby aroused the opposition of some. Holt
insisted, however, that the BGCT must conduct its work so "as not to create a feeling of permanent dependency upon the Board."[7] He vowed "to
encourage Churches and Associations to become self-sustaining as soon as
possible," and instead of being helped, become helpers of others. Holt was
more a *field* man than an *office* man. He was constantly out among the missionaries, assessing the fields first-hand, and doing the work of a missionary as well as a missions leader. He rode trains, day and night, throughout the length and breadth of the state, and spent more than a few nights
on a station bench, waiting for the next train to take him to his mission
appointment. His iron constitution and incredible energy invited comparison with his successors who could not maintain the same pace.

The mission work greatly expanded under Holt's leadership. He began 1886 with 80 missionaries at work among Anglos, and before the year
was out that number had increased to 120. In addition, cooperative work
among ethnic groups had also grown dramatically, with mission workers
among the black, Mexican, and German populations in Texas. During
1889, Holt's last year in office, only 108 missionaries worked among the
Anglo population in 550 mission stations. They baptized 1291 new converts, formed 90 churches and 211 Sunday Schools, and built 31 new
church houses on the mission fields.[8] Another 30 missionaries worked
among black people, wholly or partly sustained by the Convention. Five
preached among the Germans, and M. G. Trevino and Mina Everett continued their ministry among the Mexicans. Joseph Aden was appointed
that year as the first Baptist missionary to the Scandinavians in Texas.

Familiar complaints of neglect came to the Board during 1889, this
time from West Texas where several counties around Sweetwater felt they
were not getting their share of attention and appointments. A committee
composed of B. H. Carroll, A. M. Simms, R. C. Burleson and J. T. Harris
met with the Sweetwater Association, and agreed to form a Western
District, made up of several associations, and give them an assistant superintendent of missions for that area. In addition to Sweetwater, Cisco, Comanche, Pecan Valley, Erath County and Palo Pinto associations were
included. J. T. Harris was elected district superintendent. The district was
later enlarged to include the Panhandle.

At the Convention in 1889 the re-election of Holt, usually routine,
was challenged. Holt was nominated and so was J. B. Cranfill, giving the

new BGCT its first contested election. In addition to lingering memories of his BGA days, Holt faced two problems. He had become involved in a minor dispute in the Dallas church where he held membership and, before the difficulty was settled, he moved to another church. Some considered this disorderly conduct. A much more serious issue arose when Holt bought an interest in Hayden's *Texas Baptist Herald.* By then Hayden's contentious spirit, extremist doctrinal views, and his tactic of building subscriptions by constantly creating and fanning controversy had become obvious. For the state missions director to be linked with Hayden was simply unacceptable to most Texas Baptists. While Holt was of course very conservative, there is no reason to think he shared fully in Hayden's extreme Landmarkism. Certainly he did not share Hayden's belligerent and quarrelsome spirit. As early as 1888, Holt had been cautioned that his support among the brethren had eroded. B. H. Carroll stated bluntly that "It is not best for our Superintendent of Missions to be connected with a newspaper enterprise about which our mission constituency differ." Carroll continued,

> At the Convention last year I stated to Rev. A. J. Holt that there were obstacles in his way as superintendent of missions. That good brethren felt the obstruction and friction of certain objections. I stated them. He candidly admitted their force, but could not see a way to their removal. I then advised him to announce that his name would not go before the people another year, telling him frankly he ought to stand on his announcement if the conditions of it continued.[9]

Holt did not take Carroll's advice, but was elected and served another year. During that year he cleared up his church membership problem and sold his interest in the *Herald.* Carroll felt the difficulties were removed, and said in 1889 "because I believe the best interests of missions require his election, I do honestly, heartily and sincerely nominate A. J. Holt as Superintendent of Missions for the ensuing year."

Ordinarily, that kind of endorsement would have settled the matter. However, A. M. Simms, pastor in Cleburne and within a few months to become pastor of First Baptist Church of Dallas, introduced the following motion: "Notwithstanding the announcement just made, there are many brethren who think that the mission interests of the State require a change in the Superintendent of Missions, and we therefore nominate Bro. J. B. Cranfill to fill the place." Holt was elected by a narrow margin, but felt that his usefulness was undercut and he declined the office. Cranfill was then elected unanimously.

Holt remained in Texas for a time, but later served as Superintendent of Missions for Tennessee Baptists. A man of astute investments, Holt once owned the land where the town of Henrietta now stands. When he sold at an enormous profit, Holt decided to take a year off and travel in England, Europe, and the Holy Land. Holt later wrote,

> After I had completed my plans, I made them known to my wife. I had

not consulted her until I had perfected them. I approached her with this statement, "Darling, next Monday I will start for Europe and the Holy Land." She quickly turned her back, put her hands to her eyes a moment, then turned with a blanched face and said, "Go, darling!"[10]

Holt chose to interpret this as an expression of support from a companion who had shared the hardships of the years without a murmur. Leaving her with instructions about what to do in his absence, he departed for a grand world tour.

J. B. Cranfill (1889-1892). Cranfill's full name was James Britton Buchanan Boone Cranfill but as a boy he begged his mother to allow him to scuttle most of these family names and be known simply by two initials, though his family and close friends called him "Britt." Cranfill was a man of many abilities and, had he not been sandwiched in between such giants as B. H. Carroll, George W. Truett, and J. B. Gambrell, he would probably be regarded as one of the greatest Baptist leaders in Texas of his day. He had been a newspaper editor in Gatesville and later in Waco, served as financial agent of Baylor University, and later became the major Texas leader in the Prohibition movement. As a Prohibitionist, Cranfill attracted national attention and ran for vice-president of the United States on the Prohibitionist ticket in 1892. Cranfill attended the Convention sessions as a layman, but J. H. Stribling was so impressed with his speaking ability that he urged Cranfill to enter the ministry. His travels as financial agent for Baylor propelled Cranfill into prominence in Texas and led to his election in 1889 to succeed Holt.

Ever the newspaper man, Cranfill launched a new paper, *The State Mission Journal,* to promote the work in Texas. He also traveled extensively, attending associations and meeting with missionaries, but unlike the iron-man Holt, Cranfill could not keep up the pace. Within months his health was failing. For the two years he reported to the Convention, Cranfill showed good progress on every front in the mission work. He was a good fund-raiser and was well-liked. However, like his predecessor, Cranfill fell victim to the tensions among the Baptists and resigned under pressure.

During Cranfill's tenure the question arose as to the extent of cooperation between the BGCT and the Women Workers. Cranfill and R. C. Burleson favored cooperation with the women, but B. H. Carroll and W. H. Jenkins opposed. After an all night session, the Board voted to allow the women to cooperate with the Convention. This is how Mina Everett became a traveling agent, helping present the cause and raise money for both foreign and home missions in Texas. On one occasion, she attended a session of an association and some men challenged her right to speak. However, J. M. Carroll pointed out that the association was meeting outside, not inside the church, so Miss Everett would not stand behind a pulpit. Moreover, her message came at 10:00 A.M., the Sunday School hour, not at 11:00. Upon these grounds she was allowed to speak.

James Milton Carroll (1892-1894). J. M. Carroll, younger brother of the Texas Baptist colossus B. H. Carroll, was a substantial leader in his own right. A graduate of Baylor University, Carroll distinguished himself as pastor at Lampasas, as agent for the State Sunday School work, and as a major Texas spokesman for prohibition. He later served as president of Baptist schools, including San Marcos Academy, Howard-Payne University, and Oklahoma Baptist University. He was one of the most effective negotiators who brought about consolidation of Texas Baptist schools and conventions, and he helped create and later led the Texas Baptist Education Commission in its efforts to consolidate and pay off the accumulated debts of several Baptist colleges. Carroll was also known as an expert marksman with a rifle, and his collection of bird nests and other natural artifacts was considered the best in the nation and later sold for $5,000 when that was a lot of money.

Carroll was already serving as Texas agent for the Richmond-based Foreign Mission Board. When Cranfill resigned in February of 1892, Carroll was elected to succeed him, but to combine his responsibilities for foreign and home work in Texas. "The question of ultimately consolidating our mission work under one general management was lengthily, vigorously, seriously and exhaustively discussed," Carroll records.[11] A similar discussion was carried on in the Southern Baptist Convention, but the SBC and BGCT reached opposite conclusions. The SBC kept Foreign and Home boards separate, whereas Texas combined them in one unified work. B. H. Carroll, chairman of the Board of Directors, resigned that position when his brother took office, no doubt to avoid any appearance of nepotism.

As Superintendent of Missions, J. M. Carroll recognized that the work had grown too large for one person. The Superintendent needed to visit the associations, have contact with the missionaries, and survey the fields in person. Carroll said that the Board allotted its resources according to requests from the field. The result was that the best writers, those able to present their needs most convincingly on paper, got their requests granted, while other places of equal or greater merit got less help from lack of a persuasive writer to present their appeal. "It has frequently resulted in the best writers getting the most help. As an inevitable result, we have helped some fields too much and some too little."[12] To remedy this, Carroll appointed a series of "general missionaries," to serve in different parts of the state, to direct the work in their areas and make the on-field visits that the Superintendent could not do. However, this became a bone of contention, some urging that it was unnecessary and too expensive.

In his first report to the Convention, Carroll covered only the six months that he had been in office, noting that "the reports for the first two quarters were never turned over to the present corresponding secretary." That innocent statement later provoked no end of controversy, and resulted in S. A. Hayden leveling accusations of fraud and misappropriation of funds against Cranfill. Cranfill had the reports for the first two quarters bound, but they were lost or stolen from his buggy. These were the forms on which the missionaries reported miles traveled, sermons preached, converts baptized, churches formed, etc. The cash ledgers were not lost, and no funds were missing or unaccounted for. However, in his paper Hayden accused Cranfill of dishonesty and the Convention of covering up that dishonesty. Against all evidence, many Baptists in Texas believed those groundless accusations. To allay the rumors, four years later the same cash books were brought back to the Convention, a committee audited them, and reported the cash reports in order. However, as is often the case, simple facts could not overcome the burden of sensational accusation.

It fell Carroll's lot to lead at a time of drouth and financial recession. A report in 1894 said, "Money was scarce; the people discouraged; the times were awful."[13] Yet, despite these conditions the work progressed, and Carroll could report that "for the first time since the consolidation of the old Baptist State Convention and the Baptist General Association, we are out of debt." Carroll's last report in 1894 showed 2,567 churches in Texas, grouped into 92 associations, with 13,692 baptisms that year. Total membership was reported at 153,482, church buildings were valued at $1,190,523 and pastors' houses at $45,675.[14]

M. D. Early (1894-1896). When Carroll resigned at the end of 1894, M.D. Early was elected to finish out the year. Despite his best efforts, these were years of discouragement and decline in Texas mission work. The amount of money raised, missionaries appointed, and work accomplished all showed precipitous declines. One who was present in 1896 said,

> The report of the Board of Directors bore a discouraging aspect. There was a great falling off in mission work. For all the objects of the Convention work, the amount received from all sources was $28,813.04, and only sixty-six missionaries had been in the field, and only eight hundred and ninety-eight baptisms were reported. Comparison of the year's work with others, and contemplating the gloomy outlook, brought sadness and dark forebodings to the hearts of many a Texas Baptist.[15]

One innovation of Early's administration was the Chapel Car ministry. The American Baptist Publication Society donated to Texas a Pullman railway car especially equipped as a chapel on wheels. The spacious Pullman included seats for worshipers, hymnals, a small organ for music, and a small apartment adequate for a missionary couple. An agreement with the railroads allowed these cars to be moved free of charge from place to place, shunted off to a siding to remain a week or a year. The Chapel Car missionaries conducted Sunday Schools, won converts and in many cases formed new churches. For several years Mr. and Mrs. A. S. Stuckey served as the Chapel Car missionaries.

James Bruton Gambrell (1896-1910). After being re-elected in 1896, Early abruptly resigned, hounded out of office by the same incessant attacks of S. A. Hayden that had forced out his predecessors. This brought sadness to Texas Baptists, but it also brought something else: anger. For years the Baptists had made little response to Hayden's attacks. They just "hunkered down," tried to continue their work, and hoped the problem would subside. It did not. By 1896 Texas Baptists were ready to fight back.

J. B. Gambrell came to Texas from Georgia, and he did not come to be hounded out of office by S. A. Hayden or anybody else. Gambrell was no stranger to conflict. A scout for General Robert E. Lee, Gambrell fought at Gettysburg and was later stationed in Mississippi. After the war, Gambrell attended the University of Mississippi and served five years as pastor of the Oxford Baptist Church. In 1877 he became editor of the *Baptist Record* of Mississippi, and in 1883 was elected president of Mercer University in Georgia. He began his work as Corresponding Secretary in Texas in December 1896. He resigned in 1910 to become editor of the *Baptist Standard* and in 1912 added the duties of a professorship at Southwestern Seminary in Fort Worth. Gambrell served as president of the Southern Baptist Convention during the crucial World War I years. As Superintendent of Missions in Texas, Gambrell brought wisdom, determination and a remarkable skill in working with common people.

THE TWO BAYLORS

From the first, education was a major priority for Texas Baptists. The consolidation of the two universities at Waco and the move of the Baylor Female College to Belton gave two strong schools which they hoped all Baptists would unite in patronizing. In addition, there were numerous local and associational schools which served as feeders for the two Baylors.

Baylor University at Waco. In 1886 Rufus C. Burleson, president of the consolidated Baylor University, said "Our prospects were never so glorious nor the demand for vigilance and toil so great."[16] Layman J. W. Speight reported more cautiously for the trustees that "The uncertainty of transition and radical change . . . . was a fiery ordeal, and threatened to greatly diminish the number of students and unhinge all we did."[17] But these feared disruptions did not occur, and the university enrolled 385 students (about two-thirds of them male) who were taught by nineteen professors. New buildings grew up rapidly on the enlarged twenty-three-acre campus, and by 1887 Baylor claimed that it had the best college buildings west of the Mississippi. The students, who paid $65 a year for room and board, remained fairly healthy with only a few deaths each year from measles, whooping cough, and dengue (a severe fever). The trustees further reported that "The moral conduct and devotion to study of 98 2/3 percent of the students were never surpassed. But one- and one-third percent were deplorably bad, and required the severest discipline to maintain law and order."[18] No doubt most colleges would settle for that percentage.

In a paragraph probably aimed at the incoming people from Independence, Speight reported that "We are happy to say, our plan of coeducation, or the education of our sons and daughters in the same school, has proven in every way satisfactory." In his last report for the trustees of old Baylor, Hosea Garrett, defended the idea of single sex enrollment. Discipline was strict in the new coed environment. Students were expected to be in their rooms by dark. Causing any disturbance in class or chapel would bring demerits, and immediate suspension could result from talking back to a professor, playing cards, or drinking alcoholic beverages. Unless they lived with relatives in Waco, female students were required to live on campus under "the watchful care and counsel of the lady teachers in all the details of general deportment and social etiquette."[19] Women students were urged to keep their dresses simple and inexpensive because "simplicity saves time, thought, and money, which, to a scholar, are precious for higher uses." Full ankle-length costumes were required for Baylor girls participating in athletic programs. In 1891 the "maid" degrees of the women students were changed to "bachelor," and the older "maid of philosophy" became a "bachelor of science." Costs for women students were slightly higher because they had nicer facilities. In the 1890s men paid 80 cents a month to rent a bed, mattress, table and chair; $1 a month for room rent; and $5.50 for monthly board.[20] Academic costs varied according to courses chosen.

Baylor University received its updated charter on August 7, 1886, but full consolidation was easier to vote than to effect. There were complicated legal problems to work out, leading B. H. Carroll, trustee president of the new Baylor, to say, "Chaos, doubtful complications, past irregularities, continued drouth and invincible impecuniosity were among the formidable obstacles." Debts were present realities, while pledges of financial support "had a far-away look, misty in outline." Despite this "invincible impecuniosity," the university grew in enrollment, endowment, academic excellence and in general acceptance among Texas Baptists. "The Convention was our Pharaoh," said Carroll, "and we were the Israelites making bricks without straw. Well, we made them."[21]

However, this bright picture had its somber aspects. By 1892 Baylor University faced what was at that time a staggering debt of $92,000. Their financial agent had resigned and the trustees sought another mature and well-known leader to solicit funds for Baylor. R. F. Jenkins, pastor at White-wright, wrote to B. H. Carroll recommending the young and unknown George W. Truett. "There is one thing I do know about George Truett," Jenkins wrote. "Wherever he speaks, the people do what he asks them to do." Carroll was skeptical but agreed to interview Truett at a meeting in McKinney in the fall of 1890, and as a result asked Truett to appear before the Baylor trustees. Truett was hesitant; he pleaded his youth, the fact that he was unknown in Texas, and that he was himself as yet "uncolleged." He did meet with the trustees who were notoriously unimpressed. "George who?" they asked. "Have you ever heard of this boy?" None of them had. Then the twenty-three-year-old youth began to speak. That voice! That earnestness! The room quieted. "The people do what he asks them to do,"

Jenkins had written. Truett asked the Baylor trustees to stand behind him, to support him, to pray for him. They did.

Then began the hectic twenty-three months in which Truett criss-crossed the state, from the high plains to the Gulf Coast, from El Paso to Texarkana. He spoke at churches, association meetings, civic rallies, at country crossroads, and in civic pavilions. He traveled by train, horseback, buggy, wagons and on foot. Day and night the earnest youth pleaded for a college he had never attended, urging Texas Baptists to save Baylor. During the campaign Truett quietly gave his own check for $500, all the money he had, money saved for his education. In mid-1892 Truett brought to Carroll the check that put them over the top. They had raised over $92,000 and Baylor was saved. Carroll took the check, turned his face heavenward and, as Truett remembered it years later, said "It is finished."[22]

Truett enrolled in Baylor University that fall. Perhaps no freshman ever entered a college with more recognition. During student days, Truett lived in the B. H. Carroll home and was accepted as part of the family. He later married Josephine Jenkins, whose father was chairman of the Baylor trustees. While a student Truett pastored the East Waco Baptist Church. They enlarged the building and the membership more than doubled. Many Baylor faculty attended there during Truett's pastorate, for already he was known as an outstanding preacher. At his graduation, Truett received calls from prestigious pulpits across the nation, but accepted the call to Dallas in 1897.

Ministerial education at Baylor was no new thing, but it took a new turn after consolidation. As early as 1851 the trustees of old Baylor considered forming a Theological Department, and in 1860 laid ambitious plans in that direction which were frustrated by the war. Waco University offered studies in theology by the 1860s, and B. H. Carroll offered Bible classes for young ministers both in his home and in the university by the late 1870s. In 1890 Carroll reported twenty-six ministerial students receiving free tuition at Baylor. He said, "We have never claimed to have a theological department, nor do we issue diplomas to that effect. But we do furnish facilities for great improvement in this direction by way of preparation for a regular theological Seminary. Regular lectures are delivered, and courses of reading and study marked out to these young ministers."

In 1893 the Bible Department was formed as an integral part of the university, with Carroll as professor of Exegesis and Systematic Theology. R. C. Burleson taught Pastoral Duties and Church History and John H. Luther taught Homiletics. The department enrolled 75 students, not all of them preachers. In 1894 George W. Truett, a student in Baylor at the time, described the Bible Department as "primarily for preachers, but intended for all. . . . Under the direction of Dr. B. H. Carroll, the Bible, preeminently the preacher's book, is regularly studied in the classroom." Truett noted that non-ministerial students, including young women, were especially welcome in the Bible classes. He reported that "Forty ministerial students enjoyed such advantages last year, with perhaps as large a number of other students, not preachers.[23]

Clearly Baylor was moving toward greater involvement in theological education. A Chair of Hebrew and Greek was created in 1897, and John S. Tanner named to fill it. Next to Carroll, Tanner probably did more for early theological education in Texas than anyone else. A native of Comanche, Tanner received both B.A. and M.A. degrees from Baylor, and the Th.M. from the Southern Baptist Theological Seminary in Louisville. Since Carroll also served as a trustee at Southern, he knew of young Tanner's work in both schools. Tanner was being groomed for a faculty position at Southern, but the death of John A. Broadus changed that. After Seminary, Tanner enrolled in the University of Chicago but promised that he would not "take to the loose views reported to have a footing there." In a letter to B. H. Carroll, dated May 28, 1895, Tanner tactfully enquired about the possibility of teaching at Baylor. "I have all along entertained the feeling that my work is in Texas in connection with Baylor."[24] Two years later he came on the Baylor faculty, where he became a popular teacher. Both J. M. Dawson and W. T. Conner, later great teachers themselves, commended Tanner as one of the best teachers they ever knew.

Believing that school buildings should not sit vacant, Tanner organized a Summer Bible School at Baylor in 1896 which attracted a good enrollment. Many preachers could attend the brief summer classes who could not spare a year or even a semester. By that time Carroll was convinced that a university without a department of theology was incomplete. His own teaching at Baylor, his service as a trustee at Southern Seminary, and the situation in Texas gradually turned Carroll from the pastorate to theological education. This commitment came to fruition in the founding of the Southwestern Baptist Theological Seminary, to be recounted in the next chapter.

Baylor Female College. The Baylor school for girls moved to Belton in 1886, still under the presidency of John H. Luther. To get the college, Belton provided eleven choice acres of land, and a cash bonus of $31,000 for the first building, and cooperation in a campaign to raise $50,000 more for buildings and equipment. The new board of trustees, all men, "announced that there were fifty rooms to furnish at $40 each. The amount was raised to furnish the rooms." The college opened in Belton with 100 enrolled, of whom seven graduated the first year. Other presidents included P. H. Edgar (1891-1894), E. H. Wells (1894-1896), and W. A. Wilson (1896-1911). At Independence the men and women students used the same library. At Belton the young women had a large room designated as a library, but no books. College officials sent out an urgent appeal for persons to purchase and donate one new book, and for families to donate one or more suitable books from their home.

During the first decade in Belton, Baylor Female College developed unique programs to help poor girls who might otherwise have been unable to attend college. Eli Moore Townsend, an 1879 graduate of Baylor Female College, founded the "Cottage Home" system by which seven wooden cottages were erected adjacent to the campus. In the spartan rooms of these cottages the girls provided their own food and other needs and received a 20% discount on their tuition. The Cottage Homes operated under their own separate trustees until absorbed by the college in 1916. It was reported that over the years more than 5,000 economically disadvantaged young women were enabled to receive an education as a result of this unique system.[25]

A FLOOD OF NEW COLLEGES

College unification in Texas did not last long. No sooner were Baylor and Waco universities merged than new colleges began to spring up in many sections of the state. One could not have picked a worse time to start new schools, for the financial panic of 1893 was looming.

Howard Payne College. J. D. Robnett, pastor of First Baptist Church of Brownwood, led the Pecan Valley Baptist Association to establish a college in that town in 1889. As chairman of the first Board of Trustees, Robnett enlisted his brother-in-law, Edward Howard Payne of Missouri to make a substantial gift and the school was named for him. Howard Payne College opened in September 1890 with A. J. Emerson as president and a faculty of nine. The first classes were held in Robnett Hall, a three-story building with twenty-one rooms located where the present FBC sits. When the Main Administration Building opened in 1891, Robnett Hall became a girls' dormitory. The school was co-educational from the first. A severe drouth and the financial panic of 1893 found the infant college $30,000 in debt. Robnett took over as president and invested his own funds and life strength to keep the school open, while J. H. Grove as dean kept the classes going. In 1896 Robnett accepted a Dallas pastorate and Grove became president. Howard Payne entered the correlation system proposed by the Texas Baptist Education Commission in 1897, and ownership was transferred from the Pecan Valley Association to the BGCT. By this agreement, Howard Payne operated as a junior college, granting no degrees from 1901 to 1915.

Simmons College. Not to be outdone, the Sweetwater Baptist Association formed its own school, chartered in 1891 as Abilene Baptist College and located as the name implies in Abilene. In that early day, the Sweetwater Association reached all the way to El Paso, and Baptist leaders in the west felt that a school would help them grow. James B. Simmons, a Baptist pastor in New York, gave $5,000 to complete the first permanent building in 1891, and the trustees changed the name to Simmons University. Simmons bequeathed about $10,000 more to the school. The school was begun on a "Foundation Agreement," a statement of the purpose and philosophy of a Christian college. That document, written in part by Simmons, specified that the purpose of the school was (1) To bring young men and women to Christ, (2) To teach them of Christ, and (3) To train them for the service of Christ. In addition, the school was expected to offer the highest level instruction in academics, ethics and "liberal culture." Though distinctly Baptist, Simmons College vowed to follow "the Roger Williams doctrine of entire liberty in religious concernment" and thus "no religious test shall ever hinder any person . . . from entering and receiving instruction in said Simmons College."[26] The college began its first session in September 1892 and enjoyed rapid growth and prosperity. Simmons was the exception among Texas colleges of the time in that it was not encumbered by debt. In 1934 John Hardin and his wife Mary of Burkburnett gave the college about $1 million and the name was changed to Hardin-Simmons University.

North Texas Baptist College. An "Educational Conference" of Baptists from Jack , Wise, Parker and Montague counties formed a college in 1891. This school was named the North Texas Baptist College, and was located in Jacksboro. The college opened in 1891 and for a time reached about 350 in enrollment. However, the familiar story of drouth and debt dragged the school down, and it closed in 1897.

Northwest Baptist College. Some Wise County Baptists participated in the North Texas Baptist College at Jacksboro, but others felt they should have their own school. Therefore, a group launched the Northwest Baptist College in Decatur. The college was chartered on December 21, 1891, and held its first classes early in 1893 in a temporary building on the town square. The first commencement was held in May in a new stone three-story building. The school failed for lack of students and money, and the property was sold at auction in 1896 for $13,000.

Decatur Baptist College. In 1897 J. M. Carroll learned that the old Northwest Baptist College property in Decatur could be bought for $7,000. The Convention bought the property and established a new school under the name of Decatur Baptist College, chartered on October 29, 1898.[27] The school operated as a feeder to Baylor University, and was known as the first junior college in the world.

To what extent was Decatur College a successor of the defunct Northwest Baptist College in the same town? No doubt many of the same persons were involved in both efforts, and the two schools occupied the same property. However, the records confirm that they were definitely different schools, with different founding, different name and, most importantly, different charters. Any continuity was emotional, not organic. This school moved from Decatur to Dallas in 1965 and was renamed Dallas Baptist College.

Burleson College. Baptist educators like R. E. B. Baylor and William Carey Crane had colleges named for them, but until 1895 the great Rufus C. Burleson had none. In that year Burleson College opened as a co-educational institution in Greenville, sponsored by the Hunt County Baptist

Association. Despite its namesake, the school never prospered. It came under control of the BGCT in 1899 as part of the correlation movement and operated for a few years as a junior college.

South Texas Baptist College. South Texas Baptists felt keenly the move of Baylor University northward to Waco and the subsequent demise of William Carey Crane College. A group convened as the South Texas Educational Conference and launched a school at Waller, named the South Texas Baptist College. The school opened in 1898, but survived only two years.

What was behind this flood of new colleges? Regional pride was a factor; each locality wanted and felt it deserved its own college. Public education in Texas, even in the 1890s, was still in its infancy and many students had no other opportunity for schooling than the local church colleges. The distance from the remote areas of the state to Waco where Baylor was located seemed a far more formidable barrier then than now. Baptists had successfully planted in the Baptist mind the conviction that education was a high priority of ministry, and Baptists simply acted upon that conviction. There were also obvious economic advantages for a town to have its own college, especially if the college succeeded. Such a college would draw settlers, increase business, advance church life and even raise property values.

THE LIGHT THAT FLICKERED

J. M. Carroll in describing early efforts to unify Baptist education in Texas spoke of "a light that failed."[28] A generation later, facing a new need for correlation, Texas Baptists saw another light that flared briefly and then flickered. J. B. Gambrell, newly arrived in Texas as the Superintendent of Missions for the BGCT, saw at once what was coming gradually into focus for others. Texas Baptists had too many colleges, the colleges were poorly located, and the institutional death-rate was too high. Few of the schools could survive, and those that did could hardly flourish. Texas Baptists were pouring vast sums of money into schools, but the money was so scattered that it had little impact. Gambrell suggested that Texas Baptists form one correlated college system in Texas, with a number of regional junior colleges feeding into one major university. J. M. Carroll picked up that idea, developed it more fully, and set about one of the most ambitious projects in the history of Baptist education in Texas.

Carroll found most of the colleges deeply in debt, all of them depending upon the "agent" system of sending our fund-raisers in their areas. Naturally, these colleges did not want agents from other colleges, or even other Baptist causes in Texas, to invade their territory. Many tensions resulted from these territorial disputes. Carroll developed the plan to correlate the colleges, pay off their debts, and form one unified Baptist educational system in Texas. The idea was also greatly influenced by the

American Baptist Education Society in the North about the same time, and by the general emphasis upon correlation among Texas Baptists since the 1880s.

J. M. Carroll borrowed money to visit C. C. Slaughter who was then on what we would call a vacation in Hot Wells, South Dakota. Slaughter, a wealthy Dallas layman, agreed to give the starting gift of $25,000, an enormous sum for those days. With this encouragement, a mass meeting to discuss education was called for First Baptist Church in Fort Worth in September 1897. From that meeting came the momentum to form the Texas Baptist Educational Commission, which the Convention authorized late in 1897 and which was formed in January 1898. J. M. Carroll was head of the Commission, but a few months later persuaded his brother B. H. to take that position while he, J. M., served as assistant.

The goal of the movement was threefold. First, they would enlist all the Baptist colleges to enter into an agreement to form a "federation of our schools," in which ownership and control would pass from the local associations to the State Convention. Second, the Educational Commission would launch a massive statewide campaign to pay off all the college debts and portion out to each school funds for operation. Third, Texas Baptists would have only one major degree-granting university, Baylor, with the other colleges functioning essentially as junior colleges or preparatory schools. The regional schools would offer the usual college courses of the first two years, and offer them at the highest academic levels, but they would issue certificates and not degrees to those who finished the two years. It was expected that most students would not continue beyond the junior college level, but those who did would transfer to Baylor University in Waco. Scholarships would be available for those who needed help. Among the Baptist colleges in Texas, many would train but only Baylor would issue the standard college degrees.

Most of the colleges entered readily into this agreement. Few of them offered much beyond junior college anyway, and they were drowning in debt. Only Simmons College, which had no debt, declined to enter the agreement.

High hopes marked the beginning of the Correlation Campaign. B. H. Carroll resigned his pastorate of almost twenty-nine years in Waco to lead the campaign. He had long been involved in education, and from that time he spent the remainder of his life in that work. After the campaign was completed, B. H. Carroll accepted a professorship in the Bible Department of Baylor, all the while continuing in his role as chairman of the Baylor trustees. He also served as a trustee of the Southern Baptist Theological Seminary in Louisville. Many believe that the combined influence of these experiences led Carroll toward the founding of the Southwestern Baptist Theological Seminary in Fort Worth.

The Correlation Campaign both succeeded and failed. It succeeded in raising over $200,000 for Baptist education in Texas, saved several colleges from collapse, put added emphasis upon the importance of education, spotlighted the need for more theological education in the Southwest, and brought a number of wealthy laymen, especially C. C. Slaughter, into more generous involvement in Baptist causes. The failure lay in the fact that the schools did not long remain "confederated." Local and regional loyalties reasserted themselves, and colleges resumed their development to become four-year degree-granting institutions in their own right. Some resented the fact that Baylor got the lion's share of funds from the campaign, and the other colleges, as it turned out, were not long content to exist as feeder schools for Baylor.

BAPTIST WOMEN MISSION WORKERS

The two women's organizations connected with the Baptist State Convention and the Baptist General Convention consolidated in 1886 with minimal trauma. Their concern was less for turf protection and more for missions. The first president of the consolidated group was Mrs. Fanny B. Davis (1886-1895), followed by Mrs. W. L. Williams (1895-1906). Three corresponding secretaries served during this period, Mrs. S. J. Anderson (1886-1887), Miss Minnie Slaughter (1887-1889), and Miss Mina Everett (1889-1895). For a brief time Mrs. W. C. Luther and Miss Ella Yelvington served as corresponding secretary, until Mrs. J. B. Gambrell was elected in 1897. For a time the State Board paid the salary of the women's corresponding secretary, but that ceased in 1895.

The amounts of money raised by the women probably mattered less than did their persistent emphasis upon the missionary message of the Bible. It seems noteworthy that the Baptist women taught and practiced tithing long before most Baptist churches emphasized that plan. Each year the women prepared a detailed report of their work, but in those days the president of the Women Workers was not allowed to speak before the Convention. Instead, a committee of men analyzed the report, a man read the report before the Convention and another man took a few minutes to speak to the report. J. A. Hackett, the man appointed to read the 1886 report, said of the women "To their prayers, their sympathies and helpfulness we largely attribute the rapidly increasing mission spirit that pervades our churches."[29]

The men recommended that the women's state society "be made strictly auxiliary to our State and General Conventions," and that the women not undertake to appoint their own workers, but funnel their offerings through the State Convention. The women did funnel most of their offerings through the Convention, but they also raised enough money to build schools and orphanages in Mexico, establish missions among the Mexicans in Corpus Christi, San Antonio and Laredo, and pay a teacher for a girls' school in Mexico.

The Baptist women faced the same problems the men did: drouth, depression, and distance in Texas mission work. But they also faced an additional problem: opposition from many of the men, some of them prominent leaders. The men had an inordinate fear that the women might want to appoint their own missionaries, that they would want to speak in mixed assemblies, or that they might put a woman into the field as an effective fund-raiser. While most of the men publicly supported the formation of a state Baptist Women's Workers Society as part of the merger of 1886, privately they expressed misgivings.

Two months after consolidation, Mrs. Jennie Anderson wrote a rather snippy letter published in the *Texas Baptist and Herald,* entitled "What the Women of Texas Desire." Obviously put out with the men who publicly supported but privately opposed, Anderson sought to assure the men that the women were not trying to take over mission work in Texas. "We wish to be understood thoroughly. . . . not only by every Baptist woman in Texas, but by the united brotherhood of this state."[30] Despite public expressions of support, "we cannot say that there exists no misapprehension or alarm on the part of every brother, since such has been expressed privately and met with personally."

If the brethren had questions, better they had raised them publicly so they could be faced openly. Anderson said,

> as it is, we are using enough space for one of Spurgeon's sermons, to tell them, to assure them, of something they ought to know already, without being told, and it is this: The women of Texas do not propose—they have no desire—to control the mission work, as supposed by some. We only ask of you the uninterrupted privilege of running our part of it.[31]

Jennie Anderson defended the role of women in missions. "Some think we ought not to have organized a State Society," she said, "and let church missionary societies carry on the mission work." But if women's societies be limited to the local church, "who is going to make it his or her business to organize these societies, for there is not one of every ten, in the churches. The pastors will not do it. Who will?"

The spiritual needs in Texas are great, Anderson pointed out, "and the brethren, of themselves, do not or can not raise the necessary means required to extend the mission work as it should be." She said,

> Vast regions throughout the State are without Baptist preaching. Could the Baptist women of Texas sit quiet and see the rising generation without Christ in any part of the State, or made Catholics of? There ought to be two missionaries where there is now one, and we want to help put them there . . . .[the Baptist woman] realizes that there is no commandment in the Bible relieving her of Christian duty; that her soul has been bought with the same price as that paid for the soul of her brother.[32]

The real objection of the men, as the women clearly recognized, was not in mission work but what the women might do in the larger society. This was the day that women's rights and women's suffrage were hotly debated in America. As Jennie Anderson said,

> But some brother will say, "If we allow these women to organize a society (to advance the cause of Christ) she will soon want to organize a society

to run our government. She will be wanting to go to the ballot box next."
Well, my brother, if she does, it will be only to cast one vote, and that will
be to petition the governor to help them in some way to bring about a
general reform among the men, that they may find more time in discussing their own cause and less time in fretting and worrying over the
vexed problem, "Women's Work."

The women issued a challenge. "We want your sympathy and hearty
cooperation, brethren, and if at the end of this year's work when we meet
with you at the time and place of your Convention we cannot show that
there is more work done for the cause of Christ, by the Baptist women of
Texas, then we will cheerfully disband." Nobody asked the women to disband, and over the years opposition diminished.

The Women Workers also formed "Sunbeam Bands" to enroll children in mission studies and activities. The report for 1900 shows that the
Baptist women of Texas had raised money for foreign and home missions,
the Buckner Home, ministerial education, aged minister relief, temperance promotion, and many local projects. They also participated with
Baptist women in other states to raise funds "to be expended in the building and equipment of a Gospel boat, to be used by our unmarried women
missionaries on the rivers of Southern China, as they pursue their missionary tours."[33]

CHURCH BASED MINISTRIES

Sunday School. In 1886, the two state Sunday School conventions
merged, but did not officially become a part of the new consolidated General Convention. The Sunday School leaders believed that their work
would prosper better as a separate organization. They continued to employ "Sunday School evangelists" to travel the state, establish new schools,
conduct teacher training clinics, and in general promote the importance
of a Sunday School in every church. In their favor were the facts that suitable literature was more available, more churches had full-time preaching,
and the earlier opposition to Sunday Schools had practically disappeared.
However, they found it increasingly difficult to promote the work independently, and before the end of the period the separate organization dis-
banded and Sunday School work became a department of the state convention.

Baptist Young Peoples Union. A new organization for Baptist youth made
its appearance during this period, and it caught on like wildfire. In 1890
Anderson E. Baten, pastor of the Broadway Baptist Church in Fort Worth,
discovered to his distress that few of the young men in his church were willing or able to lead in public prayer.[34] Baten, who had shown skill in ministering to young people in his previous pastorates, conceived the idea of
forming an organization for training youth in Baptist churchmanship.

There were precedents for church organizations for youth. A young peoples' society was formed in First Baptist Church of Rochester, New York, by 1848 and in First Baptist of Charlottsville, Virginia, by 1884. Baptist young people formed statewide organizations in Nebraska in 1889 and Kansas in 1890 and other states soon followed. In July 1891 over 1600 delegates from twenty-nine states meeting at the Second Baptist Church of Chicago formed the Baptist Young Peoples Union of America, designed to include Baptist youth in the North, South and Canada.[35] Baptists in the South, however, did not participate much in this Chicago-based BYPU, despite the fact that J. B. Cranfill of Texas was named one of three vice-presidents.

In January 1891 Baten led the Broadway youth to form the "Young Christian Colabor Society." Before long other churches formed similar organizations under various names, including First Baptist, Denton and Washington Avenue (later Gaston Avenue) in Dallas. The feasibility of a statewide organization was raised, and the Broadway group posted in the two Baptist papers the following invitation, "Resolved, That we, the Young Christian Colabor Society of Broadway Baptist Church, invite all similar societies in this state to send . . . messengers to meet with us in convention on Wednesday before the second Sunday in September." In response, sixty-eight messengers from twenty-three Baptist churches in Texas met in Fort Worth and on September 10, 1891 formed the Baptist Young People's Union of Texas. They elected an executive committee, named Baten as corresponding secretary, and laid plans for an annual convention of Baptist youth. This was the first state BYPU organization in the South, but other states and the SBC soon followed.

The new organization met immediate opposition from some pastors who "feared that the tendency of the times was to get away from the churches, and to turn the main work of the churches over to various and sundry societies."[36] However, the opposition was soon quieted not by argument but by the consistent Baptist church loyalty of the BYPU members. Various churches with active BYPU groups reported that "young converts stir the baptismal waters nearly every Sunday night," that a new "devotional spirit" was evident among youth, that youth were brought more in touch with Baptist "denominational enterprises," and that "young Baptists are now studying Baptist doctrine and history as never before."[37]

The Baptist Young People's Union began in 1891 as an independent organization but in time, like the state Sunday School convention, became an agency of the BGCT.

BENEVOLENT MINISTRIES

The Buckner Orphans Home was easily the best known of many Baptist benevolent ministries in the period covered by this chapter, 1886–1900, but Baptists also stirred themselves in the care of the aged, especially "aged and decrepit" ministers, prison reform, efforts to rehabilitate ex-prisoners, both men and women, and toward the end of the period came efforts in hospital ministry, and efforts to care for the mentally ill. Space allows but a sketch of some of these benevolent ministries.

Buckner Orphan Home. A previous chapter traced the origin of the Buckner Orphan Home from the Deacons Convention in Paris in 1877. The triple unification of Baptist conventions, colleges, and newspapers in 1886 barely affected the Buckner Home, for it already enjoyed the firm support of Baptists in all sections of the state. By that time the Home had its own school, its own church and Sunday School, its own infirmary and over 65 children in residence. Needy children were admitted without regard to denominational background, and "Father Buckner" (as he was called) would not allow any pressures to make them Baptists. They heard the gospel in Sunday School and church and Buckner often baptized converts, but he would not allow evangelists to conduct meetings at the Home. With the demise of the Deacons Convention, ownership and control was placed in the hands of a self-perpetuating board of trustees, but during his lifetime of course Buckner himself was the Home.

Buckner sometimes allowed children to go out to foster care in families that passed his stringent investigation, but he always kept siblings together. He often received requests for children to work, boys on the farm and older girls to keep house and care for children. Buckner considered this little short of slavery and refused to allow the children to go. He would, however, allow the older boys to be apprenticed to learn a trade they chose and he acted the role of father in meeting, approving (and sometimes disapproving) young men who wanted to come calling upon a girl at the Home.

The Buckner Home became a family enterprise, with son Hal and grandson Robert Cooke both becoming involved in leadership. In 1887 Addie Buckner Beddoe, the founder's daughter, and her husband, Dr. Albert Beddoe, came to the Home where they remained for seventeen years. Dr. Beddoe provided medical care for the children, while Addie received the children into the Home, taught some classes, and helped administer the Home in her father's absences. On his sixty-fourth birthday, Buckner bought with his own funds but deeded to the Home the original two acres and two-story house which the Home had rented when they first came to Dallas. This was turned into a "Children's Hospital," said to be at that time the only hospital especially for children in the world.[38]

The property of the Home rapidly increased as they began to receive major donations. Additional land was bought, additional buildings went up, and better facilities for dining, schooling, laundry, and infirmary care were provided. By 1900 the Home owned 720 acres of choice land, most of it planted to wheat and corn, and over 300 children (unfortunately referred to as "inmates") lived there. The number in residence fluctuated almost daily as new children were received and others graduated, married or left for jobs. Occasionally a boy would run away, but in most cases returned a bit wiser. Buckner made it clear that the Home was not just a place to "warehouse" children. He said,

> This is not an ordinary orphanage, with a few children to be fed and clothed awhile, then passed on. It is a real home of affection and protection; where the individuality of each child is recognized, its rights regarded and all its interests looked after. It possesses, also, all the characteristics of a real school; and besides is a great Industrial School. The garden, the orchard, the stock, the mills, the shops, the steam and electric light plants, afford the means of practical training for the boys . . . . Indoor work of all kinds for the girls; cooking, house cleaning, dining room and pantry work; the proper management of milk and butter, patching, cutting, fitting and making garments, hand sewing, knitting, embroidery, crocheting, stenography, typewriting, etc., afford facilities for making useful women. . . . Add to all these advantages preaching and Sunday School, right in our own buildings, daily songs and prayers at table, and the benefits of daily association with Christian matrons, teachers, and others, and great benefits must necessarily come to the children.[39]

In 1900, Father Buckner reported the purchase of 84 acres of adjacent land, and the paying off of notes he had made in his own name to sustain the school. The Home had an orchard of 7,000 trees with a cabin, occupied by an "orchardist" who had married one of the girls from the Home. With 300 to 400 children in residence, the Home used an average of 26 bushels of fruit a week from their orchard and still had some to sell to the public.[40] Additional property had been installed in the boys' workshop, including a steam corn mill, a feed grinder, and broom-making machinery. Buckner also reported that "additional machinery has been bought for farm work, and now we have a seed drill, reaper and binder, mowers, hay rakes and baler, and everything needed on the farm unless it be a thresher."[41] During the year an additional dam had been built over Prairie Creek, creating a good sized lake which was stocked with fish by the government, and which also provided a dependable water source for the numerous livestock. The value of the entire property then exceeded $200,000.

In the midst of its growing prosperity, the Buckner Home had its share of tragedies. On the night of January 15, 1897, a fire broke out in the wood frame dormitory for boys. Mrs. Sallie Britton, the boys' matron, awoke to find the blaze already raging. She escaped and helped five boys to safety, but her own three sons were lost. Another matron also lost a son in the blaze. Adults from the Home and community rushed to help, but the fire was too far gone and fifteen boys died that night and four more in days ahead. Buckner and his daughter Addie tried to comfort the survivors, but Buckner said of that awful night, "I had no time to break down or hesitate and to weep . . . . I did not want a bite to eat for four days."[42]

When word came of the deadly hurricane at Galveston in September 1900, Buckner interrupted an engagement in Durant, Oklahoma, to rush to the stricken area. In three days he gathered over 100 orphans, mostly from the demolished Galveston Rosenburg Orphanage, and loaded them into wagons bound for Dallas. These newcomers strained the facilities, but the "Annex" was pressed into service.

To Texas Baptists, the name "Buckner" means orphanage. However, historian Karen O'Dell Bullock has shown that Buckner's social concerns and efforts reached to other needs as well. Bullock notes that "Buckner had led in championing the cause of the poor and vulnerable for many years . . . . A man of incessant activity, Buckner began a variety of campaigns for social justice."[43] These included elder care, especially for retired ministers, better race relations, prison reform, establishing "reformatories" to rehabilitate youthful offenders, better education for the poor, shelters for abused women and for newly released women prisoners, establishment of epilepsy treatment centers, special hospitals for the "feeble minded" and a humane society to "stop cruelty to children, . . . [and] to stop the beating of animals, to stop dog fights."

Clearly Buckner was a man ahead of his time, and just as clearly Baptists supported his many social ministries heartily. Many Baptists opposed the "Social Gospel" in those days but, paradoxically, heartily supported the social ministries of Father Buckner.

Care for Aged Ministers. In 1885 the Pastors' Conference of the BSC asked, "Should some plan be inaugurated for aiding our aged and disabled ministers; and if so, what plan would be best?" At that time there was no such thing as Social Security and the concept of "retirement" had not yet caught on. People simply worked until they could not work any more, and then lived on savings or were at the mercy of family and friends. Sometimes a church would voluntarily care for an aged former pastor or his widow. The answer of the Convention was affirmative and the Board of Relief for Disabled Ministers was formed and located at Lampasas. This work was continued in the consolidated Convention under the name of Ministers Relief Board, with H. M. Burroughs as Corresponding Secretary. His job was to raise money and organize a system for caring for the "aged and decrepit" Baptist ministers of Texas. His first report in 1887 shows that the Convention was assisting twenty-six destitute ministers, six widows, and a number of orphan children.[44] Several others equally deserving had applied but limited funds would stretch no further. Burroughs also sought to apply some prevention to the problem. He pointed out that hundreds of pastors and missionaries in Texas were existing on lean salaries and laying up nothing against the day of their age or disability, and he hoped the day would come that some of this problem could be prevented and the Board could have an Annuity as well as a Relief dimension. The BGCT pioneered many of the concepts and methods of the new Annuity Board of the Southern Baptist Convention, which was formed in 1918 and located in Dallas.

In 1892 the Ministers Relief Board established an "old Minister's Home and Sanitarium" at Lampasas, under private ownership, with the Convention offering moral but no financial support. The house had 15 rooms and was reported to be very comfortable. One historian, who was young and healthy at the time, wrote in surprise,

> Strange as it may seem, the three old couples, so well cared for in the "Home," were very unhappy. They were associated with old people only. They were strangers in a strange land. They were unable to go anywhere. No old or young friends came to see them. They really suffered from loneliness. They pined constantly to be back among their old friends and acquaintances. All six who were in the "Home" finally signed a petition asking that they might be returned to their old communities.[45]

Lack of funds and lack of acceptance caused the "Retirement Home" to be abandoned. In 1893 the Ministers Relief work was placed under the direct control of the Executive Board of the BGCT. By 1900 the BGCT was aiding about fifty beneficiaries, but still funds were inadequate. "We fear our pastors are not bringing this matter before their people as they should," said the committee.[46]

For a time Texas Baptists sponsored a "Minister's Life Assurance" plan which bordered on the "pyramid" concept. The plan called for each minister to pay a small entrance fee, and whenever a member died, all other members had to send in $1, which was forwarded to the family. The protection came in that any member could expect his contributions to come back manyfold to his survivors if he died. The wonder is not that the plan failed, but that it was ever tried at all.

The Great Prohibition Campaign. One of the earliest reports of the Union Association back in the 1840s spotlighted the problems caused by "demon rum." Almost every year Texas Baptists heard some report concerning the evils of beverage alcohol and promoted some plan for its control. By the late 1880s this opposition reached the level of a crusade. Prominent prohibition leaders included the Carroll brothers, B. H. and J. M., but the main leader was J. B. Cranfill who came to leadership as an editor, missions superintendent and prohibition leader. Cranfill chaired the committee in 1887 on "What Should be the Baptist Attitude toward the Liquor Traffic?" In an age of voluminous verbiage, their report was blunt and brief, only four words: *"Truceless, uncompromising, eternal war."*[47]

Cranfill, who was known to take a drop on occasion as a youth, was converted to "teetotal" prohibition when his partner in an early publishing venture was ruined by drink. Cranfill later became a lecturer for the United Friends of Temperance. When the Democratic Party rebuffed his efforts to write prohibition into their platform, he switched to the newly emerging National Prohibition Party and in fact became their nominee for Vice President of the United States in 1892. Others pitched vigorously into the prohibition campaign, including the influential Carroll brothers. B. H. took a leave of absence from his pastorate to preach, write and debate the issue, and J. M. from his base in Lampasas traveled, wrote, and campaigned. All to no avail: the wet forces won decisively. Here again we see Texas Baptists pioneering a campaign that would later involve the entire nation.

THE NEWSPAPER WARS CONTINUE

When J. B. Link's *Texas Baptist Herald* and S. A. Hayden's *Texas Baptist* were merged in 1886 to form one paper, the *Texas Baptist and Herald,* most Texas Baptists gave a sigh of relief: at last the paper wars were ended. Vain hope. With the entire field to himself, Hayden loosed all restraint in his opposition to the Convention, his attacks upon persons, and especially his war against Robert Taylor Hanks, pastor of FBC in Dallas from 1882 to 1889. Presnall Wood, historian of Texas Baptist papers and later a longtime editor of the *Baptist Standard,* summed it up: "Within a very short period of time it became obvious from the Convention point of view that Hayden was not a responsible journalist. He unleashed intemperate attacks against any who did not share his own private prejudices."[48]

Hayden's hatred for R. T. Hanks went back at least to the Live Oak church split in 1883, and had many causes, but in the 1890s the feud heated up when Hayden accused Pastor Hanks of immoral conduct. The most careful investigation by the deacons of First Baptist showed no basis for this charge and Hanks was exonerated. However, this made no difference to Hayden who kept up his constant barrage. Baptists throughout the state were increasingly embarrassed by Hayden's diatribes, and partly to counter his influence Lewis Holland launched a new paper in Honey Grove. The first issue of this paper, the *Baptist News,* came out on December 6, 1888. Holland was joined by John H. Boyet and the infant paper gained readership rapidly. In 1890 the paper was moved to Dallas, where R. T. Hanks bought in to gain a means to defend himself against the strident charges of Hayden. The name of the paper was changed to the *Western Baptist.* After he resigned the Dallas pastorate in 1889, Hanks served for a time as pastor in Abilene, where his son Bernard settled permanently. Bernard later became a partner in a communications company which owned, among other interests, the well-known paper *The Abilene Reporter-News.* R. T. Hanks later came out of retirement to serve as pastor, and for a time as head of an Old Ministers Retirement Home in Palacios. Blood clots led to amputation of both legs, and he died in Dallas in 1932, scene of his greatest ministry.

J. B. Cranfill wrote that M. V. Smith of Belton "was greatly disturbed concerning our denominational situation. He felt that the more influence Hayden secured, the worse it would ultimately be for the denomination."[49] Smith felt that Texas Baptists should establish a "peace paper," one that would promote and not attack the Convention and its leaders, one that would major on the positive and not the negative. To that end, in 1892 Cranfill and Smith bought the *Western Baptist* from Holland and Hanks, moved it to Waco and changed the name to the *Baptist Standard.* This was intended not only as an alternative to Hayden's paper, but was intended to give Waco a Baptist periodical which they felt had been stolen from them back in 1886. An early edition said, "In policy the paper will stand by every interest fostered by our people: the Baptist General Convention, our schools, our orphan's home, and every branch of our mission work."

When it appeared that J. B. Gambrell would become a joint editor of the *Standard*, Hayden sought to dissuade him. Hayden announced his intention to destroy the new paper, and if Gambrell was associated with it, he would destroy him too. This was not the approach to take with the fiery Gambrell, who concluded that the new paper must succeed "or else the work of unification so well begun would come to nothing."[50] While he did not become joint editor at that time, Gambrell soon moved to Texas and had a hand in the eventual victory over Hayden's influence. The wealthy C. C. Slaughter was enlisted as a major stockholder on condition that the *Baptist Standard* move back to Dallas where it has been ever since.

Cranfill proved to be an able editor, never hesitant to express his opinion. When President Theodore Roosevelt advocated social equality for African Americans, Cranfill editorialized: "that there can never be social equality between the races, but there can be equal rights under the law." Cranfill also complained that women should not ride bicycles and noted that the "new woman, if she keeps up her present gait, will soon be smoking, chewing, cussing and indulging in many other vices heretofore common only to men." Cranfill also came out against boxing and especially the "murderous game" of football with its "training of boys to kick and trample their fellow students to death."[51] The fact that Baylor at that time fielded a football team of sorts did not deter the opinionated editor.

TROUBLESOME DOCTRINAL ISSUES

From the days of "Wildcat" Morrell, who in the 1830s resisted Campbellism, anti-missions and extreme Calvinism, Texas Baptists have constantly wrestled with doctrinal issues. However, in the early days the problem was mostly from *outside* Baptist ranks. With unification in 1886, more problems seem to crop up from *inside*. Several doctrinal battles erupted in the 1890s and a few of them are sketched here.

Martinism. Whether M. T. Martin was guilty of heresy, minor deviation or just fuzzy thinking is not entirely clear. As a young minister of promise, a member of the First Baptist Church of Waco, Martin troubled some of his colleagues in 1889 by preaching an exaggerated emphasis upon Christian assurance. He held that God gives the Christian such positive assurance of salvation that any doubt at all indicates that a person is not saved. His preaching resulted in numerous cases of re-baptism of persons who had already been baptized once or more. In those days that practice was theologically alarming. Holt, Superintendent of Missions, urged B.H. Carroll to enter the fray since "you [Carroll] are looked upon as being thoroughly conversant with all phases of our faith."[52] Pastor B. H.

Carroll, not one to tolerate any disagreement with his own views, called a church council in March 1889 to set young Martin straight. Martin was not persuaded, and created a crisis by applying for a letter of dismission to another church.

Carroll felt the church could not grant such a letter without tacitly approving Martin's views. The deacons brought formal charges against Martin, saying

> Rev. M. T. Martin, member and ordained minister of this church, has . . . taught doctrines contrary to our acknowledged standard of faith and polity, thereby causing division and trouble in our denomination. . . . And we further charge that . . . where his doctrines have been received and his spirit imbibed, the effect has been detrimental; to prayer-meetings, Sunday-schools, mission work and other denominational activities.[53]

The Waco church revoked Martin's ordination, but granted him dismission as a layman. He moved to Georgia where he joined the Woodstock church which licensed him to preach. There the matter might have rested, but Martin returned to Texas and joined First Baptist of Marlin, in the Waco Association. The Marlin leaders asked the Waco church to rescind their action and restore Martin's ministerial credentials, and indicated if this was not done, the Marlin church would simply reordain him.

This was now more than a doctrinal question; it was an issue of *church polity*. To what extent did the Waco action bind the Marlin church, if at all? A committee of the Waco church sent word to Marlin repeating the charges against Martin and strongly implying that Marlin should follow the lead of Waco. In February 1890 the Marlin church felt they could wait no longer so they simply voted that Martin's ordination was still valid and acknowledged him as an authentic minister. B. H. Carroll led the Waco church to prefer charges against the Marlin church at the associational meeting in September, an action which offended the Marlin Baptists who felt theirs was a *church* action and was no business of the association to review.

At the association meeting, Waco deplored "the disrespect shown by [the] Marlin church in treatment of the affectionate and respectful petition and admonition of several sister churches." They alleged that "Marlin has violated Gospel order, the sanctity of discipline, the comity acknowledged and observed by the Baptist churches, Christ's law of love and fellowship, binding the churches, and has brought our form of church government into reproach." In conclusion, they said "We therefore respectfully and fraternally urge that the Association now exercise its constitutional prerogative of . . . withdrawing from and disfellowshipping a delinquent and impenitent church."

Despite their valiant defense of their freedom to decide their own issues, by vote of seventy-seven to seven the Marlin church was excluded from the Waco Association. Perhaps the action of the Marlin church was injudicious and hasty, but even worse, they had dared to challenge B. H.

Carroll and the First Baptist Church of Waco, which one did not do with impunity. When Martin charged that Texas Baptists were suffering from "a species of denominational bossism," no one doubted who he meant. Martin soon left the area and the next year the Marlin church issued an apology of sorts and was restored to fellowship. However, as late as 1895 the Waco Association and the BGCT both issued new condemnations of Martinism. The State Convention said that it would not seat messengers who were known to hold Martinist doctrines. Eventually, Texas Baptists turned their attention to other matters and Martinism receded. The same emphases, however, showed up later among some aggressive evangelists whose "converts" had already been baptized once or more.

Fortunism. George M. Fortune was at least an authentic heretic. He appeared in Paris in the fall of 1891 and, since the First Baptist Church was without a pastor, was invited to preach. He was an able preacher and after a few weeks, without any checking into his background, Fortune was called as pastor. It later appeared that his background was checkered: he had been a Methodist preacher in Illinois, a temperance lecturer in Kansas, and a Baptist preacher in Arkansas.[54] It soon became obvious that Fortune held radical views. He denied that Christ's death on the cross is effective for salvation. He also denied the existence of a personal Satan, the existence of eternal punishment, the imputation of sin in Adam's transgression, and the full inspiration of Scripture. Fortune rejected the substitutionary element of Christ's death. An influential physician in the Paris church, J. M. Fort, was a powerful ally and apparently held even more radical views than did the pastor. In addition to "heresies and vagaries," Fortune and Fort were also charged with certain "anti-Baptistic" practices: they refused to use Baptist literature, Fortune quoted no Baptist authorities in his sermons, they led the church to declare itself independent of all denominational connections, they allowed non-Baptists to take communion, and Fortune rejected the practice of an "annual call"[55] for a pastor and insisted that his own call be for an indefinite period. Dr. Fort "made the statement that the Baptist Theological Seminary at Louisville was the greatest curse upon the denomination and Christianity ever tolerated," an assessment accepted by Pastor Fortune.[56] Moral charges were raised, in light of reports that Fortune's first wife was still alive.[57]

When Fortune published his views in a widely distributed pamphlet, some members of the church protested. But the majority sustained the pastor. The minority called a council for February 11, 1896, in Paris.[58] Since their own church was barred to them, they met in the local Disciples church. The council of forty-one members included the pastors of other churches in Lamar Association plus other Baptist leaders from across the state, and was presided over by Baylor president Rufus C. Burleson. Formal charges were lodged against Fortune, and these were discussed and sustained. The council concluded that "his [Fortune's] views are, as an entirety, unscriptural, and therefore unbaptistic, and out of harmony with the universally accepted doctrine of the Baptist denomination." The substantial B. H. Carroll also weighed in, pronouncing Fortune's views "a candid, outright, downright, audacious attack on the central, vital doctrines of not only the Baptist faith, but the faith of evangelical Christendom."

Ignoring the council's verdict, Fortune continued to preach at Paris until 1897 when he left the church, repudiated the Baptist faith, and opened a law office in Indian Territory. The minority entered suit to recover the property on the grounds that they, who continued to adhere to the authentic Baptist faith, constituted the true church. However, in 1900 the Supreme Court of Texas awarded the entire property to the heretical majority. This controversy inflicted great harm to the Baptist witness, especially in North Texas.

Crawfordism. Though not centering in Texas, the views of Tarleton Perry Crawford (1821-1902) created great havoc among Texas Baptists. Crawford and his wife Martha were appointed as missionaries to China under the Foreign Mission Board. After some years in China, Crawford found himself out of agreement with the FMB about mission strategy, support and administration. Following the missionary philosophy of Presbyterian John Nevius, Crawford believed that missionaries should draw only a bare subsistence salary, and should seek to become self-supporting as soon as possible so as not to require even that. His views on missionary non-support became more pronounced after his shrewd and sometimes questionable investments in Chinese real estate gave him a measure of financial independence. Jesse C. Fletcher, who served for several years as an official of the Foreign Mission Board, says that Gospel Missionism "stirred the pot in the long simmering Landmark controversy in the Southern Baptist Convention," but did no permanent harm to the foreign mission work. By contrast, he says, "John Nevius's principles would strongly influence Mission Strategies including those of Southern Baptists in later years."[59]

Under the influence of Landmark leader J. R. Graves, Crawford also believed that missionaries should be sent out only by *churches* and not by denominational *mission boards*. This he believed was the gospel way, hence the name of the movement. Unable to dismantle the FMB, Crawford could at least ignore it. For several years he continued to receive his salary but acted independently of the Board, deciding on his own where to work, what work to do, making no reports to the FMB, and returning to the United States when he chose and for as long as he chose, without even notifying the sponsoring Board. In 1892 Crawford expressed his views in a militant booklet *Churches: To the Front!* in which he said "Baptist Churches are self-acting religious bodies . . . . [and] can never abdicate nor transfer any part of its [sic] work to the control of an outside body."[60] He felt that

This "organizational craze" has gone to great extremes, and the time has come for our people to "call a halt." . . . We have enough of General Conventions, National Societies, Central Boards, Executive Committees and

other like agencies . . . . Their very existence and course of action throw
discredit upon the Churches by taking the work out of their hands. . . .
These Boards . . . are, therefore, unlawful bodies within the Baptist fold
and should disband.[61]

Crawford felt that denominational boards usurped the prerogatives
of churches, and called for churches to regain their freedom "by casting
off this incongruous system with all its expensive adjuncts at home and
abroad." This called for nothing less than the dismantling of the Southern
Baptist Convention, and especially of the Foreign Mission Board.

Crawford also embraced the J. R. Graves version of premillennial
doctrine that shaped his understanding of missions. As understood by the
FMB, Crawford regarded Matt. 24:14

as prophetic of a time now near at hand, and propose to prepare for the
coming of the Lord by heralding the gospel among the nations. They do
not expect to gain many converts, but to evangelize the world in preparation for the millennium. These are the Premillennialists.[62]

Because of these millennial views, Crawford and his followers gave little attention to forming and developing churches, and opposed other
forms of mission work like teaching or social ministries. Their goal was not
so much to win converts as to preach the gospel in "all the world," thus
paving the way for Christ to return. On the other hand, the FMB said that
its view of missions was "to save souls, to train converts, to establish
churches as centres of influence—candlesticks in the midst of darkness."[63]
Crawford also rejected the idea of paying national pastors or helpers, and
insisted that missionaries adopt native customs of food, clothing, housing
and medical care. The Board replied that this might work in some areas,
but few missionaries would want to adopt the clothing styles where people
went naked. After years of patience, the FMB finally dismissed Crawford
from their rolls and soon afterward received with regrets the resignation
of his wife Martha.

Though not centered in Texas, the Crawford movement greatly
impacted Baptists in the Lone Star State. S. A. Hayden of the *Texas Baptist
and Herald* held many of Crawford's "Gospel Mission" views and blanketed Texas with them. He attacked the General Convention, its Executive
Board and its missionary appointment process. These attacks created suspicion, undermined confidence, and eroded financial support for the
Convention and all its various forms of ministry. Crawfordism seeped into
Texas by way of Haydenism, and created great havoc among the Texas
churches.

Whitsitism. In her definitive study, Rosalie Beck has shown that the
Whitsitt controversy revealed a denomination in crisis.[64] Of all the people
to create a crisis in Baptist life, one would never have picked William Heth
Whitsitt (1841-1911). The Whitsitt controversy of the 1890s represented
another outbreak of Landmarkism, this one centering upon views of Bap-

tist origins. Whitsitt was the scholarly professor of Baptist history at the Southern Baptist Theological Seminary who was elected president of that Seminary in 1895 at the death of Dr. Broadus. As a professor, Whitsitt's views attracted less attention, but as president he became a lightning rod for criticism. One important teaching of Landmarkism is that the Baptist denomination dates from New Testament times. According to this view, Jesus established the First Baptist Church of Jerusalem, the apostles were all Baptists, and Baptist churches have existed in unbroken continuity or succession from the days of John the Baptist to the present. Whitsitt's careful research convinced him that while Baptist *teachings* date from the New Testament, the Baptist *denomination* emerged out of the Puritan-Separatist reform movement of the English Reformation. The earliest identifiable Baptist church of modern history, Whitsitt said, was formed about 1608 or 1609 and modern Baptist churches can trace their history back to this seventeenth-century recovery of biblical teachings and practice. While baptism by immersion is taught in the New Testament, Whitsitt said, the practice was lost for centuries until modern Baptists recovered it in the 1640s. Whitsitt's views seemed controversial then, but today all reputable Baptist historians accept some version of them.

Whitsitt published his views of Baptist origins in a series of articles, and in 1896 published a book on the subject.[65] Reaction was immediate and vociferous, and much of the criticism centered in Texas. Alan Lefever says that "Carroll tried to remain a voice of moderation in the early states of the controversy," affirming that Whitsitt was dealing with historical rather than doctrinal issues and, at any rate, had denied no Baptist principles.[66] At the Wilmington meeting of the SBC in 1897, Carroll introduced a resolution calling for the Board to study Whitsitt's teachings and "pronounce upon them," but W. J. Northen, an influential Georgia trustee, offered substitute resolutions which in effect cleared Whitsitt unheard upon the grounds that the Board "cannot undertake to sit in judgment upon questions of Baptist history."[67] Northen's substitute was adopted, Whitsitt made a conciliatory statement, and many felt the controversy was over.

However, as Lefever points out, "If Whitsitt returned to Southern as the victorious warrior calling for peace, Carroll returned to Texas as the defeated knight desiring a rematch."[68] After the Wilmington meeting, Carroll led the fight against Whitsitt, both in the trustee meetings and in the Baptist press. In a biting article entitled "Theological Seminaries and Wild Gourds," Carroll noted that seminaries, like wild gourds, may look good on the outside but be worthless within.[69] Unable at first to get Whitsitt fired, Carroll led the Southern Baptist Convention to distance itself from the Seminary. This would have imperilled financial support, and in 1899 Whitsitt was forced to resign. After Whitsitt was gone, the remaining faculty at the Seminary sent Carroll a letter saying they all agreed with their embattled president and would continue to teach the same. Carroll won the battle but lost the war. Whitsitt was gone, but his views remained. Some feel this was a major factor in Carroll's desire to build a Seminary in the Southwest. J. M. Carroll added his mite to the discussion with his famous posthumous pamphlet, *The Trail of Blood,* which seeks to refute Whitsitt and reinforce the Landmark view of Baptist origins.

One might be surprised that a Kentucky controversy should create such a panic in Texas, but it did. B. H. Carroll, a trustee at Southern, was besieged by letters suggesting, among other things, that Whitsitt be fired, that Texas Baptists form their own theological Seminary, that Texas combine with others west of the Mississippi to form a new convention or all of the above. The Texas Convention in 1897 voted a resolution: "That it is the sense of this Convention, that for the sake of unity, peace and harmony, the interests of the Southern Baptist Convention and of the Seminary itself, Dr. Whitsett *[sic]* ought at once to retire from his position as president, and unless he shall voluntarily retire, the Board of Trustees ought to retire him."[70] After Whitsitt resigned, the controversy gradually subsided, but Landmark views of Baptist origins persisted especially in the Southwest.

Haydenism. Samuel A. Hayden came to Dallas in 1883 as pastor of the Live Oak Baptist Church, which had resulted from a bitter split from First Baptist. The Live Oak church held extreme Landmark views and often had J. R. Graves of Nashville as guest speaker. As pastor Hayden sought to heal the breach with FBC and by 1885 the two groups reunited, believing that Dallas could support no more than one Baptist church. It was not a happy reunion. Hayden remained in the membership, preached occasionally and perhaps expected to have some kind of role as associate pastor. However, that never worked out and before long Hayden was locked into a bitter controversy with the pastor, Robert T. Hanks. As noted earlier, Hayden used his paper, the *Texas Baptist and Herald,* to attack Pastor Hanks, prompting Hanks to buy an interest in another paper to reply to the charges.

By 1894 Hayden had broadened his attacks to include the entire Convention and especially its superintendent of missions. He charged that the superintendent was provided a handsome salary while the missionaries worked in poverty, that Convention leaders had diverted mission money to their own pockets and then covered up their embezzlement, that the Convention tried to "lord it over the churches" by assuming powers that belonged only to churches, that Convention leadership was self-serving and ineffective, and that the *churches* and not the Convention Board should direct mission work in Texas. His views were very similar to those of T. P. Crawford. Hayden persisted in describing the two factions among Texas Baptists as the "Church Party" (Hayden) and the "Board Party" (the Convention). He was essentially anti-denominational.

Repeatedly the Convention appointed committees to investigate these charges and found them baseless. It was true that the corresponding secretary was paid a larger salary than the missionaries, but the salaries for top leaders were not exhorbitant, though the "expenses" may have been generously defined at times and some of the corresponding secretaries tended to hire a lot of their relatives. However, there was then and is now no evidence whatever to sustain Hayden's charges of lavish waste, fraud, or misappropriations.

In time Hayden's attacks, accusations and innuendoes had their impact, and mission work in Texas suffered. In their 1896 report the Executive Board said,

> For several years past an agent has been at work in our state undermining the mission work, drying up the mission spirit, and sowing down our once fertile fields with salt. That agent has persistently, ruthlessly and openly, in public print attacked this board, its methods and work, charging it directly and indirectly, and by various methods of innuendo and insinuation, with misappropriation, wanton extravagance and reckless waster of public funds. . . . he has published virtual charges of embezzlement against the secretary [Corresponding Secretary] , and by fair implication the board itself. With this agent nothing pertaining to this work is sacred or ever settled. . . . [his actions] add to the general distrust, discord and divisions he himself has gendered. . . . Is there no end of patience? . . . Shall we wait until the mission cause, now bleeding, is stamped our of existence? Who, then, is this agent? His name is S. A. Hayden, of Dallas.[71]

This stern report was signed by two of the most respected men among Texas Baptists, W. H. Jenkins and George W. Truett. Truett observed that Hayden's attacks caused many to stop giving. For the most part, Truett said, "it was a waste of postage to send an appeal for help to those whose reading was confined to his distorted presentations." The Board urged that Hayden be denied a seat in the Convention, but instead the Convention issued a public reprimand to Hayden, which left him more incensed and angry than ever.

However, at the San Antonio convention in 1897 Hayden's right to a seat was again challenged. The charges against him were rehearsed, concluding that "He is a breeder of strife and dissention and contention among the brethren and associations."[72] Hayden was given forty-five minutes to defend himself, after which the Convention voted 582 to 104 to expel him.

A doctrinal issue was at stake; Hayden claimed the Convention was made up of churches and thus had no authority to expel a church. However, the Convention reaffirmed its ruling of 1895 "that the Convention is composed of persons chosen by churches, associations and missionary societies as their messengers, and that when said persons are convened they, and not the churches, are the Convention."[73] This was an important ruling, and was in accord with historic Baptist practice. About this time Landmark groups were agitating for the SBC to switch to a church basis of membership. A Landmark group in Arkansas issued an ultimatum in 1905, but the SBC adopted essentially the same decision that the BGCT had adopted ten years earlier.

In reaction to his exclusion in 1897, on April 28, 1898, Hayden filed a lawsuit in Dallas against the Convention and about thirty of its leaders by name, including J. B. Cranfill, B. H. Carroll, George W. Truett, Jeff D. Ray, J. M. Carroll, C. C. Slaughter, and R. T. Hanks. Hayden sought $100,000 in damages, alleging that they had "made his name a stench among the brethren." He later filed a separate suit for the 1898 exclusion and other suits against different individuals. For years these cases worked their weary way through the courts, inflicting untold damage to the Baptist witness in Texas, to say nothing of financial burdens for the defendants. In the first trial the court awarded Hayden a judgement of $30,000 but this verdict was set aside by the Court of Civil Appeals. The second and third trials ended in hung juries. The fourth trial awarded Hayden $15,000 in damages, but after several years of appeals the Texas Supreme Court reversed the verdict and sent the case back for retrial. At this point, Cranfill had had enough and he settled out of court for $100 in each case plus court costs.

Perhaps the low point of the entire controversy occurred on a train near Texarkana in 1904. Both Cranfill and Hayden were on board, bound for the Southern Baptist Convention. The two got into a scuffle and Cranfill fired his revolver, though no one was hit. Cranfill later issued profuse public apologies and asked First Baptist, Dallas, where he was a member, to investigate the incident. He agreed that if he was found at fault he would surrender his ministerial credentials. Deacon W. L. Williams headed the investigation, which exonerated Cranfill. Some reported, facetiously one hopes, that if Cranfill was to be disciplined, it should not be for shooting but for missing.

If these ugly lawsuits hurt Texas Baptists, they destroyed S. A. Hayden. In July 1900 his followers split off and formed an East Texas Baptist Convention at Troupe, and the next year merged with other dissidents to form the Baptist Missionary Association (BMA). This was the fourth Baptist convention formed in East Texas through the years. Their origins (Larissa, Tyler, Overton, and Troupe) lay within a twenty mile radius. This group still exists though over the years many of their churches and pastors have quietly returned to the BGCT. The *Texas Baptist and Herald*, Hayden's once influential paper, became the voice of the BMA and eventually expired. A Baptist handbook for 1995 listed for the Texas BMA 98,509 members in 498 churches.[74]

FACING A NEW CENTURY

Despite the Hayden controversy the Texas Convention ended the century intact, but the damage was immense and the scars deep. Not until the 1920s with J. Frank Norris, a disciple of Hayden, would the Convention face a similar threat. Until then, Texas Baptists enjoyed a few years of relative peace. Increasing prosperity, effective leadership, and the excitement of a new century propelled them forward to new victories. The next chapter will recount some of those achievements.

CHAPTER 7

INTO THE TWENTIETH CENTURY, 1900–1914

"A GREAT PEOPLE HAVE come to a great time." That is how J. B. Gambrell described Baptists as they entered the twentieth century. Texas Baptists in the late nineteenth century and the early twentieth hardly look like the same people. The change is incredible, as if they had walked out from dark storm clouds into bright sunlight. The outward evidence of growth in membership, missions, and money was more than matched by inward spiritual revival, renewal of spirit, and cooperation. George W. Truett, who was himself one factor in bringing these better days, said, "Rarely has the Lord's host gone afield in better conditions for spiritual conquest."[1] As if he feared he had been too optimistic, Truett added "The millennium has not arrived in Texas," but it at least seemed closer.[2]

PEACE, PROSPERITY, PROGRESS

Three words sum up Texas Baptist life early in the new century: *peace, prosperity,* and *progress.* Each word merits a brief comment.

Peace. The story of the constant bickering, infighting, accusations and damaging litigation that marked Texas Baptists during the fractious '90s has been told in the previous chapter. Almost overnight that ugly era came to an end. With his court cases settled or thrown out and his once-influential paper in eclipse, Samuel A. Hayden, Texas Baptists' chief thorn in the flesh, moved quickly from center stage to the edge of Texas Baptist life. "The difficulties which so sorely tried the faith and patience of the workers a few years ago," Truett wrote, "are becoming a memory."[3] Texas Baptists entered an era of peace, harmony and cooperation that was largely unbroken until the rise of J. Frank Norris after World War I. Where did the loud opposition of the 1890s go? How could contention give way to cooperation so quickly? The death of J. R. Graves in Memphis in 1893 deprived the Landmark movement of its founder and major spokesman, and the termination of T. P. Crawford from the Foreign Mission Board in 1894 quieted the Gospel Mission Movement. Thus the two divisive movements which had fueled a generation of unrest in Texas were quieted. Most of the remaining opposition was siphoned off by the split in 1900 which created the Baptist Missionary Association (BMA). Those who feared denominational organization, opposed organized missions, or simply could not get along with the brethren joined this ultraconservative dissident group. Their absence from the BGCT proved a blessing and allowed the Convention to get on with its work. The BMA group still exists, though remaining small. Over the years many of their pastors and churches have quietly returned to the BGCT and, in general, a more collegial spirit prevails between the two groups.

No doubt some opposition merely went underground, to surface another day over other issues. Criticism always gains more hearing when things are going badly, as they were in the 1890s. But after the turn of the century, Texas Baptist ministries of every kind went from one victory to another and the sound of success drowned out any lingering criticism. After the demise of Hayden, no leader of stature arose to galvanize the discontented until J. Frank Norris after 1915. As a result, Texas Baptists turned their attention from controversy to ministry.

Prosperity. Three things revolutionized the financial life of Texas Baptists early in the twentieth century. First, the economy improved. At long last the lingering effects of Reconstruction, persistent drouths, and low crop prices began to abate and a degree of prosperity made its appearance in the Lone Star State. Second, the churches gradually learned the grace of giving. Pastors taught stewardship, the Baptist women modeled generosity in missionary giving, and the amount of offerings in the churches, and in the Convention, shot upward. Third, both the churches and the Convention developed more order and consistency in their handling of money. Though most churches still gave only sporadically or in the two major financial "round-ups" of the year, some began to give regularly throughout the year. This allowed the Convention to plan its work with more precision, with at least some idea of how much income to expect, thus reducing the need for operating on borrowed money.

Progress. Those who like statistics would love the eye-popping annual reports of the BGCT during the years 1900 to 1914. Every unit of measurement showed incredible growth: more money for missions, more missionaries under appointment, more churches and associations formed, more converts baptized, more members added by letter, more enrollment in the colleges, more ministerial students, and more different kinds of ministry sponsored by the Convention. To list such statistics here would be tiresome but at least this much can be noted: in the fifteen years from 1900 to 1915 Texas Baptists increased from 2,740 churches to 3,623; from

190,198 members to 352,409; from 10,479 baptisms to 24,623; from a Sunday School enrollment of 57,353 to 214,687; and total gifts increased from $347,556 in 1900 to $2,021,676 in 1915.[4] This confirms the observation of an early historian who said that during these years "everything had been conspiring to the prosperity of the Baptist denomination in Texas. In God's providence everything had fallen out for their good."[5] In the heady optimism of the times it was J. B. Gambrell, "Uncle Gideon," who sounded a note of caution, urging Baptists not to jump ahead of themselves, but to learn to walk well before they tried to run.

Every believer will see in this remarkable growth ample evidence of the providence of God. From a human perspective, this growth also shows the value of good organization, effective promotion, and capable leadership. The BGCT became a major religious bureaucracy, in the good sense of that term. Baptists sponsored many forms of ministry, all correlated through the state body. The sheer size of the Convention *Annual* is revealing. A description of the work took twelve pages in 1848, but increased to 155 pages in 1898 and 268 in 1914. At a typical session, up to one hundred committees would bring reports.[6] Perhaps it was too early to refer to Dallas, where the Convention offices had been located since 1896, as "Baptist headquarters," but the trend was set. With more responsibilities and more resources, the BGCT developed a measure of power by electing the trustees and helping determine the funding of Baptist schools, missions, hospitals and other benevolences. In 1914, even the Buckner Orphans Home, long an independent Baptist agency, came under ownership and control of the State Convention.

NEW LEADERS ARISE

As Texas Baptists entered the new century some of the old giants were still active. B. H. Carroll (d.1914), Robert C. Buckner (d.1919), and Fannie Breedlove Davis (d.1915) made some of their greatest achievements after 1900. Rufus C. Burleson, M. V. Smith, and Jennie Anderson were outstanding leaders whose lives spanned the turn of the century. Others, if not giants of the order of B. H. Carroll or R. C. Buckner, were yet larger than life and provided dynamic leadership, including Jeff D. Ray, J. B. Cranfill, J. M. Carroll, R. T. Hanks and wealthy layman C. C. Slaughter. In addition to these, new leaders emerged early in the new century whose contributions to Texas Baptist life are beyond measure. No list could be long enough to include them all, but at least these come to mind: George W. Truett, L. R. Scarborough, J. B. Gambrell, J. Frank Norris, I. E. Gates, J. M. Dawson, A. J. Barton, F. M. McConnell, W. B. McGarity, J. R. Millican, J. R. Jester, Robert H. Coleman, M. H. Wolfe, and F. L. Carroll and his son George (no relation to the brothers B. H. and J. M.). Mary Hill Davis, Mary T. Gambrell (Mrs. J. B), Willie T. Dawson (Mrs. J. M.), Lucinda Williams (Mrs. W. L.), and Holly Harper Townsend (Mrs. E. G.)

were important leaders in their own right. Space will allow a brief sketch of only a few of these.

George Washington Truett. Young George Truett came to the pastorate of First Baptist Church in Dallas in 1897 with impressive credentials. He had become widely known and trusted in the successful financial campaign to save Baylor University in 1892. At his graduation from Baylor in 1897 Truett was offered strategic pulpits throughout the country, including First Baptist in Nashville. His intention to attend the Seminary in Louisville was turned aside by the invitation to come to Dallas, where he was first recommended by J. B. Cranfill. Dallas had railroads, banks and commerce, a growing population and a church of over 700 members. George and Josephine Truett, with their infant daughter, moved to Dallas in September 1897 to begin a pastorate of almost forty-seven years on a vote of seventy-four for and three against. Already Dallas had become a Baptist center, with the *Baptist Standard,* the Buckner Orphans Home, and the state convention offices located there. Quickly Truett emerged as a new star in the Baptist firmament. He preached the Convention sermon in 1898, and from that time until his death in 1944 he served on major committees, policy groups, and convention boards. George Truett was beyond question the greatest leader among Texas Baptists, and his voice carried weight. He helped reconstitute the Dallas Baptist Association and was its behind-the-scenes power for a generation. He was a major founder of the Baptist Memorial Sanitarium in 1904 (now Baylor Health Care System), and he helped create the Relief and Annuity Board of the SBC which located in Dallas in 1918.

Truett grew up in rural North Carolina where he attended the country schools. Converted at age nineteen, Truett taught school for a time and then moved with his parents to Whitewright in North Texas. He was saving money to attend law school but the church in Whitewright took the initiative in calling him to ministry and voted to ordain him. Quite early Truett became an outstanding preacher and a wise pastoral leader. He led the Dallas church to be generous in missions, loyal to denominational causes, and energetic in outreach. First Baptist became the bellwether church of the denomination, and its pastor was the acknowledged spokesman for Texas Baptists and indeed for all Southern Baptists.

Early in his Dallas pastorate came the tragedy which could have derailed Truett's entire ministry. Captain J. C. Arnold, Chief of Police in Dallas and a former Texas Ranger, invited his young pastor to join him in a quail hunt near Venus in Johnson County. They went by train to Cleburne, where they were joined by George W. Baines, pastor of FBC, Cleburne. At the close of the day's hunt on Friday, February 4, 1898, Truett shifted his borrowed shotgun from one hand to the other and it discharged, hitting Arnold in the calf. No one thought the wound serious, but Arnold died that Saturday night. Though all knew it was an accident, Truett was crushed. In an anguished letter to Mrs. Arnold, the young pastor expressed "the unutterable sympathy of my broken heart."[7] He felt that his ministry was over, that he could never preach again. However, one midnight in the depths of despair Truett gained the assurance that the Lord's hand was still upon him. One who was present in the first service Truett led after this tragedy said the pastor appeared haggard, with dark sunken eyes. "But his voice! I shall never forget his voice that night, as we heard for the first time the note of sadness and pathos which now we know so well."[8]

Truett was a strong leader in the church and the denomination but he was never dictatorial. He had a gift for inspiring others as to what needed to be done, and allowing them to carry the ball while he remained above the fray. In spirit he was magnanimous, in judgment sound, in personal integrity impeccable. It is no wonder that George W. Truett is still generally regarded as the greatest pastor Baptists in America have ever produced.

James Bruton Gambrell. Born in South Carolina, J. B. Gambrell came to Texas from Georgia where he had served as editor of the *Baptist Record* and president of Mercer University. In the Civil War Captain Gambrell served as a scout for General Robert E. Lee and later fought in the Battle of Gettysburg. In 1864 he married Mary T. Corbell, who became an outstanding Baptist leader in her own right.

Gambrell was elected Superintendent of Missions for the BGCT in 1896 in the midst of the Hayden controversy. His three predecessors had been hounded out of that office by the hostile Hayden sympathizers, and Gambrell was chosen partly because it was felt he would not be easy to run off. Gambrell served effectively until 1910, and helped bring a new spirit of unity and cooperation to Texas Baptists. In 1910 he resigned to become editor of the *Baptist Standard* where he distinguished himself for plain and powerful writing for the masses, courageous editorials, and persistent promotion of all Texas Baptist causes. In 1912 Gambrell was named a professor at the Southwestern Baptist Theological Seminary, while continuing his work as editor. In 1914 he began his second stint as Corresponding Secretary of the newly consolidated board of the BGCT, an expansion of his previous role. Gambrell later served as president of the Southern Baptist Convention during the crucial years of World War I and in that position helped to define the role of SBC president.

Known affectionately as "Uncle Gideon" and sometimes as "the Great Commoner," J. B. Gambrell had a gift for inspiring ordinary Baptists. He spoke plain language and people trusted him. He was known for his aphorisms and wise proverbs. As a Texas Baptist leader, Gambrell helped overcome the crisis of controversy of the 1890s, led the Convention to new heights of cooperation and mission work, helped define Baptist attitudes toward the ecumenical movement, and lent his considerable strength to the new Southwestern Seminary.

Lee Rutland Scarborough. Lee Scarborough grew up as a hard-riding cowboy on a Texas cattle ranch, with the nickname of "the Dogie."[9] Born in 1870, the son of a pioneer rancher and country preacher couple George W. and Martha Rutland Scarborough, young Lee cherished dreams of an education. His parents used money they had intended for building a new house to send Lee to Baylor University, where he came under the powerful influence of B. H. Carroll. Lee later attended Yale Law School, but could not escape the conviction that he was called to preach. He returned to Texas as pastor of FBC Cameron, and left there in 1899 to attend the Southern Baptist Theological Seminary in Louisville, where he came under the influence of such theological giants as E. Y. Mullins, A. T. Robertson, W. O. Carver, and J. R. Sampey. In 1901 Scarborough became pastor of FBC in Abilene at a salary of $100 a month. At this great West Texas church Scarborough proved to be an effective pastor, evangelist, and friend of Simmons College.

In the newly formed Southwestern Baptist Theological Seminary, President B. H. Carroll had instituted a professorship in evangelism, the first in the world. For two years Carroll had urged the dynamic Abilene pastor to accept this "Chair of Fire," to teach evangelism in the classroom and to model evangelism as a field evangelist for the Seminary. In 1908 Scarborough accepted. He led in the relocation of the Seminary to Fort Worth in 1910, raised money and oversaw the erection of the first building, Fort Worth Hall, and helped get the school off to a good start. It soon became obvious that the dynamic young Scarborough was the heir apparent to succeed Carroll as president, which he did in 1915. Scarborough became a major denominational leader in Texas and beyond as president of the Seminary and as director of the Seventy-five Million Campaign. With the "Chair of Fire," Scarborough helped develop the highly effective Baptist evangelism, and he also led in forming what Glenn Carson calls "a new denominationalism," including the effort to build a unified, cooperative denomination that would make a serious effort to reach the entire world with the gospel.[10]

Mary Hill Davis. Born in Georgia, Mary Hill came to Dallas as a child in 1870, where the family joined the First Baptist Church in its third year. At age twenty, she married Dallas physician F. S. Davis, and both became deeply involved in the First Baptist Church. In 1896 Mary Hill Davis was elected Recording Secretary of the Baptist Women Mission Workers (now called WMU), and served until 1906. From 1906-1931 she served as president of the Texas Woman's Missionary Union, the longest term of any president. During her tenure the name of the women's organization was changed from Baptist Women Mission Workers (BWMW) to Woman's Missionary Union (WMU), the "circle plan" for WMU meetings was begun, and an annual Week of Prayer for state missions was launched. That week of prayer and special offering in Texas now bears her name.

Known for her forward-looking enthusiasm, Davis said "Enthusiastic people make blunders, but fainthearted people never make anything."[11] Building upon the foundations laid by predecessors like Lucinda Williams, Mary Hill Davis helped awaken the missionary zeal of the "Baptist

Sisterhood of Texas," to use one of her phrases. She led in forming new WMU groups in churches, strengthened the association work, and broadened the scope of women's ministry to include mission education, offerings for all causes, sponsorship of the Woman's Missionary Training School to provide theological education for young women, aid for Buckner Orphans Home and for retired ministers and their wives. She also led in expanding the "Juvenile Bands," mission organizations for children, such as Girls' Auxiliary and Royal Ambassadors. Her first message as president in 1906 was "Onward," and her last in 1931 was "Onward, forever onward, singing all the way."[12]

Franz Marshall McConnell. By the time F. M. McConnell was elected Corresponding Secretary of the BGCT in 1910, he had already established himself as a major leader among Baptists. Born in Missouri, McConnell taught school and practiced law in Arkansas, Indian Territory (now Oklahoma), and New Mexico before moving to Texas. He was ordained at Kaufman in 1886 and after a few years as a pastor, he entered the field of full-time evangelism in 1902. He followed a path blazed by Major W. E. Penn, for full-time traveling evangelists were a rarity in those days. McConnell showed great success as an evangelist, and his travels made him well-known throughout the state. When J. B. Gambrell resigned in 1910, McConnell was immediately tapped as his successor to head up the state convention work.

McConnell was described as "sound in his preaching and sane in his methods," and "full of good common sense."[13] He brought his experience as a successful pastor and evangelist to the state office, where he served until 1914. During his years of leadership, the Baptist mission work in Texas grew rapidly. Always zealous for evangelism, he kept soul winning as the focus of the work. McConnell became superintendent of evangelism at Southwestern Baptist Seminary in Fort Worth, and later served as Corresponding Secretary of the Baptist General Convention of Oklahoma. He returned to Texas as pastor of the First Baptist Church of Bonham. Many feel that his greatest work was as editor of the *Baptist Standard* from 1928 to 1944.

Joseph Martin Dawson. Born in Ellis County in 1879, young Dawson entered Baylor University in 1899 where he was the founder and first editor of *The Lariat.* As a ministerial student, he served several pastorates, including, Red Oak, Hewitt, and Central Baptist in Italy. Though never formally enrolled in a Seminary, he studied with B. H. Carroll at Waco in the fledgling theological department that later became Southwestern Seminary. After graduation in 1904, Dawson served as pastor at Lampasas, Hillsboro and Temple, and for a short time was editor of the *Baptist Standard* when that paper was owned by his old Baylor classmate, J. Frank Norris. However, the great work of Dawson's life was as pastor of First Baptist Church in Waco for thirty-one years, from 1915 to 1946. As pastor, Dawson often spoke out against social ills such as exploitation of child labor, unfair discrimination against women, ill treatment of immigrants, excessive hours of labor, and the ravages of unrestricted capitalism.[14] From 1946 to 1964, at an age when most men are retired, Dawson served as executive director of the Washington-based Baptist Joint Committee on Public Affairs.

As a leader among Texas Baptists, Dawson was known for his blunt honesty, his commitment to religious liberty and separation of church and state, and his prophetic voice on social and moral issues, such as sharecropping, racial inequalities, and the need for education for poor youths. In 1908 he married Willie Turner, who became an outstanding Texas Baptist speaker, and even her husband acknowledged that she was the better preacher of the two.

Manson Horatio Wolfe. A successful businessman, M. H. Wolfe had a great impact upon Texas Baptist life. Born in Fannin County in 1866, he moved from Wolfe City to Dallas in 1905 where he established a number of successful enterprises. As an active Baptist layman, he served as vice-president of the Southern Baptist Convention and president of the Baptist General Convention of Texas, and chairman of its Executive Board for many years. An advocate of "more business in religion," Wolfe urged the BGCT to adopt more orderly business procedures. He was quite influential in the 1914 reorganization of the Texas Convention which, many historians believe, helped lead to formation of the Executive Committee of the SBC three years later. As chairman of deacons in FBC Dallas, Wolfe was a firm ally of his pastor George W. Truett until Wolfe's tendency to side with J. Frank Norris damaged their relationship.

Mary T. Gambrell. Often overlooked in the shadow of her famous husband, Mary T. Gambrell was an outstanding Baptist leader in her own right. When the Gambrells came to Texas in 1896 a new era began, not only for the state convention but also for the women's work. Mary was employed as office secretary at the Convention at $75 a month and worked daily alongside her husband. When she was elected Corresponding Secretary of the Baptist Women Missionary Workers she had the full support of her husband, a valuable ally since he was head of the state mission work. She brought new zeal, more effective organization, and expansion to the work. Her goal was to form a women's society in every Baptist church in Texas, and to involve women in all the mission causes in Texas and beyond. Mrs. Gambrell was fluent in Spanish and took an early interest in mission work among the Mexicans. At one convention meeting in Dallas she entertained C. D. Daniel, director of Mexican missions, and twenty Mexican preachers in her own home. She helped sponsor and also attended the Mexican Preachers Institutes, which led to formation of the Mexican Baptist Convention of Texas.

Mina S. Everett. As a youth Mina Everett was a sceptic in religion, absorbing such views from her father. While visiting a devout Baptist aunt in Dublin, Texas, she attended Sunday School as a visitor. A class of young girls, unaware of her religious doubts, asked her to be their teacher. She agreed to teach at least one Sunday, and in studying the Bible lesson she was led to conversion herself. She continued with the class until every girl in the class of fifteen was converted and baptized.

On a trip with friends to Mexico in 1885, Miss Everett witnessed the dedication of the First Baptist Church building in Monterey, and from there went on to visit the Baptist school in Saltillo. These experiences turned her heart toward Mexican missions. Back in Texas she gave her own pony and jewelry to an offering to help send a missionary to Mexico. A. T. Hawthorne, who was then serving as an agent of the Foreign Mission Board, challenged her to be that missionary and she agreed. Later, due probably to the influence of Anne Luther Bagby, she went to Brazil instead. Miss Everett's foreign mission service was cut short by severe illness, but she later worked among Mexicans in San Antonio. She remained to the end of her life an eloquent advocate of missions.

Everett was elected corresponding secretary of the Baptist Women Mission Workers in 1889, jointly supported by the FMB, HMB, and the State Board. She was offered $75 a month, but accepted only $50. Her work involved traveling among the churches, speaking to women's groups and engaging in house-to-house visitation on behalf of missions. J. M. Carroll noted that wherever Everett went, money was sent to him for missions. On one occasion, thrust unexpectedly into speaking to a large mixed audience, an eyewitness described her message: "Timidly, womanly, tearfully, prayerfully and powerfully she spoke. There was not a dry eye in that large audience. The people were strangely and mightily moved."[15] It is no wonder that she was called "the most eloquent missionary voice ever heard among Texas Baptist women."[16] In seventeen years of ministry in Texas, Everett left an indelible impact. Known for her innovative ideas, she is said to have first suggested that the state convention form a church building fund, a convention owned paper, a training school for women, and a Baptist encampment.

Other leaders of note. Any list of leaders runs the risk of leaving someone out, and this one is no exception. Other leaders of note, whose achievements are omitted here only by pressure of space, include A. J. Barton, W. L. Williams, W. C. Lattimore, Jeff D. Ray, Josephine Truett, Mrs. B. A. Copass, and Elli Moore Townsend.

STATE MISSIONS

During the year 1900, a total of 164 Baptist missionaries appointed by the state convention labored at various points in Texas, a number that increased to 482 by 1914.[17] These state missionaries held revivals, formed missions and new churches, helped weak churches obtain pastors, worked closely with associations in promoting education and stewardship, and challenged stronger churches to form missions which would eventually become new churches. A 1901 report on the general missionaries said, "Their work roundly stated, is to awaken missionary zeal and prevent waste in the denomination." No work sponsored by the Convention found more favor among the churches than that of the general missionary. The general missionary often served as a peacemaker when a church and its pastor had some difficulty A large part of the missionary's work was in helping weak churches. A 1901 report noted that

> Many of the churches built up by missionary effort and at large expense, through some misfortune become pastorless and lie waste. Perhaps there is a good house going to decay. There is everything but a united church and a godly pastor. The general missionary goes to such a place, takes hold of it, and brings the church together, induces it to call a pastor, raises his salary, and thus a church is saved and added to denominational strength.[18]

In 1901 the Convention launched a Church Building Department under the leadership of J. M. Gaddy with an initial gift of $5,000 from layman C. C. Waller. Its purpose was to help churches build suitable houses of worship, make needed repairs or expansion, and in some cases to help discharge debts on existing buildings. At that time, many Baptist churches in Texas had no building, holding their meetings in private homes, Masonic Lodge Halls, public schools, or in space borrowed from other denominations. The Board reported its conviction that a worthy house of worship was important to the vitality and growth of a church, and announced their purpose to do more such work in the future. "It is commonly known," the Board reported, "that the homeless conditions of our Churches in many places is one of the deplorable weaknesses of the situation." Further, they said, "the denomination is coming to a realization of the fact that Baptist Churches must have Baptist Meeting Houses in which to preach Baptist doctrines and grow and develop a reliable Baptist constituency."[19] Churches in disaster areas, such as Galveston during the great hurricane of 1900 and the frequent tornadoes of West Texas, received special attention from the Church Building Department. Better buildings, with more suitable space, also meant better Sunday Schools and more meaningful worship services.

Holding revivals or "protracted meetings" was an important part of the missionary's work. In the less populated areas, a suitable place for such meetings was often hard to find. Many were held out of doors, camp meeting style. In 1900 C. C. Slaughter, C. H. Briggs, and Sid Williams donated three large revival tents, which were put to frequent use. These "gospel tents" allowed the preachers to reach large crowds at a time when tent revivals were a popular part of the religious landscape of America. "We are fully persuaded of their usefulness in any complete plan for reaching and helping vast numbers of non church goers," said the Board, but they added the cautionary note that "There is danger that we may be snared by our meeting houses, as useful as they are."[20]

Practically all of the general missionaries carried religious books on their travels, especially after 1900 when the colportage work was merged into the state convention. The book display was a popular feature of associational meetings well into the modern era for Baptists who did not have access to a Baptist Book Store. In addition to the book distribution of the general missionaries, the Board employed four colporteurs in 1901, jointly supported by the state convention and the American Baptist Publication Society in Philadelphia. The Board purchased four specially equipped wagons at a cost of $220 each, described as "book-houses on wheels, with arrangements for sleeping."[21] One of these wagons was assigned to West Texas, one to East Texas, and two to Central Texas. This work proved popular, and several of the stronger associations raised money to operate their own book wagon.

Perhaps the most innovative form of mission work in Texas was the "Chapel Car" ministry. This plan was developed among Baptists in the North, and involved fitting out several large railroad Pullman cars as mobile chapels. These "churches on wheels" were complete with pews, hymnals, a small organ and pulpit, as well as living quarters for a missionary couple. The chapel cars could go wherever the railroad went and stop on sidings in communities with no permanent church for a week or several months as the needs indicated. A New York chapel car syndicate, headed by Baptist layman John D. Rockefeller, guaranteed the cooperation of the railroads, most of which moved the cars free of charge wherever they wished to go. The first car, *Evangel*, was put in service in 1891, and was soon followed by *Emmanuel, Glad Tidings, Good Will, Messenger of Peace, Herald of Hope,* and *Peace.* These cars allowed many churchless communities to have a Sunday School, revival meeting, and eventually a church.

For some years *Good Will* was assigned to Texas, with E. G. Townsend and his wife Hollie as resident missionaries. Before she married, Hollie Harper had been a "Bible woman" (a church visitor/local missionary) in Dallas. Her description of life as a mobile missionary aboard *Good Will* is so interesting as to merit quotation at some length. She wrote:

> The car is seventy-five feet long, and is a church and parsonage, all in one. The chapel is well furnished with Bibles, song books, maps, charts, tracts, etc.; also a lovely little organ, the gift of the Estey Organ Company. There is a blackboard and colored crayon for the illustrated talks, and just all one needs for convenience. The chapel will seat about 125, but I have had as many as 158 children present at children's meetings.
>
> Leaving the chapel and going through a swinging door back of the pulpit and organ you come to our living rooms. We have a combination room, I suppose you would call it. There is an upper and lower berth, as on a sleeping car, a nice library of books and a roller-top desk . . . . Two large mirrors adorn the walls. There are hooks for hanging things about the walls. The dining table is put up in this room for each meal—a folding table just like those used on buffet cars. Going out of this room (only ten feet space), there is a hall through the back door. On one side of this

hall is a little room, a doll house you would think, but it is my kitchen. Just standing room. Fitted up with refrigerator, cupboard, sink for washing dishes and a good range—missionaries cook and eat same as other folks. We have a large pantry across the hall, and next to it another closet for clothes.

There are large drawers beneath the cupboard, and in the back of the hall there is a toilet room. My porches are rather small, but my yard is as large as—Texas. . . . Come to see me and you will find that in our life "congregations ne'er break up and Sabbaths have no end."[22]

When *Good Hope* arrived in a Texas town, according to Townsend, it attracted more attention than a circus. They put out signs inviting children to an afternoon meeting with stories, songs and crafts, and conducted preaching services in the evening. Townsend was amazed to find how ignorant of the Bible the children and adults were. "Oh, the wickedness we find among the children in some of these towns," she lamented. "Little boys just out of nursery swearing great wicked words, fighting, chewing foul tobacco and sometimes drinking."[23] In addition to Sunday School, during the summer they conducted daily meetings for children, a forerunner of the Vacation Bible School. "We have the privilege of baptizing many young people, as well as converts among the older members of the family. The chapel car services have been the means of salvation to white-haired men and women. . . . who would never think of dressing up and going to a regular church." Nor was the ministry confined just to the times of services. Mrs. Townsend added that "Our private room is often turned into an inquiry room for days and days, and we can scarcely get time to eat and sleep for the troubled souls who come to us wanting to know the way of life."

An area of progress for state missions was the increasing involvement of pastors. In earlier times, it was usually paid agents rather than pastors who promoted and raised funds for Convention causes. One report noted that in earlier times "it was a rare thing that a great missionary collection was taken in any church in Texas unless some of the general workers of the Convention had a hand in it."[24] After the turn of the century, more pastors led in promoting the work of the state convention and on their own raised money for its ministries. This meant progress in all the work, with less dependence upon the financial agents of the Convention, many of whom had made themselves unpopular by their insistent appeals. The pastors also led out more in evangelism, leading to less dependence upon the general evangelists sponsored by the BGCT.

A CONVENTION PAPER

Since the 1840s Texas Baptists had tried to sponsor and sustain denominational newspapers. For awhile in the 1890s they had more than they wanted, as rival papers fanned controversy, undercut the mission work and disrupted fellowship. All of these early papers had one thing in common; they were private enterprises, not officially connected with the state convention. However, early in the twentieth century Baptist journalism in Texas took a new turn when the Convention itself owned and published its own paper.

When J. B. Gambrell became Corresponding Secretary of the BGCT in 1896, he was convinced of the importance of a paper to promote Convention causes. He had come from a newspaper background in Mississippi and well knew the value of the printed page. He led the Convention to found the *Missionary Worker,* a small monthly intended to inform, inspire, and motivate Texas Baptists. This was by no means a complete newspaper, but more of an in-house promotional piece. "This little paper belongs to the Convention," said the 1901 report. "It is devoted, with singleness of purpose, to the work of this body."[25] The Convention sent out about 7,200 copies each month, with a special issue of 20,000 to commemorate the centennial of 1900. S. A. Hayden had blanketed Texas with his paper and its criticism of Convention policies, and Gambrell used the new paper to refute false accusations, correct misinformation, and explain the Convention's work and appeal for support. For many years the paper served effectively. However, in 1910 the *Missionary Worker* was discontinued. A report at the 1910 convention said that "it has been for some time the opinion of a number of brethren that conditions had so far advanced toward a proper understanding of the policies of this Convention by the Baptists of Texas, that a special organ for the Convention was no longer a necessity."[26] The rapid growth of the *Baptist Standard* and its solid support for Convention causes with J. B. Gambrell recently installed as editor was no doubt a major factor in that decision.

At the turn of the century the *Baptist Standard* was privately owned, but was strongly supportive of Baptist work in Texas. In 1904 J. B. Cranfill, majority owner, sold his interest in the paper to Beaumont layman George W. Carroll, perhaps in reaction to the unfortunate gun incident aboard a train near Texarkana.[27] Cranfill later regretted his decision to sell the paper and tried unsuccessfully to buy it back. The new owner appointed Joel H. Gambrell, brother of the more famous J. B. and assistant editor under Cranfill, as editor in 1904. With J. B. Gambrell as corresponding secretary, his wife Mary head of the women's work and brother Joel in the editor's chair at the *Baptist Standard,* the Gambrells made a formidable leadership team for Texas Baptists. Joel Gambrell had the misfortune to be editor in a time of instability, serving under three owners within a few years. In July 1905 Carroll sold the paper to a group headed by Judge T. B. Butler, a deacon in FBC of Tyler. Two years later Butler sold the paper to J. Frank Norris, a young pastor in Dallas who had recently graduated from the Southern Baptist Theological Seminary in Louisville. Money for the purchase came from insurance proceeds from the death of J. M. Gaddy, whose daughter Lillian had married Norris in 1902. Norris and Gaddy were riding alone late at night in the back Pullman of a train to Austin when the fifty-seven-year-old Gaddy fell off the train to his death. Norris named Joseph M. Dawson, his old Baylor rival, as editor but this was not a happy arrangement and soon Norris assumed the editorial duties. Norris also used the *Baptist Standard* under the guidance of his teacher and mentor B. H. Carroll to win acceptance for the establishment of a theological seminary in Texas.

Norris brought controversy and confrontation to the pages of the *Standard* and while this increased subscriptions, it threatened the fragile peace Texas Baptists had achieved since the demise of S. A. Hayden. Apparently Norris adopted some of the Haydenite views and soon had alienated most of the influential Baptist leaders of Texas. A group of Dallas leaders, headed by George W. Truett and J. B. Cranfill, persuaded the *Standard* board of directors to dismiss Norris as editor. Hearing of this move, Norris, who was the majority stockholder as well as editor, dismissed the directors. When Norris moved from Dallas to Fort Worth in 1909 he sold the paper to a group of Dallas Baptist loyalists, including George W. Truett, J. B. Gambrell, H. Z. Duke, Charles D. Fine, R. C. Buckner, and R. H. Coleman with Gambrell installed as editor and Coleman as business manager.

The question of denominational ownership of the paper was raised again. Powerful voices that had earlier opposed the plan now came to favor it, a result perhaps of the bitter Hayden-Cranfill controversy. The obvious success of the *Missionary Worker* convinced many. Cranfill wrote, "This paper [the *Worker*], denominationally owned and controlled . . . became a mighty power for good during the days of our greatest storms and thereby greatly enlarged and strengthened the idea of denominational ownership."[28] Gambrell wrote that "The denominational paper is the denominational packhorse. It carries freight for everybody and everything."[29]

Gambrell pushed for denominational ownership when Cranfill sold the paper in 1904 but could not get it done at that time. It was probably Gambrell who persuaded the Truett group of loyalists to buy the paper from Norris in 1907, hoping it would come under Convention control. After years in Baptist journalism, Gambrell came to see the problems of private ownership. He said,

> In the personal ownership method, there is a fatal weakness, and an ever abiding peril. The weakness is that the enterprise is made personal and financial on one side and religious on the other side . . . The nearest approach we have ever known to a pope among Baptists has been a man who could buy a paper, appoint himself editor, then proceed to exploit the Baptists at will for his personal enterprise without regard to the trouble he made.[30]

Momentum was building for denominational ownership. At the Convention of 1913, records indicate that "George W. Truett spoke in the interest of the *Baptist Standard* and . . . . M.T. Andrews offered and the Convention adopted the following resolution:"

RESOLVED, That if in the wisdom of the Board of Directors of the *Baptist*

Standard it is thought well to turn the paper over to the Baptist General Convention of Texas to become its property, this Convention commits itself to such ownership and to the management of the paper in the usual way of directing its denominational enterprises.[31]

The offer was made and accepted, and ownership of the *Baptist Standard* was transferred to the BGCT in 1914, but not without lingering objections from some who feared that denominational ownership would stifle editorial freedom.

BAPTIST BENEVOLENCES

Care of orphan children, provision for aged ministers and their spouses, and sponsoring hospitals formed the bulk of organized Baptist benevolent ministries in the era covered in this chapter. In some ways these efforts were interrelated. In addition to these organized enterprises, the Baptist women regularly addressed both physical and spiritual needs of people in the churches and out. Food baskets for the poor, classes to teach such domestic skills as sewing and cooking, and efforts to help meet the needs of missionary families formed a staple of the work of the Baptist Women Mission Workers. Some advanced thinkers like R. C. Buckner also worked in prison reform, rehabilitation for "fallen women," helping ex-convicts reenter the mainstream, and efforts to persuade industry to adopt more compassionate employment practices.

Buckner Orphans Home. The child care ministry of course centered in the famous Buckner Orphans Home in Dallas, a thoroughly Baptist enterprise but not officially connected to the Convention until 1914. A few efforts to open orphan homes in other parts of the state failed to catch on.

Described in 1910 as a "great and growing institution," the Buckner Home did grow amazingly.[32] By 1906 over 600 children lived there. The Home produced much of its own food, with gardens, dairy, bakery and of course chickens, hogs and beef cattle. The school grew steadily both in attendance and academic breadth to care for children of all ages up through high school. As resources allowed, Buckner also provided a special center for infants and toddlers, accepted a number of "half-orphans" whose one surviving parent (usually a mother) could not care for them, and developed policies whereby "graduates" of the Home could make an orderly exit. After the new Baptist Sanitarium in Dallas went into operation, Buckner no longer used the "Annex," a building on property in Dallas, for a hospital but turned it into a reception center where incoming children could be kept a few days or weeks to check illnesses before they came in contact with children at the Home. Buckner learned from hard experience that even one or two children with whooping cough, measles, or diphtheria brought too quickly into the Home could have a disastrous impact. A total of 151 children passed through the Annex in 1910, most remaining for about ten days but two kept for nine weeks because of whooping cough.[33]

From time to time former residents of the Home returned for a visit, and in 1903 an official Homecoming Reunion was formed. Buckner always took great pride in the "graduates" who succeeded in life, as many of them did. Some of them became generous supporters of the Home in later years.

In forty years of caring for orphans, Buckner learned lessons which shaped his basic convictions. In the early years, faced with little children gaunt from hunger and shivering from cold, he first sought food, clothing, blankets and shelter. As he was able, Buckner also sought to provide educational, medical and dental care. Especially after the awful fire of 1897 Buckner seemed obsessed with physical safety of his large "family." After the Home became more prosperous and Buckner more experienced, he seemed to put more emphasis upon the total needs of the children, including better education, recreation, and what today would probably be called emotional nurture. Buckner believed that in addition to the physical necessities, children need love, assurance, a sense of emotional security, and a sense of self-worth. He enlisted a corps of matrons, teachers and counselors to help achieve these goals. Though emphasizing spiritual growth of the residents, Buckner refused to allow the children to be subjected to religious pressure and he kept the institution "unbounded by sect or section."

Buckner became deeply involved in the national debate of the times about whether orphan children are best cared for in foster homes or in orphan institutions. Not surprisingly, he came down squarely in favor of orphanages. As a result he faced considerable criticism from some who felt he was too reluctant to put children out to foster care, and that he did not sufficiently promote adoption. As a national authority on orphan care, whose counsel was often sought by other church and government agencies, Buckner's judgement carried considerable weight. He was adamant in refusing to turn over children to families who only wanted cheap labor, a boy to help in the field or a girl to mind the baby and carry water. "During thirty years of experience in orphan work, and out of close observation" he said, "I have formed and been thoroughly confirmed in the opinion that at least nineteen out of every twenty who seek to get possession of an orphan child, or children, are actuated by selfish motives, and that not one in a hundred mean it simply for the good of the child."[34] Buckner felt that merely putting children out in foster care or even in adoption was no guarantee that the child was better off. He insisted that his institution was a home. In one report, he seemed to respond to criticism by saying,

> Our children are not taken for the service they can render, nor as a matter of convenience, to mind the baby, to keep us from being lonesome or afraid. They are taken that they may be fed, clothed, and, thank God, that they may have protection. . . . They are not taken for the purpose of finding them homes with families . . . . I am most profoundly convinced that the best place for an orphan child is in the right kind of orphans' home; one that is not a transfer station, a labor exchange bureau, a workhouse, an almshouse, a prison, a detention station or reformatory; but a real home.[35]

The year 1914 proved a major turning point for the Buckner Home and for the Buckners personally. In June of that year Robert and Vienna Buckner celebrated their sixtieth wedding anniversary, and Vienna's health was failing. At the Abilene Convention that year the eighty-year-old veteran declined to be reelected president of the BGCT, a post he had held for twenty years. He had an unbroken record of annual Convention attendance stretching back to 1868. In a statement that caught many Texas Baptists by surprise, Buckner announced that "It is in my mind, as President and General Manager of the Buckner Orphans Home, to tender its entire property and control to the Baptist General Convention of Texas."[36] George W. Truett chaired the committee which responded to this generous offer of a property worth over $700,000, saying, "we accept that which has been tendered to us, in the same spirit of confidence, loyalty and love with which it has been offered; and that, in such acceptance, we solemly [sic] pledge that the principles and purposes set forth in its charter and by-laws shall ever be held by us as sacred and inviolable."[37] With this vote, the Buckner Home passed to the BGCT though its namesake continued for a time as general manager.

Baptist Hospitals. Between 1900 and 1914 Texas Baptists founded several hospitals, a nurses' training school and a major medical college. This venture into healing ministries, like several other Baptist benevolent ministries, stems from the vision of R. C. Buckner. His experience with the children's hospital at the Home convinced him of the need of such ministry, the available Baptist support for it, and the fact that it was a valid part of following the example of Christ. As early as 1903 Buckner wrote, "I have had a long cherished desire to see established in Dallas a general hospital."[38] This led to formation later that year of the Texas Baptist Memorial Sanitarium, with Buckner as president of its board of directors, George W. Truett as secretary and C. C. Slaughter as treasurer. Truett shared fully the vision for a great house of healing in Dallas and helped to enlist others in the venture. The Sanitarium opened in March, 1904, the third hospital in America under Baptist auspices.[39] By 1914 the Sanitarium was treating over 5,000 patients a year. By then it had moved to impressive new facilities, had achieved national and international fame as a major healing center, added a Training School for Nurses, a Pasteur Institute, and a free clinic and dispensary for the poor. It was later combined with the Baylor University College of Medicine in Dallas to form one institution, bearing the name of Baylor. C. C. Slaughter was among those who made major gifts to the hospital and some suggested it should bear his name. However, Slaughter pointed out that his might not be a suitable name for a hospital.

Dr. L. T. Mays and Pastor D. R. Peveto of Houston conceived the idea for a Baptist hospital in that city. Peveto later enlisted the influential J. L. Gross, pastor of FBC Houston, and in 1907 a Baptist group purchased a run-down seventeen-bed clinic for $18,000. From this small beginning the Houston Baptist Sanitarium developed, with Peveto as business manager.

In 1910 the trustees offered the Sanitarium to Texas Baptists, and after a cautious investigation the Convention accepted, though adding that this decision "must not be understood as setting a precedent for the indiscriminate acceptance of institutions of different sorts that may from time to time be tendered the Convention."[40]

Before the second decade of the twentieth century had run its course, Texas Baptists operated no fewer than nine Baptist hospitals in Texas, most of them under the control of associations or local Baptist groups. The West Texas Sanitarium of Abilene owes its founding to Millard A. Jenkins, pastor of FBC Abilene. Later a gift of $100,000 from Mr. and Mrs. T. G. Hendrick attached their name to the Hendrick Memorial Hospital. A small Baptist hospital was formed in Fort Worth, but it did not survive.

Ministerial Relief. In this work, as in other social ministries, Buckner was the trailblazer. Even before the consolidation of 1886, Buckner raised funds for aged ministers in the old Baptist General Association and he continued that emphasis in the BGCT. The Convention tried several means of caring for aged ministers, including dormitory-type homes in Lampasas and later in Palacios. However, none of these worked as well as the "Cottage Ministry" at the Buckner Home. In this plan a number of cottages were erected for the use of aged persons or couples, complete with garden for those able to tend it. Older children from the Home would come in occasionally to provide whatever level of assistance was needed, including cooking and housekeeping. Eligibility for these cottages was not restricted to ministers, but the Home did receive a small payment from the Convention for ministers who lived there. The Home also allowed some elderly persons who had the means to erect their own cottage on the grounds with the understanding it would eventually go to the Home. The first cottages for the aged were erected in 1905 and the first residents were retired pastor E. B. Eaken and his wife.

Buckner tried to avoid the "warehousing" atmosphere of other old folks' homes, providing privacy and whatever level of personal and household help seemed necessary. He also tried to involve the seniors in Home social and religious events. Even with best efforts, Buckner acknowledged that "Some of the aged are more or less 'cranky,' but each is permitted to turn his own crank without anybody furnishing oil for it, or grit for it to grind."[41]

BAPTIST WOMEN MISSION WORKERS

No department of Texas Baptist witness made more progress in the period 1900 to 1914 than did the BWMW group. With presidents like Lucinda Williams (1895-1906) and Mary Hill Davis (1906-1931), corresponding secretaries like Mary T. Gambrell (1897-1910) and Addie Buckner Beddoe (1910-1923), and field workers like Mina Everett and Bertha Mills the women went from victory to victory. As the wife of the state missions director, and as bookkeeper for the Convention, Mary Gambrell had an influential voice at the highest levels of Convention leadership. This could only help the women's work.

More women's societies were formed, more money was raised for missions, more missionary boxes and other assistance was sent, and Texas women participated fully in the newly formed [1888] national Woman's Missionary Union, auxiliary to the Southern Baptist Convention, including the Margaret Home[42] and the Missionary Training School in Louisville. No department of Baptist work in Texas failed to receive the prayers, efforts and contributions of the Baptist women. To balance their emphasis on foreign missions the BWMW formed a department of Personal Service in 1909 to spotlight opportunities for ministry in their own communities.

The women extended their training work to all ages through the "Juvenile Bands." The Sunbeams for small children dates as far back as 1886. Texas organizations were formed for Royal Ambassadors for boys aged 9-12 (RA) in 1908, the Girls' Auxiliary for ages 9-12 (GA) in 1913, and the Young Women's Auxiliary (YWA) in 1907.[43] In 1914 the women reported 1,304 local church societies in Texas, up from 450 in 1907.[44]

During her tenure, Mary Hill Davis streamlined the structure of BWMW. Following the lead of Lucinda Williams, she led the women to form associational unions for mutual encouragement. She extended this another step by organizing the women's societies into several "districts," each containing a number of associations. The Sunday School and Baptist Young Peoples' Union later also adopted the district plan.

No work attracted more attention and support from Texas Baptist women than did the Missionary Training School, eventually connected with Southwestern Seminary in 1911. At the Buckner Home a number of the older girls who felt called to missionary service asked Buckner if they might receive some Bible and theological training. Always progressive in spirit, Buckner approved the idea and the school opened in October 1904, the first theological school for women in the South. Dallas pastors provided the instruction. The Missionary Training School was received by Texas Baptists with great enthusiasm. Other women, not residents of the Buckner Home, were invited to attend and within a short time over a dozen young women studied in a room provided in the downtown Buckner Annex. By 1906 it was reported that two women had gone from this school as foreign missionaries, one to China and one to Mexico.[45]

Some uncertainty surfaced about the Training School. Buckner found it necessary to reassure the brethren that the women were not preparing to be preachers, but missionaries, teachers, Sunday School workers, evangelistic home visitors and, of course, potential wives for young preachers. Despite its seeming promise, the school was abruptly closed in 1907, perhaps because of an unfortunate incident described by Lucinda Williams. In a letter to her daughter, WMU historian Mrs. W. J. J. Smith, Mrs. Williams wrote,

As the story goes, the young women, one fine evening, strolled out on the streets bareheaded, about sundown. It was reported to the committee that looked after them, and they assembled promptly and delivered a severe chastisement for their having gone on the streets with uncovered heads. Next morning, Dr. Buckner came by, and they told him of the affair and asked his advice. He told them to pack their trunks and go home, and they did.[46]

For a time the Training School was connected with the Baylor Theological Seminary in Waco, and in 1910 proposed to move with the Seminary to Fort Worth. Baptist women of Texas agreed to provide a $50,000 building to house the school at Southwestern Seminary, and in 1911 the transfer was complete.

THE EDUCATION COMMISSION

Until 1897 Baptist colleges in Texas had little official relationship to the state convention. Baylor University was founded by an Education Society, but after 1848 the Baptist State Convention elected its trustees and heard reports of its progress. The BSC contributed to ministerial education but for the most part the university was expected to be self-supporting. The numerous new Baptist colleges formed in the 1890s were sponsored usually by local associations and drew their support locally. Clearly Baptists in Texas formed more colleges than they needed and certainly more than they could afford. The state was dotted with numerous "colleges," with minimal academic strength, operating on a shoestring in inadequate facilities, deeply in debt. Their financial agents swarmed over the state, with too many agents pursuing too few dollars and too few students. It was, as one historian put it, "an inefficient process characterized by wasted time, duplicated efforts, and meager collections."[47]

As recounted earlier, in 1897 the Carroll brothers, J. M. and B. H., led a move to bring some order out of the educational chaos among Texas Baptists. The San Antonio convention in 1897 voted to establish an Education Commission if at least six schools, including the two Baylors, would join the confederation. Baylor University at Waco, Baylor Female College at Belton, Howard Payne College at Brownwood, the Baptist College at Decatur, and East Texas Baptist Institute at Rusk agreed to the terms, and the Commission was put into operation in 1898. Simmons College in Abilene declined to participate in this correlation.

The Education Commission gave the BGCT, for the first time, oversight of these schools. The Convention named trustees for the "correlated schools," and they were asked not to send financial agents into the field to raise money, though that was later modified a bit. The Commission assumed responsibility for raising funds for all the colleges, helping secure their endowments, raising funds for needed buildings, and providing operating funds. Most of the schools fared better under this new system. The major drawback, however, was that only the two Baylors were four-year degree-granting institutions, while the others remained junior colleges. Gradually the Commission assumed more leadership over the colleges, though internal affairs like the election of faculty were left to local trustees. By 1908 the Commission claimed the right to review proposals for new buildings lest the colleges get deeper into debt. The Education Commission became the general oversight and advisory board for Baptist education in Texas. Its 1909 report affirmed that "The Commission is to be the voice of the Convention to the schools in all matters affecting campaigns for funds and to be the voice of the schools to the brotherhood concerning their crying needs."[48] Though trying not to meddle with internal affairs, the Commission did cite minimal academic standards which the schools were expected to maintain.

The Education Commission launched an ongoing series of financial campaigns to finance the schools. Most of these were marked by great enthusiasm, handsome pledges, and little actual cash raised. President S. P. Brooks of Baylor lamented that "The Education Commission raised large sums in promises, but as usual in such large subscriptions, much of it was not paid."[49] Of course, Baylor received the lion's share of whatever was received.

In 1914 the BGCT was reorganized and an Executive Board was formed to give oversight to all Convention ministries. Under this new structure, the Education Committee of the Executive Board gave oversight and coordination to the work of Baptist education in Texas. After 1914 most of the colleges became four-year schools, with the exception of Decatur College which remained a junior college.

Ten new Baptist schools were formed between 1900 and 1914, including Westminster Institute in Westminster in 1901 (closed in 1917); Canadian Academy, 1904 (closed in 1912); Texas Baptist University in Dallas in 1905 (closed in 1907); San Marcos Baptist Academy in San Marcos in 1907; Bryan Baptist Academy in Bryan in 1910 (closed in 1917); Wayland Literary and Technical Institute in Plainview in 1910 (now Wayland Baptist University); Palacios Baptist Academy in Palacios in 1910 (closed in 1917); the College of Marshall, 1912 (now East Texas Baptist University); and Westminster Baptist Academy in 1912 (closed in 1920). Of these, only San Marcos, Wayland and East Texas Baptist survived. Four of these schools were sold at the same time: Westminster, Canadian, Bryan, and Goodnight.

With one building costing about $100,000, thirteen teachers, and about two hundred students, the San Marcos Baptist Academy opened its doors on September 24, 1907.[50] J. M. Carroll was the primary founder of the school, and he raised most of the money for its buildings and operation. It seemed fitting that the first building, Carroll Hall, should bear his name. Before that first year was out, enrollment rose to 275 on the twenty-five-acre campus. Carroll chose the motto for the Academy, *Ad Viros Faciendos* (Toward the Making of Men) and his only daughter Edena Mae chose the school colors, the green and purple of the mountain laurel so plentiful in that area. The school newspaper was named *The Laurel.* Despite the motto, the school was coeducational from the first. The San Marcos Baptist Academy found its niche as a high quality institution, with emphasis upon strong academics, military training for boys, and strict discipline for all.

Few schools existed on the high plains when a group of Baptists in Plainview proposed to the Staked Plains Baptist Association the formation of a "college" to provide elementary and secondary education for area children. Dr. and Mrs. James Henry Wayland, pioneer physician, gave ten acres of land and $10,000 to launch what was chartered in 1908 as the Wayland Literary and Technical Institute.[51] In 1909 construction began on the first two buildings. Matador Hall, a residence for women, was financed largely by the First Baptist Church of Matador. The building for administration and instruction later took the name of the first president, I. E. Gates. Gates Hall remains as the center of a growing campus and is now recognized as one of the historic buildings on the high plains. In 1910 the name was changed to Wayland Baptist College, and that fall the school enrolled 241 students from primary to junior college grades. The college was transferred to the BGCT in 1914.

The mortality for such schools was high. Many of them originated to provide basic education such as might be found today in public school grades six through twelve. However, many Texas towns and communities had no access to public schools and these denominational schools served a need. As public education became more accessible, most of these Baptist schools fell by the wayside. Some survived and in time became colleges in fact as well as in name.

SOUTHWESTERN BAPTIST THEOLOGICAL SEMINARY

For Texas Baptists, few events can compare in importance to the formation of the Southwestern Baptist Theological Seminary in 1908. First organized as the Baylor Theological Seminary in 1905 and located in Waco as part of the university, the seminary was given a new name and its own charter on March 14, 1908. Two years later it was moved to Fort Worth where it has remained on Seminary Hill. The seminary began as a Texas Baptist institution, founded by the BGCT, and to this day provides most of the Baptist pastors and other ministers for that state. The primary founder and first president was B. H. Carroll, and the seminary is generally counted the crowning achievement of his long and productive life.

A commitment to ministerial education among Texas Baptists surfaced long before the founding of Southwestern Seminary. The Union Baptist Association formed in 1840 cited missions and education as its twin purposes. The training of ministers was one motive for the formation of Baylor University in 1845 and, though Baylor more than once declined to establish a theological department, a number of outstanding Texas ministers studied there. Most of the colleges which grew up in Texas between 1890 and 1914 had ministerial education as part of their announced purpose. A fortunate few young ministers trained at Southern

Baptists' only theological Seminary at Louisville, Kentucky, but they were the exception. Gradually it became obvious that Texas needed a theological training center along with its university and colleges.

The leader in theological education for Texas Baptists was B. H. Carroll, longtime pastor at First Baptist Church of Waco and chair of the Baylor trustees. By the 1870s Carroll had begun the practice of gathering Baylor ministerial students in his own home for reading and discussion of theological topics. Some believe that Carroll had begun this practice as early as 1873, and that William B. Bagby, who later became a well-known missionary to Brazil, was his first pupil. Bagby's daughter Helen later recalled that her father said, "Yes, Dr. Carroll and I founded the Seminary. He was the faculty and I was the student body."[52] By 1880 this "Carroll class" had become a regular feature at Baylor in which a group of fifteen to twenty ministerial students would gather on Friday evenings at the Carroll home and discuss materials they had read during the week, often from Carroll's own library. Their stated textbook was *Pendleton's Manual,* by J. M. Pendleton, one of the three primary Landmark leaders. Carroll continued to use that book in his classes a generation later at the seminary in Fort Worth. Jeff D. Ray, later a professor at Southwestern, was a member of the Friday night "embryonic Seminary" in Carroll's home. He said, "We had one small textbook, the one teacher and once a week recitations, but the instruction covered or (to speak more accurately) touched upon nearly everything taught in Seminary today."[53]

By 1893 Carroll's class had outgrown his home, and the university established a Bible Department and named Carroll to the chair of Exegesis and Systematic Theology. By 1895 Carroll was called "Principal" of the Bible Department, which by then included a number of other teachers. In 1899 Carroll resigned his pastorate to give full time to the work of education, first as head of the Education Commission of the BGCT and later as a full-time faculty member at Baylor. Oscar H. Cooper, who succeeded Rufus C. Burleson as president of Baylor in 1899, was eager to expand theological training at the university. In 1901 President Cooper announced creation of a Theological Department of Baylor, with Carroll as dean. New faculty were enlisted, including A. H. Newman and R. N. Barrett. Newman was a well-known church historian who came from McMaster University in Canada to join the Baylor faculty. He later served as dean of the faculty when Southwestern moved to Fort Worth. However, Samuel Palmer Brooks, who became president of Baylor in 1902, was less enthusiastic about expanding the Theological Department. He felt that the preacher's first need was for a general literary education. He also apparently feared that an expanded school of theology, such as Carroll contemplated, might overshadow and would certainly pull funding away from the university. Carroll continued to push for expansion of the Theological Department, and this led to tension between Carroll and Brooks. Their relationship was complicated by the fact that Carroll, a professor in the Theological Department, also served as head of the trustees. As a professor, Carroll came under the authority of President Brooks, but as trustee chairman he had, and exercised, considerable authority over Brooks.

In 1905 the Theological Department was further expanded to become the Baylor Theological Seminary. Without consulting with President Brooks who was away in Europe at the time, Carroll introduced a resolution to the Baylor trustees "that Baylor now make the Theological Department a complete School of Divinity—teaching all the courses and conferring all the degrees of a regular first class theological Seminary."[54] After a momentary stunned silence, the aged Judge W. H. Jenkins, father-in-law of George W. Truett, rose to his feet and said, "None of us is prepared for this. Humanly speaking, it seems a rash step to take. But evidently our noble brother has had a vision from God. I move that his request be granted and immediate steps be taken to launch the enterprise."[55]

Thus was born the Baylor Theological Seminary in 1905. President Brooks was decidedly displeased to discover upon his return that a department of the university had become a separate school without his knowledge or approval. However, interest in the new seminary ran high and enrollment grew rapidly. Many Texas preachers, who felt they could not move to Louisville, now had opportunity for theological training nearer at home. The 1905 session enrolled 138 students, of whom 118 were preachers, 11 were laymen, and seven were women.[56]

In a 1906 report to the BGCT, George W. Truett urged the importance of ministerial education in Texas upon which, he said, all the other ministries ultimately depend. After noting the opportunities for study in the Baptist colleges and at the Southern Baptist Theological Seminary in Louisville, Truett added

> We also have the Baylor Theological Seminary, which is now a vital part of our work, bone of our bone, the child of our labors and prayer. It has as its Dean a man whom all our great land delights to honor . . . . His ripe scholarship, his varied learning, his large experience, his splendid manhood, his unswerving devotion to the Master, and his simple, abiding, unconquerable faith in the old Book as it is written, all conspire preeminently to fit our beloved brother Carroll for the arduous responsibilities of the position that he now occupies. He has around him a corps of helpers, eminent as scholars, sound as Baptists, and efficient as teachers. The department is crowded with a most excellent student body . . . . Your committee appeals to the Brotherhood . . . [for support for] the Baylor Seminary.[57]

In his first report to the BGCT, Carroll noted that "For the first time in the history of this Convention, a Theological Seminary makes a report to the body." He spoke his "profound conviction that the necessity for this work was instant, imperious and inexorable."[58] If we wait for an ideal time to launch such a venture, he said, we would never begin. In a powerful address, later printed in the *Baptist Standard,* Carroll listed five compelling reasons for a Seminary in Texas: (1) no Seminary existed in the Southwest, (2) Many preachers who attended Southern never returned to Texas, (3) preachers "loose in doctrine" were invading the state, (4) many of the Texas preachers had no access to theological training, (5) the West was rapidly developing and needed to care for its own population.[59] Distance made the Louisville Seminary inaccessible to most Texas preachers. Carroll also insisted that a Baptist university would not be complete, and would not live up to the "University idea," if it lacked a school for the highest training in theology, as in medicine, law and other branches of learning. The influential J. B. Gambrell added his voice of support, noting that is many parts of Texas the mission work had come to "a dead standstill from the lack of trained leaders for the churches."[60] He added,

> No church is likely to go beyond its pastor, and no pastor can go beyond his conceptions and training. It is fundamental to everything we are doing in Texas, to train our ministers in large numbers—in ever increasing numbers. The Seminary is needed now, sorely, but its needs will increase with the years. . . . There is no greater nerve center in all of the denomination than the Baylor Theological Seminary.[61]

Despite such strong support, the new Seminary did not come into being without opposition, both within Texas and beyond. Some argued that Texas did not need such a school, could not afford it, that it would detract from mission giving, and that too much formal education might unfit the preachers for ministry on the rough frontier. Some college leaders and their alumni feared that the Seminary would undercut the Bible departments of those schools. Some educators, like S. P. Brooks, believed that the greatest need of pastors was for "literary" or general college training and they could add what theological knowledge they needed by private reading, as George W. Truett and Carroll himself had done.

Opposition also arose from those who feared the new school would become a rival to the Southern Seminary and siphon away students and funds that might otherwise have gone to Louisville, and of course that is what did happen. Others feared this was an effort to split the SBC with Texas as the base for a new convention. By 1901 when Baylor launched its Theology Department, some Southern partisans saw this as a bid to form a rival Seminary in the Southwest. Carroll hardly helped his cause by repeated denials that they were forming a Seminary, all the while moving in that direction. Just before the San Antonio meeting of the BGCT in 1907 some Southern partisans distributed a strong protest against the Baylor Seminary, which was printed in several state papers including the *Baptist Standard.* Carroll met the issue head-on by challenging three statements in the paper:

1. "Southern Baptists have but one theological Seminary."
2. "They desire but one."
3. "They are agreed to have just one."[62]

With impeccable logic Carroll demolished all three assertions. He acknowledged that the SBC received reports from only one Seminary, and nominated trustees for only one, but he insisted that "it is not a fact that Southern Baptists have but one Seminary," and he named other Baptist colleges which had theological study centers that amounted to seminaries. As to the second assertion, Carroll doubted that any person could speak for all Southern Baptists on this or any other issue. On the third point, Carroll said, "It is not a fact that the Southern Baptists have agreed to have just one Seminary. There is no record of any such agreement. On the contrary, the agreement was just the opposite." He then quoted from the inaugural address of James P. Boyce, founder of the Southern Seminary, that "The object is not centralization of power in a single institution, for I believe that the adoption of these changes will make many seminaries necessary."[63] Carroll concluded that "This Seminary [Southwestern] was not established as a rival of any other. . . . If it be a mere negation, let it perish. If our Father wills it to stand it must be because there is need for it and merit in it."[64]

What role did the Whitsitt controversy play in the founding of the new seminary in Texas? The issues and outcome of that controversy were sketched in a previous chapter, but a further word is needed here to show its relation to Southwestern Seminary. William Heth Whitsitt was professor of Baptist history at the Louisville Seminary and, after the death of John A. Broadus, was elected president. By diligent research in newly available primary sources, Whitsitt discovered that Baptists as a distinct denomination had originated in the early seventeenth century and recovered the biblical practice of immersion in the 1640s. This ran counter to the Landmark assertion that the denomination was founded by John the Baptist and that Baptist churches had existed in every age since the apostles. Whitsitt aroused a storm of protest when he published these views, and much of that protest centered in Texas.

As chairman of trustees at the Louisville Seminary, B. H. Carroll led the effort to have Whitsitt removed. However, it appeared that in ousting Whitsitt, Carroll won the battle but lost the war. The remaining Southern faculty members informed Carroll that they held the same views as their embattled president. Whitsitt's successor, E. Y. Mullins, also agreed with Whitsitt's views though he expressed them more discreetly.[65] By 1911 A. T. Robertson, famous Greek and New Testament professor at Southern, could affirm in an address reported in the *Baptist World* that "All our seminaries, including the one in Texas, now teach what Whitsitt claimed."[66] It is true that Albert Henry Newman, first church history professor at Baylor Theological Seminary and later at Southwestern, held essentially the same views as Whitsitt on Baptist origins. Newman, who also served as dean of the faculty at Southwestern, was fired by Carroll in 1913.

How much of Carroll's desire to found a new Seminary in Texas grew out of his disillusionment with Southern and the Whitsitt affair is impossible to determine. However, the overwhelming response of Texas Baptist pastors against Whitsitt undoubtedly helped create the climate that made possible a new seminary in the Southwest. Typical was A. B. Miller, pastor at Bonham, who wrote to Carroll that "For my part I do not think such a man [as Whitsitt] should be retained as a member of a Baptist church, much less as a professor or president of a Baptist Theological Seminary."[67]

While the Seminary and Baylor University coexisted on the same campus, relations were not cordial. The University had a president who opposed the Seminary, and the Seminary had an aggressive dean whose grand vision called for a world class school of theology far exceeding anything the president could tolerate. It was only a matter of time until the two institutions would go their separate ways. On March 14, 1908, the new school was chartered as The Southwestern Baptist Theological Seminary, with its own board of trustees distinct from Baylor. In preparing the charter, Carroll drew from three outstanding Baptists, Charles Haddon Spurgeon of London, James P. Boyce of Louisville, and Francis Wayland of Brown University. The trustees organized by electing J. B. Gambrell as the first chairman and A. J. Barton as secretary. In their first official action they elected Carroll as president at a salary of $2,500 a year and a number of professors at $2,000 a year, specifying that the president should always receive a salary 20% higher than professors.

When Southwestern Baptist Theological Seminary (SWBTS) became a separate institution, the question arose of its continued relation to Baylor. Three options were considered: the Seminary could remain in Waco on the Baylor campus, remain in Waco but not on the Baylor campus, or move to some other city. The third option prevailed. Several cities, including Dallas, Cleburne, Handley, McKinney, and Denton entered bids. Many assumed the Seminary would go to Dallas, which had long since become the Baptist center of Texas. Carroll seemed to expect that. The faculty voted unanimously to move to Dallas, just before the Seminary moved to Fort Worth. However, one influential person was not in favor of moving the Seminary to Dallas, and that was George W. Truett. His reluctance grew out of several factors. First, he really wanted the Seminary to remain in Waco in some connection with his beloved Baylor University. Second, he seemed to feel that if the Seminary came to Dallas it would compete with his efforts to build the Baylor Hospital and the Buckner Orphans Home. Truett chaired the committee that offered as a site just two small city lots in Oak Cliff, an offer which offended Carroll. In a letter Carroll curtly rejected the offer and informed Truett that he was not planning a "two by four" institution.

On a vacation trip from Waco to Mineral Wells to "take the baths," Carroll stayed overnight in Fort Worth. A delegation of leading Baptist pastors and laymen visited his hotel room and presented the claims of Fort Worth to have the Seminary. Carroll asked Lee R. Scarborough to canvas Fort Worth to see if $100,000 and a suitable site could be found, and the answer to both was yes. By late 1909 J. Frank Norris, Carroll's student at Baylor and editor/owner of the *Baptist Standard* who had helped Carroll create a climate of acceptance in Texas for the new Seminary, sold the paper and accepted the pastorate of First Baptist Church in Fort Worth. Some think he saw the handwriting on the wall that the school would move to Fort Worth and he wanted to positionize himself to become

Carroll's successor as president. On November 9, 1909, the trustees met in the parlor of the Worth Hotel and voted to move the Seminary to Fort Worth. That afternoon, they drove in automobiles, of which Fort Worth then had only a few, to visit several proposed sites in Fort Worth. They settled upon the fifty acres offered by Joe K. Winston, a deacon in the College Avenue church. This acreage, which had long been a pecan orchard, was situated on a hill about six miles south of the city. The Seminary later augmented this site with additional land obtained from H. C. McCart and other tracts.[68]

The move to Fort Worth was not easy. The Winston site, dubbed "Seminary Hill," was in open country south of Fort Worth, two miles from the nearest houses and street car lines. The faculty, who had voted unanimously that the Seminary should move to Dallas, staked out bare lots to build their houses. The first building, Fort Worth Hall, was begun in early 1910, with the hope of having it finished in time for the fall term in 1910. The building was not finished, but Seminary leaders decided to begin the fall semester anyway on October 3, 1910, with 79 students who were willing to "rough it." At the first chapel service, J. B. Gambrell "congratulated the student body on their brilliant prospects of a glorious hard time."[69] The women students shared fully in these primitive conditions, living cramped into one large room of Fort Worth Hall, but they no doubt would have agreed with B. H. Carroll who said, "We plead no baby act and play no whining role. We have camped out before."[70] Before the year was out, 126 students had enrolled. About thirty single men slept on the floor of what was intended as a library, and some of the professors, whose houses were not finished, also slept there but they at least had bedsteads. For heating that winter the entire building had only two or three coal stoves, with stovepipes run out open windows. For the hot summers the only pretense at cooling was high ceilings and large windows and, later, a few fans. There were no trees or shrubbery of any kind to adorn the Johnson grass prairie, and the dirt streets scraped out soon grew over again and horses, buggies and what few cars were around just went in whatever direction they chose. There were no stores near the Seminary, and the nearest city transportation was over two miles away. In 1913 the Seminary acquired a car, by no means dependable, which the students nicknamed "the Doodle Bug." Seminary residents counted it a great victory when a street car line at last reached the campus in 1914.

After a momentary hesitation, B. H. Carroll agreed that the Woman's Missionary Training School, which had begun in Dallas but had largely lapsed, should move to Seminary Hill and become a part of SWBTS. The urgent need for Baptist women trained in Bible, theology, missions and Sunday School work was increasingly evident, and many doors of ministry were open to such women. The women took regular Seminary classes, but in 1914 a special course in public speaking for women was added for, as Principal Mary Tupper said, "in this new and exceptional age, the well-equipped Christian woman must be able to speak the faith that is in her."[71] In 1914 the Training School enrolled 61 young women.[72] Soon their graduates were serving as "Bible women" in churches, on mission fields, and in social welfare centers. Also, as everyone hoped but few wanted to say openly, many of the young women found husbands among the preacher boys.

The Baptist women of Texas agreed to raise money for a $50,000 building to house the Training School. Ground was broken in 1913, but by the time the building was completed it cost twice that, not counting the furnishings. The building could if crowded house 112 women students, including kitchen and dining rooms, parlor, sick room, and a reading room. The widowed Lucinda Williams, known as the "Mother of the Training School," helped raise funds and in her old age lived for a time in the new building. She was an expert gardener and had students roll her around the barren campus in her wheel chair, and she would point with her walking stick where they should plant flowers, shrubbery and trees. Many of the magnificent pecan trees which grace the campus today grow where Lucinda's stick indicated.

Apparently the original plan was for the girls to take their diplomas from the Training School and not from the Seminary itself. But that is not how it worked out. In 1914 a woman enrolled for the regular degree in theology. A search of the charter showed that the Seminary had agreed "to confer upon any pupil of said Seminary . . . any of the degrees usually conferred by theological seminaries." Seminary officials concluded that they could not deny the young woman her degree, and therefore since 1914 men and women have been equally eligible for any degree offered by the Seminary.[73] Southwestern was the first Southern Baptist Seminary to admit women on an equal basis. The women also operated a nursery and kindergarten, both for the benefit of student wives and as a learning laboratory in ministry to children.

The enrollment in the fall of 1913 showed a total of 208 students, including 128 preachers, 5 laymen, and 75 women.[74] The spiritual impact of the new Seminary was immediate and intense. In Fort Worth alone, 14 new churches were added to the Tarrant Baptist Association within seven years, and Seminary students were involved in most of them.[75]

RESTRUCTURING—YET AGAIN

The Baptist General Convention of Texas of 1914 bore little resemblance to the newly merged body of 1886. There were vastly more churches, pastors, and missionaries under appointment. The number of schools had more than quadrupled, the large Buckner Orphans Home was in process of passing to the Convention, Baptist hospitals plied the healing arts, the women's work had grown geometrically, and a growing seminary flourished in Fort Worth. To sponsor these ministries, the BGCT received and disbursed vast sums of money that would have astonished the brethren of an earlier day. Clearly the informal methods, casual organization, and impromptu decisions of the past would no longer do.

Perhaps there was never a time when Baptists were not discussing some reorganization or other, but for Texas Baptists these discussions grew more intense after 1910. In a 1912 report, George W. Truett noted that

> The work of this Convention has so increased that it has become quite complex . . . We are profoundly convinced, however, that the time has come for a wise adjustment of appeals to the churches to the end that there may be no diminution in the efficiency of any department of the work. . . . your Board feels that the time has come when brethren should look to such a general plan for all the work as will promote the utmost denominational harmony, the greatest possible efficiency for each department, and the greatest prosperity for each out *[sic]* of our Baptist institutions.[76]

A Committee on Constitutional Revision was appointed in 1912, charged with devising a plan to accomplish the goals set out by Dr. Truett. The committee gave a progress report in 1913,[77] and made their final report in 1914.[78] No changes were made in Article I on name and objects of the Convention, and only minor changes in Article II on membership. The financial basis of representation was retained, with churches, associations, and missionary societies in friendly cooperation allowed a number of messengers, according to their contributions. This system allowed those who paid the bills to influence the vote. The revised constitution allowed the president to serve no more than three consecutive terms.

Article IX, which had been added during the hostility of the Hayden attacks, was dropped entirely. That article said that

> Whenever any Church, or Association, or Society, shall, by a majority vote of the Convention, be declared to be in an attitude of general or continued hostility or unfriendliness to the work or purposes of the Convention, and to be an impediment to the work of the Convention, . . . then such Church, Association, or Society, shall, by such majority vote, be denied the privilege of sending Messengers to the Convention, and such person shall, by such vote, be denied a seat as a Messenger . . .[and] the privileges so denied shall not thereafter be exercised by such Church, Association, Society or person, until granted by a majority vote of the Convention.[79]

This was obviously aimed at the Hayden disciples who so severely disrupted the Convention work in the late 1890s. However, the committee said that in the interest of greater cooperation, and the fact that disruption was greatly diminished, they could drop that article altogether. A number of churches, some of them large and influential, which had previously joined in the Hayden attacks now desired to cooperate with the Convention and this was intended to smooth the way for their realignment.

The most fundamental change came in Article V on Boards. Previously the BGCT elected annually over a dozen boards, including three boards with direct oversight of Convention work. These were the Board of Directors, the Education Board, and a Board of Trustees of the Convention to hold funds and property. The duties of these three boards often overlapped. The right hand did not always know what the left hand was doing and, when the right hand learned what the left hand was doing, did not always approve. The revised Constitution called for election of one large Executive Board of forty-five members, and directed that "The Executive Board shall have charge and control, except when otherwise directed by the Convention, of all the work of the Convention, including missions, education and beneficence, in the interim between its sessions.[80] For the first time, **all the work of the Convention** came under the supervision of one group, chosen from all sections of the state. This brought more correlation, better planning and more precise budgeting. More importantly, funding for the various ministries now had to be presented and approved through the Executive Board.

The revision further provided that "The Executive Board shall select annually a Corresponding Secretary and such assistants as may be deemed necessary, shall fix salaries, make financial arrangements, and have such other powers and authority as may be necessary to carry on the work of the Convention." Clearly this represents a major power shift in Convention work. The Convention's own interpretation of the revision was that "The Constitution of the Baptist General Convention has been so amended . . . as to place the control and management of the missionary, educational and beneficent work of the Convention under one board."[81] The Corresponding Secretary, previously elected directly by the Convention, was now elected by the Executive Board. This strengthened the hand of the Convention leadership and removed the Corresponding Secretary from the day-to-day politics that a few years earlier had driven so many of his predecessors from office in discouragement. The revision allowed the BGCT president to serve no more than three consecutive terms, so there would be no more twenty year presidencies such as Buckner served. This further strengthened the Corresponding Secretary, and it is no wonder that Gambrell agreed in 1914 to serve a second term. The Executive Board established a number of sub-committees to deal with missions, education and benevolences, so that all Convention ministries came under the oversight of the Executive Board. An exception was made in the case of Southwestern Seminary, which continued to report directly to the Convention. The new Executive Board assumed the debts and obligations of the Board of Directors and the Board of Education, which were abolished in the revision. Under the revision the BGCT continued to name a five-member Board of Trustees of the Convention, separate from the Executive Board, to "hold in trust all the property and invested funds of the Convention."[82]

The two primary advocates of the 1914 reorganization were J. B. Gambrell and layman M. H. Wolfe. Wolfe had long urged "more business in religion," to which J. B. Gambrell countered "more religion in business." Wolfe the businessman well knew the value of efficient organization, and Gambrell had pushed for a stronger state convention since he first took office in 1896. Wolfe tried to extend this unification plan to the Southern Baptist Convention, and had he succeeded the SBC would have formed one strong Executive Board and the Foreign Board, Home Board, Sunday School Board and later the Annuity Board would have been program divisions of that one central board. Wolfe's plan was narrowly defeated, but in 1917 the SBC, influenced by the Texas action, formed its first Executive Committee. Over the years that Executive Committee has gradually gained such vast power that, while the SBC boards still exist, essentially Wolfe's plan is now in effect.

Not everyone favored the ideas embodied in the Texas reorganization of 1914. Within a few years most of the other states had followed suit, which led to some grumbling. The editor of the *Baptist Courier* of South Carolina saw the Texas reorganization as revealing a massive shift of emphasis from the SBC to the state conventions. He said that between 1910 and 1915, "Home and Foreign Missions made an increase of about 7 percent; and State Missions an increase of about 50 percent. Does this not indicate that a tremendous change of emphasis is taking place. . . . The emphasis has certainly passed from Convention [SBC] over to state emphasis."[83] However, the impact of the Seventy-five Million Campaign, 1919-1924, reversed this trend and introduced a period of Southern Baptist Convention ascendancy to the distinct diminishing of the state convention work.[84]

SUMMARY

The era from 1900 to 1914 was crucial for Texas Baptists. In retrospect, the year 1914 appears as a major turning point. In that year the great B. H. Carroll died, the Buckner Orphans Home came under BGCT control, and the Convention reorganized its work for the future. Controversy simmered down and the Convention enjoyed both inner harmony and outward cooperation. The state mission work expanded rapidly, and the Baptist schools multiplied in number, enrollment, and academic strength. Texas Baptists formed a new Seminary which would undergird all their ministries, and the Baptist women sponsored a Missionary Training School for young women and kept the spotlight on mission education, missionary funding and social ministries. Even churches that had formerly stood aloof from the Convention were by 1914 lining up to support its work.

However, not all was well in the Texas Baptist Zion. Just beneath the surface of outward euphoria, an undertow of stormy water was beginning to roil. Within the next few years, the soul of Texas Baptists would be tried as never before. That story belongs to the next chapter.

CHAPTER 8

In Good Times and Bad, 1914–1929

Texas Baptists rode the same dizzy roller coaster that carried the nation through the turbulent twenties, and Baptists shared fully in both the ups and downs of that decade. Early in the period wages were high, crops were bountiful, and business was good. It is no wonder that American slogans of the time spoke of "Upward and Onward," and the still young nation breathed an air of heady optimism. World War I broke out in 1914, and America suddenly found itself catapulted into the ranks of major world leaders. The armies in Europe had to be fed and clothed. This created a vast market for American food and fiber, much of it produced in the South. Texas cotton, beef and oil propelled the Lone Star State into an era of unparalleled prosperity. When the United States entered the "war to make the world safe for democracy," American confidence and prosperity knew no bounds.

However, the war ended without making the world any safer for democracy or anything else, and the overseas hunger for American agricultural exports dried up. The end of hostilities reopened the stream of cheap European labor into this country, and wages plummeted. Cotton declined from forty cents to four cents a pound, and a combination of drouths and boll weevils further reduced Southern agriculture. Long before the stock market crash of 1929, which marked the onset of the industrial depression, the agrarian South had its own depression. In fact, Texas probably suffered less from the stock market crash of 1929 than from the agricultural crises that had been in process since the mid-twenties. Texans had little investment and less confidence in Wall Street, and manufacturing, so devastated in 1929, had only a toehold in the Lone Star State.[1]

For Texas Baptists the years 1914 to 1929 were the best of times and the worst of times. The period opened with optimism, prosperity and progress. Baptist growth took an upward spurt, and church organizations like Sunday School and the Baptist Young People's Union captured the interest and loyalty of young and old alike. The Baptist colleges mushroomed in enrollment and funding, while the Seminary in Fort Worth, still a Texas Baptist institution until 1925, set new records in training men and women for the multitudes of church and denominational positions that beckoned for them. State missions expanded dramatically, and more than a hundred associations linked Baptist efforts in evangelism and missions from El Paso to Texarkana. It appeared, as J. B. Gambrell said in 1919, "The morning light is breaking. We are at the day-dawn of the greatest day Baptists—Texas Baptists and all—ever saw."[2]

In 1914 the incomparable J. B. Gambrell began his second tenure as Corresponding Secretary, and he streamlined the Convention structure for efficiency and growth. The number of missionaries at work in Texas in 1914 reached a record high not equaled again for a generation. The amazing new technology of the age, in which a person in Dallas could call by telephone and actually be heard in New York or San Francisco, challenged Baptists to develop mission methods equal to the new age in which automobiles, radio and moving pictures transformed America. Some Texas churches began broadcasting their services over the radio during this period. The Executive Board almost got carried away in its 1915 report given under title of "A Forward Look." They said,

> The growth of Texas Baptists is almost alarming. Their numbers run into the hundreds of thousands. They hold a large part of the wealth of this rapidly growing state. They have already laid foundations upon which to build indefinitely. . . . We have attained a good degree of unity in denominational discipline. We are growing in every direction. Our preachers are growing in numbers, in preaching power and in leadership. The churches are growing, many of them into great strength. Every department of the work is growing. Enlargement is the key word to the whole situation.[3]

Alas, such heady optimism could not continue. If we fast forward to the late 1920s, we find that enlargement had given way to retrenchment, and confidence, while still present, had been severely chastened. Deepening debt cast its long shadow across the pages of annual reports from the colleges and other Texas Baptist institutions, and the Convention itself had to adopt a strictly cash policy in which they did not advance money to the institutions, even when the budget promised it, until the cash was actually in hand. In 1927 the Convention appointed a Budget Control Committee whose job was to ride herd on the institutions, especially the colleges, to see that they did not run up debts for which the Convention might share responsibility.[4] Between 1921 and 1927 the Convention reduced its ranks of appointed missionaries from 524 to 230, and its financial support for state missions fell from $367,762 to only $154,429. Baptisms for those two years dropped from 13,251 to only 7,562.[5] The first great organized financial effort of Southern Baptists, the $75 Million Campaign of 1919-1924, fell short of its financial goal and both national and state Baptist agencies fell into debilitating debt. After a prolonged agricultural decline in the 1920s, the stock market crash of 1929 plunged the nation into the Great Depression, and the despair of the country, including Texas, was complete. By January, 1929, the editor of the *Baptist Standard* no doubt spoke for many when he wrote, "Texas Baptists are getting to mortally hate two words—'deficit' and 'debt.'" Hate them or not, Baptists would have to deal with those words, and the sober realities behind them, for many years.

As if they did not have troubles enough in the aftermath of war and depression, Texas Baptists also faced the most severe controversy of their history during the 1920s. J. Frank Norris, pastor of First Baptist Church in Fort Worth, embraced and advocated a militant form of fundamentalism. When Texas Baptists refused to knuckle under to his demands to reshape the denomination and its beliefs into his extremist mold, Norris launched bitter attacks such as had not been seen since the days of S. A. Hayden in the 1890s. This constant barrage of criticism, attacking the work of the Baptist General Convention and impugning the integrity, motives and methods of its leaders, kept Texas Baptists off-balance for a generation.

However, descendants of Baptists who had lived through Comanche raids and Civil War Reconstruction survived the fortunes and misfortunes of the twenties, and they came out stronger, better organized and more united than ever. It was during those important years, 1914-1929, that the modern BGCT began to take shape.

IN GOOD HANDS

In the era between the First World War and the Great Depression, Texas Baptists were blessed with capable leadership. Three men served as Corresponding Secretary[6] during this era: James Bruton Gambrell, 1914-1918; Frank Shelby Groner, 1918-1928; and Thomas Luther Holcomb, 1928-1929. Each brought to the office significant gifts of leadership, and each faced both problems and progress.

After the restructuring of 1914 the new Executive Board in a contested election named the seventy-three year old J. B. Gambrell to his second term as Corresponding Secretary (he had also served from 1896 to 1910). Between his two terms Gambrell had served as editor of the *Baptist Standard* and as a professor at Southwestern Seminary. The "Great Commoner," as Gambrell was called, had the good fortune to preside during the best of times. Though the title was the same, the post Gambrell resigned in 1910 and the one he accepted in 1914 were far different. Before 1914 the Corresponding Secretary was elected directly by the Convention, which left him at the immediate mercy of political factions and disgruntled groups who criticized his every move. Under the old system the Convention in session approved all programs and appointments, a time-consuming micro-management process fraught with conflict. However, the constitutional revision of 1914 meant that the secretary henceforth was elected by the Executive Board, which allowed him more freedom to choose a staff and chart programs of ministry. The Board set policy but usually allowed the secretary broad discretion to allocate funds, appoint missionaries, and establish priorities. The change was dramatic.

The "Plan of Work" announced for 1914 was, "First, constant emphasis to be put on all the work all the time" and to promote four financial campaigns a year, for State Missions, Benevolence, Christian Education, and Home and Foreign Missions.[7] This continued the periodic "Round-up" method of church finance. It would be several years before the "Budget System" caught on among Texas Baptists. It is no disrespect to Gambrell to note that he basically approached the old tasks in the old ways. It remained for his successors, F. S. Groner and T. L. Holcomb, to bring innovative approaches to traditional tasks and develop new forms of ministry.

Gambrell submitted his resignation in 1917 to accept a teaching post at Southwestern Seminary. On November 24 he gave a final report to the Executive Board, and accepted a parting gift of $100 in gold.[8] In their accolades, the Board reviewed Gambrell's years of service, and noted that despite stressful days, "his face never blanched, his hand never relaxed, his heart never grew faint, his glowing optimism never failed." At the same meeting, fourteen men were nominated to succeed Gambrell but no one of them received more than six votes. Two weeks later L. R. Scarborough was elected with 35 out of 47 votes, but he declined. When several ballots failed to produce a candidate, the brethren convinced Gambrell that only he could prevent division and said that he could keep the gold gift if he would but resume his former office, which he reluctantly did. However, the next June Gambrell presented his final resignation, to take effect on September 1, 1918. He wrote to the Board,

> It is known to all of you that for years I have felt drawn to teach. I was engaged in that delightful srvice *[sic]* when the two general boards of the convention were consolidated and all of the work put under one management. In the judgment of the Board it became necessary for me to come back to the Secretarial work. I did so with the feeling that it was temporary. Every year since I have tried to find a way to return to the class room.[9]

After Gambrell's final resignation, forty-one year old Frank Shelby Groner was elected Corresponding Secretary on the fifth ballot, and his salary set at $3,600 per year. A native Texan, Groner had served as a teacher and county attorney before entering the ministry. His pastorates included Stamford (1905-1911) and Columbus Avenue Baptist Church in Waco (1911-1918). He served as Corresponding Secretary from 1918 until 1928, and as president of the College of Marshall (now East Texas Baptist University) from 1928 to his retirement in 1942. Groner was a capable and tested leader, and had been among those nominated back in 1914. He brought youthful energy, innovation, and initiative to the task. It fell his lot to preside during the heady days of the World War, the $75 Million

Campaign of 1919-1924, and the painful retrenchment of the depression years. Groner led in restructuring the Executive Board, establishing the Convention's Department of Evangelism in 1925, and launched the Baptist Foundation in 1930.

After Groner, the Board turned to T. L. Holcomb, then pastor at First Baptist, Sherman. Known as "the little big man," Holcomb was not much over five feet tall and sometimes had difficulty being seen over tall pulpits. However, he was wiry and athletic and projected an aura of strength and vitality. There was nothing small about his spirit, and his resonant voice could be heard throughout a great auditorium even without amplification. Often compared to Zacchaeus, Holcomb, like that character in Luke 19, found ways to get the job done. Holcomb graduated from Mississippi College (1904) and Southern Baptist Theological Seminary (1908), and during World War I served as religious director for the YMCA in France. Holcomb was a superb promoter who had a great capacity to enlist and motivate others. He served as Corresponding Secretary for only two years before leaving in 1929 to accept the pastorate of First Baptist Church, Oklahoma City. From 1935 to 1953 Holcomb headed the Baptist Sunday School Board in Nashville, from which position he was able to advance Sunday School work in Texas and other states.

Other capable leaders came to the fore in these years, putting Texas Baptist work in good hands. In February of 1915 Southwestern Baptist Theological Seminary elected Lee R. Scarborough as president to replace the incomparable B. H. Carroll who died November 11, 1914. George W. Truett was coming into his great strength as pastor of First Baptist Church in Dallas. S. P. Brooks, known as "the man who made modern Baylor," was in his maturity as president of the university and wielded great influence not only in his own school, but over Baptist education throughout the state. The other colleges had capable faculties and presidents, and outstanding pastors could be found from the high plains to the gulf coast. Older leaders like J. B. Cranfill, though diminished after he sold the *Baptist Standard* in 1904, continued to speak out. Young pastors like Wallace Bassett and Marshall Craig early on showed their potential for the future. The *Baptist Standard* wielded a growing influence under E. C. Routh who held the editorial pen for almost the entire period, 1914-1928. C. C. Slaughter and the wealthy Carroll family of Beaumont held their places, and younger laymen of wealth and influence came to the fore. H. L. Kokernot, M. H. Wolfe, and Pat Neff, governor of Texas 1920-1924, were but a few examples among many. Among the women Mrs. F. S. Davis, Mrs. J. M. Dawson, Mrs. Joel H. Gambrell, Mrs. A. F. Beddoe and, during her frequent furloughs, Annie Luther Bagby, provided steady leadership. Perhaps never before had Texas Baptists had such a contingent of capable and committed leaders, lay and ministerial alike. In 1914 the Executive Board organized by electing M. H. Wolfe as president, Gambrell as Corresponding Secretary, with F. M. McConnell and B. A. Copass as assistant secretaries. Surely the Baptist cause was in good hands.

GOOD NEWS ON EVERY FRONT

Reports of Baptist work in Texas after 1914 were so optimistic they might have been written by L. R. Scarborough, and indeed some of them were. Gambrell, no pessimist himself, divided the work of the Convention into three sections. In 1915 the he affirmed that

> our state mission work has its three phases, namely: 1. Evangelism—the winning of the lost. 2. Enlightenment—the teaching and training of the saved. 3. Benevolence—the touch of helpfulness to all the world.[10]

Under missions Gambrell promoted church planting, associational missions, church extension to the thinly populated high plains of West Texas, and the always persistent but never very successful missions among the European population in Texas. During his second term Gambrell continued to push missions among Hispanics, though bereft of his wife Mary, who had been such a potent force in Mexican missions before her death in 1910. He also promoted missions outside of Texas, giving major support to the two SBC boards for home and foreign missions. The church-based ministries of Sunday School, BYPU, and the women's mission work also showed remarkable advance early in this era before controversy and retrenchment threatened them.

Under education, Gambrell grouped the Baptist colleges, academies and the Seminary in Fort Worth, with its Missionary Training School. For all their loyalty to their own schools, Texas Baptists also continued to send money and students to the Southern Baptist Theological Seminary in Kentucky. Benevolence work included the Buckner Home, relief for aged ministers and their dependents, and various Good Will Centers. In an era when Baptist support for their aged ministers was more verbal than financial, Gambrell proved to be a friend to the "tottering heroes of the cross," as he called them. He helped sponsor a retirement home for aged ministers and their widows, and as president of the Southern Baptist Convention he helped bring the new Relief and Annuity Board of the SBC to Dallas in 1918.

WORLD WAR I

War broke out in Europe in 1914 and the United States was drawn into that world conflict in 1917. The war impacted Texas Baptists in several ways. Almost overnight classes were depleted in many Baptist colleges as the young men moved from campus to the military camps. The state convention geared up to minister to over 200,000 service men from all over America who did their training in Texas, and in so doing had to divert resources which might have gone to other forms of state missions. Churches near the training camps offered a multitude of ministries, from recreation to evangelism. Many Texas pastors and ministerial students served in the war, some on the front lines. A number of Texas pastors, of whom George W. Truett is the most famous, served for longer or shorter periods as chaplains to the troops in France and Germany. Wartime inflation wreaked havoc on many church building plans and put strains upon local and denominational budgets alike. When the war was over, many of the returning men created a challenge with their altered attitudes and changed outlook on life and religion. About 200,000 Texans served in the war, many of them Baptists, and of course the most poignant result of the war was the thousands who did not return at all.[11]

As it became ever more obvious that America would enter the war, some Baptists urged caution. A resolution in 1915 by J. M. Dawson to support President Woodrow Wilson survived opposition, efforts to water it down, and eventually passed in its original form.[12] However, when the chips were down, Texas Baptists supported the war effort wholeheartedly and without a murmur. The Texas historian, T. R. Fehrenbach, thinks Texas was already conditioned to war by the skirmishes along the Mexican border. From 1910 onward, the United States kept a large contingent of troops in South Texas to deal with Mexican revolutionaries like Pancho Villa who did not always stick to their side of the Rio Grande. The grandiose "Plan of San Diego," by which Mexican nationals planned to rise up in military might and retake Texas, came to light in 1917 and shortly thereafter the United States had up to 35,000 active troops in Texas, in addition to perhaps six times that number in training. Fehrenbach also believes that Texas, ripped from the national Union by the Civil War, at last fused back into the United States emotionally and politically during the patriotic fervor of World War I.[13]

While some Baptist schools were depleted by the war, others grew. By 1918 the War Department, realizing the need for trained officers, established the Students' Army Training Corps, which allowed a number of men to enlist in the army with the understanding that they were "detailed to study in college." The government paid all their college expenses, food, clothing, housing and tuition. Baylor University by 1918 had 455 of these SATC men enrolled, and their fees from the government allowed the remodeling and enlargement of facilities for their use.[14] These facilities remained after the war as college property. Other Baptist colleges developed similar military programs.

Among the most remembered training camps in Texas were Camp Bowie in Fort Worth where soldiers trained, and Kelly Field and Camp Travis in San Antonio where the "Air Brigade" learned to fly the small biplanes used in the war. Churches near these camps did yeoman service, with pastors and people doing all they could to bring a touch of home to the lonely "boys in khaki." Recreation, fellowships, pie suppers, and singings as well as Bible study and preaching were provided. The BGCT named George Green as Director of Camp Activities, to correlate efforts of the Convention and local churches. A number of Baptists served as "camp pastors," with general access to the camps similar to what a modern chaplain might have. By 1919 about 200 Baptists had served as camp pastors in the South, many of them in Texas.[15]

During the war President Woodrow Wilson invited about twenty prominent pastors to visit the front lines and minister to the troops. George W. Truett, pastor of First Baptist in Dallas, was one of those who responded. The church granted Truett a leave of absence, continued his salary and, just in case, took a large insurance policy on his life. A newspaper report said that Truett had answered the call of the government to preach to the "soldiers in the camps and in the blood sodden trenches beyond the Atlantic." Truett left Dallas on July 9, 1918, and arrived in New York in only forty-five hours, which he described as "fast travel." After training sessions with the YMCA in New York, the group sailed on July 31. In his diary, Truett wrote

> The German Bastille must fall . . . . The Am *[sic]* people have their minds made up about this war and they unhesitatingly believe that our Allied Armies are God's instruments to right the greatest wrong in all human History.[16]

Truett landed first in England where he spent several weeks visiting military camps, meeting with military commanders, and in further orientation for his ministry on the front lines. In his diary for September 22, 1918, he describes his impressions after attending a Sunday Service at Oxford. Truett wrote, "Went to Christ College Cathedral 10:30 A.M. Rec'd the clear, deep, painful impression that such religious exercises will never win the masses to Christ." Truett arrived in France in late October and spent the next several weeks in a constant round of speaking to troops in camp, in mess halls, and in the trenches near the front lines. Though his language is usually restrained, Truett got into the war spirit, referring to the Germans as "Huns."

A few lines from Truett's diary written after the Armistice was signed will illustrate his routine. On New Year's Day, 1919, he wrote, "Spoke tonight to crowded group of artillerymen—fine officers and fine men." The next day he wrote, "Spoke tonight in crowded hall, all of whom, both officers and men had been 'over the top.'" On January 3, "Spoke at three camps today, at 2 P.M., 3:30 P.M., and 7:30 P.M. Went in a motorcycle on all my rounds today, some fifty miles. . . . . [returned] in a cold biting rain. Found my bed taken by an officer, but I found another, and though I am very wet, cold and tired, I am glad to be alive." That day he had met a number of Texas men, some from Baylor. Truett always wrote to the mother or some family member of every Texas man he met in the war.

The war revealed not only Truett's patriotism, but also his warm human spirit. He lived in the primitive camps with the men, ate their food, and slogged through the cold and mud to minister to them. He experienced his share of hunger, fatigue and loneliness. However, his messages to the troops were invariably upbeat and optimistic. Along the trenches Truett saw his share of death. He later wrote, "Oh, the horribleness of this war."[17]

However tired, Truett never ended a day without writing some letter, however brief, to his wife Josephine at home, and he eagerly awaited her letters to him. After a particularly hard day, January 8, 1919, Truett wrote, "My thoughts and heart turn homeward, with inexpressible yearning. God be gracious to my loved ones, giving them every needed mercy. And to the Church, making my very absence fall out for their best good." Truett returned to Dallas in February 1919 after an absence of more than six months. His sermons, addresses, and published articles served to solidify Texas Baptists' patriotic support of the war.

As a citizen, Truett, like most Texas Baptists, strongly supported President Wilson's plans for a League of Nations. At his famous address on the east steps of the Capitol in Washington in May 1920 Truett said to a crowd of thousands that included senators and congressmen,

> I thank God that a stricken man yonder in the White House [President Wilson] pleads yet that the nation will take its part with the others in bringing a new era where shall dwell righteousness and peace. . . . the United States of America, without regard to any political party, will never rest until we have a league of nations.[18]

Other Texas Baptists, including the Corresponding Secretary, editor of the *Baptist Standard,* and prominent pastors preached sermons, wrote letters and published articles in favor of America participating in the League of Nations, but a recalcitrant congress blocked the plan.

The innocent boys who sailed to France in 1917 and 1918 came back after the war as seasoned men, toughened by hardship and in many cases with their world view enlarged. In the trenches the Baptist boys met Roman Catholics and Jews, often for the first time, along with other Protestants. The religious programs of the YMCA, along with chaplains of many denominations, gave them a glimpse of different forms of faith. The YMCA majored on recreation and offered dances and moving picture shows and, though not sponsored by the "Y," alcoholic beverages were not hard to obtain. Many of the soldiers found that they liked these, despite the fact that the folks back home vigorously opposed all three. "The dance craze is undoubtedly on the increase," said one Baptist leader. "The war programs of entertainment have done much to popularize it."[19] In an article on "After-the-War Problems for Baptists," W. A. Hamlett said the war was fought to preserve such Baptist distinctives as religious liberty, separation of church and state, and to confront the challenges of "Romanism and Unionism."[20] He said the war had made men restless, and many Baptists "were caught without a doctrinal gas mask on" and many false doctrines were "unconsciously whiffed in the battle-charged atmosphere."

Some said the returning men would change the churches. They would demand closer cooperation between denominations, perhaps even union. They would no longer tolerate doctrinal creeds, it was said, but would demand a "social gospel" form of religion. Some feared that the returning soldiers, after the YMCA dances and picture shows, would not be content with prayer meeting. David C. Gardner, later to become editor of the *Baptist Standard,* spent a few months at Kelly Field in San Antonio, in contact with airmen and YMCA leaders. They all expected a new world after the war. "They told me the boys would return from the battle front with a new vision; that Y.M.C.A. and other welfare workers would emerge from the war zone to revolutionize our churches; that creeds would no longer be endured; in fact, I was told that sectarianism and sectionalism had already appeared on the casualty list."[21]

A particular problem for Baptists was the role of the YMCA in the war. The War Department (now called State Department) decided, probably unwisely, to put the YMCA in complete charge of coordinating religious activities among the troops, both in the training camps and at the front. The YMCA adopted the now familiar three-fold designation of Catholic, Protestant, and Jew and tried, in a rather heavy-handed manner, to force all non-Catholic Christians into the "Protestant" category. The "Y" also adopted a clear and intentional policy of breaking down denominational differences among the soldiers. When the YMCA leaders later blocked admission of the Baptist "camp pastors" to the camps, Baptist indignation boiled over.

It fell the lot of J. B. Gambrell, who was then president of the Southern Baptist Convention, to deal with the War Department about Baptist concerns. Gambrell found the government policy unacceptable. He had not completely outgrown his earlier Landmark views, and he insisted that Baptists were not "Protestants." He could hardly contain his dismay that the "Y," a social organization, had been put in charge of religious activities. In a message to the SBC, Gambrell quoted an official of the War Department as saying, "The whole desire of the department [in chaplaincy] is in the interest of breaking down rather than emphasizing denominational distinctives."[22] Gambrell objected not just to the policy, but even more to the idea of the government attempting to interfere with religion. He accused the government of deliberate effort "to break down the non-Catholic denominations" and declared that "the Baptists and other great non-Catholic communions were not allowed to serve their people in their time of greatest need."

Other Texas Baptists joined in this criticism of the YMCA, though Truett attempted a few words in their defense. In addition to the anti-denominational stance to which Gambrell objected, others complained of the "social gospel" approach of the "Y." Some Baptists who had ministered to the troops complained that they had been cautioned not to tell any soldier he was lost without Christ. There is more honest Christianity, some were told, in offering a soldier a cup of hot coffee than in offering the plan of salvation. Even Gambrell praised the "Y" for its work in the canteens, but said it had no business trying to replace religion with "Sunday theatricals, 'stunts,' and sometimes Sunday dances."[23]

THE $75 MILLION CAMPAIGN

In 1919 the Southern Baptist Convention launched a great financial campaign to raise $75 million for Convention ministries over the next five years, partly to celebrate the Convention's 75th anniversary in 1920.[24] The task seemed imminently doable at the time, given the wartime prosperity and optimism. A precedent for major financial campaigns had been set with the War Bond drives and the example of other denominations which were involved in major fund drives. This was by far the greatest task ever undertaken by the SBC, and they approached it with enthusiasm. The effort was highly organized and promoted. George W. Truett was named to chair a fifteen-member Campaign Commission, and Lee R. Scarborough took a leave of absence from his post as president of Southwestern Seminary to serve as Campaign Director. Each state had a campaign director, as did each association and each church. Every week the state Baptist papers, including the *Texas Baptist Standard,* carried articles and publicity promoting the campaign and in 1920 the BGCT added to their Dallas staff a Publicity Director to help promote the total denominational program.[25] The $75 million was to be portioned out among the Baptist agencies, with education and missions getting the lion's share. Southern Baptists had never experienced such an intense effort. Scarborough worked almost day and night, so that some feared for his health. However, he responded that

> I am getting all the sleep I need, drinking buttermilk three times a day, eating three square meals. . . . My belt buckle is tight in the same hole it was when I left Texas; never felt better in my life . . . I was never a pessimist; was once a possumist; for a long time I have been an optimist, but now I am a spizzerinktumist and . . . victory is boiling in my soul.[26]

After a whirlwind seven-month effort, the campaign concluded with Victory Week, November 30—December 7, 1919. Without computers, the tally was slow, but about midnight on December 7, Scarborough telephoned from Nashville to F.S. Groner in Dallas and said, "I want some money." "How much do you want," asked Groner. "I want $600,000," the amount to reach the $75 million goal. "Well," responded the elated Groner, "You can have the $600,000 and $400,000 besides."[27] Witnesses said Scarborough's shouts of victory could be heard throughout the building.

When all reports were tallied, Southern Baptists had pledged $92,630,923. Rejoicing among Baptists knew no bounds; if they had not been Baptists, no doubt there would have been dancing in the streets. Scarborough, never one for understatement, said "God laid His big hand" on the campaign, and gave Baptists their greatest spiritual victory since Pentecost.[28]

Texas Baptists participated enthusiastically in the $75 Million Campaign, and in Truett and Scarborough Texas provided the major leadership for the drive. The goal allotted to Texas was $15 million, but state leaders bravely added $1 million extra for Texas causes. Texas churches pledged a total of $16,500,000. Truett led by example as well as precept; the First Baptist Church of Dallas, where Truett was pastor, pledged to give $606,742.50 over the five-year period.[29] Examples abound of Texas churches, large and small, that amazed even themselves with the extent of their generosity.

Unfortunately, the pledges so cheerfully given in 1919 proved difficult to collect in the 1920s in the midst of drouth, boll weevils, and the collapse of the Southern agrarian economy. The campaign was extended to 1925, but even so Southern Baptists collected only $58,591,713. Percentage wise, Texas did even worse, collecting only $8,720,060 of their $16,500,000 pledge.[30] Baptists drew no comfort from the fact that the other denominations did even worse in their financial campaigns at the same time.[31] To make matters worse, Baptist institutions had expanded rapidly on borrowed money on the expectation of large gifts, and failure to reach the goal plunged them into debt. Not until 1943 were Southern Baptists completely debt-free.

Even so, the $75 Million Campaign cannot be called a failure. Even without reaching their ambitious goal, Baptists raised more money for their ministries in five years than they ever had before. Southern Baptists became more stewardship conscious and per capita giving almost doubled.[32] The years of the campaign also brought an extensive spiritual renewal, with more converts baptized, more young people enlisted in special Christian service, and more denominational commitment on the part of churches. The Cooperative Program was adopted in 1925 as a direct result of the $75 Million Campaign. These five fateful years, especially in Texas, catapulted Baptists from the minors to the major league as one of the leading denominations in the nation. The campaign and its aftermath also helped to put Baptist churches on the "budget system" of finance.

THE NORRIS CONTROVERSY

Hard on the heels of the $75 Million Campaign, and to some extent growing out of it, came the most severe controversy Texas Baptists had faced up to that time. John Franklyn Norris was the fiery pastor of First Baptist Church in Fort Worth from 1909 until his death in 1952. Actually, the controversy erupted before the $75 Million Campaign, but Norris's refusal to honor his pledge in that campaign greatly exacerbated the situation.

Norris was born in Alabama in 1877, son of a drunken shiftless father and an intensely religious mother.[33] The family moved to Hill County, Texas, near Hubbard, when Frank was eleven, but the family fortunes did not improve. A root out of dry ground, young Frank was a brutally abused child[34] and he seemed to take refuge in his mother's religious intensity. The family was poor; Frank later recalled riding to Sunday School on a mule and having the other children make fun of his shabby clothes. At age fourteen young Frank was shot by ruffians whose real target was his father, and he went through almost three years of rehabilitation, much of which time he could not walk. Wounded in body and spirit, the boy was nursed back to health by his mother, who instilled in him the conviction that God had some mighty work for him. After a brief flirtation with the Church of Christ, Frank joined the Baptists in 1890 and was baptized by Pastor Catlow Smith in a small creek. Soon Norris felt called to preach, and for a time the militant "Cat" Smith was his role model. However, Smith apparently had second thoughts about his young protégé. Even before he entered Baylor in 1899, Norris was called as pastor of the Mt. Antioch church, but "Cat" Smith refused to participate in his ordination. Smith gave as his reasons that young Norris "was too recently from the Campbellites, and that he was a Haydenite."[35] The ordaining council was made up of BMA[36] preachers, and his next church, at Mt. Calm, was dominated by Haydenites who had just fired their previous pastor because he would not embrace Haydenite views. Though he never joined the BMA, Norris was for all his adult life a spiritual brother to Sam Hayden, and shared most of Hayden's opposition to organized Baptist ministries in Texas.

As a Baylor student, Norris was marked by good grades and a bad spirit. He barely lost out to J. M. Dawson for class valedictorian, which started his lifelong dislike of Dawson. Norris was known to ridicule students less brilliant than himself, and at times even mocked a fellow-student's halting efforts at public prayer. As a freshman, Norris led a student revolt which resulted in the forced termination of the Baylor president. He learned quite early the power of agitation. At Southern Baptist Theological Seminary in Louisville, Norris gave the class valedictory address in 1905, though some of his professors expressed reservations about his militant spirit. He returned to Texas as pastor of the McKinney Avenue (now Highland) Baptist Church in Dallas. Even then, he showed a troublesome side. A Baptist layman who knew the family well wrote from Flomont on October 27, 1922,

> I heard him [Norris] preach his first Sermon in Texas, after his graduation at Louisville, and that evening I rode with him for Several miles and he told me then that Baptist *[sic]* held to, and taught many things that was *[sic]* not contained in the Scriptures. I write in evidence that the Rev. J. Frank Norris has never been in full accord with the organized work of the Convention Baptist *[sic]* of Texas.[37]

In 1907 Norris bought a controlling interest in the *Baptist Standard* and used the paper to help B. H. Carroll, his teacher at Baylor, to win public support for establishing the Southwestern Seminary. However, he turned the paper to sensational methods to increase circulation and won the enmity of the Baptist establishment of Dallas, including the powerful George W. Truett. Truett headed a group that bought the *Baptist Standard* from Norris and conveyed it to the BGCT. Upon the strong recommendation of B. H. Carroll, his Baylor mentor, Norris accepted the pastorate of First Baptist, Fort Worth, in 1909. Some think Norris came to Fort Worth with the hope of succeeding the aged Carroll as president of the new Seminary. Certainly he had the credentials; he was perhaps the best educated Baptist pastor in Texas, was known as a powerful preacher, and had paid his dues by helping Carroll establish the institution. However, Carroll chose L. R. Scarborough, the young professor of evangelism, as his successor and Norris turned against Scarborough and the Seminary with a passion.

Over the years Norris directed his ire at three main targets: the state convention, Baylor University, and Southwestern Seminary. Like Hayden before him, Norris accused the convention leaders of receiving lavish salaries for little work, falsifying records, and fraudulent financial dealings. As in the Hayden era before him, the most careful outside auditors turned up no basis for these charges. Norris accused Baylor professors of teaching the hated theory of evolution, and eventually obtained the removal of one professor on that charge. At Southwestern Seminary Norris wanted the professors to embrace and teach the same form of militant millennialism that he himself held, and when they would not, he accused them of doctrinal liberalism and denying the Bible. With his church paper, the *Fundamentalist,* Norris regularly attacked Texas Baptist leaders and institutions, at times barely skirting libel laws. He put into practice what he had learned at the *Baptist Standard,* that controversy attracts attention and wins followers. After a traumatic experience in 1911, Norris reorganized his church. He dropped all committees, dismissed those deacons who disagreed with him, abolished the WMU and made himself virtual dictator of the church. Asked if he favored church democracy, Norris replied, "Yes, but I'm the biggest democrat of all." He said, "I prefer a good row in a church to indifference, because I am at home when they raise a row."[38]

Before Norris came as pastor, the Fort Worth church had installed a large stained glass window of a beloved former pastor who was buried directly under the window. Norris chafed under the eye of his popular predecessor. One Sunday he pointed to the portrait and remarked to Lee Scarborough, one of his members, "Lee, I can never do anything with this congregation as long as that face is looking down on me. This whole thing will have to burn down before I can do anything."[39] The next Friday night, the church burned to the ground. Norris was indicted by a grand jury and tried on a charge of arson, but he was acquitted. The church burned again in 1929 under suspicious circumstances, and Norris was questioned but not indicted. A far more serious incident occurred on July 17, 1926, when Norris shot D. E. Chips to death in his church office. The unarmed Chips was an ally of Norris's Fort Worth opposition, but his purpose in visiting the pastor's office that Saturday afternoon remains a mystery. When Norris was indicted for murder, the trial was moved to Austin where it became the most sensational murder trial in Texas history to that time. After weeks of testimony, the man called "the pistol packing parson" was acquitted. However, even his own followers seemed taken aback, and Norris never fully recovered his earlier mystique.

Despite lack of proof for his accusations against Texas Baptists,

Norris soon built up a numerous following. The BMA excision of 1900 had not removed all the disgruntled from the Convention, and Norris brought them to the fore again. To them he appeared as a champion for orthodoxy, calling Texas Baptists back from a dangerous liberalism. Some Texas Baptists felt the best way to deal with Norris was to ignore him, but not so Secretary F. S. Groner. In a hard-hitting article published in the *Baptist Standard* on July 16, 1925, Groner addressed the "discontent that may prevail with some of our brethren." He attributed much of that discontent to the fact that "we have in our midst a religious annihilist who has made it his principal employment, and in fact almost his sole business, for nearly a decade, to disseminate suspicion and circulate untruthful statements about our work with the evident design of destroying the confidence of the brotherhood in our great kingdom affairs." Finally, their patience exhausted, Texas Baptists in successive steps rose up to reject the troublemaker. In 1914 Norris was excluded from the local Pastors' Conference, and in 1922 and again in 1924 his church was excluded from the Tarrant Baptist Association. In 1924[40] and again in 1925[41] Norris and his church were refused seats at the state Convention. By the mid-1930s Norris and his church had been excluded from the Southern Baptist Convention on the grounds that he did not meet the constitutional provisions that in order to be affiliated, a church had to be "a bona fide contributor" and be "in friendly cooperation" with SBC work.

With his church in constant turmoil and with troubles in his own family, Norris spent his latter years still fulminating against Texas Baptists, but attracting less support. Even so, he created a denominational split that drew out dissident churches into his own fundamentalist denomination which he formed in 1934, inflicting gaping wounds in the Baptist body that have not healed to this day.

BAPTIST MINISTRIES MULTIPLY

During the 1920s Baptist ministries in Texas multiplied, and the employed staff at BGCT offices in Dallas reflected that expansion. The church-based ministries like Sunday School and BYPU occupied more space in Baptist budgets and reports, as did the campus based Baptist Student Union. When several of the two-year colleges expanded into four-year schools, the costs far more than doubled, offering more educational options but devouring more money. The excitement of the $75 Million Campaign and the Cooperative Program that resulted meant that Texas, along with other states, contributed more to outside causes like the Home and Foreign boards of the SBC. Previously, Texas Baptists had taken special offerings for home and foreign missions. These offerings, while usually generous, never equaled the amount of mission money spent in Texas. However, under the Cooperative Program the state sent a percentage of total receipts to Nashville. Baptist leaders like Scarborough pushed the so-called "50-50" plan, namely, that local churches should send 50% of their total receipts to the BGCT in Dallas, and in turn the BGCT should forward on to Nashville 50% of its receipts. The churches never reached their part of the goal, but for a time the state convention operated on a budget of sending to Nashville 45% of state receipts including the special missions offerings. The number of dollars spent in state mission work continued to increase, except in the retrenchment years, but the *percentage* of the churches' offerings available for work in Texas diminished sharply.

State Missions. Despite excellent progress, sections of Texas remained a virtual mission field. In West Texas, large ranches were broken up into small farms and communities emerged with no Baptist witness. During the 1920s a burst of railroad building vastly expanded the Texas rail system, bringing further settlement to what had been remote regions.

Early on, the BGCT had adapted its operation to place more responsibility on the associations. "With reference to general field workers," one report said, "we recommend that the present plan be abolished, feeling that the convention has advance *[sic]* sufficiently to do without this type of work, which in former times was prosecuted so successfully, . . . the time has arrived when the Associational Missionaries can do this work more effectively."[42] The Convention encouraged each association to elect its own local missionary or, in some cases, several associations to group together to do so. This local missionary worked to strengthen the churches, plant new churches as needed, help the churches find pastors, and lead the churches to support the various ministries of the Convention, preferably through the unified budget system. The Board also voted that "all associational missionaries shall be agents for all denominational literature and shall look out for students for all of our educational institutions."[43] The Executive Board supplemented the salaries of these local missionaries, though not always to the extent the associations desired. By 1929 the Board helped sponsor over fifty such associational missionaries, though in more prosperous times the number had been greater.[44] In addition to supplementing the associational workers, the Board continued to appoint a number of "general missionaries," strategically located throughout the state. The "general men," as they were called, bore an appointment from the BGCT, while the "associational men" were appointed by the associations. At times this resulted in overlap and not a little tension. The Board did not grant every request. In 1921 they voted "that this Board do not appropriate any money to the Parker County Baptist Association until the brethren there settle their local difficulties."[45]

By the mid-1920s churches had to meet certain qualifications to receive aid. At the beginning of 1922 J. T. Pinson, assistant Corresponding Secretary, reported that

WHEREAS, . . .there are a large number of churches which have received assistance from the state Board through a period of as long as seventeen years, and,

WHEREAS, the facts gleaned indicate that a large number of these churches have made no material progress, and in some cases have actually lost ground, and

WHEREAS, it has been revealed that there are churches receiving aid, which in no sense are co-operating with our 75 Million Campaign,

THEREFORE, be it resolved that:

FIRST, it shall be the policy of this Board to render aid to mission churches through a period not to exceed five years, and

SECOND, that it shall be the general policy of this Board to scale down the allowance to such churches not less than 25% each year after the first year. . . .

THIRD, it shall be the further policy of this Board to decline to give any aid to any church which does not in some measure co-operate with and contribute to denominational work.[46]

During these years the Convention gave more attention to the needs of about 800 "unhoused congregations" in Texas. The conviction that a church needed an adequate building in order to succeed was not new, but the financial ability to help such houseless churches greatly increased during and just after World War I. A 1922 survey showed that houseless churches did poorly in every area: almost half had no additions in a year, many had no Sunday School or BYPU, and 88% of "housed" churches subscribed to the $75 Million Campaign while only 57% of "unhoused" churches did so, and the "housed" churches contributed substantially more per capita.[47] Loans and outright gifts were extended to many unhoused churches and, in a few cases, what was intended as the former turned out to be the latter.

For all its many forms of ministry, the Executive Board pronounced state missions as the core of the Convention's work and the primary reason for its existence. State mission work, they said, "reaches out into every association, and grips the hearts of the people for everything the convention stands for. It evangelizes, baptizes, plants churches and nurtures them into self-support, then elicits, combines and directs their energies to world conquest."[48] Because they had assumed the debts of the earlier boards, the new Executive Board had to launch their work on a modest scale. For 1915 they could allow only $100,000 for state mission work. They found it hard to compress the work within that limit, but found themselves in "the iron grip of necessity." Even so, they had 332 missionaries employed in various capacities and for varying periods of time.[49]

In addition to supporting missionaries, the Executive Board also gave direct financial aid to many weak or developing churches. However, the Board voted in 1916 that no church should be aided for more than four years, with a 25% reduction in aid each year. "It should be a rule of the board," they said, "to withdraw assistance after a reasonable time" lest it become "a useless expenditure of mission funds."[50] Further, the Board would consider only written appeals from churches. They believed that some appropriations had been too generous, while other worthy causes were slighted, because some applicants made a more eloquent appeal before the Board. "It is our conviction," the Board reported, "the appropriations should be made to mission fields without reference to the eloquence exhibited in the presentation of application."[51] They also said the Board should not always wait for applications, but should seek out areas of need where overly modest brethren might not ask. The Board also bluntly affirmed that "this board was not organized for the purpose of furnishing positions or fields of labor for the brethren. . . . we can neither appoint men as missionaries under this board because we love them, nor, because of former service, nor, because they need jobs." The Board concluded that regardless of how many missionaries they have on the field, the work of Texas Baptists depends on the cooperation of pastors.[52]

By 1923 it was obvious that receipts from the $75 Million Campaign were falling short, and the BGCT had to cut back its programs. For 1924 the records note "That the Board . . . [must] adopt a policy of the strictest economy, consistent with efficiency."[53] At the same meeting they cut back on personnel in other departments, but found money to appoint two "general evangelists" and four "field secretaries," but asked the latter to "regard themselves as field secretaries instead of office secretaries." Retrenchment was essential but the Board tried to preserve stability. In July 1924 the Board said, "We recommend that in order that our Field Workers shall not be unsettled by the possibility of their positions being discontinued, and in the interest of efficiency, that it be the sense of the Executive Board that the present policy with reference to Field Secretaries, Evangelists, Stewardship Secretary and Budget Director shall continue for a period of not less than three years after the present Convention year."[54]

In 1925 the Board established a Department of Evangelism, with W. Y. Pond called from First Baptist, Hillsboro, as the first secretary at a salary of $4,500 per year plus expenses. At the Mineral Wells convention in 1925 Pond spoke against what he called "cheap-John" evangelism of those who fight the BGCT under the guise of evangelism, a thinly veiled reference to Frank Norris. Pond said, "Texas Baptists stand for a sane, constructive evangelism. Evolution is not the main trouble in Texas. Devilution is the big problem."[55] Actually, the evangelism work had been called a "department" for years, but it had no full-time leader until 1925. The pattern had been for the Executive Board to send out a number of evangelists each year who would travel the state, holding revivals, leading evangelistic rallies, and sometimes conducting evangelism workshops in the churches and associations. For most of the period, the evangelists received a salary from the BGCT, and revival offerings went into the Convention treasury, though at times offerings went to evangelists and churches could deduct that from their funds to the Convention. They noted, however, that "it is the understanding that no evangelist shall be kept on the force who fails to raise his necessary salary." In addition, Southwestern Seminary also had a corps of evangelists conducting revivals throughout the state, and also taking every opportunity to raise funds and enlist students for the seminary. With establishment of the Department of Evangelism in 1925, the seminary agreed to correlate its evangelists through the new structure. The seminary also conducted an annual Evangelism Conference, the costs for 1929 being set at $1.00 a day for room and meals, but $1.25 if the school furnished linens.[56] The staff of the Evangelism Department for 1929 included W. Y. Pond, George W. McCall, Hulon Coffman, C. Y. Dossey, and K. O. Fulgate, and it was said that "These men will go into any church without any financial obligation on the part of the church, and the free-will offering will be sent to the treasurer of our board, and the church will be given credit on State Missions."[57]

Then as now, Baptists tried to put their resources where they were most needed and would do the most good. J. M. Dawson made the interesting point in 1919 that if one should divide Texas with an East-West line drawn through Austin, three Baptist institutions with a property value of $462,000 would be found South of that line, in an area with 59,408 Baptists. North of that line one would find 336,139 Baptists and 17 Baptist institutions with property worth $4,846, 472.[58] He concluded that Baptists, like Johnson grass, would grow wherever they had a chance. "Most of our [mission] money," said one report, "is being spent now south of Dallas and west of Fort Worth."[59]

One of the most controversial proposals of the Executive Board was to revive *The Missionary Worker,* a small periodical that Gambrell had used to promote the state work and also to refute the damaging attacks of S. A. Hayden in the 1890s. That paper had been discontinued, but Secretary Groner wanted to revive it. This proposal reflects a growing dissatisfaction with the *Baptist Standard,* whose editor, E. C. Routh, felt the best way to deal with Frank Norris was to ignore him. Groner did not share that view, but felt that the extravagant accusations printed in Norris's *Fundamentalist* should be vigorously refuted. In 1921 Groner proposed "to revive *The Missionary Worker,* to be conducted on the well known policy of that publication in promoting, exploiting and defending the organized work and institutions of Texas Baptists."[60] However, the Board advised delay, "provided The *Baptist Standard* shall give sufficient space, editorially and in its news columns, to the adequate setting forth of the great interests of the convention and shall meet the high demand for correcting misinformation, and a vigorous constructive way for handling criticisms concerning the work and workers." Editor Routh promised to do better, since the Board cautioned him that "We need our great paper now to hearken with hope, to stabilize with sanity, to defend our Redeemer's cause against unjust and unfriendly criticisms." However, Groner persisted and a revised *Missionary Worker* was launched later, and its columns, under Groner's control, gave vigorous response to Norris.

The Executive Board itself underwent change during this period. The Convention turned aside proposals that members of the Executive Board be elected by the associations, but did agree to the enlargement of the Board. In 1925 Pastor R. F. Stokes of Jasper introduced a resolution to enlarge the Board from 45 to 68 members, elected to three year terms with one third rotating off each year. "Some good men feel left out," said Stokes, and he offered this plan to "iron out the kinks in our work." Stokes noted that "We have made pack horses of a few of our brethren, while others, who are abundantly able to carry heavy burdens, have not been trusted with any." Stokes said that "With this change of our Constitution put into practice, I feel sure many of our troubles among Texas Baptists will disappear."[61] The change was voted, with the one man opposing later moving to make it unanimous.

Sunday School. Such "auxiliary organizations" as Sunday School, Baptist Young People's Union, and the Baptist Women Mission Worker organizations were considered "effective arms of mission power." Sunday School and BYPU came directly under control of the Executive Board. The BWMW, while independent, always worked in close harmony with the Board and, in turn, were always treated with respect, courtesy and appreciation.

In 1915 the Board noted that "in nothing are Texas Baptists doing better than in Sunday School development." Baptist attitudes had changed dramatically, with churches that formerly spurned the "new fangled" classes now clamoring for help in setting up schools, training teachers, and obtaining literature for Bible study. The state convention employed W. E. Foster as their state "Sunday School missionary" for three years until his resignation in 1915. His successor was William P. Phillips who served from 1916-1926. Phillips had studied Sunday School pedagogy at the Louisville Seminary and later worked with Lewis Entzminger in Kentucky. He came to Texas as Sunday School and BYPU leader for Tarrant Baptist Association, and later went to First Baptist Church in Tyler as one of the first paid Sunday School superintendents in the state. This office was a forerunner of what is now called Minister of Education. These leaders worked not only with churches directly, but also conducted associational workshops. Early on, Foster launched annual associational Sunday School "conventions" which were a mixture of training, inspiration and evangelism. While emphasizing enlistment, Bible teaching and stewardship, the Sunday Schools kept the focus on soul winning. Foster sought to form schools in churches that yet lacked them, led the churches to adopt a standard grading system, and helped the churches obtain suitable Baptist materials for study.

One of the problems facing Texas Baptists was the image of Sunday School as a children's exercise. The idea of all-age Sunday School had not yet caught on. In 1919 Phillips reported that about 70% of Baptists in Texas were over the age of sixteen, but the Sunday School had concentrated its work on the 30% under that age.[62] Phillips lamented that efforts to enroll adults had been "very negligible." For a time Texas Baptists promoted the "Organized Class Movement," involving large Baracca classes for men and Philathea classes for women. These classes were helpful in getting adults involved, but later created problems when such large classes became almost separate organizations from the church and, at times, created tensions with their independent and nondenominational flavor. Later, with the help of the Sunday School Board in Nashville, Texas moved to a plan which brought adult as well as children's classes into closer cooperation with the churches. Reports for 1919 show a total of 3,709 Baptist churches in Texas, with 383,774 members. Only 2,234 churches had a Sunday School, and these enrolled 225,002 pupils. This left 1,475 churches with no school, a situation which Phillips successfully addressed in the next years. Most of the churches with no Sunday School were in rural areas with half-time or quarter-time preaching. Phillips urged such churches to form an every Sunday meeting centered around Sunday School.

The Baptist Sunday School Board in Nashville also helped promote Sunday School in the states, including Texas. Their agents traveled the state, working with Phillips to conduct workshops. The BSSB also provided for new Sunday Schools three months of free literature. The Nashville board also developed certain "standards" for how a Baptist Sunday School should be organized and how it should relate to the church. An ongoing promotion in Texas sought to lead more churches to develop a standard Sunday School. Many older Baptists in Texas to this day remember the large banner that hung on the wall of many a rural church proclaiming the methods and virtues of a Standard Sunday School.

Baptist Young People's Union. When it was first formed in the Broadway Baptist Church in Fort Worth back in 1891, the Baptist Young People's Union, forerunner of the Baptist Training Union, faced immediate opposition throughout the state. However, those objections soon melted away as Baptists saw the power of the BYPU to enlist youth in church life, and to train them in evangelism, stewardship and Christian living. For a time J. R. Magill had served as state BYPU secretary, though at first he had to combine that with his regular job as an accountant in the BGCT office in Dallas.[63] Magill resigned the BYPU job in 1914, and the next year T. C. Gardner, then president of the College of Marshall, was elected the state BYPU Secretary. No better choice could have been made. He brought fresh ideas, aggressive leadership and, above all, a contagious enthusiasm which quickly transformed the new organization into a statewide power in Baptist life.

As the name implies, the BYPU began as an organization for youth. However, when youth who had been active in BYPU reached their mid-20s, they did not want to drop out. The younger children also wanted to share in the new excitement. By 1919 the BYPU was graded on a departmental basis, with Unions for Primary (6-8), Juniors (9-12), Intermediates (13-16), and Youth (17-24). The first Adult Unions were formed in 1921, thus completing what they called the "five-department plan." Some of these groups were further sub-divided. In BYPU work, as so many areas, Texas Baptists pioneered paths later followed by other states. Gardner reported in 1929 that Texas had 4,431 unions (classes), with 121,083 members. More than 20% of all BYPU members among Southern Baptists were in Texas by the end of this period.[64] The unions promoted steward-ship, tithing and missions and already they were promoting the Junior Memory Contest and the Intermediate Sword Drill.

Baptist Women Mission Workers. The Baptist Women Mission Workers usually abbreviated their long name as BWMW, an alphabetical designa-tion which many did not understand. These letters "stare us in the face in denominational literature," said an early report.[65] In 1919 the women voted to take back their original and less complicated name, Woman's Missionary Union, the name the women of the Baptist State Convention yielded up in 1886 as the price of merger with women from the Baptist General Association. Taking back their "maiden name" also brought the Texas women into line with the national WMU. But under whatever name, Texas Baptist women continued their ministry during good times and bad. Though structurally independent of the BGCT, the WMU "every-where follows the lines of work laid out by this Convention." The WMU occupied rooms in the Slaughter Building in Dallas alongside BGCT offices, and the Executive Board paid their administrative expenses and provided a salary for the Corresponding Secretary. Nowhere else, said the Board, did they receive greater return for their money. For their part, the women were so pleased with results of their work in 1919 that they said it would take three women all talking at once to do justice to their report.[66]

For many years the WMU had divided their work in Texas into a number of regional districts. Beginning with twelve districts, they eventu-ally expanded to seventeen. Their goal was to have an active WMU in each church, an associational organization to correlate promotion, and a series of district WMU conventions made up of representatives from several associations to feed directly into the state organization. Each district had its own WMU organization, leaders, and promotional plans. Both the Sunday School and Baptist Young People's Union organizations adopted similar regional divisions. In 1927 J. Howard Williams, director of budget promotion, led the Executive Board to adopt this "district plan" for its state mission work. The Executive Board began with fourteen districts and in 1929 expanded to seventeen to match the number and boundaries of the WMU organizations. The Board intended to place a "district mission-ary" in each region, whose ministry would be to encourage the associations and churches, promote the total program of the Convention, and serve as a close-up liaison with pastors and churches to whom the state convention headquarters in Dallas seemed quite distant. In time many credited Wil-liams with inventing the district plan which, in reality, he had adopted from the WMU.

Assemblies. A new form of ministry appeared among Baptists early in the twentieth century: the summer encampment or assembly. In this work Texas pioneered, especially through the BYPU, blazing the trail which others followed. Actually the idea of meeting for a few days in an outdoor setting during the summer for fellowship, study and worship is at least as old as the frontier camp meetings and probably older. For Southern Baptists, B. W. Spilman founded the Ridgecrest Conference Center in 1907 essentially as a training ground for Sunday School teachers. However, the Baptist encampment as it developed in Texas was a twentieth-century innovation. The first encampment among Texas Baptists was at LaPorte in 1902, but a few years later more suitable property was obtained at Palacios, on Matagorda Bay not far from Corpus Christi.[67] By 1915 Texas Baptists had three active summer assemblies, at Palacios, Christoval, and Lampasas. With over twenty acres fronting the gulf, and with cabins, assembly rooms, and dining facilities Palacios was the most popular. At Lampasas Baptists obtained about 100 acres with a river running through it, providing "an unlimited amount of water for bathing."[68] The Christoval Baptist Encampment was located about twenty miles south of San Angelo on the Concho River, shaded with large trees and providing comfortable cabins, meeting rooms and separate lodgings for men and women speakers. These encampments, it was affirmed, "furnish the opportunity for recreation and rest, and at the same time study and instruction in the Word of God, training in Sunday school and B.Y.P.U. work, and all phases of the work of our Baptist women."[69]

During World War I programs at the encampments were curtailed due to high transportation costs, and some even advocated selling the properties, but wiser heads prevailed. Within a few years the summer camps multiplied and proved their value. In addition to the pioneer three, by 1926 encampments are listed for Buckner's Home, Fellowship, Hill County, Paisano, Driftwood, Rivera Beech, Leonard, Two-Draw Creek near Post, Woodlake, Lueders, Panhandle, Menard, and Canadian. The Paisano Assembly, located in the Davis Mountains just west of Alpine, achieved prominence for its annual "Cowboy Camp Meeting" where George W. Truett preached each summer to the cowboys. When Southern Baptists planned a second national assembly to go with Ridgecrest, Paisano was briefly considered as a site before Glorieta was selected.

In addition to fun and fellowship, the summer camps featured the best preachers and teachers in Texas. Sunday School, BYPU, WMU, Evangelism, and State Missions would each be assigned a week at various camps, and often the workers would trek from one camp to another for most of the summer. The few complaints about the camps, not surprisingly, alleged that not enough time was allowed for recreation. However, all ages flocked to the camps. Many who attended were converted or renewed in their faith, and specific training was offered for Sunday School teachers, BYPU workers, deacons, and soul winners. Classes in Baptist doctrine, Bible studies, and missionary challenges were provided. Some camps even offered studies for pastors in sermon preparation and church leadership. On a less inspirational level, some camps provided remedial summer school studies for children. And always the work of the state convention was presented and promoted. Countless young people were led to recognize the call of God to special Christian service at the assemblies and, if reports be credited, not a few found marriage partners there.

Baptist Student Union. The increased college enrollment of Baptist youth called forth a new form of student ministry during this period, the Baptist Student Union. The BSU provided a way for Baptist students to express their faith on campus while separated from their home churches. Like the BYPU, the BSU had ties back to earlier non-denominational movements, especially to the YMCA and Student Volunteer Movement for Foreign Missions. In 1903 the Student Department of the YMCA called for a conference of Christian youth from the southwestern states to meet in Ruston, Louisiana. Joseph P. Boone and two other young men from Baylor attended that meeting and became interested in forming a campus organization to practice and deepen their faith. On October 21, 1905, six Baylor students and graduates formed a Prayer Covenant. The six "Covenanters" were Basil Lee Lockett, who became a missionary to Africa; Harry H. Muirhead, who became a missionary to Brazil; Julian H. Pace; Tandy Y. Adams; Joseph M. Dawson, who later became pastor of First Baptist Waco; and Joseph P. Boone. Boone was offered a job as Texas director of the YMCA campus program, but declined in hope that Baptists would soon form their own student ministry. For this he had to wait a number of years.

Interest in foreign missions also played a role in calling forth a Baptist student organization. By 1909 the Foreign Mission Board was sending speakers to Baptist colleges to give lectures on missions, and in 1910 the WMU of the Southern Baptist Convention created a special division of the Young Women's Auxiliary to work in the colleges and to organize YWA circles on campus.[70] Charles T. Ball, professor of missions at Southwestern Seminary, called a conference to meet on the Seminary campus where, on November 9, 1914, the Baptist Student Missionary Movement was formed. The movement spread and soon "Volunteer Bands" sprang up on many college campuses. At the Southern Baptist Convention meeting in Houston in 1915 S. J. Porter of Texas was appointed to chair a committee to report on the new organization. His report said,

> Many Baptists throughout North America have felt for some time the need of a more definite cooperative effort to inspire and enlist more thoroughly the Baptist students in the interest of world-wide missions. It is with pleasure, therefore, that we report to this Convention the organization of the Baptist Student Missionary Movement, and the favor which is being accorded to it throughout the entire country.[71]

In time the BGCT became convinced of the need for an organized work among Baptist students in Texas. In 1919 the Convention adopted a resolution presented by the BYPU which called for the election of a "Baptist Student Secretary for Students of Texas." This person would "give his entire time among the Baptist Students of Texas emphasizing Baptist principles, interpreting Baptist life, creating and sustaining Baptist loyalty, enlisting and crystallizing a denominational spirit; virile, consecrated, and active and that shall express itself through the local churches where students hold membership."[72] The same resolution expressed approval of the

Baptist Student Missionary Movement and assured the Convention there would be no conflict between the older foreign mission body and the proposed more general student organization. In fact, the more missionary student groups were later absorbed into the more general body. Joseph P. Boone was named the first Baptist Student Secretary, and began his work April 1, 1920.[73]

Boone was the first full-time Baptist student worker among Southern Baptists. He began with little job description, and it took time for the new structure to coalesce. Boone led a meeting of about fifteen students and five faculty from six colleges at the Palacios Encampment in July 1920. He later called this "a history-making event" where the shape of the future BSU was determined.[74] There they chose a name one word at a time. They agreed the new organization should be distinctly "Baptist," that it should concentrate on the "Student," and that "Union" described their intended structure. Their purpose statement emphasized evangelism, missions, stewardship, denominational loyalty, and "calling out the called for special service." The first statewide convocation of Baptist students met at Howard Payne College, Brownwood, October 22-24, 1920. There over 300 students from twenty schools enthusiastically adopted the name "Baptist Student Union." The next statewide conference was held at Baylor College for Women in Belton, and part of the program was to show a local BSU program in full operation. Frank H. Leavell, who later became the Southwide director of the BSU work, attended that meeting. The first BSU Manual was published by Boone in 1922. When Boone began his work in 1920, the Convention said, "Brother Boone has been given a number of helpers who are located in connection with our state schools." These included O. P. Campbell, teacher in the Townes Bible Chair at the University of Texas; R. L. Brown, Baptist Student Secretary at A&M College; Elva Fronabarger, at Northwest Normal College in Canyon; Edna Belle O'Neal at San Marcos; and Leon M. Gambrell at the North Texas Normal College in Denton.[75]

Three facts emerge from this story. First, Texas students led the way and pioneered a student ministry which was later picked up by other states and by the SBC. Second, Baptists preferred a more denominational approach to student ministry than was available through the earlier YMCA and Student Volunteer Movement. Third, the Baptist Student Missionary Movement, which originated at Southwestern Seminary in 1914, ceased to function after 1920 and its emphases were absorbed into the more comprehensive goals of the new Baptist Student Union formed in 1920.

Daily Vacation Bible School. The Vacation Bible School made its appearance among Texas Baptists during this period. One of the earliest such schools in Texas was held at the Seminary Hill Baptist Church in Fort Worth (now Gambrell Street) in 1916. Fifteen Texas Baptist churches conducted a VBS in the summer of 1926, and that number steadily increased to 30 in 1927 and 47 in 1928.

Education. Texas Baptists gave such support to schools during this period that some complained they had abandoned state missions in favor of colleges.[76] It must not have seemed so to the colleges, where most struggled against rising costs, mounting debts, and overcrowded facilities. No doubt most of the colleges could have offered a report similar to that of Howard Payne in 1929 which showed that college students were a major factor in evangelism in Texas.[77]

In his 1915 report to the Convention, Secretary J. B. Gambrell minced no words. Under the heading of "The Educational Situation," he said "We are in an educational jam."[78] He concluded that "By far the most serious situation confronting this Convention is the education situation." Several elements combined to create that jam. Before the war the colleges had enlarged both faculties and facilities in expectation of rapidly growing enrollments. However, the war drew young men away from campus into the army camps and the rapid rise of state schools provided stiff competition for the Baptist schools in recruitment. The result, Gambrell said, was to "reduce the patronage of the schools below self-support." As the student population diminished, the debts increased. In the reorganization of 1914, the old Education Board was abolished and oversight of Texas Baptist schools passed to the new Executive Board. The old board was not only deeply in debt, but had made pledges to the various colleges totaling almost $48,000.[79] The colleges had already expanded their work on the strength of these pledges, thus contracting debts of their own. Gambrell concluded that these pledges somehow had to be paid "to save the schools from a break-down."

Gambrell warned those who felt the denomination could abandon the schools and continue to prosper. "Education is working at the roots," he said, while "Collecting is pulling at the top." He had no intention to abandon the roots of Texas Baptist achievements. However, he did challenge Baptists to face some facts. "The time has come," he said, "for this Convention to face the education problem and discuss it down to the bone." Gambrell said bluntly that "Denominational education must face the competition of state schools, with the taxing power of the state behind them. This is true of every grade of education, from kindergarten to university. . . .Let us not blink at these facts."[80]

In the same report on competition, Gambrell asked "Can we meet it? And, if so, how?" Meet it they must, for "We cannot maintain a single school without competition by the state, by other denominations, and by the secular spirit within our own ranks." To assure the ongoing success of Baptist colleges, Gambrell urged that the schools be unapologetically Christian, strongly Baptist, loyal to the Convention and all its work, contact high school seniors more diligently, and above all make "our schools represent a type of education different from the state schools or any other."

When Gambrell gave this blunt report, Texas Baptists had some degree of sponsorship over nineteen schools, counting one university, six colleges, six academies, one theological seminary, one medical college, two training schools for nurses, and schools of pharmacy and dentistry.[81] The basic question was how to finance this growing educational empire. They could tighten the correlation, allowing the Convention more control over the college funds, faculties and curriculum, or they could go in the opposite direction and "take the bridle off and let each board [of trustees] be free to handle its own affairs." This would mean that the state once again would "swarm with agents" as each college competed for support. The course actually chosen lay between these extremes.

During this period educational standards were rising, and the Baptist schools participated in this increasing academic strength. In addition to the several academies which did not pretend to be colleges, all the colleges included an academy or "preparatory school" division. Some of the college academy divisions admitted students as low as fifth and sixth grades, others offered what we would call junior high work and all of them provided high school studies. Baylor University dropped its academy program in 1915, not without severe criticism from some who felt they were unduly exclusive in admitting only college level students. For many of the colleges, the academy division was their bread and butter and their main source of recruits for the college courses. In a way, the very success of the Baptist colleges created some of their problems. As Gambrell's report pointed out, the higher the level of instruction the higher the cost per student. Academies, he said, can live on tuition but colleges and universities will die without endowment. Texas Baptists were not prepared for the escalation of costs as the academic levels of their schools increased. By the late 1920s, records show, most of the colleges were operating in the red (and all of the athletic departments were).

The Baptist colleges made a great contribution in providing teachers for the burgeoning public schools of Texas. Prospective teachers accounted for a large part of the enrollment of the colleges, perhaps nowhere more than in the Baylor College for Women at Belton. Herein lay both an opportunity and a challenge. At that time, the state would give full certification to teachers who had completed two years of college. Baylor College expanded its "Summer Normal" to include a full term, so a young woman could attend two summer sessions and the two regular semesters between, and thus complete two years of college studies in fifteen months. College officials rejoiced in 1915 that while overall enrollment had increased 50% the freshmen class had increased over 500%. They worried, however, that

> Our greatest weakness therefore is in not being able to carry a sufficiently large per cent of the freshmen into the sophomore class. . . . Too many of our girls want to commercialize their education and their lives, and come to college merely for a certificate with which to teach. When this certificate has been received, the purpose of their educational effort has been fulfilled, and they leave college and college life, nevermore to return.[82]

The location of Texas Baptist colleges came in for much discussion during this period. The schools had grown up much like Topsy, with little overall planning. Even so, they were fairly spaced out in most major sections of the state. Baptist leaders then operated on the assumption that more is better, for they assumed that most Baptist youths would not go more than a hundred miles from home to attend college. Almost all the colleges at some time considered moving to a new location where, they hoped, they would find more dollars and more students. On the question of relocation there was more talk than action, though a few schools actually did move. One Baptist school, however, refused to be moved.

By the mid-1920s a number of influential Texas Baptists proposed that Baylor University be moved from Waco to Dallas. For reasons not unlike the earlier arguments which led to the removal of Baylor from Independence to Waco, some pointed out that Dallas was nearer the heart of Baptist population. The rich city on the Trinity, they argued, could offer more money, better facilities, more students and more prestige than could the smaller city on the Brazos. Besides, the vast Baylor Hospital complex was already in Dallas, along with its cluster of "healing schools" of medicine, nursing, pharmacy, and dentistry, all of which had attracted favorable national attention and large funds. Meantime, the city of Waco seemed dormant, the university plant deteriorated, and inadequate facilities acted to cap university enrollment. This gave an enterprising Dallas group the opening to grab a great university, or to make a good university great, depending upon one's viewpoint.

At Wichita Falls in 1927 the Convention authorized the formation of an Education Commission, to have broad jurisdiction over Texas Baptist schools. Some of the most influential Texas Baptists leaders were included among the sixteen members of this body. H. L. Kokernot was named chairman, and the committee included George W. Truett, L. R. Scarborough, former governor Pat Neff, A. D. Foreman, wealthy layman Carr P. Collins, O. S. Lattimore, Earl B. Smyth and others.[83] Immediately upon their organization, the suggestion surfaced to move Baylor to Dallas or, as they put it, "a proposal for the consolidation of all the departments of Baylor University in the City of Dallas."[84] Dallas offered impressive "inducements," including large tracts of well-located land without cost, additional tracts for future expansion, a promise to build a campus second to none in the South, and a covenant from the Chamber of Commerce to provide large endowments to guarantee the future of the university. "Texas Baptists desire a real university of first rank," said the Commission, subtly implying they did not yet have one. On April 28, 1928, the Commission met in Dallas and voted thirteen to three to accept the following recommendation:

> WHEREAS, the Commission has considered especially the welfare of Baylor University, mindful of its long history and its mission in the world.
> . . .
> WHEREAS, it is believed that the future growth, development and usefulness of its various departments will be best conserved by a consolidation of its various departments in one city, . . .

NOW, THEREFORE, BE IT RESOLVED, that this body recommends (1) that the foregoing offers be accepted, . . . (2) that all departments of Baylor University now located at Waco, Texas, be removed to Dallas and consolidated with the departments now located in Dallas, Texas.[85]

This recommendation seems to have caught the Waco business community by surprise, but their reaction was swift and militant. Just two weeks after the recommendation was passed, a delegation from the Waco Chamber of Commerce met with the Commission in Dallas, "submitting a challenge to the Baptist denomination of Texas for the permanent retention of Baylor University in Waco." They presented a nine-point statement, offering to raise a $1,000,000 endowment fund if Texas Baptists would match that amount, and promising funds for several major new buildings and renovations on campus, additional lands for expansion, and an open-ended promise for any future improvements and expansions as needed. In return, the Waco leaders wanted a promise that Baylor would remain permanently in Waco.

The Commission seemed surprised by the hornets' nest of controversy their proposal raised. "We find the denomination profoundly stirred by intense agitation for and against removal," they reported. They denied that their recommendation arose from inter-city rivalry, real estate schemes that might profit Commission members, or any other "sordid motive." They particularly rejected the idea that the removal of Baylor represented a "moral wrong." They took note of several warnings of "the possible consequences to the Baptist denomination and to Baylor University by reason of the probable division resulting from the present agitation." Clearly, a contingent of Baylor leaders intended to remain in Waco whatever the Convention voted. The Convention could recommend, but only the trustees could decide. President S. P. Brooks was apparently willing to discuss the move until the Waco community rose up with promises of massive support, which may have been his true motive. He also concluded that the Dallas inducements did not measure up to expectations, and he came out strongly against the move.[86] Brooks believed, rightly, that an aroused Waco business community would come to the rescue of Baylor. "I firmly confidently believe," he said, "that when the donations available from Waco are known, the glamour of the Dallas gift will fade to its proper proportions and that the Convention will keep the school in Waco."[87]

Stung by criticism, shocked by the depth of resistance, and fearful of division the Commission backed down. They voted unanimously to rescind their former action, recommending instead that Baylor remain in Waco. The statewide reaction was so enormous that it was felt necessary to call a special meeting of the Convention for the fall of 1927 to confirm this decision. Leaders felt it would not be possible to collect the sums pledged until the Convention had spoken officially and the future site of Baylor was settled.

With their emphasis upon colleges, Texas Baptists did not neglect the cause of ministerial education. In 1915 they reported about 500 ministerial students in Texas Baptist schools, and said this number could be doubled if scholarship aid were available. Most of the colleges, including Baylor, waived tuition for ministers, ministers' wives, foreign missionaries on furlough, and provided half-tuition for the sons and daughters of active Baptist pastors in Texas. The schools regularly complained to the Convention that they were carrying more than their share of the cost of ministerial education, and asked the Convention for more help to defray these costs. From time to time the BGCT had a committee to solicit funds for ministerial scholarships, but the funds were never adequate and some claimed they were not allotted equitably. A few colleges had some scholarship plan, but others made what was called "a sympathetic but desultory, somewhat aimless and almost despairing effort." A 1915 report says the result of "these unorganized, unrelated divergent and sometimes friction-breeding policies has been confusion, waste of energy and needless, not to say sinful, hindrance to the work." This report recommended the Board try for more equity and fairness in its aid.[88] Despite these problems, the number of ministerial students steadily increased.

In its concern for Baptist students in Texas the Convention did not overlook those enrolled in the state colleges. A group of students from the First Baptist Church in Austin formed a mission near the University, and by 1908 that mission became the University Baptist Church.[89] In 1915 the Convention sponsored a Bible chair at the University of Texas at Austin where over 400 Baptist students were enrolled.[90] The University Baptist Church in Austin, overwhelmed by the influx of students, asked and received help from the BGCT in obtaining additional land and erecting a building to accommodate the students. By 1929 Texas Baptists had about 8,000 students in their own colleges and about 9,000 in state schools. The Convention sponsored student workers at Huntsville, Nacogdoches, Commerce, and Stephenville. Some colleges employed their own BSU workers, like Mrs. B. W. Vining at Baylor and J. A. Lovell at Simmons. The BGCT helped provide BSU workers at Texas A&M and University of Texas at Austin. At UT, the Convention sponsored the John C. Townes Bible Chair, with a full-time teacher in the person of W. C. Raines.[91]

Southwestern Baptist Theological Seminary. In 1915 the Seminary brought J. M. Price to the faculty to start a "Department of Christian Education and Religious Pedagogy." The stated purpose was to train Sunday School teachers and workers, pastors' assistants, "and to build a strong school of religious education." The same year came I. E. Reynolds, "a thoroughly equipped gospel singer," to launch a "Department of Gospel Singing." With these new music courses, Seminary officials hoped it would no longer be necessary for those who wished "to gospelize the great message in song" to go outside the South for their training.[92] Also in 1915 President Scarborough established a Department of Field Evangelism, with F. M. McConnell as Superintendent. This department was not for teaching but for modeling good evangelism. The several "field evangelists" were commended to the churches as men who practiced a "sane" evangelism, sound in the faith and thoroughly Baptist. "We believe they are resurrection preachers," said Scarborough. "We do not wish our Seminary to be a theological refrigerator. We want it to be a spiritual power house."[93]

In his first report to the Convention as president, Scarborough set out "Five Marks of the Efficient Minister," which revealed his goals for the Seminary.[94] The school, he said, would try "to make it impossible for a ministerial degenerate, a moral marplot, a designing, spiritual imposter, to get through our seminaries to the churches." He also expected the graduates to show spiritual power. "We believe that a theological Seminary should not be a cold storage for the preserving of theological eggs, but rather a warm incubator for the hatching out of living, flaming, shining evangels of Christ, hot with zeal and full of power." Though he paid lip service to scholarship, the president declared that, "We need great souls with spiritual power in our pulpits and pastorates far more than we need great scholars with profound learning." The Seminary, according to the new president, would turn out "an indoctrinated ministry," who would reflect "militant orthodoxy," all within a context of denominational loyalty.

The Missionary Training School, the women's division of Southwestern Seminary, reported in 1915 that since it opened they had enrolled 428 women, but had graduated only forty-six. Of the 428 total, 263 were preachers' wives, 160 were unmarried, forty-three took their diplomas from the Training School and only three from the Seminary. The Training School offered two diplomas, the Bachelor of Missionary Training and, for an extra year of study, a Master of Missionary Training, which was intended "to train the women in all the activities of the kingdom of God, except in preaching."[95] In 1915 the school had a faculty of four, Mrs. Alma Lile, Superintendent; Miss Leota Turner in piano; Mrs. W. R. Lambert, kindergarten work; and Miss Myrtle Dockery, in expression. Mrs. W. L. Williams was named Assistant Superintendent and described as "mother over all."[96] It was "Mother Williams," an expert gardener in her time, who was rolled around campus in her wheel chair, pointing with her cane where the now huge and stately pecan trees should be planted. Taking on a big challenge, she was determined to "make our campus one of the beauty spots of the South. . . . making Seminary Hill a rose-smile to God and man."[97]

Both for training and as a ministry project, students with the help of local churches established "a settlement work" in North Fort Worth. This "Goodwill Center," as they called it, included child care and kindergarten for working mothers, and a boarding house for single young women within walking distance of the packing plants where most of them worked. The center also included a night school for young women of the area. Their purpose was to provide a clean, safe, wholesome place for the single girls to live, and to bring them under evangelistic influence. Several baptisms resulted from their work. In 1916 they obtained a larger house with room for twenty girls plus the resident director. The BWMW helped sponsor the home, though four Fort Worth laymen bought the house and held it in trust for the Training School. In addition to ministry, this provided training for the students. "In this institution our training school girls have experimental work in that phase of practical endeavor," said the report. Two serious problems later led to abandonment of the Goodwill Center: the rising costs, and the difficulty of the young women finding transportation from the Seminary campus to the Northside.

The women's building at Southwestern, still a magnificent structure today, was completed in 1915 at a total cost of $104,720 plus $45,000 for furnishings. The Baptist women of Texas raised most of this money, though the Baptist Sunday School Board in Nashville contributed some. For many years the women continued to struggle with unpaid pledges on the building. Most of the operating expenses came from the room and board paid by the students, but they had to canvas women's groups in churches and associations to raise money to pay the teachers. In addition to funds, the most urgent need of the Training School was more students. They were pleased to have preachers' wives enroll, but felt it important to enlist more single women who would be available for employment in the churches, denominational agencies, and in missionary appointment. They also asked Baptists to put on their calendar a Missionary Training School Day for a Sunday in January or February.

The Southwestern Seminary charter of 1908 gave ownership and control to the Baptist General Convention of Texas, though by the 1920s ten other states contributed funds and elected some of the trustees. However, in 1925 ownership and control of the Seminary was transferred to the Southern Baptist Convention. In the optimism of the $75 Million Campaign, President Scarborough and others came to believe that the Seminary could attract more students and funding under sponsorship of the larger SBC. An idea also took root that the state conventions could appropriately sponsor colleges, but the SBC should sponsor theological education. At a trustee meeting on February 15, 1923, "a motion was unanimously passed tendering the ownership and control of this institution to the Southern Baptist Convention."[98] This offer was made on condition that the BGCT, which held title to the property, would approve. On March 20, 1923, the Executive Board voted that we "do hereby authorize the Board of Trustees of the Southwestern Baptist Theological Seminary . . . to proceed in tentatively offering the ownership and control of said Seminary to the Southern Baptist Conventions." The BGCT in session also voted approval, and the transfer was completed 1925. The SBC also assumed ownership of the New Orleans Baptist Theological Seminary, previously a Louisiana institution, the same year.

The expected benefits of SBC sponsorship did not materialize. The SBC assumed control, elected trustees, and offered best wishes but little else in terms of support. Southwestern Seminary entered a period of severe financial crisis in the late 1920s when the very existence of the school was in doubt.

Benevolence. As noted earlier, the Buckner Orphans Home was given to the state convention in 1914, but it continued largely as a Buckner enterprise. Upon the death of Father Buckner in 1919, two of his sons Joe and Hal, assumed joint leadership.[99] During the consolidation of the 1920s, the Buckners successfully avoided having the Home come under the Convention budget as other agencies did. For obvious reasons they preferred to continue to stand alone as a separate object of church and individual contributions. During these years the Home continued its solid claims upon the benevolence of Baptists, and was able to expand its campus, population and programs. "Care for more children and do more for those children," was their goal, and Karen Bullock has shown that they achieved it.[100] Under the younger Buckners, the Home overcame setbacks, fires, the flu epidemic of 1918, and survived the depression of the late 1920s better than most Baptist groups.

Another benevolence of importance concerned the "decrepit ministers," as the retirees were called. As noted earlier, the Convention founded a series of retirement homes for ministers, none of which succeeded greatly, scrounged up money to provide $10 a month pension for some retirees, but helped far more by cooperating with the new Relief and Annuity Board of the SBC. This board was formed in 1918 and located in Dallas. By the 1920s the BGCT had largely turned over to the new board the responsibility for aged ministers and their widows. When the Palacios Academy failed, the property was turned into an Old Ministers Home under the superintendency of R. T. Hanks. However, in 1920 the Board voted to "close the Old Ministers Home at Palacios, and see that the inmates are properly cared for" in other ways.[101]

Moral and Social Concerns. Though their primary focus was evangelism, church growth and education, Texas Baptists were not oblivious to social concerns. They spoke out, preached, wrote and otherwise promoted women's suffrage; the prohibition of alcoholic beverages; opposition to lynchings, still too prevalent in Texas; and opposition to divorce. Texas Baptists, following the lead of J. B. Cranfill, played a major role in the Eighteenth Amendment for prohibition, and labored hard and, in the end, unsuccessfully to preserve it. By the late 1920s when it was clear that Prohibition was losing national support, Baptists spoke out urgently, charging that government officials had made no serious effort to enforce the law. When it appeared that Governor Al Smith of New York, both a Roman Catholic and a "wet" (who favored repeal of Prohibition) would be nominated for president of the United States, Baptist concerns mushroomed. Even George W. Truett, who never allowed partisan politics to intrude into the pulpit, preached a militant sermon at the state convention of 1927 saying that he and other Baptists would never support any candidate who favored repeal of Prohibition. Though he did not endorse the "dry" candidate, Herbert Hoover, Truett, a life-long Democrat, left no doubt of his intentions.

Miscellaneous Concerns. Records of this period reveal a variety of concerns among Texas Baptists, as various as college football, social dancing, chaplains in the military, the desire for better church music in the worship services, whether churches should use the "annual call" with pastors and the Clinton Carnes affair.[102]

One important concern was the the Confession of Faith adopted by the SBC in 1925. In an editorial, E.C. Routh allowed it would do no harm for the SBC to devise such a confession, so long as it was not allowed to become a creed.[103] At first Routh had no idea that the SBC itself would adopt the confession; he expected them simply to draw it up and leave it to the local churches to adopt or not as they chose. He conceded that the Convention might require its employees, especially professors, to affirm such a confession but he concluded "I do not believe that such ought to be done." Three weeks later L. R. Scarborough wrote a strong article in favor of the confession, while on the same page, John E. White argued that such a confession was unwise and, at any rate, was outside the purpose of the SBC. He feared that such a confession would compromise Baptists' commitment to Scripture and would inevitably become creedal. White said,

> Historically the foundation and record of Southern Baptists is absolutely against the exercise of the function of doctrinal standardization. Not until quite recently has the Convention entertained the idea that it should assume to make official pronouncements of Biblical interpretation.[104]

Once adopted, the confession attracted little further attention, but some felt the camel's nose was in the tent. The 1925 statement, named the "Baptist Faith and Message," did not speak on evolution, but in 1926 that was remedied as a strong anti-evolution statement was added. The SBC voted that the confession should not be used as a creed or to restrict investigation into any subject, and should never be circulated without these restrictions attached. However, over the years that caution receded into the background, and the confession has indeed been used as a creed by some Southern Baptists.

THE END OF AN ERA

In 1929 Texas was in the depths of depression. Even those banks not robbed by the outlaw couple, Clyde Barrow and Bonnie Parker, or their friend "Pretty Boy" Floyd, tended to go broke and deprive people of their savings. Farms were foreclosed, jobs were scarce, and already the beginnings of the great dust bowl were evident. Many homeless families, including Baptists, joined the migrant trail westward toward California, so vividly described by John Steinbeck in his *Grapes of Wrath*. Baptist churches in Texas shared fully in the hard times. Not only did offerings plummet, but the number of baptisms and other signs of spiritual vitality also declined. Many people blithely assume that hard times are good for the soul, but the evidence in America is rather that economic and spiritual depression go hand in hand.

During his last year as Corresponding Secretary, T. L. Holcomb reported that "The work of the year has been conducted along lines of strict economy." The Convention allowed $36,000 for administrative expenses in 1928, but they spent only $24,534.[105] They also operated on a strictly cash basis, making no new debts and distributing only such money as they had already in hand. Holcomb resigned in 1929, to accept the pastorate of First Baptist Church in Oklahoma City. As a parting gift, the Board gave Holcomb "a pig skin case costing $40," and passed resolutions of appreciation for his brief but effective service.

However, better days were ahead for Texas Baptists. They elected courageous new leaders, stretched the few dollars they had, and kept heroically to the task. That story belongs to the next chapter.

TEXAS
BAPTIST
PIONEERS

R. E. B. Baylor

Z. N. Morrell

J. W. D. Creath

James Huckins

Noah T. Byars

Noah Hill

R. C. Burleson

J. B. Link

William Evander Penn

L. R. Millican

William B. Bagby

Anne Luther Bagby

CHAPTER 9

DEPRESSION AND DELIVERANCE, 1929–1945

"NO GROUP OF TEXAS Baptists ever faced a more serious hour." That was the conclusion at a meeting of the Executive Board of the Baptist General Convention of Texas in 1932 during the depths of the great depression. "This is a life and death meeting. . . . Depressing conditions, diminishing income, [and] increasing obligations have cornered us," said W. R. White, pastor of the Broadway Baptist Church in Fort Worth and chairman of the influential Finance Committee. The chairman had made many committee reports but, he said, never one he so dreaded as this one. In the midst of economic collapse such as the nation had rarely seen, White said "We must reduce our budget to match our income or completely collapse within five or six months. . . . The issues of this hour will take our measure. What we write will be written."[1]

At that somber meeting, the Board voted to cut salaries severely for all Convention employees, lay off some staff members, cut the Sunday School and Baptist Training Union appropriations by 50%, reduce WMU funds by more than a third, and abolish the position of Baptist Student Union worker entirely. All the state mission workers faced a salary cut, and those whose jobs were abolished entirely got two months severance notice. Later the Board called upon a select few strong churches for immediate emergency aid, and set a special day of prayer concerning "the awful calamity which now desolates the land."[2]

Life looked bleak in the early 1930s as the nation lay in the grip of a devastating depression whose cause and cure seemed equally elusive. Yet, in the worst of times Texas Baptists never lost faith and they never doubted that these desperate times were temporary. They could say with the Apostle Paul, "We are troubled on every side, yet not distressed; we are perplexed, but not in despair."[3]

If we fast forward to a few years later, we see a different picture. The same Executive Board heard a report from J. M. Dawson, who said "Texas

189

Baptists have emerged from the grievous period of depression, and we are convinced that insofar as our denominational affairs are concerned, we have come upon the hour of recovery."[4] As the 1930s gave way to the 1940s, Texas Baptists resumed their remarkable growth, with more converts baptized, more churches growing, more people enlisted in service and more money for missions, evangelism and Christian education. "There is undoubted improvement," reported the Board. "Our educational and benevolent institutions, having weathered the storm on scanty support, are now expanding beyond all expectation."[5]

The twin factors of depression decline and World War II recovery provide the framework for this chapter in the Texas Baptist story. Several other highlights mark the decade and a half from 1929 to 1945.

* Texas Baptists fell dangerously deep into debt and it took heroic measures to dig out of the hole and become "debt free by '43."
* After several false starts, Texas Baptist men formed a statewide Brotherhood organization, and elected a full-time state secretary in 1945.
* Enrollment of Baptist college students, in both Baptist and state schools, mushroomed and work among the students emerged as one of the most challenging forms of ministry.
* As the Convention ministries expanded, so did the professional staff, with workers for budget promotion, publicity, rural church development, a director of inter-racial relations, and enlargement of the evangelism division.
* The "District Plan" was inaugurated, whereby Texas was divided into seventeen districts of five or six associations, with a "district missionary" in each area acting as a sort of assistant to the General Secretary for promotion and enlistment.
* The Baptist colleges grew rapidly in enrollment, academic strength, accreditation and budget needs, and in 1945 the two Baylors (Baylor University at Waco, and Baylor College for Women at Belton)[6] celebrated their centennial anniversary.
* During this period the Convention formed a Church Music Department, with a state worker teaching and promoting better worship in the churches.
* Baptists participated in the Texas Centennial observance of 1936, formed a committee to collect and preserve Texas Baptist historical records, and published a history of Texas Baptists up to that time.[7]
* Toward the end of this period a major trend toward centralization emerged, with many institutions like hospitals, schools, and assemblies that had been locally sponsored coming under ownership and control of the state convention.

FOUR SECRETARIES

Four men served as General Secretary of the Executive Board of the BGCT from 1930 to 1945. They were W. R. White (1930-1931), J. Howard Williams (1931-1936), R. C. Campbell (1936-1941), and W. W. Melton (1941-1945).

Since 1914 the General Secretary was elected by open ballot without any search committee recommendation or nomination from the floor. When a vacancy occurred the Executive Committee would assemble for the announced purpose of electing a Secretary. After a season of earnest prayer, committee members would write on a slip of paper the name of the person they felt should be elected. Often as many as a dozen or more names would show up on at least one or two ballots, but usually one person would emerge as the leading candidate. If that person received a majority of the votes, he was elected. If no one received a majority, another ballot would be taken. Sometimes it would take two or three ballots for a clear winner to emerge. At that point some committee member, usually one who had voted for another candidate, would move that the election be made unanimous, which was invariably done. In the weeks before an election, those who aspired to the Secretary's chair had ways to make their availability known, and no doubt Board members talked among themselves and with others about likely candidates. However, the actual election was marked more by prayer than by politics. Unlike the contentious days of the 1880s and 1890s, the four Secretaries of this period received the loyal support and cooperation of Texas Baptists.

William Richardson White. In 1930 W. R. White was elected to lead the Executive Board, and thus became the top leader of Baptist convention ministries in Texas. White came from the pastorate of First Baptist Church in Lubbock, and after serving only a year he resigned to become pastor at Broadway Church in Fort Worth. After leaving office White remained active in state work, serving as chairman of the influential Finance Committee. From Broadway Church he moved to Oklahoma City as pastor of First Baptist Church, and in 1943 became president of Hardin-Simmons University in Abilene. He served briefly as editorial secretary for the Baptist Sunday School Board in Nashville, but returned to Texas in 1945 as pastor of First Baptist, Austin. "Billy" White was one of three finalists considered for the pulpit of First Baptist in Dallas after Dr. Truett died,[8] but he is perhaps best remembered in Texas for his distinguished service as president of Baylor University from 1948 to 1961. He was named chancellor of the university in 1961.

It was White's lot to serve during tough times. Depression, debt and decline marked his year in office, due to no fault of his own and no lack of diligent effort on his part. He enjoyed the respect and affection of Texas Baptist leaders who said of him, "W. R White knows how to build the Brotherhood."[9] At his resignation in 1930, the brethren said "our Secretary has directed the finances, . . . in a most acceptable manner during one of the greatest financial depressions any of us have ever seen." Then they voted to cut the salary for his successor by 20%.[10]

John Howard Williams. J. Howard Williams, a native of Dallas, was elected Executive Secretary on August 1, 1931. In Dallas he grew up under the ministry of George W. Truett, and was licensed to preach at the age of sixteen and served for a time as a mission pastor in Dallas. He later graduated from Baylor University and Southwestern Seminary, and studied for two terms in the doctoral program at Southern Seminary in Louisville while pastoring a Kentucky church. In 1918 Williams volunteered as an army chaplain and spent several months with the troops in Europe. He later distinguished himself as a pastor in Venus, Sulphur Springs and Corsicana. Williams had been an active and effective leader on the Executive Board for some years, directing the budget promotion campaign of the state convention in 1929. He also introduced the "Williams Plan" of district missionaries in Texas before he became Secretary.

It fell the lot of Williams to lead Texas Baptists during the depths of the Depression when money was short, programs had to be curtailed, salaries cut and the number of state missionaries reduced. Williams and those who worked with him instituted the most rigorous economies in the state convention work and labored to keep at least the essential ministries intact. Despite the dark clouds on the horizon, Williams never lost hope and never allowed his associates to do so. He kept an upbeat, optimistic spirit and above all, urged Texas Baptists to keep a strong faith in God.

Despite the Depression, Williams led Texas Baptists in some major new initiatives. He led a new push for support of the Cooperative Program in Texas, and made a major emphasis upon leading the churches to adopt the budget system and to use the every member canvass. He launched major new summer evangelistic campaigns, and formed Pastors' Retreats over the state for the enlistment and encouragement of pastors. The rural churches of Texas never had a better friend than J. Howard Williams, who despite the stringent times managed to keep a "rural evangelist" in the field to head up "the work of country church rehabilitation and enlistment."[11]

When Williams resigned in 1936, the Board spoke of his "distinguished services" during his five year tenure and said, "From the hour he entered upon his responsible duties in the leadership of this Board, he has demonstrated a rare administrative ability, particularly in his capacity for organizing, inspiring and directing our forces." They added, "Coupled with this has been a statesmanlike vision and utterance, at all times progressive and constructive."[12]

Williams served as pastor of First Baptist, Amarillo from 1936 to 1940, when he moved to Oklahoma City as pastor at First Baptist Church. He returned to Dallas for his second term as Executive Secretary, serving from 1946-1953. Williams had proven himself as an effective leader, a man of vision and with a remarkable ability to unify and motivate Texas Baptists. In 1953 he was elected to succeed Eldred Douglas Head as president of Southwestern Baptist Theological Seminary in Fort Worth. Williams's imminently successful presidency was cut short by his death in 1958.[13]

Robert Clifford Campbell. On the same day that J. Howard Williams resigned, R. C. Campbell was elected General Secretary on the first ballot with a slim majority of 30 votes out of 59 cast. He was the second pastor of First Baptist, Lubbock, to be called to the Secretary's chair, after W. R. White in 1930. Born in North Carolina, Campbell graduated from Carson-Newman College in Tennessee and attended Southwestern Seminary in Fort Worth. Campbell was also a writer of some note, with six books to his credit.[14]

By the time Campbell came to leadership, the Depression had eased considerably and Texas Baptist ministries showed remarkable progress on every hand. Campbell was a major leader in developing Southern Baptists' emphasis upon stewardship and tithing. His popular booklet *God's Plan* sold over 500,000 copies and helped shape Southern Baptist teaching and practice of stewardship. Campbell also launched the annual statewide Evangelism Conference which still ranks as one of the most important meetings of Texas Baptists. He said Baptist work in Texas could go forward on two legs, stewardship and soul-winning, and as General Secretary he emphasized both legs. He was an early advocate that Texas Baptists have their own headquarters building, and in the state work he established new departments for the Brotherhood, Endowment, and for ministries among the soldiers. He reestablished the Baptist Student Union Department which had lapsed some years earlier. He also led in promoting the Ministers Retirement Plan which by the end of his tenure included more than 1000 participating Texas Baptist churches.[15]

Campbell was an outstanding preacher, and churches were always after him to become their pastor. He abruptly resigned in 1938 to accept the pastorate of Immanuel Baptist in Little Rock, but apparently George W. Truett talked him out of it. A month later, Truett suggested that Campbell be re-elected with a salary raise, which was done, and Campbell remained another three years. However, in 1941 he did leave to accept the historic First Baptist Church of Columbia, South Carolina. In 1953 he was elected vice-president of the Southern Baptist Convention.

William Walter Melton. In 1941 the popular pastor who had served twenty-nine years at Seventh and James Church in Waco, W. W. Melton, was elected to succeed Campbell as Executive Secretary, after E. D. Head had declined the post. J. M. Dawson of Waco was among those who sought to change the election procedure by having the Executive Board appoint a search committee to bring a recommendation to the Board. This was voted down, and Melton was elected with 30 votes out of 47 cast, the other 17 votes being divided among 13 other nominees.[16]

Melton grew up as a West Texas cowboy, without formal education. He entered the junior college at Decatur at age twenty-two, and later earned a degree from Baylor University at age forty. He brought stability and maturity to the Convention work, strengthening several areas of ministry that had been curtailed during the Depression. It was Melton's good fortune to serve in days of prosperity, but much of that prosperity was bought at the price of World War II which brought its own problems to Texas Baptist churches. At the end of 1945 Melton resigned to return to Waco, this time as pastor of the Columbus Avenue Church where he served until his retirement in 1957 at age seventy-eight.

THE GREAT DEPRESSION

The American economy has had several periods of recession in the twentieth century, but The Depression of the early 1930s stands out for its severity and its indelible mark upon the nation's psyche. Those who lived through those terrible years were imprinted with a distinctive outlook and found their attitudes and actions permanently shaped by the hardships of that era. This was true among the churches as well as other institutions of society.

Among Texas Baptists, many churches had difficulty keeping a pastor on the field. The rural churches suffered most, some of them in effect lapsing. A number of churches stopped sending their mission offerings to the state convention, and examples are not lacking of pastors and treasurers who simply stopped sending their offerings without bothering to get approval or even inform the church.[17] Enrollment in the Baptist colleges and the Seminary in Fort Worth declined and even the popular Buckner Orphans Home had to scramble to care for its large family.

As a result of the Depression, the available ministry resources of the Executive Board diminished sharply. In 1930 W. R. White spoke of "the terrific financial adjustments that have characterized this year," and noted that falling prices and rising unemployment worsened daily.[18] The Executive Board had to take emergency action. In what the *Baptist Standard* called "Drastic Reductions," the Board cut salaries by 10%, and later cut another 10%.[19] These reductions included the top man, J. Howard Williams, whose $6,000 salary went to $5,400 and then to $4,800. Appropriations for the Sunday School and Training Union departments were cut by 50% and the WMU annual allocation was reduced from $9,500 to $6,000. The BSU work was dropped entirely. In 1933 the Convention had to discontinue aid to the associational missionaries, but Williams persuaded the Board to allow them a sixty-day grace period to try to find other employment.[20]

Even with these drastic measures, the Board continued to fall about $5,000 a month short of meeting expenses. Debts increased and Convention leaders had to struggle to renew the bank notes, though they often got more favorable interest rates. Responding to a resolution from FBC, El Paso, the Board set a day of special prayer concerning the "awful calamity" they were facing. The Board also made a special appeal to 100 strong churches to send immediate emergency offerings in addition to their regular contributions to offset the $5,000 a month shortfall.[21] They also appealed to wealthy donors, like John and Mary Hardin of Burk-burnett.

At the Convention office in Dallas no penny was spent without good reason. The office staff was greatly reduced, and expenses for office supplies and printing were cut to the bone. When Secretary Williams and Treasurer George Mason found it necessary to travel by train about the state on Convention business, they rented only one Pullman bed, where one of them slept a part of the night and then arose and let the other one sleep the remainder of the night in the same bed.[22]

Despite the Depression Texas Baptists continued to send a significant portion of their money outside the state. At the first meeting of the Baptist State Convention back in 1848 offerings were taken for foreign and home missions, and through the years Texas Baptists continued to give loyally for witness beyond their borders. However, one result of the heady days of the $75 Million Campaign and the resulting Cooperative Program was that Texas Baptist churches sent a much larger percentage of their total contributions to Nashville for SBC work and relatively less to Dallas for ministries within the borders of Texas. The Convention reported that despite depression and debts, in 1930 "more than 30 per cent of the total receipts coming to our office were sent to Southwide causes."[23] In 1938 that ratio had risen to 43% of Texas receipts going outside the state.[24] Fifty years later that had increased to over 48%.

Even the Great Depression did not last forever. The federal government passed legislation known collectively as the "New Deal," including the National Recovery Act which, according to many observers, helped to jolt the nation out of its economic doldrums. As jobs became available more people moved from the soup lines to the assembly lines, but at the same time ominous war clouds gathered over Europe. By 1936 the Executive Board could report that "Texas Baptists have emerged from the grievous period of depression, and we are convinced that insofar as our denominational affairs are concerned, we have come upon the hour of recovery."[25] Texas leaders noted such hopeful signs as "a wider enlistment of our people," "a genuine and deepening spirit of unity and cooperation," and "everywhere a heartening hopefulness." The same 1936 report affirmed that

> It appears that not only do our people possess the will to give, but that they have to a gratifying degree recovered the power to give, by reason of more stabilized incomes or improved economic conditions. While there is yet much distress among certain groups, on the whole there is undoubted improvement, for which we thank God and take courage.[26]

More churches could maintain full-time pastors, and the BGCT could sustain more missionaries. The departments for Sunday School, Training Union and Baptist Student Union were restored to their former strength, as was the Women's Missionary Union. Salary cuts were restored, and ministries that went dormant during the Depression were revived. What a contrast between the early and later 1930s! In the early 1930s the General Secretary had his salary cut by 20% to $4,800 and the Convention could not afford to furnish him a Pullman sleeper for a full night while he was traveling on official business; by the late 1930s his successor had his salary increased to $6,600 and the Board sent him on a full month of vacation to "New York or some other interesting place," with all expenses paid.[27] While the actual figures bear little resemblance to those of today, the annual receipts of the state convention in the 1940s were several times that of the early 1930s. Total receipts for 1931 were $435,255, about $55,000 under budget, and the Convention faced a debt well over $1 million. In 1946, the Convention received almost $3 million, all debts were paid, leaving a reserve in bonds. The BGCT met its goal of "debt-free by '43." On April 6, 1943, while Secretary Melton and board members McConnell, White, Williams, Groner, Springer, and Mrs. B. A. Copass watched, Treasurer George Mason held a facsimile copy of the last note paid off and Judge E. E. Cummings, president of the Baptist Brotherhood of Texas, put a match to it.[28]

THE DISTRICT PLAN

While pastor at Corsicana, J. Howard Williams had a growing conviction that Texas Baptists needed a better organization to do their work better. As director of budget promotion for the state convention he was keenly aware that in 1928 only 414 churches out of 3105 gave monthly to state mission causes.[29] "It is our belief, " he said, "that our organization is not such at the present time as best to enlist the leadership nor our people as a whole." The state is so large and Baptist ministries so extensive, Williams noted, that many churches lacked information about the overall ministries. He concluded that, "It is our belief that a plan is needed which will get closer to the people and tend to localize responsibility upon them."[30] "Closer to the people" is the key phrase here. For many pastors and even more laypeople, the Convention office in Dallas seemed distant indeed. Many of them never attended a state convention, and lines of communication were often weak. The result was that while the Dallas leaders planned their ministries, the churches out in the remote regions either never heard of these plans or felt little responsibility for work which seemed so distant. Clearly Williams had in mind far-reaching changes. He said, "This old high powered collection and round-up system has made Texas famous and perhaps I had better say infamous and it has been a most difficult thing for many of the brethren to believe that the work could be carried on under any other plan."[31]

Williams, who had a gift for enlistment and promotion, came up with a plan to bring all the churches into a closer cooperation with the state convention. He chaired the "Committee on Plans for Better Enlistment of our Associations and Churches" which reported to the BGCT in 1930.

Their proposals, later known as "the Williams Plan," suggested that the state convention adopt seventeen regions or "districts" in Texas as the basis for promotion and enlistment. Each district would be headed by a "district missionary," elected by a committee from the associations but partially supported by the state convention. The report said,

> Let us accept as a working basis the seventeen districts into which Texas has been divided, each being composed of five to ten associations. Make the associations units of operation for the districts and the districts units of operation next to the Baptist General Convention of Texas for all of our work, including the co-operative program, evangelism, the W.M.U., the Sunday School, the B.Y.P.U., and the Laymen's Union. The territorial boundaries of all these departments should, of course, coincide.[32]

Such district divisions were of course not new to Texas Baptists. In 1908 the Baptist Women Mission Workers divided the state into districts for the better promotion of their work. That year only the Central District and the Southwest District were formed but other districts followed: East (Palestine), Northeast (Winnsboro), North (Gainsville), Panhandle (Goodnight), West (El Paso), United (Houston), Central West (Abilene), and Central South (Temple).[33] In time the women formed seventeen districts in their effort to bring their work closer to the churches. The BYPU and Sunday School leaders later adopted the same "co-terminous" district boundaries as the basis for their work. The obvious success of this plan in bringing the work closer to the churches attracted the interest of the state convention. Williams is often credited with inventing the district plan, but the record shows that instead he adopted and adapted a plan that had been pioneered and proven by the Baptist women. This was neither the first nor last time Baptist women pioneered plans which were later adopted by the entire denomination with little acknowledgment of their origins.[34]

The "district missionary" formed a liaison between the associations and the state convention. He was elected by a committee from the associations (with input from the state office) and received one-fourth of his salary from the state office. The district missionaries functioned largely as regional deputies of the General Secretary and thus could be counted on to promote the state convention program vigorously. "We recommend," said the Convention, "that it be understood that these men employed [district missionaries] shall work in closest harmony with the executive Board and the General Secretary in promoting all the work of the Convention."[35] Before the district plan was inaugurated, the associational leaders could promote the state program or not as they chose. Williams pointed out as one of the "glaring weaknesses" of the old plan that "The Association is not directly responsible to any other organization."[36] Under the new plan, Williams noted, "the churches report to the Associations, the Associations to the Districts and the Districts to the Convention." Each district would hold its annual convention in the fall, which in effect provided a "mini-convention" in many parts of the state. This involved pastors and laymen who would never have had any opportunity for leadership in the state body, and it brought Baptist meetings to many parts of the state that could not host a state convention. Some districts and associations engaged in friendly rivalry, provoking one another to good works, as they strove to outdo one another in enlistment, evangelism, and financial support for Baptist work in Texas. The *Baptist Standard* regularly published reports from various districts showing the number of baptisms, the number of churches giving to missions monthly, the percentage of churches in the district giving, the number of churches not giving all year, and the amounts given. The result, whether intended or not, was to put each district missionary under pressure to produce.

The head of the district was called a "missionary," but his work was quite different from the "general missionaries" appointed earlier by the state convention. Though still involved in evangelism and church planting, the district missionary was primarily a representative of the state convention to promote the overall program, enlist cooperation among the churches and pastors, and to lead the churches to adopt the budget system and contribute to missions monthly through the Dallas office. W. W. Melton later described the district missionaries as "pastors at large." He said, "What the teacher is to a class, what the superintendent is to the school, what the pastor is to the church, what the General Secretary is to the work of our State—that the District Missionary is to his district. . . . It is their business to promote every interest of the Kingdom of God, and to keep all of the churches, so far as it is within his power, in accord with the general plan of our denominational work."[37] The district missionary always attended the various associational meetings, where he shared information, inspiration, and promotional emphases. He also carried a display of Bibles and books, which he set up for sale on a table or church pew, an important ministry for churches far removed from a Baptist or any other kind of book store.[38]

Though both Convention and Executive Board expressed approval of the new district plan, it was put into effect slowly and over some opposition. It was not until Williams was elected General Secretary in 1931 that the plan was assured of acceptance. Even so, some parts of the plan were never inaugurated, such as moving the state convention meeting to January. The general consensus was that the district plan, once in full operation, was an overwhelming success, though in time tensions developed between the district and state leaders. The district plan remained in operation until 1963 when it was replaced by the smaller "Area" divisions.

A NEAR MISS

In 1933 the Convention voted to seek reconciliation with the Baptist Missionary Association (BMA), the dissident group that split off at the turn of the century in the Hayden controversy. The BGCT appointed a twenty-five member committee, headed by Walter H. McKenzie, chairman of the Executive Board, and the BMA appointed a like committee headed by A. O. Hinkle.[39] Negotiations went well when the two committees met and a joint meeting of Baptists from both groups convened in 1934 at the FBC of Oak Cliff in Dallas and pronounced that "Misunderstandings, misconceptions and prejudices have been removed." At their November convention in 1934 the BGCT readily revised their constitution to welcome the BMA churches into affiliation. At an emotional service, with tears of joy and messages from both groups, George Truett led the prayer of reconciliation and the entire convention "began to sing 'Amazing Grace' and rejoiced greatly."

It looked like a done deal, but the reconciliation never came off. In 1935 the BMA convention not only voted down the reconciliation, but also voted to end all discussions. Despite efforts by the Executive Board to minimize objections, there was considerable opposition on both sides.[40] Some BMA people objected to terminology from the BGCT side that implied this was not really a merger of two groups but the absorption of one group by another. When official reconciliation failed, the steady stream of individual BMA churches transferring their affiliation to the BGCT increased.

THE COUNTRY CHURCHES

The Great Depression was damaging for all Baptist work in Texas, but it was devastating for the country churches. In the 1930s about 2,400 Texas Baptist churches were in open country or in villages of fewer than 500 population. Most of the 700 churches then classified as urban, in towns of over 500, would today be considered rural. Already social and demographic changes were underway which would change forever the shape of rural America. The government estimate for average annual income in Texas at that time was $1,017 per family, but farm income was far below that.[41] Few of the country churches could maintain a pastor. Many closed entirely, while some tried to maintain Sunday School with occasional preaching whenever a preacher happened through the community. Of course, missionary contributions from the country churches declined radically.

The country churches never had a better friend than J. Howard Williams, General Secretary of the Executive Board. He saw at once that the future of Baptist life in Texas was inseparably intertwined with their base in the country churches. Williams asked for and received approval to employ a "rural evangelist" to travel among the country churches. F. V. McFatridge, pastor at Llano, commenced "the work of country church rehabilitation and enlistment" on January 1, 1934. Since the work was new, nobody knew for sure what the rural evangelist was to do, and Williams was given the greatest freedom in defining the work. Even so, the actual work on the field did not always match entirely the duties discussed in the Dallas board room. McFatridge traveled among the country churches, encouraging those that lived, trying to gather the remnant of members to reconstitute those that had lapsed, working out plans for at least occasional preaching by pastors of neighboring churches, and helping weak churches obtain pastors. He attended countless associational workers' conferences, spoke in district conventions, and attended the national Rural Church Conference held at Texas A&M University in 1934. He wrote many articles for the papers and held revivals in rural communities. In some cases, McFatridge led contiguous rural churches to merge and for those that could not maintain a full-time pastor, he encouraged neighboring churches to call a pastor whom they shared from Sunday to Sunday. One of his most effective innovations was the state-wide Rural Pastors' Conference held at Mt. Calm in December, 1934. The Executive Board was pleased with the results of the rural church ministry. They noted that in one year largely as a result of McFatridge's ministry, 1,339 rural churches contributed to missions compared to only 952 the year before.[42]

For a time Willis J. Ray served as "Superintendent of Rural Evangelism," but resigned in 1944 to become the first Executive Secretary-Treasurer of the newly formed Baptist General Convention of Arizona. His successor in the rural ministry was A. B. White, pastor at Paris, who received one-half of his salary from the Home Mission Board in Atlanta.[43] However, by then the approach to rural church ministry had changed, with the districts assuming more of the responsibility. As part of his duties White also served as assistant to the General Secretary, especially as liaison between the state office and the districts.

Laudable as the work among rural churches appeared, not everyone approved of the way it was done. R. R. Cumbie, a rural pastor, wrote in 1932 of his resentment of the constant reference to "the rural church problem."[44] Cumbie had been a rural pastor since 1906 and he said the problems of rural churches were no different from those of churches everywhere. He complained that many preachers were not willing to serve the rural churches or, if they did, they lived somewhere else. He noted that few rural pastors live on the field, and said, "Brother, you may do the preaching for your church and not live on the field, but you certainly can't do the pastoral work and not live on the field." Warming to his subject, Cumbie said "Another problem in the country church is the lack of cooperation on the part of our 'big brothers.' They will not go out to the country churches for meetings for lack of funds at the close of the meeting. They seek the larger centers where there is more wealth, and hence, a larger offering at the close of the meeting." If many people shared Cumbie's complaints, the records do not reveal it.

THE TEXAS CENTENNIAL

In 1936 the Lone Star State celebrated the one-hundred year anniversary of its freedom from Mexico. Texans from the state house to the courthouse went all-out to recount their past, magnify the present, and look forward confidently to the future. Pageants, historical dramas, displays of Texanic memorabilia, essay contests, interviews with old people who had lived through the pioneer days, and publication of articles, books, and collections of photographs marked this year-long celebration. The Texas legislature, universities and colleges, businesses, historical societies, and public schools were all involved in this year of remembrance and anticipation. The churches were also involved. All the major denominations in Texas participated in the celebration, including the Baptists.

Perhaps the major public event in this centennial year was the Centennial Central Exposition which opened at the state fair grounds in Dallas on June 6, 1936. Lone Star Gas Company gave $50,000, a considerable sum in 1936, to erect a Hall of Religions at the Exposition, which was open to displays by the various denominations in the state. What was called "the Baptist Booth" in the Hall of Religions was far more than the word "booth" may imply today.

Early on the Executive Board elected Earl B. Smyth to chair the Baptist Centennial Committee and that committee named the creative T. C. Gardner, head of the Baptist Training Union of Texas, as Director of Centennial Activities, assisted by W. W. Chancellor of Mineral Wells, C. S. McKinney of San Benito, C. E. Lancaster of Pampa, and Mrs. R. T. Wilson of Austin.[45] In time the Centennial Committee was enlarged to include L. R. Scarborough, Fort Worth; Wallace Bassett, Dallas; William Fleming, Fort Worth; J. F. Kimball, Dallas; J. Howard Williams, Amarillo; Cullen F. Thomas, Dallas; Millard A. Jenkins, Abilene; J. B. Tidwell, Waco; J. M. Dawson, Waco; J. C. Hardy, Belton; and R. C. Campbell, Dallas.[46] Gardner was released from his BTU duties to devote one half of his time to the centennial project.

Extensive displays in the Baptist Booth of the Hall of Religions spotlighted the Baptist role in early Texas history. The displays told of Baptist martyrs at the Alamo and Goliad and Baptists who fought at San Jacinto. Baptists helped populate the new state, and established schools, colleges, newspapers, and churches. The display included "balopticon pictures" of Baptist pioneers, sites and institutions, including the blacksmith shop of Noah Byars, a picture of the first Primitive Baptist church in Texas in 1834, a picture of Rock Creek near Independence where R. C Burleson baptized General Sam Houston in 1854, the historic old church at Independence, pictures of Baylor University and Baylor College for Women, along with Texas Baptist leaders past and present.[47] Murals around the walls depicted historical scenes and glass cases displayed historical photographs, rare books and Bibles, along with documents, diaries and parchments. Amidst all this remarkable exhibition in the summer of 1936, many Baptists seemed most impressed with the air-conditioning of the building (by what method is not stated). It was reported that about 600,000 persons visited the Baptist exhibit in Dallas.[48]

Besides the exhibits, Baptists presented over a two-week period six outstanding speakers, several musical events, and a widely acclaimed historical drama. "Give Me Texas" was written by J. M. Dawson and presented by the Baylor University Little Theater with the help of a generous grant from Fort Worth oil man William H. Fleming. Speakers included George W. Truett, pastor in Dallas and president of the Baptist World Alliance; Robert G. Lee, pastor of Bellevue Baptist Church in Memphis, Tennessee; Pat M. Neff, president of Baylor University and former governor of Texas; M. E. Dodd, then pastor of First Baptist Church in Shreveport, Louisiana; C. Oscar Johnson, pastor of Third Baptist Church in St. Louis, Missouri; and L. K. Williams, pastor of the Olivet Baptist Church in Chicago and president of the National Baptist Convention, USA, the major convention of African-American churches in America. Baptist churches in and around Dallas made up choirs of 700 to 800 voices, directed on different evenings by Robert H. Coleman, pastor's assistant at FBC in Dallas; Harry P. Wootan, educational director at the Gaston Avenue Baptist Church in Dallas; J. B. Christian, music director of the Cliff Temple Baptist Church in Dallas; Shelby Collier, music director at the Ervay Street Baptist Church in Dallas; and C. S. Cadwallader, pastor of the East Dallas Baptist Church. When Dr. L. K. Williams spoke on "The Contribution of Baptist Negroes to the Growth and Development of Texas," the Choir was directed by the famous African-American contralto soloist, Lula Hurst of Kansas City.[49]

In addition to its premier presentation at the Dallas Exhibition, Dawson's drama, "Give Me Texas," also played to rave reviews at the BGCT meeting in Mineral Wells and at Southwestern Seminary in Fort Worth. Paul Baker, professor in the Baylor University Speech Department directed the drama, and Kathleen Cole played the lead role of Mrs. Sam Houston. Scores of local plays, dramas, and musicals were presented at churches, colleges, and other public occasions. Special publications during 1936 included a centennial issue of the *Baptist Standard,* highly prized today, "The Texas Baptist Centennial," a twenty-four-page booklet by T. C. Gardner, and *The Centennial Story of Texas Baptists,* a 434 page book edited by L. R. Elliott of Southwestern Seminary.

For Baptists, one important by-product of the centennial was an upsurge of interest in their own history. As early as March, 1933, the BGCT appointed a Committee on the Preservation of Baptist History, led by Harlan J. Matthews, chairman, and Alvin Swindell and W. E. B. Lockridge. The committee suggested that the library of Southwestern Seminary, presided over by L. R. Elliott, be designated as the official depository for Texas Baptist historical materials. The committee visited the Seminary Library and found a great deal of Texas historical data already on hand, including rare books, minutes, photographs, periodicals, the papers of both B. H. and J. M. Carroll, and extensive materials from J. R. Graves of Tennessee given by his son-in-law O. L. Hailey. Much of the material was not yet properly bound and catalogued. The committee report merits quotation at length.

> Your committee therefore makes the following recommendations:
> (1). That the Baptist General Convention of Texas officially designate a place which shall be known as the depository for Baptist historical materials for Texas.

(2). That a suitable person be appointed for superintendency over this matter, who shall be responsible for such historical materials and for the labors which may be performed upon the same.

(3). We recommend, inasmuch as the Seminary is the place where, and largely the agent whereby the above mentioned materials are now assembled, that the relation between the Convention and the Seminary on this matter be definitely defined.

(4). That this [Executive] Board recommend that the Convention take, or authorize to be taken, the steps necessary for the maintenance of such depository as suggested above, and in whatsoever measure as in the judgment of the Convention may seem wise.[50]

Further emphasis upon heritage came from George Truett's address in 1933 on "One Hundred Years of Baptist Growth in Texas." In 1934 J. Howard Williams discovered stacks of Baptist papers and records housed at the Ross Avenue church in Dallas, and had them moved to the newly designated state convention depository at Southwestern Seminary. At the convention meeting in 1935, J. B. Tidwell read a telegram calling for Baptists to raise $1,500 to save the ruined walls of the old Independence church, cradle of Texas Baptist history and "oldest Baptist church shrine in Texas."[51] This renewed interest of Texas Baptists in their heritage led to formation of the Texas Baptist Historical Society on November 11, 1938 with thirty charter members by 1939.[52] However, by far the most ambitious result of Texas Baptists' renewed interest in their history during the 1930s was *The Centennial Story of Texas Baptists,* published by the Executive Board in 1936. This topical approach was concluded with charts, photographs, and a list of Texas Baptist foreign missionaries.

HOW SHALL THEY HEAR?

By the 1930s Texas Baptists had a growing bureaucracy of agencies, committees, and boards but the focus remained upon the spiritual needs of individuals. From the crowded coastal cities to the remote Davis Mountains of the Big Bend area, spiritual needs and opportunities beckoned, and Texas Baptists tried heroically to respond to those needs. If they failed to address all of them adequately, it was not for lack of trying. During the depression year of 1931, the Executive Board supported a total of 155 state mission workers, including 34 associational missionaries, 75 missionary pastors, 21 workers among the foreign speaking population of Texas, seven full-time evangelists, and 18 state workers in Sunday School, Baptist Young Peoples work, and Woman's Missionary Union.[53] These numbers expanded dramatically after recovery from the depression.

In addition to the Anglo population, Texas Baptists also sought to address the spiritual needs of other groups within the state.

European Texans. From the beginning Texas had a sizeable population of immigrants from Europe, most of whom sought to hold on to their language, general culture and especially their religion. Texas Baptists seemed fascinated by these non-English speakers and made ongoing efforts to evangelize them to the Baptist way. A 1930 report said, "Secretary White discussed the foreign population in our midst and asked the Board for authority to employ Jno. A. Held for a brief period, in order that he might make a complete survey of the foreign population of our state, with a view to meeting as early as possible, our missionary obligation to these people."[54] Held's preliminary survey showed about 500,000 Europeans in the state, concentrated primarily in South Texas; Lavaca County, for example, was made up of about 90% Europeans, with Bohemians predominating.[55] Held was employed to direct the Baptist mission work among the Europeans, and at one time he had as many as twenty-one fellow missionaries in the task. In 1936 Held asked for and received an allotment of $325 to purchase a large gospel tent for use in revivals in the European communities.[56] At the same time the Board declined the request of Harry S. Bernabey, an itinerant Italian preacher, for $250 to purchase an automobile with a loud speaker for street preaching.

By far the most extensive survey of Europeans in Texas came in 1936. Whether the result of growth, better statistics or both, that survey, supplemented by statistics from government sources, showed 747,714 Europeans in Texas, about half of them foreign born.[57] The largest numbers came from, in descending order, Germany, Bohemia, Italy, Scandinavia, Austria, France, Poland, and Russia. Texas cities with large European populations included Houston (41,212); Galveston (26,204); San Antonio (34,397); Dallas (33,263); Austin (9,923); Fort Worth (12,087); Waco (10,040); and Beaumont (7,014).[58] This meant that about 17% of all white Texans were of European origin. "Unless we enter these fields now," said the report, "we are sure to lose out." Held remained as director of Texas Baptists' ministry among Europeans until his retirement in 1940.

African Texans. The spiritual needs of the large black population of Texas claimed the attention of the BGCT, though it appears that when all was said and done, much was said and little done. Most black Texans who were church members were Baptists, with most non-members at least predisposed toward Baptists. The picture was complicated by the fact that black Baptist churches were divided into three overlapping state conventions all doing similar kinds of work. Partly at the request of black leaders, Charles T. Alexander was appointed in early 1936 to correlate BGCT cooperative ministries with black Baptists in Texas. In reporting on his first year, Alexander said that "the work has been inter-racial and co-operative."[59] Hitherto, most BGCT ministries had been aimed at the masses, but Alexander pioneered a program trying to bring together the pastors and lay leaders of the two races. "The two races, and our two Baptist groups, do not know each other today as they should," he said. "Our future with them must be built on a new and better understanding."

Alexander concentrated more on teaching and training than upon direct evangelism, which he felt could best be done by black pastors. He conducted numerous Bible Conferences and Workers Institutes involving both black and white leaders. His description of several regional Workers Institutes is instructive:

> Our programs usually run from Monday night to Friday night, with three meetings each day after Monday. We have thus used about 60 Negro speakers, and about 30 white speakers. We have thus brought together 90 leaders in mutual conference and fellowship. As to my own part on programs, I have delivered 70 doctrinal and expository addresses concerning our work to white and colored churches, and 10 addresses before colored state and district conventions. I have had part in the ordination of 7 deacons and four candidates for the ministry; and in each case I conducted the examination and then delivered an address. I have thus delivered about 100 addresses in all; and this does not include regular sermons delivered in white churches.[60]

Alexander also distributed to black pastors and church leaders large quantities of books, Study Course materials, and Sunday School and BYPU literature provided by the Sunday School Board in Nashville.

The two main objectives of Alexander's ministry were: first, to strengthen the black churches by educational efforts among their leader and, second, to change the attitudes of white Baptists toward their black fellow-believers. "The enlightenment of our own white people concerning the present status of the Negro race in America, and at our own door, and the character of cooperative service we can render with them, is one of our heaviest tasks of the present hour,"Alexander said. He urged Texas Baptists to imagine what one million Texas Baptists, 400,000 black and 600,000 white, could do in ministry together "as a common fellowship in a common cause."

The response of black Baptists to these efforts was generally receptive, but cautious. "Their whole-hearted response has been a matter of hesitation," Alexander noted. "They must first be convinced that we are sincerely wanting to help and to cooperate with them, and not dictate or try to rule them. Who can blame them?"

Upon Alexander's retirement in 1943, the work changed and expanded as the Executive Board called for a Superintendent of Inter-Racial Work whose ministry would include evangelistic efforts among the Jews in Texas.

Mexicans in Texas. In 1910 the *Convención Bautista Mexicana de Texas* was formed in San Antonio, but the work progressed slowly. The Great Depression called new attention to the plight of Mexicans in Texas. In 1930 Secretary W. R. White "presented the Mexican situation and asked that Paul C. Bell be employed to make a survey of the Mexican population in our state."[61] The challenge of what Bell found led to the appointment of E. J. Gregory of San Antonio by the Executive Board as their "Missionary to the Mexicans" of Texas.[62] The 1934 session of the Mexican Convention received messengers from thirty-one churches, and planned evangelistic campaigns, took an offering for the local Baptist hospital, and heard the plan of the Mexican WMU, led by Mrs. Jovita Delgado, to launch a ministry to Mexican orphans in Texas.[63] Five years later, in 1939, the *Convencion* meeting in Harlingen, reported a total of 100 churches, plus fifty missions, with a baptized membership over 7,000, plus thousands of interested hearers. At that meeting the Mexican Baptists agreed to translate R. C. Campbell's book *God's Plan* to promote stewardship. They launched a new periodical, *El Bautista Mexicano,* with the first issue appearing on July 10, 1939. They also reported 1,500 baptisms for the year. Some Mexican churches formed their own *associaciones* while others affiliated with the predominantly Anglo associations.

A number of other missionaries worked with Gregory, including some sponsored in Texas by the Home Mission Board in Atlanta. When the political situation in Mexico forced the Foreign Mission Board to curtail their work there they redirected four of their missionaries to work in Texas, provided only that the BGCT pay their relocation costs.[64]

Mexican Baptists in Texas had a long history of itinerant Bible study sessions, in which they held regional study groups in various locations for a few days or a few weeks. However, many longed for more permanent training opportunities. Paul C. Bell had the unique role for several years of serving as pastor of both the Anglo and Mexican churches in Bastrop, dividing his time between them. He resigned the Anglo church to devote his full time to educational ministry among the Mexicans. He led in forming the *Instituto Bautista Mexicana de Bastrop,* emphasizing both secular and religious training. The first building was erected on a site donated by Mrs. S. J. Orgain, an Anglo member of FBC Bastrop. She also gave $700 to start the building. Bell won the support of Mexicans and partial support from the Home Mission Board but, for some reason, the BGCT never looked with any great favor upon his school. The Mexican Baptist Institute was closed in 1941 when Bell, whose wife had just died, left to become a missionary in Panama.

In 1936 the Mexican Baptist Seminary opened in San Antonio, led by J. H. Benson, for thirty years a missionary to Mexico. The Seminary was delayed somewhat by the resignation of Secretary J. Howard Williams, but eventually opened with twenty students. Most of the students received scholarships from the Foreign Mission Board, Home Mission Board, the Baptist Convention of Old Mexico, the Texas Baptist WMU or from some local church. Later the Seminary was moved to El Paso, then to Torreón and eventually to Mexico City. A third school operated at El Paso under the direction of A. Vélez, the *Instituto Anglo-Americana.*

Prominent Mexican Baptist leaders in Texas during the 1930s included Jorge B. Mixim, Hattie Amelia Greenlaw Pierson, Adelina V. García and his wife Matías, and Emetrio V. Rodríguez. Mexican Baptists grew rapidly, with many responsive revivals in the churches. However, their relation to Anglo Baptists, while mostly cordial, had its tensions. Mexicans, many of whom sprang from ancestors who had been in Texas long before the Anglos came, resented being considered a part of the "foreign population." The label *Chicano* originated as a blending of the words *chihuahua* and *Mexicano*. The term embodies an economic and cultural protest, in what Mexican Baptists called a "battle for identification."[65]

MINISTRY DEPARTMENTS

The departments for Sunday School, Baptist Young People's Union, and Woman's Missionary Union all faced financial crises during the depression, but with reduced staff and less money they kept their essential ministries alive and, in fact, experienced some increase in enrollment in the churches. The Baptist Student Union did not fare so well; during the worst of the depression the BSU was abolished and its ministries assigned directly to the General Secretary. Toward the end of this period the Baptist Brotherhood, an organization for men, was formed and in 1945 they elected a full-time director.

Sunday School. In the years between the two World Wars, the Sunday School rapidly assumed larger functions among Baptists. In addition to teaching the Bible, the Sunday School became the major engine for enlistment, evangelism, and stewardship in the local church. Described as a "great agency for finding, teaching and winning people," the Sunday School was also regarded as a way to improve worship, increase prayer, and encourage righteous living.[66] As more churches went on the budget system and the old "Roundup" method of one or two special collections a year diminished, the Sunday School became the major collection agency for the local church. With its emphasis upon making regular offerings every week, not just to raise money but as a part of worship, and its teaching on tithing, the Sunday School helped to transform Texas Baptists' understanding and practice of stewardship. "We have largely assigned the colossal and blessed task of financing the work of Christ at home and abroad to the Sunday school," said a 1933 report. "The teacher therefore must not only convince the student of the Bible doctrine of tithes and offerings but he must lead the student to bring these 'tithes and offerings' into the storehouse that they may be used for the spread of the gospel around the world."[67]

In the 1930s the Sunday School Department of the state convention promoted the work vigorously. The "Sunday School missionary" in charge of the department was Granville Shelby Hopkins, who had served since 1925. Most Baptist churches in Texas had Sunday Schools; a 1934 report, for example, showed a few more Sunday Schools than churches and a total enrollment of 441,000.[68] There were seventeen district Sunday School conventions, each with its organization, promotion and annual convention. This extensive organizational network culminated in a statewide Sunday School convention. Hopkins and his associate, Andrew Allen, traveled constantly about the state conducting training workshops, leading summer assemblies, and directing enlargement campaigns in the churches. Andrew Allen, who later worked for the Sunday School Board in Nashville, served as associate from 1930 to 1934. W. J. Lites left his position as educational director for FBC, Galveston, to become associate in the state Sunday School department in 1934 and served until his resignation in 1945 to become state Sunday School secretary of New Mexico.[69]

Until the depression curtailed their work, the Sunday School Department had a fairly generous annual allotment for their work. The Sunday School Board in Nashville contributed $7,400 to their work in 1930 and for several years thereafter which, the department reported, "makes possible the great increase in rural work."[70] The Nashville Board sent many of its top workers to Texas to promote the work, including such stalwarts as J. N. Barnette, Harold E. Ingraham, Mary Alice Biby, and Sibley Burnett. T. A. Holcomb, head of the Sunday School Board and former General Secretary of the BGCT Executive Board, was also a frequent visitor to Texas. Gone were the days when Texas Sunday Schools had to search for suitable lesson study materials. The Nashville Board produced and marketed aggressively an excellent line of literature geared to all ages from the cradle to the grave, with helpful publications for teachers and superintendents. There soon developed a conviction that for a Southern Baptist church to use other than the Southern Baptist literature out of Nashville would be tantamount to denominational disloyalty. Use of a common study materials by all the churches led to a common outlook and even a degree of uniformity among Baptist churches and certainly helped promote denominational identity and loyalty.

Like other Southern Baptists, Texas churches resisted the large independent classes like Baracca for men and Philalethia for women. These large classes operated as independent organizations, elected their own officers and teachers, and kept their own budget and ministry projects separate from the churches. At times the classes promoted their own projects to the neglect of the church, and tension and conflict between church and class often resulted. Texas Baptist leaders consistently promoted the church connected classes which made the Sunday School an ally rather than a competitor of the church. One emphasis of the 1930 report was that the Sunday School "should be controlled by the church, and is entitled to the support of the church."[71]

By the 1940s Texas had a number of churches with Sunday School weekly attendance of more than fifteen hundred. The largest was Cliff Temple Baptist Church in Dallas with 2121 attending on January 14, 1945.[72] Other churches with over 1,500 attending that Sunday included FBC, Dallas (1,916); Travis Avenue, Fort Worth (1,625); and FBC, San Antonio (1,626); and FBC, Amarillo (1,659). Those with more than a thousand included FBC, Austin (1,167 on January 21); FBC, Beaumont (1,030); Gaston Avenue, Dallas (1,484); Broadway, Fort Worth (1,299); FBC, Galveston (1,042); FBC, Houston (1,218); Second Baptist, Houston (1,225); South Main, Houston (1,292); FBC, Lubbock (1,401); and FBC, Wichita Falls (1,017).

Another dimension of Sunday School ministry that grew rapidly during these years was the Daily Vacation Bible School. The VBS was an effort to extend the work of the Sunday School on weekdays during the summer when the children were out of school. Homer Grice, first VBS director at the Sunday School Board in Nashville, with his wife pioneered in creating a Southern Baptist literature for study in these weekday schools. Texas churches reported seventy such weekday schools in 1934, but that number mushroomed to 364 in 1939.[73] By 1945 Texas had twenty-two teams of "Invincibles," teams of young people, going about the state conducting VBS, taking census, enlisting workers, and teaching study course books.

Baptist Young People's Union. Thurman Cleveland Gardner served as state director of the BYPU work from 1916 to 1956. He guided many changes not only in BYPU, but in all dimensions of Texas Baptist religious education in the churches. He developed the eight-point record system which was widely used in Baptist churches, and he published many books on Training Union work. Gardner served as president of the College of Marshall from 1913 to 1916, and after his retirement from the Training Union work forty years later he returned as vice-president of that college, by then named East Texas Baptist College at Marshall.[74] A man of vision and creativity, Gardner was at the forefront of many advances in religious education in the churches. His influence reached far beyond Texas; his pioneering work helped shape the Baptist Training Union for all Southern Baptists.

The BYPU work grew rapidly under Gardner's leadership. In the decade from 1920 to 1930, the number of unions (classes) increased from 2193 to 4648 and the enrollment from 64,121 to 122,774.[75] By the time of Gardner's retirement, enrollment had reached 400,000. Gardner was a passionate apostle of the training ministry in the churches. He defined the three-fold purpose of the BYPU as soul winning, training in church membership, and missions. "The missionaries of tomorrow," he said, "are in the B.Y.P.U. of today."[76] The state work was organized into at least ninety-two associational and seventeen district BYPU conventions, culminating in a popular and well-attended state convention. Like the Sunday Schools, the BYPU made a concerted effort to reach the rural churches. Until depression budget cuts hit them, the BYPU department received about $7,500 annually from the state convention and a like amount of supplement from the Sunday School Board in Nashville.

One avid advocate of the training work was W.W. Melton, pastor of the influential Seventh and James church in Waco, and later General Secretary of the Executive Board. Melton said of the BYPU, "It has discovered our leaders, and has trained them for service, and has turned them over to the church capable of carrying on every department of church work."[77] Melton noted that

> Formerly churches were made up of older people almost altogether, there being no place for young people; but this movement [BYPU] has opened the doors of the church to younger people, who come with their

zeal, their vision, and their vigor. . . . They have driven back the prevailing spirit of Hardshellism and have given us a program of evangelism and missions. . . . We hail this movement as a blessing from Heaven.[78]

The name of the Baptist Young People's Union fit very well so long as it remained an organization for youth. But, as sketched in an earlier chapter, the unions became so popular that younger children as well as adults wanted to participate. Expansion to include all age groups led to the need for a name change. The matter was under discussion by 1927 and in 1931 the name was changed to Baptist Training Service (BTS), though the Primary and Junior Unions retained the name of BYPU.[79] In 1934 the SBC adopted the name of Baptist Training Union (BTU) and urged all states to fall into line with a common name, which Texas did in December, 1934.[80] Despite the official change, many older Baptists continued to use the familiar BYPU even to recent years. Some larger churches created separate departments for Young Adults and Senior Adults, and some added a separate "junior-adult" department to distinguish young marrieds from young singles. Gardner said, "The young married people need to be enlisted and trained. They will not enroll in an adult union if the majority of the adults are considered 'old' people."[81]

In November 1934 Gardner reported that 250 Texas churches had more in attendance in the evening BTU than in the morning Sunday School. However, that was hardly the norm. On the high attendance day of January 14, 1945, only three churches reported more than 500 in BTU. First Baptist, San Antonio, led with 642, followed by FBC, Amarillo (538) and FBC, Dallas (516), though Travis Avenue, Fort Worth, came close with 491.[82]

For the most part a sympathetic, even symbiotic, relationship existed between the ministry departments of SS, BTU, BSU and WMU. The Sunday School Department workers regarded theirs as the lead organization in the churches, and at times they chafed under the aggressive and successful advances of the Training Union Department. Tension surfaced occasionally over budget allocations and who was allowed more office staff and field workers. The relationship between BTU in the churches and BSU on the college campuses was especially close. Despite their various acronyms, most of these organizations did similar work. All majored on evangelism, missions and training in church membership. In the summer of 1934 the BTU sponsored 487 students from Texas Baptist colleges for eight days of evangelism in churches throughout the state, with no expenses to the churches except travel and hospitality for the youth. This was quite similar to the effort of the Invincibles sponsored by the Sunday School.

Woman's Missionary Union. Baptist women in Texas in the 1930s spent little time contemplating their own personal and spiritual enrichment. Instead, their eyes looked outward upon the needs of others and their hearts and hands united in efforts to help the poor, minister to children, support the missionaries and share the gospel with all. As the name implied, the WMU was a *missionary* group.

In 1931 Mrs. F. S. Davis completed twenty-five years as president of the Texas WMU and in that time had never missed a meeting of the Executive Board or the state convention. Cricket Keys Copass was elected president and continued in office until 1946. Cricket Keys was born in Alabama but moved to Johnson County, Texas, as a child. After graduation from Baylor she taught at Waxahachie where she also served as organist at First Baptist Church. The pastor at Waxahachie was B. A. Copass, a young widower. He and Cricket were married in 1904, and they later moved to Fort Worth where he served as a professor at the Southwestern Seminary.[83] Other officers during this period were Mrs. W. D. Howell, Recording Secretary (1926-1947); Mrs. Olivia Davis, Treasurer (1925-1945); and Corresponding Secretaries Mrs. J. E. Leigh (1923-1938) and Mrs. E. F. Lyon (1938-1942). Leaders in the young people's work (YWA) included Mrs. T. C. Jester (1926-1935), Mrs. J. E. Williamson (1936-1937), Miss Ann Hasselstine Stallworth (1937-1938), and Marie (Mrs. R. L.) Mathis (1938-1945).[84]

Marie Wiley grew up in Wichita Falls and attended Midwestern State Teachers College there. After she married Robert L. Mathis, a young pastor, Marie became active in WMU work. In 1936 she was elected state Benevolence Chair and two years later became YWA director. After her husband's death, Mrs. Mathis served for a time on staff at FBC, Dallas, and later as BSU director for Baylor University. She would later serve as president of both the Texas WMU (1949-1955) and the Southwide WMU (1956-1963) and as second vice-president of the Southern Baptist Convention (1963).[85] Mathis, like her predecessors, brought great vision and energy to the WMU work in Texas.

The WMU pioneered the division of Texas into seventeen districts, each headed by a vice-president. They also had a large executive committee, and standing committees on missions, benevolence, education, young people, mission study, periodicals, personal service, and stewardship organization for promotion of its ministries. Another committee worked with Mrs. W. B. Garrity, superintendent of the Woman's Missionary Training School at the Southwestern Seminary in Fort Worth. The state WMU also had representatives to report for the Baptist Bible Institute in New Orleans, the Woman's Training School at Louisville, and the Margaret Fund of the Foreign Mission Board. The Margaret Fund was designed to provide aid (especially scholarship help) for the children of foreign missionaries back in the states to attend college. In 1933 Cricket Copass presented three Margaret Fund students from Texas, Eloise and Lois Glass, daughters of veteran China missionary W.B. Glass, and Marian Morgan, whose parents were missionaries in South America.[86] Eloise Glass later married Baker James Cauthen and the two served as missionaries to China until Cauthen became head of the Foreign Mission Board in Richmond.

President Davis reported in 1930 that she had attended all seventeen district meetings and many of the associations and had been able to speak in more churches than ever before. Her report concluded, "Pulpits filled on Sunday, 29."[87] That year they listed 2,568 organizations for youth, of which 212 were new that year, and 1,689 organizations for adult women, 86 of them new. The Young Women's Auxiliary (YWA) reported 526 groups; the Girls' Auxiliary (GA), 719; the Royal Ambassadors for boys (RA), 412; and the Sunbeams for small children, 911.

Mission study was a large part of the WMU work. They were convinced that mission action follows from mission *information*. They sponsored mission study groups, mission Bible study, missionary study courses. For 1937 the Texas WMU sponsored 3813 mission study classes with 37,995 women in attendance. They also conducted 1,638 classes for young people, with 15,641 enrolled. They conducted 136 schools of missions in the churches, and held sixty-five mission institutes. To lead these groups they enlisted pastors, professors in the Baptist schools, leaders from the state office and especially missionaries on furlough. Pastor Paul A. McCasland at Wilson, south of Lubbock, reported in 1937 on an eight-day school of missions for the Brownfield Association led by General Secretary R. C. Campbell and other missionary speakers. "Yes, the sand blows, and the north wind brings her blizzards to the Plains territory, but the truth remains that the South Plains section of Texas is one of the most religiously energetic parts of the state."[88] Certainly the WMU kept the subject of missions before the churches.

Stewardship was never far from the minds of WMU leaders. They taught that giving of one's money was a part of worship, and they encouraged weekly offerings no matter how small. The women picked up and popularized the practice of placing one's Sunday offering in a small envelope, an idea derived from Methodist women. Most importantly, the women seemed to grasp the biblical doctrine of tithing long before most of the men, and their consistent teaching and practice on this subject bore fruit. "I am happy to say," Mrs. Davis wrote, "that many men have become tithers on account of the women's zeal in following the biblical plan."[89] They vigorously promoted the Lottie Moon Christmas Offering for Foreign Missions. The state goal for 1930 was $45,000, a sizeable sum in those days, and despite what one woman called "the fearful financial depression," they lacked only a few hundred dollars in meeting that goal. This amount was more remarkable in that the women raised this money virtually alone; in those days the Lottie Moon Offering was not church wide and men hardly participated at all. For 1945 that offering in Texas reached $383,296.69.[90] Even during the depression, the women promoted their work vigorously. In 1933 upon a motion by Josephine Truett they raised their Lottie Moon Offering goal from $30,000 to $35,000. Their recent historian, Inez B. Hunt, noted that "The early 1930s were years of bitter economic depression, but the women acted as if there were no such thing as bank failures."[91]

Before 1933 no woman had served on the Executive Board of the BGCT, though the WMU president by virtue of office attended its meetings. Several women and even some of the men came to feel that, in light of all they did for Texas Baptists, women should be represented on this important policy-making group. In 1933 the Executive Board adopted the following statement:

> WHEREAS, the Executive Board of the Baptist General Convention of Texas is now composed entirely of men and there never has been a woman elected by the Convention as a member of the Board, and,
>
> WHEREAS, there is nothing in the Constitution of said Convention pertaining to the Executive Board which would forbid the election of women as members of the Board, and inasmuch as there are as many faithful, competent, loyal women in the membership of our cooperating churches as there are men, be it
>
> RESOLVED, that the Executive Board in session in Dallas, September 12, 1933, express itself as favoring the election of women to its membership at the annual Convention each year, and that the attention of the committee, which shall be named to recommend the membership of the Executive Board to the next annual session of the Baptist General Convention, be called to this resolution.

The minutes state that "Upon motion and second this paper was adopted." If there was any discussion or opposition, there is no record of it. However, misunderstanding soon developed. Apparently the WMU thought they would choose the women to serve on the Executive Board, but the Board felt this might make the women members representatives of the WMU rather than the churches of Texas. At the fall convention of 1933 two women were elected to the Board, but they were not the two who had been nominated by the WMU. Shortly after the November convention meeting, the WMU directed a rather pointed letter to the Executive Board, signed by two of its vice-presidents. The women thanked the Board for including women in the membership, commended the women elected, but complained that their own nominations were ignored. "The Woman's Missionary Union has through the years been in heartiest accord and fullest cooperation with every movement sponsored or promoted by the Baptist General Convention and has been met with the same spirit and sympathetic interest on the part of the Baptist General Convention in any project undertaken by the W.M.U.," the letter pointed out. "So we find it difficult to understand the action of your nominating committee in this matter."[92]

Walter H. McKenzie, chairman, was given the thankless task of replying to this letter. His undated letter, reprinted in the Executive Board minutes of December 12, 1933, merits quotation at some length.

> Dear Friends:
>
> Your communication . . . was read to the Executive Board in annual session Tuesday, December 12, 1933, and I was asked to reply to same. I am now complying with that instruction and would remind you and your women of the following facts:

214 TEXAS BAPTISTS: A Sesquicentennial History

1. When the motion was made . . . that women should be placed on our Executive Board, it was made perfectly clear that such representation should not be from the W.M.U. of the state as an organization, but should be from the great body of loyal women holding membership in our churches and in our Convention.

2. It was my privilege and honor to make the motion, and I sought to make it very clear that in my judgment, it would be unwise for us to select women from the W.M.U. Statewide organization, from the Sunday School Statewide organization or from the B.Y.P.U. Statewide organization; but since more than one-half of our constituent membership in the Convention was women, it would be fair and right for some women to be chosen. . . .

3. Since no protest was made in the convention when the report of the nominating committee was read, and since the 75 recommended were elected, the Executive Board would not feel that it was within our province to take any action whatever concerning the matter.

Two women among seventy-five members may not seem like fair representation, but by 1945 there were still only two women on the Executive Board, Mrs. B. A. Copass and Mrs. J. R. Chilcoat.[93]

Baptist Student Union. The BSU was designed to minister to college students, to keep them tied to the local church and develop them into loyal Baptist adults. A 1930 report showed 22,867 Baptist college students in Texas, 9,001 of them in Baptist schools.[94] The BSU Department had to extend their work to the state campuses because most of the Baptist students were there. In 1930 John Caylor became full-time secretary of the state BSU; previously he had divided his time between the BSU and his post as president of Burleson College. Described as "the Premier of Student Secretaries," Caylor had an annual budget of $6,500 (of which $500 was given by the Sunday School Board in Nashville). His job called for him to devote most of his time each fall to promoting the Every Member Canvas in the churches. Caylor called for "a more sympathetic understanding of the Baptist Student Union on the part of the denomination," and urged "that the B.S.U. be given a place in our denominational life equal to the other departments [of Sunday School and Training Union]."[95]

Some of the Baptist colleges employed their own BSU directors, usually assisted by local churches, and the churches sometimes banded together to sponsor a BSU director on state campuses. In the early 1930s these included Mrs. B.W. Vining at Baylor University; Miss A. M. Carpenter of the faculty of Simmons College along with J. A. Lovell, student leader; and Elizabeth Barton at Baylor College for Women. Taylor Pickett, a senior medical student at Baylor University in Dallas, was employed by the medical school to lead religious programs for both faculty and students. At Lubbock, Hazel Kokanour was employed by FBC to enlist students from Texas Tech University. A number of BSU directors served on state campuses, including Earl W. Rogers at Commerce; W. W. Earnest at Canyon; Mrs. H. C. Osborne at Nacogdoches; Tom E. Vaughan at Teachers

College in Huntsville; Mildred Wheeler at Rice Institute in Houston; and Miss Grace Allen, president of the state BSU was employed by FBC Denton to work with students in both colleges in Denton. University towns like Austin and College Station also had BSU workers, usually employed jointly by the state BSU Department and by local churches.[96] Such workers had to be acceptable to local pastors, which occasionally led to tension.

By 1933 the Depression took its toll, and the BSU Department was abolished as part of severe downsizing of the BGCT. In addition to his other duties, Secretary J. Howard Williams, assumed the duties of the BSU. He was assisted occasionally by Robert Fling, a student who was paid a small stipend to travel among the colleges. However, the work continued with more burden shifted to the churches in the college towns. In 1934 C. Roy Angell, chairman of the committee on BSU work, reported that student work was "firmly rooted" in Texas, with functioning BSU units at ten Baptist colleges, ten state colleges, and two private schools in Texas.[97]

After several years without a full-time state secretary, in 1938 the Executive Board elected J. W. Marshall to head the work. Marshall had served as pastor of the University Baptist Church in Fort Worth, and after five years resigned to work for the Foreign Mission Board. He later served as president of Wayland Baptist College (now University) in Plainview. In 1943 Marshall was succeeded by William F. Howard, whose name has become legendary among Baptists for his creative ministry to students.

Another dimension of the BSU work was the Bible Chairs in several state universities. Of course the Baptist colleges had faculty members who taught Bible, and several state schools allowed college credit for Bible classes taught by accredited teachers chosen by their denominations. The oldest of these chairs dates from 1919 at the University of Texas in Austin with O. P. Campbell as teacher. In 1925 W. C. Raines assumed the double duty of BSU director at the university and teacher in the Bible chair. In 1931 the BSU and Bible chair work was separated and Raines continued as teacher of Bible. By 1936 Baptists had Bible chairs at state colleges in Denton, Lubbock, and Huntsville.[98]

Useful as they appeared, the Bible Chairs also caused controversy. The Bible teachers were of course active in local churches, but the pastors had little or no control over them. In 1941 E. D. Head, pastor of FBC Houston, chaired a committee which recommended abolishing the Bible chairs. After his committee made an extensive study, Head reported[99]

> Our findings are revealing. . . . These [Bible] courses are mainly factual, giving little or no emphasis to distinctive Baptist principles or to materials of study which are calculated to produce unswerving adhesion to our Baptist faith. Our investigations also seem to show that these Bible classes do not fruit in enlarged religious activities on the part of the class members. In fact, it appears that the percentage of Christian activity favors the students not registered in these classes.

In light of this sharp criticism of the Bible chairs, the Head committee (which also included J. B. Tidwell and E. T. Miller) concluded:

Your committee, therefore, does not believe we should go any further in this present program; first, because we are not in a position to do it adequately; second, because we should endeavor to find a better way of dealing with the problem. Therefore, we recommend that we discontinue the Bible Chair plan and try to do our work through the local churches and the B.S.U. of the colleges and universities concerned. [We believe] this line would bring better results for Baptists.

This bombshell recommendation was adopted despite valiant efforts by Joseph P. Boone, the BSU pioneer in Texas, to derail it. However, Boone managed to get another committee appointed for further study with himself as chair and including J. M. Price, S. G. Posey, and G. Kearnie Keegan. The new committee brought back a more favorable report in 1942 which recommended that the Bible Chair ministry not only be continued but expanded. The new report was unanimously adopted.[100]

Baptist Brotherhood. Baptist men of Texas were slow to realize they needed, or had time for, a special organization for themselves, busy as they were being deacons and teachers in church, trustees in the schools, and leaders in the denomination. However, the Southern Baptist Convention had sponsored a men's movement since 1907 and by the 1930s several states had men's organizations, some with paid directors. For a time in the 1920s Texas had a Baptist Layman's Union, a BLU sort of parallel to the WMU, but it did not endure. Some churches and associations had men's groups, but their meetings were sporadic and no statewide structures linked them. However, the men noticed the achievements of the Baptist women (WMU), young people (BYPU), and college students (BSU). A Committee on Layman's Work reported in 1933 that "the laymen have as much right to have a representative upon the field as the women or young people," and recommended "employing a Christian layman as Brotherhood State Secretary."[101] The Depression prevented that, but in March 1935 a statewide laymen's conference was held in Dallas and a statewide organization grew out of that, with Earl B. Smyth as president. Three years later, in July 1938, R. A. Springer was employed as "State Leader of Laymen" in addition to his regular job as treasurer for the BGCT.

The Baptist men wanted a state organization, but were not always clear on what it would do. One report said, "it is the judgment of your committee that the real cause of the failure in the development of the layman's program is: *lack of a definite objective.*" (Emphasis theirs)[102] By 1938 the men had their statewide organization, and they hoped to form Brotherhood groups in all the churches, associations and districts. It was an uphill struggle for, as one report acknowledged, "Some of our local churches and pastors do not see for the moment wherein the organization of laymen is desirable and workable." Though not always clear on the purpose for the Brotherhood, they said "Let it be perfectly clear that in speaking of organizing our Baptist laymen, we are not for a moment thinking of a social organization."[103] The Brotherhood, it was hoped, would develop better deacons, teachers, fathers, husbands and would solve the financial problems in church and denomination. By 1939 about 700 Texas churches had organized Brotherhoods, enrolling over 15,000 men, but one report lamented that "some of them have majored on fellowship and food."[104] Some prayer breakfasts, they complained, had more breakfast than prayer, and before long the annual fish fry became Brotherhood's most familiar activity.

The first full-time Brotherhood Director in Texas was L. H. Tapscott who took office on March 15, 1945 at a salary of $4,500 per year. The tall layman known affectionately as "Mr. Tap," was a graduate of Auburn University and had served since 1937 as Educational Director for FBC, Dallas, where he had revitalized the Sunday School, totally reorganized the BYPU into an all-age organization, and made the summer Vacation Bible School a regular feature of church life. In the years to come, Mr. Tap would bring the same energy and creativity to the state Brotherhood.

Church Music Department. What was called "the song service" varied considerably in Texas Baptist churches in the 1930s. R. H. Coleman, assistant to Dr. Truett at FBC, Dallas, formed a company to publish songbooks. By 1939 Coleman had published thirty-three different songbooks which greatly influenced music among Baptists in Texas and the Southwest. However, by the 1920s strong sentiment emerged for improving church music. The Southern Baptist Convention appointed I. E. Reynolds, church music professor at Southwestern Seminary, to head a "Committee on Better Church Music." Out of this, the BSSB brought B. B. McKinney from Fort Worth to Nashville to serve as "Music Editor," and six years later elevated that work to department status.

The Southwide movement for better music spilled over into Texas. At the BGCT meeting in 1934, I. E. Reynolds brought a report on the importance of music as a part of Christian worship.[105] The report said, "There is a dire need for improving the music program in the average church, in respect to the grade of music and its rendition." Few argued with this conclusion but, Reynolds noted, "Nothing is being done by the denomination in an educational way to assist the local churches with their music programs." In light of these needs, the report suggested "That this Convention ask its Executive Board at its next session to give prayerful consideration to the establishment of some agency for the purpose of aiding the churches of this Convention in improving their music programs." The Board appointed J. M. Dawson, E. D. Head, and J. A. Ellis a committee to study "the question of Church Music with a view to improving the quality, spirituality and effectiveness of its rendition in our worship." Their goal was to guide the churches in "the selection and use of such music as would fit the genius of our faith and express more nearly the spirit of a true Baptist Church, avoiding on the one hand the music which conforms to the highly formalistic music of strictly ritualistic churches, and on the other hand the cheap, tawdry, glitterbug swing of nondescript cults and sects."[106] In 1940 Dawson moved that the Music Committee make its report directly to the Convention instead of to the Board.

A major milestone in Southern Baptist church music came in 1940 when the Sunday School Board issued the *Broadman Hymnal,* edited by the incomparable B. B. McKinney. This hymnal probably shaped Southern Baptist worship more than any other book except the Bible. With a happy balance of gospel songs and more stately hymns, along with benedictions and choral responses, the *Broadman Hymnal* fixed upon Baptists what McKinney called "heart music for the masses."[107] This hymnal greatly influenced Texas Baptists.

In 1945 the Executive Board formed a new Department of Church Music, and elected J. D. Riddle to head it at a salary of $4,500 per year plus travel. The BSSB in Nashville was asked to supply $1,200 of this amount. Riddle traveled extensively throughout the state conducting music workshops, helping train choirs, encouraging churches to employ music directors and, not incidentally, promoting the *Broadman Hymnal.*

THE BAPTIST BUILDING

For many years the BGCT had rented office space on the seventh floor of the R. E. Burt Building in downtown Dallas. From the 1920s there had been suggestions that Baptists should build their own headquarters building, but debt and depression delayed that action. When the worst of the depression was over, Secretary R. C. Campbell raised the question again and this time the Board moved from talk to action. Minutes show that in March, 1940, "Doctor R. C. Campbell brought the matter of a Baptist Building before the Board." He reported that the BGCT was paying about $15,000 a year in rent and this would increase because they needed more space.

At the meeting of the Executive Board on September 10, 1940, "The first consideration was the matter of a Baptist Building to house all of the Baptist work," and "Dr. C. B. Jackson moved that we look with favor on uniting in a Building." R. C. Campbell and Cricket Copass (Mrs. B. A.) were appointed a committee, they to choose five others, to draw up plans. Property was obtained at the corner of Ervay and Pacific in Dallas and, jointly with the Relief and Annuity Board, a Baptist Building was erected. Baptists entered the new building on July 15, 1941, when the Executive Board met there, having postponed their meeting from June so they could use the new building.[108]

BAPTIST COLLEGES

In 1930 Texas Baptists operated nine colleges, though they did not then elect trustees for Simmons College in Abilene.[109] Baptists gave strong verbal support to education, affirming that colleges were "building the builders of the Kingdom," and "wherever Baptist schools have prospered there Baptists have flourished." Financial support, however, lagged. In

1930 the Executive Board set as a minimum standard that the colleges should have $3,000 in endowment for each student in senior college. At that time, Texas Baptist colleges had about $3 million in endowment and they would have needed $18 million to meet this minimum standard.[110] Texas Baptists offered education at three levels, academy, junior college, and senior college. Of course, the senior college was far more expensive.

In 1939 Baptists reported 6,113 students in Texas Baptist colleges, plus 125 nurses at Baylor Memorial Hospital in Dallas and 60 at Hendricks Memorial in Abilene. Of the 6,113 college students, 3,225 were men and 2,888 women. Total college professors, not including the medical schools, was 305 (60 with PhD degrees and 122 with Masters).[111] Most students received some kind of scholarship aid, but only about 30% of entering freshmen remained to graduate. The Convention reported that "The salary schedule of the teachers in our schools is pitifully small and inadequate," with teachers receiving an average of $1,600 a year.[112]

Ministerial scholarships created some problems. When granted by the colleges, the amounts were not uniform which led to some shopping around. It soon became evident that some candidates came from out of state to benefit from the scholarships and immediately upon graduation returned to their home states. Also the colleges found that much of their scholarship aid was going to "those not in accord with our General Convention principles."[113] In 1943 the BGCT changed the plan to have scholarships granted not by individual schools but by the Convention, and applicants had to meet certain standards of affiliation and loyalty to Baptist work. The Convention also granted Mary Hardin Baylor $10,000 a year to make up for the fact that they received no ministerial scholarship money.

The colleges suffered of course during the depression, with decreasing enrollment and mounting indebtedness. By the late 1930s the schools shared in the general recovery, and many launched extensive building campaigns. Many of the colleges qualified for full accreditation, and their curricula expanded greatly. Some of the colleges, like the College of Marshall, moved from junior to senior college status and others, like Simmons College, underwent a name change. The Convention designated June 25, 1945, as "Christian Education Day," with statewide emphasis. In 1945 the college presidents included Pat M. Neff, Baylor; Gordon G. Singleton, Mary Hardin-Baylor; Rupert N. Richardson, Hardin-Simmons; George W. McDonald, Wayland; H. D. Bruce, East Texas Baptist College; J. L. Ward, Decatur; Thomas H. Taylor, Howard Payne; and R. R. Ray, San Marcos Academy.

SOUTHWESTERN BAPTIST THEOLOGICAL SEMINARY

Though no longer owned by the Texas Convention, Southwestern Seminary in Fort remained a vital part of Texas Baptist life. No Baptist institution suffered more than Southwestern during the Great Depression. President Scarborough wrote in 1932,

In these tragically depressing times, we have made heroic reductions, both in force and salaries. Since the depression came we have left off four in the administrative force, two in the School of Religious Education, three in the School of Gospel Music, one Missionary Training, one in the School of Theology, and have reduced salaries since 1929 fifty per cent. . . . and in the last year we have gotten only about 50 percent after reductions were made, bringing our income down to a place of real sacrifice.[114]

Scarborough continued, "We have doubled up, put more work on our teachers. . . . We raise the question of whether or not it is fair for this Seminary to suffer in this regard more than others." At times professors received no salary, for there was no money, and some families faced genuine crisis. Learning of this crisis situation, J. Frank Norris, pastor of Fort Worth's FBC and longtime foe of Southwestern Seminary, distributed bags of groceries to Southwestern faculty families. He then used his paper *The Fundamentalist* and his radio station to gain publicity, saying that while the Seminary fought him he in turn offered them food. Some faculty refused the food; one report says that W. T. Conner, professor of theology, threw the sack over the yard fence where it burst and spilled food on the ground. W. W. Barnes, professor of church history, on the other hand said "Food is food. Let us cook and eat."[115] The Southern Baptist Convention allocated $152,000 to the Seminary in 1931 but actually paid only $46,941, a pattern of reduction repeated for several years.[116] The Seminary also faced reduced enrollment during the Depression.

However, better times returned and gradually the Seminary recovered. In 1945 G. Kearnie Keegan, president of the SWBTS Alumni Association, led in planning a central Memorial Building at Southwestern. The name was to commemorate three outstanding Texas Baptists: George W. Truett, the incomparable pastor who had died the year before; L. R. Scarborough, the flaming evangelist-president who had retired in 1942; and William H. Fleming, wealthy layman of Fort Worth who gave generously to the Seminary. This familiar domed building opened in 1945 with Scarborough Hall for administrative offices and classrooms, Fleming Library, and Truett Auditorium. The Central Rotunda has an outline map of the world embedded in the floor to commemorate "the Baptist World Alliance and [with] special relation to Dr. Truett's connection with this world-girdling organization."[117]

During the 1930s and 1940s the Missionary Training School came into closer affiliation with the Seminary. In 1930 Mrs. W. B. Garrity, Superintendent, reported 235 women enrolled in the Seminary, 11 in theology, 40 in missionary training, 100 in religious education, and 85 in sacred music.[118] Ninety-two young women lived in the dormitory, most of them with scholarships from a church, a WMU or an association. In addition to scholarships, the Seminary on occasion presented the young women with boxes of grapefruit from the Seminary farm in the Valley, referring to the fruit as "globes of gold from the Magic Valley." In addition to study, the young women engaged in ministry, visiting hospitals and jails and working among Fort Worth's Mexican population, Chinese, deaf and the Union Gospel Mission. Many of the girls also had places of responsibility in the Gambrell Street Baptist Church adjacent to the campus.

WORLD WAR—AGAIN

When the Japanese bombed Pearl Harbor on December 7, 1941, life in America changed forever. Already deeply concerned about Hitler's advances in Europe, America was already edging closer to war. College men left their classes to enlist and, like in the First World War, the Baptist colleges adjusted to offer training suited to the war endeavor. Many pastors volunteered for appointment as chaplains and almost every Baptist church displayed a banner showing a silver star for each service man or woman from that church.

Although the chaplains did not bless the weapons, as some were reported to have done in World War I, clearly the churches supported the war effort wholeheartedly. Every service included prayers for the troops and when silver stars turned gold to represent church members fallen in battle the churches ministered to the grieving families. Yet through it all, there was unwavering church support for the war effort, for Americans deeply believed that Hitler had to be stopped.

In 1941 Acker C. Miller was appointed to head the "soldier work," and a generous funding was allowed. Miller reported that most of the training camps in Texas would be located in San Antonio, Palacios, Camp Bowie in Fort Worth, Brownwood, and El Paso's Fort Bliss. His ministry involved strengthening the churches near these camps, and where no churches existed he would rent a building and hold services. He sought to cooperate with others, especially the Baptist Sunday School Board, the Home Mission Board, and the American Bible Society. Miller reported in 1945 that 2196 servicemen had been won to faith in Christ and over 200 baptized into Texas churches.[119]

James F. Byrnes, the government's War Mobilization Director, asked that all conventions after February 1, 1945, be canceled to conserve fuel. The SBC did cancel its 1945 meeting but by the time of the Texas state convention that fall the restriction had been lifted. The BGCT met in 1945, not in Waco as first planned, but in Fort Worth.

During the war church building came to a virtual standstill for lack of materials, especially steel. After the war came a burst of church building as the pent-up demand for new and larger buildings could be addressed. America experienced a religious revival during and after the war, and the service men and women came back from the conflict with a new spiritual hunger. Sunday School enrollment skyrocketed, and church membership increased. The famous G.I. Bill helped finance college studies for the veterans and in the process changed the face of America and, not incidentally, led to a burgeoning enrollment at the Baptist colleges.

In the context of war, the Executive Board made a strong defense of complete religious liberty, guaranteed by separation of church and state.

In a letter to Texas Senator Tom Connally, dated March 13, 1945, they said, "The Texas Baptist Executive Board, in behalf of nearly one million church members in the state, feeling there is occasion for the utmost vigilance at this time for safe-guarding full religious liberty including complete separation of church and state, want to express deep appreciation for your public utterances and private assurances in support of [these principles].[120]

A NEW DAY

The Texas Baptist situation in 1945 was vastly different from that of 1929. The Baptists emerged tested by depression, encouraged by innovative new structures and approaches to ministry, led by creative and energetic leaders, and energized by a far-reaching spiritual revival. With over a century of history behind them, Texas Baptists were just beginning.

CHAPTER 10

READY TO GO FORWARD, 1945–1953

ON JANUARY 1, 1946 John Howard Williams began his second term as Executive Secretary for Texas Baptists. He held the same post before, from 1931-1936, but both the times and the man were different. In his first term during the depths of depression, Texas Baptists faced financial crises that crippled their ministries. His second term came during post-war prosperity which made possible advance on all fronts. During his first term Williams was a capable but relatively inexperienced young pastor. He came to his second term wiser, more mature, and seasoned by a decade as pastor of two of the largest churches in the SBC, the FBC in Amarillo and Oklahoma City.

In his acceptance, Williams said he could "feel the pulsebeat of thousands of Texas Baptists who in my judgment are ready to go forward."[1] Certainly Williams had read the pulsebeat correctly, for Texas Baptists were indeed "ready to go forward." And forward they went! However, even the optimistic Williams could never have dreamed what incredible growth and progress would mark Texas Baptist work over the next several years.

THE SECOND TIME AROUND

When the sixty-seven year old W.W. Melton resigned during the state convention of 1945 to accept a pastorate in Waco, the eyes of Texas Baptists turned immediately to J. Howard Williams. They did not have to look far, since Williams, then pastor of FBC, Oklahoma City, was an invited speaker at that same convention. Williams brought a powerful message about the potential for advance in Texas. His five-year absence from the state had made him appreciate Texas Baptists even more. He said, "Your large numbers, your outstanding achievements in so many realms of life, your marvelous spirit, your blessed fellowship, your staggering possibilities for future development are things which cause many outsiders to stand in amazement."[2]

At a meeting called to elect a new Secretary, C. Y. Dossey, Perry F. Webb and C. E. Matthews led an effort to change the election procedure and have a search committee nominate a new leader, but this lost by a large majority. Bassett called for a season of prayer, the group sang "Have Thine Own Way," and then proceeded to ballot without nominations as they had since 1914. On the first ballot, Williams received a majority of 49 votes, with 33 votes scattered among thirteen other men. The tellers declared Williams duly elected, and a motion to make the vote unanimous passed enthusiastically.

A NEW DAY

With the return of J. Howard Williams, an exciting new day dawned for Texas Baptists. And what a day it was! Williams brought to the state office ten valuable years experience in the pastorate, in which he had successfully implemented programs he would emphasize as executive secretary. He served seven and a half years, until his resignation in July, 1953, to become president of Southwestern Baptist Theological Seminary in Fort Worth, where the irenic E. D. Head had been pressured to resign. Several features mark the second Williams administration.

* The first post-war year, 1946, saw rapid changes in America. Factories converted from making war materials to providing goods to meet the pent-up demands of American families, and rising wages allowed them to buy these goods. New consumer goods made their appearance, such as white margarine with little packets of yellow powder to stir in to make it look and taste more like butter.
* For the first time in four years, new automobiles were available for civilian purchase, and gasoline and tires were no longer rationed.
* The famous GI Bill filled the colleges, including Baptist colleges, and changed the future of America as thousands of young men and women were able to get an education, many of them from families for whom higher education had previously been largely impossible.
* Marriages delayed or interrupted by the war blossomed and new households provided a ready market for American industry, and the flood of new babies born in America was nicknamed the "baby boom."
* A spiritual revival marked the land, symbolized by the rise of a dynamic Youth for Christ evangelist named Billy Graham..The returning GI's brought home from the war a deep spiritual hunger; they wanted religious nurture for themselves and they especially wanted it for their baby-boom children. Churches were filled and Sunday School enrollment mushroomed.
* The pent-up demand for new or enlarged buildings led to a Baptist

church building boom, as money and materials became available and allowed churches to address space needs long delayed. So great was the demand for new, enlarged and remodeled buildings that the BGCT founded a church loan department.

* For a few years Texas Baptists enjoyed peace as well as prosperity. No major controversies rocked the Baptist boat. Fundamentalist Frank Norris, still pastor in Fort Worth until his death in 1952, had come to a bitter old age but his fulminations provided more distraction than real damage. Even Lester L. Roloff of Corpus Christi cooperated with the BGCT in those days, though he later created his share of havoc among Baptists in the Valley.

* During the second Williams administration, under the leadership of C. E. Matthews and C. Wade Freeman, Texas Baptists put new emphasis upon evangelism and devised new forms of revivalism, particularly the simultaneous revivals, that proved unusually effective.

A FIVE YEAR PLAN

As part of the "Centennial Convention" of 1948 a Committee on Survey, chaired by Perry F. Webb, reported on Texas Baptist achievements of the past and prospects for the future. Out of this grew a Five-Year Plan to pursue advance on six fronts: evangelism, missions, Christian education, benevolence, hospitals, and finances.[3] The details of this Plan show not only the aggressive spirit of Texas Baptists for advance on all fronts, but also the organizational genius of J. Howard Williams. The five years goals were set out in increments, with progress monitored along the way.

Evangelism was listed first because it was first in the work of Texas Baptists. The Department of Evangelism reported over 50,000 baptized each year in 1946 and 1947, and predicted the number would reach 60,000 in 1948. They emphasized simultaneous revivals because "we believe there is great value in concerted effort."[4] In the Five-Year Plan, missions was divided into two sections: state missions and southwide missions. In state missions, challenging goals were set for rural and city missions, ministries with minorities, and the vital contributions of Woman's Missionary Union were recognized.

For 1948 the eight Texas Baptist colleges and one academy reported a record enrollment of 16,005, including 2,634 ministerial students and 1,073 mission volunteers.[5] Goals for education included enlarged facilities, more endowment and continuing attention to accreditation. The Five-Year Plan said "Benevolence should be a part of the total ministry of any Christian group," and on that basis Baptists announced goals of enlarging Buckner Benevolence to care for up to 1,000 boys and girls. They also planned to establish a Boys' Ranch, a home for unwed mothers, another home for the aged and continuing support for the Mexican orphanage in San Antonio.

At the beginning of their second century of organized convention work, Texas Baptists owned and operated five hospitals. In 1947 these houses of healing ministered to 57,401 patients, recorded 10,893 births, and 343 conversions. A total of 14,559 charity patients were treated at a cost of $320,119.97.[6] By the end of Williams's second tenure, the number of hospitals had risen to seven and all the statistics had mushroomed.

In finances, the Five-Year Plan set out an ambitious goal of raising $50 million for Texas Baptist causes between 1948-1953. Of this they expected $25 million to come from the churches in budget giving, and $25 million from major gifts. The Endowment Department, headed by J. W. Bruner, and the Baptist Foundation, headed by George J. Mason, sought and received major gifts. The Convention urged both churches and individuals to make their gifts undesignated, but recognized that many would prefer to designate large gifts to some specific cause.

Just when things were going well, Williams suffered a heart attack in late 1948 and was out of the office for about three months. The Board named A. B. White to serve as interim executive secretary. Fearing that Williams's heavy work load contributed to his health problems, the Board appointed a committee of James H. Landes, W. Boyd Hunt, and Wallace Bassett to recommend an associate executive secretary to take some of the load off Williams. With blunt candor, the committee reported that they could not afford the man they wanted so they recommended Floyd Chafin instead.[7] Williams attended his first Board meeting after his illness on March 8, 1949. As he made his way to the front of the meeting room, all present rose and sang the Doxology.

DOLLARS AND SENSE

J. Howard Williams was especially capable in the ministry of fund-raising, a gift he had shown as a pastor before he became executive secretary. His was not a heavy-handed high-pressure tactic. Instead, he preached stewardship as a part of the Christian life and taught tithing as the minimum standard of giving for Christians. Williams believed that undesignated giving through the Cooperative Program was the best way to conduct kingdom enterprises. He particularly disliked the frequent high-pressure campaigns, but reluctantly acknowledged the need for some of them. His only point of tension with the WMU was his fear that their several statewide special campaigns might detract from regular budget giving. "We have serious misgivings," said one report, "about the many campaigns for funds now being conducted. . . . The undesignated cooperative program is our life line."[8]

For 1946, the first year of Williams's second term, the Convention budget was set for $3.3 million, to be divided into three equal amounts for state causes, southwide causes, and for enlargement and endowment of Texas Baptist institutions.[9] For his last full year, the state budget called for $12 million, with $6 million from the churches and an expected $6 million from major gifts. The $6 million from the churches was to be divided 50/50 between Texas and Southwide causes.[10]

Texas Baptist Foundation. It was not enough, Texas Baptist leaders felt, to raise large sums of money; Christian stewardship also required that this money be managed well and directed faithfully to the purposes for which it was given. To this end, Texas Baptists pioneered in forming the Texas Baptist Foundation, a pattern later adopted by other states and by the SBC. By 1946 George Mason, head of the Foundation, reported about $13 million in endowment for Texas Baptist institutions.[11] That year Mason completed twenty-five years of service to Texas Baptists. He started in 1920 as field secretary for the $75 Million Campaign, becoming state convention treasurer in 1923. In 1931 the work of heading up the Foundation was added to his treasurer task, but in 1938 he devoted full-time to the Foundation, being succeeded as treasurer by Rudolph A. Springer. The Foundation made careful investments, including high quality stocks and A-1 bonds. They once bought some promising drug store stock but, finding the stores sold liquor, sold immediately. A. B. Culbertson succeeded Mason as head of the Baptist Foundation in 1950.

Endowment Department. The BGCT formed an Endowment Department in 1938 to seek major gifts from wealthy donors. Such a department was new; no other denomination to that time had tried such a plan, but by 1952 the Executive Board reported that "Many other states have followed the Texas example and have established endowment departments for themselves."[12] When J. W. Bruner became head of the Endowment Department in early 1940, they had only $6.5 million, but by the end of 1952 that amount had increased to $22.5 million. Though not wealthy himself, Bruner related well to wealthy people, easily winning their confidence. He became a recognized expert on tax and inheritance laws and helped people see how they could make the most of their estates. As a result of his work millions more came to Baptist causes later as a result of wills, trusts and bequests made during his tenure. Bruner was persuaded to delay his retirement because no suitable replacement could be found. For a time the Endowment work was combined with the Baptist Foundation but that did not work well and was discontinued after one year. Finally in 1953, L. Taylor Daniel, a successful businessman as well as pastor, was named to head the Endowment Department. The department sponsored two special days a year, a Make Your Will day in January and a Christian Education Day in June.

ON THE FIELD

Baptist activity picked up considerably in the post-war years, and not all of it was confined to the Baptist Building in Dallas. Out among the churches new vitality was evident as attendance increased, more converts were baptized, and participation mushroomed in Sunday School and other church organizations.

For years many churches had needed new or enlarged buildings but were held back in the 1930s by lack of money and in the early 1940s by the shortage of materials needed for the war effort. When both money and materials became available after the war, and the widespread revivals further crowded the churches, the 1950s brought a boom in church building such as the nation had rarely seen. Some even cautioned that the churches might be overbuilding and taking on too much debt, while others warned that prosperity might threaten spiritual values even more than depression had. Population growth led to a need for new churches and the state missions department was in position to offer help in pastoral salary supplements. This allowed many churches to have resident pastors which would not otherwise have been able to do so. For years the majority of Texas Baptist churches had been "part-time," that is, having preaching only one or, more commonly, two Sundays a month. With the post-war growth in members and money, many of these "quarter-time" and "half-time" churches went "full-time" and some even had a resident pastor on the field. These growing churches also tended to complete their church organizations. While most churches had Sunday Schools, in the late 1940s and 1950s more of them formed Baptist Training Unions, Woman's Missionary Unions and related organizations for children, some began mid-week prayer meetings and a few formed a Baptist Brotherhood for the men.

For years it was customary among Baptist churches to renew the pastor's call every year. This "annual call" meant that the pastor's tenure extended for only one year with no assurance it would continue. It was also common at the time for employees of the Convention, professors in the schools, and even the executive secretary to be reelected annually. However, in time the "annual call" gave way to the "indefinite call" in which pastors had no predetermined time limit set on their tenure. Baptist leaders encouraged this new call in the belief that pastors could give more vigorous leadership if they could be relieved of pressure from powerful church members or groups who might be disgruntled.

MINISTRY DEPARTMENTS

All the church-related organizations shared in the post-war growth and prosperity of Texas Baptists. At a time when spiritual interest was high, money was available to provide personnel to promote and enlist, and enrollments mushrooming, it is not surprising that state leaders could report in 1946 that "Victory has been the order of the day in our work during the past year."[13] With this optimistic assessment of the past, they also challenged the future. "The Lord may return today, but as a group we must . . . plan our work with the same thoroughness as if we knew He would delay His coming for a thousand years." This sheds light not only upon Baptist beliefs in eschatology, but also their aggressive ministry plans.

Sunday School. For years the state Sunday School and Training Union conventions had met in alternate years, but in 1948 they asked and received approval to meet annually. When G. S. Hopkins, who had led the Sunday School Department in Texas since 1926, retired in 1949 W. A. Criswell chaired the committee that recommended Andrew Q. Allen as his successor. Allen had served for some years as associate director of the department. Russell Hooper Dilday, Sr., joined the department as associate director on June 1, 1953, after ten years as Minister of Education at FBC, Wichita Falls. Dilday later headed the state Training Union department.

In the summers of 1946 and 1947 many churches had to curtail their Sunday Schools severely, and some shut down entirely, because of the polio epidemic. Hundreds of children came down with the dread paralytic disease and doctors felt that exposure to crowds, as in Sunday School, increased the risks of contracting the disease. Among those taken ill were children of some prominent Baptist families.[14] Texas Baptists mounted a massive prayer support for these and other families, and the *Baptist Standard* gave weekly updates on their condition. Some churches mailed Sunday School quarterlies to the children and set up a plan of home Bible study. Some kept in touch with pupils by mail and telephone, and some teachers visited their pupils at home. After a time the polio epidemic subsided and later the development of an effective vaccine greatly allayed parental fears.

For many years the Baptist Sunday School Board in Nashville parceled out funds each year to the Sunday School, Training Union, and Baptist student ministries in Texas. However, beginning in 1950 they appropriated a lump sum and allowed the BGCT to determine how to divide it among the agencies. The amount for 1950 was $29,150.[15] In addition to the ministry angle, this was obviously good business for the Nashville board, for the more Sunday Schools and Training Unions formed in Texas, the more Nashville literature the churches would buy. Statistics alone tell a scant story, but it is instructive to note that Sunday School enrollment in Texas stood at 711,801 in 1948 but when Williams ended his tenure as executive secretary in 1953 it has risen to about one million.[16]

The Daily Vacation Bible School grew rapidly in Texas. A total of 3,014 such schools were reported for 1952, with enrollment at 325,512, and 7,728 conversions.[17] The Invincibles, volunteer college students, were active in leading the VBS program under the leadership of Winifred L. "Wimpy" Smith who also served as Student Secretary and Bible Teacher at the college in Commerce. Winnie Dudley, a worker with the Invincibles, tells of about twenty college girls who spent eight weeks on the High Plains in the summer of 1946 conducting 108 Vacation Bible Schools, mostly in rural churches that would not otherwise have had them. They enrolled 7,361 children and registered 505 conversions. They also took religious census, taught Sunday School classes, and led study courses. The spirit of the group was illustrated by two college girls who visited a rural church that had voted not to have a VBS and persuaded them to change their mind. They put on one of the summer's best schools while the pastor was away, closing before he returned.[18] Some of the girls met rattlesnakes, sandstorms, and tumble weeds for the first time.

A new form of ministry for Texas Baptists, the weekday school, appeared during the Williams years, correlated through the Sunday School Department. The Lakeview church of San Antonio started a parochial day school in September 1946, one of the first such schools among Baptists in Texas. They erected a four room building to accommodate 120 students, and opened with 77 pupils in grades 1 through 6.[19] The church employed four teachers, each with college degrees and teacher certification. The same textbooks used in the public schools were provided by the church without cost to the children. A nominal fee of $1.00 per week per child was charged, but this met only about 20% of the costs of the school. In addition to the regular school subjects, "Bible lessons are taught by consecrated teachers every day in every grade of the school. This is the outstanding feature of our school. These teachers have free and unshackled privilege to teach the Bible and its truths as Baptists believe, and this is an important part of the curriculum." The Lakeview church was neither large nor wealthy, but they felt that day school was part of their ministry. The church reported that "This school was born out of the conviction that a better education should be given the children than the public schools are giving them; better in this way, that the Bible can and will be taught." The church concluded that "We can unhesitatingly commend it [the day school] to our sister churches. The day school and all our regular church services are now combined to the one end and purpose to teach children the way of life."[20]

In 1950 the Executive Board heard a lengthy report from a committee, chaired by J. M. Price, head of the School of Religious Education at Southwestern Seminary, on the prospects for weekday religious instruction.[21] Price noted that many Protestants were entering the field of parochial education, an area largely left to Catholics before. The National Association for Evangelicals (NAE) was promoting the idea. Price traced the increasing secularization of public education, the limitations of Sunday religious instruction, and moral conditions calling for more religious training of children. The committee pointed out advantages of weekday instruction, recommended greater use of the VBS, but closed with only one recommendation, that Secretary Andrew Allen continue to study the need for Baptist day schools. Soon thereafter the Baptist Sunday School Board in Nashville made plans to provide suitable instructional materials for Bible study in such day schools.

However, for all the publicity, Baptist parochial schools gained little headway until the turbulent 1960s when secularization, court cases restricting school sponsored prayer, and tensions over racial integration led to an upsurge in such schools.

Baptist Training Union. In 1946, T. C. Gardner, head of the Training Union Department, said "If we are properly interpreting the signs of the times, a commanding day has dawned for the Baptist Training Union."[22] These signs included heightened interest, increased enrollment, and vibrant enthusiasm. During the years of J. Howard Williams's second tenure as executive secretary, BTU enrollment almost doubled from 183,607 members in 1946 to 346,125 in 1953.[23] The BTU sponsored all kinds of training, including missions, stewardship (they formed Tithers Leagues and Tithers Bands in the churches), doctrinal studies, evangelism and personal witnessing. Gardner affirmed that "manifold blessings" had come "to our great denomination because of the enlistment, training, indoctrination and development of a vast army of Baptists who received their training through the Training Union."[24] Warming to his subject, Gardner continued: "From whence cometh our personal soul winners, tithers, Sunday School teachers and officers, deacons, missionaries, church leaders and preachers? That is the big question. The answer is the Baptist Training Union."

Gardner and his associates carried on an aggressive program of enlistment and training of workers in the 17 districts and 114 associations. The state BTU convention which, like the Sunday School group, met on alternate years, began holding annual sessions in 1949. The 1949 convention in Abilene illustrates the enthusiasm of the group. They expected about 6,000 to attend, but 7,667 registered.[25] Decked out in western garb, host pastor Jesse J. Northcutt welcomed the enthusiastic youth to Abilene. Sessions were held in the auditorium of Hardin-Simmons University.

A popular new BTU program was the Saturday Night Youth Meetings sponsored in many churches and associations throughout the state. In 1946 Gardner was allotted an extra $2,500 to publicize and promote these youth meetings, which combined fellowship and inspiration. "Baptist youth are on the march for Christ and the church. Saturday Night Youth Meetings are being conducted in literally hundreds of churches throughout the state of Texas."[26] "Our youth are being challenged to live and to witness for Christ. All meetings are both Christ centered and church centered." The motto for these youth meetings was "Adventurers for Christ," and the slogan was "Straight from the bow of God into the heart of the world."[27] These meetings were a sort of Texas Baptist version of the popular "Youth for Christ" movement on the national scene, from whose ranks evangelist Billy Graham emerged.

Gardner's report asserted that "the purpose of the Saturday night youth movement is to deepen the spiritual lives of our youth, to inspire them to win their friends and loved ones to Christ, to challenge them to find God's will concerning their life's work, and to encourage them to be loyal and faithful upon the attendance of all the services of their church." Reports confirm that many young people were converted in these meetings, scores made decisions to enter some phase of Christian ministry, and not a few found marriage partners from the crowds of youth attending from different churches. The Saturday night youth meetings proved a major stimulus to the famous "youth revival" movement of the times. On one Saturday night (September 28, 1946) over 40,000 youth had attended approximately 200 meetings throughout the state.[28]

Not surprisingly, the BTU had an impact upon Baptist church architecture, for activities in a building will inevitably influence the shape of the building. In their efforts to parallel the BTU organizations with similar divisions in Sunday School, BTU leaders said "Educational buildings should be erected to take care of both training and teaching needs. This calls for a new type of an educational building."[29]

The Training Union Department sponsored the first Baptist assemblies in Texas, and they continued to promote assemblies, but in time the work outgrew any one department. In the summer of 1946, Texas Baptists sponsored twelve encampments, with between 12,000 and 15,000 attending. A *Baptist Standard* editorial noted that "Texas Baptists have invested considerable money in camp grounds and buildings. Regardless of the amount of money involved, we are convinced that the investment is declaring large dividends for the spiritual enrichment of our people."[30]

In the post-war years the idea of a summer family vacation became popular, and this tended to increase the assembly attendance. Some assemblies grew so rapidly they had to employ full-time directors. In 1947 the Latham Springs Assembly employed J. E. Roth, former pastor of FBC, West, to direct their camp. They had several buildings, a modern cafeteria that could feed 600 people in 45 minutes, and comfortable dormitory and meeting rooms. During the summer of 1948, Latham Springs held 22 camps, with 5,107 attending, with 97 conversions and 913 rededications to Christ. Receipts for the summer were about $38,000.[31]

Due to a long series of events, the BGCT held title to the property of two encampments, those at Palacios on the coast and Paisano in the Davis Mountains of West Texas. However, the Convention itself did not plan, finance or supervise the programs conducted at these camps. In 1947 a move developed to get the Convention to elect trustees for the Palacios assembly, but a partisan of Paisano objected, saying "We have two encampments." J. Howard Williams responded by saying, "In reality we have sixteen encampments and if we [as a state convention] operated two, we were in competition with the other fourteen."[32] Some suggested the BGCT set up its own state assembly, but the Executive Board declined. By 1952 Texas Baptists had a total of fourteen assemblies, including Alto Frio (Leaky); Bell County (Belton); Copass (Denton); Daingerfield (District 1); East Texas (Newton); Latham Springs (Aquilla); Lueders; Mt. Lebanon (Dallas County); North Texas (Sherman); Paisano (Alpine); Plains (Floydada); and Texas (Palacios).[33]

Baptist Student Union. Increased college enrollment in the post-war years brought new challenges to the work of the BSU and to the churches in college towns. Reports in November 1946 showed 6,068 Baptist students in the various Baptist colleges in Texas, along with 13,888 Baptists attending one of the fifteen state senior colleges. Additional Baptist students attended union colleges, schools of other denominations, and various kinds of business colleges. Under the leadership of W. F. Howard, the state BSU Department sponsored thirty-seven active BSU groups on various campuses in Texas. Religious interest was high, and at that time no non-denominational or para-church groups competed for the spiritual allegiance of Baptist students.

The BSU sought to link their ministries to the local churches, but Baptist churches in the college towns faced severe challenges. When hundreds and in some cases thousands (Austin, College Station) of Baptist students showed up for the school term, the churches were overwhelmed. For years a part of the ministry of W. F. Howard's department was to assist the college churches to erect buildings and secure church staff to minister to these mobile congregations. This help was not restricted to churches near Baptist colleges. Many agreed with R. L. Brown, pastor of FBC, College Station, that "we should give attention to state schools as well as denominational schools or we will lose the Baptists in our state schools."[34] In 1946 the Executive Board advanced $150,000 to help FBC, Denton, erect an educational building. With two universities in town, during the school term students composed more than half of the total population of Denton.[35] One of those Denton students active in BSU was Keith Parks, who headed a statewide drive to increase subscriptions to the *Baptist Student*, the southwide student magazine. Parks and his wife later served as SBC missionaries in Indonesia, and he headed the Foreign Mission Board from 1979 to 1992. Aid to college churches included grants to Seventh and James in Waco, Highland in Denton, and FBC in College Station. The Executive Board also voted to pay 25% of the cost for a building at the Gambrell Street church adjacent to the campus of Southwestern Seminary in Fort Worth, up to a maximum of $37,000. Burns K. Selph, pastor at Gambrell Street, "spoke his appreciation and assured the Executive Board of the cooperation of his church in all of the denominational activities."[36]

In 1946 the BSU Department conducted Bible Chair classes at four state schools: University of Texas at Austin (teacher, W. C. Raines); Texas Women's College and North Texas State Teachers College (now University of North Texas) in Denton (D. B. Lloyd); Sam Houston State Teachers College in Huntsville (T. B. Prescott); and East Texas State Teachers College in Commerce (Nat C. Bettis). These were aimed to minister especially to future public school teachers in Texas. Meeting on the Seminary campus in Fort Worth in February, 1946, the committee on Bible chairs voted to establish another chair, at the West Texas State Teachers College in Canyon.[37] James H. Landes, then pastor of FBC, Wichita Falls, recommended the founding of a Bible Chair at Hardin College there (now Midwestern University), with Harold Diggs as teacher. In time the BSU expected to establish several other chairs at different schools. J. P. Boone, chair of the committee, reported that the Bible chair classes enrolled about 700 students who received college credit for Bible classes. These chairs, he reported, "have met with ever increasing favor with the Presidents and students" of the colleges where they are located.[38]

In late 1946 the Executive Board, noting that the Bible Chair work was growing rapidly, agreed that this work needed a fulltime director. J. Howard Williams "stated that he thought we needed a Secretary for the Bible Chair division of the student work—one who could help organize these Bible Chairs, standardize their courses of study and get them functioning."[39] He recommended J. P. Boone, the pioneer of Baptist student work in Texas, who was then pastor of FBC, Waxahachie. W. F. Howard would continue as Secretary of the BSU department, with oversight of all its work, with Boone as a colleague for a limited time. In light of the growing importance of the Bible chairs, the committee was enlarged in 1946 to include a representative pastor from each town with a state college. The Executive Board, in authorizing expansion of the chairs, cautioned, "We further recommend that they [the committee] give careful consideration to the orthodoxy and spirit of cooperation of the men who teach these courses."[40] In the early years all the teachers were men, but women were later appointed as teachers.

In 1945 the state board of University Regents voted that they could no longer provide state facilities for the teaching of religion. The colleges would continue to grant credit for the Bible classes, but would no longer permit any denominations to use college facilities. They asked the denominational groups, including the BSU, to "work out arrangements within a reasonable time to bring about compliance." That reasonable time turned out to be September 1, 1946. The Executive Board noted that holding Bible classes in state facilities was always a temporary measure which, if made permanent, would violate the cherished Baptist doctrine of separation of church and state. However, it was the state and not the denominations which took the initiative in halting the practice. The records note that, "The Executive Board of the Baptist General Convention of Texas commit[s] itself to a program including the purchasing of property adjacent to campuses of state schools and the establishment of student centers to be used for the housing of both the Bible Chairs and all student activities of the Baptist Student Union."[41]

This resolution, unanimously voted, proved difficult to carry out. Good property adjacent to the campuses was at a premium, if available at all, and building costs were rising. Baptists felt that an effective witness required that their buildings compare favorably with the college facilities and the buildings of other denominations. Within a few years Baptists had a number of well-equipped Student Centers near college campus in Texas.

By 1953 the BSU Department, led by W. F. Howard and Ross C. Coggins, associate, conducted sixty active student unions emphasizing "Christian studentship," and they offered credit Bible classes on seventeen campuses with more than 2,000 enrolled.[42] The list of student directors of these local BSU groups reads like a Who's Who of future Baptist leaders in Texas and beyond.[43] By then Baptists had ten permanent Student Centers near college campuses, seven temporary centers, plus several centers locally owned. At the request of the BGCT, the BSU department also conducted an annual ministerial student orientation on various campuses.

Woman's Missionary Union. During the second tenure of Williams, Texas Baptist women did what they always had—they taught mission studies, raised money for missions, conducted organizations to involve youth and children in missions, provided leadership and funds for both rural and city missions, and raised both funds and goods for the Buckner Home and other state and local benevolences.

In 1946 the WMU officers included Mrs. Earl B. (Rosalind) Smyth who in 1946 succeeded Crickett Keys Copass as president and editor of *The Helper;* Mrs. R. L. Mathis (Marie), Executive Secretary-Treasurer, who had succeeded Olivia Davis in 1945; Eula Mae Henderson of Oklahoma who succeeded Virginia Ely as Young People's Secretary in 1946; Mrs. W. D. Powell, Recording Secretary; and Mrs. Carlton R. Winn, Assistant Recording Secretary.[44] Rosalind Smyth was a widow when she came to office in 1946, but her husband had been a leading layman among Texas Baptists, being especially influential in forming the Baptist Brotherhood. In May 1947 Marie Mathis resigned to accept a position on staff at FBC, Dallas, and was succeeded by Eula Mae Henderson who served until 1977. Ruth Thornton (Prichett) served as Young Peoples Secretary from 1948-1953, when she was succeeded by Amelia Morton (Bishop). Mrs. Mathis continued active in the Texas WMU, succeeding Rosalind Smyth as president and serving from 1949-1955. She proved to be an effective leader, in Texas and beyond. She served as president of the southwide WMU 1956-1963 and 1969-75. She was named President of the Women's Department of the Baptist World Alliance in 1970, and as vice-president of the BWA 1965-1970. She was the first woman to serve as vice-president of the SBC, elected in 1963. The WMU sponsored the Royal Ambassador work, the mission organization for boys, until 1954 when they reluctantly transferred this work to the Brotherhood. In 1948 Jimmy Allen was named director of the state R.A. work, succeeding C. W. Farrar.[45] Allen later headed the Christian Life Commission of Texas, and served as president of the BGCT and in 1979 was elected president of the SBC. After a pastorate of FBC, San Antonio, Allen headed the SBC Radio and Television Commission.

In a presentation to the Executive Board, Marie Mathis said the WMU "had pledged themselves to four love Offerings each year, the Mary Hill Davis Offering [state missions], Annie Armstrong [home missions], Old Ministers Relief, and Lottie Moon [foreign missions], and that their desire was to give full attention to these offerings and no others."[46] The women felt they were being asked for too many impromptu offerings throughout the year, often for projects their group had not voted on. In 1950 when the southwide WMU had an opportunity to purchase a new headquarters, Mrs. Mathis asked each WMU member of Texas to give $1.00 to this special project.

One special project in which the Texas WMU gladly participated was the World Relief Offering in 1946. President Harry S. Truman called for a "Share the Food Program" because, he noted, more people faced actual starvation in 1946 than during any of the war years.[47] The Southern

Baptist Convention adopted a goal to raise $3.5 million for this Relief Offering, to be coordinated through the Foreign Mission Board. Texas Baptists were assigned a goal of $458,000.[48] The offering was so vigorously promoted in Texas, especially by the WMU and Brotherhood, that some dared to hope Texas would exceed a half million dollars. Marie Mathis was one of those who had seen with her own eyes the devastation caused by the war in Europe, and she promoted the Relief Offering vigorously. July 21, 1946 was designated as World Relief Sunday, and a month later Texas Baptists had in hand $479,448.07 for this cause. By the close of the campaign in November, Texas Baptists had given $725,140.50, far exceeding their original goal.[49] In what was called a "Texanic Victory," Texas Baptists amazed even themselves by what they could accomplish if all pulled together. The import of this great victory was not lost on J. Howard Williams, who used it as a springboard for other financial challenges for Texas Baptists.

The Texas WMU was carefully organized, with functioning units not only in local churches but also at associational, district and state levels. A favorite meeting was the House Party, a kind of overnight retreat, which began as a one-time gathering at Baylor University. However, it became so popular that it was made an annual event, with up to 2,000 attending.

In their 1953 report to the BGCT, the Baptist women reported that "Another year has passed. Another record has been made."[50] Every statistic of membership, new WMU's in the churches, increased membership in both the WMU and the youth organizations, and mission offerings set new records. That year the major offering totals show: Lottie Moon, $1,254,938.25; Annie Armstrong, $233,105.63; Mary Hill Davis, $313,729.39; and Ministerial Relief, $41,663.60.[51] The report also showed a total of 2,606 WMUs in Texas (279 new that year); 506 circles for business women; 767 Young Women's groups (138 new); 1,761 R.A. groups (367 new); 2,810 Girls' Auxiliary groups (504 new), and 1,841 Sunbeam Bands for younger children (364 new that year).[52]

Men's Brotherhood. J. Howard Williams was a great believer in the value of mobilizing Baptist manpower and he warmly supported the Brotherhood. In his pastorates in Amarillo and Oklahoma City he formed Brotherhoods and saw firsthand how the men could strengthen the life of the church. This support from the executive secretary, combined with the capable leadership of L. H. Tapscott, Brotherhood secretary, brought an era of growth and acceptance for this organization. In earlier years the Brotherhood had to struggle for existence, but that was assured with the election of R. A. Springer as part-time secretary in 1938. During Williams's second tenure, the Brotherhood still struggled, this time for a role. The function of Brotherhood was less sharply focused than the WMU; Tapscott said that whatever the church was doing the men wanted to help do it. While quite laudable, this goal was so general that some had little idea what it meant. In 1946 Tapscott said the Brotherhood was ready to take "its rightful place as one of the four strong agencies carrying on the work of the church," along with Sunday School, Training Union, and WMU.[53]

Perhaps the greatest contributions of the Brotherhood lay in the area of stewardship. Through the work of Tapscott, literature they produced, and conferences sponsored in churches, associations, and districts, the men emphasized tithing. They also urged individuals and churches to make more of their giving undesignated. The Brotherhood also took on such varied tasks as evangelistic witnessing assignments, took an active role in the summer encampments, took as a special project helping returning military veterans to find jobs, led a campaign to increase the circulation of the *Baptist Standard,* sponsored doctrinal study courses, and busied themselves with local mission projects. For example, the Brotherhood of FBC, Plainview, helped plant the Date Street church in 1941. The men took a religious census, bought a lot, and while Pastor L. B. Reavis was away they erected a building. On the first Sunday the Date Street Church had 49 in Sunday School and within weeks had almost 200 members.[54] The annual Brotherhood convention, held at the same time as the state WMU convention in conjunction with the state convention, offered such programs as "How to start a new church," "Millions for Christ in Stewardship," and "Laymen's Revivals."

The Brotherhood also sponsored an annual Laymen's Day in the churches and some of these special programs were broadcast on the radio. Some Brotherhoods sponsored "Friendship Centers" to help migrant farm workers in Texas. Ivy Boggs originated the "Men and Boys Movement," whose purpose was to get more boys involved in church life and was, in fact, a precursor to the switching of the Royal Ambassador Program from WMU to the Brotherhood in 1954. By 1953 about 25 churches had formed a Young Men's Brotherhood for men aged 17 to 24. State Brotherhood presidents included E. S. Cummins, Abilene, 1941-1944; Grover C. Cole, Fort Worth, 1945-1947; Thomas J. Pitts, Odessa, 1948-1949; Clifton J. Brannon, Longview, 1950; F. Ivy Boggs, Dallas, 1951-1952; and T. Gordon Ryan, Fort Worth, 1953-1954.[55] By November, 1953, the Brotherhood Department reported 1,679 church Brotherhoods in Texas, 155 of them new that year. A total of 74 layman-led revivals were reported for that year.[56]

Church Music Department. "Music is the language of the soul. God is the author of music." So said J. D. Riddle, Secretary of the BGCT Church Music Department, in a 1946 promotional article.[57] He affirmed that music can teach, inspire, motivate, and even brings rest to the weary. Above all, "Music brings us into fellowship with each other and with God."

With such convictions, one is not surprised that J. D. Riddle vigorously promoted music in the churches. Assisted by a host of volunteer workers and, after 1952, by department associate director Raymond D. Jones, the Church Music Department staff conducted music training workshops and clinics in hundreds of Texas Baptist churches, organized adult, youth and children's choirs, and urged the use of better music in the churches. Riddle warned the churches against two extremes in church music: first, what Riddle called "lighter type of semi-jazz music" (what B. B. McKinney called "heel music" from his dance band days), and second, what Riddle called "a trend toward cold formalism and ritualism." Riddle warned Baptists as a free and non-liturgical people to steer clear of both of these extremes.[58] For all the use of solos, quartets, and choral groups, Riddle insisted that the heart of worship music was congregational singing. The department gave vigorous endorsement to the new *Broadman Hymnal* in 1941 and encouraged churches to buy it.

The Church Music Department also served as a clearing house for revival singers, helping bring together churches seeking evangelistic music leaders and singers open to engagement. They also helped churches find permanent ministers of music. One report said, "Pastors, churches, and evangelists are requested to use our office for any service where music is concerned. We have names, addresses, and records of open dates of some fifteen full-time evangelistic singers, some eight qualified summer field workers in music education, and the schedules of the full-time music department staff."[59]

Riddle developed courses of study for local churches that were later adopted by the Music Department of the BSSB in Nashville.[60] Always the primary concern was music in the churches. In 1946 the Music Department asked the Executive Board for an extra $3,000 to sponsor "summer singing schools particularly to combat the commercial type of music now being presented over most of our states," but the Board deferred action on the request.[61]

NEW DEPARTMENTS AND COMMISSIONS

When Williams began his second term as executive secretary in 1946, the BGCT had thirteen departments and agencies connected with Baptist witness in Texas. Two new departments, Endowment (1938) and Church Music (1944) had been formed between Williams's two terms. Williams had worked with an Executive Board of no more than 68 members, but that number had increased to 105 by 1945 and to 150 by the end of 1946.[62] When Williams resigned in 1936, the Executive Board did its work through four standing committees, but upon his return in 1946 Convention ministries had so grown in size and complexity that the work was distributed among twelve standing committees. During the second Williams tenure a number of new Convention departments and agencies were formed. Some, like the Radio Department, launched new forms of ministry while others, like the Christian Education Commission, sought to do the same or similar tasks more efficiently.

Department of Evangelism. Evangelism was identified as "the primary task of Texas Baptists,"[63] but except for a brief time in the 1920s the Convention had no specific department for that task. One of the first actions of Williams upon his return to Texas was to appoint a large State Committee on Evangelism, headed by Charles Everett Matthews, long time pastor of Travis Avenue Baptist Church in Fort Worth. Matthews announced plans for evangelistic rallies, simultaneous revivals, and renewed emphasis upon a statewide evangelism conference. He said, "Evangelism is the purifier of the bloodstream of Christianity. It abolishes heresies from teaching and preaching. It excludes worldliness from our churches. It prevents our worship from being stifled with cold, clammy formalism."[64]

The total revamping of the evangelism work of Texas Baptists which the Matthews committee called for indicated some dissatisfaction with the way the work had been done previously. Previous BGCT evangelists had concentrated on rural work, but they were notified that their employment would not continue beyond May 1, 1946. "The reason for this change," the committee reported, "is that the new program of evangelism contemplated will require a different personnel on the part of evangelists in the future." They later agreed to keep on two evangelists who were slated to retire within a year, but reaffirmed "the decision to build a new staff of evangelists in line with the changed needs."[65]

Moving rapidly, on March 5, 1946, the Executive Board created a Department of Evangelism and named Matthews to head it. This was the first state evangelism department among Southern Baptists, but other states and the HMB soon followed. Williams pointed out that other aspects of ministry had departments and personnel to plan, pray and promote "and yet, evangelism, which is one of the supreme tasks of any Christian group, was not so positionized in our thinking, or in the denominational program."[66] One feature of the Evangelism Department is that it came directly under the jurisdiction of the Executive Committee, not the entire Executive Board as was the case with other departments. Matthews took office on May 1, 1946, at a salary of $6,000 plus freedom to hold two revivals a year outside of Texas. The first staff evangelists were carefully chosen by Williams, Matthews and Wallace Bassett, chair of the Executive Board. They included C. Y. Dossey, the first one chosen, C. B. Jackson, J. Frank Weedon, and Jesse Yelvington. One of Matthews's first actions as director of the new department was to move the annual Evangelism Conference to January in order to give more time for planning evangelistic campaigns in the churches later in the year. Described as "a state-wide rally for preachers and singers," the Evangelism Conference soon became one of the largest gatherings of Texas Baptists.

The new department showed remarkable achievements. "The Department is encouraging all methods of evangelism—individual church revivals, personal and conversational soul winning, youth revivals, etc., but the emphasis is placed mainly on the association-wide simultaneous crusade."[67] A total of 107 of the 114 associations in Texas, including about 3,000 churches, had committed themselves to simultaneous revivals in 1947, a method by which all the churches in an area would have their revivals at the same time, thus allowing them to share in prayer, publicity, and promotion.

Within six months C. E. Matthews, who came to office with much fan-fare, resigned to accept a similar position with the HMB. His replacement was Clifford Wade Freeman, pastor at Sulphur Springs who took office in early 1947 and served until his retirement in 1974. Freeman, a successful pastor and evangelist in his own right, shaped the evangelism ministry of Texas Baptists. The "department" he inherited was scarcely more than a group of self-directed evangelists holding revivals across the state. Free-man brought more organization, planned evangelism training and clinics, created a literature to help pastors plan for effective evangelism, and greatly expanded the January Evangelism Conference held in Fort Worth.

By far the most ambitious project undertaken in evangelism during Williams's tenure was the effort to win 250,000 new converts in 1951. The Billy Graham revival in Fort Worth in 1950 inspired William Fleming, wealthy Fort Worth oilman, to pray about the unchurched multitudes in Texas. Fleming and his wife felt the Lord had revealed to them that Texas Baptists should plan a special evangelistic campaign. Mrs. Fleming want-ed to set the goal at one million, but William scaled it back to one quarter of that. Fleming had just been reelected president of the BGCT, and he approached J. Howard Williams and C. Wade Freeman about this goal, almost five times as many converts as Texas Baptists had won in any one year. Williams was hesitant, but Fleming was insistent. The result was that the Convention adopted the goal. Williams and C. Wade Freeman planned the most intensive evangelistic campaign in Baptist history. There is no space here to tell of all the prayer meetings, inspirational rallies, organi-zational meetings, district and associational conferences, personal soul winning clinics, posters, *Baptist Standard* promotional pieces, and person-al testimonies that went into that campaign. Freeman enlisted the per-sonnel of all the other ministry departments in full cooperation. At the end of the year they had not met this ambitious goal, but they did baptize 62,086 new converts, about 5,000 more than the year before.[68]

Radio Department. For many years Texas Baptists had a growing inter-est in radio as a means to share the gospel, and some churches had begun to broadcast their Sunday services as early as the 1920s. J. Howard Wil-liams felt radio had great potential. As a pastor in Amarillo and Okla-homa, he had some experience with radio, and he served on the SBC com-mittee which pioneered the Baptist Hour broadcasts.

The BGCT had a Radio Committee by 1944 but they faced problems. The powerful AM stations were all booked up and local Baptist churches could hardly get air time at any price, and favorable time slots were not to be had. The Radio Committee reported in 1946 that

> Since the Texas Radio Committee was formed their biggest problem has been to get on the best stations in the state, that is, those that have power enough to command a listening audience [emphasis theirs]. In these two years we have been able to get on only one station with any coverage, KWFT in Wichita Falls. The only time we could obtain on this station was 4:00 o'clock on Saturday afternoon. This is a very poor hour.[69]

Unable to get on existing stations, Baptists began to consider founding their own stations and perhaps even a Baptist radio network in
Texas.[70] At the 1946 Convention meeting in Mineral Wells, R. Alton Reed,
chairman of the Radio Committee, proposed a project of setting up FM
stations throughout the state. Reed had worked in radio before entering
the ministry. The Convention asked the Executive Board to consider setting up a Texas Baptist Network of FM stations which would provide 100
hours of broadcast time per week, fifteen hours for six days and ten hours
on Sundays with no commercials. They hoped churches, groups of individuals and colleges might band together to set up stations. The cost for
setting up individual stations was estimated at $11,000 to $40,000 but,
once in operation, they expected that revenue from advertising would
defray costs.[71] Far less powerful than the AM stations, the FM broadcasts
would reach out only about 35 to 75 miles. The Board voted to appropriate $175,000 to be used over a five-year period to establish such a net-
work.

By 1947 the work of the Radio Committee had grown so that the
Executive Board felt it could no longer be carried on by volunteer effort.
They had already eight programs on the air regularly, with Norvelle Slater
of Dallas providing some of the music. Slater later became well-known on
Texas radio for his Sunday morning "Hymns We Love" program. On May
1, 1947 the Radio Department was formed and R. Alton Reed was named
its first paid director. In 1949 the Executive Board voted to construct a
90,000 watt FM station on the Dallas Baptist Encampment grounds, with
the transmitter to be between Fort Worth and Dallas. This station was to
be known as KYBS (Your Baptist Station). Baptist groups in Brownwood,
Fort Worth, Beaumont, San Antonio, Plainview and Abilene also held per-
mits to build stations, and one was already in operation in Belton.[72] Assisting Reed in this work was a committee, which included Julian Atwood,
Odell Jamison, W. A. Criswell, C. E.Colton, C. Wade Freeman, T. Hollis
Epton, Earl Hanamaker, and James N. Morgan.

These ambitious plans never worked out well. Problems surfaced
from the first and they refused to go away. The programming on some of
the early stations, much of it by volunteers, did little to convince Baptists
of its permanent value. Some cared little for the FM technology and, like
most projects, the costs kept escalating. The entire radio venture faced the
strong and continuing opposition of Carr P. Collins, powerful layman of
Dallas, and those who agreed with him. Executive Board Minutes state
that "Mr. Carr Collins expressed forcefully his objections to our erecting
an FM station or entering the FM field."[73] The advent of television was
probably the deciding factor in the demise of Texas Baptists' ambitious
radio plans. Already by 1949 Forrest Feezor, chair of a large committee to
study the radio situation, concluded that "The radio picture now is not too
clear. Television is entering in."[74]

Reed resigned as head of the Radio Commission in 1952 to accept a
position with the SBC Annuity Board, and he was succeeded briefly by
Leonard L. Holloway who had been public relations officer for the Shep-

pard Air Force Base in Wichita Falls. Some Baptist churches made their own arrangements with radio stations to broadcast their services but the idea of a vast Baptist Radio Network for Texas faded. Holloway later taught at Wayland Baptist College (now University), and served brief terms as president of Mary Hardin-Baylor University and the University of Corpus Christi.

Publicity Department. As BGCT programs grew larger and more complex the need for clear communications increased lest the left hand misunderstand what the right hand was doing. Not only was there need for internal communication among the various departments, but with the general public there was a growing need to explain, clarify, promote and sometimes defend what the Convention was trying to do. Like any successful organization, the BGCT wanted to present itself and its work in the most favorable light possible. Early in his second tenure Williams recommended the employment of a publicity director "to interpret us to the press and interpret the press to us." The Department of Publicity was set up in June 1947 with Andrew Q. Allen named as the first director. When Allen succeeded the veteran G. S. Hopkins as head of the Sunday School Department in 1949, the Department of Publicity was combined with the Radio Department under the leadership of R. Alton Reed. By that time there was little radio work left and the combined department was named the Public Relations Department.[75]

Church Loan Department. Through the years the BGCT had sought ways to help churches to enlarge and improve their buildings. In 1951 a committee chaired by A. B. White reported that over 300 churches in the 25 largest cities of Texas, and many more in rural areas, needed aid but had insufficient collateral to go to the banks. In response, the Executive Board voted to establish "The Church Building and Loan Association" and appropriated $250,000 to get started plus an additional $750,000 line of credit.[76] This was a separate corporation from the BGCT, under its own board of directors. Later the words "Building and" were omitted from the title to avoid coming under the jurisdiction of the state Banking Commission. The purpose statement, adopted upon motion of W. A. Criswell, said the new corporation was intended "for the purpose of administering funds entrusted to it, and from such funds to make loans to Baptist churches cooperating with and having the official sanction of The Baptist General Convention of Texas, to aid such churches in constructing buildings and improving existing buildings for public worship and religious education."[77] By the end of 1952 the Church Loan Association had closed twenty-eight loans in Texas for a total of $611,785 and was dealing with several other churches.[78]

Western Missions. Texas Baptists became interested in western missions partly, no doubt, because the opening of the Glorieta Baptist Assembly near Santa Fe, New Mexico, brought more Baptists to the west, and partly because so many of the pastors in the west were from Texas. Those who traveled to other western states, especially Arizona, California, Washington and Oregon saw that Southern Baptist work in those areas was in its infancy. Some felt that the inability of churches in these pioneer areas to provide adequate facilities was a major factor in slowing their growth. In 1952 a Texas group, headed by A. B. Culbertson, William Fleming and J.Howard Williams, approached the Home Mission Board about helping the western churches to obtain building grants and loans, but got little encouragement. Rebuffed in Atlanta, a group of Texas Baptist "laymen of large financial means" set out to raise a fund of $1 million to help SBC churches in the west. William Fleming, who believed deeply in the potential of the western churches and backed up that belief with his checkbook, agreed to provide the first $250,000 to get the project started. The Executive Board agreed to form a new non-profit corporation to work closely with (but not merge with) the Church Loan Association. A group of laymen agreed to give $500,000 if Texas Baptists would raise another $1 million, giving a beginning capital of $1.5 million.

In meeting with Baptist leaders in the western states, it was noted that "We [BGCT] anticipate the necessity of establishing a man of sound judgment and seasoned experience in the Western territory to make personal inspection of each application for loan and to give his attention to each loan after it has been made."[79] Qualifications for aid under this program were stringent.

> A church making application for loans must be located in a community which presents opportunities for building and maintaining a church, based upon a religious census made during the ninety day period preceding the application for loan. Such locations are to be agreed upon by representatives of the state convention and by the Loan Association. It is necessary for churches to be well located in their communities and on ample space sufficient for contemplated expansion.[80]

Not only must the location be acceptable, but any aided church must be distinctly Southern Baptist in its affiliations and sympathies. The Board specified that:

> The church making application for loan must be in full fellowship and cooperation with an association which is affiliated with a state Baptist Convention and with the Southern Baptist Convention. Such church must be contributing to or agree to contribute to missions through the Cooperative Program regularly and systematically. . . . Non-cooperation shall be determined by the association and the state convention with which the church is affiliated or by the Church Loan Department of the Baptist General Convention of Texas.[81]

Texas Baptists wanted to be sure their aid went to churches that were truly Baptist. "We recognize the freedom and absolute autonomy of each Baptist Church," said the Board, "and would in no sense encroach upon the liberties of any church and yet we must acknowledge the importance of proper pastoral leadership." With this in mind they concluded that "preference will be given to applications for loans where pastors are well balanced in their doctrine, thoroughly cooperative and in complete accord with their state convention and with the Southern Baptist Convention."

This building program for the west was the first major out of state mission project for Texas Baptists. Churches aided included the First Southern Baptist Church of Seattle, the First Southern Baptist Church of Hollywood, and the Parkview Baptist Church in Phoenix, which for months had been meeting in a tent.[82]

Christian Life Commission. Off and on over the years the BGCT had adopted resolutions on various moral issues, especially alcohol, gambling and movie theaters, and sometimes the *Baptist Standard* carried articles or editorials against such practices as professional boxing, college football and women riding men's bicycles. However, Texas Baptists had no organization to follow up on these issues, no continuing effort to educate or motivate Texas Baptists on moral issues, though Acker C. Miller's Department of Ministry with Minorities had since 1944 spoken out on race relations. Secretary Williams had something more in mind. He wrote:

> I missed the convention at Houston last year [1948] because of illness. As I listened to the proceedings by radio, I saw our work more objectively than ever I had before. I rejoiced in the fine work that was reported, but I was disappointed in much that we did not do. The followers of Christ in our day are pressed on every side with problems and movements which pull at the anchors of their faith and call for Christian interpretation. It is my conviction that this convention should initiate some plan by which we can help our people to understand the grave issues of our day in terms of Christian faith and practice.[83]

This started the ball rolling. Both T. B. Maston and A. C. Miller regarded J. Howard Williams as the primary founder of the CLC, but they modestly downplayed their own crucial role in that development. In his oral memoirs, Miller recalled Williams saying, "we go along here preaching what we call the gospel, but we leave out the help that we can give to labor, we leave out the help that we might give to race, . . . We ought to have some agency by which we could promote this phase of the Christian life."[84] The 1949 convention appointed a Committee of Seven to study the needs and bring a recommendation as to how to help people to understand and apply the principles of Christian living to issues of daily life. The committee consisted of J. A. Ellis, Herbert Howard, A. C. Miller, Jesse J. Northcutt, Arthur Rutledge, W. R. White, and Thomas B. Maston. They were assisted by Ralph Phelps and also by Hugh Brimm, head of the Social Service Commission of the SBC (forerunner of the SBC Christian Life Commission).

The report of the Committee of Seven in 1950 said "the major need of our day is an effective working combination of a conservative theology, an aggressive, constructive evangelism and a progressive application of the spirit and teachings of Jesus to every area of life."[85] They recommended that the BGCT form a "Commission on Problems in Christian Living" to work in cooperation with the already existing Department of Ministry to Minorities.[86] The Executive Board accepted the recommendation, but the name came out different. While members discussed the proposal, an opponent inadvertently named the commission. He warned of the dangers of "this commission on the Christian life." A. C. Miller, who was sitting next to T. B. Maston, exclaimed "That's our name, Maston. That's our name, the Christian Life Commission."[87] According to J. Howard Williams, the new commission was created for two purposes: (1) to help create an awareness of the many areas of daily life in which specific Christian principles apply, and (2) to point out ways to make that witness more effective.[88] Texas was the first state convention to form an agency to speak on moral concerns, but other states and the SBC soon followed and the name chosen in Texas, Christian Life Commission, was also adopted throughout the SBC.

A. C. Miller was named to head the new commission, which began with an annual budget of $19,557. Since 1944 Miller had been director of the Ministry with Minorities, with responsibility to preach the gospel and develop fellowship with five minority groups in Texas (African-Americans, Mexicans, Asians, Europeans, and Jews). During World War II Miller directed ministries among the soldiers in Texas. In both his military and minority ministries, Miller ventured beyond the traditional approach to address the social and moral needs of the people. In addition to saved souls, he sought restored lives. As a student in Southern Seminary in Louisville, Miller had gained a wide reading in social problems, to which he added his own experiences as a pastor in Cleveland, Oklahoma, and in Cisco and Belton, Texas. T. B. Maston, the respected professor of Christian ethics at Southwestern Seminary and one of the founding fathers of the CLC, said "Dr. Miller was an older, more mature man, and I have the feeling that he knew a little better how to get along, maybe, with folks that opposed him."[89]

When the commission held its first meeting in 1951 under Miller's leadership, it laid out six distinct areas for research, writing and emphasis. They were: (1) scriptural basis and approach to moral issues, (2) the family, (3) race relations, (4) public morals, (5) economic life, and (6) world order. The next year the first area was dropped as a separate division and instead integrated as the basis of work in all the other areas.

In 1953 Miller resigned to become head of the CLC of the Southern Baptist Convention, thus perpetuating a pattern that was becoming familiar, that is, Texas Baptists pioneering a new ministry only to have the national convention lure the pioneer leader to Nashville to head a similar program for the SBC. Miller's successor was thirty-year-old Foy D. Valentine, pastor at Gonzales. He was a graduate of Baylor University and a doctoral graduate of Southwestern Seminary, majoring with Maston in Christian ethics. Valentine had twelve years experience as a pastor, and had been one of the first workers in the youth evangelism movement in Texas. He had been a field worker with the CLC, and had been the first BSU director at Prairie View A&M, a black college near Houston. He spent the summer of 1944 at Clarence Jordan's Koinonia Farm in Georgia, but returned to Texas convinced that a more church-centered moral emphasis would be more effective.[90] Williams said, "Most of you know Brother Valentine, and our recommendation is unanimous and hearty that we elect him to this office at a salary of $7,200.00 per year, plus necessary traveling expenses."[91] Valentine served until 1960 when he, like his predecessor, resigned to head the CLC of the SBC.

Under Miller and Valentine, the Texas CLC developed a literature to point out Bible teachings on various social and moral issues. Miller developed a highly effective series of pamphlets entitled "The Bible Speaks," spotlighting various moral issues. Valentine developed the annual Christian Life Workshop, a meeting to consider moral issues. During his seven years of leadership, Valentine was assisted by Browning Ware (1956) and William M. Pinson, Jr. (1957).

At first the CLC was assigned to work under the State Missions Commission, and heads of the other BGCT departments were members of the CLC. This meant, according to its historian, that the early CLC "had the name of a commission but was a stepsister of the other commissions."[92] Later the CLC achieved full commission status in fact as well as in name.

The Christian Education Commission. The last new BGCT commission formed during Williams's second tenure was the Christian Education Commission, created in 1952. With some exceptions, most Baptist colleges in Texas served regional constituencies and efforts to correlate their curricula, fund-raising, and building programs into one state-wide program proved elusive. Since the 1890s efforts to bring some unity to the Baptist educational program in Texas had worked better on paper than in reality.

In 1950 a BGCT Committee on Christian Education recommended "that the Executive Board be instructed to examine very carefully the feasibility of giving the Executive Secretary a special assistant who shall be a professional school man, and shall give his time to studying the educational problems in Texas and their effect upon Baptist schools." This educational specialist would advise the Executive Secretary and "spend a generous portion of his time actually out on the field 'selling' Christian education to our whole Baptist constituency."[93] However, the Board voted to hold the matter "in abeyance" until 1952 when they appointed a Committee of Fifteen to study Baptist education in Texas.[94] In addition to Secretary Williams, this committee included James H. Landes, chair; Carl Bates; James L. Sullivan; Guy Newman; Kyle Yates; Carlyle Marney; Arthur B. Rutledge; Grady Metcalf; H. C. Bennett; E. S. James; F. B. Malone; William Fleming; George Mason; Howard E. Butt; and Ross Sams.

The committee enlisted R. Orin Cornett, head of the Southern Baptist Education Commission, to head a group of educators to make a survey of Baptist education in Texas. From this group, "teams of specialists" made an extensive survey, sent questionnaires, visited campuses and got fairly complete information on academic, administrative, and financial life of the schools. All this data was digested by the Committee of Fifteen, who made their report to the Executive Board in December 1952. This was perhaps the most thorough study ever undertaken on Texas Baptist schools and the results led to significant changes.

The survey found and commended some points of strength in the Texas colleges. They were reasonably well distributed regionally, except there was none in the Dallas-Fort Worth metroplex or in Houston; they showed rising academic standards; and most were judged to have effective faculty and administrative leadership. However, these strengths were offset by points of weakness. The junior college (Decatur) and three of the senior colleges lacked full regional accreditation; there was a serious lack of coordination among the schools; and there was, the survey concluded, "a great deal of needless and expensive duplication." Each school acted independently and "the absence of a united front for Christian education is one of the most serious weaknesses of the Christian education program of Texas Baptists."[95]

The committee also noted that the relation between the BGCT and the colleges was not spelled out, with the result that the BGCT was called upon to help fund programs it had not approved. "Another serious problem," said the committee, "is the lack of a plan of basic appropriations to the several institutions based on quantitative factors such as cost of instruction, enrolment, tuition and fees, etc. It is the opinion of your committee that serious consideration should be given to the working out of a formula for basic appropriations for operating expenses." For Texas to operate seven senior colleges without any correlation of their curricula "is needlessly expensive and unwise," said the committee.

The Committee of Fifteen recommended that the BGCT create a Christian Education Commission and "employ an Executive Co-ordinator" who would be "a man of background and capabilities which will command the respect and confidence of the presidents of the colleges, the leaders of the convention and the Baptist constituency at large." This leader should understand college finance, academics and public relations and should be paid commensurate with his abilities.

The report was adopted with only one change: Mrs. Theron Fouts moved that the word "men" be changed to "members," which unanimously passed. The Board named Harold A. Haswell, president of Ouachita Baptist University in Arkadelphia, Arkansas, as the first head of the Christian Education Commission. He took office in August 1953 just as J. Howard Williams was leaving the BGCT to become president of Southwestern Seminary.

UNIVERSITY OF CORPUS CHRISTI

Only one new Baptist college was formed during the second tenure of Secretary Williams. For years Baptists in South Texas had chafed at the absence of any Baptist school in their area, and in 1946 they saw an opportunity to remedy that lack. On November 12, 1946, the Executive Board had a called meeting to consider an offer from the United States Navy to turn over Chase Field, a 1,062 acre training facility six miles from Beeville. The property had cost over $8 million and was set up to handle about 3,000 trainees. The Navy offered to lease Chase Field for $1.00 a year and later give the property outright when all threat of war had diminished. Baptists readily accepted and formed the Arts and Technological College. The college existed on paper but never held classes at Chase Field. E. S. Hutcherson, pastor in Houston, was elected president and Raymond M. Cavness served as dean until succeeded by John W. Cobb. W. R. White chaired the building committee and sought to elicit support for the new school.

The offer of Chase Field seemed too good to be true and, as it turned out, it was. The vast facility was not suited for use as a college and remodeling cost far more than expected. Local support in Beeville was lukewarm at best, though the citizens raised $37,000 of a $50,000 pledge and forgave a $38,000 bonded indebtedness.[96] In 1947 it was voted to move the college to Cuddihy Field in Corpus Christi, another surplus military site, with promises of firm support from the Baptists and other citizens of South Texas. On short notice, the school opened in September, 1947, with 321 students. Four months later over the Christmas holidays the college moved yet again, this time to the surplus Navy Technical Air Training Center on Ward Island. In October, 1947, the college board voted to change the name of the school from Arts and Technological College (ATC) to University of Corpus Christi (UCC).

From the first the college was problem plagued. In its first two years of life, it moved three times, tried to shape a curriculum under three different deans, tried to adapt to unsuitable military surplus buildings, and struggled for identity and financial resources under two presidents.[97] Internal tensions grew between those who wanted to emphasize liberal arts and those who preferred a more technical or business orientation. Enrollment lagged and financial support failed to develop as hoped. Support from the BGCT, never enthusiastic or generous, further diminished as did support from South Texas Baptists. In 1971 the college trustees asked the BGCT to release the school from its denominational ties, and UCC continued as an independent school until it was closed in May 1973.*

ASSEMBLY IN THE WEST

The Ridgecrest Baptist Assembly (now Conference Center) in North Carolina proved its value to Southern Baptists and by the late 1930s there was talk of forming another such center in the West. For Baptists west of the Mississippi attendance at Ridgecrest was difficult given the condition of roads and cars at the time. There was also an undercurrent of concern, seldom mentioned openly, that Baptist churches in the West needed to be more firmly anchored to the SBC, which at that time was still centered in the Southeast. In time talk led to action and the SBC appointed a Committee on Southwestern Assembly to report in 1947. Several states made a bid for the new assembly, including Arkansas, Missouri, Texas and New Mexico.

Texas Baptists pushed hard for their Paisano Assembly in the Davis Mountains of far west Texas as the second SBC assembly. Paisano, named for the "road runner" bird common in the area, had been the site of the famous Texas "Cowboy Camp Meeting," and had become well-known for the preaching of George W. Truett each summer. Advocates of Paisano noted that it was close to the Rio Grande, with high altitude and cool brisk air, not far from such attractions as Carlsbad National Caverns, the Big Bend National Park, old Fort Davis and the modern McDonald Observatory. Nearby were Indian villages, cattle ranches, and dude ranches. Descriptions of the charming scenic beauty of the area, one suspects, might have been written by an eager publicist who had never actually visited the site.[98]

Even so, Texas convinced the committee if not the SBC. Minutes from 1947 record that, "The report of the Committee on Southwestern Assembly recommending the immediate acceptance of the Paisano Assembly was not approved."[99] Instead, another committee, headed by Perry F. Webb of San Antonio, made further studies and on a split vote recommended a site in the Ozarks near Harrison, Arkansas, and even took an option on property there. However, in a stunning reversal, the SBC meeting at Oklahoma City in 1949 rejected the committee's majority report for Harrison, and instead accepted the minority report for a little-known site at Glorieta, New Mexico.[100] Having lost their bid to become the second SBC assembly, Texas Baptists determined to develop Paisano on their own, but the popularity of nearby Glorieta which opened in 1952 attracted so much Texas attendance that Paisano declined.

BENEVOLENCE MINISTRIES

While expanding the BGCT structures and building institutions, Texas Baptists did not neglect the needs of people around them, especially the neediest and most helpless.

The Orphans. Since the days of Robert Cooke Buckner in the 1870s, the name of Buckner has linked Texas Baptists with child care for orphans. In 1948 the Buckner Home expanded to include a broader range of ministries and changed its name to Buckner Baptist Benevolences. A report to the Executive Board noted that "three additional social institutions shall be established under the Buckner Baptist Benevolences."[101] These included a home for the aged (Houston), a Welfare Mission for unwed mothers (San Antonio), and a Baptist Boys' Ranch (South Texas). However, it appeared that over time Texas Baptists, many of whom had never known old Father Buckner, felt less loyalty to the Buckner Home and some even regarded it as more a family than a Texas Baptist enterprise.[102] In 1951 Robert C. Buckner, grandson of the founder, warned that while they must guard against Texas Baptists losing the home, "Buckner must see to it that it does not lose Texas Baptists."[103] In 1952 in what one historian calls "Buckner's New Day,"[104] Ellis L. Carnett was elected president of Buckner Baptist Benevolences. For the first time in its long life the institution was headed by someone outside the Buckner family. Carnett had taught music at Southwestern Seminary and for a time served as Director of the School of Music at the New Orleans Baptist Theological Seminary. In 1945 upon the death of I. E. Reynolds, Carnett became head of the church music school at Southwestern Seminary. He left that post to be pastor at the Travis Avenue church in Fort Worth, from which post be was elected president of Buckners. Carnett led the institution in new directions, not entirely free of friction. Not fully sympathetic with these new directions, Robert Cooke Buckner resigned as vice-president in 1954, after serving eighteen years. The tie between the institution and the Buckner family was further loosened.

Additional orphanages under some degree of BGCT sponsorship were founded at San Antonio (1944), Round Rock (1950) and Beeville (1952). On January 13, 1946 ground was broken in San Antonio for the Mexican Baptist Orphanage, led by E. J. Gregory, superintendent. M. C. Garcia, pastor of Calvary Mexican Baptist Church, turned the first dirt. The new home dedicated two cottages in September, 1946, one given by the Texas WMU and one given by the Buckner Home in Dallas.[105] By 1949 this home had four cottages and 46 children in residence. It was located nine miles west of San Antonio on Highway 90, and was the only orphanage in Texas ministering exclusively to Mexican children.

In 1950 Mr. and Mrs. L. B. Henna of Round Rock offered to the BGCT a home built and furnished to house 50 to 60 children with no strings attached other than that it be used as an orphanage. The Board accepted and named Herbert Dollahite as superintendent. The home was in operation later that same year. In 1952 a "Mrs. Booth" gave a ranch near Beeville to be used as an orphanage. The institution, under the leadership of J. M. Lunsford, was accepted by the BGCT in December 1952.

Retired Ministers. The work of the SBC Annuity Board, located in Dallas, took much of the pressure off caring for elderly and "decrepit" ministers in Texas. Even so, many did not join the program of that Board and, in old age, became dependent upon the mercies of the BGCT. In 1952 the Executive Board voted that after July 1, 1953, it would no longer aid ministers who could have joined the Annuity Board, were urged to do so, but did not. It was said that even with as little as three years of active ministry remaining, participation in the Annuity Board program would provide a retirement income far beyond the amount usually received in relief. The policy was stern, but its enforcement was gentle. Twice the deadline was extended and it was never rigidly enforced.

The Sick. "Texas Baptists have every reason to be grateful to God for the great teaching and healing ministry of their seven hospitals," said a report at the end of 1952.[106] These hospitals included Baylor Hospital, Dallas; Memorial Hospital, Houston; Hendrick Hospital, Abilene; Hillcrest Hospital, Waco; Valley Baptist Hospital, Harlingen; Southeastern Texas Baptist Hospital, Beaumont; and Baptist Memorial Hospital, San Antonio. Five of the seven included schools of nursing. These seven institutions had a total bed capacity of 1,789 and 319 bassinets. In 1952 they treated 88,522 patients, of whom 17,832 were charity patients. The hospitals gave over a half million dollars of charity care plus $86,554 in discounts. Total income for all the hospitals that year exceeded $11 million.

While the BGCT operated seven hospitals they could have had a dozen or more. Other cities clamored for a hospital and numerous towns that had a community hospital desperately wanted to give it to the BGCT or to anyone. Places wanting a Baptist hospital, or wanting Baptists to take over an existing hospital, included Rusk, Greenville, Tyler, Denison, Sherman, Big Spring, Lubbock, and Littlefield. A committee which studied the matter, recommended that in light of the expense involved that "no further hospitals shall be established by the Convention at this time."[107] However, in time the Convention did establish others.

The Displaced. Texas Baptists agreed to work with a committee of the SBC in helping to relocate persons, mostly Europeans, displaced by World War II. By 1950 Texas Baptists had 43 sponsors who agreed to settle 124 persons, and hoped eventually to settle 300 in Texas. Sponsors must guarantee that potential settlers would have a job, decent housing, and would not become public charges.[108]

THE BAPTIST BUILDING

From the beginning the BGCT and its predecessors, the BSA and BGA, made their headquarters in rented office space. In the affluent 1920s there was talk of building their own headquarters but the Depression quieted that. However, the idea of their own building simmered on the back burner of Baptist consciousness, awaiting the right time to flame up again. In the early 1950s three factors converged to move this idea to the front burner: more BGCT departments and larger programs that called for more space, financial ability to build, and the presence of a trusted leader who could bring it about. Williams, the "Mr. Can Do" of Texas Baptists, believed that no institution can do its best work until it is adequately housed. He also applied this conviction to churches; it is no happenstance that the Church Loan Association originated during his tenure. Williams believed Texas Baptists *should* have their own headquarters building, he believed they *could* do it, and so he determined they *would* do it.

By 1948 The Executive Board had determined to erect a Baptist Building but the path from the idea to blueprints, and from blueprints to a completed building was lengthy. Endless details had to be debated, decided and, in some cases, re-debated and re-decided. In 1949 a Texas couple offered the bulk of their substantial property to the BGCT, on condition that the first $400,000 go toward a new Baptist Building.[109] The Board voted to accept this gift and appointed a committee to seek a site for the proposed building. In March, 1949, Williams informed the Executive Board that "It seems now that the building where we are now located will be sold. We will have to find someplace to go."[110] This pending sale was probably fortuitous for it required the Board to move beyond endless discussion to specific action. Williams suggested that since the BGCT already owned property at Ervay and San Jacinto, across from the First Baptist Church, that "we look with favor on the erection of our own building, and get into it as soon as we can."

The building, long delayed, cost far more when it was completed in 1952 than expected when it was planned in 1948. In October, 1950, the committee called a halt because bids were so much higher than expected. The Board authorized them to proceed, up to a maximum of $1.2 million. In 1951 the Board conveyed to the SBC Relief and Annuity Board and the Texas Baptist Foundation a one-fourth interest in the building site, with the understanding they would share in the cost and ownership of the building.

Dedication for the spacious and attractive new Baptist Building at Ervay and San Jacinto came on June 3, 1952. In describing the new facility, Williams said Texas Baptists "could be justly proud without having to apologize either for its elaborateness or for its modesty."[111]

CONCLUSION

On June 9, 1953, J. Howard Williams resigned as executive secretary, effective August 1, to become president of the Southwestern Seminary in Fort Worth. In two terms he had served for twelve and a half years as the leader of Texas Baptists. Always on the cutting edge, Williams periodically "re-potted" himself in new soil to accept new challenges. His pastorates were always successful but never lengthy, and his two terms at the helm of Texas Baptist life lasted five and seven years respectively. His term as president of Southwestern Seminary was imminently successful but he was felled by a heart attack in 1958 just before he reached his fifth anniversary.

With Williams's resignation came the end of an era in Texas Baptist history. Perhaps more than any of his predecessors, Williams combined all the best gifts for effective leadership. He was a man of vision who saw what *could* be done, and he could enable others to see that vision. He was also a man of action who could bring the vision to reality. Finance Committee minutes record that Williams "gave a heartening report about our entire work and spoke enthusiastically about our great opportunities."[112] That statement happens to come from 1947, but it could have come from any time, for Williams was always upbeat and optimistic. He was extraordinarily gifted as a fund-raiser and administrator. Williams genuinely liked people and people liked him. He related well to students, pastors, BGCT staff, poor people, wealthy people. People trusted him. During his tenure as executive secretary Texas Baptist fellowship was not marred by distrust, theological bickering, or backroom sniping. In 1953 J. Ralph Grant, pastor of FBC Lubbock and chair of the Executive Board, referred to "the great spirit of Texas Baptists and said it was due in large part to Dr. Williams."[113]

Upon a motion by W. A. Criswell, Williams was given the entire month of July 1953 as paid vacation and was given the Convention car he was driving. Woodrow Fuller was named interim executive secretary and served until September 1, 1953, when Forrest C. Feezor took over.

CHAPTER 11

NEW DIRECTIONS, 1953–1960

"OUR WORK CONTINUES TO prosper. The Lord is blessing it. The people are supporting it."[1] This report by Grady Metcalf to the Executive Board of the Baptist General Convention in late 1953 sounds too optimistic, but the facts bear out Metcalf's assessment. For Texas Baptists, as for the nation, the 1950s proved to be a time of growth, prosperity, and self-confidence that bordered at times on smugness.

When has the country seen a decade like the 1950s? This was a "golden age" for America, economically, culturally and socially. The rise of the Billy Graham revivals brought a spirit of renewal and the churches shared generously in the spiritual advances of the age. The American industrial machine which had become so productive during the war was almost overnight converted to producing consumer goods. These goods were distributed not only in America but to the ends of the earth, making America the dominant industrial power as it had already become the dominant military power.

Rising wages swelled the middle class, a group with affinity for Baptist affiliation, giving Baptists vastly more "prospects" for addition to the churches. A powerful new medium of communication became popular during the 1950s, the television.[2] No one could then have predicted what a dominating influence the new "one-eyed monster" would become. To a large extent the decade of the 1950s was also a time of conformity. Millions of American "dream homes" in suburbia looked surprisingly alike; cars, refrigerators, and clothing looked much alike, and even human behavior was expected to follow a uniform pattern. This widely accepted cultural behavior pattern included religious participation; to be active in church was an "in thing" and membership rolls of both Protestant and Roman Catholic churches reflected that trend.

Texas Baptists shared generously in the surge of membership, church attendance, and financial contributions. The simplest programs succeeded beyond all expectation but, like the shallow soil in the parable, much of this growth was too shallow to stand the heat which arose in later less favorable times.

FORREST C. FEEZOR

After the shock of J. Howard Williams's resignation, the Executive Board met on July 10, 1953 to choose his successor. During the interim, J. Woodrow Fuller, the Associate Executive Secretary, was put in charge. In their time-honored method the Board met, prayed earnestly, and without any nominating speeches members wrote on blank ballots the name of the person they felt should be elected to lead Texas Baptists. The first ballot showed that fifteen men had been nominated. Because they represent a Who's Who of Texas Baptist leadership at the time, it seems appropriate to list their names. They were A. B. Rutledge, Forrest C. Feezor, E. S. James, James H. Landes, Floyd Chafin, E. H. Westmoreland, J. Ralph Grant, A. B. White, J. Woodrow Fuller, Thomas A. Patterson, Andrew Q. Allen, A. C. Donath, R. A. Springer, E. Douglas Carver, and C. Wade Freeman. Of these, six were already on the staff of the BGCT, and one, E. S. James would soon be elected editor of the *Baptist Standard*. Three of these nominees would indeed serve as Executive Secretary for Texas Baptists (Feezor, Patterson, and Landes) and one (Fuller) would hold the same office for Florida Baptists.

Several of the nominees asked that their names be removed from consideration (Landes, White, Freeman, Springer, Grant) and the second ballot removed others. The third ballot showed the election was basically between Forrest C. Feezor and E. S. James, and on the fifth ballot the vote went 47 to 40 for the sixty-one year old Feezor. James then moved that the election be declared unanimous for Feezor, which was done.[3] Feezor appeared reluctant to accept the post and reported that he had been on the verge of withdrawing his name after the third ballot but a friend talked him out of it. He had been a pastor for twenty-seven years in North Carolina and Texas, the last seven years at FBC, Waco. He seemed particularly apprehensive about the "arrows of criticism" that some Baptist leaders had to endure, but noted hopefully that Texas had recently had little of that. R. A. Springer noted that, going back to the old Baptist State Convention of 1848, Feezor was the fourteenth man chosen to lead Texas Baptists. Standing well over six feet tall, Feezor was also one of the biggest leaders and the first to make a full medical exam a prerequisite of his acceptance.

Two weeks after his election, Feezor announced his acceptance, to begin September 1, 1953. He said, "I feel honored in your having elected me beyond anything I could say. I wish you had not done it. I do not think I have ever felt weaker in my life." He affirmed that "After days of seeking the Lord's will as to this office, there came a sense of peace and a feeling that here was offered an opportunity for service to the Lord and that

I must answer. . . . I am here to do the best I can."[4] Feezor resigned his pastorate and as president of the BGCT. He also resigned from the trustee boards of Baylor University, Hillcrest Memorial Hospital in Waco, and the Southern Baptist Theological Seminary in Louisville. James N. Morgan, first vice-president of the BGCT, assumed the presidency when Feezor resigned.

Before he accepted, Feezor said "I wrote all the former secretaries living and asked them for advice," and apparently they gave plenty. They said the secretary needs to arrange his schedule so as to be in the office as much as possible, but during his first week Feezor received fifty-seven requests to give a speech somewhere. He worried publicly if he would have enough time for his family, and he said "I come to this office with the conviction that I belong to this office and to the Lord." The advice most frequently given by former secretaries, Feezor said, was "Don't kill yourself."[5]

Who was this big man who came somewhat hesitantly to office in 1953? Feezor was born July 1, 1892, near Lexington, North Carolina. As one of eight children he grew up in poverty, had little educational advantages, and never saw a newspaper until he was eighteen. Feezor's parents were nominal Christians but the family seldom attended church. Young Forrest was converted from reading a book from his grandparents, *The Story of the Bible,* and publicly confessed his faith at age fourteen. His only schooling was in a one-room log cabin, but at that time his county had no public high school. Forrest determined to attend a boarding school some miles away but, lacking money for room and board, the teenager gathered the rudiments of housekeeping ("a discarded stove, a bedstead, and other things") and made out the best he could in a one room shack without electricity, running water or indoor plumbing. After five years of hard work, he graduated from this high school at the age of twenty-three, the first high school graduate in his family's history.[6] In 1915 on borrowed money Feezor entered Wake Forest College at Wake Forest, North Carolina.

Feezor felt a call to preach and his first pastorate was somewhat impromptu. One Sunday he attended the Stoner's Grove Baptist Church only to learn that the pastor was absent that day. Three laymen asked Feezor to preach, which he did. The next Sunday the pastor resigned and the church immediately called Feezor in his stead. Stoner's Grove was a "quarter-time" church (with preaching only one Sunday a month) and before long Feezor accepted two other part-time churches as well. He also became a teacher in a country school much like the one he had attended. Feezor was ordained on June 30, 1916, and returned to Wake Forest with more purpose to his studies. He graduated from Wake Forest in 1920 and enrolled in Southern Seminary in Louisville, receiving his Master of Theology degree in 1923 at the age of thirty-one. For three years, 1923-1926, Feezor taught Bible (and served as chair of the Bible Department) at William Jewell College in Liberty, Missouri, and during the summer of 1925 studied in the divinity school of the prestigious University of Chicago. He returned to the pastorate in 1926, serving five years at Second Baptist, Liberty. In 1927 Feezor was married to Jessie Ray Fuller of Dallas, whom he had met at the 1926 SBC in Houston. Miss Fuller had grown up in FBC, Dallas, and the wedding ceremony was performed by Pastor Truett. For twelve years, 1931-1943 Feezor served as pastor of the Tabernacle Church in Raleigh, North Carolina, his home state, where he was active in denominational work. His alma mater, Wake Forest, conferred upon him the honorary Doctor of Divinity degree in 1934. He served two Texas pastorates, Broadway in Fort Worth (1943-1946) and FBC, Waco (1946-1953). Always active in denominational work, Feezor served as state convention president in both North Carolina and Texas. He was also a member of the Masonic Lodge.[7]

CHANGE AND CONTINUITY

In December, 1953, the powerful Plans and Policies Committee of the Executive Board nominated staff members for the new church year. Because this provides a microcosm of the BGCT at the time, it seems good to list these as they appear in the records.[8]

Your committee on Plans and Policies desires to submit for your consideration the following report:

I. EMPLOYEES
In the light of effective and far reaching work done by our co-laborers, we both commend their constructive work and recommend the following employees of this Board with salaries as indicated:

GENERAL ADMINISTRATION
1. That Dr. Forrest C. Feezor be reelected as Executive Secretary at a salary of $12,900.00 per year.
2. That Rev. J. Woodrow Fuller be reelected as Assistant Executive Secretary at a salary of $9,200.00 per year.
3. That Dr. R. A. Springer be reelected Treasurer of the Board at a salary of $8,500.00 per year.

DEPARTMENT ADMINISTRATION
4. That Mr. Andrew Q. Allen be reelected as Sunday School Missionary at a salary of $7,800.00 per year.
5. That Dr. L. T. Daniel be reelected as Endowment Secretary at a salary of $7,800.00 per year.
6. That Dr. C. Wade Freeman be reelected as Superintendent of the Department of Evangelism at a salary of $8,900.00 per year. Since the election of the Evangelistic Staff members has always been under the Executive Committee of this Board, we recommend that this matter be referred to the Executive Committee.
7. That Dr. T. C. Gardner be reelected as Baptist Training Union Missionary at a salary of $7,800.00 per year.
8. That Dr. Harold A. Haswell be reelected as Executive Coordinator of the Education Commission at a salary set by the Education Commission. [The Education Commission provided a somewhat larger salary than did the other departments].

9. That Rev. Leonard Holloway be reelected as Director of Public Relations of the Board at a salary of $7,800.00 per year.

10. That Dr. W. F. Howard be reelected as Baptist Student Union missionary at a salary of $7,800.00 per year.

11. That Dr. J. D. Riddle be reelected as Missionary of the Department of Church Music at a salary of $7,500.00 per year.

12. That Dr. L. H. Tapscott be reelected as Brotherhood Missionary at a salary of $7,500.00 per year.

13. That Dr. Foy Valentine be reelected as Director of the Christian Life Commission at a salary of $7,500.00 per year.

This was the crew Feezor inherited from J. Howard Williams. Five years later most of these were still at their posts.[9] Arthur B. Rutledge had been added to the General Administration staff as Secretary of Stewardship and Direct Missions. Russell Hooper Dilday, Sr. had succeeded T. C. Gardner as BTU Secretary in 1956 and when J. D. Riddle died, he was succeeded as head of the church music department by V. F. Forderhase. George Shearin had become Endowment Secretry in the place of L. T. Daniel. In those five years, salaries for most department heads were lowered slightly, by about $300 per year, but the Board added a tax-exempt $1,800 housing allowance, so overall compensation rose.

COMMENDATIONS AND CAUTIONS

In beginning a new year (1954) with a new Executive Secretary, the Plans and Policies Committee voiced both commendations and cautions. They noted that "The people are supporting it [our work] through their churches because they believe in the plan of work and in the workers who are leading."[10] In light of this trust, the Committee called on department heads to observe all prudent economy in budgeting their work. They specifically applauded the plan to combine evangelism and stewardship as the twin emphases for 1954, for "indeed, these two go together."[11] They commended the "Million More in '54'" campaign of the Nashville Sunday School Board, and urged Texas churches to participate. This was an effort to increase Baptist Sunday School enrollment by one million in 1954.

The P&P Committee called for renewed emphasis upon urban churches. "In recent years," they observed, "marked progress has been made by this Board in rehabilitating rural church buildings, assistance in salary supplements in needy and worthy situations. As the peak of need appears to have been passed in these two areas," they recommend that the Direct Missions Department redirect its attention and resources to cities where population growth made new churches necessary. "We now have nine of these city mission programs" with more needed. They had in mind grants for new churches, not for relocation of existing churches. The growth of the BGCT in size and complexity has made the work of the district and associational missionaries even more important, the Committee said. "We are depending more and more upon responsible District and Associational leaders in matters of planning and promotion. These leaders are close to the pastors and people in the churches. Their generous operation is invaluable in every phase of the work." In the past, the Executive Board supplemented the salaries of some district and associational workers more than others, depending on the number of churches in the area and the level of perceived need. However, the P&P Committee said, "We recommend a uniform policy be set up by which this Board will supplement the salaries of associational missionaries, city Superintendents and District Missionaries." For associational missionaries the Board would provide annual supplements of $900; for superintendents of city missions, $1,500; and for district missionaries, $2,100. With these limits, the associational and district boards were free to set total salaries. The Board agreed to pay $900 annually toward secretarial help for the district missionary offices.[12]

The Committee commended David M. Gardner, editor of the *Baptist Standard,* for helping military chaplains as they sought to return to Texas pastorates. Gardner chaired the Texas Baptist Chaplains Association and also used his paper to publicize the availability of ministers who had been out of the pastorate while serving as chaplains and who wished to return.

The P&P Committee urged restraint in founding new institutions, particularly if the Convention was expected to help support them. "In time of prosperity it is easy for new institutions to be born," they pointed out, "but it is always much easier to start an institution than it is to sustain it." On this point they were insistent. "We believe, therefore, that no . . . institution should be alunched [sic] without the recommendation of the proper committee and the approval of the Convention or its Executive Board." They asked that the established policy be continued that no grants of funds should be made apart from the recommendation of the Finance Committee.

A problem in budgeting arose from the tendency of the Board to make grants to institutions on an ongoing basis, to continue so much a year for many years into the future. Because the annual amount was smaller, some members tended to forget how much the Board was obligated for years to come. Some suggested that before any more ongoing grants were voted, all those already approved and the total amounts already promised be read out in open meeting. The Finance Committee, it was reported, "faces an exceedingly difficult task of working out an equitable budget due to current operation demands and these long term commitments." These long term promises could endanger other work of the Board. "The time is near at hand when State Missions and mission causes beyond Texas cannot go forward but will rather be forced to greatly reduce their ministry and missionary forces in order to honorably uphold the continuing commitments made by this Board."

One happy result of Baptist growth in Texas was that the supply of capable leaders greatly increased. The Executive Board recognized this and said, "In view of the fact that we have many valuable men for committee service and that such responsibility should be widely distributed, we recommend that beginning with this year all standing committees be divided into three groups."[13] The first group would serve one year, the second two years and the third group would serve three year terms. After serving for three consecutive years, a committee member would be ineligible for reelection until at least one year had elapsed. This not only passed the leadership around but could also prevent some person from becoming entrenched on a committee and dominating its decisions for years. Another change in the committee structure related to benevolence work and orphanages. In the past one committee had provided oversight for both forms of ministry, but beginning in 1954 it was recommended that the Board appoint a separate Committee on Benevolence and a Committee on Orphanages.

THE NEW ADVANCE COMMITTEE

The Executive Board had long planned and promoted Texas Baptist ministries in five-year segments. They set goals for evangelism, stewardship and other areas of ministry, monitored progress, and reported their achievements at the end of the period. As the latest of these five-year plans, 1948-1953, was concluding, the Board appointed a strong committee to draw up goals for 1954 through 1958. Members included J. Ralph Grant, Louis Henna, E.S. James, James H. Landes, Marie Mathis, T. A. Patterson, Gordon Ryan, and John Wright, with E. Herman Westmoreland as chair.[14] At first called a Survey Committee, J. Howard Williams by April 1953 gave it the name of New Advance Committee.[15] The group divided into sub-committees on Benevolences (Patterson, chair), Education (Landes), and State Missions (Westmoreland). Because the ambitious goals presented by the New Advance Committee, and their adoption by the Executive Board, tell so much about the spirit of Texas Baptists in that optimistic age, they are listed here.[16] Under heading of "GOALS FOR THE NEXT FIVE YEARS," they listed:

	1954	1955	1956	1957	1958
Baptisms	65,000	70,000	75,000	80,000	85,000
New Churches	100	100	100	100	100
Total Church Mem.	1,400,000	1,550,000	1,700,000	1,850,000	2,000,000
S.S. Enrolment	1,000,000	1,050,000	1,100,000	1,150,000	1,200,000
S.S. Awards	125,000	125,000	125,000	125,000	125,000
Vacation Bible Sch.	3,100	3,200	3,300	3,400	3,500
T.U. Enrolment	400,000	450,000	500,000	550,000	600,000
T.U. Awards	175,000	175,000	175,000	175,000	175,000
Brotherhood Enr.	61,000	67,000	73,000	79,000	85,000
New Bro'hoods	135	135	135	135	135
W.M.U. Members	160,000	170,000	180,000	190,000	200,000
W.M.U. Organizations	8,400	8,800	9,200	9,600	10,000
Baptist Student Unions	70	75	80	85	90
New Student Centers	2	3	4	5	6

FINANCIAL
Total All Gifts	58,000,000	62,000,000	66,000,000	70,000,000	74,000,000

Undesignated	5,500,000	6,000,000	6,500,000	7,000,000	7,500,000
Designated	2,500,000	2,500,000	2,500,000	2,500,000	2,500,000
Major Gifts	7,000,000	7,500,000	8,000,000	8,500,000	9,000,000
Total Missions	15,000,000	16,000,000	17,000,000	18,000,000	19,000,000

These represented ambitious goals, but most of them were met or exceeded. The success in meeting these goals, however, presented new problems. As the work of the Convention grew and became more complex, with more money to manage and more personnel to supervise, the simple administrative structures of the past came under increasing pressures.

CHANGES IN STATE MISSIONS

For a generation the "district missionary" had been a part of Baptist work in Texas and the term had become entrenched in Baptist vocabulary. Both title and work changed in 1955, and the changes proved surprisingly controversial. In 1955 the Executive Board authorized a Mission Study Committee, chaired by M.B. Carroll, to consider any needed adjustments "in view of the expansion and development of our Baptist life in all promotional phases."[17] That committee brought recommendation for sweeping changes. The district missionary's title would be changed to "district secretary," and his salary would be paid 50/50 by the district executive board and the state executive board. The new district secretary would be elected by a committee made up of members of both district and state boards, but clearly the balance of power would be with the state board. "His election will be accomplished by the District Board and ratified by the State Executive Board." Duties would remain much the same, to promote the entire Baptist program of ministries, maintain good public relations, and be available to help churches, especially pastorless ones.

The title change tacitly acknowledged that the district missionary had become more an office administrator and less an actual missionary on the field. In response to a question, the committee said the reason for these changes was "to move the District Secretary closer to the State Secretary's office."[18] Another person asked, "Will this be thought of as centralization of authority?" The committee's response was vague, but public response quickly answered the question in the affirmative. When the issue came up again a few weeks later Feezor, clearly put on the defensive by public response, acknowledged that they had not consulted adequately with the "district men" before recommending the changes. Some objected that the new title sounded too bureaucratic, while others objected that districts lost all initiative if the state board had to "ratify" everything they did. "There was some question," the minutes state, "about whether the District Missionary was to be a [sic] office man or a field man." Some objected even to providing full-time office secretarial help lest this reinforce the idea that the district missionary was expected to remain mostly in the office. The vote on the changes passed by only 47 to 38.[19]

J. Ralph Grant, chairman of the Executive Board, said "I do not think we should leave with a vote like this." He agreed with Robert E. Naylor, pastor at Travis Avenue in Fort Worth, who called for a new committee to make a new study. Judge Frank M. Ryburn chaired the new committee, which brought its report in September, 1956. They used more felicitous language, but the substance of the old report survived. The new title would be "district missions secretary," and election would be "by joint agreement of the District Executive Board and the State Executive Board." The term "ratify" did not occur in the new report, though the salary was still to be paid 50/50 between district and state boards. Their report passed readily, and a committee was appointed to put the changes into effect. The Correlation Committee concluded that "the very genius of our work is found in the one word cooperation," and predicted that "the whole work of our Convention would find a happy coordination and it would be done without the sacrifice of soul freedom and independence of the local church."[20]

MISSIONS BEYOND TEXAS

For much of the nineteenth century Texas Baptists were dependent upon missionary help from outside, but their growth in the twentieth century was such that other states began to call upon Texas for help. Most of these requests came from the West and from states like Wisconsin and Minnesota where Baptist work was new. Texas Baptists contributed generously to build Texas Hall at the Glorieta Conference Center, and continued the annual appropriation for a time even after the building was paid off. They also helped from time to time with grants to the struggling new Arizona state convention and to Grand Canyon College at Phoenix. When the Colorado convention was formed in 1954, Texas Baptists helped by sending money and manpower to help the churches get a toe-hold. Oil man William Fleming of Fort Worth, according to one report, "had a passion" for western missions. He backed his convictions with his checkbook and also used his considerable clout to get the BGCT to underwrite a fund for western missions. The attitude of the Executive Board is seen in the minutes of March 5, 1956, which state that "it is altogether fitting for us to extend some financial assistance to them in the crisis they face in Arizona and in the beginning of the new Convention in Colorado. . . . we designate $10,000 for the Arizona Convention and $10,000 for the Colorado Convention as a meager but altogether worthy expression of our assistance to them in the marvelous missionary activities that these brethren are taking in the West." Frequently Willis J. Ray and R. E. Milam, leaders of new conventions in Arizona and Washington-Oregon respectively, along with the president of Grand Canyon College, would appear before the Executive Board to make a direct appeal for aid. The Board always made some grant, but usually only about half of what was asked.

When Roy L. Johnson, BGCT recording secretary for many years, left to become superintendent of missions for the Interstate Baptist Association in Oregon, the Finance Committee of the Executive Board agreed to provide funds to equip his office with desks, typewriter, mimeograph machine and other office needs. In 1958 the Executive Board sent a cement mixer, along with money for cement, to Jamaica to help rebuild churches wrecked by volcano and storms. Many individual Texas church budgets included a monthly amount for some church in the West. A committee chaired by Lee Hemphill reported in 1959 that "We have polled the churches of Texas and find much interest among our churches in the work in pioneer areas." Of churches that responded to this survey, 28% were already giving assistance to some western church or mission, 12% expressed willingness to underwrite loans for new churches, and 50% were willing to send their pastor for mission revivals.[21] The Executive Board was generous in sending its staff members to other states, and other nations, for various mission projects.

A different form of out of state missions arose in 1956 when a number of Southern Baptist churches in Wisconsin and Minnesota applied for affiliation with the Texas convention. Feezor said, "Many of our Southern Baptists in Minnesota and Wisconsin cannot find a church that conforms to their denominational belief; therefore, they organize and start new work." Home Mission Board policy was to aid only those churches affiliated with a state convention, and these churches had no access to a state convention in their area. A committee studied the application and members visited the churches and reported favorably. Feezor said, "We are possessed of a deep conviction that we would forfeit one of the greatest evangelistic and missionary opportunities if we do not approve the petitionary letters of these churches."[22] J. Ralph Grant moved that the churches be received into affiliation and said, "It will be . . . healthy for our Convention to have a part in it." Once affiliated with the BGCT, these churches were also eligible for aid from the HMB. For the next several years "Minnesota Missions" became a mainstay of Texas Baptist ministries.

CHRISTIAN EDUCATION

In the 1950s Texas Baptists sponsored seven senior colleges, one academy and one junior college, with aggregate assets of about $64 million and annual operating budgets for all of them amounting to about $14 million (1956-57 figures).[23] Under the leadership of Harold A. Haswell, education secretary, these schools had made remarkable progress in budgets, buildings, enrollments and especially in improving accreditation. The Executive Board had already served notice that any school that had not received accreditation by 1960 would no longer receive funds from the Cooperative Program. For the fall of 1957, the eight Baptist colleges enrolled 10,514 students, which represented about 20% of the Baptist college students in Texas. A look at these students yields some interesting facts. About 74% of them were Baptist, 23% some other denomination, and 3% registered no religious preference. The colleges retained a strong regional flavor, with well over half of their students coming from a radius of 100 miles or less (except for Baylor University, which drew only 41% from a 100 mile radius).[24] For the ten years ending in 1954, the BGCT had given about $10,300,000 to the schools, a little over $1 million a year.[25] In 1955 the Mary Hill Davis offering for state missions and the offering for Christian Education were combined, but nobody liked that arrangement and it was not continued.

About one out of seven students in the Baptist colleges was a ministerial student, and of the others about one out of fifteen was training for some other Baptist church position. Thus it appears that over 20% of Baptist college students were preparing for some kind ministry within the denomination. Even so, Baptists could not afford to ignore the 80% of Baptist students who attended non-Baptist colleges, for most of their lay leadership in the years to come would be drawn from that group. Of the 602 faculty members in the fall of 1957, 73% were Baptist and of course all the presidents and administrative officers were. For their highest degree, 31% of the professors at Texas Baptist colleges held doctorates while 56% held master's degrees.[26]

By 1959 the Baptist Student Union sponsored 65 active BSU groups and operated 24 Student Centers on state campuses in Texas. They had a total of 40 campus directors, of whom 19 also taught college Bible courses for college credit in addition to their other BSU duties. In 1955 the BSU Department moved to sponsor a Bible chair at Texas Southern University, a predominantly African-American school near Houston. About 60% of the 3500 students there were Baptists. In 1956 Bill Lawson, a gifted young black minister who later achieved great prominence in Baptist life in the Houston area, appeared before the Executive Board. He was a graduate of Tennessee State University and the Central Baptist Seminary in Kansas City. With rare good humor, Lawson said "I count it a privilege to come in and add some color to your program."[27] Lawson reported that the BSU on the Texas Southern campus was well underway, though at this point "we have not so much to report this time by way of actual achievement as by way of hope." He said,

> We have found that when we came to Texas the Negro students were not encouraged to go to church and had little Christian devotion. Their own missionary responsibility was something of which they were not even aware. The Baptist Student Union has changed a great deal of that this year. They now dedicate their lives to Christian service. There are fewer than one dozen Negro missionaries in the world. We want them to see their responsibility.[28]

In their beginnings the Texas Baptist colleges grew up much like Topsy, largely regional enterprises with no statewide planning as to location. Such planning might have done little good when most of the colleges were formed, since the population patterns of the state were not yet evident. However, by the 1950s it became obvious that Baptists had no col-

leges in the major metropolitan centers where over 50% of Texas Baptist people lived. In 1956 the Finance Committee voted to "express itself as looking with favor upon . . . the establishment of new Baptist Colleges in the heavily populated and rapidly growing metropolitan areas." James H. Landes, chairman of the Executive Board, reported in 1956 that in ten years the number of Baptist collegians in Texas would double, and he moved "to continue studying the possibilities of expansion into metropolitan areas not adequately served by existing institutions."[29] Major Texas cities without a Baptist college included Dallas, Houston and San Antonio, along with smaller but growing cities like Lubbock and Amarillo. To address this need, the Board discussed plans to establish junior colleges in Dallas and Houston, while Mary Hardin-Baylor considered starting a coeducational branch campus in San Antonio. The Board established stringent minimum requirements for site and local funding; after the University of Corpus Christi they wanted no more "shoe string" colleges. Further study led the Board to turn away from the concept of junior colleges on the grounds that they would not really meet the needs of the denomination, and that it would be better to launch senior colleges from the first.

In 1952 the Houston Baptist Association had a special committee, chaired by William E. Denham, to study the possibility of a Baptist college in that city.[30] By 1956 it was agreed that the school would be a coeducational, liberal arts college with special emphasis upon religion and the natural sciences, and that it would open with a freshman class and add a class each year until it reached a standard four-year curriculum, offering standard degrees. All thought of starting with a junior college or of making the Houston school a branch of Baylor University had by then been dropped. By 1957 Houston Baptists had raised substantial funds and had obtained a choice 390-acre tract of land in southwest Houston. In time, the Executive Board approved these plans and appointed a board of trustees for the new Houston Baptist University. The school was chartered on November 15, 1960, and held a ground breaking ceremony on May 20, 1962 with Governor Price Daniel, a Baptist layman, as speaker. The college opened for classes in 1963 under the presidency of W. H. Hinton.

From the 1860s onward Baptists had tried to sponsor a college in Dallas. Several such schools were founded and as promptly failed. In the 1950s a plan was discussed, but not enacted, to establish a Baptist college in Dallas as a branch of Baylor. For many years it had been obvious that the Decatur Junior College must move or die, and President Otis Strickland engineered a move to a new two-hundred acre campus overlooking Mountain Creek Lake in southwest Dallas. Fred A. White, pastor of FBC, Carrollton, played a leading role in moving the college from Decatur to Dallas, changing its name, and raising the college from junior to senior status. White later served as head of the Bible Department of the Dallas Baptist College. Ground breaking on the new campus came on May 3, 1964.[31]

Colleges are expensive and quality colleges even more so, and Texas Baptists struggled to maintain adequate financing for their several schools in the face of rapidly rising costs. Unfortunately, few of the schools had

enough endowment to make any great difference. All together, in 1957 the colleges received 45% of their total support from tuition and fees, and only 8% from endowment. The BGCT contributed 14% of total support and auxiliary enterprises and gifts provided the remainder.[32] Clearly this was not a recipe for stability or strength in the colleges. Layman Ben Wooten said "we are facing a new crisis in Christian education. Sputnik has changed things." Carr P. Collins pointed out that "our schools must have more support or they will deteriorate." He urged that Texas Baptists reexamine their entire budget with a view to keeping more Texas money in Texas. "The institutions of the Southern Baptist Convention," Collins said, "were in better shape than our Texas Baptist schools."[33] Some voiced fears that the declining percentage of Baptist students choosing to enroll in Texas Baptist colleges was both cause and effect of failure of the schools to maintain adequate facilities and strong academic programs.

BAPTIST BENEVOLENCES

The vast changes in American society in the 1950s affected Texas Baptists' efforts to minister to people in need. Prosperity caused some problems to diminish, but others equally serious emerged.

Child Care. Perhaps no benevolent work changed more than child care. Advances in health care meant that fewer adults died in their 30s or 40s, and thus fewer children were true orphans, though a number of "half-orphans" had only one surviving parent. More of the children in Baptist homes were there because of broken homes, abuse or abandonment. However, for whatever reasons, these children did not engage the strong emotional reaction and financial support that the true orphans had in Buckner's day. In an effort to appeal to a wider support base, the Buckner charter was changed in 1958 to allow women and ministers to serve as trustees (previously all trustees had been laymen), but this came too late to help much. There was also a basic shift in the concept of child care. The institutional orphanage, such as Buckner established, had gone out of style, to be replaced by adoptions and "foster care" that placed children in families. Studies indicated that in the future, the need for adoption and placement services would increase, but institutional child care would be increasingly restricted to temporary care or long-term care of the handi-capped.[34] These predictions, so confidently announced in the 1950s, have not proven entirely accurate.

Despite these changes, Texas Baptists by 1959 supported six homes for children (up from four in 1956), and one maternity home for unwed mothers. The Buckner Home in Dallas remained the flagship of Texas child care facilities, and Buckner also operated the Buckner Boys Ranch near Austin, the Milam Girls Home in Lubbock, and the Bethesda Maternity Home in San Antonio. In addition to these, the BGCT also operated the South Texas Children's Home at Beeville, the Texas Baptist

Children's Home at Round Rock, and the Mexican Baptist Orphans Home in San Antonio. The total capacity for the six children's homes was 1156, and average occupancy in 1957 was 1012.[35] Total operating expense for that year was about $1,367,000, about half of which came from the churches in direct offerings. Only Buckners in Dallas had enough endowment to produce significant income.

Up to 1960 the children's homes had not been included in Cooperative Program funds. At first the homes resisted being brought into the Cooperative Program, feeling they could do better by appealing directly to the churches. Some in the BGCT missions department also opposed, fearing that if the CP pie was sliced any thinner there would be less money for missions. A special committee on orphanages, reporting to the Executive Board in 1956, said, "In view of some discussion to put these four homes in the cooperative program, we studied this matter in our survey. We do not believe this is the solution to the financing of these homes at the present time." However, some felt it was time to bring the children's homes into the Cooperative Program. Robert E. Naylor of Fort Worth said,

> The report concludes that we cannot put our Homes in the Cooperative Program. If that is the finished report of the committee, I think it should be referred for further study. My feeling is that our Homes ought to be in the Cooperative Program. I believe the Cooperative Program suffers more by this [exclusion] than the Homes suffer by it. I just believe that the cost of one million dollars for operating them is not a valid ground for the conclusion that they cannot be in it. It would produce twice as much. I will be glad to make a motion that we refer this to the committee for further study.[36]

Ralph Grant of Lubbock chaired the new Benevolent Homes committee that took a survey of Texas Baptists and determined that most wanted the children's homes in the CP along with other ministry causes. After about two years of study, the Executive Board voted to bring the homes into CP support.[37] Even then, opposition lingered. Roy Johnson "expressed his fear that if the homes were included in the Cooperative Program, it might mean a decrease of the 37% budgeted toward Southern Convention causes." However, his motion to reject the committee report died for lack of a second.[38] E. L. Carnett, president of Buckners in Dallas, asked for and received assurance that while the homes would no longer appeal directly to the churches for money, they could continue to ask for canned goods and good used clothing.

Churches near the children's homes, like those near colleges, often had trouble providing facilities for the large numbers who attended but had little money to give. For example, FBC of Round Rock had 176 children from the home enrolled in Sunday School, and fully 53% of their total attendance was from children of the home. The church asked for help in providing space for these crowds. The Executive Board granted some help, though not nearly as much as the church asked.[39]

Homes for Aged. The Buckner Home in Dallas continued to provide a few cottages for retired people, and over the years the state convention operated retirement homes in different parts of the state, none of which succeeded very well. In 1956 two wealthy laymen, Carr P. Collins and Earl Hankamer, suggested the BGCT purchase two hotels, the Crazy Waters in Mineral Wells and the Paisano in Marfa, and operate them as homes for the aged on a self-sustaining basis. Both of these had been luxury hotels according by the standards of their day but both had, like their intended residents, aged and fallen into disrepair. The laymen agreed to pay half the cost of buying the properties if the Convention would pay the rest.[40] This proposal was referred to the Benevolence Committee which recommended against it.

Another offer came in 1957 that seemed more attractive. The owners of the Memorials Hospital in San Angelo offered their entire property to the BGCT. Though called a hospital, this included living quarters for retired persons all the way from independent living to various stages of assisted living. Ralph Grant, chairman of the Benevolence Committee and James Basden, subcommittee chair, went to San Angelo to inspect the property and were favorably impressed. Keenly aware they had just declined hotels in Mineral Wells and Marfa, Grant reported "We believe the offer [in San Angelo] is different to any offers heretofore."[41] After cautious consideration, the Executive Board voted to accept the property and renamed it to include "Baptist" in the name. The facilities included medical care at different levels, including care for the mental patients, the chronically ill and different levels of assisted living. "It is a place," said the committee, "where old people who are chronically ill can live. It is more of a home in that they reside there. But they are equipped to take care of sick, aged people."[42] Baptists agreed that if they should ever sell the property, they would devote at least $400,000 to a similar facility in Tom Green County.

The Baptist Memorial Geriatrics Hospital in San Angelo proved to be one of the more successful benevolent efforts of Texas Baptists. After taking control of the property, Baptists spent a great deal of money in repairs, remodeling and enlargement. The new Baptist trustees retained Mrs. Louis Gayer, administrator. Soon after Baptists took over, they had hundreds of new applications for admission with over 200 on a waiting list by 1958. Residents formed a Baptist church, which met in a large assembly room though they hoped soon to build a chapel. In 1960 the Executive Board deeded the property to the trustees, but it has continued as a Baptist institution, including separate houses for independent living, a high rise apartment with kitchens and a well-equipped cafeteria, and facilities for the most intense hospital care.

In 1959 the BGCT voted to accept the offer of a home in McAllen for "a multi-function geriatrics center," based on a firm offer of 15 acres of land and $100,000 in cash from Mrs. Virginia Anderson, and the raising of another $200,000 from residents of McAllen and adjacent towns. This home provided for about forty residents. Baptists also operated the Mary E. Trew Home for the Aged in Dallas and Texas Baptist Haven for the Aged in Houston, both connected to the Buckner Home in Dallas. By 1959 these several homes for the aged had about 300 on waiting lists for admission.

Hospitals. Wallace Bassett reported in 1954 that "We are going to have to do something in the very near future about our hospitals. . . . The hospitals have been having the hot end of the poker for a good while."[43] Most Baptists agreed that something had to be done, but they did not agree on what. Should Baptists get out of the hospital business? Or should they expand their healing ministry? If they continued, could Baptists borrow money, or even accept grants, from the government? There were advocates for all of these positions. By 1959 the BGCT sponsored seven general hospitals (at Beaumont, San Antonio, Abilene, Waco, Houston, Dallas, and Harlingen) and one geriatrics hospital (San Angelo), with a total capacity of 2,135 beds. The Convention supplied about 15% of the operating costs of these institutions.

Costs for everything were rising in the 1950s, but costs for operating hospitals shot up dramatically. By then it was becoming obvious, especially to the business and medical communities, that it was no longer feasible or even possible to operate a modern hospital as a business and hope to break even. A report to the Executive Board in 1959 said, "The need for hospital services can no longer be met by private enterprise," and added, "The modern hospital cannot be understood in terms of a business enterprise."[44] Scores of smaller hospitals across the state were going under, and the Hospital Commission reported that they were constantly being offered hospitals if only they would take them over and run them. Most such offers they promptly declined, but one in Texarkana offered such a unique situation that Baptists were inclined to accept. This provoked an intense controversy that merits a more extended description.

THE WADLEY MEMORIAL HOSPITAL

Citizens of Texarkana, located in a prosperous and growing section of the state, banded together to build a modern state of the art hospital in the 1950s. Led by Mr. and Mrs. J. K. Wadley, devout Baptists who gave almost $2 million to the project, the new institution was designed to serve an area with few existing hospitals. The Wadleys also gave the Wadley Blood Center in Dallas, which is named for them. The Texarkana hospital was located on a choice acreage. Of the total cost of about $4 million, the federal government provided about $1.6 million in Hill-Burton funds. Hill-Burton was a program by which the federal government tried to assure its citizens of medical care by helping build hospitals in communities which otherwise could not have had them. Such grants were available to both church and public hospitals, and many denominations readily accepted them. Other than requiring that the hospitals be operated as a public service and not for profit, and requiring that church-sponsored hospitals admit patients of all denominations or none, the government placed few restrictions.

James E. Coggin, the Wadleys' pastor at FBC in Texarkana, influenced the community leaders to offer the hospital to Texas Baptists in 1957. Since Baptists were the leading denomination in that part of the state, much of the private money that built the hospital came from Baptists, and Texas Baptists had a good record in running hospitals. In 1957 the Texarkana group offered the entire hospital, with land and modern equipment, debt-free to the BGCT. This offer was referred to a committee headed by Robert E. Naylor, who was then pastor at Travis Avenue church in Fort Worth and who continued on the committee after becoming president of Southwestern Seminary in 1958. Others on the committee included J. Howard Williams (later replaced by E. H. Westmoreland), Judge Frank M. Ryburn, James K. Crawley, and Vernon Elmore.

The Naylor committee moved cautiously. The offer came while the facility was under construction and the committee delayed a final answer until all construction was completed and all equipment in place. After two years of study, the committee in 1959 recommended to the Executive Board that Baptists accept the Wadley hospital offer with the condition that if the federal government ever attempted to exercise any control over operations they could give the facility back to the Texarkana group without liability to Baptists. Executive Secretary Feezor felt this was the right move and that it would greatly enhance Baptists' benevolent ministry. He told Board members that by accepting, "you will be doing one of the finest things for the Baptist denomination you could do."[45] James Coggin, who later succeeded Naylor as pastor at Travis Avenue, strongly supported the recommendation to accept, pointing out that most of the private money in the project came from Baptists.

However, strong opposition surfaced, led by Sterling Price, W. Fred Swank, L. L. Morriss, Herbert Howard and above all by E. S. James, powerful editor of the *Baptist Standard*. Even J. M. Dawson, longtime Texas Baptist leader who by then headed the Baptist Joint Committee in Washington, D.C., entered the fray against the proposal.

The problem was the Hill-Burton money. Many Baptists felt it was a violation of the principle of separation of church and state for the government to provide money to any church project. They made no distinction between a public service agency, like a hospital, and helping finance a church building for worship. In several strong editorials, E. S. James fought the proposal. He wrote, "Our forefathers have lived and died by the principle that church and state must be kept forever separate. The moment we accept a gift from the government to our denomination we will in that moment forever nullify every argument we have ever offered in defense of the principle."[46] No denomination had appeared more eager to accept Hill-Burton money than Roman Catholics, and Baptists had in effect painted themselves into a corner by their loud protests. James said, "We have cried out against the effort of Roman Catholicism to finance its institutions with government aid. . . . How can we turn right around in the face of all this and retreat from our own time-honored position?" The only way Baptists could accept the hospital, according to James, was to return all the government funds. Better, he said, that Baptists should pay out $50 million that accept even $50 in government grants. "If Baptists cannot pay for their own work," the editor concluded, "then they are just trying to do too much work." Some Southern Baptists east of the River referred to this intense opposition as "Texas fever." Whether fever or fervor, there is little doubt that the James editorials turned the tide against accepting the hospital.

However, there was also strong support for the proposal. Loud discussions aside, every actual *vote* on the matter favored acceptance. Nobody believed in separation of church and state more strongly than Naylor but he believed that accepting the Wadley hospital represented no threat to that cherished principle. He was quoted as saying, "I feel that Texas Baptists should accept the hospital. . . . There would be no more government control than if we built the hospital ourselves." Naylor continued, "May I add that I think we would be remiss in our obligation if we failed to do so as long as we give support to a hospital ministry in the earth."[47] James Coggin said, "It is my conviction that there would be no violation of the Baptist principle of separation of church and state in having our state convention accept the Wadley hospital in Texarkana. . . . What a tragedy it would be to lose such an opportunity on the basis of such a highly questionable subject."[48]

For weeks the debate raged, reaching far beyond the borders of Texas. The Executive Board asked its Christian Life Commission, the agency designated to speak on matters of religious liberty, to prepare materials to help Texans understand better the doctrine of religious liberty and separation of church and state. The CLC produced three pamphlets on the historical, biblical and constitutional bases of this doctrine and the substance of these was published in successive issues of the *Baptist Standard*. The head of the CLC, Jimmy Allen, also wrote an article, "The Texarkana Hospital: A Decision in Gray," in which he acknowledged this was not a clear-cut decision but had strong arguments on both sides.[49]

When the objections intensified the Naylor committee was asked in 1958 to restudy the matter. They brought a new recommendation to the Executive Board in 1959 that instead of accepting the hospital outright the Baptists *lease* it for 99 years at $25 per year. After long debate, with a flurry of motions, substitute motions and amendments, the Executive Board finally voted to approve the lease proposal by a margin of 74 to 71. The lease idea was acceptable to the Texarkana group and many hoped the vexed question had been put to rest. However, E. S. James would not be mollified. On the leasing proposal he sternly pronounced that, "Such a procedure would be nothing but salve to satisfy the consciences of some of us."

Between the Board vote in September, 1959, and the Convention meeting in November, James continued his strong editorials against the Wadley hospital. This had the effect of greatly increasing the attendance at the convention meeting in Corpus Christi, where C. E. Colton said "It is evident that hundreds of messengers have come to this convention for the express purpose of voting against the acceptance of the Texarkana hospital which the Executive Board had voted 74-71."[50] However, the Texarkana group had had enough and in a letter dated October 22, 1959, withdrew their offer. Even so, the messengers were not to be denied their chance to speak on this volatile issue. Though acceptance of the hospital was no longer an issue, the Convention voted a motion by C. E. Colton that, "this convention express its kind but firm opposition to the position taken on the matter by the Executive Board . . . and that we hereby announce to the world that this convention looks with disfavor upon any future move by our Executive Board, or any committee appointed by it, to accept as a gift or on a lease basis any institution financed in whole or in part by a gift or grant from the government."[51] Feezor tried to get a substitute motion that softened this rebuke by affirming that the Executive Board members who voted for the proposal had acted in good faith, though "mistaken in judgment," but even this failed and the strong rebuke was voted overwhelmingly. In the entire two-year debate, perhaps the strangest motion was offered by Stanley White, who moved that "As members of the Executive Board of the Baptist General Convention of Texas we must confess that we are confused on the interpretation of principles of separation of church and state. We do, however, purpose to move in the right direction" if we can ever figure out what it is. This motion died for lack of a second.[52]

THE SHAPE OF THE FUTURE

From 1957 to 1959 the Baptist General Convention of Texas conducted a massive survey of its organizational structure, methods of work, and prospects for the future. What exactly is the denomination trying to accomplish, they asked, and what are the best ways of accomplishing those goals? This was by far the most intensive self-study Texas Baptists ever attempted. The results of this study shaped the denomination for the remainder of the twentieth century.

Texas Baptists reported a 51% increase in church membership and a 130% increase in giving in the decade between 1949-1959.[53] As the ministry programs of the Texas convention became larger and more complex, the organizational structures which had evolved in simpler times were strained to keep up with new demands. There was much talk about the need for new colleges, more hospitals, more child care institutions, and care for the aged was also receiving more attention. How far could and should the BGCT extend its efforts? In 1957 Secretary Feezor proposed a major study for Texas Baptist hospitals and schools "and possibly for our total convention work."[54] The Plans and Policies Committee authorized such a study, and the chairman of the Executive Board (Arthur B. Rutledge) and the president of the BGCT (E. H. Westmoreland) jointly appointed a twenty-five member Survey Committee, headed by T. A. Patterson, pastor in Beaumont. Feezor said, "I do feel that this is needed. I believe it will enable us to do our work more efficiently." The Baptist Survey Committee was divided into four sub-committees: Universities, Colleges and Schools (Grady Metcalf, chair); Hospitals and Benevolences (Orba Lee Malone); State Missions General (W. M. Shamburger); and Executive Board Administration (Elwin Skiles). Probably no one at first knew how important this study would turn out to be. Their report led to the most fundamental and far-reaching restructuring of the Texas convention since 1914.

The Booz, Allen, Hamilton Report. On December 3, 1957, the Plans and Policies Committee recommended the employment of the Booz, Allen, Hamilton firm to assist with the survey. Booz, Allen, Hamilton (BAH) was a highly respected management consultant firm based in Chicago. Founded in 1914, the firm had impressive credentials including charter membership in the Association of Consulting Management Engineers. They had a professional staff of 260 persons, and a specialized Department of Institutional Management to work with nonprofit groups such as religious, educational and health care organizations. In the 1950s this firm did major studies of both the Southern Baptist Convention and the Baptist Sunday School Board in Nashville, both of which led to major restructuring of those bodies. Arnold F. Emch was the "general partner" of the firm who directed the Texas study. Citing the social and demographic changes expected in Texas, he pointed out the urgent need for advance planning if the BGCT were to meet the new challenges. Emch promised that Texas Baptists "would be provided with a master plan worked out step by step, which would include a management guide, a general plan of organization, and recommendations for strengthening your administrative features." In their proposal, the firm said "the total cost of the survey will be somewhere between $80,000 and $90,000."[55] Treasurer R. A. Springer later reported that the cost of implementing the recommended changes would run about $125,000.[56]

Under heading of "How We Will Conduct the Survey," the BAH officials proposed to do seven things: (1) Develop a clear statement of objectives of the Convention, (2) Develop estimates of future growth in the number of churches and members to be served by the Convention, (3) Prepare a master plan for the development of Convention programs, (4) Develop a plan of organization which will assure the most effective possible conduct of programs and attainment of Convention objectives, (5) Develop a personnel administration program for the staff of the Executive Board, (6) Conduct a management audit of the Convention's administrative services, and (7) Prepare a plan of action.[57] To accomplish these things, a number of BAH professional staff spent months in Texas visiting churches, colleges, children's homes and interviewing pastors, professors, presidents, and lay persons. Their massive study was completed by mid-1959 and presented to the Survey Committee in five bound volumes with over a thousand pages total.

First, the management consultants sought to determine and state clearly the objectives of the BGCT. They began by asking, "What is the [Texas] denomination as a whole trying to accomplish? What are its primary purposes?"[58] They concluded that "The basic objective of the denomination as a whole is to bring men into a right relationship with God through Jesus Christ," and that this evangelistic purpose included a spiritual development dimension of "bringing the saved to an increasingly greater knowledge and commitment to the will of God through Jesus Christ."[59] They developed similar purpose statements for the colleges, hospitals, benevolent homes, and program departments such as Sunday School and Training Union.

Second, with these objectives clearly defined, the survey next asked "How well is the Convention (and its ministry departments) achieving these goals?"This led to an extensive analysis of the current Convention structure, program, procedures and personnel. Reports in this part of the study included two categories: "Favorable Aspects," and "Aspects Requiring Attention." The survey found much in the favorable category, including zeal and commitment of Baptist people and leaders, steady growth, and a high degree of overall success despite some clumsy methods and structures. They also found plenty of less favorable aspects: unclear (and often ineffective) lines of administrative authority; outmoded organizational structures which did not directly address objectives; lack of any overall plan of how to cope with future growth; financial allotments to the various agencies without any overall system of priority; board members and trustees chosen without much regard for their qualifications; failure to group related ministries (except in the case of the Christian Education Commission); and several cases of duplication because the right hand did not know what the left hand was doing and other cases of neglect where neither hand was doing much. The survey showed that *twenty-two* organizations reported directly to the Executive Secretary, far more than any one person could oversee adequately.

Third, the survey leaders came up with a recommended action plan which included a far-reaching reorganization of the BGCT, its Executive Board, committee structure, and especially of the various ministry departments. It would be fair to say the BAH report called for more bureaucracy, a tighter organization, and more authority for the Executive Board and for the Executive Secretary. A glance at the earlier BAH studies of the SBC and the Sunday School Board give a preview of the additional layers of bureaucracy that the firm was likely to recommend in Texas.

The Chicago consultants who spent months in Texas expressed continued amazement at the sheer size and complexity of Baptist work in the Lone Star State. The total assets of the BGCT ranked it as one of the 230 largest corporations in America and, standing alone, it would rank as one of the nation's larger denominations. Feezor noted that "In some respects Texas Baptists have a larger operation than the Southern Baptist Convention."[60]

Using sophisticated techniques, the consulting firm estimated population growth in Texas for the next fifteen years, and used that to project Baptist ministry needs. They concluded that general population, and Baptist population, would increase dramatically, especially in the cities and in both younger and older age groups. If aggressive evangelism continued, they said, the proportion of Baptists in the Anglo population could be increased from about 25% in 1959 to about 33% by 1975.[61]

Just because the BAH firm made recommendations did not guarantee that the Convention would accept them all. Quite the contrary. T. A. Patterson, chair of the Survey Committee, made it clear that "whatever is recommended will have to clear the committee of twenty-five, then the Executive Board, and then the convention."[62] The Survey Committee received the 1000 page BAH report, ran the report and its recommendations through its own Baptist filter, and issued its own 148 page summary. Some of the strong criticisms were omitted and others toned down. Most of the major recommendations were accepted, though some were delayed, others modified to make them fit better with Baptist terminology and procedure, and some were rejected outright.[63] The final report was the report of the Convention's own Survey Committee, with the BAH report as background material. Acceptance did not of course mean immediate implementation; in some cases, it took years to gradually work in the changes. Texas Baptists rejected some recommendations not because they opposed them, but because they could not afford them. Some of the BAH suggestions read like a wish list for a denomination with unlimited funds.

General Administration. The Survey Committee concluded that the Executive Board should be elected in a way to assure better representation from all parts of the state, and that it should deal more with policy and turn most administration over the the committees and commissions. "The Executive Board," the Committee said, "tends to make too many specific operating decisions. Not enough responsibility is delegated to committees, commissions and staff."[64] Definite qualifications should be established to assure better qualified members named to trustee boards of the colleges, hospitals and child care homes. The Executive Board, said the Survey Committee, should consider carefully how much of its receipts to keep in Texas and how much to forward on to the SBC, always keeping in mind where the money could do the most good for the cause of Christ.[65] They urged that allocations be made on the basis of need, and how the money would be used, and not just on some percentage basis that floated all ships alike. The Committee also called for more research as the basis for detailed denominational planning in the future.

The Convention had become far too large for careful deliberation, and even the Executive Board had to rely on committee and staff to do much of its work. The survey group felt that far too many programs reported directly to the Executive Secretary and they suggested that another layer of leadership be installed to free up the Executive Secretary for overall guidance of the entire program. The consultants also found that lines of communication and authority were often unclear and, in some cases, too few people exercised too much authority.

The heart of the Booz, Allen, Hamilton report was in its recommendations for restructuring the work of the Executive Board, its agencies and committees, and the Survey Committee accepted most of these changes. They suggested a four-fold division: a *State Missions Commission* (including all the ministries that related directly to the churches); a *Christian Education Commission* (already in place, to correlate the work of all the schools); a *Human Welfare Commission* (to correlate the work of the children's homes, homes for aged, hospitals and any work that involved Christian ministry to persons in need); and a *Program Coordinating Committee* (which would absorb functions previously done by the Plans and Policies Committee, Finance Committee and Appropriations Committee). The Convention treasurer would relate to a new Business Administration and Audit Committee, and the public relations director would work with a Public Relations Advisory Committee. With high praise for the effectiveness of the *Baptist Standard,* the Texas Baptist weekly news magazine, the BAH officials recommended that it remain under its own board of directors but cautioned against allowing the editor too much freedom.

State Missions Commission. The greatest change came in the State Missions area. The study revealed that their work had evolved gradually over the years, more in response to situations as they arose than with any systematic plan. The Survey concluded that, "The organizational structure is not patterned after our basic objectives. The main streams of activity do not stand out."[66] The Survey Committee recommended that all ministries that related directly to the churches be grouped in a new section to be called the State Missions Commission. This new body would "be responsible for those activities primarily concerned with facilitating and supplementing the work of Texas Baptist churches."[67] Specifically, they would lead in work to strengthen existing churches, plant new churches and missions, and encourage the practice of biblical stewardship in the churches.

The State Missions Commission would have three subdivisions: *Church Services Division* (including Sunday School, Training Union, Brotherhood, WMU, Church Music Department, and Evangelism Department); *Stewardship Division* (including the Church Finance Department and Capital Gifts Department); and the *Missions Division* (including departments for work with Latin Americans in Texas, Church Building Department, Direct Missions Department, and Wisconsin-Minnesota Missions Department). The entire State Missions Commission was to be headed by a State Missions Secretary, who would report to the Executive Secretary of the Executive Board. Each *Division* would be headed by an assistant state missions secretary, and each *department* would have its own director. The director and professional staff of each group would also be assisted by a volunteer advisory committee made up of both pastors and lay persons. The staff would report to the department director, who would report to the assistant state missions secretary over that division, who would report to the state missions secretary, who would report to the Executive Secretary, who would report to the Executive Board, which would report to the BGCT, which presumably would report only to God.

The Christian Education Commission. The Christian Education Commission (CEC), formed in 1953, was already in place and had proven its value. It no doubt provided a pattern for the other newly formed commissions. The CEC was also less bureaucratic, including only an Executive Secretary and one professional assistant secretary to correlate the work of one university, seven colleges, and one academy. Already the colleges had made progress in moving toward more cooperation and less competition.

By far the largest part of the BAH survey dealt with Baptist schools. Under the category of "Favorable Aspects," the consultants found the colleges had dedicated presidents, committed faculties, and a generally positive Christian environment on campuses. However, under "Aspects Requiring Attention," the BAH study listed unusually severe criticisms of the Baptist colleges in Texas. The denomination had no clear concept of exactly what they expected the colleges to accomplish, though "Some Texas Baptists look on the Baptist schools as primarily devices for preventing the exposure of Baptist students to outside ideas that mighty destroy their faith."[68] The report claimed that there was wasteful duplication and overlapping between the colleges, many of the schools were poorly located outside of major population centers, some lacked accreditation, some compromised academic freedom, and all provided faculty salaries too low to recruit or retain competent teachers.[69] "The quality of the facilities in Texas Baptist institutions is consistently substandard," the report said, and the schools were often served by trustees who had little concept of the task of an educational institution.[70] In one particularly biting section, the BAH report said

> Most of the Convention institutions are smaller than the minimum (80 faculty members, 1000 to 1200 students) required to support a quality program. . . . The physical facilities at most Texas Baptist schools are of substandard quality. . . . Many of the institutions do not have the financial strength to support high quality education, and most of them are seriously dependent upon the Convention for financial help. . . . As a group, the Texas Baptist schools have a great distance to go before they will be able to provide genuinely high quality education.[71]

To address these problems, the BAH report recommended that the colleges try to develop more community support and become less dependent upon the Convention. They also recommended the Convention abandon sponsorship of junior colleges, concentrate on liberal arts programs, seek to recruit and retain better teachers, make specific plans to recruit the more promising Baptist students, and move some of the colleges to better locations. They especially recommended moving Howard Payne College to Dallas, Wayland College to Lubbock or Amarillo, and Mary Hardin-Baylor to San Antonio. "Baptist liberal arts colleges should be established in all major metropolitan areas of Texas by 1975. . . . Every metropolitan area of over 100,000 population should have a Baptist college," concluded the report.[72] This hardly seems realistic in view of the fact that Texas then had twelve such areas without a Baptist school. Further, the report said, "The Convention should promote full academic freedom for its institutions and should guard them against restrictive denominational controls over subject matter, teaching methods, or research studies."[73]

In reaching their own recommendations, the Baptist Survey Committee filtered out some of this severe criticism. Goals to improve funding, facilities, and faculties were couched in more general terms. Whatever else these stinging criticisms may have accomplished, they apparently motivated the BGCT to make major improvements in their colleges.

One important recommendation which the Survey Committee accepted was to bring the Baptist Student Union, which had previously reported directly to the Executive Secretary, into the Christian Education Commission on the grounds that it was logically related to the educational enterprise. "There is need," the Committee concluded, "for a unified approach to all Christian education efforts and to all work with Baptist college students." The Survey Committee cited "needs for future leadership in the form of well-educated Baptists in many fields. Our primary need is for active full-time leaders of regular denominational activities. Our secondary need is for Baptist leaders who will exert an important Christian influence in nondenominational areas and who will furnish strong lay leadership within the denomination."[74] To provide these leaders, the Committee recommended that Texas Baptists concentrate on standard four-year colleges, that they discontinue work with junior colleges, and that they maintain only one major research university (Baylor). They recommended that the colleges seek to recruit the most promising Baptist students, raise faculty salaries in order to recruit and retain a competent faculty, and give attention to academic as well as spiritual strength. They also recommended that the Christian Education Commission set up Texas Graduate Fellowship Program to provide up to 25 graduate fellowships to encourage and enable outstanding Baptist students to complete advanced degrees in various fields.

In contrast to the BAH report, the Baptist Survey Committee did not recommend moving any colleges, though they acknowledged that "the Convention's present institutions are not well-located."[75] Of fourteen Texas cities with over 100,000 population, where over half the Baptist population lived, twelve had no Baptist college (though Houston and Dallas had plans underway for schools). Four of the colleges were located within a 90 mile radius, and "only three of the Convention's eight institutions are in communities that are unquestionably large enough to supply adequate amounts of qualified student material, trustee leadership and financial support for quality educational programs."[76]

The Survey Committee noted that the proportion of Baptists among the state's college students had for many years remained steady at about 30%. However, in one decade "the proportion of Baptist students attending Baptist institutions has dropped from 25% to 18%. The Committee finds this decline both significant and alarming." Clearly the majority of Baptist leaders of the future must come from the 82% attending non-Baptist schools. That brought a new spotlight to the BSU program. In 1959, the BGCT sponsored 65 Baptist Student Unions in Texas and had 24 Convention-sponsored student centers on non-Baptist campuses. There were 40 campus directors, 19 of whom taught credit Bible courses as part of their student work. They recommended more staff and more budget for the BSU work.

Drawing upon the BAH survey, which was especially critical of Texas Baptist colleges, the Survey Committee acknowledged that "As a group, the Texas Baptist schools have a great distance to go before they will be able to provide genuinely high quality education for their students." All the Baptist colleges should maintain a strong Christian environment, but that could not substitute for academic excellence. "Every effort should be made to greatly increase the quality of education provided by our Baptist schools in Texas. To increase quality, first emphasis should be placed on improving the quality of the schools faculties. . . . Faculty salaries in Baptist institutions should gradually be raised until they reach at least the top median level of southern colleges and universities."[77] With these improvements, they hoped to continue to attract at least 20% of Texas Baptist college students.

Human Welfare Commission. The BAH study concluded that ministry to help persons in need was a valid part of the objectives of the BGCT. They suggested combining all the various forms of helping ministries into a Human Welfare Commission. "It should combine for purposes of planning, sponsorship, and financial support all programs that assume a primary responsibility to render some form of service to individuals who are in need of help."[78] Thus the Baptist hospitals, children's homes, homes for the aged and the maternity home, which had previously operated separately, would be combined into one program category. The fifteen-member Human Welfare Commission should include, the BAH report suggests, "at least one lawyer, one physician, one educator, one banker, one engineer, and one individual with background in public administration."[79] The Commission would be led by an executive secretary, one associate secretary and two clerical secretaries.

The report calls on the BGCT to state clearly its reasons for conducting hospitals, children's homes and homes for the aged and suggests that making "an organized effort to apply the teachings of Jesus Christ to modern society" should be a part of that rationale. The consulting firm also pointed out the need for flexibility in methods and programs since "the general character of human need has radically changed, [and] there has been a revolution in the techniques of helping people."[80] Though the shape of the needs was changing, with development of an industrialized society, the needs could only increase especially from "the increasing hazards of urban living." They predicted, and recommended, that practically all healthy orphan children should be placed in adoptive or foster homes rather than in institutional orphanages. "Institutional child care," they confidently predicted, "will either be temporary or limited to the care of the handicapped."[81] The demographics of an aging population, they said, will require more future attention to homes for the care of the elderly.

The study distinguished sharply between the need for *sponsorship, control, and financing* of the human welfare institutions. The primary responsibility of the Convention was *sponsorship,* but this did not imply the Convention should exercise total control or provide the majority of funding.

Concerning hospitals, the BAH study noted that Texas Baptists as of 1957 sponsored seven general hospitals (Dallas, Houston, San Antonio, Beaumont, Waco, Abilene, Harlingen) and one geriatrics hospital (San Angelo). In light of increasing health care needs, they recommended that Baptists establish five additional hospitals by 1975, more than double total bed capacity, and provide more facilities for psychiatric and long-term care. The cost of such expansion, estimated the Chicago consultants, would be about $59,000,000, a sum they admitted "may appear staggering when first considered."[82]

The Chicago experts argued strongly that Baptists should reconsider their refusal to accept government grants for human welfare work, especially in hospitals. The denomination, they said, "should restudy the whole question of relationships between church and state as they affect human welfare institutions. It should include a careful reconsideration of the Hill-Burton program dealing with the contribution of capital funds for the construction of hospitals."[83] They recognized Baptists' commitment to the separation of church and state, but insisted that accepting government grants for hospitals and other welfare institutions represented a service to citizens and not a subsidy to a church. "It is important, however, to recognize that human welfare programs are not purely religious programs but are, rather, community service programs sponsored by a religious group." They said that accepting such grants would not give the government undue control or compromise the freedom of the sponsoring denomination. If refusal of such grants deprived citizens of needed health care, moral questions might be raised "if a real injustice to individuals is allowed to occur because of a theoretical risk that is not only remote but of such a nature that adequate precautionary measures can be taken to eliminate that risk."[84] However, the chaplaincy programs in the hospitals, being purely religious in nature, should be paid for by the denomination.

Texas Baptists generally did not buy these arguments, as the Wadley hospital flap in Texarkana had clearly revealed. The Baptist Survey Committee received the extensive BAH report, but significantly they did not report out this recommendation about government funds.

Program Coordinating Committee. This committee would oversee no ministry programs of its own but, as the name implies, would facilitate, coordinate programs and calendars, and manage the flow of funds to the various commissions which would, in turn, disperse funds to the departments.

The three Commissions and the Program Coordinating Committee would relate to the Executive Board, not directly to the Convention. In addition, the Convention itself would set up a number of necessary committees, including a Committee on Committees, a Committee on Nominations for the Executive Board, and others for nominations for institutional boards, credentials, convention arrangements, order of business, resolutions and memorials and any special ad hoc committees.

In Perspective. Clearly the Survey Committee's work led to the most significant changes in the shape of the Convention and its agencies since 1914. In addition to citing the details, how can these changes be put into some perspective?

The adoption of the basic recommendations of the Booz, Allen, Hamilton study represents acceptance of a new level of secular, corporate methodology in Convention life. What the BAH study recommended for the BGCT they might also have recommended for General Motors or any major secular corporation in America. To an extent previously unknown in the BGCT, the *spirit* and *methods* of secular America were brought into the Convention. The Chicago consultants felt they were helping to bring the BGCT into the twentieth century; at times, they seemed genuinely surprised that the Convention, with such unsophisticated methods, had achieved so much.

This restructuring, which was guided more by T. A. Patterson as chairman than by Secretary Feezor, also brought a significant increase in bureaucracy in the BGCT and its work. The staff at the Baptist Building multiplied as a result of these changes and the proportion of workers in the Dallas office as compared to workers out on the field tipped toward the Baptist Building. The end result was to augment the power of the Executive Board and its Executive Secretary, add layers of leadership, and demote the ministry departments further back into the organizational charts. Executive Board minutes state that all personnel in all the Commissions must "be presented to the Executive Board for approval."[85] The new Program Coordinating Committee also established a salary schedule for all Board employees, including a minimum for new staff, a mid-range for "an entirely competent person doing a satisfactory job," and an upper range for "above average performance and exceptional ability." Most of the salaries were set rather low, including the Executive Secretary though his range was later increased.

On the positive side, these changes also streamlined the work of Texas Baptists and paved the way for an era of rapid growth. By whatever measure, whether members, money or missions, the generation following the restructuring of 1959 saw new records set in every category. The criticisms raised by the consultants, which seemed so severe at the time, provoked Texas Baptists into making needed improvements, especially in their colleges.

Baptist reaction to the study was generally positive, though a lot of wrangling took place over the details. It would be as pointless now to describe all the motions, substitute motions and amendments which came out of the Survey as it was pointless to make them then. No doubt E. S. James spoke for most Texas Baptists when he said "The report is tremendously important . . . . [and] may determine the course of Texas Baptists until the Lord shall come again." He later editorialized that the study, though not perfect and subject to further fine-tuning, "will clear the way for a mighty forward movement of organized Baptist work." The report, he said, "appears to be sound, reasonable, and potentially powerful in expanded Christian service."[86] Time has validated this assessment. The changes resulting from the Booz, Allen, Hamilton study helped Texas Baptists gear up for one of the greatest periods of progress in their history.

Implementation of the changes took time, but the three major commissions were in place by the end of 1959. The State Missions Commission, chaired by W. E. Denham, recommended J. Woodrow Fuller as State Missions Secretary, R. H. Dilday, Sr. as Secretary of the Church Services Division, George L. Shearin as Secretary of the Stewardship Division. James Basden, Chairman of the Human Welfare Commission, presented the recommendation that Walter R. Delamarter be elected Interim Secretary of the new Human Welfare Commission. They delayed naming a Secretary for the Education Commission. Most of the personnel in the departments remained the same, with people doing much the same work but sometimes under different titles.

THE END OF AN ERA

Forrest C. Feezor had early on announced his intention to retire on December 31, 1960. He concluded his ministry with a four-fold challenge to Texas Baptists, that they would win and baptize 100,000 new converts in 1960, have every church affiliated with the BGCT giving regularly to Baptist missionary programs, have at least 3500 Texas Baptist churches giving through the Cooperative Program, and have every department and agency of the BGCT devoted not only to winning new converts but also to training the converts toward more mature Christian living and responsible churchmanship.[87]

Before stepping down, Feezor's parting words were "Finally, brethren, be strong in the Lord." In the years to come, Texas Baptists would need that strength to face new challenges and opportunities.

CHAPTER 12

ONWARD AND (SOMETIMES) UPWARD, 1961–1973

A RESPECTED YALE HISTORIAN, Sydney E. Ahlstrom, said the 1960s brought "a fundamental shift in American moral and religious attitudes," and he concluded that "this turbulent decade" will be remembered as a decisive turning point in American history."[1] Such terms as "post-Protestant" and even "post-Christian" were used to describe America. Ahlstrom described this "decisive decade" as a "watershed" for all American institutions and especially for the church in which traditional values, beliefs and behavior were all challenged.

Texas Baptists, like other Americans, were deeply affected by the rapid changes which swept in like a tornado as the placid 1950s gave way to the tumults of the 1960s. The old certainties suddenly seemed less certain, moral convictions which once seemed absolute became relative, and traditional patterns of church life almost overnight looked outmoded. Like others, Texas Baptists struggled to meet the challenges of the strange new times.

STRANGE NEW DAY

No one who lived through the sixties could doubt that America had entered a strange new era. It is no wonder that John Jeter Hurt, laconic Georgia layman who succeeded E. S. James as editor of the *Baptist Standard,* could editorialize about "a new day" in America.

New Day for America. In the 1960s American society was in turmoil. The assassination of President John F. Kennedy in 1963, followed by the killing of Robert F. Kennedy and Martin Luther King, Jr., cast a dark shadow over the nation. America lost, or at least failed to win, two wars: the military war in Vietnam and President Lyndon B. Johnson's "war on poverty." The promise of the Brown decision of the Supreme Court in 1954 desegregating public schools had not been fulfilled and the country erupted in the worst race riots in its history. After King's death (and to some extent before) the Civil Rights Movement took a radical turn to "Black Power" which further divided the nation. In *Engle v. Vitale* (1963) the Supreme Court ruled that government officials could not compose or impose prayers for public schools, a decision which was widely misinterpreted as "kicking God out of the schools." Homosexual people in America got a new nickname, "gay," and more of them "came out of the closet" to challenge traditional moral concepts. The war in Vietnam escalated to become America's longest, least understood, and most devastating in both casualties and costs. It drove one president from office, depleted the nation's treasury, and further divided the American people. Narcotic drugs, which had not been unknown in America, reached epidemic proportion as a generation heeded the call to "turn on and tune out." Crime reached new heights as fear gripped American families who often barricaded themselves behind triple-locked doors in the "home of the brave and land of the free." The much-discussed "sexual revolution," whether real or imagined, added to the volatile mix of American culture in the 1960s. "There are good reasons for believing," said Ahlstrom, "that the decade of the sixties, even at the profoundest ethical and religious levels, will take a distinctive place in American history."[2]

A New Day for American Religion. The revolution in the country was matched by a revolution in the churches. Many observers thought the election of a Roman Catholic as president of the United States in 1960 underscored the fact that America was no longer a Protestant nation. The death of President Kennedy in 1963 was followed quickly by the "death of God" as radical Protestant theologians in 1965 proclaimed the demise of the "western deity." The ecumenical movement gained new ground as the old denominational loyalties weakened. Interdenominational and "parachurch" organizations thrived and, in many cases, challenged the historic denominations. New ways of grouping believers, such as "evangelicals," "charismatics," and "fundamentalists," gradually became more important to many than the old denominational labels. The moral and religious crises of the 1960s left deep scars. "The legacy of these contentious times," says Wheaton College historian Mark Noll, "was a pervasive division between liberal and conservative approaches to both public issues and the life of faith. This division came to dwarf the significance of the traditional denominations."[3]

A New Day for Southern Baptists. Texas Baptist leader T. A. Patterson said candidly, "Trends during the sixties were disturbing to Southern Baptists. Almost everything but giving was on the decline. During this period, numerous surveys and analyses were made in an effort to determine the causes for the reverses and to suggest possible remedies."[4] Editor Hurt noted that the number of baptisms was down, Sunday School attendance had dropped, and "budgets no longer skyrocketed as in previous decades."[5] The Training Union came up with a catchy new promotion of "Church: The Sunday Night Place," but many found other places to be on Sunday nights. Even Woman's Missionary Union showed strain; the usual explanation was that women employed outside the home were too busy for the traditional WMU "circle" meetings. This is no doubt true, but one cannot totally rule out another contributing factor: a cooling of missionary fervor among Baptists. Professional sports on television on Sunday afternoons wreaked havoc on Sunday night church attendance, and when it became almost impossible to recruit enough teachers for the traditional two weeks Vacation Bible School many churches shortened the VBS to one week and some even had it at night.

In the 1960s Southern Baptists were caught up in the most devastating controversy they had faced in the twentieth century, and the subsequent convulsions greatly affected Texas Baptists. Accusations of "liberalism" in the Baptist schools divided brethren, undermined the confidence of the people, and threatened the cohesion of Southern Baptists. Texas Baptists were right in the middle of this great controversy and many of its most prominent leaders on both sides were Texans.

Despite the challenges of this "new day," some of Texas Baptists' greatest victories were reached during the sixties and seventies. New programs of ministry appeared and old programs reached new heights. Texas Baptists were chastened by the recurring crises of this troubled time, but they did not retreat. Like the Apostle Paul, they were "troubled on every side, yet not distressed . . . perplexed but not in despair" (2 Cor. 4:8, KJV).

THOMAS ARMOUR PATTERSON

The man whose destiny it was to lead Texas Baptists in the sixties and into the seventies was T. A. Patterson, who served as executive secretary from 1961 to 1973. Patterson came to the Baptist Building with thirty years experience as a pastor, the last fourteen at FBC, Beaumont. He had long been active in Texas Baptist life and was thrust into prominence as chairman of the important Survey Committee that received the Booz, Allen, Hamilton report in 1959. Patterson was probably the most influential Texas Baptist in the restructuring of the Convention beginning in 1959. When Forrest C. Feezor announced his intention to retire on December 31, 1960, Patterson was elected in September, 1960, to allow him a few months to work with Feezor before assuming the office.

Born in the tiny community of Floyd, in Hunt County, young Patterson spent most of his growing up years in West Texas in the Winters area. He attended rural schools and later graduated from Eastland High School. The Patterson family was Baptist, though religion was seldom mentioned at home. Young Thomas made a profession of faith as a boy but did not join a church until his college days. He earned a B.A. degree from Hardin-Simmons University in 1927, the same school which conferred upon him an honorary doctorate in 1950. After college, Patterson taught history and English for two years at Sylvester High School, where he also served as principal during the second year. Hungry for more education, Patterson enrolled in a Masters program at the University of Texas in Austin. He attended for two summer terms but did not complete the degree. Instead, he enrolled in Southwestern Baptist Theological Seminary in Fort Worth where he studied under the famed W.T. Conner in theology, W. W. Barnes in church history, L. R. Scarborough in evangelism, and Jeff D. Ray in preaching. Patterson completed both Th.M. (1932) and Th.D. (1945) degrees at Southwestern. He credited these teachers and his boyhood pastor, a Brother Nicholson, with shaping his theological conservatism and his evangelistic commitment. In his doctoral studies, Patterson majored in theology and served as assistant to Professor Conner. However, he wrote his doctoral dissertation on the theology of Landmark leader J. R. Graves. His favorable assessment of some points of Graves' theology led many to conclude later that Patterson had adopted some Landmark doctrines.

One of Patterson's college classmates, Roberta Mae Turner, was hired to teach home economics at Sylvester High where Patterson also taught. The friendship of these two young teachers blossomed and they were married in 1930. This gifted daughter of an Abilene pastor also attended the Seminary with her husband but did not complete a degree. At that time, she and Eloise Glass (Mrs. Baker James Cauthen) were said to be the only women enrolled in the School of Theology.[6] Jeff Ray nicknamed the young couple "Pat" and "Pet."

It was no secret that the 55 year old Patterson was considered a likely choice to succeed Feezor. He was elected on the fifth ballot over Carl Bates, James Landes, Ralph Grant and E. H. Westmoreland. Patterson, often known as "Dr. Pat," was the last executive secretary elected under the old open ballot system in use since 1914. He headed a Baptist Building team which included R. A. Springer, treasurer; Lloyd Wright, public relations director; Jimmy Allen, director of Christian Life Commission with associate William M. Pinson, Jr.; A. B. White, head of the Church Loan Association; Edward N. Jones, head of the Christian Education Commission, with W. F. Howard as head of the Baptist Student Union; James Basden, secretary of the Human Welfare Commission; J. Woodrow Fuller, secretary of the State Missions Commission. In addition, James C. Cantrell headed the Baptist Foundation of Texas. E. S. James edited the *Baptist Standard,* and Eula Mae Henderson was executive secretary-treasurer of the state WMU, but these did not come under the direct authority of the Executive Board. By the time Patterson laid down the mantle twelve years later, this staff had changed considerably.

Patterson was a far more activistic leader than Feezor had been. Feezor, it was said, did little actual "administering," preferring to concentrate on prayer and spiritual growth. Though sparing in his criticism of his predecessor, Patterson did say "I do not see how on earth he got the job done." Patterson concluded that the answer was in the person of

J. Woodrow Fuller, associate executive secretary, to whom Feezor delegated most of the leadership tasks.[7] When he assumed the top post, Patterson
neither had nor wanted such an associate. Patterson's first priority as executive secretary was evangelism, but he later reflected that he spent more
time on stewardship than anything else. He recalled, "I spent more time
traveling with Cecil Ray [stewardship director] than I even did with Wade
Freeman of the Evangelism Division."[8] Though supportive of the institutions, Patterson kept the focus upon church growth. "We have grown a
great denomination in Texas because of church extension," he said.[9]
Churches build institutions, so the best way to strengthen the institutions
is to strengthen the churches.

As chairman of the Survey Committee that restructured the Convention's work in 1959, Patterson had in effect shaped his own working conditions, and he must have had a strong inkling that he would administer
the new programs resulting from that study. He was generally pleased
with the results, saying "the work was organized for the first time in the
way in which I feel that it should have been organized."[10] Plans that look
good on paper do not always work out in reality, and Patterson found that
many adjustments had to be made He felt the actual authority of the executive secretary had been diminished and the commission secretaries had
a bit too much independence.

One area in which Patterson was disappointed with the results of the
Survey Committee was in relation to the *Baptist Standard*. This weekly news
magazine had reached a circulation approaching 400,000 and it was estimated that it had about a million readers. It was by far the largest and
most influential Baptist paper in the world. Though a vital part of Texas
Baptist life, the *Standard* was not under the authority of the Executive
Board. From its early beginnings the paper had a tradition of independence. After it was acquired by the BGCT, the *Standard* continued to nurture its tradition of editorial independence. It operated under the authority of its own board of directors, elected by the Convention and not the
Executive Board. The directors chose the editor, set overall policy, and
left the editor free to determine the content and emphases of the paper.
The Executive Board had no voice in choosing the editor, setting editorial policy, or determining the content of the paper. Most Texas Baptists
liked it that way. For all their editorial freedom, the editors were loyal
team players who did all they could to advance the ministries of Texas
Baptists. Some strong-minded editors, like E. S. James, often took strong
editorial stances that not all agreed with. As executive secretary, Patterson
wrote a weekly article for the *Standard* and, it appears, Editor James did
not always approve of its content. James felt that Patterson should write
promotional articles, not opinion pieces which might conflict with the editorials. Patterson insisted he should write whatever he felt like, and he did.
He later reflected, "I think that he [James] felt like he, and not the
Executive Secretary, was the spokesman for Baptists."

In his *Memoirs* recorded after his retirement, Patterson cited the
Booz, Allen, Hamilton report that cautioned against allowing the editor of

the *Baptist Standard* too much freedom, concluding that "the concentration of so much responsibility on one individual poses dangers for the future." Patterson added, "I was in agreement with their findings."[11] The final Survey Committee report specified that the editor, the Program Coordinating Committee, and the executive secretary should jointly establish editorial policy. This policy was never implemented, though Patterson wanted it done. He said "I never did get a Program Coordinating Committee that had the nerve to invite the editor of the *Standard* to come in—to give any consideration to editorial policy. . . . they just didn't have the courage to buck the press."[12] In one of the rare times that Patterson allowed his frustration at the *Baptist Standard* to show, he said,

> I do think the recommendations of the Survey Committee were right. But, they've never been followed and apparently they will not be. The recommendations were that the PCC and the Executive Secretary sit down with the Editor of the *Baptist Standard* and together work out the editorial policies for the *Standard*. . . . I often thought at the time, I wish I were back as a pastor and serving on this committee [PCC]. This is one time we would see to it that a recommendation approved by the Convention is carried out, because this doesn't take away from editorial freedom at all.[13]

Even while seeking to gain more control over the paper, Patterson advocated editorial freedom for the editor and apparently saw no contradiction in his position. He also would have preferred for the paper to have offices in the Baptist Building rather than in their own separate building some distance away. "Frankly, my feeling was that it would be much better if all of our offices were together, and I never could see that as any threat to editorial freedom."[14] When the Baptist Building became overcrowded, Patterson put forward a plan to build a "Baptist Complex" on some Buckner property in East Dallas. This Complex would include the BGCT Executive Board staff, the various commissions, the *Baptist Standard*, the Annuity Board, and the Radio and Television Commission then housed in Fort Worth. Some urged delay to see where the new International Airport would be located and the moment of opportunity passed. The heads of the other agencies showed no enthusiasm about being domiciled with the powerful BGCT.

BOARDS AND BUDGETS

The Executive Board was made up of 180 members chosen from different parts of the state, including both pastors and laymen and, after 1932, women. Women also served on the Administrative Committee of the Board (later renamed the Program Coordinating Committee), and the Executive Board included ethnic members in 1956 and thereafter. Board members served on a volunteer basis, and not even their expenses to meetings were paid. They met quarterly for only a half-day, though that had to be generously defined since they often continued until around

3:00 P.M. Their main tasks were to elect the executive secretary, set general policy, approve the annual budget to be presented for final vote at the Convention, review and approve (or very rarely reject) reports of the various commissions, elect or in some cases ratify employment of Board staff, oversee the public relations office of the Board, and try to keep peace among the sometimes overlapping agencies of the Convention.

At times board members felt that their discussion and vote amounted to little since most major decisions were made in committees. When they did attend meetings, some complained, their questions were barely tolerated more as interruptions than a seeking of information. In 1972 Chairman Travis Berry appointed a Committee on Executive Board Members' Involvement, chaired by Gordon Bays. Their assignment was to "find ways for the Executive Board to be more involved in the decision-making process," and to "find ways for Executive Board members to better represent the Executive Board and the Convention to the Associations and the churches."[15] After study, the committee recommended that board members be provided printed reports earlier, that they be invited to attend commission meetings in "a systematic plan of observation," that new board members receive more thorough orientation, and that the board consider paying the expenses of board members to necessary meetings.

A more serious problem emerged from this study. It appeared that churches where board members were pastors or, in the case of laymen, members, the percentage giving to the Cooperative Program had declined over the period 1968-1971. While 38% of Texas churches increased their percentage of giving during that time, only 26% of churches with executive board members did so. Of churches represented by Convention officers, 18% had a percentage increase while 61% declined.[16] "The causes for these variations are many," said the report, "but one thing it clearly indicates is the <u>urgent need of a leadership commitment</u>."[17] Among the reasons suggested for these trends were: inflation, pastor-laymen conflicts in the denomination, lack of effective communication, crises in the churches, and adverse reactions to the unceasing call for more funds by the institutions (especially the colleges). They might also have cited studies showing that the churches were spending more of their money for buildings, church staff and local mission projects.

In his 1961 report, R. A. Springer reported the first budget shortfall the BGCT had faced in many years. The shortfall was only about $600,000, not much out of a $13.5 million budget, but the trend was ominous and it continued for several years. Springer pronounced the obvious when he said, "Our budget may be a little high."[18] Budget problems carried over to 1962 despite the fact that the BGCT was receiving more dollars than ever before. That year the convention received from the churches a total of $14,341,444 which was distributed as follows: 48.5% was sent to Baptist causes outside Texas, and 51.5% was used for ministries within the state. These amounts of course included the two major mission offerings, Lottie Moon and Annie Armstrong, in addition to budget gifts. Springer noted later that the BGCT first received $1 million for missions in one year back in 1944, but by 1964 they adopted a budget calling for $1 million a month.[19] In 1963 Springer completed twenty-five years as treasurer, and reported that during that time over $150 million in mission money had passed through his hands to ministry causes in Texas and beyond.

In 1962 Cecil Ray, director of Cooperative Program (CP) promotion in Texas, presented a Seven Year Plan to lead the churches to gradually increase their gifts through the CP and at the same time lead the BGCT to increase its percentages to SBC causes. The plan asked the churches to increase their gifts by .05% each year until the average rose from 10.65% in 1961 to 14.5% by 1970. The goal was for the BGCT to pass on to Nashville an additional .75% each year until gifts increased from 32.8% in 1962 to 38.2% by 1970. Ray assigned categories for the churches according to what percentage of their undesignated receipts they forwarded on to Nashville: churches that gave at least 10% were *Keeping Faith with World Needs;* those that gave at least 25% were *Reaching Missionary Maturity;* and those that gave 33% or more were *Rising to Missionary Greatness.*[20] Churches had always been recognized for the total *amount* they gave, but Ray wanted also to recognize them for their *percentage* of gifts.

The projected budget for 1966, which might be considered a typical year, called for a total of $12 million through the Cooperative Program.[21] Of this amount, $3,892,636 would be sent on to Nashville, with $7,785,256 used for ministries within Texas. The two major mission offerings (Lottie Moon and Annie Armstrong) were projected to raise an additional $4 million. "If these offerings are realized," said the report, "it will make the worldwide proportion approximately 50%."

For 1966, the Texas portion of the mission money would be allocated as follows: $1,542,912 for State Missions; $3,157,500 for Christian Education; $1,889,000 for Human Welfare; and $70,132 for the Christian Life Commission.[22] General administrative expenses would take $348,261 and Ministers Retirement would consume another $480,000. The Public Relations Department, Bishop College, and miscellaneous expenses would round out the total. This budget shows rather clearly where Texas Baptists placed their priorities. Those who like statistics will be interested in a report to the Executive Board comparing Texas Baptist financial life in 1956 and 1966. In that decade, total income for Texas Baptist churches increased by 55.96%, from $71,960,879 (1956) to $112,323,333 (1966). For the same period, gifts through the CP went from $7,100,764 to $11,960,914 for a healthy 68.44% increase. The average percentage of church income sent on to the Cooperative Program rose slightly from 9.8% to 10.66%.[23]

During Patterson's last year at the helm, the budget had increased considerably. For whatever reasons, giving continued strong while other dimensions of Baptist life showed decline. For 1972, the projected budget called for $15,250,000 total Cooperative Program, with the mission offerings expected to raise an additional $4,800,000. This grand total of almost $20 million would still be divided about 50/50 between ministry needs in

Texas and beyond.[24] These amounts sound impressive, but Patterson noted that in 1967 Texas Baptists gave an average per capita of only 14 cents a week through the Cooperative Program.[25] A study of CP giving by the churches from 1925-1971 showed that 1967 was the turning point, with percentage giving increasing before that date and steadily decreasing afterward.[26]

When Springer retired at the end of 1970 after 32½ years as treasurer, only T. C. Gardner had served longer. Springer had served with five executive secretaries, 18 executive board chairmen, and 17 BGCT presidents. There was never a breath of impropriety in his handling of millions of dollars during that third of a century. He was succeeded by Jay Skaggs who had served some years as controller.

THE COMMISSIONS

"The work of the Executive Board is channeled through four commissions," said a report in 1962.[27] This was an effort to group the various ministries according to the nature of their work. The State Missions Commission (SMC) related to the churches, the Christian Education Commission (CEC) to the schools, the Human Welfare Commission (HWC) to the helping institutions like hospitals and child care homes, and the Christian Life Commission (CLC) spoke out on moral issues. However, the Commissions were not equal. The giant among them was the SMC, with eleven different programs of ministry. The CEC got the lion's share of the budget, while the CLC had to struggle for its existence. Some even referred to the "three commissions," omitting the CLC, and others referred to "the three major commissions," implying the CLC was minor. One historian of the CLC said "the CLC remained secondary in status in relationship to other BGCT commissions."[28]

THE STATE MISSIONS COMMISSION

J. Woodrow Fuller headed the State Missions Commission (SMC) from its beginning in 1959 until 1964, when he resigned to become associate pastor at FBC, Dallas. He had served the BGCT for eleven years, under Secretaries Williams, Feezor and Patterson. As a youth, Fuller had been known as the "boy preacher from Memphis." Major Fuller had been a pilot in the military and later a flight instructor. He had been pastor at Diamond Hill in Fort Worth and superintendent of missions for the Tarrant Baptist Association. Later he served as executive secretary of the Florida Baptist Convention. His successor as head of the SMC was Charles McLaughlin who had served eight years at the Sagamore Hill church in Fort Worth when his pastor, W. Fred Swank, was chairman of the SMC board. McLaughlin had also served as Education Director and Superintendent of Missions of the Tarrant Association and for almost five years had headed the Direct Missions Division of the SMC. E. Eugene Greer served for several years as an associate in the SMC, responsible for program planning. The SMC was divided into four divisions.

Evangelism Division. The work of evangelism was headed by C. Wade Freeman from 1954 until his retirement in 1974. His was the only department that had the same number of personnel after twenty-five years; six evangelists on staff. However, by about 1960 they had evolved from a staff of *general* evangelists to a staff of *specialists,* with workers who led in local church revivals, language and ethnic revivals, city crusade evangelism, personal witnessing and those who taught evangelism methods in the churches. The staff in 1965 included Theron V. "Corky" Farris, Rudy A. Hernandez, Ralph W. Neighbor, Jr., O. Byron Richardson. Cecil E. Sherman served as a staff evangelist in 1963.[29]

A major event for the Evangelism Division, and for all Texas Baptists, was the annual Evangelism Conference held in January in Fort Worth. This conference originated years earlier on the campus of Southwestern Seminary and was held alternately in Fort Worth and Dallas before settling in its present time and place. This conference features some of the finest preaching to be heard anywhere and for some years was the largest annual gathering of Southern Baptists, with more attendance than the Southern Baptist Convention. Freeman steadfastly guarded the conference against becoming politicized; winning the lost was the Northstar by which he guided the Evangelism Conference. The planning, promotion and inspiration of this vast gathering helped set the spiritual tone for Texas Baptists for the remainder of the year. It became a common saying that Baptist laymen wanted to make sure their pastor attended this conference, for he always came home spiritually invigorated and with several new sermons!

If the goal of evangelism remained constant, methods changed. When the department was formed back in the 1950s, "simultaneous revivals" were popular. As these lost their appeal, along came "Encounter Crusades," "Evangelism in Depth," "Youth Encounters" (growing out of the Jesus Movement of the 1960s), Lay Renewal Weekends, and more use of television in evangelism. The work of the Evangelism Division, said Freeman, is two-fold: to create a favorable spiritual environment for evangelism, and to test and demonstrate effective methods of evangelism.[30]

A major concern for Texas Baptists was the decline in baptisms in the 1960s. Baptism of new converts fell from a high of 64,817 in 1959 to a low of 53,538 in 1966.[31] Patterson described this decline as "the greatest crisis we face."[32] Baptists responded with "Faith in Action" and "Evangelism in Depth," intensified evangelistic programs designed to reverse this trend. Not until 1980 did baptisms (67,138) again top the 60,000 mark.

Church Services Division. This division covered a multitude of ministries including Sunday School, Training Union, Church Music, and Brotherhood. The division was headed by Russell Hooper Dilday, Sr. until his retirement in 1972 due to bad health. Four major functions of the department were: (1) Develop materials, training opportunities, and field services to help the churches in developing and strengthening church library work, (2) Provide material and assistance to churches in developing a church recreation program, (3) Provide material and counsel to churches in the area of church administration, (4) Serve as a liaison between the BGCT and the 23 Baptist encampments.[33] Though most of the encampments were owned and operated by local groups, associations, or districts, they were very important to the overall life of Texas Baptists. The 1968 report, for example, shows a summer attendance at the various camps of 120,188. They registered 4036 conversions, 7418 rededications, and 1811 commitments for Christian service.[34]

In the 1960s audio and visual media, while growing in importance, had not yet pushed print media to the sidelines. Therefore, church libraries were a major emphasis of those days. In 1968 the Church Services division helped 316 churches expand and improve their libraries, and helped another 119 churches to begin a library. They conducted three statewide workshops on church library work, and worked with the Church Library Department of the Sunday School Board in Nashville on a Free Library Offer of a set of books for a beginning library. They also helped Latin American churches in Texas to collect suitable books in Spanish for beginning a church library. In time, print media diminished and the church library emphasis, while it did not disappear, was greatly muted. Many church libraries put more emphasis upon audiovisuals and less upon books.

Churches do sometimes have problems in organizing their work, managing promotion and publicity, and it is not unknown for churches to have interpersonal tensions between members or staff workers. When asked, the Church Services Division tried to help such churches by personal visits, workshops and/or by providing written guidance materials. In this area, Dilday drew upon his own local church experience.

Sunday School Department. For several years the Sunday School Department, once a division on its own, functioned as a subgroup of the Church Services Division. William R. Bumpas headed the department for seven years until he resigned in 1967 to return to FBC, Midland, the same church he had served before accepting the Sunday School post. Bumpas was succeeded by James E. Frost. Associates included, over the decade, Harold G. Hanson, William R. Cox, Nelda P. Williams, Karl Bozeman, Cecil Roenfeldt, and Richard Sims. Their main work included helping the churches to enlist more people of all ages in Bible study. To this end, they conducted "enlargement campaigns" in churches and associations, led workshops and clinics for training Sunday School teachers and workers, and held age group conferences for workers in elementary, youth and adult divisions.

In addition to Sunday School, this department also had responsibility for the Vacation Bible School and the Invincibles. For example, in one typical year the department conducted VBS clinics in 84 associations to train workers. That year they reported 2270 VBS schools in the churches, with 518,173 children enrolled and 8264 conversions.[35] That same year, 1968, the department enlisted and trained 90 Invincibles, college students who volunteered for summer work in the churches. The Invincibles that year conducted 188 Vacation Bible Schools, with 14,434 enrolled and 934 conversions.

The Texas Sunday School Department, like other departments in the Church Services Division, also extended their ministries to the new Southern Baptist churches in Minnesota-Wisconsin that were related to the Texas convention.

Training Union Department. For most of Patterson's tenure, Edward E. Laux headed the Training Union Department. During the 1960s his associates included Thomas A. Dempsey, R. Clyde Hall, Lee E. Garner, Tommy Dixon, and Bill D. King. Their emphases included, in addition to helping churches strengthen their overall training ministries, promoting the Bible Sword Drills and Speakers' Tournaments, developing materials and promotion for New Member Orientation, sponsoring various youth rallies over the state with special emphasis upon challenging youth to consider a church related vocation, promoted and conducted "M Night" (Mobilization) meetings to strengthen the Training Union, led the churches to sponsor an annual doctrinal study course, and of course promoted the Baptist encampments in Texas. They also conducted workshops and provided materials for such specialized ministries with the deaf and with mentally retarded persons and their families.

For all their helpful ministries, dedicated workers and creative programs, the Training Union faced hard times in the 1960s. The increasing secularization of the South rapidly turned the Sunday "holy day" into a "holiday," and churches found their Sunday night attendance plummeting. Already in many parts of the nation the churches had abandoned Sunday night services entirely. While few Texas Baptist churches voted to skip Sunday night services, many of the members voted with their feet. Many churches found that their two main services of the week were Sunday morning and Wednesday night. In this new format, Training Union faced an uphill pull.

Church Music Department. V. F. "Pete" Forderhase headed the Church Music Department until 1971 when he was succeeded by Sam W. Prestridge who had been an associate in the department since 1961. "The objective of the Church Music Department," according to a 1972 report, "is to assist churches in establishing, conducting, enlarging and improving a music program which (1) teaches music to members (2) trains persons to lead, sing and play music (3) provides music in the church and community (4) provides and interprets information regarding the work of the churches and denomination."[36]

A candid observer would readily acknowledge that music was an area in which many Texas Baptist churches needed help, not that all of them would admit it. Too many churches used unsuitable selections from unsuitable hymnals, had the music led by indifferent persons with limited aptitude, offered no training to help people learn to sing, and often regarded the "song service" as a casual "preliminary" before the real service of preaching. True understanding and appreciation of the spiritual and biblical role of singing as a vital part of worship was not always present. The Church Music Department set out to change all this, and to a remarkable degree did so. The department staff, along with countless volunteer workers, conducted workshops in churches, associations and districts where they taught music, modeled appropriate music, helped form choirs, led churches to obtain better pianos and organs, and encouraged leaders to outfit their churches with the *Baptist Hymnal* of 1956. They also conducted summer music camps for all ages and provided a number of college students who served as volunteer "summer workers" in music in the smaller churches. Jack Terrell led in efforts to help the smaller churches improve their worship through music. They also encouraged the churches to provide choir robes to lend dignity to the services.

A major emphasis of the music ministry in the churches was in forming choirs. To this end, the department sponsored a number of age-group choral clinics and choir festivals. Somewhat like the Protestant reformer John Calvin, who in the sixteenth century led the emerging Protestant churches to sing by beginning with the children, the Baptists felt that by teaching the children they could develop a singing church. Parents saw the value of having their children in a good music program and this also encouraged participation. In 1965 the department sponsored 16 "Junior Choir" festivals and clinics (ages 9-12), with almost 7,000 children participating, representing 199 choirs.[37] Choir enrollment continued to grow, reaching a total of 136,737 in 1965 and 167,381 in 1972.[38] It is safe to say that any Baptist church in Texas that wanted to improve its music had ample opportunity to participate in training workshops in their part of the state. The department also sponsored an annual retreat for full-time ministers of music in Texas churches.

Another dimension of the music ministry was to help Latin American churches to improve their worship with better music and better performance. Each year they conducted a number of clinics and workshops led by Latin Americans who had been trained by the Church Music Department. A helpful leaflet, *Las Funciones del Ministerio de la Music,* was distributed. They also helped the Latin churches form choirs, and conducted a Music Conference at the annual Mexican Baptist Departmental Convention and launched plans for a statewide Latin American Music Festival for 1973. In all this, the department used Latin leaders as much as possible and tried to be sensitive to the fact that Latin Americans had their own heritage and preferences in church music.

The Brotherhood Department. L. H. Tapscott, "Mr. Brotherhood" in Texas, headed the department until December 31, 1963, when he resigned to become Minister of Education at Cliff Temple church in Dallas. His successor was William L. "Wimpy" Smith who had been a missionary to Argentina. Smith is not to be confused with A. C. Wimpee, who had been an associate in the department until his resignation in 1963. Robert E. Dixon joined the department in 1961 as head of the Royal Ambassador work. In 1969 the Brotherhood name was changed to Baptist Men of Texas. Dixon has headed the group since 1969.

The 1963 resignations of both the secretary and associate no doubt reflects a sense of frustration at the failure of the Brotherhood to thrive. This department of work had not found ready acceptance in the churches and enrollment and participation lagged far behind the Sunday School, Training Union and Woman's Missionary Union. Brotherhood enrollment dropped from 72,660 in 1961 to 60,074 in 1972.[39] Even so, the department sponsored a number of creative and worthwhile projects in missions, evangelism and church building. In 1966 the Brotherhood declined to enter into any organic relationship with Boy Scouts of America, but received commendations from the Executive Board "for the new image of Royal Ambassadors."[40] Hispanic churches reported a total of 151 Brotherhoods by 1962. In 1966 Charles McLaughlin, head of the SMC, noting that since the Brotherhood work has "increasingly taken the shape of missions," majoring in mission education and activities, recommended that for administrative oversight the Brotherhood be transferred to the Missions Division of the SMC.[41]

One of the most successful Brotherhood projects was the promotion of Layman's Day in the churches, a day which spotlighted the responsibilities and contributions of Baptist laymen. Often a layman filled the pulpit and men filled the choir. The men also were involved in promoting the church budget, establishing local missions, and training laymen in personal witnessing.

The Missions Division. Everything the SMC did was somehow related to "missions," but the division that bore that name sought to help the churches through three departments: the Church Building Department, the Direct Missions Department, and the Language Missions Department. The division director was Charles McLaughlin until he was chosen to succeed Woodrow Fuller as Secretary of the SMC. McLaughlin's successor as head of the Missions Division was Harold C. Bennett, who served in Texas from 1965 to 1967. Bennett resigned in 1967 to be Executive Secretary for Florida Baptists and later was named Executive Secretary of the SBC Executive Committee. To succeed Bennett as head of this important department, the Executive Board named Charles Lee Williamson who came from significant leadership in both local church and association posts. Texas participated in the SBC "30,000 movement," an effort launched in 1954 to establish that many new churches and missions in America. That movement concluded at the end of 1964, by which time Texas had established 448 new churches and 971 new missions.[42]

The Church Building Department. H. Taylor Pendley headed this department for many years, with Ed Clark as associate. Operating on the assumption that an adequate building is essential for a church to reach its full potential, this department sought to help smaller Texas churches to build, expand or improve their facilities. They also consulted with small churches to help them design their building for maximum usefulness. "Poorly arranged buildings tend to bring about confusion," said their report, "while well-arranged buildings lend themselves to well-ordered worship experiences."[43] Money from the Mary Hill Davis offering for home missions helped fund this program, and some of the money went not just for buildings but also for suitable furnishings for the buildings. An important part of their work was the "Pastor-Builder Program," in which a pastor who was also a skilled builder would accept a call to be pastor and during that pastorate would also lead the church in a building program. This was especially helpful among the Hispanic churches. The department also provided an award for third-year architecture students in Texas universities to help them become acquainted with the architectural needs of Texas Baptist churches.

Direct Missions Department. Darwin Farmer directed this department for many years, succeeding Roy A. Lambert in that post. Associates in the department included Paul Aiken, Frank Burress, Lloyd Henderson, J V Thomas, Clinton Watson and others. Their work was as varied as it was important, including pioneer missions in Wisconsin-Minnesota, church development in Texas, and missionary extension in which they conducted schools of missions utilizing the witness of missionaries on furlough. They also oversaw the Goodwill Center ministry, promotion of evangelism among the Jewish population, a juvenile rehabilitation ministry, and cooperative work with four National Baptist groups (African-American). On May 1, 1965, Paul Aiken was elected director for the work with National Baptists. His task was to promote interracial fellowship and mutual understanding, channel financial aid to African-American colleges like Butler in Tyler and Bishop in Dallas, and sponsor Seminary Extension classes in Amarillo, Austin, College Station, Dallas, Fort Worth, Galveston, Houston, Lubbock, Odessa, Port Arthur and Waco. During the first year of Aiken's work, 1036 students were enrolled in 81 such courses. They also sponsored weekday programs in the inner cities to help latchkey children.

Language Missions. As the name implies, this department sought to minister to the growing number of Texans whose primary language was other than English. Of course, most of these spoke Spanish, but a goodly number of Chinese, Japanese, and various European groups lived here and, like the disciples at Pentecost, the Language Missions Department sought to help them hear the gospel in their own tongues. Dallas P. Lee was longtime director of this department, assisted at various times by John R. McLaughlin, Rudy Hernandez, Rudy Sanchez, Daniel Aleman, Roberto Garcia, Oscar Romo, Martha Ellis, Noemi Cuevas and others. An important part of their work was offering of scholarships, funded by the Mary Hill Davis offering, for promising students. By 1963 more than $200,000 had provided scholarships for 247 Latin students, and that fall 92 Latino students were enrolled in Texas Baptist colleges, many of them receiving some scholarship aid.

By 1963 Dallas Lee reported 475 Spanish-speaking Baptist churches in Texas with a membership over 30,000.[44] Patterson pointed out that more than half of all Mexican Baptist churches in the United States were in Texas.[45] To keep the pastors of these churches informed, the department published a monthly, *El Bautista Mexicano,* mailed to 3,000 homes. They also helped sponsor the broadcast of *La Hora Bautista* and *La Voz del Evangelio* over thirteen stations with Leo Estrada as principal speaker. The Language Missions Department also sponsored ministry to Chinese, Japanese, the deaf, and migrants, sometimes with help from the Home Mission Board. The department also offered salary supplements to a number of small Mexican church and mission pastors as well as a few teachers.

Providing leadership for the Mexican churches was no small task. Two schools trained pastors, the Valley Baptist Academy in Harlingen, owned and operated by District 5, and the Mexican Baptist Bible Institute in San Antonio, sponsored by the San Antonio Association. Both of these schools were adopted by the state convention in 1962, which placed them on steadier financial footing. Both schools increased their enrollment, raised academic standards, and improved their facilities. The Mexican Baptist Bible Institute (H. B. Ramsour, president) broke ground in 1963 for their handsome new campus located on a choice 12 acre tract in San Antonio. In 1965 the Bible Institute reported 120 students and 7 teachers, while the Academy (Howard E. Gary, president) reported 60 students and ten teachers. The Academy was in process of moving to their new 40 acre campus. As schools, these might have come under the umbrella of the Christian Education Commission, but they were assigned instead to the Language Missions Department.

Stewardship Division. Though only one division in the SMC, the Stewardship Division undergirded the total ministries of Texas Baptists. Under the capable direction of O. D. Martin, former pastor and associational missionary, the division sought to lead individuals to give generously to their churches and churches to give generously to denominational ministries. They not only emphasized the giving of money, but also the Christian responsibility to make proper use of the remainder of one's income. They also made a major emphasis upon leading people to make their wills and trusts to see that their possessions continued to serve God after they were gone.

Cooperative Program and Church Finance Department. For many years this department was headed by Cecil A. Ray, and emphasized the teaching of tithing as the minimum of Christian stewardship. Ray developed a resource kit called "Tithe Now Planning Kit," and led a number of "Tithe Now Clinics" attended by pastors and lay persons from over 2,000 churches. He also developed and led a Faith in Action program with twin goals of increasing members giving to the churches and the churches' giving through the Cooperative Program.

Endowment and Capital Giving Department. Heading this department in 1965 was Frank Denton, with Oswin Chrisman as staff attorney. Their emphasis was to lead Baptists to arrange their wills, trusts, annuities, insurance and other properties in such a way as to benefit not only their own families and heirs, but also the Lord's work. They were well informed on estate and tax laws and were able to counsel people to make wise plans for the future.

From District to Area Plan. One of the most significant structural changes in Baptist mission work during this period was the switch from the old District organization to the new Area. W. E. Denham headed a Missions Study Committee which recommended that we "ask the associations to group themselves in smaller units (one to four associations to an Area)" with an Area Missionary serving in each such Area.[46] Several factors led to this change. Charles Lee Williamson, an authority on associational life among Baptists, points out that as early as 1941, the Union Association of Houston launched a City Missions program that provided a viable alternative to the district plan. The election of Elmer Dunham as City Missionary for Tarrant County in 1946 provided another precedent. Durham's associates included Woodrow Fuller and Charles P. McLaughlin, both of whom would come to leadership in the State Missions Commission and emphasize the importance and priority of the association in Baptist polity. Williamson notes that the Gulfshore Conference of 1962, convened by the Home Mission Board, "was a defining point in associational life in the SBC."[47] The Gulfshore Conference reasserted the historic autonomy of the association, rejecting the modern notion that the association was a creature of the state convention. In the old plan, money went from the churches to the state, then back to the districts and associations, thus giving the state undue control.

From a theological perspective, the switch to the Area plan reaffirmed the historic importance and autonomy of the associations. From a practical perspective, it meant that mission planning and promotion came from the churches and associations upward, not from the Convention downward. This led to a greater spirit of cooperation, less tension, and in the judgment of some helped to keep doctrinal controversy at a minimum in Texas until recent years.

The districts had been successful in their day, especially with promotion of CP giving. In effect, the district missionary was an extension of the executive secretary into the different regions. In time, the district missionary began to help place pastors and thus functioned as a kind of "bishop" for his district. When a prominent church in West Texas became disillusioned with a district missionary who could not be removed, they simply stopped supporting the program. This dollar protest attracted attention and led to the study committee of 1962.

Despite the admitted contributions of the old plan over the years, the study committee found growing dissatisfaction among the churches and associations. "There is some confusion," the committee reported, "regarding the organization and purpose of the district and of the paid personnel involved," and they also reported that they found some "ineffective personnel and poor programs."[48] They also found a certain paternalism in the districts which, whether or not intended, diminished the role of the associations. "Texas broke away from that paternalism," says Williamson, and reaffirmed "that associational autonomy was rooted in history and [was] ecclesiastically sound doctrine." With former associational ministers like Fuller and McLaughlin now in power, the new idea "had sympathy in high places in the convention."[49] The Area plan was implemented in 1964.

The new Area plan ended supervisory ties between the associations and the state convention and reaffirmed the autonomy of the association. It also removed the state from Director of Missions (DOM) selection and removed all supervisory relationships between state and area employees. The DOMs were no longer regarded as state employees.

CHRISTIAN EDUCATION COMMISSION

Since the formation of Baylor University in 1845, Texas Baptists have had an ongoing commitment to higher education. That was no less true during the 1960s and 1970s when the Christian Education Commission (CEC) helped correlate the work of eight Baptist colleges and one academy in Texas, 26 Bible Chairs at state universities, and Baptist Student Union programs on over 80 campuses. In 1960 Edward N. Jones was elected as executive secretary of the CEC and served until his retirement in 1967. Jones was a layman and a capable school man. He had taught at the Midwestern University in Wichita Falls, and later served as a professor and dean at Baylor University. Most recently he had served as president at Texas Tech University in Lubbock. C. Eugene Kratz served as coordinator of institutional programs and W. F. Howard continued to head up the BSU division. The Commission worked in three areas: the institutional program (the colleges), the student program (BSU), and dealing with faculty in administering scholarships, grants, and other faculty improvement activities.

Communication, correlation and budgeting were important in the ministry of the CEC. The CEC provided a forum in which college leaders could talk to each other, talk to the denomination, and hear from denominational leaders. Ever since Baptists had more than one college in Texas they have talked about *correlating* the educational program to avoid costly duplication, but mostly the college leaders gave lip service to that idea while in reality going their own ways. The CEC once again attempted to lead the colleges to cooperate more fully and develop one unified system of Baptist education in Texas. While the idea was popular, little actual correlation took place. As for budgeting, the colleges received only a small portion of their total income from the BGCT, but the CEC had clout because they shaped the formula for parceling out those funds.

Institutional Program. Inflation drove up all costs during the 1960s, but the cost of running schools skyrocketed. One study showed that in one decade, 1957 to 1967, costs at Texas Baptist colleges increased by 107.2%.[50] During that decade the total value of college property increased by 141.6%, and tuition rose by 110.3%, five times faster than the general cost of living. During the same decade, allocations from the BGCT as a percentage of total costs steadily decreased, leaving the colleges under necessity of raising their own funds. The colleges found themselves scrambling to make ends meet, to keep buildings in repair and erect needed new ones, to recruit and retain a competent faculty, and to provide dormitory space for students. The annual BGCT budget put the lion's share of its money into the schools, but it was never enough. The projected budget for 1969, for example, provided over $3.5 million for the schools, as compared to only $1.85 million for the State Missions Commission and $2.2 million for the Human Welfare Commission.[51] Baptist college enrollments grew from about 12,000 in 1960 to 20,042 in 1972.[52]

Soon after signing on as secretary of the CEC, Jones reported that "We [the colleges] are approaching bankruptcy. . . . both financially and in terms of adequate trained personnel and physical facilities . . . . The inadequacies of our institutions are overwhelming."[53] Later reports make this sound almost cheerful, as a steady stream of dire warnings about the colleges used such terms as "crisis," "collapse," and "failure." A 1961 report pointed out that "Our schools are all in dire need of improved and expanded facilities."[54] Perhaps the most blistering indictment came in the Carden Report of 1968, which emphasized the shortcomings of Texas Baptist colleges in libraries, laboratories, classrooms, dormitories, and especially in budgets.

In 1960 the BGCT launched a major campaign to raise $28 million to strengthen the colleges. With this money, the colleges expected to erect 36 new buildings, renovate some existing buildings, and strengthen libraries. The plan also called for "upgrading our schools academically and above all a deepening of spiritual resources and attitudes." The plan called for 1961 to be used for preparation, with the campaign itself launched in 1962, pressed in 1963 and 1964, and concluded in 1965.

Problems developed almost immediately. Many assumed this would be an "in house" campaign led by the Board's own staff. However, when the Stewardship Division was asked to "organize and direct" the effort, they begged off, pleading overwork and shortage of staff. Between the lines one reads a pronounced lack of enthusiasm for the campaign from the first. Over the protests of many, the Board employed the professional firm of Ward, Dreshman and Reinhardt to run the campaign. Their fee would be $275,000 with expenses of about $300,000, to be paid regardless of how much money they raised.[55] Herbert Howard said, "I think you are going to find some discouragement on the part of some people because of the large expense of this campaign. . . . I think we are deceiving ourselves if we think we are going to get $28,000,000 out of Texas Baptists and get the same amount of money we have always received, and hope to receive from our people, in their regular tithes and offerings."[56] This expressed the two major complaints, that the campaign was too costly and that it would eat into mission funds. Harry Wofford, a layman, said "Fred Swank asked what an ordinary church member would think about this. Well, I am an ordinary church member and I doubt the wisdom of the employment of this firm to conduct the campaign." Wofford's motion to table the proposal was defeated, partly at the insistence of H. E. Butt, Sr. Secretary Patterson inherited the campaign since it was voted a few weeks before he took office. He later reflected that "When I came as Executive Secretary they had approved this crusade for Christian education. I realized soon after we got into it that the guidelines were all wrong, it would never work. It had been approved; we had to see it through."[57]

Fred Swank pinpointed another problem for the campaign. Some complained that the schools had, at best, diminished their Baptist emphases or, at worst, had fallen into doctrinal liberalism. If we raise the $28 million, Swank demanded, what assurance can we have "that our schools are going to turn more Baptistic and more Christian and more fundamental in the Baptist word?" Secretary Jones responded by admitting that the colleges might have a few problems, but "the best way to reduce the small number of 'off color' situations that we might have now is for us to restore in the minds of college faculties, to whatever extent it has slipped, a feeling of confidence in our schools." He concluded that, "The more we do for our schools the more we have the right and privilege of requiring these things of them." In his roundabout way, Jones said Baptists would have to support their schools in order to control them.

Needless to say, the campaign did not go well. After three years they had received only $2,327,918 in cash plus some pledges of uncertain value.[58] In September, 1964, the campaign was completely reorganized to make a final push in 1965. The consulting firm was long gone by then, and the campaign was brought back in house. Patterson brought O. D. Martin in to head the Stewardship Division partly to oversee the remnants of the $28 Million Campaign. Instead of a general appeal for "Christian education," Martin tailored school-specific campaigns to appeal to alumni and partisans of individual colleges. In one year Martin raised more money than the professional firm had in three, but in the final analysis only a fraction of the hoped for goal was received.

The failure of the $28 Million Campaign convinced the schools that they could no longer look to the BGCT for financial support but must find alternate sources of income. This came at a time when the federal government was making more money available in the form of grants and low-interest loans to make educational opportunities available for their young citizens. The Baptist colleges tried for a decade to convince the BGCT to allow them to receive government loans, but the Convention adamantly refused. They also refused to allow the colleges to approach churches directly to ask to be included in local church budgets. Convention leaders, especially T. A. Patterson and O. D. Martin, suggested instead that the colleges become more aggressive in raising their own funds from foundations and wealthy donors.

When the Executive Board in 1961 voted to ask the Baptist colleges in Texas to increase their Bible course requirements for graduation from six to twelve semester hours, many no doubt regarded it as a routine request. Some board members were distressed that Baptist colleges required so little in the way of religious studies, and complained that the six hours was mostly introductory Bible survey courses which "are not making the greatest possible contribution to a well indoctrinated Baptist leadership and constituency for the future."[59] However, this proposal to double the religion requirement in the standard degree program proved surprisingly controversial. The college leaders objected that a non-academic body, the Executive Board, seemed willing to meddle with academic matters. College business managers said they could not afford the extra faculty needed to carry out this request; W. R. White estimated it would cost an extra $100,000 per year at Baylor alone. E. N. Jones said in some schools the standard four-year degree would become four and a half years, and others feared that the enrollment of non-Baptist students would diminish. Wayne Evans made the motion to refer the request back to the CEC for further study.

After a year of study, the CEC reported that they could not comply with the request and listed a number of reasons. Charles Wellborn, pastor of Seventh and James Baptist Church hard by the Baylor campus, introduced an alternate proposal: that the semester hours be kept at six, but one course (three semester hours) be used for introductory Bible survey and one course (3 hours) include more in-depth studies of Christian doctrine and be offered at the junior or senior level. In addition, the alternate proposal included a plan to improve college chapel services and form a Christian Maturity Council on each campus to bring faculty and students together for serious discussion of religious topics. The CEC professed themselves to be "heart to heart and shoulder to shoulder" with the Board in the original proposal, but simply could not do it. However, they felt the alternate proposal met the spirit and purpose of the original proposal.

Not everyone agreed. Many Baptists thought if the schools wanted to add the hours they would simply do so. William Fleming could not attend the meeting but sent a telegram "protesting this recommendation" [the alternate proposal]. Public response was so negative that in 1963 the CEC recommended that all the colleges increase their offerings to at least nine hours, but most of them responded by keeping the six hours required and adding a third course on an elective basis.

The Survey Committee of 1959 had specified that one purpose of the Baptist colleges was to provide a dependable source of trained ministers for the churches and denomination. In light of this expectation, many were concerned to see the enrollment of ministerial students steadily declining from a peak of 1891 in 1955 to only 881 in 1969.[60] Over the years the Convention adopted various methods to help ministerial students by providing scholarship aid. In 1963 Lee Ramsour chaired a Ministerial Aid Study Committee that recommended a new program called "Reciprocal Service Program."[61] This committee reported that ministerial aid is "an investment of the denomination in its own future," but proposed that the "tuition assistance program of the Convention be limited to the assistance of persons preparing for the preaching ministry only." Students preparing to serve as ministers of education or ministers of music would not qualify for scholarship aid. To receive aid, a student must enroll for full-time studies, maintain a grade of C or better, present a statement each year from the church where he held membership, and "demonstrate continued loyalty to, and willingness to cooperate with, the Baptist General Convention of Texas." The aided student must also covenant to serve as a Southern Baptist pastor after graduation, or else pay back the tuition. "The service obligation of the student will be relieved," said the report, "on the basis of two months in ministerial service for every one month in school while receiving ministerial scholarship assistance." A student who received four years of scholarship would be obligated to serve as a Southern Baptist pastor for at least eight years, or pay back the scholarship. However, the committee graciously specified that "Should a participant in this program die. . . . any outstanding amount of indebtedness will automatically be canceled, and no continued payment will be requested or required from his estate."[62] The student who met these qualifications would continue to pay regular tuition, but could apply for a $5 per semester hour refund. The committee hoped that could be raised to $10 but CEC officials said they could not afford that.

The Carden Report. In 1967 the CEC, with Executive Board approval, employed William H. Carden to make a year-long study of Texas Baptist colleges. This "Carden Report" was presented in 1968. Perhaps no study in Texas Baptist history raised so many questions, caused so much dissension, and did so little good. However, its story must be sketched here.

By the mid-1960s Texas Baptist colleges were reeling from one crisis to another. Perhaps the CEC thought that a detailed study of the schools, with statistical analysis of enrollment, courses offered, and costs involved would persuade Texas Baptists to increase their support. Bill Carden, lately of Stetson University, was a superb school man and nobody doubted his credentials to make the study. He amassed a huge report of several hundred pages, with minute reports of every statistical dimension that one could imagine, producing reams of detailed analysis whose accuracy need not be doubted but whose relevance is not immediately apparent.[63]

Carden did the study virtually alone, traveling about the state to visit the schools. He kept his own counsel and until he released the report, few had any inkling what he would recommend. The report turned out to be quite radical, with the most blistering indictment of the deficiencies of the Texas Baptist colleges to be found anywhere. According to the Stetson educator, the physical plants were deplorable; the faculties underpaid and rarely measured up even to mediocre quality; the libraries in most cases could not compare with the high school libraries in their cities; the colleges were poorly located and competed with one another for students and dollars; they were not able to recruit the better students and teachers; costs in Baptist colleges were too high in comparison to state schools; and even worse, Baptist colleges may have outlived their usefulness. He said that the Baptist schools suffer a "quality gap" of at least $10 million annually, and would require $35 million at once to bring the campuses up to par. Noting that the relationship between the denomination and its colleges in recent years "has not been completely harmonious," Carden concluded that tensions have arisen from three factors: (1) an underlying concern that the colleges are slowly drifting away from denominational sponsorship and affiliation, (2) a troubled feeling that no real differences, other than six hours of required Bible courses and a few indifferent chapel services, exists between the state and denominational schools, and (3) a growing split between those who identify the purpose of the colleges as another form of evangelism and those who say the college's role is primarily academic.[64]

If Carden's analysis was radical, his recommendations were even more so. He recommended that Baptists sell Howard Payne College (Brownwood) and Wayland Baptist College (Plainview) to the local tax districts to make them into state community colleges; that Mary Hardin-Baylor at Belton become a branch of Baylor University; that East Texas Baptist College (Marshall) revert to junior college status; that the University of Corpus Christi be released outright; that Hardin-Simmons University (Abilene) continue in existence but drop most of its graduate programs; that colleges continue in Dallas and Houston, and that Baylor remain as the only Baptist university in the state.[65] The report also urged that the BGCT reverse its stand and allow the colleges to accept government loans.

Not only was the report shocking in its content, but its presentation could hardly have been worse. It was first unveiled at a closed meeting in Salado on July 22, 1968, before CEC members and staff, a few college trustees, and other denominational leaders. Realizing that this report would raise a furor among Texas Baptists, especially supporters of the schools marked for demise, the CEC unwisely decided not to release it. Instead, they appointed a twelve member committee to study the report for a year and bring recommendations of what parts of the report, if any, to recommend for adoption. It should be emphasized that the report was just that, a report, until it was officially acted upon by the CEC, the Executive Board, and the BGCT. What was presented in Salado may have sounded shocking, but it was far from being actually accepted.

Of course, those who attended the Salado meeting did not, as requested, keep the information confidential; within days details of the report circulated throughout the state. Editor Hurt wrote a sharp editorial on "Efforts for Secrecy," in which he decried what he called an effort to keep the report from Texas Baptists. Why, he asked, should not the report be released at once? Cannot Texas Baptists be trusted? "We have faith," the editor said, "that Texas Baptists, given all the information, will do their best to vote their honest convictions."[66] T. A. Patterson, a shrewd denominational leader, saw at once that the report was fatally flawed and he was carefully noncommittal about it. He did, however, in the only article he wrote on the subject, try (without complete success) to defend the decision not to release the report.[67]

What became of the report? A Committee of Twelve studied it, reported on it, and then let it lie. No group ever adopted it. The Carden Report turned out to be much ado about not much. It did, however, convince many Texas Baptists that they must support their schools or run the danger of losing them.

HUMAN WELFARE COMMISSION

As the name implies, those institutions devoted to helping people were grouped into the category of "Human Welfare." In 1961 this agency worked with four child care homes, eight hospitals, two homes for the aged, and a home for unwed mothers. Over the next decades the number of hospitals remained at eight, though not the same ones in every case. The number of child care homes also remained constant, but the homes for the aged had increased to five. Disaster relief efforts began under the Human Welfare Commission (HWC) but was later switched to the State Missions Commission. In 1961 James Basden was named Secretary of the HWC.

Child care homes. Gone were the days when the Buckner Orphans' Home was one of the biggest ministries of Texas Baptists. By the 1960s and 1970s changes in society, changes among Baptists, and changes in the American family had drastically changed child care needs in Texas. R. C. Campbell served as president of Buckner Benevolences, which covered a multitude of ministries. The Buckner Baptist Children's Home in Dallas was headed by Harold H. Hime, which housed an average of 374 children in 1973.[68] Most of these children lived in family-style cottages, with house-parents seeking to provide a home atmosphere. Whenever possible, the children were placed in actual families by adoption and by foster-care. The BGCT continued to sponsor the Buckner Baptist Children's Home in Lubbock (established 1957), Buckner Baptist Boys Ranch near Burnet (1951), Mexican Baptist Children's Home in San Antonio (1944), South Texas Children's Home in Beeville (1952), and Texas Baptist Children's Home in Round Rock (1956). Two of these, Buckner's in Dallas and the home the Mexican home in San Antonio had ethnic restrictions in their charters; Dallas restricted admission to children of "Anglo-Saxon parentage" and San Antonio to children of "Mexican parentage." Both of these restrictions were removed, though not without opposition in the case of Dallas. When opponents could not prevent removal of the restriction, they asked that the change not be publicized. Lloyd Wright, director of public relations for the Executive Board, refused to cover up the news.[69]

The 1973 statistics give an interesting picture of the child care homes, which that year housed 1438 children.[70] Of these, only 30 were full orphans and 217 were half-orphans; 146 were adopted out, and 72 adoptions were pending; 220 were placed in foster homes and 928 were returned to their parents or other kinfolk; applications for admission which could not be accepted were received from 519 children; and 128 conversions were reported. Of 661 employees, only 97 were Baptist. Total operating expenses for the homes came to $5,944,995, of which $1,167,958 or less than 20% came from the Cooperative Program.

Hospitals. In 1973 the BGCT sponsored hospitals at Beaumont (Guy Dalrymple, administrator); San Angelo (Taylor Henley); San Antonio (David A. Garrett); Dallas (Boone Powell); Abilene (Boone Powell, Jr.); Amarillo (Emmett R. Johnson); Waco (Alton Pearson); and Harlingen (T. H. Morrison, Jr.). It would be too much to say the BGCT "owned" these hospitals, for in some cases they owned neither the land, buildings or equipment. Instead, they "sponsored" the hospitals, and provided only a fraction of their operating costs.

By the nature of their work, the hospitals were much involved with the government. "Hospitals are subject to a multitude of licensing agencies, government regulations, accreditation groups, professional associations, social and health agencies, group purchasers of hospital services, and others, all of which have some influence on decision making in the hospital," and these combine, one report said, to "make hospitals one of the most difficult of all enterprises to manage successfully."[71] The rise of Medicare further entwined the hospitals with government regulations.

At their best, the hospitals provided spiritual as well as physical healing. In addition to the Baptist hospitals, the BGCT also sponsored chaplaincy programs in several non-Baptist hospitals including, for a time, the Mayo Clinic. "The hospital ministry provides vast opportunities for reaching people to whom our churches have little or no access," said a study committee. In 1973 the hospitals reported 861 professions of faith, 3532 rededications to Jesus Christ, and 12 nurses preparing for foreign mission service.[72]

The hospitals, like the colleges, faced constant crises of funding. Total expenditures for all the hospitals in 1973 came to $118,825,548, of which the convention provided $1,138,219, or less than 1%.[73] Much of this 1% went to pay costs of the chaplaincy programs. Unlike the colleges, however, Texas Baptists seemed to have less objections to the hospitals receiving some forms of government aid. John Bagwell chaired a major Hospital Study Committee which reported in 1971. The committee was charged to "focus on the needs, problems, and alternatives faced by the hospitals and the Convention in ownership of these hospitals," because they said, all of the Baptist hospitals are "pointing to a true crisis."[74]

The Bagwell committee came up with four far-reaching recommendations, two of which passed and two of which failed. Recommendations to allow hospital trustees to elect some of their successors, including non-Baptists, failed 59 to 47, and a proposal to ease the way for a Baptist hospital to drop its Baptist ties failed 59 to 57. However, a proposal to allow Baptist hospitals to accept both federal and state funds passed 66 to 50 and a recommendation that the hospitals be allowed to apply for and accept government loans passed 67-59.[75] The hospitals were allowed to do what the colleges were specifically forbidden to do. James H. Semple, pastor of FBC Paris and a strong advocate of separation of church and state, brought a minority report but he could not stem the tide. By the 1970s the blazing fervor of the church-state debate had cooled. Many Baptists were convinced that the hospitals could not survive without government aid, and many perceived them to be more Baptist in name than reality. The doughty old *Baptist Standard* editor E. S. James, who carried the fight against accepting the Wadley Hospital in Texarkana in the 1950s because of government money in it, was gone. His successor, Georgia layman John J. Hurt, was no less Baptist but took a much more relaxed attitude toward government aid for humanitarian purposes.

Homes for the aged. By the 1970s, Texas Baptists had more widows than orphans. The HWC oversaw five homes for the aged, including the Mary E. Trew Home in Dallas (established 1954), the Frank M. Ryburn Home in Dallas (1966), Buckner Baptist Haven in Houston (1955), and the Buckner-Monte Siesta and Buckner-Villa Siesta Retirement Homes in Austin (1970). These homes were supposed to be self-supporting and mostly they were. In addition, one of the hospitals, Baptist Memorials Geriatric Center in San Angelo provided living arrangements for elderly persons from independent living to all stages of assisted living and nursing home care. Many prominent Texas Baptists retired to the San Angelo center, including (among others) E. D. Head, the Robert L. Dobsons, and Ray and Jester Summers.

By 1973 the home for unwed mothers in Dallas was closed for lack of patronage, but the Buckner Maternity Home in San Antonio was still maintained. Births at the Dallas home had declined from about 230 a year to fewer than 40 by 1972, a trend which some attributed to the lessening of the stigma to bearing an out of wedlock child, meaning the girls did not have to flee to a secluded home.

CHRISTIAN LIFE COMMISSION

Though the smallest Commission, there was nothing small about the CLC task or their efforts to fulfill that assignment. Jimmy R. Allen headed the Commission until 1967 when he resigned to become pastor of FBC, San Antonio. He was succeeded by James M. Dunn. William M. Pinson served for six years as associate secretary until his resignation in 1963 to accept a professorship at Southwestern Seminary. Other associates in the

Commission included, at different times, Weston Ware, who succeeded Pinson but later resigned to join the Peace Corps, Phil D. Strickland, Director of Citizenship Education, and Ben E. Loring, Director of Research.

The CLC was assigned to speak out on moral issues, such as family life, Christian citizenship, race relations, moral issues like gambling and alcohol use, and daily work. From time to time, they also addressed such issues as capital punishment, church-state issues, and the fire-bombing of black churches. They also monitored the Texas legislature concerning laws that might affect the moral climate of Texas. They did their work through publication and distribution of various kinds of literature, conducting regional and state-wide workshops on moral issues, providing sermon and illustrative materials to encourage pastors to preach on moral issues, and lobbying the legislature in Austin. They also held district youth conferences, held conferences in local churches, and conducted summer camps emphasizing moral issues.

To the surprise of no one, the work of the CLC proved controversial, especially in the realm of race relations. However, the leaders never budged from their insistence that all persons are created in the image of God, that all persons have infinite value because Christ died for them, and all American citizens are entitled to basic constitutional rights. Ideas that seem a given today were often challenged in the 1960s and many opposed the CLC, called for its meager funding to be cut, or advocated that it be abolished entirely. Some were not thrilled when after the Dallas assassination of President Kennedy, the CLC spoke out for peaceful toleration in an increasingly lawless society. "We have been made keenly conscious," one report said, "of those elements in our society who despise law and create disorder . . . [and we] urge our people to a prayerful support of our national leaders in these critical days."[76]

The CLC was perfectly clear on one issue: their assignment was to speak TO Texas Baptists, not FOR them. In no way were the positions on issues taken by the CLC the official position of Texas Baptists, the BGCT, or the Executive Board. Many misunderstood this distinction, a fact that kept the leaders in hot water.

For all their boldness on moral issues, the CLC never fared well in the budget battles in the Baptist Building. Their projected 1962 allocation was less than $60,000. By 1973 that modest amount had risen to $114,186.[77]

CRUSADE EVANGELISM

By far the largest effort of the Evangelism Division during these years was the Japan New Life Crusade of 1963. When Patterson visited Japan in 1959, then FMB missionary W. H. "Dub" Jackson suggested that a new approach, a nationwide crusade, might advance the gospel in that land. Patterson was receptive to the idea, and later the FMB agreed to the Texas request to give it a try. J. Ralph Grant, influential Lubbock pastor, urged the BGCT to approve Patterson's proposal. "This may be God's way,"

Grant said, "of giving us the opportunity of carrying our General MacArthur's request after World War II for 1,000 missionaries for the Orient and Far East. I feel this is an opportunity to redeem the time we have let go by."[78] Recognizing the proposed crusade as "one of the great missionary opportunities in the world today," the Executive Board assigned the task of planning and promotion to the Evangelism Division, though the task eventually involved the entire convention. Working with Secretary Freeman was a Crusade Committee, with K. Owen White (chair), Dub Jackson, James H. Landes, A. J. Kincaid and Mrs. Bert Black. Roberta Patterson, wife of the Executive Secretary, served as Prayer Chairman and coordinated prayers throughout the state involving WMU groups, churches, and associations as well as countless individuals. Costs of the crusade were first projected at about $300,000 but when the project was expanded beyond Japan to other nations in Southeast Asia expenses rose to $677,690. When only $571,447 came in for this purpose, the Executive Board appropriated an extra $100,000 to make up the shortfall.[79]

In 1962 the Board sent Patterson and Freeman to Japan to spy out the land and they returned full of enthusiasm. They reported that a few reluctant Japanese Baptists had changed their attitudes completely and were now cooperating heartily. An Amarillo layman, C. J. Humphrey, had attended the Japanese Baptist Convention and returned to urge laymen to enlist the support of their pastors and churches. A number of laymen participated in the crusade. Patterson hoped the churches would send their pastors and that laymen would pay their own way and that some men of means would help underwrite the crusade.

Freeman reported that in April and May, 1963, a total of 156 teams of Texas Baptist pastors, musicians, and laymen conducted revivals in Japan, with over 23,000 recorded decisions, about 98% of them conversions.[80] The famous Cowboy Band of Hardin-Simmons University made their own tour of Japan and performed at many of the crusades. Patterson noted that news of the Japan Crusade attracted attention throughout Southeast Asia and requests came for Texas Baptists to conduct similar crusades elsewhere. As a result, Texas teams conducted 10 revivals in Okinawa with 1,108 decisions; 26 revivals in Hawaii with 527 decisions; 47 revivals in Hong Kong with 2,000 decisions; 28 revivals in Taiwan with 2,500 decisions; and a citywide revival in Singapore with 300 decisions. Altogether, Texas teams conducted about 350 revivals in the Orient, with 39,636 decisions reported.[81] Texas Baptists also sponsored a number of other crusades, both in America and overseas, culminating in the Crusade of the Americas in 1969.

Patterson became an enthusiastic advocate of the crusade as a means of missions and evangelism. "With the resources we have as Texas Baptists," he said, " it seems to me we ought to think seriously and prayerfully about a major crusade somewhere every year." The Executive Board shared this enthusiasm. They passed a resolution that "We recommend to the Foreign Mission Board that the Board consider prayerfully the New

Life [crusade] movement as a possible program for a world evangelistic emphasis."[82]

Years later Patterson said the Japan crusade "was one of the most significant developments in the field of missions," and he predicted that "Ultimately the [Baptist] denomination will come fully to this program. I think it's inevitable."[83]

Jesse Fletcher, who served as an associate secretary of the FMB under Baker James Cauthen, thinks Patterson's prediction was right on target. Fletcher says that Cauthen reluctantly agreed to participate in the Japan crusade despite the recommendation of his staff, and he concluded that "Cauthen's intuition was good."[84] Fletcher tended to identify the crusade with the views of the old China hand, John Nevius, who influenced the Landmarker, T. P. Crawford. R. Cal Guy, longtime professor of missions at Southwestern Seminary, was also influenced by Nevius. Cauthen held to traditional Baptist missionary policy, but Fletcher says "It was his successor who changed the paradigm under which the mission board worked and moved more toward the Patterson-Guy emphases."[85]

Despite widespread enthusiasm, the crusade was not without its tensions. A few Japanese Baptist pastors at first withheld their support. A few American pastors complained about their revival assignments, and some FMB missionaries wondered (mostly in private) if the enterprise involved as much zeal for tourism as for missions. One clear implication of the new crusaders was that a group of pastors with no training, no facility with the language, and with little or no awareness of Japanese culture could accomplish in a few days what career missionaries had not accomplished in a lifetime. Sensitive to this criticism, Patterson said "this [crusade] is a pilot project and we are trying to demonstrate whether or not this new approach can be made to make an impact for Christ and to speed up this effort to touch the world for Christ."[86]

As a follow up to the crusade, Patterson arranged for a number of Japanese pastors to visit Texas to see how churches operate here. How much of the Texas methods would translate back into the Japanese culture was not entirely clear, though the pastors did request that musicians and religious education leaders, as well as preachers, be sent to visit Japan.

The *Cruzada Bautista Nueva Vida* for Latin Americans in Texas was planned for the fall of 1964. Like the Japan Crusade, this was assigned to the Evangelism Division. L. L. Morris, pastor in Midland, chaired the Latin American New Life Crusade Committee. The Executive Board called for a minimum of $500,000 for publicity and promotion, rental of stadiums and auditoriums, and for newspaper, radio and television promotion, and for massive distributions of scripture. Freeman defended the use of stadiums rather than churches for the meetings by quoting Billy Graham who said that they could reach about 40% of the unchurched population in stadiums but only about 2% in churches.[87] A film spotlighting the growing Mexican population in Texas, called "a state within a state," was widely used among the churches and every Anglo church was teamed with a Mexican church as prayer partners for the crusade.

The crusade took about six weeks in the fall of 1964 with about 2,500 preachers and musicians, both Latin and Anglo, taking part. According to one report, about 500 revivals were held, with about 12,000 decisions of which 7,500 were conversions.[88] "The Latin American Crusade was the greatest single undertaking in the history of our Texas Baptist life," said one report.[89] Even so, compared to the reams of reports on the Japan New Life Crusade, the Latin American Crusade was reported in the 1964 BGCT Annual in only nine lines.

Perhaps even Patterson did not fully realize what force he had unleashed in the New Life Crusade. This marked a major new motif in Southern Baptist missions. There was more focus on volunteers rather than career missionaries, more emphasis upon short-term crusades than lifetime appointments, and more opportunity for personal involvement in missions rather than merely giving to a cause. The later development of such programs as Partnership Missions, the Mission Service Corps, and even the Texas River Ministry grew to a large extent from the precedent set in the Japan New Life Crusade.

CHURCH—STATE ISSUES

One major "hot-button" for Texas Baptists in the 1960s was the relationship of church and state, specifically whether Baptist institutions could accept long-term government loans for construction. The controversy centered mostly around the colleges which needed funding to build dormitories for the increased enrollments. Almost all Texas Baptists agreed that it would be improper for the Baptist colleges to accept outright grants from the government, but a growing number saw no great problem in accepting long-term low-interest loans, so long as those loans were repaid. But the majority of those who attended the state conventions would not agree even to that.

Several factors combined to intensify the debate in the 1960s. College enrollment in America mushroomed and the schools scrambled to build classrooms and dormitories to accommodate the incoming crowds. Inflation drove up construction costs just when the colleges needed new buildings. Several government programs made funds readily available to colleges, both for loans and outright grants, in order to assure American youth of an opportunity for education. Most colleges and universities took all the government aid they could get and new science buildings, libraries, laboratories and dormitories sprang up in one of the greatest building booms in college history.

The term for the government loans was forty years, while loans from banks had to be repaid in twenty years. This duration was far more important to the Baptist colleges than the interest rate. A dorm built with a forty year loan could be paid off from income from room rent, but that was not the case with a twenty year loan. The Education Commission wanted to accept the loans. The Survey Committee of 1957-1959 had bludgeoned the colleges with candid reports of inadequate facilities, crowded class-rooms, deficient libraries, and outdated dorms. They had insisted that in order to be viable, a college should have a minimum enrollment of 1,000 to 1,200 and several of the Texas schools fell below that. However, the schools maintained that they were unable to provide the facilities that would attract and support such enrollments. Secretary Jones said in 1961 that Texas Baptist colleges needed 15 new dormitories immediately and there simply was no money to build them. He led the CEC to launch a campaign to persuade Texas Baptists to allow the schools to accept government loans.

Never loath to appoint a committee and launch a study, the Executive Board appointed a series of committees during the 1960s to study the church-state issue. The first was chaired by James Basden and made its report in 1961. After reviewing the biblical and historical basis for separation of church and state, the committee brought several recommendations, the most basic being "That the Executive Board . . . oppose the securing of loans from public funds for the construction of church schools, church college buildings, hospitals, and other church institutional buildings."[90] The Board amended the report by adding to this sentence the words, "or for any other purpose under any circumstance." The committee argued that if Baptists would reject government loans to build churches they should also reject them for a college since there can be no distinction between a Baptist church and a Baptist university. "To accept long-term low-interest loans is to obligate churches and their institutions to the state. Such an obligation Baptists must refuse to accept." They saw no problem with tax exemption for church property and had no objection to grants and loans to individual students. They agreed that churches could use a Non-Profit Second Class Mailing Permit, though they acknowledged that this was a clear government subsidy. The committee also said, "That the Executive Board of the Baptist General Convention of Texas does not consider the military chaplaincy a violation of the church-state principle," though they acknowledged that the government employed and paid ministers to advance the cause of religion. The Board approved this statement.

Several argued against the recommendations, pointing out that the loans would be repaid in full, that such loans would not breach the wall of separation, that the loans would not enable the government to control the colleges and that, objectionable as government loans might be to some, the prospects of closing the colleges was even more objectionable.

In 1965 the Board appointed yet another Church-State Committee, this one chaired by W. Morris Ford. T. A. Patterson said, "I think all of us are aware of the fact that we are facing some very complicated problems. No generation has ever confronted what we are facing and most everything we have stood for is being tested now."[91] The Ford committee reported in 1966, beginning with the usual reaffirmation of the Baptist principle of church state separation, but pointing out that new circumstances required a new look at the issues. "Rapid changes in the nature of our society, increased participation by government in the fields of education and human welfare, and new kinds of tax supported programs demand a constant re-evaluation of Baptist institutional programs and policies," they said.[92] The heart of the report said, "We recommend that the Baptist General Convention of Texas approve the securing of long-term low interest loans from public funds for construction of buildings by Texas Baptist institutions provided the institution voluntarily reimburses the government annually the additional mount of interest which will cover the government subsidy involved in the loan."[93] This was exactly opposite of the recommendation five years earlier. In defending their recommendation, the Ford committee said

> Long-term, low interest loans are available under several government programs to church-related institutions of education and welfare. The chief advantage of this financing is that loans are available for such a long period of time that they can be self-amortizing. There is no question that the current interest charged involves some government subsidy. However, the fact that the principal of the loan is to be repaid by the institutions makes the subsidy minimal.
>
> The desire of Baptists to pay their own way in the propagation of their faith through institutional ministries can be fulfilled by a voluntary repayment of the amount of the subsidy involved according to the method recommended by the President's Committee on Federal Credit Program (February 11, 1963). This will remove objections based on tax subsidy within the loan. It would mean that the institutions are taking advantage of the longer term of credit but at the same time are paying their own way in order to fulfill their religious function without a violation of religious conscience."[94]

The committee recommended that such loans, if accepted, be buttressed with additional safeguards: that they be used sparingly, that no Baptist school become overly dependent upon them, and that no loan be accepted if accompanied with any efforts at control. They also okayed government support of military, prison and state hospital chaplains "though this does involve some government support of the ministry."

This 1966 report represents a complete reversal of the recommendation in 1961. However, in the fall of 1966 by a ballot vote of 739 to 536 the Convention defeated the proposal to accept government loans under any conditions.[95] Three times in eight years the BGCT soundly rejected the idea of government loans for Baptist institutions. Even so, only weeks after the latest rejection, the CEC geared up for another try, partly on the grounds that the 1966 convention vote was taken late in the session when many messengers had already left. Editor Hurt urged the CEC to back off since the Convention had spoken decisively. In a statement that might have put his predecessor into apoplexy, Hurt said, "We have no quarrel with the proposal [to accept government loans]. Involvement with government loans, in our opinion, adds little if anything to current involvement with a thousand government regulations."[96]

The church-state issue provoked an intense statewide debate. This debate was capsuled by facing full-page articles in the *Baptist Standard* (June 26, 1967) in which two of the big guns, Abner McCall of Baylor University and E. S. James, recently retired editor of the *Standard,* faced off. McCall's article, "Southern Baptists TAXED; Others get GRANTS," argued that government aid is essential to having quality colleges; that government had been aiding colleges for decades without trying to exert control; that government loans which are repaid represent no subsidy and thus do not compromise the separation of church and state; that colleges are already involved with the government in countless regulations; that Baptist schools in other states have received such aid with no adverse effect; and that, in effect, Baptists are providing the taxes to build up the colleges of other denominations while their own languish. James countered with "Tithes and Taxes Just Don't Mix," in which he argued that government loans do represent a subsidy and should be rejected. James acknowledged that government loans were available only for "non-religious" studies like math and science, but he insisted that "If any part of a Baptist school is not thoroughly Christian, it has no right to expect Baptist support. If every part is altogether Christian, it has no right to expect compulsory support by non-Baptists." He concluded that "Tithes and taxes just don't mix. . . . These grants are not right."

Practically all of the school leaders agreed with McCall, as apparently did most laymen. Preachers more generally agreed with James, and they had a dominant voice in the state convention.

The issues were vividly illustrated in the case of three church colleges in Abilene: Hardin-Simmons University (Baptist), McMurray College (Methodist) and Abilene Christian College (Church of Christ, now University) all of whom erected new science buildings in the middle 1960s. McMurray received an outright grant of $296,893 and a 40 year loan $374,000 at 3% for a total aid of $670,893. Abilene Christian received a grant of $564,824 and a loan of $711,000 for a total assistance on their science building of $1,163,272. On a physical education building ACC received a grant of $443,736 and a loan of $559,000, making in three years a total assistance to ACC of $3,431,832. Meantime, Hardin-Simmons borrowed $600,000 from commercial sources at 6% to build a small science building. Elwin Skiles, president of HSU, said "As it is now Baptists are paying taxes to make other schools stronger while denying our own schools like resources with which to do a better job."[97]

In 1969 the CEC tried another tack, to allow the board of trustees of each school to decide whether or not to accept government loans. Woodson Armes, who had succeeded James Basden as Secretary of the CEC, doubted whether the Convention would let them get by with this "back door" approach and he was correct in that.

By the 1970s it was clear that the BGCT would not allow its colleges to accept government loans, and would not allow them to approach churches to be included in the budget. It was also clear that with other pressing ministry needs in Texas, the schools could not expect a larger percentage of the annual Convention budget. However, several decades of prosperity had produced a large number of wealthy individuals who in turn had created a number of charitable foundations. The Baptist colleges established their own development offices and approached such individuals and foundations with considerable success. Whether being beholden to wealthy individuals or restricted foundations cost the Baptist schools more in independence than the government loans would have could be debated and often was. The upshot of that decade of decision was that Texas Baptists had less confidence in their schools and the schools felt less anchored to the denomination.

After he had retired and the issue was long since settled, Patterson came out in favor of accepting government loans. But during the decade of decision when Texas Baptists debated the most crucial issue of the times, their top leader gave no leadership on this important question. He said of the church-state debate, "I don't think I ever made any public statement. . . . I felt that in view of a divided constituency it would not be wise for me to positionize myself with either side."[98]

THE CHURCH LOAN ASSOCIATION

Since its formation in 1951, the Church Loan Association had helped churches, especially the smaller and newer ones, to erect or improve their buildings. Under the direction of businessmen, this agency usually operated both quietly and efficiently, but in the 1960s a scandal erupted which threatened its very existence. A. B. White, head of the CLA, bought up large tracts of California real estate when the market was high, hoping to sell the land to developers for huge profits, which would be used to build more churches. While the motive was laudable, the investments turned out to be bad. When real estate prices in California crashed, the Loan Association was left holding the bag. Some California Baptists raised questions about Texas investing in "worthless real estate," and rumors flew about missing funds, fraud and possible embezzlement. Some called for the agency to be abolished.

In 1967 the Executive Board took over operation of the agency from its board of directors and appointed a committee headed by Fort Worth businessman J. T. Luther to investigate the rumors. After thorough investigation, the Luther committee found mismanagement, bad judgment, loose record keeping and a string of bad investments, but no fraud or dishonesty. As it turned out, rumors of "missing money" were just that, baseless rumors. In what he called a "post-mortem," Luther said the Loan Board had "made some investments in real estate which we consider not good judgment, but to be unimpeachable as far as honesty and integrity is concerned."[99] The Church Loan work was reorganized, placed under a new board of directors and headed up by Don S. Singletary, a respected Fort Worth banker. White was relieved of his duties but kept on the payroll for over a year until he reached age sixty-five.

One major criticism of the old board was not just their bad investments, but their departure from (or at least skirting) their charter purpose. The new board agreed to stick to their purpose, providing money to churches for building, and to avoid speculative investments. However, in time, what looked like huge financial losses on the California real estate actually turned a profit. Baptist first sold the land at a loss, collected a generous down payment, but had to foreclose when the buyer forfeited. They sold again, repeating the process, and after selling and reselling eventually came out ahead.

COMMITTEE OF 100

One of the most important of a long string of study committees of the 1960s was called the Committee of 100. Appointed at the Convention in 1966 by the president J. Carroll Chadwick and vice-presidents Bruce McIver and Gordon Clinard, the committee consisted of 50 pastors and 50 laymen. The chairman was E. H. Westmoreland of Houston. Their assignment was twofold: first, to review and evaluate "all of the work of the Baptist General Convention of Texas, its boards, agencies, commissions, committees and institutions," and, second, to "explore ways and means of enlisting the total resources of Texas Baptists in the implementation of the Great Commission through our churches and convention."[100] One purpose of their work was to find ways for more participation by laymen for, said Chadwick, "We don't want to be a preacher-dominated convention."

At least to some extent, this committee grew out of frustration. In the mid-1960s baptisms were down, Sunday School enrollment and attendance were in decline, Training Union had dropped and the Brotherhood had gone into steep decline. The bitter church-state controversy had to some extent divided laymen (who generally favored government loans) and preachers (who generally opposed). There was a vague feeling that the restructuring resulting from the Booz, Allen, Hamilton study was not working well, and the Church Loan debacle had tongues wagging. This was, significantly, a committee of the Convention and not the Executive Board and they were asked to do their study without employing any professional consultants and at minimum expense, perhaps in reaction to the huge fees paid to outside consultants in recent years. The role of lay persons on the committee was mandated. Robert M. Foley, leading layman from Wichita Falls and chairman of one of the sub-committees, said

> I suppose the single underlying cause for the committee [of 100] to be formed had to do with an action taken by the then Executive Secretary, Dr. Patterson, who had the treasurer, Dr. Springer, transfer a huge sum of money from the general budget funds as a 'temporary loan' for a highly speculative real estate purchase in Southern California. This was promoted by a high flying preacher in Colorado who convinced Dr. Patterson that this property could be resold at a profit . . . . As it turned

out this 'temporary loan' wasn't so temporary and Patterson and the Executive Committee *[sic]* were out on a limb.[101]

Foley amply documents, and perhaps did his bit to contribute to, the growing tensions between preachers and laymen. This tension was all the talk at Lubbock in 1967. Editor John J. Hurt wrote that "The pastor-layman issue in the Texas Baptist Convention's 1967 session had some sounds of the Arab-Israeli debate in the United Nations," and he called for an end to Baptist "jabber" which served only to escalate the conflict.[102]

Miffed perhaps at being left off the committee, Carr P. Collins of Dallas and Luman W. Holman of Jacksonville signed a letter calling a mass meeting of Texas laymen for April 5, 1967, in Dallas.[103] Their purpose was to give greater weight to the layman's viewpoint in denominational life. Preachers were not excluded, though it was made clear that the meeting was primarily for laymen. The year before Collins had proposed a Texas Baptist Layman's Association, but had been talked out of it. This was not unlike what the Committee of 100 eventually proposed. About 125 men attended this meeting, and apparently they circulated many of the unfavorable rumors concerning the problems of the Church Loan Association.

The Committee of 100 made its first report in Lubbock in 1967 and everyone seemed shocked at how controversial it proved. They reversed many of the recommendations which had come out of the BAH study a few years earlier, and recommended that: Baptist colleges and hospitals be allowed to accept government loans; the Church Services Division of the SMC be dismantled, with Sunday School, Training Union, and Church Music elevated to division status as they had been before 1959; and that the Brotherhood be removed from the SMC entirely and reorganized as Texas Baptist Men, auxiliary to the BGCT much as the WMU was. They also recommended that the Christian Life Commission be expanded and be related to the Executive Board directly rather than through the SMC. They recommended more lay participation in Convention work, including a provision that at least one of the top three elected officers of the Convention (president or one of two vice-presidents) be a lay person. Concerning the colleges, they called for a new study of the question about including the colleges in local church budgets.[104] They also recommended that the SMC "inform Negro Baptist churches how we receive churches into the fellowship and encourage those desiring to do so to participate with the Baptist General Convention of Texas in our work." The committee was ready to recommend total reorganization of the Church Loan Association only to find that the Executive Board had beat them to it.

Practically all of these recommendations were rejected, some of them in a late session after many messengers had already left. The proposed reorganization of the SMC was turned down; it turned out that the Church Services Division, which was to be dismantled, had not even been consulted about the proposed changes. Of course, the recommendation to accept government loans was voted down, but the proposal to reorganize the Brotherhood passed by a slim margin.

WOMAN'S MISSIONARY UNION

One could not name an important dimension of Texas Baptist ministry in which the WMU was not significantly involved. The women helped plan the projects, raise the money, and keep the attention of Texas Baptists fixed upon their ministry. The women, as usual, had less controversy, less distraction, and less wasted motion. They had more focus, more concentration upon their ministry tasks and more sense of purpose by far than did some of the men. It was said the first task of the Baptist Men after the demise of the old Brotherhood was to rebuild their damaged image; the WMU had no such problem, for their image was never better.

Officers of the WMU during the 1960s and early 1970s included presidents Mrs. Clem Hardy (1955-1961), Mrs. Bert Black 1961-1963, Mrs. C. J. Humphrey, 1964-1968, and Mrs. H. C. Hunt, 1968-1972. Mrs. Eula Mae Henderson served from 1947 to 1980 as Executive Secretary-Treasurer (the exact title varied). Mrs. Verney Townes of Muleshoe and Mrs. C. J. Humphrey of Amarillo participated in the Japan New Life Crusade of 1963.[105] Two of the most popular WMU speakers during these years, in addition to Mrs. Henderson, were Mrs. Woodson (Sybil) Armes and Mrs. Charles (Marge) Caldwell.

The women contributed greatly, both in money and personal ministry, to work among the Latins in Texas. They helped form women's groups in the Mexican churches and in 1964 helped raise the money to sponsor the Latin American Evangelistic Crusade. Through the Mary Hill Davis offering, they helped launch the famed River Ministry project and in 1969 helped promote interest in the area through a chartered bus tour with 34 persons, including Elmin Howell and Charles McLaughlin. They helped observe the fiftieth anniversary of WMU work among the Mexican churches of Texas in 1967, and sponsored a number of scholarships for Latin American students in Texas. They also formed a partnership with the women in the Minnesota-Wisconsin churches to strengthen mission work in that area.

TEXAS BAPTIST MEN

One of the most significant results of the Committee of 100 was the reorganization of the Brotherhood, which had been a minor department buried deep within the Church Services Division of the SMC. The Convention in 1967 voted for "the creation of a new organization for men to be known as Texas Baptist Men, an auxiliary of the Baptist General Convention of Texas. This new organization would replace the Brotherhood department that now operates as a part of the State Missions Commission."[106] This change was to become effective in 1969. Some compared this new relationship to the WMU and spoke, some disparagingly, of the "Men's auxiliary" or the "MMU." There was an unsuccessful effort to exclude the new men's group from receiving any CP funds.

Some felt that the change from Brotherhood to Baptist Men was an expression of the preacher-layman tension so prevalent at the time. Editor John J. Hurt denied this, insisting that the move "has the one and only purpose of enlisting men. Brotherhood needed more than a transfusion. This is a new body with somewhat the same alignment as the Woman's Missionary Union. We have something if it succeeds. We are none the worse if it fails."[107] After the favorable convention vote, Roy Akers, Brotherhood president, called a meeting for January 15, 1968, at FBC Dallas to adopt a constitution for the new body.

The change went deeper than just a name change. There were also changes in leadership and in basic outlook for ministry. Robert E. Dixon became executive secretary in 1969 and under his dynamic leadership the men's group took a far more active role in hands-on ministry projects. After a period of what John Hurt called "a bit of wandering in the desert of confusion," the men found their role and a dynamic role it turned out to be.[108] The new Baptist men's emphasis is best captured by a cartoon in the *Baptist Standard* in which a wife says to her husband who was putting on a suit and tie, "If you're heading for Baptist men's meeting, you'd better wear these work clothes instead."[109]

In an editorial on "New Day for Men," Hurt said, "There is a new day dawning for laymen who want a bit of action in their church and denomination. . . . The old Brotherhood structure is dead. Those who want to linger for an autopsy will probably find church suppers and speeches, even good speeches, no longer generate much activity. Skidding enrollment figures told their own story."[110] Instead of holding meetings to talk about ministry, the men would form work groups to do ministry. Thus began the call for volunteers for manual labor projects in building churches and missions. This was an important new direction for Texas Baptist men. They led the way in turning the men's organization toward actual involvement in missions, building, and eventually to disaster relief. As they had in so many areas, once again Texas Baptists blazed the trail that others followed.

MINISTERS COUNSELING SERVICE

Ministers were not exempt from the tensions of the 1960s. Church expectations for the pastor and his family were sometimes unrealistic, and the term "burn-out" came to be applied to pastors. Already by the 1960s the scandal of forced termination of pastors, which became an epidemic later, was in evidence. Clearly the pastors needed a pastor with whom they could talk candidly about hopes, fears, problems and solutions.

At the 1970 Convention Charles Miller of Wharton introduced a motion that the president appoint a committee "to study the feasibility of our having an office of Pastoral Care in our Baptist General Convention to help pastors and other full time staff members who find themselves in need of counseling."[111] This passed unanimously, provoked perhaps by the widely publicized nervous breakdown of the dynamic pastor of a prominent Texas Baptist church. The resulting committee, chaired by Darold H. Morgan, first took a survey to determine the extent of personal problems among pastors and their families. What they found could fill a volume.[112] At least 57% of respondents indicated that they or some family member needed, or had needed, psychological help. The survey showed that a third of Texas Baptist pastors had seriously considered leaving the ministry. Tensions of the parsonage affected the entire family, with marriages undermined and many children damaged by the intense pressures of life in the parsonage fishbowl. "Many of our ministers and their families today are in dire need of professional counsel and are unable to afford it . . . they are caught in the crossfires of a lonely calling." Another problem which surfaced was reluctance to admit to any problem "because they fear that the denominational structure will ostracize one who is frank enough" to admit to a problem. Repeatedly, some version of the following surfaced in this anonymous survey, "Someone in my family needs counseling, but if others find out, it will ruin me."

Growing out of this committee survey, the Convention in 1972 named James L. Cooper as Coordinator of Ministers Counseling, a new ministry of the Executive Board. Cooper had served for 16 years as pastor at the First Baptist Church of Oak Cliff in Dallas, and had specific training in clinical pastoral education, a masters degree in counseling from East Texas State University, and extensive experience in pastoral counseling. Cooper not only did counseling, he also set up a network of doctors, psychiatrists and other counselors throughout the state who could accept Baptist ministers or their family members. The BGCT provided a modest fund for this work. "The goal," said Cooper, "is to have a counselor to whom cases may be referred within easy driving distance of all points within our state."[113] Cooper also set up retreats, workshops and seminars throughout the state to deal with problems and try to catch problems before they became serious. Many of these were marriage enrichment retreats for, Cooper found, "strange as it may seem, marriage and family relationships constitute some of the greatest problems" of Texas Baptist pastors and their families. This service was not provided for all Baptists, but just for ministers and their families. The service was limited to counseling and did not include any effort to help with pastoral placement, which was another area of need.

In order to maintain privacy and anonymity, Cooper's office was located in the Bank Tower at Exchange Park in Dallas, far from the Baptist Building. Cooper assured Texas Baptists that "The files of this office are not available to anyone else."[114]

THE RIVER MINISTRY

One of the most dynamic new forms of ministry Texas Baptists developed in the 1960s had to do with ministry along the 800 miles of the Rio

Grande River which provides the boundary between Texas and Mexico. It was estimated that in the 1960s over two million people lived along both sides of this great river. To a large extent, the River Ministry grew out of the Latin New Life Crusade of 1964 which focused the attention of Texas Baptists on the population along the river border as never before. When Charles McLaughlin was named to head the SMC in 1964 he brought a new emphasis on ministry to Latin Americans in Texas. Two couples, Dr. and Mrs. Patterson and Dr. and Mrs. McLaughlin, made a two-week tour of the Rio Grande from El Paso-Juarez to Brownsville-Matamoros, visiting both sides of the river to listen and observe. Patterson said, "We felt very definitely there was the greatest neglect there of any place on earth— higher infant mortality rate than any other place in the world—villages along there, not one Christian, nobody working there, no health programs—you couldn't even find a box of aspirin."[115] Because this would be an international ministry, Patterson and McLaughlin conferred with the Foreign Mission Board, the Home Mission Board, and with SBC foreign missionaries in Mexico City. At first the foreign missionaries, Patterson said, "were scared to death of it," fearing it would threaten their tenuous toehold in Mexico.

When Patterson was pastor in Beaumont, he brought on staff a gifted layman named Elmin Howell and in 1967, Patterson encouraged McLaughlin to bring Howell on board to head up the River Ministry. At that time, Howell was Minister of Activities of FBC, Shreveport, Louisiana.

To a large extent, the River Ministry depended on volunteer workers. Already a number of churches sent youth teams to conduct VBS there, and for years the BSU had sent summer missionaries to that area. In 1969 more than 10,000 laymen and young people from 275 churches were involved in ministry along the River; some taught VBS, some erected or repaired buildings, some did public health service. At least 5,000 persons were seen professionally that summer by the many doctors, nurses, and dentists who volunteered their services. Some churches donated medical supplies as well as other needed materials. One of the most unusual projects of the River Ministry was the Christmas airdrop in 1970. Baptists received official permission to fly over isolated villages along the River and drop bundles of Christmas gifts to people who might otherwise have been forgotten.[116]

This work was not without its tensions. Most of the needy people on both sides of the River were only too glad for whatever help they received, but some radical political groups sought to restrict the Baptists' activity.

The River Ministry could never have succeeded without the powerful assistance of the WMU. It was the annual Mary Hill Davis Offering for home missions that financed the project and the WMU provided more than their share of volunteers, materials, and promotion that helped this work catch the imagination of Texas Baptists.

CONTROVERSY IN THE SOUTHERN BAPTIST CONVENTION

In the 1960s the SBC was caught up in a divisive controversy which intensified in 1961 when Ralph H. Elliott, young professor at the Midwestern Baptist Theological Seminary in Kansas City published his *Message of Genesis.*[117] Described as a theological commentary on the first book of the Bible and intended for academic study, some readers felt Elliott's book questioned the final authority of some Genesis passages. Much of the resulting uproar centered in Texas.

E. S. James, editor of the *Baptist Standard,* criticized the book in several articles and editorials, and gave space for other writers to do the same. He assumed that since the book bore the stamp of Broadman Press, the publishing arm of the Baptist Sunday School Board, it represented or at least would be taken to represent an official expression of Southern Baptist views.

One of those who spoke out sharply against the book was K. Owen White, pastor of FBC in Houston, who published an article entitled "Death in the Pot."[118] White quoted several selections from the offending book (out of context, some said) and concluded that "The book in question is 'poison.'" This article was picked up by several other Baptist papers and helped make the "Elliott Controversy" a major issue among Southern Baptists. So much did the Baptist papers keep the conflict before their readers that some referred to "the newspaper controversy." White was then serving as chairman of the Executive Board and when the article was published, he offered to resign. He said he had expressed his own views, but had not tried to involve his church or the BGCT. Board minutes say that "By silent consent board members assured Chairman White that they had no misgivings over his protest in print of the book 'The Message of Genesis.'"[119] If White did not want to involve the BGCT, others did. The El Paso Association passed a resolution asking the Executive Board to take a stand against Elliott's book, but the Board replied that the El Paso brethren should address their concerns directly to the Midwestern trustees.

White's "Death in the Pot" was the first major critique of the book and it propelled White into prominence in the SBC. He was elected president of the SBC in San Francisco in 1962, a meeting where Elliott's book was the major issue discussed, thus beginning the trend of electing SBC presidents on the basis of their conservative theological views. At first the Sunday School Board defended their right to publish views of different groups of Southern Baptists but later agreed not to publish a second edition. A committee of trustees at the Midwestern Seminary asked Elliott not to seek another publisher. He agreed that he would not do so if the entire board of trustees asked him not to, but he would not be bound by the request of only a few trustees on the committee. As a result, Elliott was fired from his professorship in late 1962. He was not fired for heresy, indeed was never charged with heresy, but was fired for insubordination. His termination escalated the controversy.

T. A. Patterson took a strong stand against Elliott's book. His article on the issue was picked up by others and circulated in booklet form throughout the convention, a fact which Patterson did not fully approve.[120] Patterson was somewhat involved in the Midwestern crisis. He said, "I recommended a man from Texas to serve on their board who would help them to work that thing out. Of course, (chuckling) this is behind-the-scenes activities."[121]

CLOSE OF THE PATTERSON ERA

T. A. Patterson, at age sixty-seven and still in vigorous health, retired as Executive Secretary at the end of 1973, caught in the mandatory retirement policy he had helped to devise. By his own admission, Patterson had not faced retirement with any great enthusiasm. He retired from the Executive Board on December 31, 1973 and began on January 1, 1974 as executive vice-president of Dub Jackson's World Evangelism Foundation in Dallas. This not only gave Patterson an ongoing ministry, but pointedly reaffirmed his growing commitment to new forms of missions and evangelism.

Executive Officers

of the

Baptist General Convention

of Texas

1886-1998

Adoniram Judson Holt
Mission Secretary 1886-1888

Wilder Richard Maxwell
Mission Secretary 1888

James Britton Cranfill
Mission Secretary 1889-1891, 1893

James Milton Carroll
Mission Secretary 1892, 1894

M. D. Early
Mission Secretary 1895-1896

James Bruton Gambrell
Corresponding Secretary 1897-1909

Franz Marshall McConnell
Corresponding Secretary 1910-1914

James Bruton Gambrell
Corresponding Secretary 1914-1918

Frank S. Groner
Corresponding Secretary 1918-1928

Thomas Luther Holcomb
Executive Secretary 1928-1929

William Richardson White
Executive Secretary 1929-1931

J. Howard Williams
Executive Secretary 1931-1936

Robert Clifford Campbell
Executive Secretary 1936-1941

William Walter Melton
Executive Secretary 1941-1945

J. Howard Williams
Executive Secretary 1946-1952

Forrest C. Feezor
Executive Secretary 1953-1960

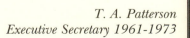

T. A. Patterson
Executive Secretary 1961-1973

James H. Landes
Executive Director 1974-1982

William M. Pinson
Executive Director 1983-Present

CHAPTER 13

FOCUS ON TEXAS, 1974–1982

Jesus COMMISSIONED HIS DISCIPLES to *"be witnesses unto me both in Jerusalem, and in all Judea, and in Samaria, and unto the uttermost part of the earth."* (Acts 1:8, KJV) Texas Baptists have not found it easy to maintain balance between the demands of local (Jerusalem), regional (Judea-Samaria), and world (uttermost part) ministries, any one of which could absorb their entire energy and resources. In Texas the burgeoning cities offered great evangelistic challenge and promise, while population growth along the Gulf Coast, in the Valley and along the Mexican border, and on the High Plains all called for more effort to win these broad regions for Christ. Meanwhile, Texas Baptists could not forget that Christ also called them to witness to the whole world. How could they balance the urgent needs of so many areas and allot their limited resources accordingly?

Many Baptists felt that in the 1960s the Texas convention had gradually put more emphasis upon "all the world" and less upon "Jerusalem and Judea." The Japan New Life Crusade of 1963 put the BGCT directly into foreign mission work and, some felt, intruded into the proper sphere of the Foreign Mission Board. Meanwhile, ministries in Texas did not seem to receive quite their share of emphasis. This was especially true of the Texas Baptist colleges, which received an ever diminishing slice of the budgetary pie. By the 1970s some influential Texas Baptist leaders wanted to see a shift of focus back to the urgent needs and challenges closer to home. The consensus was that James H. Landes, popular pastor and former college president, both could and would lead this effort to refocus the Baptist spotlight on Texas. Dewey Presley, a leading Dallas layman, told Landes, "We are going to elect you executive director, and I need to ask you right now if you can take the heat for some of the institutions and from the mission division and from the other divisions of the convention. Can you take the heat to raise the money, the level, the percentage of money going to the [Texas] institutions?" To these questions Landes replied, "Yeah, I can do that."[1]

Clearly those who nominated Landes hoped for a change of direction in the state convention, and he did not disappoint them. When asked to summarize differences between himself and his predecessor, Landes said Patterson put the focus on foreign missions while Landes turned the spotlight back to Texas missions.[2]

A NEW LEADER

James Henry Landes, Jr. was elected as Executive Secretary for Texas Baptists in September 1973, to take office the following January 1. The popular pastor of FBC, Richardson, was a natural choice. Twice nominated under the old open ballot system, Landes was the first Secretary elected under the new plan of working through a nominating committee. His engaging personality, proven ability to work with people, and his unswerving commitment to Texas Baptist ministries had not gone unnoticed. As far back as the 1950s, J. Howard Williams urged Landes to go into denominational work, and over the years the young pastor had served on every significant board, committee and commission in the denomination. Jimmy Allen chaired the committee that nominated the sixty-one-year-old Landes.

Jimmy Landes was born in Lewisville, Arkansas, on August 24, 1912, the youngest of six children. He came from a strong Baptist family. His mother taught the women's Bible class at their church, and was known as a woman of prayer. His father was a country lawyer and merchant who served his church as deacon, teacher of the men's Bible class, and music director. He became one of the most prominent Baptist lay preachers of South Arkansas. Jimmy had one brother and a brother-in-law who were preachers.

After high school, Jimmy got an appointment to the Naval Academy at Annapolis but his mother persuaded him not to accept. Largely at her urging, he enrolled at a local college, Magnolia A&M, where he attended one year. He then entered Rice University in Houston for a year, where he enjoyed the academic challenge but felt lonely and missed the warm spiritual atmosphere in which he had grown up. It was at Rice, young Landes said, that he learned to study. He returned to Arkansas to enroll in Ouachita University at Arkadelphia where he graduated two years later with a degree in chemistry. At Ouachita Landes was not a ministerial student, and he made it a point not to join the BSU or similar campus religious organizations. Upon graduation, he received a Mobil Oil Fellowship to study chemical engineering in a masters program at the University of Arkansas at Fayetteville. He never finished that degree, dropping out when his father became ill. Landes returned home and for a year he taught English and coached basketball at nearby Magnolia High School. While in Fayetteville, Landes became active in University Baptist Church where Irene Pearson was secretary to pastor Blake Smith and also served as church organist. Jimmy Landes, who had a good singing voice, joined the choir partly to become acquainted with her. Their friendship blossomed and they were married during his second year in Seminary.

There never was a time in his conscious memory, Landes said, when he did not know that he was called to preach. Yet he had difficulty accepting that call, trying instead to become a chemical engineer. His mother helped him work through, and pray through, his feelings until he could joyfully accept the call to be a minister. Most of his pastors had been graduates of Southern Seminary in Louisville, but Jimmy entered Southwestern in Fort Worth, partly at the influence of his brother-in-law who was pastor in Texas. Landes also knew Professor W. T. Conner, who was an Arkansas man and a friend of Landes' father. Young Landes turned down an invitation to teach at Ouachita to enroll in Southwestern.

At the Seminary, the friendly and outgoing Landes quickly made friends, including James G. Harris who had come to Southwestern the year before. James and Tunis Harris became close friends with James and Irene Landes, a bond that endured the rest of their lives. Landes later said, "James [Harris] was the closest friend I ever had outside of my own family. . . . He was an all-around good leader."[3] Harris also became an influential leader among Texas Baptists, serving on various boards and commissions and as chairman of the Executive Board. At the time of his death, Harris was president of the BGCT and chairman of the Foreign Mission Board. He was for twenty-five years pastor of the University Baptist Church in Fort Worth. Harris was one of those who influenced the nomination and election of Landes in 1973.

During his second week at Seminary, Landes preached at the Baptist church in Floyd, the tiny community where T. A. Patterson had been born, and they called him as pastor for two Sundays a month. He later accepted another "half-time" church at Dial, near Honey Grove where his sister and her pastor husband served. When Jimmy and Irene were married she joined him in the weekend trips to Floyd where the cultured young church organist had her first experience with a rural church whose music style ran to Stamps-Baxter. Jimmy described her first reaction as "stunned," but she later adjusted and won the hearts of the people. After their marriage, the Floyd church doubled their salary from $10 to $20 a week.

While more of an activist than a reflective scholar, Landes made good marks at the Seminary where he came under the influence of professors like Jeff Ray in preaching, W.W. Barnes in Baptist history, and especially W. T. Conner in theology. He served as assistant to Conner for a time and taught classes to good acceptance during the professor's absences. Landes recalled that upon his graduation from Southwestern, President L. R. Scarborough called him in and offered him a teaching post at the then handsome salary of $150 a month.[4] However, Landes was committed to the pastorate and accepted the pulpit of FBC, Eagle Lake, a small but well-to-do congregation that emphasized orderly worship and good preaching. Landes later described them as "Episcopal Baptists."[5] From there he went to Central Baptist Church in Bryan, 1941-45; FBC, Wichita Falls, 1945-63; president of Hardin-Simmons University in Abilene, 1963-66; pastor of FBC Birmingham, Alabama, 1966–68; and pastor of FBC, Richardson, 1968-73.

While still in his 20s, Landes was elected to serve on the Executive Board and there attracted the favorable attention of the primary leaders among Texas Baptists. He served for ten years as chairman of the Christian Education Commission and was twice elected, 1961 and 1962, as president of the state convention. He served on every significant board, committee, and commission of the denomination. He later recalled that, "Dr. Williams kept me driving back and forth to Dallas all the time he was executive secretary."[6] Though much involved, Landes professed no great love for denominational work. He recalled that "Years ago, Dr. Howard Williams talked to me about my life and wondered if I would not like to follow in this kind of train. And I very frankly said . . . Dr. Williams, denominational work is distasteful to me. I don't like the politics of it; I don't like the pressures of it."[7]

Landes was elected in September in time to work with T. A. Patterson who continued with full authority as secretary until December 31. During that interim, Patterson agreed to make no major staff changes without consulting Landes. The secretary-elect used most of that time to travel about the state, visiting the Baptist pastors, associational and area missionaries, and leaders in the colleges, hospitals and child-care homes. He wanted to feel the pulse of Texas Baptists, to come to know them better and allow them to know him. He moved into a temporary office in the Baptist Building on December 1 and began the process of meeting with as many of the approximately 165 employees as he could, but especially with Level II and Level III workers (the heads of departments and divisions). The secretary and his immediate staff, including treasurer and public relations director, were designated as Level I.

Landes brought Doris Ann Tinker to the Baptist Building as administrative assistant to the executive secretary. She had served for ten years as pastor's secretary at FBC, Richardson, 5½ of them with Landes. She grew up in Jonesboro, Arkansas, where she attended Arkansas State University. She later took additional training at the Pan American Business University in Miami, Florida. It was not an easy transition for either Landes or Tinker. Both had become accustomed and committed to local church ministry with close contact with people, and the Baptist Building with its constant meetings seemed so different. Landes had been in office some time before Lloyd Elder joined the staff as associate executive director. During that time Doris Tinker actually performed much of the work later assigned to that office. She knew better than anyone else the kinds of ministry assistance the executive director needed, so she helped define the office of associate executive director and helped write the job description. Observers credit her for helping create a pleasant environment in the Baptist Building, for detailed knowledge of the BGCT and its work, and for her can-do competency and overall efficiency. Doris and husband Bill have a son and two grandchildren. She continues in office as executive associate to Bill Pinson.

Landes made a habit of meeting each week with department heads, often at a working luncheon. Concerning his predecessor, Landes offered his opinion that "as an administrator, he operated in a pretty lonely fashion," leaving department heads "anxious for a personal relationship with the executive secretary."[8] Landes felt that one of his own contributions was to bring back a "family concept" to the Baptist Building, which he defined as "a spirit of everybody for everything within our Texas Baptist convention agencies and the institutions." He wanted the leaders of *each* agency to be committed to the work of *all* the agencies. With echoes of the spirit of J. Howard Williams, Landes urged Texas Baptists to "Get back together and everybody push everything together."[9]

The new secretary came to office with four major goals: 1. To unite the Convention and "bring peace between brethren;" 2. To raise Cooperative Program giving overall and increase the allocation to Texas ministries, especially the colleges; 3. To improve relations between the Texas convention and the SBC; and 4. To improve the image of Texas Baptists, which he felt had suffered in recent years.[10] Landes felt that he achieved at least three of these goals but regretted that over the years Texas Baptists showed more tendency to division than to unity.

Prior executive secretaries carefully avoided criticizing their predecessors or at least couched their criticisms in vague terms. Landes was much more candid, and at times caustic, in his comments on the tenure of T. A. Patterson. He blamed Patterson for adding to Texas Baptist disunity and for damaging relations with the two SBC mission boards. "By the very nature of his [Patterson's] emphases, we were a divided people," Landes said.[11] Landes traced much of the problem to the shift of emphasis which followed the Japan Crusade of 1963. Landes was among a group of powerful Texas Baptists who either did not favor the crusade, felt it diverted too much money away from Texas causes, or felt it intruded into the proper work of the FMB. As president of HSU at the time, Landes described himself as the only Baptist college president in Texas who still supported Patterson. He regarded Patterson as a "Landmarker"[12] who diminished the role of denominational agencies, especially the colleges, which he [Patterson] considered too liberal. "He [Patterson] feels that all missions should be tied a little closer to the church; and he was not a traditional denominationalist." Landes said, "His J. R. Gravesism was very strong. . . . He was very independent with reference to missionary action. And he was not particularly in love with the institutional life of Texas [Baptists], not very supportive, really, of the schools," and as a result "the institutional life had suffered at that particular time."[13] Patterson so concentrated on world evangelism, said Landes, that "the man who follows him goes around and he picks up the loose pieces for about four or five years. . . . He was a man with one mind and one purpose, . . . He left the schools to run themselves, he left the other institutions to run themselves."[14]

One of the first things Landes did as secretary was bring in a Dallas management consultant to work with him for the first six months, to help him get a handle on his task, evaluate personnel, and suggest any needed reorganization. Most of the departments pleaded overwork and asked for more personnel. The chairman of the Executive Board when Landes was elected was Lloyd Elder, popular young pastor of the Gambrell Street Church in Fort Worth. Landes liked Elder's style of leadership and offered him the post of assistant to the executive secretary. Elder served in this capacity until 1978 when he became executive vice-president at Southwestern Seminary. He was succeeded at the Baptist Building by Edward Schmeltekopf who continues in that role at the present writing.

INSTITUTION STUDY COMMITTEE

Important changes in convention operation came out of the work of the Institution Study Committee. The twenty-five member committee was appointed in 1972 and made its final report in 1974. After chairman E. H. Westmoreland became ill, William H. Shamburger took over as chair. The committee resulted from questions about the severance of Memorial Baptist Hospital of Houston from BGCT sponsorship. This combined with severance of another hospital and closure of the University of Corpus Christi raised questions about the Baptist institutions and their relation to the BGCT. Roy E. Ladd, pastor at Baptist Temple in Houston, wrote a letter to the Executive Board which was approved by his church in conference protesting not only the dropping of the hospital but also the manner in which it was done, rather suddenly and with little advance notice.[15] "A part of the grief stems from the almost complete lack of opportunity to be heard regarding the proposed release," wrote Ladd. "This procedure has caused some to question seriously the efficiency of our denominational operation, the dependability of the administration of our institutions, and the effectiveness of our Cooperative Program endeavor." Ladd called for a moratorium on the release of any more Texas Baptist institutions while a special committee studied the matter. Discussion in the Executive Board revealed that at least some Baptists believed poor management had contributed to the financial distress of Texas Baptist institutions. Some Baptists decried the "giving away" of a multimillion dollar institution, not realizing that while Baptists sponsored the hospital, they did not actually own the land, buildings or equipment.

Harold V. Freeman, pastor at Highland Church in Dallas, moved "That a special committee be appointed to study and make recommendations concerning the role and place of our institutions in the life of the Baptist General Convention of Texas. Such a study schoul [sic] include a philosophy of institutional ministry, a strategy for attainment of the objectives, an administrative structure which will assist the Convention toward the implementation of that strategy, (a restudy of the debt limitation structure,) and effective methods for the support of the Convention's institutional ministry as well as the development of a deliberate procedure for consideration of requests for release and an equitable procedure for the achievement of the release of an institution should the Convention so decide."[16] Freeman persisted in his motion for a total study despite efforts by L. L. Morriss and others to limit the committee. Members were divided into five subcommittees: Philosophy and Objectives (Harold Freeman, chair); Debt Limitation Structure (Alvin Burns); Procedures for Release (John Rasco); Strategy and Structure (Travis Berry); and Methods of Support (Dewey Presley).[17]

The Freeman subcommittee on philosophy asked essentially why Texas Baptists sponsored institutions, how the institutions fit into the larger picture of Convention objectives, and what kind of institutions help the Convention achieve its larger purposes. They affirmed many of the objectives which grew out of the earlier Booz, Allen, Hamilton report and concluded that Texas Baptist schools and human welfare institutions were appropriate channels through which Texas Baptists could pursue their mission. They insisted that every institution be "distinctly Christian in purpose and accomplishment," maintain their Baptist identity, and "maintain mutually loyal and cooperative working relations with the Baptist General Convention of Texas."[18] The Travis Berry subcommittee on structure recommended that names of the Christian Education Commission and the Human Welfare Commission be changed to Coordinating Boards, with slightly different functions. Previously the Commissions had little power to do more than referee hassles among the institutions, but this report asked that more teeth be put into the boards. The coordinating boards were to report to the Executive Board rather than directly to the Convention.

It was also decided that the child care and retirement homes would not only meet but exceed government standards.[19] Previously the commissions had elected their professional staff and reported it to the Executive Board. Under the new plan, they elected upon recommendation of the Executive Secretary, with elections ratified by the Executive Board. The commissions had been operating in relative independence, but this brought them under the authority of the Board and, not incidentally, the executive secretary. The Debt Limitation group made a fundamental change. Previously, Texas Baptist institutions were forbidden to contract any debts beyond 25% of their total assets, which severely hampered their expansion. The committee voted to remove that limitation gradually over a period of years.

The subcommittee on Procedures for Release specified that a Texas Baptist institution might be severed from the Convention for any one of three reasons: if the institution no longer fulfills the objectives of the BGCT; the institution requests release so it can seek wider support beyond the Convention; or the institution is not being adequately supported from Convention sources and must go its own way to seek support or cease to exist.[20] They recommended the following procedure:

If an institution desires release, it would bring such a request to the appropriate Coordinating Board. If the Coordinating Board believed the point well taken, they would then present the request to the Executive Board. If the Executive Board decides that the matter should be investigated, then the committee would be formed and elected by the Convention with instructions to report at the next annual session. If the committee is to recommend release, this report must be made to the Executive Board at least 90 days before the Convention. . . . The purpose of the preceding plan of release is to prevent undue haste and to give adequate time for sober reflection. Institutions are not grown in a year or even a decade.[21]

As a matter of fact, very few institutions have been released under these guidelines.

The Presley subcommittee on Methods of Support made a detailed study of the Texas economy, how much money the churches received, how much they sent to the BGCT in Dallas, and how the BGCT used the money. What they discovered raised some serious questions. "The trend for total receipts, Cooperative Program receipts, and designated receipts," they said, "is steadily moving in the wrong direction. It is pretty obvious that the Convention program has 'lost ground' when you look at the gains made in the total receipts by all the churches."[22] With a series of detailed charts, the committee showed that in the period of 1963 to 1972, the total receipts of the churches increased by 75%, while the portion they sent on to the Convention increased only 44%. In other words, the churches were keeping more of their money at home. Looked at another way, in 1963 the churches sent to the Convention an average of $8.74 per member, and in 1972 that had increased to $10.96 per member, a 25% increase while the income of churches had increased by 75%. This amounted to an increase of about five cents per member per year for the Christian education work, and only about two cents a year per member increase for the hospitals and child care homes. "When you break it down on these terms," said the committee, "it's pretty disappointing."[23]

Clearly the churches were keeping more of their money at home; other studies showed that costs of buildings and staff increased rapidly, leaving the churches with less money to contribute to denominational causes either in Texas or beyond. The colleges and child care homes were hit especially hard. While they received more total dollars, they received a steadily diminishing percentage of Convention resources. The committee asked Texas Baptists to decide "whether or not the downward trend of support so clearly evident in these charts was to continue." The answer of the executive board was no. With the help of Landes, who had been a college president, an effort was made to increase funding for Christian education gradually until it comprised 30% of total Convention receipts. By 1976, it had reached 27.8%.[24] The effort to fund the colleges better grew to some extent also out of financial crises at Howard Payne and Dallas Baptist colleges. Landes said, "We decided to try to get back to the place where we were a number of years ago, percentage-wise, for our educational institutions who have to have more help than a hospital, for example; the hospital can charge the legitimate amounts that it costs, whereas a school can't begin to charge enough. A Baptist school can't anyway—to pay the freight."[25] Whether fairly or not, Landes largely blamed T. A. Patterson for this decade of diminished support for Texas Baptist schools.

The Institution Study Committee also redefined the role of the top leader, whose title was changed from "executive secretary" to "executive director." James G. Harris was one of the influential voices which called for this title change. This was more than semantics; as the name implied, the "director" had a great deal more actual authority. Landes also led in changing the titles of the heads of all commissions and coordinating boards to director.

MANIFOLD MINISTRIES

Space is too sparse here to describe all the manifold ministries conducted in the 1970s by the BGCT and its various agencies. Suffice to say that *whatever a church attempted to do, a Convention agency was ready to help them do it.* Whether the church attempted to win a convert, teach the Bible, train people in church membership, promote missions, educate a volunteer for ministry, call a pastor, erect or improve a building, improve their choir and total music and worship program, start a local mission, minister to ethnic groups, care for needy children, provide home and care for elderly people, provide retirement income for ministers, provide ongoing news and information about Texas Baptists, heal the sick, counsel ministers with problems, offer emergency help in time of crises like floods and storms, send children and adults to summer camp, offer moral guidance for daily life, plan and conduct a revival meeting, promote and raise a church budget, guide persons to prepare a will that reflects their Christian values—for all of these and more, the BGCT had some department to help the churches to accomplish their objectives.

MINISTRY TO MINISTERS

The Baptist General Convention of Texas felt a growing responsibility for the total welfare of the more than four thousand pastors in Texas, plus a number of evangelists, Convention employees and other church staff members. Just as the Convention sought to help the churches accomplish their objectives, they also sought to help the ministers with their personal and family needs.

Ministers Counseling Service. The ministry of counseling for pastors and their families, begun in 1967, not only continued but grew in scope and personnel with James L. Cooper in charge. The need was acute. Many of the personal and family crises grew out of the pervasive insecurity of the

Baptist parsonage. Perhaps Jimmy Landes expressed it best: he said a Baptist pastor never knew on Wednesday if he would still be pastor on Sunday.[26] The number of pastors fired from their churches was on the increase, and many who were thus forcibly terminated had difficulty finding another pulpit or, indeed, any employment. This was especially tough for younger pastors, Landes said, for "Stress for numbers and stress for commercial world success" put extra burdens upon the pastor to "produce."

Cooper reported that the "Crisis Intervention Ministry" had established a statewide network of psychiatrists, psychologists, and clinical pastoral education specialists to whom people could be referred. The BGCT provided a modest financial subsidy to compensate such counselors. In his report to the Executive Board in 1974, Cooper said they had a total of 265 counselors available statewide, and they had dealt with 250 clients. These clients included 91 pastors, 55 pastors' wives, 14 pastors' children, 25 staff ministers, 15 staff ministers' wives, 1 staff minister's child, 13 denominational workers, 16 denominational workers' wives and children, and 20 others (ministerial students, special service volunteers and former staff ministers).[27] Increasingly all the problems of society showed up in the pastors' families.

Cooper conducted each year a number of retreats for ministers and wives, and special retreats for wives only were also scheduled. The department also conducted a number of annual workshops for marriage enrichment, grief therapy, pastoral care and career assessment. Regional Family Life Conferences also proved popular.

Ministerial Placement. One of the most persistent needs of the Baptist pastor is for help in moving from one pastorate to another. This is also the source of much tension in pastors' families. The problem is more acute in light of Baptists' heritage of local church autonomy since the denomination cannot "place" or "assign" pastors. For years the associational and district missionaries had served as *de facto* placement offices, though they would not have used that term. Churches seeking a pastor and pastors seeking a church, or a move, often sought a "recommendation" from their associational missionary. However, the Convention felt that more could be done.

In 1971 the BGCT established a Church/Staff Information Service, an innovation that other state conventions soon followed. This was during the "pre-computer" age and the work was limited; only $5,000 was budgeted for this purpose in 1978.[28] In 1977 James Cooper recommended that the office, previously voted but not fully activated, be launched and that W. E. Norman be engaged as director along with his regular duties as Convention statistician. This office was intended "for the purpose of offering a liaison service between the Baptist General Convention of Texas churches and ministers, upon request, in the form of information and counsel." The service was by necessity merely voluntary. The Convention said, "It is thoroughly understood that the principles of the sovereignty of God, the leadership of the Holy Spirit, the autonomy of the local church, and the freedom and responsibility of both ministers and churches be respected."[29]

Forms were devised to be filled out by churches and pastors seeking information, but little came of the work for some years. By far the most influential person in pastoral placement among Texas Baptists remained the directors of missions.

Ministers' Retirement. By mid-century the concept of "retirement," almost unknown in early America, had firmly caught hold. Aged ministers were no longer referred to as "decrepit ministers" nor their widows as "relicts," but the state convention had an eye on their needs. As noted earlier, in 1918 the SBC formed its Relief and Annuity Board (now Annuity Board) to encourage pastors to participate in retirement planning by setting aside a percentage of their income to build up savings against the day of their retirement or disability. For some years it was not clear if pastors were eligible to participate in Social Security. When that question was settled, the government made a provision that ministers who had a conscientious objection to participating in a government retirement program like Social Security could opt out, which many Baptists pastors did. Research showed that about 1,500 Texas pastors did not participate in any of the Annuity Board plans and others participated only at minimal levels. The state conventions, including Texas, sought to address this need. In September, 1974, the Executive Board in Texas voted to establish a permanent Annuity Committee. The Baptist heritage of independence of the church (and the pastor) meant they could only encourage. The committee recognized up front that "pastors and other church staff and employees are employed by the church and that each church is an autonomous body."[30] In light of this basic principle, the committee recommended that the Convention "Encourage the churches and staff members in a program of increased participation in the retirement and insurance programs administered by the Annuity Board." However, the committee had agreed that the BGCT should encourage "all churches to enter their pastor and staff members as repidly as possible." They also agreed that the BGCT should fulfil "its role of responsible assistance to the churches because of the voluntary ties of denominational life."[31]

The Texas plan called for the pastors to put up a percentage of their salary, that amount to be matched by the church (hopefully, 10%), and augmented by the Convention. The BGCT budget for 1975 provided $620,000 to supplement the contributions of ministers and churches.[32] Of course that amount increased over the years. The plan was also extended to ministers other than pastors. The committee recommended that churches and pastors participate in the health insurance programs offered by the Annuity Board, and urged the churches to pay 50% of premiums.

THE RIVER MINISTRY

The "River Ministry" on both sides of the Rio Grande began in 1967 when T. A. Patterson brought Elmin K. Howell to direct the work. Over the years the River Ministry expanded and took on a life of its own. Jimmy Landes is probably correct that the River Ministry may be the most significant and enduring legacy of the ministry of T. A. Patterson.

Baptists study the Bible message on missions, preach about missions, and give to missions. But the River Ministry allowed Baptists, at least for a time, to BE missionaries. Though quite accessible to most Texas churches, the Rio Grande area provided an authentic atmosphere of genuinely foreign missions. In an age when church people, Baptists included, were showing a hunger not only for *programs* about ministry but for *actual hands-on experience* in ministry, the River work provided a ready outlet for Christian zeal. A number of volunteer workers ended up as fulltime ministers. It is amazing how many people were involved, and how extensive the work became, not only in evangelism but also in medical and dental care, instruction and demonstration of agricultural methods and irrigation, drilling water wells and piping water to homes, instruction in crafts and light industry for economic development. The cars and church buses of early years were augmented by the semi-trucks and cargo planes better to transport materials. Howell said, "We're trying to carry the gospel on the —on the wings of medical services, through agriculaural services, through a leadership training [program], through handcraft training, and through an economic awareness development."[33]

Justice Anderson, professor of missisons at Southwestern Baptist Seminary and for many years a missionary in Argentina, spent a few weeks on the River in 1978 and pronounced it one of the greatest missionary laboratories available for students to learn first-hand about missions. He worked out a program at the Seminary whereby students could get six hours of academic credit for ten weeks' work on the River Ministry. Some colleges worked out similar arrangements for credit.

From the early days an organization called *Amigos Internationales*, led by John LaNoue, sponsored medical missions on the River. They first used a converted school bus but when the rough roads (and in places, no roads) shook that to pieces, they replaced it with an eighteen-wheeler, complete with medical and dental rooms. Within a few years they had six mobile clinics in service at various places along the Rio Grande.

However, mobile clinics proved less than satisfactory due to bad roads and the uncertainty of where the clinic might show up next. John Bagwell, a Dallas physician, led the transition from mobile to permanent clinic sites but continued to use both for some years. When Joann Goatcher, a physician from Van Horn, became medical services director for the River Ministry in 1977 she retired the beat up medical buses. She had worked for years as a volunteer with the mobile clinics and knew their drawbacks. She knew the roads soon destroyed the clinic buses, and they often lacked mechanics to keep them running. It was frustrating, she pointed out, to persuade busy Texas doctors and dentists to donate a few days of their time only to find when they arrived they could do nothing because the clinic had a dead battery. By 1980 Baptists sponsored 21 permanent clinics on the Mexican side of the River. These were not large, mostly 24' by 20' buildings, with four small rooms for reception, a dental chair, medical examination room, and a conference room. Some clinics had electricity, while others worked off generators. With volunteer labor, often from Texas Baptist Men, it took only about three days to put up the clinic building.

The clinics of course could not operate fulltime. The goal was to have volunteer doctors and dentists at each clinic for three to five days a month. The buildings did not remain vacant, however, for a fulltime nurse employed by the BGCT made rounds treating minor wounds, mid-wifing and dispensing such medications as the rules allowed. Texas Baptists appealed, with considerable success, for medical schools in Mexico to send their student doctors to the clinics on occasion to observe and assist. Many of these apprentice doctors spoke well of the clinics and some even said that the clinics served to stimulate better overall medical care in Mexico.

Most of the clinics were on the Mexican side of the Rio Grande, not that the population along the Texas side had no medical needs. Texas Baptists faced some opposition to their medical work inside the Texas boundary because, it turned out, such medical facilities as already operated there depended upon federal subsidies for their existence. Some regarded the Texas Baptist medical work as competition which might endanger their own programs.

One reason the FMB missionaries in Mexico were originally leary of Texas Baptists' River Ministry is that they feared that the best and brightest of the young pastors would be lured to Texas to serve Mexican Baptist churches stateside. Howell was sensitive to their fear of skimming off the cream of Mexican pastors and he got to the point that he would hardly recommend a Mexican pastor even to come to Texas to preach a revival.[34] Some directors of missions in South Texas became upset because Howell would not encourage Mexican pastors to migrate to Texas.

PERSONAL INVOLVEMENT IN MISSIONS

The Japan New Life Crusade and the Texas River Ministry gave Texas Baptists a taste of personal involvement in missions and they liked it. People who had preached missions and prayed for missions had now *practiced* missions and they could not go back to the old passive ways. The clamor for more on the field experiences kept pressure both on the BGCT and the FMB to come up with more such opportunities. In response three separate but interrelated programs emerged.

Mission to Brazil. For Texas Baptists the first great work of partnership evangelism in another country was the Mission to Brazil. It was much like the Rio Grande River Ministry, but a little further south. By the mid-1970s Executive Director James Landes was seeking an overseas mission to challenge the resources, as well as the restless spirit, of Texas Baptists as a part of the SBC Bold Mission Thrust emphasis. He talked with Joe Underwood, the FMB consultant on evangelism and a former missionary to

Brazil, who suggested that this land of the Southern Cross might be an eligible place for a special mission project.

Meanwhile, events were also moving in Brazil. As Brazilian Baptists moved toward their centennial in 1982, they came up with the idea of a great nationwide evangelistic crusade to plant new churches, increase their membership to one million, and strengthen their witness. Rubens Lopes, a warm-hearted Brazilian pastor, had led a nationwide crusade in 1965 with good results, and had also led out in the Crusade of the Americas in 1969. It was his dream to celebrate the centennial with another such crusade. Landes approached the FMB about a Texas mission to Brazil and received a favorable response from Frank Means, the board's Area Director for Eastern South America which included Brazil. After a momentary hesitation, fueled mostly by American missionaries in Brazil, the Brazilian Baptist Convention and several of their state conventions joined in an invitation to Texas Baptists to participate with them in a Mission to Brazil to span the years 1978-1981. The Executive Board voted "That Texas Baptists accept the invitation of the Brazilian Baptists and of our Foreign Mission Board. . . . [and] That coordination of Texas Baptist involvement in the Brazilian Campaign remain the responsibility of the Foreign Mission Board."[35] Unlike his predecessor, Landes was careful not to appear to usurp the FMB.

Brazilian Baptists cooperated fully, including Nilson Fanini, president, and Joao Faclao, executive secretary of the Brazilian convention. Thurmon Bryant, missionary to Brazil who succeeded Means as Area Director, also gave full support to the project. It was Bryant who suggested the need for a coordinator for the project in Texas, and suggested Ronald Boswell for that job. Boswell served from 1978 to 1980, when he went with the FMB as a missionary to Brazil. He was succeeded as coordinator by William J. Damon who served from 1980 to 1982.

In his helpful history of the movement, Damon says there were at least four factors that led to the Brazil-Texas partnership mission. These were: 1. A growing interest on the part of Texas pastors and lay persons for direct and personal involvement in missions, 2. A bold evangelistic movement in Brazil which welcomed outside help and involvement, 3. Increasing pressure on the FMB to provide channels for lay persons to be involved in foreign missions, and 4. The increasing involvement of parachurch organizations in Partnership Evangelism.[36] A major example of the latter would be W. H. "Dub" Jackson's World Evangelism Foundation.

James Landes reported the Brazilian invitation to the state convention meeting in Fort Worth in 1977. He said, "They want a few of us down there in 1978. They want a lot of us down there in '79. They want even more of us down there in 1980 and they want a great group to follow-up in 1981." The Brazilians had asked Landes to "promise us that you can furnish us 1500 trained workers, who will pay their own way down to Brazil and work there during the next four years." Nilson Fanini, well-known Brazilian evangelist who is often called the "Billy Graham of Brazil," is a graduate of Southwestern Seminary. He spoke at the Texas convention in

1978 and promoted the Brazilian campaign. He concluded his message with a quotation from William B. Bagby, pioneer Southern Baptist missionary to Brazil, who said, "There is a mine in Brazil richer than her gold mines, more precious than her diamonds. Who will come down to illuminate the darkness and gather the jewels for the Master?"[37]

Early on Bryant and Boswell established the principle that Texas teams would go to Brazil only in response to invitations to specific projects. At first there were more volunteers than projects, but when the Brazilian churches caught on to the possibilities the requests mushroomed. Projects might include an evangelistic campaign, a crusade to establish new churches, Bible schools for children, training for Christian workers, or construction of new buildings. The teams included both pastors and lay persons. The construction crews perfected a plan whereby they could erect a chapel seating 200 in two weeks at a total materials cost of $5,000.

By 1979 the idea surfaced of linking ten major cities of Brazil with specific areas of Texas in a "Sister Cities" program. Instead of teams from somewhere in Texas going somewhere in Brazil, the plan was to link specific Brazilian cities with specific cities or associations in Texas. This, it was hoped, would bring more order to the work. The Brazilian city of Curitiba was linked with El Paso and Grayson Association; Sao Paulo with Houston and the Gulf Coast Association; Rio de Janeiro with Dallas Association; Vitoria with Golden Triangle Association; Belo Horizonte with Tarrant Association; Brazilia with Midland-Odessa Area; Salvador with Waco, San Antonio and Austin; Recife with the Panhandle and South Plains; Fortaleza with Big Springs and San Angelo; and Belem with the Wichita-Archer City Association. Damon said this linkage saved the program from chaos and was "the key factor that enabled us to handle such a large number of projects and people."[38] By 1982, 3750 Texas Baptists served in Brazil, some more than once, and about 95,000 conversions were reported.[39] Some of these volunteers included special groups such as BSU, Acteens, the Singing Men of Texas, Texas Baptist Men and others.

Texas Baptists had little precedent for such massive volunteer efforts and therefore had little printed materials to guide the training of volunteers. Damon called Dub Jackson, head of World Evangelism Foundation, for advice. Jackson not only gave counsel, but shared a complete set of his group's guidebooks for selection, training, and conduct of partnership evangelism. "Many of these materials," said Damon, "and many of W.E.F.'s procedures served as the basis for the Mission to Brazil operation."[40] One of the most helpful aids to witnessing proved to be the personal testimony, which each volunteer had written and had translated into Portuguese.

From the first, Landes had a clear understanding with the FMB and Brazilian leaders that Texas Baptists would provide volunteer workers who would pay their own expenses to/from Brazil, while Brazilian Baptists would provide food and lodging for the volunteers and would underwrite the financial costs of the campaign. Brazilian Baptists agreed to these terms, affirming they were well able to bear such costs. However, the over-ail Mission to Brazil proved such a success that it expanded beyond the original parameters. The final budget came to $6.3 million and Brazilian Baptists felt they could come up with about $2.3 million of that amount. The FMB kicked in $500,000 and Texas Baptists were asked to raise $3.5 million. This put Landes in an awkward spot, given his earlier firm assurances that Texas would provide personnel but not funding. A conference with FMB and Texas leaders resulted in a plan (over some FMB objections) to promote a special "Lottie Moon Plus" offering in 1980, that is, to combine the usual Lottie Moon offering for foreign missions with a special over and above offering for Brazil. That offering raised an extra $768,486 for Brazil which, combined with other Texas funds already set aside, provided about $1.5 more. The final reports showed that Brazilian Baptists bore about 37% of the total costs.[41] This does not include the uncounted (and often unreported) contributions of money and materials from individuals and churches. Jerold McBride, pastor of FBC, San Angelo and volunteers from his church determined that they would spend at least as much for building materials in Brazil as they spent for airplane fares.[42]

One important aspect of the Mission to Brazil was the "Prayer Life" campaign, led by wives of BGCT leaders. Eula Mae Henderson, head of Texas WMU, and Sophia Nichols, WMU director for Brazil, helped coordinate the effort. Mrs. James Landes, Mrs. Charles McLaughlin, Mrs. Carlos McLeod in Texas and Mrs. Nilson Fanini and Mrs. Olinda Lopes in Brazil also led.

After the campaign concluded, Texas leaders conducted an extensive survey to assess the results. With questionaires for Texas Baptist campaign leaders, Texas Baptist volunteer workers, and Brazilian Baptists, the survey showed that most people considered the campaign a success. The three groups showed similar response on most questions, but the Texas leaders tended to assign a more optimistic rating to their work than did the Brazilians. On the overall campaign, almost 87% of Texas campaign leaders thought the results were "Very Good to Excellent," while 68% of Brazilians and 57% of volunteers gave that rating. The results were good enough to encourage similar efforts in other countries.[43]

Mission Service Corps (MSC). Two presidents who were close friends pushed for formation of the Mission Service Corps of the SBC in 1977: Jimmy Allen, pastor of FBC San Antonio and president of the SBC, and Jimmy Carter, Southern Baptist layman and president of the United States. President Carter had suggested even earlier that Southern Baptists form a service agency similar to the Mormon system of youth on mission in which Southern Baptist youth could give a year or two in voluntary missionary service. President Carter had been active in volunteer mission projects as a layman, and his mother had served as a Peace Corps volunteer in India at age 67.[44] Jimmy Allen had been active in the Texas River Ministry and knew first-hand the power of volunteerism. President Carter invited a group of Southern Baptist leaders to the White House on June 7, 1977, to discuss plans for a new volunteer effort, to involve not only youth but retired persons as well. Also attending that conference was lay-man Fred Gregg, teacher of the president's adult Bible class at FBC, Washington, where a discussion had sparked the idea for such a confer-ence. The result was the Mission Service Corps, a kind of Baptist version of the Peace Corps.

At its Kansas City meeting meeting in 1977, the SBC officially found-ed the Mission Service Corps and agreed "to enlist by 1982 five thousand persons, groups of churches, or churches who will agree to provide and fund 5,000 mission volunteers to serve for one or two years, either in the United States or overseas."[45] They asked the state conventions to lead out in enlisting and training volunteers, which the BGCT agreed to do. The Executive Board set up a department for this work and enlisted D. Eugene Strahan as coordinator. The Texas goal was 1,000 volunteers, and response was enthusiastic. Strahan said, "Mission Service Corps response in Texas continues to be the pace-setter for Southern Baptists."[46] By 1982, MSC had volunteers at work in 20 states and 13 foreign countries. Strahan and sev-eral regional regional consultants conducted six orientation/training con-ferences for volunteers in 1982. Other groups closely involved in the work included the Texas WMU, Texas Baptist Men, and BSU. Retired mission-aries in Texas helped form and staff a prayer chain and put out a "Prayer and Praise Newsletter." By 1982, 45% of the volunteers were men and 55% women, 24% were under thirty years of age and 31% were above 60.[47]

Partnership Missions (PM). On December 9, 1980, the Foreign Mission Board voted to engage in a program of partnership missions. Pressures from Dub Jackson's World Evangelism Foundation and the successful example of the Texas River Ministry and the Mission to Brazil helped move them in the direction of formalizing what had long been practiced, namely, short-term mission volunteers working in various countries. In light of this FMB action, the World Evangelism Foundation was disband-ed and turned over to the Partnership Mission program all of its projects for 1982 and beyond.

Texas Baptists formed a Partnership Missions Study Committee which recommended that the BGCT form a Partnership Missions Office, staffed by a coordinator and office secretary, with field consultants enlist-ed as needed.[48] This office was established effective January 1, 1983, and William H. Gray, Jr. was named coordinator. The WMU (who else?) was asked to fund the office through the Mary Hill Davis offering. The announced objective was "To promote and coordinate the response of Texas Baptists through the Foreign Mission Board of the Southern Baptist Convention to invitations received from Baptist entities of other countries to cooperate in partnership mission efforts." The plan specified that "Volunteer participants will arrange financing for their own expens-es relating to plane passages, hotel, meals, ground transfers, insurance, airport taxes and some incidental expenses." Already Texas Baptists had invitations from Mexico, Senegal, and Australia and others would follow. The Executive Board set out ten goals for the PM program, along with strategies for meeting each goal, all of which are too tedious to recount here.[49]

The 1982 report of the PM program says rightly that "Partnership Missions is an extension of the Mission to Brazil" applied to other countries.[50] The Texas River Ministry had developed on an impromptu basis, and the Mission to Brazil was an extension of the same ideas further south. The Partnership Missions program gathered up the pattern of these earlier efforts into one unified program of short-term volunteer mission service in many parts of the world, though it was agreed that the River Ministry would continue as a separate Texas program.

In perspective. These various interrelated programs to provide short-term missionary service for Southern Baptist volunteers and the favorable response in Texas are quite revealing. First, Baptist preaching about missions had clearly taken deep root; Texas Baptists really wanted to have a share in the missionary task. Second, the new affluence of Baptists made these world ventures possible. In earlier times Baptists could never have mounted such an expensive undertaking. If this was good for Baptists, it was also good for the airlines. With 3,750 volunteers paying their own way to Brazil, for example, with untold donations of materials, this was quite an expensive undertaking. Third, despite Landes' protestations to the contrary, there is no concealing the fact that the Mission to Brazil and other similar efforts expressed a growing disenchantment with the slow-moving methods of the Foreign Mission Board. The Executive Board voted that "Texas Baptists subscribe to the philosophy that career missionaries living and ministering in foreign cultures on a long term basis is the primary methodology for doing foreign mission work."[51] No doubt this expressed the view of most of the leadership, but not all agreed.

Unfortunately, some of the highly opinionated volunteers came home with criticisms. This was especially the case in Brazil, where a few short-termers after a few days in the country felt qualified to give advice. Fearing that some missionaries might be living too comfortably, their complaints may have helped lead the Foreign Mission Board to adopt stricter limits on the size of house its missionary families could occupy on the mission field. It was not unknown for various missions to spend sizeable sums to remodel missionary houses to make them smaller.

GOOD NEWS TEXAS

In 1977 the Texas Convention launched a major statewide evangelistic campaign, called "Good News Texas." Described as "the most extensive evangelical undertaking in the history of our state," the purpose of GNT was to share the gospel with every person in Texas during this year-long effort. Landes described this program as "the boldest of the bold programs for reaching out in the name of Christ."[52] Lloyd Elder, associate executive director and L. L. Morriss, chairman of the evangelism department, served as co-chairs of the Steering Committee, and George Worrell, associate in the evangelism department, was Prayer Chairman. Landes said, "My hope and prayer is that we will have Good News Texas with an evangelistic thrust, Good News Texas with a discipleship thrust, and Good News Texas with a maturation thrust. For that reason we have involved everybody. . . the totality of our denominational life."[53]

The Steering Committee began by engaging a public relations firm to survey the Texas population to find out, first, what people thought about Texas Baptists, and second, given this public image, what kind of campaign would work in presenting the gospel. The firm surveyed non-church people, church dropouts, and faithful members. They found, to the surprise of some, that Baptists had the best public image of any denomination in the state.[54] On the basis of this survey, Baptists employed the Bloom Advertising Agency of Dallas to devise a million dollar media blitz, including television and radio spots, newspaper ads, and testimony from well-known personalities telling how their lives were changed by Jesus Christ. It was estimated that the average Texan would see this publicity about forty times during the Spring of 1977.[55] The media portion of the campaign was called "Living Proof," and Mrs. John Gilliam of FBC, Valley Mills, composed and often sang a song of the same title. The state was divided into different zones, each with a zone chairman, and the amount and nature of the promotion and publicity was adjusted for the specific needs of each zone.

The month-long Living Proof media campaign, "designed to present the gospel to 4.7 million unsaved Texans through radio and television testimonies and newspaper ads," began February 21 in North Texas, March 7 in South Texas, and March 26 in West Texas.[56] Living Proof testimonies about the dramatic difference Christ can make in a life were given by such diverse persons as Rebecca Ann Reid, Miss Teenage America; Eldridge Cleaver, former Black Panther leader; Connie Smith, country and western recording artist; Billy "White Shoes" Johnson, professional football player; Dean Jones, professional actor; Rosargentina Pinel, Consul General, Republic of Honduras; Jeanie C. Riley, country and western recording artist, and many others.[57] Neal Jeffrey, former Baylor University football quarterback and in 1977 backup quarterback for the San Diego Chargers, also found time to give his testimony in Texas. Lloyd Elder, director of the GNT project, appeared on the popular Phil Donahue talk show where he was able to explain the purpose of the campaign to a national audience. Thereafter the number of letters of inquiry to the Dallas "Living Proof" office picked up sharply, but still fell far short of the 200,000 the Bloom Agency predicted.[58]

The Convention provided each pastor with a "Good News Texas Pastor's Kit," with guidance for the correlation of Sunday School, campus evangelism, use of local media, and the promotion of local revivals with the overall GNT campaign, and a lapel pin to initiate witnessing opportunities. The approach, as Landes emphasized, was not to ask people to help the church but to ask, "Can we help you? Is there any way that we can render service to you?" In El Paso, members of FBC pledged themselves to the ambitious task of telephoning every family in the city to offer ministry in Christ's name.

The Good News Texas campaign came at a time when Texas Baptist church membership and offerings were at an all-time high, but the number of new converts was lagging. Landes regarded the GNT as a "back to basics" program. He said that when he was a pastor, it seemed that every year the Convention came up with a new theme, a new slogan, a new approach. By the time he came to understand the new program, the Convention had already gone on to some new emphasis. As a result, he felt that the catchy new slogans rarely made it to the membership of the local church. In the GNT, Landes said, "We are moving back to stress Bible study, church training, Biblical music, Biblical missionary work at home and around the world. And we're forgetting all these extra titles; we are forgetting all these themes." He asked the SBC leaders, "For heaven's sake, don't be sending us a new theme every year. Bold Mission [Thrust] is fine if you stay with it for five years." Texas Baptists, he said, "are back at the fundamental point of teaching, preaching, discipling, and missionizing."[59] The Texas WMU provided $575,000 of the overall $1.4 million cost of the GNT campaign. This represented the most extensive use of television, radio and other media that Texas Baptists had ever attempted.

At the conclusion of the GNT campaign, Convention officials enaged a Dallas research and management firm, Louis, Bowles and Grove, Inc., to evaluate the campaign and its results. They found that about half of adult Texans had seen or heard one or more of the ads, that nine out of ten found the spots "believable," and the already good image of Texas Baptists was further improved. Only half of those surveyed remembered that GNT was sponsored by Texas Baptists, and only half of Baptist respondents who had seen the ads knew they were sponsored by their own denomination.[60] However, the evangelistic results were disappointing. The number of new converts still lagged, with only 52,599 baptisms reported for 1977.[61]

CHURCH-STATE ISSUES IN THE 1970S

One might think that Texas Baptists could debate and decide their stance on church-state issues and move on to other things. Not so. The landscape kept shifting and Baptist viewpoints showed a little shift of their own. As the programs and institutions of both church and government multiplied, they tended to overlap in new ways that often produced friction. When government and church were both relatively small, with limited funds, and with little involvement in social ministries they seldom touched each other and conflict was rare. However, in the twentieth century both government and church became more deeply involved in education, health care, care for children and the elderly, welfare or relief efforts for the needy, regulation of hospitals, and even vaccinations for school children, and both government and church agencies had vastly more money to invest in these endeavors. This created a crowded field in which the civil and spiritual forces had vastly more contact, with every contact providing a potential conflict.

For Texas Baptists, the main church-state question of the 1960s was whether or not to accept government loans for their colleges and they answered decisively in the negative (although a few of the colleges found creative ways around this roadblock). However, in the 1970s the shoe was on the other foot, as Baptists tried to cope with excessive government intrusion into the rightful affairs of the church. The government, primarily at the federal level, presumed the power to regulate enrollment and hiring practices of Baptist institutions, even those that had specifically declined the government handouts. Donald Anthony, for years chairman of the Christian Education Coordinating Board and later elected its coordinator, pointed out in 1976 that "The coin of church-state separation has another side to it. I refer specifically to the matter of recognition by the state, of the right of the church and its institutions, to exercise their historic role in our society without undue government interference." Anthony had adequate reasons for his concern, having observed over a period of years the increasing government interference in Baptist colleges. "Our convention has in the past voiced its concern that the church by its actions not intrude upon the proper role of the state," he said. "I believe that we now need to speak with a loud and clear voice against the tendency of the state to intrude unduly upon the proper role of the church and its institutions."[62]

Landes shared these concerns, speaking of "the lengthening arm of the federal government over our institutions . . . . [and] their continued interference with our affairs."[63] Baptists took the interpretation that since their institutions had not received federal funds, they were not subject to federal requirements about employment and turning in reports. The Equal Employment Opportunity Commission (EEOC), a federal agency, took the approach that if even one student in a Baptist college had received a federal grant or loan, the college was thereby obliged to abide by all the attending government regulations. These regulations involved equal opportunity for enrollment and employment of persons of all religions and races. Most of the Baptist schools already met or exceeded these standards but they resented the reams of reports they had to make. Landes complained that, "What we do have is a nuisance and an expense for every institution that we have because of extra bookkeeping related to the red tape of government interference."[64] On January 4, 1977, the Internal Revenue Service (IRS) issued new rules defining an "integrated auxiliary" of a church, thus in effect determining what constitutes Christian ministry. The Executive Board adopted resolutions of protest, to no avail. Large churches with numerous staff also found their hiring practices scrutinized by the government. Nor was Washington the only source of problems; the Texas legislature in Austin passed new laws in 1981 on how nonprofit organizations, including churches, could qualify for exemption from ad valorem taxes. Many Texas Baptist institutions had to make hasty charter changes to qualify for provisions they had long been granted routinely.

Much more than a nuisance was the effort of the EEOC as well as the IRS to define what did or did not constitute a "ministry" position. It was agreed that a Baptist church, college, or theological seminary could hire only Baptists for "ministry" positions like pastor, minister of music or teachers of religion. However, the hiring of persons for "non-ministry" positions, such as church custodial and secretarial staff and college professors of subjects other than religion, must come under government guidelines. The difference in pastor and custodian is fairly clear, but Baptists considered many other positions in a church, college, or Seminary to be a "ministry." This issue came to a crux in Texas when the EEOC demanded that Southwestern Baptist Seminary in Fort Worth submit records to determine if they were in compliance with federal hiring practices. Southwestern claimed that the school already followed fair hiring practices but refused to turn over their records. After many weary and expensive years of litigation, the Supreme Court ruled substantially (though not completely) in favor of the Seminary.

Faced with these new crises, Texas Baptists did what they always did; they appointed a committee. The CECB recommended that "In view of the changing complexity of the church-state issue, . . . that the President of the Convention and the Chairman of the Executive Board appoint a committee to study and update convention guidlelines concerning church-state relations."[65] President James G. Harris and Chairman Grayson Glass appointed a Special Church-State Study Committee, naming Lester B. Collins as chairman. Other members included Carlos McLeod, William M. Pinson, Jr., Browning Ware, Donald Anthony, Orba Lee Malone, and Irving Dawson. Anthony resigned to join the BGCT staff and Pinson resigned to become president of the Golden Gate Baptist Seminary in California, and they were replaced by David Slover and James Semple.

The Collins committee made its final report on September 12, 1978, reaffirming the historic Baptist principle of church-state separation but acknowledging that "The concept of separation has become increasingly complex. Government programs have become more diverse, and church ministries have grown in scope and in nature. . . . As society has become more complex the church and government have found themselves involved in the same efforts."[66] They also reaffirmed the findings of prior committees of 1961 and 1966, and bluntly declared opposition to the increasingly intrusive demands of government agencies. Noting that "controls have increased markedly in recent years," the committee claimed that the government has no need and no right to the information in the many records and reports they demanded. They also recommended that Baptist agencies be cautious about entering into any contracts to provide services to the government and to avoid any contract that would give the government more "control of its personnel policies." They strongly opposed the idea of Baptist parochial schools in Texas accepting any aid or supplement from government sources. However, the committee acknowledged that the government has a valid concern for the well-being of its citizens and therefore has a right "to protect the health, safety and welfare of its citizens," and urged all Baptist institutions to meet or exceed government standards in these areas.[67]

The Collins committee mentioned, but left unchanged, Baptist acceptance of such government perks as minister's housing allowance, postal rate subsidy for church papers and mailouts, tax exemption for churches and church property, tuition equalization grants for Baptist college students, sales tax exemptions for churches, and medicare and medicaid for ministers.[68]

CONVENTION STUDY COMMITTEE, 1979

Texas Baptists were always on the lookout for better ways of doing things, and in 1979 it appeared they might have found some. The imminent retirement of Executive Director Landes, the growth of BGCT programs, and the hard lessons of experience gave opportunity to make some changes. What began as a sub-committee of the Administrative Committee was enlarged and charged to make yet another study of the entire BGCT program, with Winfred Moore of FBC, Amarillo, as chairman. The committee organized itself to work through four sub-committees on the Role of the Executive Director as related to the staff, commissions, coordinating boards, executive board and BGCT (D. L. Lowrie, chair); Energy Usage (Paul Teague); Present and Future Space Needs of the Executive Board (Dewey Presley); Organization and Structure (W. M. Shamburger).

The Lowrie sub-committee clarified and strengthened the role of the executive director. They specified that he supervises and provides administrative guidance to the associate executive director, public relations director, ministers' counseling coordinator, the heads of commissions and coordinating boards, and the head of the Church Loan Corporation. The executive director personally names the associate executive director, treasurer, public relations director and the coordinator of ministers' counseling. He may nominate other department heads but their election must be confirmed by the executive board. Not a part of the original report but added later was the specific statement that the executive director does not formulate policy or exercise oversight of the *Baptist Standard*. The sub-committee recommended nineteen statements outlining the executive director's responsibilities, all of which were adopted.[69] The overall impact was to clarify, define and extend the authority of the office.

The committee's report came during the oil embargo and consequent energy crisis in the United States. Energy shortages, especially of gasoline, and radically increased energy costs had to be faced. National policy called for reduced driving to save gasoline, the national highway speed limit was lowered for the same reason, and President Carter made a speech to the nation wearing a sweater and asking Americans to turn down the thermostat. Texas Baptists reduced staff travel by making more use of the telephone and printed materials, reviewed the heating and cooling of the Baptist Building, and prepared materials suggesting ways for churches to conserve energy. Some churches consolidated services to prevent families from making so many trips to the church and others made contingency plans to do so if necessary.

The Shamburger sub-committee on structure left many things the same for the simple reason that they were working well and offered no need for change. They did, however, suggest that Executive Board members be divided into geographical groups and be more directly involved with the reports of the commissisons and other agencies. In order to prevent proliferation of professional staff, they also specified "that there be no associates added to serve with the directors of the coordinating boards."

More important changes were suggested for the State Missions Commission, where the number of divisions were reduced from five to four by combining the Special Services Division and Stewardship Division into a new Church Services Division, including responsibliity for stewardship, church music, and church training.[70] They also recommended that the office of Coordinator of the Area/Associational Liason Work be reestablished and given division status; that the Office of Language Coordination be elevated from section to division level; that the Mission to Brazil and Mission Service Corps be assigned to the oversight of the SMC and the associate executive director; that the River Ministry be assigned to the Missions Division; that Church Building be recognized as a separate section; and that the Minnesota/Wisconsin Baptist Fellowship be removed from the oversight of the Missions Division and instead relate to the SMC through the office of the Program Planning Director. Other than the people directly involved, the average Texas Baptist probably did not feel the effects of any of these changes, but they represent efforts to streamline the work.

The Presley sub-committee on space had a tough task. The Executive Board and its various agencies had seriously outgrown their office facilities; one professional staff member, for example, had his desk in a hallway. The sub-committee recommended that the Executive Board sell its Baptist Building at 703 N. Akard in downtown Dallas and move in with the Annuity Board at 511 N. Akard, after remodeling the available space in the Annuity Board building. The Annuity Board agreed to provide a favorable lease rate and, far more important as it turned out, included an option whereby the Executive Board could later purchase the building *at market value established at the time of the lease.* They further agreed to pay one-half the cost of remodeling, provide 101 parking spaces, and change the name to Baptist Building after the move was completed.[71]

This agreement seemed simple and straightforward, but Murphy's law that whatever *can* go wrong *will* came into play. The costs of remodeling far exceeded the original estimates and both the Annuity Board and Excecutive Board balked, placing Landes in an extremely awkward position and delaying the move for a time. Despite soaring real estate prices in Dallas, the sale of the old building proved both difficult and controversial. W. A. Criswell, pastor of FBC, Dallas, put pressure on Landes to get the building but the board had a firm offer for several times what Criswell offered.[72] Eventually the building was sold and the Executive Board staff occupied a portion of the Annuity Board building.

The Executive Board was not without resources to provide their space needs. When the old Baptist Building was paid off in 1960 the board continued to set aside the $62,500 annual payments into a special fund invested to provide for future space expansion. When the vote on how to provide for long-term space needs proved too close for comfort, or for action, the board called for a long-range planning committee, including Dallas Baptist business and real estate leaders, to study the matter. Under the chairmanship of Fred Roach, this committee recommended that the board exercise its option to purchase the Annuity Board building. One morning the board purchased the building at the value established at the time of the lease agreement, and that afternoon sold the same property in a highly inflated Dallas real estate market for about a $3 million profit. This and other prudent measures provided the money for the present Baptist Building on Washington Avenue without using any Cooperative Program funds.

TENSIONS IN TEXAS

Like Baptists everywhere, Texas Baptists have never been without their conflicts and controversies, but some seasons have been worse than others. Storm clouds appeared on the Baptist horizon during Patterson's time in the 1960s and the deluge began during the Landes era in the late 1970s. Some of the issues were as old as the first Baptist church in early Texas (missions), while others were more recent (the charismatic movement); some remained fairly constant (college funding), while others were constantly changing (the role of the association). In a 1989 interview long after he had left office, Landes was asked what were his greatest disappointments as executive director. He replied that, "In the convention as such, I've been disappointed in myself that I've not been able to bring together in the finest bonds of fellowship certain sections of the convention, I have tried; I judge that we will always have groups that do not relate to other groups because of their ideas and their ideals." He said, "I have tried awfully hard to eliminate politics from the convention. . . . I wanted to see all these guys get on the same team." However, he concluded that "I have come to see that certainly I can't get them all on the same team and I hope that God will."[73] After nine years in office, Landes reluctantly concluded that "We have two groups in our midst—or three."[74]

Missionary Priorities. Only a minority of Baptists in Texas actually opposed missions, but many disagreed on what missions involves and how to conduct the work. Some leaders (like T. A. Patterson) tended to spotlight evangelism and emphasize the direct role of churches and individu-

als; while others (like J. Howard Williams and James H. Landes) emphasized education and the helping ministries along with evangelism and
allowed more room for denominational mission boards and church institutions like colleges. It was a significant difference.

Rightly or not, Landes traced a portion of Texas Baptist tensions to
the Japan New Life Crusade of 1963. He regarded the movement as divisive, and said "He [Patterson] took money away from a lot of the programs
in order to have this Japan crusade."[75] While Landes quietly opposed, or
at least did not support, the Japan crusade, he later became an enthusiastic supporter of Partnership Missions which embodies many of the same
concepts.

Role of the Association. No organization beyond the local church has
been more vital to Baptists than the association. The earliest Texas association dates from 1840 (the Union Association, Houston) but its role has
taken many turns since then. The development of the District Missionary
plan in the 1930s and the change to Area Directors in the 1960s added to
the mix. Over the years the power of the Executive Board and especially the
executive director of that board continued to grow in function and extent.
The increasing funds at the control of the board further increased its clout.
During the 1970s there erupted a mini-power struggle between the Area
Missionaries (Directors of Missions, or DOMs) and the Executive Board.

Specifically, the DOMs wanted more of a voice in decisions affecting
Texas Baptists and especially their own work. Some of the more powerful
associations were sore because the state convention did not always do what
they wanted. For example, it was reported that some leaders of the Dallas
Association were miffed when the Convention did not follow immediately
their lead on the charismatic movement.[76]

There had been many suggestions for enlarging the Executive Board
to assure a broader representation, and the suggestion for more input
from the influential DOMs hardly seems radical. However, Landes
seemed to regard that request as a challenge to his leadership. He said,
"Those association missionaries wanted to become a part of the Executive
Board and tell the Executive Board of the Baptist General Convention of
Texas how to run *[sic]*." Landes would have none of that. He said, "The
stand was finally taken, and I had to take it. It was not a very pleasant
stand to take. I had to say, 'As long as we are providing anywhere from 30
to 70 percent of the money you are receiving, you are not to determine
what the Executive Board is to do.'"[77] One could hardly find a better example of the old adage that "money talks." The occasional disagreement,
however, could not obscure the longterm cooperative relationship between the executive board and the area missionaries. A bit later a committee chaired by Miller Robinson reaffirmed the association as the basic
unit of Baptist cooperation. Significantly, the report was approved by the
DOMs before it was presented to the executive board.[78]

The Charismatic Movement. Back in 1654 a Baptist association in Wales faced the controversial issue of "diversities of tongues" and other miracles and concluded that "All of those officers and gifts were extraordinary, and therefore are now ceased."[79] Two years later the Abingdon Association in England, one of the oldest such associations in history, said, "We doe not now expect, nor sue for [pray for], the gift of tongues" which, they said, were given only to the apostolic age and were not intended to continue in the church.[80] That has been essentially the Baptist position from the beginning. In the United States, many have "sued" for these dramatic gifts and claimed to receive them.. The modern "pentecostal movement," however, grew up mostly in the twentieth century, stemming largely from the famous Azusa Street revival in Los Angeles, which followed the great earthquake in San Francisco in 1906. Several pentecostal denominations were formed and flourished. By the 1950s and 1960s the pentecostal stream overflowed its banks and seeped into many of the "mainline" denominations, Baptists included. Several important events marked (and stimulated) the emergence of pentecostal beliefs and behavior in the mainline denominations, such as formation of the Full Gospel Businessmen's Fellowship International (1953); the "coming out of the closet" of a secretly charismatic pastor of an Episcopal church in Van Nuys, California, and subsequent nationwide publicity (1960); and the decision of pentecostal evangelist Oral Roberts to join the United Methodist Church without changing his beliefs or practices (1968). Southern Baptists were less affected than most of the mainline groups, but by the mid-1970s the charismatic movement had showed up among Texas Baptists.

The Beverly Hills Baptist Church in Dallas and the Shady Grove Baptist Church of Grand Prairie adopted some charismatic practices, including the practice of "glossalalia," or speaking in "unknown tongues." They not only followed such practices but were said to send out individuals and small groups to join other churches to seek to seduce them to similar practices. These controversial practices were widely discussed by Texas Baptists. A motion was presented at the 1975 Convention asking for a statewide "polling [of] the churches in fellowship with the Baptist General Convention of Texas as to their acceptance or rejection of neo-pentecostalism doctrinal practice as a valid tenet of Baptist life." The messengers were not inclined to open that can of worms and the motion was defeated.[81] After due investigation, the Dallas Baptist Association excluded the churches in 1976, *not for their worship practices, but for "unbrotherly conduct"* in introducing disharmony and conflict into sister churches in the association.

This dramatic development came to the notice of the state convention in 1976. A messenger from the North Temple Baptist Church of Dallas challenged the seating of messengers from the two churches. The Credentials Committee reviewed the challenge and Presnall Wood, chairman of that committee, made a motion that "the challenge be denied and the messengers be seated."[82] However, after long discussion that motion was defeated by a two-thirds vote, which in effect excluded the messengers.

The 1976 convention also received the report of a special committee, appointed the year before, "to study the historical and doctrinal positions as to what constitutes a 'regular, missionary Baptist church' as set forth in Article III of our constitution." Not everyone wanted to do that, and the vote was too close to call by a show of hands but passed on written ballot. That committee, headed by Kenneth Chafin, reaffirmed the historic Baptist church/convention relationships: that each Baptist church is autonomous; that denominational relationships and cooperation are voluntary; that representation in one Baptist body (such as an association) does not automatically carry with it representation in another (as a state convention), nor would loss of representation in one automatically bring exclusion from another. Thus the exclusion of the charismatic churches from Dallas Baptist Association did not mean they were automatically excluded from the BGCT or, for that matter, the SBC. For a general discussion of what Baptists believe and practice, the committee referred to the Baptist Faith and Message statement adopted by the SBC in 1963.

The committee emphatically reaffirmed the report of the 1969 Constitution Study Committee which concluded that "the Convention is defined primarily in functional terms," rather than creedal terms. That is, affiliation of churches with the BGCT is determined more by whether they cooperate in the missions, education and evangelism tasks of the Convention than where they may agree on every doctrinal belief.

The Convention is not without recourse, the committee pointed out, in maintaining the integrity of the body. "Messengers from any church which brings serious disharmony, disturbs fellowship, or undermines the work and programs of this Convention may be excluded from fellowship."[83] Several examples were given of the kinds of offenses which might lead to exclusion. A church could be excluded for maintaining only a token relation to the Convention when "it is clear that their main allegiance, practices, and objectives are out of harmony with those of the Convention," or if the church adopts beliefs and practices which have more in common with some other denomination, or "if a church maintains a relationship to the Convention but uses that relationship to undermine the work of the Convention or its cooperating churches, or to make converts to beliefs, practices, and affiliations 'out of harmony with the Convention.'"

The report did not specifically mention charismatic practices, but the committee strongly believed that the two excluded churches had committed many of the offenses listed as worthy of exclusion.[84] The charismatic question was a hot topic for a time but, like a fever that passes its crisis and then ebbs, the charismatic movement quickly faded and no longer troubled Baptists very much. James Landes had an interesting explanation for the fact that charismatic practices never proved much of a problem to Texas Baptists. Most of the Texas Baptist pastors, he said, had attended Baptist colleges and studied under Baptist professors and therefore "They've [charismatics] never been a great problem to us."[85]

Funding for Colleges. From 1845 when Baylor University was founded, Baptist colleges in Texas have struggled for adequate funding. During the

1960s Baptists decided not to accept government loans or grants, and the colleges learned to look elewhere than the Convention for financial support. They learned they could raise more money with less effort, and with fewer strings attached, from other sources. However, the policy of Landes, who had been a college president, to raise the funding of Texas Baptist schools proved controversial at times. This was especially true in connection with Dallas Baptist College.

When Decatur Junior College moved to Dallas in 1965 and took the new name of Dallas Baptist College, financial problems were built in from the first. Not enough money was provided for the move, nor was funding adequate for the transition from junior to senior college status. A number of buildings were erected on the new Dallas campus, including a state of the art learning center with modern technology which proved quite expensive and which, some said, was not fully utilized at first. When expected enrollment did not materialize, the infant school was left with a large number of faculty and few students. For many years the school operated on the very edge of bankruptcy. Some suggested that Dallas Baptist merge with an existing school and become the Dallas branch of either Baylor or Hardin-Simmons. The presidents and trustees of those schools, however, showed no great enthusiasm for that idea. Wealthy donors, particularly A. Webb Roberts, Kenneth Burg, and Mary Crowley at times bailed the school out, but it was never enough. At one point W. A. Criswell, pastor of FBC in Dallas, sent the trustees a crisp one-line letter asking if they would simply give the school to him for the debt against it. They said no. "No one thought we as a Convention ought to give up Christian education in the Metroplex area."[86]

Almost every year brought a new crisis at DBC, and repeatedly the CECB and Executive Board struggled with what to do. Repeatedly the Executive Board was asked to advance a few hundred thousand dollars over and above, always with the firm promise that the school would not have to ask for special help again. The board always complained loudly and just as regularly came through with the emergency appropriation, and warned sternly that they would not bail the school out again. Just as regularly, the school faced new crises and again appealed for emergency aid, sometimes in the millions.

The ongoing debate revealed and exacerbated deep fissures in Texas between people with differing viewpoints of what the priorities of the BGCT ought to be. The crisis of 1982 is particularly revealing. The college once again faced bankruptcy and came to the Executive Board asking for a $3 million loan, on the expectation that they would receive a promised $1 million gift from Mary Crowley and $3 million, partly in gifts and partly in longterm loans, from anonymous donors who made the offer contingent upon an expected favorable tax ruling by the IRS. This was a lot of "ifs." Ralph Smith, pastor at Hyde Park Baptist Church in Austin and former president of the BGCT, spoke strongly against the proposal. Smith was no disgruntled critic; his loyalty to Texas Baptists had been proven and his church was one of the most generous in the state. However, he gave a blistering indictment, in which he said

> When we come to these Executive Board meetings to talk about DBC, it is always thrust upon us as a crisis that must be met immediately and if we don't meet it immediately, then the school is going to fold, or our credit is going to be no good, or something is going to happen. . . . It really matters very little if we pay off this present debt, for we are going to be faced with the very same crisis again in 2-3 years. . . . He reminded the group that this was the sixth time DBC has come to the Executive Board at the eleventh hour: 1968, 1971, 1972, 1974 (twice). . . . I regret I feel this way. If I owe you an apology, I want to apologize right now before I say this. But, I feel now in this meeting the integrity of the Executive Board is on the line. And I feel like that we are about to vote to determine if we mean what we say when we have said to DBC the last three times. Don't come to us at the 11th hour with a crisis—we are not going to respond.[87]

The crux of the conflict was revealed in Smith's comment, "Don't care how you cut it, this is mission money that we are using." He noted that his church was trying to start a new mission in Austin and could obtain a building loan only at high interest. He urged that, "If we have $2,500,000 that we can loan debt free, for God's sake let's take that kind of money and build New Testament churches . . . because that is the way our Lord told us to win the world for him."

Feelings ran high. Dan Moore, a layman on the Executive Board, echoed Smith's opposition. He noted that he had urged his church to raise its Cooperative Program gifts to 22%, but was ready to go back to his church and tell them the money was not being wisely used. "I am beginning to question why we use some of our money as we do," he said. "I am opposed to pouring money, like water, down a rat hole. Folks, the well is going to run dry. . . . I am ashamed sometimes at the way we spend our money as Texas Baptists." The irate layman also complained that he was not furnished adequate information before the board meeting. "I don't know what you think a Board member is for," he huffed, "but I'm getting tired of giving up a day's work and about $100 in expenses to come up here to find out what you have already decided we're going to do."[88] Not many, perhaps, agreed with these extreme remarks, though the minutes record that he was greeted by "amens and applause."

After long and sometimes confrontive discussion the board voted 63 to 40 to advance the money to DBC. After the vote, which made the deal contingent upon the $1 million gift and $3 million gift and loan coming through, Wayne Allen said, "Now that the Proposal has been approved, we would ask you as a [Trustee] Board to delete three words, 'and contingent upon.'" This would allow the college to receive the help immediately so they could pay off their debt and save about $1,343 a day in interest payments. Opposition to this motion was immediate and impassioned. "I feel somewhat insulted by the motion," said one Executive Board member. "I think it raises a grave amount of questions about the integrity of the trustees to present a motion of this nature. Having withheld that information prior to and having full knowledge that this body was going to vote. This is an insult to me personally—to bring this information after the fact." Ralph Smith said, "We're down to a matter of truthfulness and integrity. We talked about 'contingent' and now we're changing the motion after the fact." Browning Ware perhaps spoke for most when he said, "I voted for the original motion but I do believe this action changes the meaning of it."[89] Opposition was so heated that Allen withdrew his motion.

Clearly this 1982 debate involved far more than the question of funding for a college. Already a division among Texas Baptists was evident, with pastors and people lining up on different sides of the question of what is the denominational mission. In the years to come, these divisions would deepen.

Relation to the Southern Baptist Convention. What is and ought to be the relationship between the state conventions and the national body, the SBC? When he first came to office, Landes complained that the SBC took the state conventions for granted and at times seemed to regard them as subordinate branches of the national body. Landes distinctly did not regard the BGCT as a kind of minor league "farm club" of the national body. He said, "I hadn't been in this office but six months before I was firey mad because the Home Mission Board was sending a lot of stuff to the pastors and none of it was crossing my desk. The same thing was true of the Sunday School Board; same thing was true of several other boards."[90] Landes wrote to the leaders of the SBC boards and suggested that "You'll do a lot better job in Texas if you let me know what you're doing."

On one occasion Landes became quite angry with the Executive Committee in Nashville. Early in his tenure he had occasion to sign a check to the Executive Committee for $840,000. Since this was a sizeable amount, Landes wanted to get some promotional value from it and perhaps use the incident to increase gifts in Texas. Jay Skaggs, treasurer for the Texas board, suggested they deliver the check in person at the next meeting. When the Texas men got to Nashville, they found the Nashville group irate because the check was a few days late. Landes said, "I walked into a group of stinging bees, the killer bees, when I went into Nashville. They said, Texas is not going to do this and Texas is not going to do that, and everyone was questioning some of the things that Dr. Patterson had done."[91] Landes remarked that "Jay [Skaggs] was angrier than I; we were both pretty upset about it."

However, Landes stood his ground and refused to be pushed around by the national body. As the leader of a strong state convention that provided major funding to the SBC, he was not without clout of his own. He said, "Texas is first, always, among the Southern Baptist Convention, you know. They are the innovators. They are the ones who have led the way. That sounds braggadocio *[sic]*, doesn't it? But it's true."[92]

The Fundamentalist Resurgence. From the day in 1835 when the pioneer Baptist Z. N. "Wildcat" Morrell first crossed the Sabine and saw that Texas would "blossom as the rose," Texas Baptists have continued to be Bible-believing, conservative, evangelistic, mission-minded, church-building, gospel-preaching people. At times, however, a faction of Texas Baptists have wanted to go beyond Bible conservatism to an ultraconservative or fundamentalist stance. Issues varied from time to time, but this tendency to extremism can be seen in such diverse movements as Landmarkism (1860s), Haydenism (1890s), Norrisism (1920s and 1930s).[93] All of these movements were marked by a bitter spirit, narrow extremism, and all left hurtful scars upon the Baptist body in Texas. However, in every case the Texas convention resisted and, in time, overcame these movements and refused to succumb to their divisive ways.

However, a new wave of ultra-conservatism arose in the 1960s which threatened to engulf not only the SBC but the state conventions as well. Many people date the rise of this new movement from the divisive Houston SBC meeting in 1979, but in *A Messenger's Memoirs* (Providence House Publishers, 1995), Robert E. Naylor, who lived through the Norris era, shows that the seeds of fundamentalism had been nurtured long before that. Historians have debated the causes of this resurgence of intense conservatism among Baptists, attributing it variously to changes in Southern culture (Leonard and Rosenbaum);[94] the development of liberalism among Southern Baptist schools (Hefley),[95] and the fact that a few Southern Baptist educators earned doctorates in northern schools (Noll.)[96] Others regarded the new conservatism as the Baptist equivalent of the new conservatism in American politics and society. Whatever the causes, accusations of liberalism in the colleges and seminaries increased, some ultra churches reduced their gifts to the Cooperative Program or escrowed the funds to bring pressure on the Convention, some churches stopped using SBC Sunday School literature and larger churches with resources made their own Bible study curricula.

Two Texans led the new fundamentalist resurgence: Paige Patterson, president of the Criswell Bible College in Dallas and son of the former executive secretary, and Paul Pressler, a layman who was a judge in Houston. It is generally agreed that Pressler provided the political know-how to organize Southern Baptist protests at the grassroots level, and Patterson provided the theological basis for the movement. At first, most Texas Baptists knew nothing of what was going on. "The real tipoff in Texas," said Landes, "was in 1978 when Jaroy Webber [an ultra-conservative] was elected president of the SBC. Everybody thought Landrum Leavell would be elected but he wasn't. . . . And so its right at this time that we became aware that something was happening, but . . . we didn't know, yet, how much had happened."[97] What had happened was the skillful political organization of Texas Baptist dissidents in a virulent protest against the denominational program and leadership. Landes received a letter from Paige Patterson warning him that Texas Baptists were ready to erupt in protest. Landes said he mistakenly showed the letter to W. A.

Criswell, only to learn that "He [Criswell] was the head of the thing."[98] The Pressler-Patterson movement was imminently successful. Since 1979 their party has consistently elected the SBC president who, in turn, has made the appointments which have given the fundamentalists complete control of the SBC and all its agencies.

However, the right-wing group has not fared so well in the state conventions, particularly in Texas. Landes was concerned to keep the controversy at bay. He objected to what he regarded as their extremist views, their lack (in his view) of denominational loyalty, and especially to their harsh and divisive spirit. "They just cut your head off if you don't agree with them," he said.[99] This group did gain a toehold in Texas when a committee appointed by BGCT president Carlos McLeod brought several militant conservatives onto the Baylor trustee board in the early 1980s. This intensified the uneasiness at Baylor which led by 1990 to a change in their relationship to the BGCT. The Baylor alumni, who held significant leadership posts in Texas Baptist churches, led the resistance to the fundamentalist efforts to extend their takeover of the SBC to the BGCT. They felt that Baylor would have much to lose if any extremist group gained control. The Baylor loyalists organized their own skilled precinct-like organization. They set up a computer network at Baylor to keep tabs and drum up support. "We have captains; we have co-captains; we have colonels; we have lieutenants," one leader conceded.[100] They were ready if necessary to fight fire with fire.

THE END OF THE LANDES ERA

Jimmy Landes was sixty-one years old when he was elected executive secretary and he was expected to serve only four years. However, his health was good, the work was going well and, perhaps most importantly, Landes wanted to continue. Moreover, federal law had changed in 1979 to prevent employers from enforcing mandatory retirement at age sixty-five. The Executive Board had twice extended Landes' tenure by secret ballot, the last to the end of 1982 when Landes would turn seventy. In asking him to continue, the board noted that Landes had brought unity, had helped smooth over controversy, and that all factions of Texas Baptists wanted him to continue. He retired as of December 31, 1982, after nine of the most productive years in Texas Baptist history.

After retirement, Landes continued active in Baptist life. For a time he taught on the religion faculty of Baylor University, but continued to live in Dallas. He died in 1996.

CHAPTER 14

CONTINUITY AMIDST CHANGE, 1983–1998

AMERICA IN THE 1980s and 1990s faced unprecedented new opportunities along with plenty of challenges. In the 1980s, still suffering a national hangover from Watergate and the forced resignation of President Nixon, the nation faced a combination of economic recession, rising crime rate, and further weakening of the family. The election of President Ronald Reagan in 1980 over Southern Baptist layman Jimmy Carter signaled a sharp turn toward conservatism, with building up America's military might despite the mushrooming of the national debt. The fall of the infamous Berlin Wall in 1989 and the subsequent dramatic breakup of the old Soviet Union left the United States as the only world superpower. America flexed its military muscles in successfully resisting the aggression of Iraq's Saddam Hussein in Kuwait, and engaged in several quasi-military "peace keeping" missions in other world trouble spots. The election of another Southern Baptist layman, President Bill Clinton in 1992 indicated, some said, a desire for change and his reelection in 1996 confirmed the national confidence in the improving economy. Texas was especially hard hit by the economic slowdown of the late 80s, with a recession in agriculture and a virtual collapse of the oil industry. By the '90s, Texas was booming again with the lowest unemployment rate in a generation.

Development of the microchip led to incredible advances in technology and introduced what some called the "information age." Americans went "on line" in computer networks, communicated by "fax" and "e-mail," formed "web sites," and carried telephones in their pockets. The stock markets recovered from their blahs of the 1970s and, despite a sharp downturn in 1987, roared back in the 1990s with the greatest "bull market" in history. In 1997, almost exactly ten years after the 1987 mini-crash, the markets took another sharp downturn, despite a generally strong American economy. The 1997 drop was fueled largely by economic woes in the Pacific Rim countries and illustrated the close interconnectedness

358

of the global economy. Unlike the old days when only rich people invested in the stock market, in recent years most Americans were directly affected because their retirement funds were invested in the stock market. Texas Baptists of course were directly affected by all these trends.

In these challenging and changing times, Texas Baptists not only continued their traditional work but also pioneered a number of innovative ministries to address the needs of churches and their members. The last two decades of the twentieth century proved to be a time of incredible growth for Texas Baptists, and unprecedented expansion of their evangelistic, missionary, and educational ministries. The Baptist General Convention of Texas that entered the twentieth century, small, always short of money, and with limited ministries, bears little resemblance to the strong and confident BGCT with its extensive programs of ministry at the close of the century. With over 5,700 churches and missions gathered into 113 associations; sponsoring 29 Baptist universities, hospitals, child care homes and retirement facilities; with over 2.7 million members who give annually to their churches over $1.1 *billion*; and with an annual Convention budget over $70 million, the BGCT forms one of the strongest units of the Baptist family worldwide.

PASSING THE BATON

Like members of a relay team who run alongside each other for a time and then pass off the baton without breaking stride, the seventy-year old Jimmy Landes passed the baton of Texas Baptist leadership to forty-eight year old Bill Pinson on January 1, 1983. Like the relay team, the change of leadership in the Executive Board of the Baptist General Convention of Texas came off without a hitch and without disruption in the work. When Pinson took over the office which Landes had held for nine years, the primary leadership team remained intact, the basic ministry programs continued and, above all, the same spirit of cooperation which Landes had nurtured remained in evidence and, over the years, was strengthened.

Landes and Pinson had a great deal in common. Both had been pastors of the same great church, FBC Wichita Falls, and both had been school presidents, Landes at Hardin-Simmons University in Abilene and Pinson at the Golden Gate Baptist Theological Seminary in San Francisco. Both served as teachers in Baptist schools, Pinson at Southwestern Seminary before his election as Executive Director, and Landes at Baylor University after his retirement. Though different personalities, the two men shared basic convictions and leadership emphases. A new leader always brings some change, but there was no radical break in the rhythm of Texas Baptist convention work in 1983 when Landes passed the baton to Pinson as there had been back in 1974 when Landes took over from T.A. Patterson. In the era from 1983 to 1990 *continuity* seemed to predominate over change in Texas Baptist life, while *change* predominated from 1990 to 1998. The story of this continuity and change will be sketched out in two chapters.

WILLIAM M. PINSON, JR.

In late 1981 the Executive Board appointed a search committee to recommend a new Executive Director when Landes, who had twice postponed his retirement, said he would definitely step down at the end of 1982. The BGCT president, Carlos McLeod, appointed the committee in consultation with James Landes. They wanted a strong conservative voice on the committee and agreed that James T. Draper, then pastor of FBC Euless, was the man. The committee elected its own chairman in the person of Dallas layman Dewey Presley. The committee developed a "Prospective Profile" of what they expected of the new leader.[1] They said he must take "a theological stance in the mainstream of Southern Baptist life," must have a history of faithful involvement in local church life, a sound mind and body confirmed by comprehensive medical exams, and be old enough to have significant experience but not so close to retirement that effective service would be diminished. They wanted a strong administrator but "a leader-servant who excels in interpersonal relations." The profile also called for a person who could listen as well as speak, one who could relate to persons of all cultural, social and ethnic backgrounds, and who had a thorough understanding of SBC and BGCT policy, structure, agencies and constitutions. The new leader, the committee agreed, must also be able to represent Baptists favorably in the general public and with other religious groups.

Finding a person to fit even most of these ideals proved no easy task. The committee met frequently, sifted through more than 100 names, cut that list to 33, then to 16, and to 7. They named a final four to be interviewed, only three of whom consented: Darold Morgan, Lloyd Elder, and Bill Pinson.[2] At first most people assumed that Lloyd Elder, the popular associate to Landes, would be the choice: Landes seemingly thought that would be the case, as did many of the search committee.[3] At one point Pinson asked that his name be dropped but later agreed that he would accept if elected. After the first interview, there was no doubt that Pinson would be the committee's choice. He and his wife Bobbie were invited back for a second interview and he was elected unanimously at a called meeting of the Executive Board on May 18, 1982. They were especially impressed with his ability to relate to young ministers. In an increasingly urban world, the committee said, "[Bill Pinson] is perhaps the finest urban strategist we have in our convention. . . . This man can deal with the present and pave the way for the future denominationally."

In his acceptance Pinson told the Executive Board, "This is without doubt the most humbling and terrifying moment of my life." Pinson had a deep conviction that it was God's will for him to accept the Texas office. Without that conviction, he said, "I would stay in California regardless of the threat of earthquake!" He was named Executive Director-Elect as of July 1, 1982. The Pinsons moved to Dallas and for six months he worked alongside Landes. All agreed that the 1982 state convention should be Landes' convention, and Pinson would take over officially on January 1, 1983. Actually, he began to assume more leadership after the November convention. Pinson spent the intervening months working with Landes, traveling throughout the state, meeting with and listening to Baptist leaders in churches, colleges, and other institutions. He got a good "feel" for the needs and challenges of Texas Baptists. He said, "I come therefore on mission . . . . I see Texas as the cornerstone of our mission to the world."[4]

The new executive director comes from a family with deep roots in Texas Baptist history. Josiah F. Pinson, great great grandfather to Bill, was a close associate of R. C. Buckner, and gave the land on which the original buildings of Buckner Orphans Home were placed.[5] The same Josiah F. Pinson helped form a church in Dallas in 1860, which took the name of First Baptist Church of Dallas.[6] Like its two predecessors, this church did not prosper in Dallas and later moved to the Pleasant View community near the present White Rock Lake. In 1863, with Pinson still an active participant, the church changed its name to Pleasant View Baptist Church.[7] Josiah F. Pinson also served for a time as pastor of FBC, Richardson. Another kinsman of Bill Pinson, J. T. Pinson, was one of the first to serve as associate executive secretary, though he did not carry that exact title. One who knew him described J. T. Pinson as an "all around assistant" to several executive secretaries.[8]

William Meredith Pinson, Jr., was born August 3, 1934, in Fort Worth, and grew up in Lancaster, just south of Dallas. He attended North Texas State University (now University of North Texas) where he served as president of the Baptist Student Union and of the student body. He graduated with the B.A. degree in 1955, and received both masters (1959) and doctors degrees (1963) from Southwestern Seminary in Fort Worth. He served as professor of Christian Ethics at Southwestern Seminary from 1963-1975 as successor to the famed T. B. Maston. Prior to that, Pinson was associate secretary of the BGCT Christian Life Commission from 1957-1963. He was married to Bobbie Ruth Judd of Lancaster in 1955, a gifted leader in her own right. They have two daughters, Meredith Pinson Creasey and Allison Pinson Hopgood, and presently have three grandchildren.

Pinson has served in a variety of leadership roles in Baptist life. From 1975-1977 he was pastor of FBC, Wichita Falls, a church that has provided so many top leaders for Baptists in Texas and beyond. In 1977 he was named president of the Golden Gate Baptist Theological Seminary in San Francisco, and served there until his election to lead the BGCT Executive Board in 1982. A many-talented person, Pinson has also proven to be a writer of note, having published eighteen books and countless articles. With Clyde E. Fant, Jr., Pinson co-authored the thirteen-volume reference work, *Twenty Centuries of Great Preaching*. He holds honorary degrees from four Baptist universities, and has preached in many countries around the world. As early as 1965 he was named one of the "outstanding young men in America," and since then has received honors, awards, and recognitions too numerous to list. He has participated in, and often led, conferences on various moral issues all the way from country churches to the White House, and has delivered lectureships at more than fifty universities. In his denominational leadership role, Pinson has served on many committees, commissions and boards of trustees, culminating in his election as president of the Association of Southern Baptist State Executive Directors, 1996-1997.

After careful investigation, the search committee concluded that with all his academic and administrative achievements, Bill Pinson remained a deeply spiritual person, a man of prayer, firmly committed to the fundamental doctrines of Baptists and the primary tasks of evangelism, missions and Christian education and benevolence. In 150 years of convention life perhaps Texas Baptists have never had a leader more prepared for the task by conviction, experience and temperament.

A LEADERSHIP TEAM

"My work is primarily to coordinate a team effort," said Pinson at his first official meeting of the Executive Board. Other team members in the Administrative Section included Doris Ann Tinker, executive associate; Ed Schmeltekopf, associate executive director; Jay Skaggs, treasurer; and Thomas J. Brannon, director of public relations.

Doris Tinker came to the Baptist Building on December 1, 1973 as administrative assistant to James H. Landes. She continued on the Pinson team where over the years her experience and competence led to several promotions. She presently serves as executive associate to the executive director, one of the most responsible positions in the Building. After a quarter century of leadership in the Baptist Building at the highest levels, few if any have a more detailed knowledge of the BGCT and its manifold ministries than Doris Tinker.

E. Edward Schmeltekopf was born in Kyle, Texas, to a family with deep roots in German Baptist life in early Texas. He holds a bachelors degree from Southwest Texas State University in San Marcos, and both masters and doctoral degrees from Southwestern Seminary in Fort Worth. He has also done graduate study at the Hankamer School of Business at Baylor University. After a year as a high school coach, young Schmeltekopf served as pastor of several Texas churches, most recently at FBC, Burleson (1961-1980). He and his wife Lilla have a son and a daughter, and four grandchildren. Schmeltekopf was named associate executive director in April, 1980, and continues in office at this writing.

Four areas of work fell under the supervision of the associate director in 1983: Cooperative Program promotion, personnel administration, Partnership Missions, and Missions Service Corps. William Jan Daehnert later joined the staff as coordinator of work with personnel as well as convention committees, and Bobbie Burkett later became director of the Office of Human Resources. It was her assignment to oversee the recruitment and employment of personnel for the Baptist Building, and oversee plans for the management, training and development, health and safety, wage and salary administration, benefit provisions, and employee relations. Her office also provides assistance to more than one thousand members who serve on various committees of the Convention and its agencies.[9] In the 1990s, the office of Cooperative Program Promotion was created (the first such office in a state convention). It has been served by Robert Polk, Bill V. Cathey, and Glenn Majors.

Jay L. Skaggs retired at the end of 1983 after nineteen years as treasurer for the BGCT. A native of rural Oklahoma, Skaggs served as business administrator for the Cliff Temple church in Dallas from 1958-1964, and began work with the Executive Board in 1964 as controller. He succeeded R. A. Springer as treasurer in 1971. Noted for his quick wit and careful management, Skaggs was sometimes known as the "watchdog" of Baptist funds.

Roger W. Hall was named treasurer in late 1983, and continues as Chief Financial Officer/Treasurer of the BGCT. Hall is a graduate of Southwest Missouri State University and Midwestern Baptist Theological Seminary. He served in the army in Viet Nam in 1968-1969 with the rank of captain. A Certified Public Accountant since 1973, Hall served at Southwest Baptist University in Missouri as a professor of accounting and also as vice-president for Development-Planned Giving. For five years he was Director of Business Services for the Missouri Baptist Convention, and for one year was Vice-President of Financial Services for the Midwestern Baptist Seminary. Hall and his wife Donna have two daughters and two grandchildren. They live in Duncanville, and are active in the First Baptist Church of Oak Cliff where Hall serves as a deacon and Sunday School teacher. He is a member of several professional financial management groups. He annually receives and disburses millions of dollars for Texas Baptists. These funds are accounted for and audited in the most thorough and professional manner.

As CFO/Treasurer, Hall manages the Convention's properties, serves as liaison with the Convention's legal advisors, and oversees the extensive insurance needs of the BGCT. He also helps plan and administer the annual budget of the Convention, and oversees the Management Information Systems (data processing) at the Baptist Building.

The Office of Public Relations, directed by Thomas J. Brannon, had a name change in 1994 to the Office of Communications.[10] They felt that the former name had negative connotations of trying to control or "spin" the Baptist news to outsiders, whereas the office primarily addressed Texas Baptists rather than the general public. Brannon said, "We feel that 'communications' more accurately describes the work that we do and frees us of the negative perceptions that the term public relations often carried."[11] Brannon and his staff regularly churn out newspaper articles, press releases, films, and photographs to explain and promote the various ministries in which Texas Baptists are active. Their materials appear in secular papers, the *Baptist Standard,* and various radio and television programs. In 1994, for example, news stories about Texas Baptists were distributed to 625 Texas newspapers, and nearly 200 articles were carried in the *Baptist Standard,* and 65 stories appeared in Baptist Press and Associated Baptist Press. As the name implies, this office *communicates* by keeping Texas Baptists informed about the various ministries in Texas and beyond.

RECESSION

By the mid-80s the Texas economy was in severe distress. For several years the BGCT had modest budget shortfalls, though the dollar amounts they received were still impressive. Some felt they simply set the budget too high. In 1983 for the first time Texas Cooperative Program giving exceeded $50 million. In March, 1984, Roger Hall reported that Cooperative Program receipts were 6% above the year before, and for the first quarter of 1984 gifts were running about 8.8% above 1983.[12] Changes in the Texas economy, however, did not allow these positive reports to continue. Economic slowdowns in the cattle and agriculture sectors and virtual collapse in the oil-patch put thousands out of work. Prosperous oil towns like Midland and Odessa lost population, leaving hundreds of vacant houses whose owners could not sell. Treasurer Hall referred to 1986 as "a character builder year," with budget shortfalls for the BGCT. Texas Governor Mark White had to call a special session of the state legislature that year to deal with the slumping Texas economy.

As late as 1988 Pinson's report to the Executive Board included the reminder that "the economy is still in a crisis stage" and Hall reported for that year that the BGCT budget receipts were running at 91.1% of budget, with expenses held to 88.5% of the budgeted amounts.[13] However, the BGCT leadership remained confident that there would be a turnaround and that the hard times would prove temporary. Pinson said that "during these months of difficult financial crises that Texas Baptists are seeking to: 1) Get the job done, 2) Live within the income, and 3) Keep up the morale."[14] Records show that they achieved all three of these goals. Though they fell somewhat short of budget for some years, their ministry achievement did not appear to suffer. By careful management they remained in the black and kept an optimistic spirit.

MISSION TEXAS, 1985-1990

Often written in capital letters, MISSION TEXAS was the theme for all the work of the BGCT for the five year period, 1985-1990. Since the 1930s, the BGCT has planned and promoted its work in five-year cycles, but only recently has assigned theme names to those periods. MISSION

TEXAS included goals for evangelism, enlistment and training in Christian living, and missionary giving in Texas Baptist churches. A vital part of this five-year plan was a statewide soul-winning campaign, "Share Jesus Now." The goal was to have 89,000 trained witnesses from 3,000 churches sharing the gospel with a million Texans during February and March of 1989 leading up to the "Here's Hope" simultaneous revivals in March and April. This part of the program was led by Carlos McLeod, director of the Evangelism Department. The promotion included training people in the "Roman Road" plan of witnessing, Lay Renewal Weekends, and sixty days of special evangelistic emphasis preceding the revivals. Every agency of the BGCT was directly involved and MISSION TEXAS became the undergirding theme for the work of every agency of the BGCT. Charles McLaughlin reached the retirement age of sixty-five in 1984 but Pinson asked him to stay on at least through 1987 to direct the program.

This five year program was launched at the state Evangelism Conference in January, 1986. Pinson said, "There are hundreds of tasks for us, but only one hammers at us: to tell the Good News."[15] At that Evangelism Conference, Governor Mark White, a Baptist layman, was introduced by his pastor Ralph Smith of the Hyde Park church in Austin. Governor White gave his personal testimony, and noted the rising crime rate in Texas. He said, "Strong laws are not enough. . . . We must have moral guideposts that only Christian commitment can provide. Christ in the lives of individuals is the difference. . . . The old time religion still works."[16]

Part of the urgency of this massive effort was the realization that the Lone Star State had undergone significant changes in population. "Today's Texas," said one report, "is a multi-cultural, religiously pluralistic, greatly diverse state. It is also a largely unchurched state. At least half of its population claims no church affiliation whatsoever."[17] With floods of new immigrants, whether legal or illegal, more than 100 languages and dialects were spoken in Texas. By the 1990s Texas passed New York to become the second most populous state, surpassed only by California. It was expected that by the turn of the century the Texas population would reach twenty million, at least half of them not related to any church. This made Texas truly one of the great mission fields of the world.

Four facets of MISSION TEXAS were: Reaching People, Developing Believers, Strengthening Missions, and Spiritual Awakening. One goal was to increase baptisms by 10% a year, and start 2,000 new churches by 1990. Baptisms fell a bit short of that goal but they did record 318,643 new baptisms for the five year period, including 68,046 in 1986 for a 5.52% increase, but only 60,590 in 1987 for a 10.96% decrease.[18] At the end of the period, new congregations totaled 2,078, of which 760 began without BGCT financial aid. Sunday School enrollment grew from 1,304,138 in 1985 to 1,346,482 in 1990, a bit short of its goal of a 4% annual increase, and in the same period enrollment in Discipleship Training increased from 257,911 to 295,341. Students in the BSU increased from 36,000 to 38,700, but the percentage of Baptist students enrolled in Texas Baptist schools decreased somewhat. Cooperative Program giving increased, but the Texas offering for World Hunger decreased from about $1.5 million in 1985 to $919,695 in 1990. Enrollment in WMU and Texas Baptist Men increased, and the number of Texans engaged in some form of volunteer missions rose dramatically. The Mary Hill Davis offering for state missions averaged nearly $5 million a year, but in the special emphasis of 1986 reached the incredible total of $8.3 million.

Many of the results of MISSION TEXAS are quantifiable; one can cite numbers to show the goals that were reached. However, the spiritual renewal of these years of special emphasis is not easily tabulated, but is very real nevertheless. Every evidence suggests that these were years of increasing spiritual maturity for Texas Baptists, for their churches, and for the denomination as a whole. The emphasis upon prayer, the continued cooperative spirit, and the evidences of vitality in the churches, add to the impact of this program.

THE BAPTIST BUILDING

Since the Convention moved its offices to Dallas in 1896, they have occupied space in various rented buildings until acquiring their own facility in 1952. However, they soon outgrew that building and by the 1980s they were considering other options. In 1981 the Executive Board appointed a Long Range Property Study Committee, chaired by Dallas businessman Fred Roach, to study space needs. That committee recommended in 1983 that they exercise their option to purchase the lot next to the Annuity Board on Akard and enter into a contract with a Dallas developer to erect a 21 story office building with 275 parking spaces. That plan fell through when the development company could not raise adequate financing.[19]

In 1985 the Board appointed a Facility Study Committee, with Dallas businessman Dewey Presley as chair and pastor D. L. Lowrie as vice-chair. The committee included leading real estate leaders of Dallas, with the BGCT president, and chairmen of the Executive Board and its Administrative Committee as ex officio members, with Roger Hall as the primary staff liaison. After considering several approaches such as leasing, minority interest in a larger facility, renovation or buying an existing building, the committee recommended that the BGCT erect a new building located at the corner of Washington and Race, next to the Baylor Medical Center. The land of this choice site was leased from Baylor Health Care System with an option to purchase later. Roger Hall and the committee engaged the architectural firm of F & S Partners, Inc., to draw plans for a four story 98,000 square foot building with two levels of underground parking and with warehouse and storage space. These plans were approved by the Facilities Study Committee, the Administrative Committee, and by the full Executive Board. The J. W. Bateson Company was contracted to construct the building, to begin in 1987 with completion scheduled for late 1988.

The timing for the Baptist Building seems providential. For some years the Executive Board occupied several floors of the Annuity Board building which they leased. At the time of the lease they also obtained an option to buy that portion of the building at the price then current. Years later they exercised that option. On the same day, Pinson signed two contracts: one to purchase the Annuity Board property at the price established years before, and another contract to sell that same property at its current higher price. They sold at the peak of the Dallas real estate market, at the highest per foot sale in Dallas up to that time. With those two contracts, the BGCT cleared enough money, combined with trust funds already on hand and careful management by Roger Hall, to construct the $11.5 million Baptist Building free and clear without using any Cooperative Program or mission money. Just after they completed the purchase/sale, the Dallas real estate market collapsed. They got out just in time—the old Annuity Board building still sat vacant in 1997. When they contracted for the new building, construction costs were down and contractors were willing to lower their bids drastically just to keep their crews busy. The foundation will support two additional levels if that expansion should ever become necessary. In March 1989, Hall reported that all construction costs had been paid and all liens released.

In the May 19, 1998 meeting of the Executive Board, Pinson announced that the Board of Directors of the Baylor Health Care System had voted to give the land on which the Baptist Building is located to the Executive Board, a gift valued at $2.5 million. The Executive Board expressed appreciation to the BHCS board, to Boone Powell, Jr., BHCS CEO, and to Judge Oswin Chrisman, BHCS board chair.

This pink granite building provides attractive office space for the WMU of Texas, Texas Baptist Men, and the Executive Board staff such as the Baptist Church Loan Corporation, the State Missions Commission, the Christian Life Commission, the Christian Education Coordinating Board, the Human Welfare Coordinating Board, the director of Church/Minister Relations, the director of Black Church Development, the computer-technology department which undergirds the computer needs of all the offices, the Baptist Leadership Center and many other BGCT offices and agencies. The building also includes conference rooms, storage, catering and dining facilities, and a recording studio. Crowds thronged the new building for the dedication and open house on December 6, 1988. Former leaders T. A. Patterson and James H. Landes with their families attended the dedication.

The location adjacent to the Baylor facility has several advantages for persons who work in the Baptist Building. They have access to the several acres of beautifully landscaped park around the hospital, and access to the renowned Tom Landry Fitness Center which many of the Baptist Building personnel use regularly. Baylor Hospital also gave ongoing permission for the Executive Board to meet in its Beasley Auditorium at no cost, since the new building has no room able to accommodate the more than 200 persons who attend that meeting. The building is easily accessible from the adjacent Interstate 30. About 30,000 people a year visit the Baptist Building, and approximately 9,000 meals are served for working members of committees, commissions and study groups.

Perhaps no state convention, and no Baptist organization anywhere, has a more attractive, functional and totally acceptable building in which to conduct its work. Several people played leading roles in bringing this to fruition. Bill Pinson gave wise overall planning, and Treasurer Roger Hall was the "money man" who managed the construction and financing, seeing that things were done properly and within budget. In a large measure, the building is his achievement. The help of competent business men and real estate leaders like Dewey Presley and Fred Roach of Dallas and J. T. Luther of Fort Worth was invaluable. D. L. Lowrie, pastor of FBC Lubbock, served on the Facilities Study Committee, and Ed Rogers, pastor of FBC, Dumas, had the considerable task of chairing the Building Committee. Texas Baptists took justifiable pride in the new structure. Presnall W. Wood, editor of the *Baptist Standard,* joined others in celebrating the new building but reminded his readers that "It is not Baptist headquarters. Headquarters for Baptists is the local church."[20]

TECHNOLOGY AT THE BAPTIST BUILDING

Like all organizations, the BGCT has to deal with far more forms of information today and they are, like other organizations, increasingly dependent upon computers. Convention workers who at the turn of the century were thrilled when someone donated a used "typewriting machine" would be astonished at the vast computer network which connects the Baptist Building to the churches, denominational offices and agencies, the Internet, an "Intranet" that links their own staff, and indeed puts them in direct touch with the whole world. When Roger Hall came as chief financial officer in 1983, the building had only one small computer to handle financial records, accounting and mailing lists.

One priority of Hall's leadership, a priority fully supported by Pinson, was to automate the Baptist Building as a way to increase the effectiveness of the staff. An outside consultant was engaged in 1984 to make a study of computer needs and potential and, as a result, by 1985 the Baptist Building entered the Personal Computer (PC) network era. Over the years as needs increased, the system grew. The Management Information Services Department was formed in the 1980s to manage records like the annual church uniform letter reports, mailouts, records of financial contributions from the churches, and the computer needs of the individual offices in the Baptist Building. Jim Tillery, who has worked with computers for over thirty years, has headed the department since 1989, having succeeded Bob Darling in that work. Tillery heads a complex operation which involves not only the purchase, maintenance and repair of computer equipment, but also the operation of a vast information management, printing and mailing enterprise.

In 1997, the computer systems consisted of a mainframe (IBM AS-400 Model 310-2043) which had been upgraded four times, 170 PC units and 73 laptops. The MIS department does about 95% of their own computer repair work. Tillery's department also conducts a regular program to train new employees, to bring existing staff up to speed on new programs, and to find new and better ways to do their work. The MIS department operates its own research and analysis work, surveying modern trends, demographics, and shifts in society. This work is headed by research analyst Clay Price, and the data he generates is used for planning, locating new churches, and evaluating the needs for new programs of ministry in the future. Computer skills are considered important not just for clerical staff but also for department heads, all the way to Hall and Pinson. However, clerical staff and department heads attend different training sessions in order, it was reported, to protect the egos of some high level executives who cannot keep up with their own office staff in learning the latest computer skills.

The funding changes effected by the BGCT in 1995, by which churches could direct their gifts in any one of four channels or some combination thereof, greatly increased the task of financial record keeping at the BGCT. The treasurer's office handles over $100 million a year, and crunches about 3 million pieces of data daily. Cooperative Program funds are directed to about 80 different objects, and the computers keep track of BGCT funds which are deposited temporarily in numerous banks while in transit to the various institutions and agencies for whom they are intended. On a given day near the first of a month, the Baptist Building may receive, deposit, and direct several million dollars, and everything must be accurate to the penny, able to withstand the most intense audit. Of course, safeguards are in place and, so far, the system has suffered no breach of security.

Most of the Directors of Missions are "on line" and communicate with the Executive Board by Internet. Many churches do the same, and use e-mail to receive reports, review their contribution records, and to order printed materials. The Baptist Student directors are also on line, and communicate among themselves and with the BSM Department electronically. The BGCT also has a "Web Page" to share information with Baptists and the public, and to offer a witness to the gospel.

VOLUNTEERS ON MISSION

In recent years volunteerism has become an ever more important part of American society. With many people retiring earlier and living longer, retirees find they still have much to give and time in which to give it. One of the candidates in the presidential election of 1988 emphasized the importance of private citizen volunteer efforts in society with his reference to "a thousand points of light." Texas Baptists provided their full share of these volunteers.

Rio Grande River Ministry. Charles Lee Williamson was right when he said "River Ministry captured the imagination of Texas Baptists early and never lost it."[21] Williamson should know—from 1968 to his retirement in 1992 he headed the Missions Division of SMC which oversaw the River Ministry work. Since the 1960s Texas Baptists have worked along both sides of the over 800 miles the *Rio Grande* winds its way along the border between Texas and Mexico, engaged in a combination of evangelistic, church-planting, medical and social ministries. This work not only captured the heart of Texas Baptists, but also helped introduce a new way of doing global missions. Elmin K. Howell was coordinator of the RM department for twenty-eight years until his retirement in 1995 when he was named Founding Director Emeritus. By the conclusion of Howell's fruitful ministry, the work was supported not only through the BGCT, but also through seven stateside associations along the border and by seven Mexican Baptist Regional Conventions (formerly associations) south of the River. Howell listed the top four priorities of the program as leadership training for lay persons, basic theological education for pastors (many of them bivocational), starting new churches, and maintaining the health care programs.[22]

The achievements of the first 25 years of River Ministry are impressive: more than 500 new churches, 67 medical/dental clinics treating an average of about 25,000 people a year, over 200,000 pairs of eye glasses prepared and fitted, and about $6.1 million given to RM causes from the Mary Hill Davis Offering.[23] By 1996, the number of new churches formed and functioning had risen to 639, with 67 medical/dental on-site clinics in operation with eight health care professionals, six theological training centers on the Mexican side of the border, six children's homes, and summer missions programs involving more than 800 students, many of whom later entered full-time missions service, and thousands of new converts who might not otherwise have heard the gospel. In time the National Baptist Convention of Mexico has assumed more leadership and involvement in the River Ministry, and has adopted many of the principles used there in their own ministry efforts along their borders with Guatemala and Belize. They have proclaimed 1998 as "the Year of Border Missions."[24] The Mexican Convention also formed a Theological Training Center Commission to help sponsor the training of teachers and overseeing the curriculum for the training centers.

Howell's successor as head of the River Ministry Department was Lynn Eckeberger, a graduate of East Texas Baptist University in Marshall, and with both masters and doctors degrees from Southwestern Seminary in Fort Worth. Before assuming the River assignment, Eckeberger was Director of Missions for the Concho Valley Baptist Association in San Angelo. Eckeberger's father was director of the *Los Hermanos de la Frontera*, a subsidiary of the River Ministry, with offices in Van Horn. Young Eckeberger grew up speaking Spanish and understanding the challenges of the River Ministry. He had been a pastor, associate pastor of missions, administration and education in four churches, and associate director of missions in the Lubbock Baptist Association. He had also served for two years with the Home Mission Board in the western states. He brought a wealth of experience in mission work which seemed to make him a logical successor to pioneer Howell.

The crisis caused by Hurricane Beulah in 1967 hastened the development of RM. Two subsequent crises, the earthquake in Mexico City in 1985 and Hurricane Gilbert in 1988 left hundreds dead, and thousands homeless and hungry. Texas Baptists responded to these disasters primarily through Partnership Missions and Texas Baptist Men. Despite some initial hesitation by Mexican officials, TBM was welcomed and they performed heroic service in Mexico City. As always, the TBM disaster teams trained local Baptists quickly to cook and deliver food, distribute water, and hand out simple medical supplies so the relief efforts could be identified in the public mind with Mexican Baptists. Over the years, specific ministries have changed as needs changed but, the underlying motive remained an unwavering commitment to evangelism.

With their River Ministry, Texas Baptists helped pioneer the concept of volunteers engaging in missionary work, and the concept succeeded beyond all expectation. When this program emerged in the 1960s, it provided virtually the only opportunity of its kind for volunteer missions. Since then many similar opportunities have opened up, both for service in this country and overseas. At some time, Baptist volunteers from about 30 other states have participated in the Texas River Ministry, but now many of those states have developed their own unique ministries, such as Mississippi River Ministry (MRM) for states which border that great river.

Partnership Missions. William H. Gray served as Director of Partnership Missions for the BGCT from the origin of the program in 1983 until his retirement in 1997. A graduate of Baylor University and Southwestern Seminary, Gray and his wife Amy Nadine ("Pinkie") had been missionaries in Mexico under the FMB for twenty-two years. They had been involved in RM from the Mexican side, and Gray had also taught at the Hispanic Baptist Seminary in San Antonio. Because of his long experience in Mexico, Gray was able to make the partnership with Mexico one of the most fruitful. In 1983 there were fifty-eight partnership projects in various parts of Mexico, and about 100 Hispanic pastors from Texas went to Mexico to lead revivals.[25] In 1997 Donald E. Sewell succeeded Gray as director of Partnership Missions for the BGCT.

In "Partnership Missions Guidelines," adopted by the Executive Board in 1988, it was specified that partnerships would be set for three years, with the possibility of renewal for another three years for a maximum of six years. In one or two cases a seventh year was added, and in at least one case after a few years had elapsed a second cycle of partnership was approved. The Board gave two reasons for this limitation. First, they said, "Volunteer partnerships seem to lose some of their challenge for state conventions after several years of joint effort." Second, "The Baptist General Convention of Texas does not wish to establish a long-term official 'partnership' with any Baptist entity in a foreign country because of the possibility that the state convention be perceived as another foreign mission agency."[26] However, when a partnership with the BGCT was completed, other states sometimes took up a partnership with the same area. Partnership Missions was "project oriented," in that volunteers were enlisted for short periods to work on specific projects.

When some Baptist group, whether in this country or overseas, requested to form a partnership the BGCT would send some representative to "spy out the land" and assess the possibilities. If the potential seemed favorable and the Executive Board felt it had resources and personnel to meet the needs, the agreement would be finalized. Usually one full year of preparation was necessary before the three years of partnership began. Leaders would identify specific needs or "projects" in the host country, and Texas associations or churches would be recruited to send volunteers to achieve those projects. In this way, the BGCT opened partnerships in Brazil, Mexico, Australia, Senegal/The Gambia in West Africa, Romania, Estonia and the English-speaking churches of the European Baptist Convention.

By 1987 the Partnership Missions office had requests from 58 churches in several countries of western Europe, most of them located near U.S. military bases. Terry G. Carter, a Texan who was then pastor of the Immanuel Baptist Church in Weisbaden, West Germany, was chairman of the European Baptist Convention's Partnership Missions Committee. He coordinated the efforts in Germany, especially the effort to match American pastors to European churches for terms of service. Carter said in 1990 that seventeen EBC churches were seeking English-speaking pastors. The work in Europe greatly expanded after the fall of the Berlin Wall and the opening of Eastern Europe. In Senegal, a largely Moslem country, Texas volunteers erected a cultural center which was visited by thousands and which gave an open door to make the gospel known. Gray reported in 1984 that over two thousand volunteers were at work in three foreign countries.

In 1997 plans finalized for a Texas partnership with Germany to work with the churches of the German Baptist Union. In late 1997 Jerry F. Dawson and his wife Margie spent several weeks in Germany working out details for the partnership. Dawson was assigned this planning task partly because he had time, having recently retired as head of the Christian Education Coordinating Board, and partly because of his fluency in the German language. Currently other Texas partnerships in the United States and beyond are in the planning stage.

Partnerships were also formed with Baptist groups in this country, including the Baptist Convention of Washington, D.C. and with the Northwest Baptist Convention, which includes Washington, Oregon and the panhandle of Idaho. The plan of operation was not greatly different from that used overseas. The host area helped identify specific tasks that needed to be done, and volunteers were matched to those tasks, whether conducting revivals, holding home Bible studies to form the nucleus of new churches, helping to build or remodel church buildings, leading Vacation Bible Schools, or helping with Sunday School enlargement campaigns. Other partnership volunteers worked in Texas in associations, camps, apartment evangelism, in Baptist Mission Centers, and in the Baptist Building. In addition to the PM volunteers, more than 400 MSC volunteers worked in Texas in 1989 while providing their own support. Of these, 38 served on associational staff positions, seven served on BGCT camp staffs, 45 helped start new churches and apartment ministries, nine were assigned to Texas Baptist schools, 17 worked in the Baptist Building, and 18 were on staff in Baptist Mission Centers. Multitudes of students served through the BSU, and 2,410 students participated that summer in mission trips.[27]

By 1997 it was clear that Partnership Missions offered Texas Baptists a new missions paradigm, or an additional way of doing missions, both home and foreign. The new director, Don Sewell, said "Texas Baptists should lend great attention to reaching the masses of Texans for Christ." That spotlights the "home" mission part of the task. But Sewell added, "At the same time, we rightfully have accepted our role in taking the good news beyond the state boundaries."[28] With partnerships in several foreign countries and more in planning, this spotlights the "foreign" missions aspect of Partnership Missions.

Mission Service Corps. More opportunities for volunteer mission service were provided by the Mission Service Corps (MSC) which was modeled partly on the Peace Corps. There was some overlap with the other volunteer agencies since their work was so similar, but in 1984 the duties of the MSC were spelled out. They would enlist volunteers for mission service in Texas, the USA, and overseas, long and short term, but would not be involved in the River Ministry, Partnership Missions, Resort Missions, student ministries, or with TBM Retiree Builders. All of these agencies conducted their own volunteer recruitment and assignments. Unlike the Partnership Ministry volunteers, the MSC workers served for longer periods, up to a year or two and sometimes longer.

In 1978 the Executive Board created the position of Mission Service Corps Coordinator and enlisted Dallas biology teacher Bill Barnett to fill that position. He served until 1980 when he was succeeded by D. Eugene (Gene) Strahan who had been a home missionary in Iowa and Minnesota. Strahan had also served on the BGCT staff assigned to the Minnesota-Wisconsin Baptist Fellowship as their first director of Church Services before retiring in Texas in 1979. It was Strahan who first saw the need and developed the system of "consultants" for the MSC to give the organization a presence in all parts of the state. Sam Pearis later said, "This concept of using consultants is the primary reason for the growth of MSC in Texas. It was later adopted for use throughout the entire Southern Baptist Convention."[29]

Samuel P. Pearis IV, a retired Air Force colonel, has headed the MSC since 1984. Pearis is a graduate of Alderson Broaddus College in West

Virginia with a masters degree in management. As an Air Force pilot, he flew 175 combat missions in Southeast Asia. He was later assigned to head up the Air Force re-enlistment program, excellent experience for his work in enlisting MSC volunteers. Sam and Polly Pearis became Southern Baptists while living on Okinawa. After retirement they worked as MSC volunteers with the San Antonio Association for three years. With creative innovation they developed many of the concepts later used by the MSC in Texas and other states. In working with about thirty trained consultants across Texas, all of whom are themselves volunteers, Pearis keeps a list of needs in Texas, the USA, and across the world and seeks to direct volunteers to the places where their gifts will count for the most.

Pearis reported that as of January 1996 there were 1,172 Texans serving in volunteer MSC posts. Of these, 206 were serving overseas in connection with the Foreign Mission Board, 806 were serving in Texas, and 160 were posted to states outside of Texas. Local churches had 375 volunteers assigned to them, while 140 had positions in Baptist associations and 220 were assigned to or related to the BGCT or its agencies. Others were assigned to work in Baptist encampments, in apartment ministries, and in the criminal justice system. Some volunteers were assigned to schools, especially Hispanic Baptist Theological Seminary. Bill Robbins, a retired professor at Howard Payne College and his wife Ruth were assigned to the small Yellowstone Baptist College in Montana where Robbins served for a time as president. One report said, "The 806 MSCs serving in Texas provide almost $25 million annually in ministry and service."[30] From the first, over 40% of MSC volunteers in the entire SBC came from Texas, and in some years that figure approached 50%.[31] Despite the vast growth in the number of volunteers, Pearis reported that there were 400 unfilled requests for volunteers in Texas alone at the end of 1995.[32]

A part of MSC work from 1982 through 1987 was "Laity Abroad," an effort to identify those persons, especially military personnel, whose work took them overseas. The plan was to enlist and train these persons to share their Christian faith. Another dimension of this was called "God's New Envoys," which involved persons who sought to live and work overseas with the specific intent to start churches. They would be trained as missionaries but also trained in some secular occupation. It was hoped that they could go to some countries where missionaries were not allowed. A similar effort was renamed "Baptists Living/Traveling Abroad" in 1990 and continued until 1992 when the FMB backed off from the idea. The HMB's "Tentmaker" program is a stateside version of this plan for missionaries to work at secular occupations while doing mission work, and it has grown rapidly. By 1997, fully one-third of Baptist home missionaries at work in America were volunteers with Mission Service Corps.[33] The oldest known MSC volunteer was 95 year old Lola Mae Daniel. "It's never too late to serve if the Lord is calling," said the former missionary to China, who in 1997 was teaching English and the Bible to a group of Chinese women in the international department of Austin's Hyde Park Baptist Church.[34]

Jewette McLaughlin (Mrs. Charles) in 1985 coordinated the overseas MSC assignments. She was followed by Re Jackson (1987), Dorothy Miller (1988), Jacque Hughes (1988-1995), and Barbette Ganza (after 1995). A major part of the overseas assignments involved the ESL program (English as a second language), especially in China.

A unique feature of the MSC volunteer program was Volunteers in Annuity and Stewardship Planning (VASP). In the 1980s Pearis was troubled by the low retirement income of church staff members, and by the fact that in Texas many ministers still did not participate in the Annuity Board retirement plans. In consultation with Ed Schmeltekopf, associate executive director of the Executive Board, and Frank Schwall of the Annuity Board, it was decided to develop a network of MSC volunteers seeking to promote the Annuity Board's retirement plans and enlist more Texas ministers to participate. The volunteers met with ministers at association meetings, worked with local church committees, and consulted with churches that wanted to participate but felt they could not afford it. Charles McLaughlin, retired Director of the SMC, was enlisted to direct the program and the first VASP volunteers were trained in 1990.

The MSC program grew so rapidly that the work load could no longer be handled with only two full-time paid staff and seven volunteers in the MSC office in the Baptist Building. In 1993 the Board approved the addition of two more paid staff, with salaries to come from the Mary Hill Davis offering.

New Paradigms for Global Missions. By the 1990s it was obvious that Baptists were developing new ways for doing global missions and Texas was leading the way. There was a growing feeling that traditional "board missions" was not the only way to share the gospel. Many were no longer content just to write a check, to give "at long distance" and never see directly the results of their gifts. More people wanted to become personally involved, to go on mission, and take a "hands on" approach. T. A. Patterson launched the Japan New Life Crusade in 1963 and the Rio Grande River Ministry in 1967, both of which depended upon volunteers going in person to a mission field. These two experiments in new ways of doing "foreign" and "home" missions had far-reaching influence upon Baptists, and may go down as Patterson's greatest achievements. They demonstrated that people will go when the opportunity is presented, that volunteers can make a worthwhile contribution on the field, and that churches will respond to an exciting new form of missions with people, money, and enthusiasm. Changes in society also facilitated the new methods. Better travel makes the entire world more accessible, economic prosperity gave the people more resources to work with, and people who retire in good health with a secure pension provide a ready pool of volunteers. The new missions paradigms mushroomed and within a few years several avenues of volunteer missions had emerged, and more are in the works.

Texas has long provided almost half the MSC volunteers, but other states and even some associations have followed. By 1997 several other

Baptist state conventions had entered partnerships with a number of nations in Europe and Latin America. Clearly there is a new burst of interest and excitement in this new approach to global missions.

Still another approach to global missions, as old as the Apostle Paul but receiving more attention lately, is the local church sending its own missionaries. In a day of affluence, when even a moderately sized church may have a multiple staff, adding an overseas missionary to the local church staff is entirely feasible and more churches are doing just that. In 1997 Michael Stroope, a twenty-year veteran with the IMB (the old FMB), resigned to start a new missions agency to help local churches appoint and send their own missionaries.[35] Stroope and his wife Kay are native Texans. The new agency, called All Peoples, will not be a sending agency but will, according to Stroope, "assist churches to send out their own long-term missionary teams" by helping make legal, travel and living arrangements for the new appointees. By cutting out some of the red tape of the more traditional mission boards, All Peoples hopes to increase the number of Christian witnesses on foreign fields. "What we've learned in the past 10 years," said Stroope, "is that the whole thing (sharing the gospel) won't be done by 4,000 or 6,000 missionaries. We must mobilize the whole church. The money is there, the personnel are there, but the commission is no longer owned by the church. It's been given to a centralized board. The church must take back its [Great] Commission."[36] Stroope seemed to regard this as a supplement rather than a replacement for traditional missions, but critics profess to hear in the All Peoples group echoes from the "Gospel Mission" movement of T.P. Crawford from a century ago.

SCHOOLS AND STUDENTS

The Christian Education Coordinating Board (CECB) was the agency responsible to oversee the work and funding of eight colleges and universities, one academy, and the extensive Baptist Student ministries on well over 100 campuses in Texas. For many years the head of the CECB was Lester L. Morriss who served Texas Baptists in several leadership posts for a half-century. He was pastor of FBC, Midland before becoming Director of the Evangelism Division for the BGCT. He had also been chairman of the Executive Board, president of the Texas Baptist Training Union Convention, and a member of significant committees. Largely at the initiative of Jimmy Landes, who wanted a change of leadership in the Evangelism Department, Morriss was named to succeed Woodson Armes as head of the Christian Education Coordinating Board, though Morriss's ministry had never put him in close connection with Texas Baptist colleges.

When Morriss retired in 1985, Bill Pinson and the search committee looked immediately to a popular and gifted young educator, Jerry F. Dawson, president of East Texas Baptist University in Marshall. A native of the Panhandle town of Borger, Dawson attended Wayland Baptist College (now University) in Plainview, and later received a B.A. degree from Mississippi College. He also earned the M.A. (1958) and Ph.D. (1964) from the University of Texas in Austin. A historian by training, Dawson has taught at Mississippi College, the University of Texas, and the University of Northern Colorado. From 1960-1968 he was chairman of the history department of Wayland Baptist College, and from 1968-1971 was professor of history at Texas A&M University in College Station. In 1971 he accepted the position of dean of the graduate school and professor of history at Southwest Texas State University, where he served until he became president of East Texas Baptist in 1976. Dawson was the first professional educator to head the Christian Education Coordinating Board. While leading the CECB, Dawson also served for a time as interim president of Dallas Baptist University in 1987-1988. An ordained minister, Dawson served student pastorates while he was in college and has been interim pastor of more than 60 churches since 1960. His professional memberships and honors are numerous. A recognized scholar as well as skilled administrator, Dawson is fluent in the German language and has delivered over twenty lectureships at universities and professional societies, has written numerous articles, and is author of five books. Dawson and his wife Margie have two sons and a daughter.

Upon recommendation by the search committee, Dawson was elected unanimously by the Executive Board on September 10, 1985. In secret ballot, committee members were asked to write their first choice for the office of CECB coordinator and, according to the minutes, "Each person had as number one the name of Dr. Jerry Dawson. He is a preacher, teacher, administrator, president—a gifted individual who is a Christian gentleman."[37] The supportive personality and mission interests of Mrs. Dawson, Margie, were also noted. Dawson headed the CECB during a time of unusual challenge and progress. After eleven years as head of the CECB, Dawson retired in 1997 but remained on call as a consultant.

Despite recommendations of the ill-fated Carden Report in 1968, the universities have remained fixed with none closed and no new ones formed. The Texas Baptist schools and their presidents in this period included: Baylor University at Waco, Herbert H. Reynolds, 1981-1995; Robert B. Sloan, Jr., since 1995; Dallas Baptist University, Dallas, W. Marvin Watson, 1979-1987; Gary R. Cook, since 1988; East Texas Baptist University, Marshall, Jerry F. Dawson, 1976-1985; Harvey D. Lewis, acting president 1985-1986, 1992; Robert F. Craig, 1986-1992; Bob F. Riley, since 1992; Hardin-Simmons University, Abilene, Jesse C. Fletcher, 1977-1991; Lanny Hall, since 1991; Houston Baptist University, Houston, William H. Hinton, 1960-1987; E. D. Hodo, since 1987; Howard Payne University, Brownwood, Ralph A. Phelps, Jr., 1980-1985; Don Newbury, 1985-1997; Rick Gregory, since 1997; University of Mary Hardin-Baylor, Belton, Bobby E. Parker, 1971-1991; Jerry G. Bawcom, since 1991; Wayland Baptist University, Plainview, David L. Jester, 1981-1987; Glenn E. Barnett, acting president 1988-1989; Lanny Hall, 1989-1991; Wallace E. Davis, since 1991; and San Marcos Baptist Academy, San Marcos, Jack E. Byrom, 1965-1996; Paul W. Armes, since 1996.

These presidents were elected by, and were responsible to, their own university trustees, but occasionally others put in an opinion. A few zealous brethren tried to deny funding to Wayland Baptist University during the eighteen months that Glenn E. Barnett served as acting president. Their complaint was that Barnett, who had served 16 years as Dean of the School of Education at Texas Tech University in Lubbock, was a Methodist layman. Their mini-protest lost steam, however, when the Executive Board refused to intervene and when it became obvious that Barnett had done an excellent job, helping put the Plainview school back on a solid footing after several disastrous years.

In the minutes of the Executive Board for September 9, 1988, one reads that "Jerry Dawson reported that the [educational] institutions are in good shape." Coming to head the CECB in 1985, Dawson had the good fortune to work with the Texas Baptist universities during some of their best years. His optimistic assessment in 1988 could apply equally to the entire last quarter of the twentieth century.

Several factors combined to improve the situation of the schools. First, they enjoyed the confidence of the Baptist public as never before. A survey conducted by the CECB in 1984 showed that an overwhelming 99% of Texas Baptists surveyed said that Christian education should remain a high priority for Texas Baptists.[38] Gone were the days when many Baptists, even some of their prominent leaders, publicly questioned the value of the Baptist colleges, suggesting that with ready availability of public colleges, denominational schools had outlived their usefulness. Second, the enrollment of the Baptist universities increased substantially. When Pinson assumed office in 1983, the eight Baptist universities in Texas reported a total enrollment of 28,701 which, combined with 652 students enrolled in the San Marcos Baptist Academy, brought the student population of Texas Baptist schools to 29,353.[39] For the fall semester of 1997, the universities enrolled 31,028, plus 437 in two academies and 373 in Hispanic Baptist Seminary in San Antonio, bringing the total to 31,838.[40] In the 1990s, enrollment in Texas public colleges declined slightly, while junior college enrollments held steady. The only increases came in private schools, and Baptist schools registered about 60% of the growth in private college enrollments in Texas from 1993 to 1997. Counting the number of semester credit hours completed, Baptist university enrollment increased about 6% annually in the 1990s.

Third, and partly as a result of the two factors just cited, the Baptist schools enjoyed a better level of financial support. As noted in a previous chapter, BGCT budgets in the 1960s had diverted funds from the schools to other ministries, but Jimmy Landes and Bill Pinson reversed that trend and helped restore the importance of Christian education in the BGCT budget. Though the Convention allotted a greater percentage of its budget and vastly more dollars to the schools, the Convention funds provided an ever diminishing portion of the annual operating costs of the schools. Their own development departments conducted successful capital funds drives among alumni, wealthy benefactors and benevolent foundations. Better funding allowed the schools to increase the number and quality of faculty, grow in academic strength, offer more study programs and degrees, and provide better facilities. This new prosperity did not put the schools on easy street for, as Dawson reported, "there is a fine line that separates existence from disaster for all our educational institutions except Baylor [which has a greater endowment]."[41] Even so, in the 1980s and 1990s the records are not crowded with crisis accounts of some Baptist school in a financial emergency which threatens to close its doors, as was true in some earlier times. For most parents the old rule of thumb held true, that while the dollar amounts might change over the years, it took just about the cost of a new Buick to send a young person through four years at a Texas Baptist university. Of course, various kinds of scholarships help reduce that cost and, unlike the Buick, the students did not depreciate in value.

Some of the enrollment increases came from ethnic students. From 1992 to 1996 there was a 38% increase in the number of ethnic and minority students enrolled in Texas Baptist colleges, according to Keith Bruce, who succeeded Dawson as head of the CECB in 1997. By 1997, ethnic and minority students made up fully 23% of the enrollment in Texas Baptist schools.[42] Jerry Dawson maintains that the key to a rising enrollment in Texas Baptist universities is the number of new churches started in the state. New churches usually have a higher ratio of members in the 16 to 21 age group and, for whatever reasons, young people from new churches are more likely to attend a Baptist school. He maintains there is a direct link between new churches and Baptist college enrollments, especially for ethnic students. "Take out the students who come from the new churches," said Dawson, "and our Baptist schools in Texas would be in modest decline."[43]

Most of the universities also established satellite branches in other cities. This followed a trend toward decentralization of American education, and enabled some students to enroll who might not otherwise have been able to do so. In some cases regular faculty commuted to teach in the satellite centers, but some schools employed a resident faculty at the study centers. The accrediting agencies established standards for class instruction, library access, and academic procedures but often made generous allowances to accommodate the universities and accredit their programs. Many of these satellite centers were for specific study programs, such as Wayland's police training academy. Mostly the universities established study centers in adjoining cities, but some reached out to other states and even to Hawaii. Some of the satellites put financial strain on the universities (and indirectly on the CECB) but most of them were self-sustaining.

Ministerial Students. Training for ministerial students has always been a high priority for Texas Baptist colleges, and in the last two decades of the twentieth century they had far more such students to educate. By the fall of 1997, about 3,500 students in Texas Baptist schools were preparing for some form of Christian ministry, up from 3,259 in 1996 and 3,033 in

1995.[44] Of the 1997 enrollment, only 1,689 received tuition grants from the BGCT. Thus Texas Baptists have more ministerial students, but fewer who receive tuition aid from the Convention. The ministerial aid amounts to only $40 per semester hour and carries stringent eligibility requirements. Many students can receive far more tuition aid from other grants and scholarships and with less red tape and hoops to jump through. If they sign up for the BGCT grants, they become ineligible for other forms of aid. The tuition grant was raised from $10 to $40 per semester hour in 1989 and has not changed since then.

Several factors help account for the increase in ministerial students from the late 1960s when fewer than 1,000 were reported. The prayerful and persistent seeking for spiritual renewal, so much a part of the leadership plan of Executive Director Bill Pinson, no doubt played a role. The number of ministerial students and their level of commitment provides one helpful barometer of the spiritual health of the churches. There has also been a change in how to define a ministerial student. In the past, only those preparing to be preachers were considered to be ministerial students, but now students preparing for music, educational, or youth ministries are also counted. The BGCT also increased substantially the different kinds of financial aid to black ministerial students and, of course, the Texas WMU continued its practice of providing scholarships for ethnic students.

From time to time questions have been raised as to who is eligible for ministerial tuition grants in Texas Baptist schools, whether "ministers" in the larger sense or only "preacher boys." In 1989 the question took a new turn; would young women students, preparing for some form of ministry be eligible and, if so, would they have to be ordained? C. W. Bess, chairman of the Executive Board, appointed a committee to study "Ministerial Tuition [to determine] if it included men or women who are studying to be missionaries, youth ministers, etc., that do not anticipate ever being licensed or ordained." Julian Shaddix chaired the committee, which included Ophelia Humphrey, David Slover, Leroy Fenton and James Puckett.[45] Jerry Dawson also worked with the committee.

The Shaddix committee asked two questions: (1) Did current practices allow the local church complete autonomy in recognizing divine gifts and call to ministry in individuals in its membership and in certifying those persons as ministerial students? (2) Did current practices provide fairness in providing assistance to all individuals certified as ministerial students by the churches? The committee firmly agreed that it was the *churches,* and not the Convention or the colleges, that determined who was a ministerial student. "Without question," they said, "it was the local church that was the certifying authority as to the divine call of any individual from its membership." The Convention may provide tuition assistance and the university may provide training, but they cannot determine who is and is not a Texas Baptist ministerial student. Only the churches have that prerogative. Applicants for tuition aid must furnish to the university an affirmation of a call to ministry approved by a local church, a written testimony of a call to ministry, and must participate in a testing and counseling program at the university in cooperation with the In-Service Guidance Office of the BGCT. The qualification for aid is reviewed regularly, and its renewal requires that the candidate maintain a Christian lifestyle, participate actively in local church life, and make satisfactory progress toward a degree program.

Some feared that this policy of leaving the certification of ministerial students to the churches might open the door to the ordination of women. The committee report, and the vote of the Executive Board, made it clear that women who met the criteria of a credible call to ministry and certification by their local church would be eligible for ministerial tuition aid on the same basis as men, but that neither men nor women were required to be ordained to qualify. The Board made it clear that they were not advocating the ordination of women, since decisions about ordination belong to the church and not the denomination.

Baptist Student Union. Since 1920 the BSU has addressed the spiritual needs of Baptist students in Texas. Since 1959 the CECB has had oversight of the Division of Student Work, which includes the BSU. Chet Reames succeeded the legendary W. F. Howard as Director of the Division of Student Work and when Reames was killed in an automobile accident, his successor was Jack Greever who served until his retirement in 1995. Tom Ruane, who had been an associate in the department, became Director in 1995 and continues in office at this writing. As of 1996 the department reported 137 Baptist Student Ministry units located in eight Baptist universities, 97 state and community colleges, 16 medical, dental and nursing schools, and 13 private or other denomination schools. Staff for this extensive ministry to students included 55 full-time student directors, five full-time associates, 35 part-time directors and many volunteers. Of the 55 Baptist Student Center buildings on or adjacent to Texas campuses, 24 were owned by the BGCT, 25 by Baptist associations and four by Baptist universities. For the 1995-96 church year, the student department reported 2,591 college students baptized in Texas Baptist churches, over 2,200 involved in student mission ministries, 7,800 participating in Bible study programs, 3,750 in Christian witness training programs, and 150 college campuses reporting an evangelistic emphasis in 1996. For years the students had been an integral part of volunteer missions in Texas and beyond, in the River Ministry, Partnership Missions, and other student projects.[46]

One interesting student department program was called BEACH REACH, in which students took special training to prepare them to witness and minister to the crowds of college students who crowded the Texas beaches during Spring Break, especially at Padre Island. In the summer of 1996 they reported 121 professed conversions at Padre Island.[47] Texas students are also expected to be deeply involved in the Baptist World Alliance Youth Conference, scheduled for Houston in 1998.

The Bible Chairs, long a basic part of the BSU campus ministry, faced new challenges in the 1980s. Texas Attorney General Jim Mattox issued a

382 TEXAS BAPTISTS: A Sesquicentennial History

ruling in 1985 that state colleges could no longer offer Bible classes for credit. On the basis of that ruling, several state universities canceled the denominational Bible chairs and others planned to do so. However, Mattox, a Southern Baptist layman, later reversed this ruling and held out "the possibility that, within certain guidelines to preserve the separation of church and state, 'Bible Chair' programs may continue to offer religious courses to state college and university students."[48]

Despite its capable leadership and solid programs, the public image of BSU suffered somewhat in modern times and it never involved a majority of Baptist students on Texas campuses. The BSU was sometimes perceived as *traditional* in a non-traditional time and it was distinctly *denominational* in an era increasingly ecumenical. Several non-denominational groups competed on campus for student affiliation and some of them seemed exciting and innovative. A committee chaired by Michael Dean, pastor at Travis Avenue church in Fort Worth, made a year-long study of the BSU and came up with far-reaching recommendations, including a name change. The Baptist Student Union (BSU) became the Department of Student Ministry (BSM) and its work and relationship to churches and associations was more sharply defined. Changing the name, the committee said, would help change the image. "The term 'union,'" they said, "is no longer in contemporary usage on college campuses." They wanted a more inclusive name, reflecting ministries to Baptist and non-Baptist students. In 1994 the Executive Board also authorized an ongoing Student Ministry Committee "to give leadership and direction" to the BSM."[49]

Since the Dean committee study, BSM has made a considerable turnaround. Student participation is up and more students volunteer for summer mission activities. According to a recent UCLA survey, the number of American college students listing a "Baptist preference" in religion increased from 14% to 19% between 1990 and 1997, and those answering yes to the question "Are you a born again Christian" increased from about 19% to 29% during the same years. Leaders of the Texas Baptist student work interpret these as promising trends.

HOSPITALS AND HOMES

By 1994 the Human Welfare Coordinating Board (HWCB) gave oversight to seven hospitals, four children's homes and five homes for the aged.[50] When Bill Pinson took office in 1983, Max L. Brown was the Coordinator of this Board. He was succeeded in 1988 by Dwayne Martin, who served until 1994. In 1994, the Executive Board named A. Edward Rogers to head the HWCB and he continues in office at this writing. A graduate of Howard Payne University, and with both masters and doctors degrees from Southwestern Seminary, Rogers served for 34 years as pastor of FBC in Dumas, during which time he held many Texas Baptist leadership posts, including chairman of the trustees of the HWCB, member of the Executive Director Search Committee that recommended Bill Pinson, and chairman of the building committee that erected the present magnificent Baptist Building. Rogers reported that in 1996 these hospitals and homes gave some form of care to almost two million persons. Almost 25,000 employees staffed the institutions, which were directed by twelve dedicated administrators and 241 trustees.

Hospitals. As noted earlier, the BGCT did not so much *own* the hospitals as *sponsor* them. Most of them received an ever diminishing share of their annual operating expenses ($2.6 billion in 1996) from the denomination, though the Convention did pay for the chaplaincy programs involving more than fifty chaplains in the hospitals and homes.

The increase in the number of public hospitals after World War II led some to doubt the need for Baptists to continue their involvement in hospital ministry. However, by the 1990s the Baptist hospitals seemed to supply an urgent need in American health care that made them at least as relevant to Christian ministry as ever. The rapidly changing conditions of American health care raised serious moral concerns. More people realized the human body is more than an intricate network of "physical plumbing," and that physical and spiritual wellness are related. Profound ethical questions are faced daily in any major hospital, and almost all hospitals, church related and public, have an ethics committee whatever its exact name. Important as the chaplaincy programs are, not all moral and religious concerns are limited to the chaplain's office. In this supercharged atmosphere of both ancient and modern moral concerns, the Christian stance and Christian values of the Baptist hospital seem even more relevant and necessary than ever.

One persistent moral issue that has affected the hospitals, as it has the CLC and every aspect of Baptist life, is the question of abortion. A motion was offered at the 1995 Texas Convention to forbid any abortion to be performed "on the premises of, or under the auspices or authority or tolerance of, any Texas Baptist medical institution or agency, except where such abortion is necessary to save the life of the mother." This motion was referred to the HWCB, which reported in 1996 that they had been essentially following this policy already. "The Baptist General Convention of Texas has repeatedly stated its belief in the sanctity of life and its opposition to abortion on demand," the HWCB reported. However, they said, "there has been the allowance for the rare exception of termination of the pregnancy in the case of rape, incest, or the imminent danger to the life of the mother." In the rare crisis cases where abortion is considered, they reported, there is an extensive review of the case by both chaplains and medical personnel.[51]

Child Care Homes. Reports that Texas Baptists sponsored four children's homes could be misleading, for some of the homes, especially Buckner Baptist Benevolences, operated several campuses reported as one unit. In recent years the homes deal more with neglected and dependent children rather than true orphans. For 1996 the cost of operation of the homes came to $25.9 million, of which about $3.2 million came from the BGCT. That year the homes had 689 employees, of whom three were chaplains. In 1996 the homes completed only 16 adoptions, and reported 446 professions of faith.[52]

In its second century, Buckner Baptist Benevolences developed into one of the most far-reaching and effective social ministry agencies in the nation with an extensive network of institutions. These included, of course, children's homes but ranged far beyond that. They included several homes for the aged, family services programs, assessment centers, client assistance programs, foster care programs, counseling centers, maternity and adoption services, along with Camp Buckner in Burnet, a unique Christian summer camp for children ages 6 to 14. They also branched overseas, with child care ministries in some of the war-torn countries of Eastern Europe where children bore so much of the pain of war.

Homes for the Aged. One of the most rapidly growing segments of the American population is the over 65 group, and Texas Baptists have moved to help meet their physical and spiritual needs. In 1996 the HWCB reported 2,998 residents and patients cared for in the five homes for the aged, of whom 1,723 were resident retirees, 735 receiving intermediate care and 540 skilled nursing care. Texas Baptists also established homes for physically and mentally challenged persons, seeking always to identify people needs and in the spirit of Christ trying to meet those needs.

In the 1980s the Baptist homes for the aged teetered on the brink of bankruptcy, but in the 1990s they are fiscally sound. They have proven their value, offering secure living conditions in pleasant surroundings and with appropriate levels of medical care and assisted living.

Special Needs. In 1997 the San Antonio based Baptist Children's Home launched a new venture, Breckenridge Village in Tyler, to care for "individuals between 18 and 50 who are mildly to moderately retarded." Such persons comprise a significant sub-group in the population and their ministry needs are substantial. The San Antonio home received a favorable vote of the Executive Board to enter this new field, and to adopt a new umbrella name to accommodate it. Obviously it would sound awkward for a "children's home" to operate a facility for adults, so the Baptist Child and Family Services was created, and the Baptist Children's Home Ministries (BCHM) and Breckenridge Village will operate as subsidiaries.

Breckenridge Village is named for Mrs. Jean Breckenridge who donated the land and other gifts in honor of her son Jimmy who was born with Down Syndrome. The plan calls for several residences, each housing about eight adults and a house parent in a Christian home environment. To the extent they are able, residents will participate in household chores, hold outside employment, and participate in community activities such as church, movies, dining, and shopping. Even before the facility is fully operational, widespread interest has created a lengthy waiting list. Breckenridge Village is no doubt a sign of things to come as Texas Baptists respond to the specialized needs of different segments of the population.

FACING MORAL CONCERNS

The Christian Life Commission (CLC) is the BGCT agency responsible to speak on the issues of moral concern, with emphasis on applying the Christian faith to the issues of daily life. Certainly the 1980s and 1990s provided no shortage of challenges for Christians who wanted to practice the teachings of Jesus Monday through Saturday, as well as on Sunday. "Our culture is having foundation problems with hairline cracks," said one report, while another noted that "Quarter-horse ranches were going up everywhere in the Hill Country" preparing for the debut of horse-race gambling in Texas.[53]

Phil D. Strickland has been on the CLC staff since 1967, and head of the commission since 1980. An Abilene native, Strickland did undergraduate study at both Baylor and the University of Texas, and received his law degree from the UT Law School in 1966. He later did graduate study in theology at the Southwestern Seminary in Fort Worth. Before joining the CLC staff, he served as legislative assistant to the Lieutenant Governor of Texas, did legal work for Southwestern Seminary, and practiced law in Fort Worth. He served as an official consultant to the White House and has been active in community, educational and benevolence causes in Texas and beyond. Strickland has been recognized for outstanding work in relation to children, in seeking to combat child abuse, promote child protective services, and seeking to achieve adequate nutrition, medical care, and emotional support for poor children in Texas. He and his wife Carolyn live in Dallas, where they are active in the Wilshire Baptist Church.

The six areas of responsibility assigned to the CLC are family life, race relations, Christian citizenship, daily work, moral issues and religious liberty. The CLC has led major programs in each of these areas. Strickland has led the CLC to monitor the state legislature on laws affecting the moral and physical well being of Texans. They have maintained an active lobby against gambling, the liquor traffic, race discrimination, the narcotics problem, gang violence, abortion on demand and all forms of child abuse. Currently, Strickland serves as chairman of CARE, a coalition of over fifty organizations that address the needs of children in Texas. Not content just to oppose evil, they have also promoted positive and redemptive steps to help counteract these problems. With his legal background, Strickland has emphasized public issues, especially religious liberty, separation of church and state, fairness in employment and housing, and world hunger. In 1986 the CLC helped sponsor the Texas Baptist Farm Crisis Task Force to deal with the economic crisis of the farming economy.

From their early days, Texas Baptists have spoken out on issues of personal moral conduct. In modern times they have not neglected the importance of individuals behaving morally, but have added to that an emphasis upon *public* morality. Leaders like Jimmy Allen, James Dunn, and especially Phil Strickland have emphasized not only the moral behavior of individuals but have also opposed immoral and damaging conditions in society that damage people's lives. The Texas CLC has maintained a presence in Austin to lobby for laws that help people, especially children, and to oppose laws and social conditions that hurt people, weaken families, and increase conflict.

As a part of Texas 2000, the CLC launched "Hope for Home," a major emphasis on improving family life. Citing frightful statistics on problems facing Texas families, Phil Strickland and Mike Lundy, who is in charge of the family life section, obtained additional funding to train about 100 Certified Family Ministry Consultants. These consultants will in turn enlist and train hundreds of Texas Baptist church members as Family Ministry Corps to work with troubled families in trying to help them deal with problems that already exist and seeking to make decisions to prevent future problems. The goal is to have in place by A.D. 2000 a force of 750 Family Ministry Corps with ongoing ministries in 800 churches. These highly trained volunteers are expected to work in such areas as marriage counseling, helping people move off welfare into the work force, helping young couples learn parenting skills, work with youth to reduce teen pregnancy, helping senior adults who find themselves rearing their grandchildren, and developing programs of guidance for latchkey children.

Because of the nature of their work, especially in the realm of public morality, the CLC has been a lightning rod in Baptist life, attracting their share of opposition. They have been sorely criticized at times for what they did and what they did not do. Perhaps the moral dilemma of abortion has led to as many criticisms, Convention resolutions, and efforts to chastise or defund the CLC as any other issue. In a major statement on "The Sanctity of Life," the CLC strongly defended the principle that all life is a gift of God and therefore infinitely precious, and they strongly condemned abortion on demand, abortion for trivial reasons like gender preference or for birth control, and late term abortions. However, following the historic position of Southern Baptists, in extremely rare crisis cases like rape, incest and imminent threat to the life of the mother, the Texas CLC refused to condemn all abortions without any possibility of exception. Those who oppose any abortion for any reason have been unsparing in their criticism of the Texas CLC.

Southern Baptists have always opposed abortion, but have usually allowed some possibility of exception under certain crisis conditions. Not many years ago this was the usual stance of the most conservative as well as less conservative Southern Baptists. Even W. A. Criswell, longtime pastor of FBC in Dallas and a major architect of the rightward tilt of the SBC, expressed approval of the 1973 *Roe v Wade* Supreme Court ruling permitting abortion. In his sesquicentennial history of Southern Baptists, Jesse C. Fletcher quoted David Beale, a fundamentalist historian, who said, "Following the 1973 pro-abortion ruling of the U.S. Supreme Court, Dr. Criswell publicly expressed satisfaction." A Religious News Service in Dallas quoted Criswell as saying, "I have always felt that it was only after a child was born and had life separate from the mother, that it became an individual person, and it has always, therefore, seemed to me that what is best for the mother and for the future should be allowed." Beale says that Criswell confirmed to him by telephone that this was indeed his view. An authorized biography of Criswell, published with his cooperation and approval, also confirms Criswell's approval at that time of abortion under some circumstances.[54]

Relations between the Texas CLC and their national counterpart at the SBC in Nashville have been more distant since the ultraconservatives took control of the SBC. The Texas and national bodies take different views on several topics, especially on religious liberty and separation of church and state. In 1988 the Texas CLC took strong exception to published statements from the annual meeting of the national CLC, labeling Martin Luther King, Jr. as a "fraud," affirming that "apartheid in South Africa . . . doesn't exist anymore and was beneficial when it did," and implying a cynical view of world hunger by the statement of one CLC trustee that "starvation has been used since time immemorial to control people."[55] These harsh views were expressed by individual trustees and never represented official policy of the national body. The Texas CLC expressed serious concern about these views, which they called "a radical departure from the historic positions of both the Southern Baptist Convention and the Texas Baptist Christian Life Commissions." In a bit of unsolicited advice, the Texas group urged the SBC body "to express their support of policies that reflect clear opposition to racism, support of peace with justice, commitment to minister to the poor and hungry and affirmation of the historic Baptist understanding of church-state separation."[56]

The Texas CLC has become known for the excellence and depth of its research. Not content merely to "speak out" on issues, Strickland and his associates gather and analyze extensive data on specific moral problems and how they affect the citizens of Texas. Public officials have been known to call upon the research and statistics gathered by the CLC in helping to shape legislation and public polity in Texas. This research also strengthens the printed educational materials the CLC issues for the churches.

STRENGTHENING TEXAS CHURCHES

The State Missions Commission of the Executive Board relates most directly to the churches, with the twin assignment to help strengthen existing churches and start new ones. The largest of the Board's several agencies, the SMC provided overall guidance for the work of direct missions, church extension, church building planning, Black church development, the Rio Grande River Ministry, evangelism, Sunday School and Discipleship training, church music ministries, stewardship emphases, and coordination of ministries with various ethnic groups. The SMC also coordinates the disaster relief services which includes family assistance, church building assistance, counseling, and the mobile feeding units provided by Texas Baptist Men. This commission also provides a point of contact between the BGCT and the Minnesota-Wisconsin Convention, and serves as a channel of communication and correlation between the BGCT and the 113 Baptist associations and their associational and area directors of missions (DOMs). They also provide communication in cooperative efforts with the Texas Baptist Men, the Texas Woman's Missionary Union, Partnership Missions and Mission Service Corps.

The remarkably gifted Charles P. McLaughlin worked in the SMC for almost thirty years, heading the agency from 1964 to 1988. Born in Rotan, Texas, "Charlie" McLaughlin graduated from Hardin-Simmons University in Abilene, and completed studies in religious education and church music at Southwestern Seminary in Fort Worth. From 1941 to 1950 he served as minister of music and education at three churches, including Sagamore Hill in Fort Worth. During World War II McLaughlin was a B-24 pilot, flying combat missions out of England. He was interned as a POW for a time in Sweden. After the war McLaughlin spent ten years on the staff of Tarrant Baptist Association, first as director of education and later as superintendent of missions. This gave him invaluable experience for work with the state convention beginning in 1960. McLaughlin's denominational service and work on various committees are too extensive to list. He and his wife Jewette have been a part of almost every good thing Texas Baptists have done over the past forty years. After retirement from the SMC, McLaughlin served as minister of education of FBC in Dallas and continued to take occasional denominational assignments. He is still referred to as "Mr. State Missions" in Texas. When the BGCT met in El Paso in 1937, "Cowboy" Joe Evans, a prominent West Texas layman, rode a horse into the meeting hall; in 1986 they drove a car into the meeting place, a gift to retiring Charles McLaughlin.[57]

In 1988 the Executive Board turned to the popular pastor of FBC, Lubbock, to succeed McLaughlin as head of the SMC. D. L. Lowrie was a Tennessee native, but most of his pastorates were in Texas, including FBC, Lorenzo, 1962-1964; Calvary, Lubbock, 1964-67; North Fort Worth, 1967-1976; FBC, Texarkana, 1976-1980; and FBC, Lubbock, 1980-1988. Lowrie brought extensive denominational experience to his new work, having served as chairman of the Executive Board, 1980-1981, and president of the BGCT, 1982-1984. He resigned as head of the SMC in 1988 to become executive director/treasurer of the state convention in his native Tennessee. Presently he is back in Texas in a second tenure as pastor of FBC, Lubbock.

When the State Missions Commission sought a new leader in 1988 only one person was interviewed: James H. Semple, pastor of FBC, Paris, for twenty-five years. As a successful Texas pastor since 1953, Semple had proven himself to be an effective leader, a loyal denominationalist, and a Baptist statesman of stature. He was unanimously recommended by the search committee, the Administrative Committee, and by the Executive Board, and took office on January 1, 1989. Semple's ministry in Paris from 1963-1988 helped draw the attention of the Executive Board. In Paris, the church gave 20% of receipts through the Cooperative Program despite extensive building projects, increased Sunday School enrollment by 130%, and showed strong growth through evangelism. A recognized leader, Semple has over the years served on most of the major Convention boards and committees. In 1987 Semple received the Home Mission Board award as Outstanding Evangelistic Pastor of a Multi-Staff Church. His various denominational assignments have also included being parliamentarian for the SBC and also for the BGCT. Semple is a native of Miami, Florida, and graduated from Stetson University and he holds both masters and doctoral degrees from Southwestern Seminary. He and his wife Betty, who is also from Miami, have six children.

E. Eugene Greer served in the important post of Program Planning Director of the SMC from 1974 until his retirement in 1992. He then became a special consultant for the Church Recreation Department and a MSC volunteer. An avid sportsman and runner, Greer also served as a Sports Evangelism Consultant. A multi-talented man whose knowledge of the inner workings of the BGCT and the Executive Board are extensive, Greer continues since 1997 as special assistant to the executive director.

Other leaders in the SMC as of 1996 included Jimmy Garcia III, Ethnic Missions Coordinator; Omar Pachecano, President, Hispanic Baptist Theological Seminary; Daniel J. Rivera, President, Valley Baptist Academy; H. Bailey Stone, Jr., Director, Evangelism Division; Herbert L. Pedersen, Director, Missions Division Administration; James W. Culp, Sr., Coordinator, Black Church Development; W. L. Walters, Director, Church Building Planning Department; E. B. Brooks, Director, Church Extension Department; Milfred Minatrea, Director, Church Ministries Department; Winford Oakes, Director, Creative Church Development Department; Lynn Eckeberger, Director, Rio Grande River Ministry Department; Richard Faling, Director, Church Services Division, William Jan Daehnert, Director, Bivocational/Smaller Church Development; Don McCall, Director, Church Music Department; Bobby L. Eklund, Director, Church Stewardship Department; Bernard M. Spooner, Director, Sunday School/ Discipleship Division; and Bill Arnold, President, Texas Baptist Missions Foundation.[58] The State Missions Commission also works closely with two auxiliaries, the Woman's Missionary Union and Texas Baptist Men.

NEW CHURCHES IN TEXAS

During Bill Pinson's administration, "the churches first" has been more than a motto; it has undergirded every agency and action. The Convention exists to help the churches, not the other way around. However, by the 1980s Pinson became convinced that the Convention needed to put more emphasis on starting new churches. In 1985 he said, "Most of the [BGCT] budget presently goes for helping existing churches. Strengthening their programs, ministering to them in training. We are doing all that is possible to see that they are equipped to do the tasks to which they have been called." He had no intention to diminish that work, but added, "There must be an emphasis for starting new churches in Texas. There is daily evidence that this is the course to follow."[59] Not all agreed. A prominent Texas pastor said at the Evangelism Conference, "Texas Baptists don't need new churches. We need to fill up the churches we have." However, many of the churches proved difficult to fill because the people moved away, and at the same time countless new communities have grown up with no Baptist church.

Pinson persisted in his relentless drive to start new churches, leading the BGCT to direct more personnel and funds to that effort. The new church emphasis has become a major feature, and a major success story, of Pinson's administration. MISSION TEXAS (1985-1990) had a goal to start 2000 new churches, which was exceeded, and Texas 2000 (1995-2000) has a goal of starting at least 1,400 new churches by A.D. 2000, or about 300 new churches per year. As of 1997, they were ahead of schedule.

Texas was the first Baptist state convention to have a Church Extension Department with a full-time director in charge of starting new churches, preceding even the Home Mission Board in that work. The "Key Church" program was also pioneered in Texas. J V Thomas came to head the new department in 1969 and helped determine where new churches were needed, obtained sites, and helped get the new work launched. With the beginning of MISSION TEXAS in 1985 church planting was greatly accelerated. The new churches were largely funded through the Mary Hill Davis offering, and about half of the new starts were ethnic churches. The Baptist Church Loan Corporation helped with the financing. The WMU sponsored a special "way above normal" Mary Hill Davis centennial offering in 1985 which sought to triple the offering given in 1984, and triple again in 1986, to raise $30 million for new church starts. The SMC helped set up a MHD Centennial Offering Coordinating office to guide this massive effort.[60] Starting new churches preceded so rapidly that the SMC experienced a temporary cash flow shortage. They agreed to limit property purchases to no more than five acres and agreed to provide financial supplements to new churches for no more than five years. J V Thomas reported that in 1985 there were 99 sites for new churches that had loans with the Baptist Church Loan Corporation. They were using the "Key Church" concept by which strong churches agreed to sponsor several missions each.[61] By 1997 there were 144 such key churches in Texas.

An expansion of the "Key Church" concept led to a new department called the Creative Church Development. The plan, it was said, grew out of a coffee shop conversation in Fort Worth between J V Thomas and Joel Gregory, then pastor at Travis Avenue. The idea was that if churches can employ church staff ministers to help bring people into the church, why not develop staff specialists to send people out of church, that is, to go out intentionally to start new churches. A new department was formed to do just that, headed by Win Oakes from 1993 until his retirement in 1997. His successor was Jim Burgin, former minister of missions in Georgia and Texas. A graduate of Baylor University and Southwestern Seminary,

Burgin was previously active in Mission Arlington. His mother, Tillie, is Minister of Missions (MOM) at FBC Arlington, and has received national recognition for her work in apartment ministry. The three program assignments of this department are Key Churches, Multi-housing, and Missions Development. Burgin seeks to lead churches to add a "minister of missions" on their staff, and he helps train these mission specialists, providing encouragement and materials for their use. The BGCT also helps supplement the salaries of these church starting specialists on a reducing scale for up to three years. Burgin reports that presently Key Churches with a minister of missions on staff make up only about 2% of Texas Baptist churches, but those churches start about 40% of the new churches in Texas.

Changes in the Texas population came so rapidly that many had trouble keeping up with the new landscape. Many assumed that Texas was largely a Christian state, but by the 1990s at least half the population was not related to any church. Others assumed that Texas was predominantly Baptist, and sometimes called it the Baptist Zion. That was never really accurate, and by the 1990s Baptists related to the BGCT composed less than 14% of the state's population, and in the large cities much less. With 5,695 congregations reported in 1996[62] one might assume that Texas was well blanketed with Baptist churches, but that was not the case. Many of the churches were small and declining because of population shifts. Countless villages and towns which once had flourishing Baptist churches by the 1990s found those churches struggling to maintain attendance and programs. Meantime, new suburbs sprang up almost overnight and the cities expanded in every direction, creating new communities with no Baptist church.

Untold thousands of immigrants from all parts of the world swarmed into Texas, creating a vast need for additional witness and new churches. Demographic experts predicted that Anglos would make up only 55% of the state's population by 2000 A.D., and that Hispanics would outnumber Anglos by A.D. 2025.[63] A *Baptist Standard* article said, "Today's Texas is a multi-cultural, religiously pluralistic, greatly diverse state. It is also a largely unchurched state. At least half of its population claims no church affiliation whatsoever. Reaching out with the gospel to the Texan of today means speaking in more than 100 different languages and dialects. It means crossing cultural, racial and economic barriers."[64] Bill Arnold, president of the Texas Baptist Missions Foundation, pointed out that in 1960 Texas Baptists had 45 Baptist churches for every 100,000 population, but by 1995 that ratio had dropped to 30 churches per 100,000.[65] Despite the numbers of new churches formed, the state's population growth was even more rapid. Pinson and Semple certainly recognized these needs, and the SMC devoted money and manpower to make church planting a major priority.

E. B. Brooks has been director of the BGCT Church Extension Department in the Missions Division of the SMC since 1989. Before that he was Director of Weekday Ministries for the Dallas Baptist Association (1977-1978) and consultant in Christian Social Ministries and Interfaith

Witness (1979-1988). Brooks directs the work of nine field consultants who help churches and associations to start new churches, and he also supervises four "Catalytic Missionaries" who specialize in beginning new churches among various ethnic groups. He oversees the Land Site Purchase Program and the No Interest Loan Program for the development of facilities for new and low income churches.

Brooks reported that 160 new churches had been started in the first half of 1997, with over twice as many Hispanic as Anglo new church starts. For the 1996-1997 church year, Brooks reported 73 new Hispanic churches, compared to 48 Anglo, 30 African-American and three Korean. Other church starts included Arabic, Chinese, Filipino, Russian and Vietnamese. Among more than 62,000 Indians in Texas, Baptists had about 15 congregations by 1997, some of them dating from the 1960s. There are six new missions among the Indians, including the American Indian Christian Fellowship in Lubbock.[66] The other recently formed Indian missions are in Fort Worth, Dallas, Houston, Waco and Abilene.

One report shows that the BGCT assisted in forming 3,177 new churches from 1980 to 1997.[67] These included 1,104 Anglo, 928 Hispanic, 344 African American, 103 Korean, 46 mixed or multiethnic, 23 Chinese, 16 Vietnamese, 13 Deaf, 10 Ethiopian, 10 Laotian, 9 Filipino, 8 Cambodian, 7 each of Arabic, Asian, Native American, and Russian, 6 African National, 4 Japanese, 4 Jewish Christian, 2 Romanian, 2 Russian, and one each of Haitian, English Hispanic, English Korean, Khurdish, Liberian, Micronesian, Nigerian, and Polish. These were not all the church starts. Many began with no Convention involvement.

Not all new churches survive. The mortality rate in Texas is about 30%, compared to the national average of about 50%. Newly founded ethnic churches tend to be especially fragile. Brooks tries to reduce the mortality rate by good feasibility studies to see where churches are really needed, by enlisting capable leadership, and by careful financial help that avoids creating dependency.

CRIMINAL JUSTICE MINISTRIES

"I was in prison and you came to me" (Mt. 25:36, RSV). With this example, Jesus included prisoners in his redemptive circle and showed his disciples that ministering to them is a form of ministry to Christ. When Texas Baptists say that by A.D. 2000 they intend to share the gospel with every person in the state, they mean *every* person and that includes almost a quarter of a million inmates in Texas reform schools, jails, and prisons. It is commonly reported that Texas has the third largest prison system in the world, behind only China and the former Soviet Union. Texas locks up a higher percentage of its citizens than any other society on earth. Texas Baptists have long sought to minister to the prison population and their families, by providing chaplains and sponsoring various religious and social ministries both inside and outside the prison walls. One of the pio-

neer ministries in this area was sponsored by Bill Glass, a graduate of Baylor University and Southwestern Seminary, and former professional football player.

A serious problem in Texas prisons, as elsewhere, is recidivism or repeat offenders. Some contend that prisons turn convicts into more hardened criminals and no amount of secular counseling seems to help much. However, recent studies show that "faith-based programs," or counseling that includes an authentic religious experience and training does help to reduce the amount of repeat offences. Studies show that through faith-based programs, many prisoners turn their lives around and become productive citizens. These studies attracted the attention not only of churches but also government officials. The Texas Department of Corrections (TDC) not only allowed but encouraged religious programs in the prisons. Byron Johnson, Director of the Center for Justice Research and Education at Lamar University in Beaumont, says it is a "no brainer" that authentic religious faith helps in prisoner rehabilitation.[68] Johnson said that prison recidivism is a serious problem, but "once you put religion into the equation it changes everything." He also noted that Texas had the most extensive network of faith-based prison ministries in the nation. Texas governor George Bush has shown considerable interest, and appointed a Task Force on Faith-Based Community Service to explore the role of religion in addressing the Texas prison problem.

In the past decade there has been a virtual explosion of faith-based prison ministries. Almost every denomination has been involved, but the work is largely inter-denominational. There are so many groups doing some form of prison ministry, that some major simply on correlating the groups and resources that are available. For example, INFORMS (Inmate Family Organization Relation Management System), has the announced purpose "to network the thousands of Texas citizens who are currently doing Criminal Justice Ministry." They emphasize the role of religious faith in prisoner rehabilitation, publish a newspaper, conduct statewide conferences and seminars, and encourage churches to get involved in ministry to prisoners and their families. They correlate the work of dozens of prison ministry groups, including the Bill Glass Ministries, Mike Barber Ministries, and Paul Carlin's Prisoners Bible Institute.

Texas Baptists have been in the forefront of this new wave prison ministries. In 1990 more than 200 inmates in 15 Texas prisons were involved in MasterLife, an intensive 26 week Christian discipleship program. This program was led by Don Dennis, who knew prison life firsthand from nearly 20 years behind bars before he received Christ and got his life turned around. He later formed Don Dennis Ministries, Inc., an interdenominational prison ministry that was partially sponsored by the BGCT. The Don Dennis group included an entire section of Juvenile Justice Ministry. Part of Dennis's ministry was to enlist churches, especially in inner cities, in a "covenant agreement" to receive persons who come out of prison and help them get a place to live, a job, and get integrated back into society.[69] Don Dennis deceased in April 1998.

The BGCT formed a new department of Criminal Justice Ministries (CJM), headed by Milfred Minatrea. The new department was listed in the Church Ministries Department, but in fact almost every Baptist group was involved in some way. The department was jointly sponsored by WMU and TBM, and funding came from the Mary Hill Davis offering. Don Gibson, Director of Lay Ministries with Texas Baptist Men, was especially involved. They enlist and train volunteer chaplains and also work in "after care" ministry to help people coming out of prison. Exodus Ministry, Inc. of Dallas was established to help ex-offenders and their families to become productive, cohesive and law-abiding again. It was jointly sponsored by the HMB, BGCT, and Dallas Baptist Association. The number of women in prison tripled between 1987-1997, and the Texas WMU has been greatly involved in ministry to that group.[70]

The "Hospitality House" near Huntsville prison, which opened in 1986, was sponsored by Baptists and built by Texas Baptist Men retiree builders. It was intended to provide a temporary lodging place for families who came to Huntsville to visit their family member in prison. Hospitality House provided lodging, food, and in some cases child care during family visits. Directed by Bob and Nelda Norris, the house is governed by the board of the Texas Baptist Prison Family Ministry Foundation, a board which includes representatives from the State Missions Commission, Texas Baptist Men, and the Tryon-Evergreen Baptist Association. In its first four years Hospitality House had in some way touched the lives of over 16,000 people, and similar houses were being planned for other prison locations.[71]

Through their Criminal Justice Ministries, Texas Baptists work on many fronts. They work directly with the prisoners in evangelism, education, and counseling. The average education level of inmates in the TDC is sixth grade, and 88% are high school dropouts. Many lack basic skills in reading and writing and, for many, even speaking English is a barrier. Trained MSC volunteers teach in Literacy Missions ministries behind the walls. Of course, MasterLife is still popular, jointly sponsored by TBM and Discipleship Training. MasterLife is currently conducted at 18 different prisons in Texas. The CJM department also works with prisoners' families, conducts "exit ministries" to help prisoners reenter the community, does job search and job training, sponsors "mentoring" programs to assure that each person who comes out of prison has some sympathetic friend, conducts family financial planning seminars, teaches homemaking skills and English as a second language (ESL). They also provide gifts for children of inmates at Christmas and other special occasions through programs like Angel Tree, and sometimes help organize transportation for families to visit their loved one in prison. Whatever the form of ministry, the basic motivation is evangelism.

Texas Baptist Men have led out in prison ministry but others have also participated. In 1990 TBM sponsored the first Criminal Justice Awareness Meeting in Belton to help churches see the potential for ministry behind the walls. Similar meetings were held elsewhere around the state. In 1994 the men were asked to pilot the Experiencing God Weekends, a devotional approach pioneered by Henry Blackaby, in selected prisons. These weekends have enlisted scores of new volunteers for prison ministry.

RESPONSIBLE STEWARDSHIP

In the 1990s Bobby L. Eklund headed the Church Stewardship Division of the SMC and it was his task to lead the churches to give generously through the Cooperative Program. To this end his department conducted over 50 associational stewardship conferences, distributed over 250,000 pieces of stewardship materials, and prepared sermon aids for busy pastors to use in preaching on stewardship.[72] To some extent, the entire Executive Board staff was involved in stewardship work, from executive director Bill Pinson and chief financial officer Roger Hall to the newest staff member in the smallest department. Though the churches continued to give large dollar amounts, the *percentage* of their income sent on through the Cooperative Program continued to decline.

BGCT Budget. The budget adopted for 1997 may be taken as typical. The BGCT projected a total $43.5 million for Texas missions and ministries, a 1.9% increase over 1996.[73] An even greater percentage increase was projected for 1998. The 1997 budget was divided into four sections: Strengthen and Start Churches, $11,635,484 or 26.75%; Minister to Human Needs, $5,613,444 or 12.90%; Equip God's People and Develop Christian Families, $20,160,741 or 46.35%; and Missions and Mission Support, $6,090,331 or 14%. This included a significant increase for new church starts. This budget does not include the three major mission offerings, Lottie Moon (foreign missions), Annie Armstrong (home missions), and Mary Hill Davis (state missions), nor funds directed through the Cooperative Program for worldwide Baptist causes. When these special offerings are included, the total Texas Baptist giving approaches $70 million, about half of which goes to ministries outside the state. The 1997 BGCT receipts broke all records, exceeding the budget by an impressive margin. The budget adopted for 1998 shows modest increases, with more funds allotted to new church starts.[74]

Baptist Church Loan Corporation. The BCLC was formed in 1952 to help Baptist churches to obtain loans to build or enlarge their facilities. At the time many banks and other commercial agencies were reluctant to lend money to churches. Three men have headed the corporation: A.B. White, 1951-1967; D. J. Singletary, 1967-1972; and Bruce W. Bowles, since 1973. Before coming to the BCLC Bowles was vice-president of a Dallas bank and, from 1969-73, was director of development for Mary Hardin-Baylor College in Belton. He received his BBA degree from Baylor in 1960 and has earned additional degrees and professional certifications since then. The BCLC has succeeded beyond all expectations. As of April 30, 1997, they had loaned over $294 million to help 2,249 churches. By judicious management, the corporation earns an income on its funds which are awaiting distribution, and their losses over the years have been minimal. The BCLC ended 1997 with total assets of $107.7 million, with $101 million out in loans to churches. Net earnings for 1996 amounted to $3.9 million.[75] The first woman to serve on the BCLC board of directors was Beatrice Martin in 1971. Other women directors have included Linda Lyle of Plainview and Joan Taylor Trew of Fort Worth.

In a further effort to serve the churches, Bowles led in forming Texas Baptist Financial Services in 1996, of which he is president. Though separate from the BCLC, the TBFS works in close cooperation, helping Texas churches to obtain needed funds through bond programs.

Baptist Foundation of Texas. Another success story has been the Baptist Foundation of Texas. Texas pioneered in this work. When the TBF was formed in 1930, neither the SBC nor any other state convention had such a foundation, and now practically all have. Since 1976 the president and CEO of the Foundation has been Lynn Craft. Craft is a Dallas native who was greatly influenced by James C. Cantrell, who was president of the Foundation from 1954 to 1976. Dewey Presley, who had worked with the Foundation since the 1950s, said Cantrell was wise enough to know he needed to build an expert staff. "In Lynn Craft, he found an outstanding young man and developed him. There is no question in my mind but that is the key to the Foundation's success in recent years."[76] Discerning unusual promise in young Craft, Cantrell quietly financed the young man's education at Baylor University. After a stint in the Coast Guard, young Craft earned his CPA certificate and in April, 1968, he came to work for the Baptist Foundation in the accounting department. Eight years later he was named to succeed his old mentor as president, and has served in that post since 1976. Without sacrificing stability, Craft has adopted a bit more aggressive investment policy and led the board to contract with an outside investment advisor. Craft's first annual report in 1977 showed total assets of the Baptist Foundation at $131 million. In 1995 this figure first surpassed the *one billion dollar* mark and in 1997 stood at $1.3 billion.

Martin Lovvorn, Dallas developer and home builder and banker, was elected a member of the Foundation board in 1965 in the seat made vacant by the resignation of Dewey Presley. After three terms as a director, Lovvorn was named chairman of the board in 1977 to succeed Carr P. Collins. Collins during his chairmanship practically ran the Foundation, functioning almost as a CEO in fact if not in name. Lovvorn returned the board to its historic function as overseers and policy makers. Lovvorn had been Lynn Craft's Sunday School teacher at FBC, Dallas, when the department director was James C. Cantrell. These three men out of the same Sunday School department provided leadership for the Baptist Foundation for more than a generation.[77] Over the years some of the most prominent Texas Baptist laymen have been associated with the Foundation.

    The Baptist Foundation is essentially an investment firm. Baptist agencies in Texas, including universities, children's homes and other agencies deposit their reserve funds into the Foundation which, in turn, invests them. Upon call, the Foundation returns to the agencies the earnings on their funds and as much of the principal as they may call for. By pooling Texas Baptist funds, and by careful professional management and investment, the Foundation enables the Baptist agencies to earn a better return on their money and at less risk. The present financial health and stability of Texas Baptist institutions is due in no small part to the outstanding work of the Baptist Foundation since 1930. During the 1990s, Texas Baptist institutions received about as much income from earnings on their funds at the Baptist Foundation as from the Cooperative Program.

    Texas Baptist Missions Foundation. The drive to establish 2000 new churches as part of MISSION TEXAS (1985-1900) called for a major budget commitment. BGCT leaders estimated that it would take twenty to thirty million dollars to meet that goal. With all the other ongoing Convention ministries, where would this new money come from? Pinson enlisted Fred and Gloria Roach of Dallas to lead out in seeking lay-persons to raise support this massive church-planting effort. A plan evolved to develop a "far above normal" challenge through the Mary Hill Davis Offering for 1985 and 1986. The "Triple-Triple" emphasis called upon individuals and churches to triple their MHD offering in 1985 and again in 1986. Response was overwhelming, with the MHD offering for 1985 reaching over $6 million, and almost $8.5 million for 1986. All the extra money not already committed to other ministry programs was directed to new church starts. This was followed by the "God's Two Hundred" plan, which was very simple. The Roaches would seek to enlist 200 individuals who would give or raise $15,000 a year for five years to start new churches. Thus the funds for new churches continued to grow.
    After the MISSION TEXAS program was completed, the need for new churches continued. Bill Pinson has made planting new churches a major hallmark of his administration. Up to that time the Executive Board had not sought endowment funds of its own, leaving that primarily to the institutions. However, Pinson felt so deeply about the need for new churches that in 1993 he led the Board to establish the Texas Baptist Missions Foundation to provide ongoing financial support to this vital ministry. William M. "Bill" Arnold was named the first president of the new Foundation, with Fred Roach as the first chairman of its Board of Advisors. Arnold has been with the BGCT since 1980, serving in the Sunday School Division and as Missions Promotion Coordinator. Previously he was on the staff at the Dallas Baptist Association and at Willow Meadows Baptist Church in Houston. Other board members included Charles Avery, Sugarland; Virginia Connally, Abilene; Ramona Daniel, Wichita Falls; Arnold Maeker, Lubbock; Earl Patrick, Waco; Ramiro Peña, Holland; Malcolm Watson, Dallas; and David Wicker, Dallas.
    In one of its first actions, the Texas Baptist Missions Foundation cre-

ated the New Church Fund as a permanent endowment, launched with $1 million gift from Temple businessman Drayton McLane. By the end of 1997, the Fund had about $10 million in assets and its growth was accelerating. Earnings from this fund are ploughed directly into new church starts, while the corpus is used as a guarantee by the Church Loan Corporation when they advance funds for new church buildings. In 1996 the Foundation was expanded to seek endowment funds for other BGCT ministries. The staff was enlarged, with Don Cramer named as vice-president. In succeeding years, endowment funds also benefitted student ministries, the River Ministry, disaster relief, churches in crisis, and other ministries.

WOMAN'S MISSIONARY UNION

The WMU forms the rudder of the BGCT, steering Texas Baptists on a steady course of missions and evangelism. That was the description applied to WMU by Herbert Reynolds, president of Baylor University.[78] Certainly the Baptist women have lived up to that description in recent years as they have guided their own organization into innovative new ministries. The influence of Texas Baptist women may be seen in every program and every progress of the BGCT. The Mary Hill Davis state offering for missions has grown dramatically and has undergirded a multitude of Texas ministries.

Since January 1, 1981, Joy Lynn Phillips Fenner has been Executive Director-Treasurer of the Woman's Missionary Union of Texas. She grew up in Avinger, in Cass County, and attended Paris Junior College and East Texas Baptist College (now University) in Marshall. Always interested in missions, Miss Phillips served as Girls' Auxiliary Director of Texas WMU from 1956-1959. She married Charlie W. Fenner in 1966, and the couple served as missionaries in Japan from 1967-1980 until her election to head the Texas WMU. Presidents of the Texas WMU in recent years have included Mauriece Johnston, 1980- 84; Amelia Bishop, 1984-88; Gerry Dunkin, 1988-92; Mary Humphries, 1992-96; and Jeane Law, since 1996.

Joy Fenner has brought dynamic new vision and energy to the WMU and has kept them in the forefront of innovative new ministries in Texas. Gone are the days when WMU meant "circle meetings" to hear programs. They continue to do missionary education, but they are much more "doers of missions" and not just hearers. The enrollment has declined somewhat in recent years, due primarily to women's employment outside the home, but many observers feel the Texas WMU is presently at its peak in influence and creativity. In recent years they have developed radically new approaches. Some of their ministries include Baptist Nursing Fellowship, to provide for continuing education and fellowship for Texas Baptist nurses, and to encourage their participation in medical missions at home and overseas. Criminal Justice Ministries provides a way for women to minister to inmates within prison walls, especially women prisoners, and also to work with prisoners' families, with wardens, chaplains, and guards.

Hope for Home provides opportunities for witness through Family Ministry Consultants and the Family Ministry Corps. Ministers Wives Fellowship exists to encourage and direct the witness zeal of this important part of the Texas Baptist family. Women on Mission is an adult organization of WMU which leads women to grow in spiritual maturity and express their faith through volunteer mission projects. Women Reaching Texas, a ministry of the Evangelism Division of the BGCT in cooperation with the WMU, acts as a catalyst to focus on women praying for the lost, witnessing in personal evangelism, and using literature prepared by women to reach women for Christ. Women Strengthening Hispanic Families holds an annual convocation, *Celebrating the Hispanic Woman,* in an effort to identify, focus upon, and meet some of the most pressing needs of Hispanic families in Texas. They feel that strengthening the Hispanic woman will strengthen the home, and stronger homes will result in stronger churches. Women of Purpose (WOP) provides an overall umbrella group to network and correlate the various forms of ministry available to Baptist women of Texas.[79]

The WMU leaders discovered, not to their great surprise, that most Texas Baptist programs to reach new people for Christ were male oriented. They worked with veteran evangelist Ted Elmore, on the staff of the Evangelism Division of the SMC, to pinpoint male bias in the programs and with WMU specialists to learn how to target women for evangelism. Beyond this purpose, they also sought ways to address the gospel effectively to other specific target groups.

The Mary Hill Davis offering for state missions has grown dramatically in recent years, and has undergirded a multitude of Texas ministries. Gloria Roach and her husband Fred have been leaders in WMU work and they served as co-chairs of the MHD Centennial Offering. Roach reported that Texas Baptists gave $3.2 million to the MHD offering in 1984 and $7.6 million in 1985, for a 235% increase.[80] In 1985, 494 churches gave to the offering for the first time, and 879 churches tripled their 1985 offering over 1984. The 1986 offering was also successful, enabling Baptist women to raise over $15 million for Texas mission projects in the two years of 1985 and 1986.[81] In addition the WMU, with Gloria and Fred Roach, launched a special emphasis called "God's Two Hundred," an effort to identify 200 persons of means in Texas who would give substantial gifts to sponsor new church starts in Texas. They only had to find 199 more, for the Roaches were people of substantial means and they gave generously both in time and money.

TEXAS BAPTIST MEN

Tennessee native Robert E. Dixon has headed Texas Baptist Men (TBM) since 1970. A graduate of a Chattanooga business college and Southwestern Seminary, Dixon has been a pioneer for most of his life. He was the first person to serve full-time in a Baptist church in the field of youth and recreation in Mississippi and Tennessee. He was Minister of Youth and Recreation at FBC in Nashville and later in Memphis, the first such staff member in the state. He came to work for TBM in 1966 as director of Royal Ambassadors. Dixon has probably pioneered and developed more different forms of ministry among Southern Baptist men than any other person. Many of the innovative ministries that he "invented" in Texas have been picked up by other states and by the national SBC organization for men. He has led Texas Baptist Men to pioneer in disaster relief, retirees on mission, day camping, Royal Ambassador Camping, and Church Renewal Journey as well as the retiree builders and relief work in other countries. In 1996 the Executive Board adopted a Resolution of Appreciation for Dixon in which they recognized his outstanding contributions. Other leaders of TBM include Don Gibson, director of Lay Ministries; John LaNoue, director of Baptist Men; and John M. Bullock, director of the Royal Ambassadors/Challengers. Recent presidents of TBM have included Olen Miles, 1979-81; Joe Lenaman, 1982-84; Wilton Davis, 1986-88 and 1992-94; George Crews, 1989-91; George Andreason, 1995-98.

The TBM ministries, once largely confined to Texas, have in recent years expanded literally worldwide. Especially in cases of natural disasters like floods, tornadoes, or hurricanes, or human disasters like famine or disease epidemic, Texas Baptist men are equipped and ready to go anywhere in the world to help meet human needs in Jesus' name. They have an extensive array of equipment, including 18 wheeler cargo trucks, mobile kitchens and clinics, and even their own huge cargo airplane. They have enlisted men of every imaginable skill, from engineers, truck drivers, airplane pilots, physicians and others who are able to deal with almost any situation which may arise. As Texas Baptist Men and their work become better known, they are often the first outside group invited to assist at disaster areas. Such is their influence and clout, that in addition to cooking meals for a few hundred, they also sometimes deal with huge agricultural corporations and even overseas governments to direct hundreds of tons of grain to famine areas.

Some areas where Texas Baptist Men have ministered include Honduras, Mexico, the Caribbean, northern Iraq, the Ukraine and several others. They airlifted medical supplies and food to the Kurds in northern Iraq and Iran; airlifted medical supplies to stem a cholera epidemic in Peru; airlifted food and blankets to Bosnia; and sent a water purifier system and well digger to Kenya, as well as food for Somalian relief.

John LaNoue, Director of Baptist Men, spent over three months in Korea in 1997 to coordinate relief efforts in the famine there. Texas Baptists provided 130 tons of food to North Korea, along with 5,500 children's coats and $71,000 in cash to buy more coats at a favorable price in China to distribute to children in Korea.[82] Just two days before LaNoue arrived in China in January 1998, a major earthquake near China's Great Wall left over a half million people homeless in sub-zero weather. Texas Baptist men received a request to provide immediately about 2,000 tents, each capable of housing 10 to 15 people. These examples are typical of the growing international ministry of Texas Baptist Men.

Meanwhile, the men certainly do not neglect the needs in the Lone Star State. Wherever in Texas a tornado strikes, a flood occurs, or a hurricane blows in, literally before the wind dies down Texas Baptist Men are already on the move. Their trucks loaded with food, medicines, and blankets are on the highway within hours, and volunteers gather from all parts of the state to do whatever is needed to help people in crisis. Their work is more than humanitarian; it is ministry in Jesus' name.

In addition to disaster relief, perhaps the Texas Baptist Men are best known for their building projects in which volunteers erect church buildings in Texas and other states, sometimes also furnishing the materials. Wilton Davis, coordinator of Texas Baptist Men Builders, reported that they had built 41 churches in 1997, and over 400 over the past twenty years.[83] Most of these churches could not otherwise have had buildings. In addition to churches, TBM also builds other facilities for retreats, camps, and schools, both in this country and overseas. In 1997 they completed a $1 million classroom and office building for the new Southern Baptist Seminary in Cochrane, Alberta, where Richard Blackaby is president.

Nobody knows for sure how many men are enrolled in the TBM organization, and they don't seem to worry much about it. There are so many different groups, with different skills and expertise, doing so many different kinds of ministries that, were it not for the overall coordination of Bob Dixon, the left hand would hardly know what the right hand was doing. There are also many women involved in the men's organization, with couples participating in almost all the various ministries. Some of the women, it is said, are excellent builders and can swing a hammer as well as a paint brush.

Though they are mostly doers, TBM are also hearers. They sponsor spiritual renewal programs in churches, prisons, camps, and for their own members. Their annual Labor Day "Cedars of Lebanon" retreat, held at the Mt. Lebanon Encampment near Dallas, draws several hundred men and women. The emphasis is on prayer, Bible study, and seeking God's will, but in 1996 a Congregational minister, Richard Owens Roberts, raised some concerns by remarks which some interpreted as right-wing partisan politics. A few days after the Cedars of Lebanon incident, the Executive Board passed a resolution asking its agencies to caution invited speakers to refrain from endorsing political parties or candidates, defaming any elected official, questioning the salvation of a political candidate, or "engaging in partisan politics which hinders the ability of the BGCT to reach people for Christ."[84] At the same meeting the Board also adopted a lengthy resolution commending Dixon for his effective leadership of Texas Baptist men for thirty years.

In response to the criticism, Bob Dixon said, "Texas Baptist Men are not and should not be considered a political party. We do not endorse political parties." He also said the organization included men of different political views, but when they come to meetings "we've told them to leave their [political] views at the door, and they have."[85] Dixon announced his retirement for 1998. Jim Furgerson, with the International Mission Board, Richmond, Virginia, has been elected to succeed Dixon, effective September 6, 1998.

CHALLENGE AND RESPONSE

A number of new issues arose in the 1980s and 1990s to challenge Texas Baptists. This section names some of those issues and briefly describes how Texas Baptists responded.

Convention "Ownership" or "Affiliation?" For many years and for good reasons, the Executive Board had placed limits on the amount of debt the institutions, especially the colleges, could assume. However, those restrictions later proved too strict. In 1984 James H. Semple, chairman of the Administrative Committee, said "Texas Baptist institutions are continuing to develop and grow. Their growth frequently creates the need for expansion of facilities, the acquisition of new property, and the provision of new equipment."[86] The Debt Limitation Committee named to study the matter was chaired by Dewey Presley. The committee was also much concerned about the issue of "ascending liability," by which the debts of the colleges, or other BGCT related institutions, might legally become the debts of the Convention. Also, if one of the institutions became the object of a lawsuit, it was feared that the assets of the entire Convention and not just that institution could be at risk. To address this risk, the committee recommended a change in the BGCT constitution that describes the institutions as "owned or controlled by this Convention" (Article VIII, Section 3) to say instead that the institutions are "affiliated with this Convention." The Executive Board spelled out clearly that the debts of the institutions belonged solely to that institution and are not guaranteed by the BGCT. They also asked each institution in contracting debts to spell out clearly on the contract that no liability for the debt extends beyond that institution.

Whether this change would have provided any legal protection is not known, for on a close ballot the Convention rejected the committee's report. Some messengers felt that "affiliated with" significantly changed the relationship of the Convention and the institutions, and in fact represented a weakening of Convention control over the institutions. Perhaps many would have agreed with D. L. Lowrie, BGCT president at the time, who said, "If I have to make a choice on liability and control, I'll assume liability and keep control."[87] By the 1990s the matter of control was assuming more importance among some Baptists.

The matter was referred back to the Executive Board, which appointed a new Constitution Review Committee, headed by James H. Semple. The Board made it clear that the committee was not charged to *rewrite* the constitution, but to review it and make only those changes that were essential. They were also instructed to "make the meaning of any changes clear to Texas Baptists," a hint perhaps that the previous committee had not done that.[88] The new committee concluded that since the Convention exercises its control through funding, approving charter changes, and election of trustees, the term "affiliated with" would not affect Convention control. However, in light of widespread perception to the contrary, the committee recommended to keep the existing terminology of "ownership or control." They made it clear, however, that "each institution is liable for its own obligations." If BGCT "control" of its related institutions was in fact weakening, it was not caused by any particular terms in the constitution.

The committee also recommended a loosening of the debt restrictions, which the previous committee had also recommended. That was part of the original intent, and it was not controversial.

Associational Study Committee, 1994. Texas Baptists formed their first association in 1840, eight years before they had a state convention. The association, the oldest Baptist body beyond the local church, has had a major role in the growth of Texas Baptists in the past century and a half. Important as both are to Baptist advance, the relationship between associations and the state convention has not always been smooth. Some seemed to regard the associations as subordinate to the Convention, or even as regional branches of the state body. In earlier times, the association was sometimes regarded as a "denominational marketer" to promote programs originated by the state convention.

In time, the associations rebelled against this plan as demeaning and out of harmony with Baptist polity and began to assert more autonomy in seeking to meet the needs of churches in their area. As more churches placed the association in the church budget for a definite percentage, the larger associations had their own money to fund their own programs. The smaller associations, however, remained more dependent upon supplemental funds from the state convention to fund their local programs. When both state and association shared in promoting some ministry project, there often arose misunderstanding about how much of the cost would be borne by the state and how much by the association. Some felt the state convention did not always treat the associations alike, and some complained the state was often heavy-handed in pressuring the associations into conformity. Over the years, tensions have arisen, most recently in the early 1990s. The relationship of convention and association has been a growing, evolving relationship. Bill Pinson, helped by such state mission leaders as James Semple and Ken Coffee, has led in pioneering a partnership relationship between state and associations that is somewhat different from that of other states.

In an effort to further define and strengthen the relationship between the BGCT and the 113 Baptist associations in Texas, the SMC authorized a study committee composed of nine directors of missions, eight pastors, five BGCT staff members, and one staff member from the Texas WMU. The committee was chaired by Paul Armes, then pastor of FBC, Corpus Christi, and made their report in 1994. The committee began with "basic presuppositions," that both BGCT and associations exist by the will of the churches and for the benefit of the churches, and that "The Convention and the Associations affirm each other's autonomy as well as that of every church." Convention and association are voluntary partners, working together to advance the gospel. Neither partner controls the other. Any financial contribution from the state to the associations is not intended to guarantee that the associations will promote or cooperate with BGCT projects.

The report recognizes that associations differ in size and structure from mega-associations, metropolitan associations, and town and country associations. However, they recommend that all relate to the BGCT through one office. Previously, metropolitan associations coordinated directly through the Missions Division of the SMC while all others related through the SMC administration. Some area DOMs felt this gave the metro associations an undue advantage. The committee recommended "that area and associational coordination be in one office at the convention level, and that office be sensitive to and plan for the differing needs of associations of varying sizes." They also recommended that the BGCT "develop a system of relating to associations by Cooperative Agreement." In these written covenants, associations and the BGCT would spell out agreements about funding, promotion and the role of BGCT personnel in the associations. Such written agreements, they said, would help prevent misunderstandings and foster healthy relationships.

Texas Baptists have pioneered a cooperative relationship between Convention and associations that differs somewhat from other states. In a 1997 address to DOMs from across the nation, Bill Pinson described the relationship of convention and associations as a voluntary partnership of equals.[89] The state convention does not "own" or "control" the associations; the associations are not "members" of the state convention. Neither is the state convention a creature of the associations. The two kinds of Baptist organizations cooperate in a voluntary partnership because they choose to do so. Necessary ingredients for an effective partnership, Pinson said, include appreciation for each other, commitment to a common task, cooperation, mutual support, and ongoing dialogue. To work together effectively, both must understand and accept Baptist polity. Pinson said,

> In Baptist polity the local church is basic to all other entities. A church relates directly to the association, directly to the state convention, and directly to any other Baptist entity. The churches do not need to go through any of these to the other nor do any of these need to go through the other to the churches. Thus it is inappropriate to speak of 'levels' of Baptist organization—the associational level, the state convention level, the national convention level. Apart from the churches all are on the same level. Each is equal to the other. None is more important than the other. . . . The relationship among them is voluntary. Failure to be committed to this bedrock Baptist principle is to endanger the nature of our partnerships. . . . Each Baptist entity is autonomous and relates to others only through voluntary cooperation.[90]

Many DOMs came to regard themselves more as consultants to the churches than as administrators, thus following a "church first" policy. In changing times, Pinson noted, new complexities emerge. Some churches have multiple alignments with several state and national bodies, some associations may be formed not on the basis of geography but on the basis of racial, cultural, political or theological affinity, and more than one Baptist association or state convention may emerge in the same area. How will the weakening of the Cooperative Program and resurgence of the "society plan" affect Baptists? Pinson pointed out that "The Cooperative Program has never provided adequate funding for state or national work in spite of numerous modifications and heavy promotion," and thus Baptists have always created "societies" to raise funds for various causes. "There is a resurgence of the 'society' approach with resulting multiple appeals for funds."[91] No one claims that all tensions are gone or that all problems have been solved. However, it appears that the voluntary partnership between the BGCT and the 113 associations in Texas is healthy, growing and productive.

Task Force for Small Churches, 1990. The majority of Texas Baptist churches have always been small and that is still the case. In 1994 it was reported that 52% of all Texas Baptist churches fall into the category of "smaller membership," defined as having fewer than 199 members, many of them much fewer. By another measure, about 70% of BGCT affiliated churches have an average Sunday School attendance of fewer than 100. In recent years these churches have faced unusual problems, and many have not shared in the general growth and vitality of Texas Baptists. Many of these churches are in rural areas or villages where the population is diminishing. Social and economic changes which transformed the face of rural America have greatly undermined these churches. Some of them have part-time or bivocational pastors, while others have difficulty maintaining any pastor at all. In some small churches, a new form of bivocationalism emerged in which a wife worked full-time to allow her husband to continue in a pastorate that could not financially support them. It was inevitable, the Task Force acknowledged, that some of the smaller churches would simply have to close.

In an effort to help strengthen the smaller churches, a Smaller Membership Church Task Force was named in 1989, to report in 1990. Richard Faling, director of the Church Ministries Department of SMC, chaired the group. The Task Force began by affirming the importance of the smaller churches and their historic contribution to the life of Texas Baptists. In words that evoke the memory of J. Howard Williams in the 1950s, who cared deeply about the rural churches, Bill Pinson asked the Task Force to study three things: the needs of the smaller churches, what was currently being done to help them, and what more could and should be done. Some noted that the church literature seemed geared to the larger churches "and smaller membership churches are overwhelmed by it all. The smaller churches need help, the pastor needs help."

The study group agreed that in Baptist churches, large or small, the pastor is the key leader. They set about finding ways to help the pastors, to encourage them, affirm them, train them. They also sought to work with the churches to instill enthusiasm, to provide attractive programs that would enlist people, and to train lay people to perform some ministry tasks when no resident pastor was available. Faling prepared materials for the smaller churches, including "Church Achievement" in English and *"el Plan de Avance de la Iglesia"* in Spanish.[92] They also planned conferences for bivocational pastors. Pinson asked that a cross section of Texas Baptists leaders help the smaller churches, including WMU, TBM, and he particularly asked the DOMs to conduct a series of "Listen/Talk Back Sessions" throughout the state to hear directly from pastors and members of smaller churches.

By 1994 the Bivocational/Smaller Church Development Department was in full operation, headed by Jan Daehnert. This department worked with the growing number of bivocational pastors in Texas, offering workshops, conferences and materials, but more especially offering affirmation and admiration for the heroic ministers who could maintain both a secular career and a pastoral ministry.

Task Force for Cooperative Program Promotion. Each year the BGCT received more dollars from the churches to use for ministries within the state and beyond. Because of that increase, some may not have noticed that for many years the churches gave an ever diminishing *per cent* of their income for work beyond their own community. While the income of the churches increased dramatically, the income of the Convention increased more modestly. This trend was not limited to Texas, but was true of all Southern Baptists. The churches simply used more of their money at home, for increasingly elaborate buildings and for more paid staff members. Even in fairly small churches, it became customary to have a multiple staff. Also, by the 1990s (and even before) many churches sponsored mission projects on their own apart from the BGCT. The River Ministry, Partnership Missions, and the Mission Service Corps were only the most prominent of many such opportunities. Some churches formed mission churches in nearby communities, others adopted or even sent their own foreign missionary, while many contributed to popular non-denominational or "parachurch" mission groups. Already Baptist churches had discovered alternate forms of mission work, outside traditional denominational channels, a trend that escalated as the new century drew nearer.

As a part of the Long Range Plan for 1990-1995, the Executive Board appointed a Task Force for Cooperative Program Promotion. "New approaches are needed," said the committee, "to reverse the downward trend in percentage of undesignated receipts given by churches through the Cooperative Program."[93] However, the work of the Task Force showed not so much new approaches as a reinforcement of the old ones. They reaffirmed the value of the Cooperative Program as the best avenue for Baptist giving, and discouraged the practice of designated giving. They said "there will be no effort [by the BGCT] to promote designated giving." Affirming a promotional emphasis upon "One for All," that a gift through the CP is a gift to all Baptist ministries, they reaffirmed that the CP "is still the basic and best way to fund mission work."

True to their Baptist convictions, the Task Force also strongly reaffirmed the freedom and autonomy of every church to decide for themselves how they would use their money, what missionary causes they would support and in what measure. They insisted that "the right of the individual churches must be affirmed."[94] In the 1990s the income of the BGCT increased sharply, not because the churches increased their percentage of giving, but because the income of the churches increased even more sharply.

Broadening the Leadership Base. From time to time, the BGCT has taken specific and intentional steps to broaden the base of leadership among Texas Baptists. At times this has taken the form of enlarging the Executive Board so more people could serve or altering the makeup of Convention committees to assure that both men and women, both ministers and lay persons, and persons from all regions of the state have a voice. In December 1988 upon the recommendation of Bill Pinson, the Executive Board authorized a "Council of Consultants." This was an effort to involve more young people, women and ethnics in leadership among Texas Baptists, and also to discover and develop potential leaders for the future.

The plan called for the two commissions (SMC and CLC) and the two coordinating boards (CECB and HWCB) each to enlist six young people under thirty to serve as "consultants." Of these 24 young leaders, at least 12 would be pastors or other church ministers and the other 12 would be lay persons. They would include women, ethnic and racial minorities, and lay persons from different secular occupations. These consultants would serve a two year term, not repeatable, and would attend all the meetings of their sponsoring board or commission, and all meetings of the Executive Board. Their expenses would be paid but they would receive no stipend. The idea was to help them become familiar with how Texas Baptists work together, to allow them to glimpse the great challenge of the Texas task, and to develop their leadership potential and give them name recognition for the future. This experiment has proven its value and is still in operation.

Pre-Convention Meetings. For many years the BGCT started its annual meeting on Tuesday afternoon. When auto travel was mostly by two-lane highways, messengers needed Monday to get to the meeting site. Then travel changed. With better cars and better roads, auto travel was much faster, and more messengers traveled by airplane which was even faster. A widespread practice developed for messengers to leave for the Convention meeting after the Sunday morning service, thus arriving in the convention city on Sunday night. Some Convention committees and work groups began to hold Sunday night meetings. For years the Woman's Missionary

Union and Texas Baptist Men held their annual meetings on Monday afternoon, but messengers not involved with those groups had time on their hands.

For some time, pastors who wanted to move the BGCT in a more conservative direction, as the SBC had already moved, eyed the Monday time slot as an opportunity. A group of ultra-conservatives, led by Richard L. Scarborough and Miles L. Seaborn, Jr., formed a Pastors Conference to meet on Monday, a Texas equivalent of the national Pastors Conference preceding the Southern Baptist Convention. Many years earlier Texas had a Pastors Conference but it was discontinued by vote of the Convention and a Pastors and Laymens Conference was established, a forerunner of the annual convention meeting of Texas Baptist Men. It was widely believed that the SBC Pastors' Conference had become the major platform for giving fundamentalist pastors exposure to help them get elected to SBC office and also for drumming up support for their agenda at the Convention. The politicizing of the Pastors' Conference was a major factor in the politicizing of the SBC and was clearly one decisive factor in the ultra conservative group gaining control of the SBC.

Sensing the political divisiveness of such meetings, the BGCT on a motion by James Pleitz called for a Committee on Convention Related Meetings to study the issue.[95] The committee was chaired by Wayne L. Allen, conservative pastor of FBC in Carrolton, and the 29 members included a wide range of Texas Baptist theological and political viewpoints, including both Scarborough and Seaborn. After extensive study, the committee made its recommendations with only one negative vote and one abstention.

They recommended that the BGCT annual meeting begin on Monday at 2:00 P.M., and "that no pre-Convention general meetings by any groups be held except the Semi-annual Business Sessions of the Executive Boards of WMU/TBM," and "that interest groups meet at their choice of free times on Monday night following the Convention session, Tuesday breakfast, Tuesday lunch, Tuesday night following the Convention session, Wednesday breakfast, and Wednesday morning."[96] They urged that "other groups, such as pastors; ministers of education, music, youth and other church staff; ministers' wives; Seminary alumni; annuitants; Baptist Historical Society; Texas Baptist Public Relations Association; Texas Baptist Development Officers Association; and others find a time slot, in a cooperative pattern with the general schedule." The committee felt this new format would give priority to the Convention rather than have attention diverted to the satellite meetings, and that reducing the sessions from five to four and thus cutting out one day, might encourage more attendance by lay persons and bivocational pastors and allow people to visit the exhibits area without the distraction of meetings. They recommended that the new format be tried for two years before a final decision was made. After the 1991 and 1992 sessions, the BGCT voted to adopt the new format permanently with minor changes.

The committee made it clear that "it does not have the authority to require all groups to meet at particular times. . . . Baptists can and will meet whenever they desire." However, in an appeal for voluntary cooperation, they said "the Committee appeals to all individuals and groups to cooperate in a spirit of Christian love and harmony with this recommendation believing it is indeed in the best interest of the whole Texas Baptist family."

This compacted schedule was quite acceptable to most of these groups, and would have been fine for pastors to meet for inspiration, fellowship and the enjoyment of good preaching. However, all of these times come after the election of officers and the primary business session of the Convention and thus give no opportunity for affecting the outcome of major votes. The Pastors Conference continues to meet prior to the business sessions despite the official Convention vote asking them not to do so, and while the meetings emphasize prayer and biblical preaching there is also a clear political agenda.

HELPING THE HELPERS

The BGCT has been keenly sensitive to the needs of Baptist ministers in Texas and has done what it could to see that those needs are met. Of course, the Convention has respected the autonomy of the churches, who employ the pastors, and respects the freedom of individual pastors. Three of the ways in which the BGCT has sought to help are Ministers Counseling Service, the Minister/Church Relations Office, and in negotiating with the Annuity Board of the SBC about ministers' insurance and retirement benefits.

Ministers' Counseling Service. In 1997 the Ministers' Counseling Service observed its twenty-fifth anniversary. James Cooper was the first coordinator, serving 16 years, and Glenn Booth has served since 1988. Hundreds of ministers and their families have received help from this ministry. The MCS program offers counseling in Dallas, referrals for counseling elsewhere throughout the state, retreats, workshops for ministers and their families, and limited financial aid to ministers who have been terminated by their churches. This office also administers a program of psychological testing of all ministerial students in the eight Texas Baptist universities and, as a result, some problems are spotted early and students receive needed help.[97] As a result of insights gained through these tests, a few students have made their own decision not to continue in ministry.

Minister/Church Relations Office. In 1994 the BGCT formed a new ministry to work with churches and ministers to resolve conflicts and, when possible, avoid them. In some ways, it was an effort to identify ahead of time the problems that the Ministers' Counseling Service met after the fact. The Executive Board formed the Office of Ministers/Church Relationship and enlisted James Richard (Dick) Maples, popular pastor of

FBC, Bryan, to head up the new work beginning April 5, 1995. Maples works closely with Glenn Booth, coordinator of the Ministers' Counseling Service and Richard Faling, coordinator of the Church Services Division. Faling leads the Church Information Services (CIS) which sends out information on available pastors to churches seeking pastors. Maples also works closely with the Area and Association DOMs, who understand the local pastors' situation perhaps better than most.

In 1992 Levi Price, Jr., chairman of the Executive Board, appointed a committee to study the growing problem of conflict between ministers and churches. The resulting Minister/Church Relations Committee, chaired by Bennie Slack, made an extensive survey which revealed the problem was even worse than first thought. "There is a growing crisis of staggering proportions in Southern Baptist and Texas Baptist churches which is undermining the denomination's effectiveness," said the report. "The crisis is the destructive conflict within many of our congregations which threatens to shatter the fragile fellowships and impair or end the careers of faithful, God-called ministers of the gospel."[98] The Sunday School Board reported that about 2,000 Southern Baptist ministers a year are fired, and that Board often receives up to 50 telephone calls a day from ministers in distress, suffering burnout, or who are facing forced termination. In 1996, 172 Texas Baptist pastors and 122 other staff ministers were fired. The committee found not only an epidemic of forced terminations, but also a high level of anxiety, discouragement and depression among ministers, even those not in obvious danger of termination.

> We have discovered a growing erosion of trust and a lack of communication between ministers and their congregations. We have found churches in turmoil and communities where the good name "Baptist" has been the object of ridicule and contempt. We have discovered an epidemic of forced terminations of ministers and widespread discouragement and disillusionment among ministers in all size churches, even those who are in no apparent danger of termination.
>
> We have found that the average church member does not begin to understand the pain and grief which a terminated minister and family experiences, nor the tremendous difficulty a terminated minister faces in being called to another church. For many good and dedicated ministers termination means the end of their ministry.[99]

All agreed that the upsurge in forced terminations of ministers in Texas had reached crisis proportions, but there was less agreement about the causes. Some churches have unrealistic expectations or demand perfection in the pastor and his family. Some churches have a history of mistreating their pastors, and in some a clique of entrenched lay leaders seek to dominate the pastor and, in time, to dismiss him. Many churches are "repeat offenders" with an ongoing history of firing ministers. A recent survey showed that 62% of fired pastors said their church had previously fired a pastor, and 41% said the church had fired two or more in succession.[100] Whatever the announced reasons, some pastors are fired for failure to grow the church numerically; some corporate minded lay leaders operate on the philosophy of "grow or go." Pastors may inherit long-standing problems which existed long before they came, and frequently church members import into the church the residue of their own life problems and disappointments.

Not all the fault lies with the churches. Some pastors may have sincerity and zeal, but are poor in "people skills" or relating to people. The tendency of some pastors in recent years to assume dictatorial power cost some their position. H. H. Hobbs said, "pastors consider themselves 'rulers' and the people aren't taking it."[101] Some pastors lack personal and spiritual maturity, and some cannot tolerate any disagreement with their views. In addition to leadership style and poor interpersonal relationships, the fifth most frequently mentioned reason for termination was moral failure. Not all ministerial moral failure was sexual in nature: misappropriation of church funds and "inability to tell the truth" were often cited.

Most lay persons, even the leaders, appear to have little concept of the devastation inflicted upon the minister and his family by forced termination. Studies show the damage is usually worse for family members, especially children who often turn against God and the church entirely.

The new department sought not only to address the problems that surfaced, but also to spot the potential problems before they emerged. When a problem developed, they worked at both ends: with the pastor who was terminated and with the church that terminated him. The program of "Intentional Interims" sought to enlist and train a group of experienced ministers who could be available to serve as interim pastors of churches that have a history of problems. The Intentional Interims receive over 60 hours of intensive training and serve six months under supervision. The interim serves as pastor for at least a year, helping the church to review their expectations and their relationship to their pastor. In working with terminated pastors, the department helps them reaffirm their call, assess their leadership skills, and provides refresher training in relationship skills. As of 1997, a total of 72 persons had been trained in conflict mediation and were available to consult with ministers and/or churches in conflict. One church in Euless which had a troubled history of conflict worked with an Intentional Interim and faced up to their faults. They posted a public sign, "Forgive Us," and sought to contact former pastors and members who had been hurt by the church.[102] The Interim led the church in a study of Matthew 18 where Jesus taught his followers how to deal with personal conflict and as a result church leaders feel they are in position to overcome their troubled past and become a peaceful and loving church fellowship.

Maples also developed a "Churches of Refuge" program that has attracted a great deal of attention. In response to the growing problem of forced resignations and involuntary terminations of ministers, Texas Baptist churches are being enlisted to agree to become a "Church of Refuge." The idea is based upon the cities of refuge in the Old Testament to which

Israelites could flee in times of danger or stress. Churches agreeing to participate in the program would agree "to love and sustain ministers and their families who have been bruised by an unfortunate experience with the church they were serving." The Church of Refuge agrees to provide housing and utilities for the displaced family for up to one year. Some provide a part-time ministry post in the church, either volunteer or at a modest stipend. They also assist the displaced minister and/or spouse to find secular employment. However, the ultimate purpose is to help the family recover and reenter ministry. There is a "House of Refuge" at Big Country Retreat Center to help in the retreat ministry to terminated ministers, and another at Circle Six Ranch Camp.

"Mediation " and "Mentoring" are other aspects of Maples' work. Both of them seek to prevent problems or catch them early. In mediation, counselors meet with pastor and church leaders in conflict and seek to help them work out their problem. If severance is the best solution, they seek to make it amicable and fair to all. While new to the BGCT, this is an ancient form of ministry in Baptist church life. In the 17th and 18th centuries Baptist churches with internal conflicts often called for "helps" from neighboring churches, that is, a visitation of members from other churches to help them work through their conflicts. The BGCT "mediators," who include both men and women, receive 40 hours of training in mediation methods. Nancy Ferrell, a former church staff member who holds a PhD. in Adult Education, is the primary trainer for the Minister/Church Relation department.

In mentoring, an experienced pastor agrees to work with a new pastor for up to two years. The mentor meets with the new minister not less than monthly, listens a lot and offers friendship and encouragement. The mentor may also offer counsel as needed, but often just serving as a listening ear is what the young minister needs most.

Maples was also working on a plan to develop regular "sabbaticals" for ministers at intervals to allow the pastor several weeks to get away for refresher studies, to reassess oneself and one's ministry, and to seek the kind of personal, spiritual and family renewal that can counteract the problems of burnout. Many churches already provide such a "time out" for harried ministers. Maples is convinced that such a program would have great benefits for both churches and ministers.

Church/Staff Information Service. One of the great needs of Baptists is to find some way, within their theology of autonomous churches, to bring pastorless churches and churchless pastors together. Historically, the DOM has been the primary human agent in bringing pastors and churches together. The BGCT, like other state conventions, is moving cautiously into that area. Richard Faling is director of the Church/Staff Information Service. Unlike some other denominations, Baptist polity does not allow the "placement" of pastors and that term is carefully avoided by Faling and his associates. They respect the freedom of the churches to call whom they will as ministers, but they do keep an active file of biographical information on Texas Baptist ministers who wish to participate, and they will upon request send this information without endorsement or recommendation to churches seeking ministers. From there it is up to the churches and ministers to get together or not.

Texas Baptist Leadership Center, Inc. Growing out of the survey taken by the Church/Ministers Relations Committee came the stark evidence that too many Texas Baptist pastors faced conflict in their churches because they lacked adequate leadership skills or used inappropriate leadership styles. Many of these were highly educated persons who could conjugate a Greek verb at the drop of a hat or explain predestination but could not promote a church budget successfully, cope with a disagreeable deacon, or motivate a church committee to work harmoniously. They concluded that the typical seminary education is stronger on academics than upon the practical "how to" skills of daily ministry. Pinson once remarked that as a seminary president he attempted to introduce more practical studies only to find that students who had not yet faced such actual situations were not able to benefit much. It is the student who is five years out of seminary who has faced real life problems in the church who is crying out for help, and who is at last in a teachable frame of mind. The Leadership Center hopes to strengthen churches by addressing potential problems before they surface, and thus reduce the work load of the Ministers Counseling Service and the Church/Ministers Relation Office.

To meet this need for updated or refresher training of a practical nature, the BGCT formed a new ministry called Texas Baptist Leadership Center, Inc. Its purpose statement says, "The Texas Baptist Leadership Center has been created to address critical leadership issues facing Texas Baptist pastors, staff, and churches entering the 21st century." Planning had been underway since 1994 when Pinson led the Executive Board to begin discussing the kind of leadership Texas Baptists will need for the 21st century. In 1995 Pinson assembled a staff leadership team at the Baptist Building to determine how the BGCT could help provide the needed leadership for Texas Baptist churches in the new century. The team was led by Richard Faling, director of the Church Services Division, and included Glenn Booth, E. B. Brooks, Ken Coffee, Jim Culp, William Jan Daehnert, Jimmy Garcia, Patty Lane, Dick Maples, James Semple, and Nelda Williams. Ex-officio participants included Bill Pinson, Roger Hall, Tom Brannon, Lloyd Elder, and Art Hodge as Consultant. In 1996 the group contracted with Lloyd Elder, former associate executive director, and then head of the Moench Center for Church Leadership at Belmont University in Nashville, to author the first five leadership seminars. In 1997 the Leadership Center began its first full year of operation. This endeavor, like all the work of the BGCT, involved a partnership of many groups. The participation of the DOMs will be crucial to the success of the Leadership Center.

The TBLC is not a "school" with a campus, but a series of specialized seminars offered at different points around the state, led by experienced ministers who teach not only out of extensive training but also out of their own personal experience. In 1997 Robert B. Cavin was named as director of the Leadership Center and Paul Powell, the highly respected and recently retired head of the SBC Annuity Board, was enlisted to chair the advisory committee that oversees the enterprise.

By 1997 seminars were offered on Practicing Servant Leadership, Shaping the Mountain of Change, Managing Stress in Ministry, and Trans-forming Conflict. The cost of each seminar is $80, of which $40 is provided by the BGCT as a scholarship. In addition to the seminar, participants also receive a notebook of materials for future reference. Other seminars on Interpersonal Skills and Church Unity are in the planning stage and will be offered at different locations both in English and Spanish.

Retirement and Insurance Benefits. Baptist ministers are employed by churches and not by the Convention, but the BGCT works with the churches and the SBC Annuity Board to provide at least a modest safety net for ministers and their families. This safety net includes both health insurance and retirement benefits. Realizing that ministers' retirement benefits were too low, the BGCT in 1984 adopted the New Church Annu-ity Plan. A further advance was made in 1986 when the BGCT worked with the Annuity Board to develop the Expanded Church Annuity Plan. This plan called for ministers to contribute by salary reduction (usually about 5%), while the church contributes double what the pastor does, up to a maximum of 10% of salary. Some churches also give the minister's por-tion. The BGCT then contributes one-half the amount the church does, up to a maximum of $420 per year. This plan includes not just pastors, but other staff members and area Directors of Missions. Participation is voluntary and as late as 1986, only about 60% of Texas Baptist churches and only about 21% of ministers and staff members were enrolled.

The amount of BGCT contribution to the ministers' retirement plan rose from $410,000 in 1963 to $968,000 in 1987, and in 16 years the BGCT had put $16,307,692 into their share of the retirement funds for ministers.[103] However, the Convention's income rose so rapidly that the *percentage* of total income funneled to the ministers' retirement plan de-creased from 3.42% in 1963 to 1.6% in 1987.[104] In the last decade, howev-er, that percentage has risen significantly.

PUBLISH AND CONCEAL NOT

On a plaque in the foyer of the *Baptist Standard* building in Dallas is a citation from Jeremiah 50:2, which reads *"Declare ye among the nations, and publish, and set up a standard; publish and conceal not."* Publish and conceal not. This text describes the role of the *Baptist Standard,* the widely read and highly respected weekly newsjournal of Texas Baptists. Since its ori-gin in 1892 the *Standard* has grown to become the most widely circulated and probably the most influential paper in Baptist history.

For years the *Baptist Standard* was privately owned, but was given debt-free to the BGCT in 1914. It is governed by a board of directors elected by the Convention. The board elects the editor, oversees general editorial policy, and within that context leaves the editor free to do his job. Probably no Baptist paper in America has the degree of editorial freedom that the *Baptist Standard* does and that, no doubt, is one reason the paper is highly regarded as an authentic voice of Baptist conviction and not merely a parroting of some party line dictated by Convention bureaucrats. Some of Pinson's predecessors have chafed over the editorial freedom of the *Standard,* and one or two executive secretaries tried to bring the paper under the control of the Executive Board but those efforts failed. Pinson has consistently supported the present relationship. Currently the board chairman is Danny Andrews, a Baptist layman who is editor of the *Plainview Daily Herald* in Plainview. Other board members include Larry C. Ashlock, Nell Bowles, Mark Bumpas, Sammye Cottle, Leroy Fenton, Kenneth W. Flowers, Jerold McBride, James R. Moore, James Nelson, Charles Risinger, Bennie Slack, Margarita Trevino, Charles D. Walton, and Billie Wilks.

The paper regularly carries news stories about Baptist events, articles on Baptist doctrines and church practice, and notices of staff changes among the churches. The executive director, Bill Pinson, has a regular article emphasizing some phase of Texas Baptist work. One popular feature is the page of "Letters to the Editor," which allows readers to offer their own comment on any aspect of Texas Baptist life or any article appearing in the paper, whether they agree or not. Of course, the highlight of each issue is the editorial page in which the editor offers his insights and judgments on any current events, trends, or developments affecting Baptists.

Presnall H. Wood served as editor of the *Baptist Standard* for over eighteen years (1977-1996), the longest tenure in the paper's history. He succeeded layman John Jeter Hurt, who held the editor's pen for twelve years. The man who modestly signed himself as "PHW" is Baptist to the bone. A native of Vernon, Texas, Wood grew up under the ministry of E. S. James who later edited the *Standard* from 1954-1966. A graduate of Baylor University and Southwestern Seminary, Wood earned a doctorate in Baptist history under the famed Robert A. Baker. He served a number of Texas churches as pastor, most recently the Park Place Church in Houston. His doctoral dissertation on the *Baptist Standard* was later published under the title of *Prophets With Pens* (1969), and he was a member of the paper's board of directors before assuming the editor's chair in 1977. He retired in 1996 and was named Editor Emeritus.

During his two decades at the helm of this influential paper, Editor Wood became known for his clear and straightforward writing, his firm commitment to telling the news about Baptists in Texas and beyond, and his absolute honesty and integrity. He operated on the conviction that "an informed Baptist is a better Baptist," and he did his part to keep Baptists informed about what was going on in their own churches and denomination. He often said, "One can inform the unenlisted, but one cannot enlist the uninformed."

During its peak in the late 1970s the paper reached a circulation of almost 400,000 and an estimated readership of about one million. Many churches used the back page of the *Standard* for their church newsletter, and mailed the paper to all the church families. Fewer churches do that today, and instead of sending the paper to all church families, many churches subscribe to a number of copies and members who want a copy pick it up at church. Circulation is down to about half of what it was during the peak. Leaders at the *Standard* and the BGCT have analyzed that decline, and have named several contributing causes.

In the new age of visual media, more people get their news from "sound bites" and less from print media. All print media in America face severe competition; some even suggest that the "age of Gutenburg" (whose invention made printing feasible) is drawing to a close. Most people watch more visual images and read less. While the *Standard* faithfully emphasizes Baptist doctrines, many Baptists in a more ecumenical age seem less concerned about denominational distinctives.

Cost is probably one factor in the decline. The cost of paper and postal rates have both skyrocketed in recent years. Presnall Wood recalled that when he became editor the cost of mailing the paper was about $8000 a week, but by the end of his tenure that had risen to over $25,000 a week.[105] The cost of paper and post have forced the paper to raise its subscription rates. Like most newspapers in America, the *Standard* earns its own way with subscriptions and advertising. The paper receives no Cooperative Program funds except to pay for the several pages of financial reports from the churches published quarterly. For almost 50 years the paper had been published in a magazine format, but in 1996 they switched back to a tabloid format which the paper had used in its earlier history. The tabloid was cheaper to produce and allowed more space.

Without doubt the theological controversy has also contributed to the *Standard's* drop in circulation. From the first, Wood determined to tell Baptists what was going on. The news coverage was extensive, and PHW used his editorial page to speak forcefully about the painful division and the dangers it posed for Baptists. It turned out that not all agreed with him, and others did not really want to know. Some thought the controversy would go away if it was ignored, and others would have been only too glad to silence his pungent editorials. Wood often harked back to an earlier crisis in Baptist history when J. B. Lawrence, then head of the HMB, coined a phrase: "Trust the Lord and tell the people." Wood continued the policy, which had been set by his predecessors and which has been continued by his successor, to have enough confidence in Baptists to tell them the truth. He was deeply convinced that Baptists have a right to know what is going on in their denomination. "The right to know," he wrote, "is at the heart of Baptist polity."[106] Baptists can be trusted with the truth, he maintained, and "there is more unity in Baptists knowing than in not knowing."

Toby Allen Druin was elected editor of the *Standard* effective January 1, 1996. A native of Amarillo, Druin is a journalist by training and has been in newspaper work most of his adult life. He joined the staff as associate editor in April 1976. Before that he was associate editor of the *Biblical Recorder,* the newsmagazine of North Carolina Baptists, for seven years, and editor of news services for the HMB in Atlanta for three years. A graduate of Baylor with a degree in journalism, Druin was named director of the university's news service after graduation. He has worked for a number of Texas newspapers as reporter, sports writer, and city editor. He is the author of *Step Over the Line,* the Home Mission study book for 1975. An excellent athlete, in high school in Amarillo Druin was an all-state catcher and was considered a good prospect for a career in professional baseball. An arm injury ended his tryout with the Baltimore organization. Toby and wife Larra are members of FBC in Duncanville.

In June 1998 Toby Druin announced his retirement as editor effective January 1, 1999.

In 1996 John A. Welch resigned as business manager of the *Standard.* He had been employed by the paper for 48 years, believed to be a record among Texas Baptist entities. He was succeeded by Gary L. Phillips.

In June 1998 Marv Knox was named editor-elect until January 1, 1999, when he will assume editorship formally. Knox, a native of Fort Worth who grew up in the Texas Panhandle, joined the *Standard* staff as associate editor in 1995. He earned degrees from Hardin-Simmons University in Abilene and Southern Baptist Theological Seminary in Louisville, Kentucky. An experienced journalist, Knox served as editor of the *Western Recorder,* the Baptist paper of Kentucky from 1990-1995. Before that he was associate editor of the *Baptist Message* of Louisiana, director of news and information at Southern Seminary, and assistant news director of the Home Mission Board in Atlanta. Knox and his wife Joanna have two daughters. The family is active in FBC, Lewisville, where Marv is a deacon and Sunday School teacher and Joanna is financial secretary for the church.

One could hardly find a better example of "continuity amidst change" than in the Baptist "people's paper" in Texas. Its assignment from the Convention is "to aid and support the Baptist General Convention of Texas and to interpret events and movements that affect the welfare of the people of God."[107] The editors have faithfully followed the officially adopted policy of "promoting all phases of work sponsored and promoted by the denomination and cooperating churches, the dissemination of all information relevant to the growth and welfare of these Baptist people, the development of fuller understanding of Baptist doctrines by all who bear the name Baptist, the evangelization of all persons within the reach of this convention and the encouragement to high moral standards and living among all peoples."[108]

PRESERVING THE RECORDS

In recent years BGCT leaders have shown a great deal more interest in preserving the historical records of the Convention and its agencies. Even before the first state convention was formed in 1848, leaders like Z. N. Morrell, Judge Baylor, and William Tryon took pains to keep an account of early churches and ministers. In 1848 the infant Baptist State Convention named a committee to collect and preserve historical records, and they made sure that their annual report contained a full account of their work. However, later leaders took a more casual approach to Texas Baptist history and, unfortunately, it appears that the minutes of the BSC Board of Directors from 1848 to the merger of 1886 have been lost.

In the 1930s Executive Secretary J. Howard Williams saw the importance of preserving historical records. He rescued several boxes of data that were about to be discarded, and in 1933 he led the Executive Board to designate the library of Southwestern Seminary in Fort Worth as the official depository of the Convention's historical materials. By that time the Seminary, which was a Texas Baptist institution from 1908 to 1925, had already collected a significant amount of Texas Baptist historical books, minutes and papers of important Texas Baptist leaders like the Carroll brothers, B. H. and J. M. From time to time, the BGCT sent materials to this depository, along with very modest amounts of money for cataloging. Meantime, the Seminary continued to collect materials on its own. These historical materials came to be called the *Texas Baptist Historical Collection*. In 1970 there was a proposal to move the collection to Baylor University, but the Texas Baptist Historical Committee recommended unanimously that it remain at the Seminary. The Convention continued sporadically to send materials to the Collection, and increased their financial supplement for their care and preservation.

Bill Pinson, whose lot it has been to lead Texas Baptists as they approach the sesquicentennial anniversary of convention life in Texas, has shown a keen awareness of the importance of history. He has done more to collect, preserve, and utilize the historical records of the BGCT than any of his predecessors. In the late 1990s, Pinson led the BGCT to develop plans to create its own historical archives at the Baptist Building in Dallas, possibly to be combined later with a historical museum. This was intended to give greater focus to the heritage of Texas Baptists and to become a part of their witness to the thousands of people who visit the Baptist Building each year. In early 1998 the BGCT employed Alan Lefever, who had served as archivist at Southwestern Seminary and specifically as director of the Texas Baptist Historical Collection, as the new archivist to help the Convention establish and maintain its archives in Dallas.

The BGCT request to have the Collection moved to Dallas created some confusion. It appears that the Seminary librarians who served as curators of the material never clearly distinguished between materials sent by the Convention, and thus belonging to the BGCT, and materials gathered over the years by the Seminary on its own both before and after the depository was formed in 1933. The confusion developed about the division of materials and the question of who owned what. To complicate the matter further, some churches had deposited their own records in the Seminary library but these records continued to belong to the churches. Representatives from the Convention and Seminary met several times to discuss the matter and agreed they needed the wisdom of Solomon who had offered to divide a baby between two mothers both of whom claimed it (1 Kings 3:16-28).

By early 1998 an amicable solution had been found. However the materials are divided, both institutions have agreed to provide the other with copies of any materials they want from the Collection. The name, *Texas Baptist Historical Collection,* will go with the archives to Dallas, but of course Southwestern Seminary will continue to collect, preserve, and make use of historical data relating to Baptists everywhere in the world, including Texas.

CONCLUSION

The ministry achievements of Texas Baptists since 1983 have been impressive. By whatever measure is applied, the work has been strengthened and extended. The records reveal more converts, more churches, more Baptist students, more ministerial volunteers, more overall gifts and mission contributions, and more volunteers on mission in Texas and beyond. In addition to statistical growth, there is ample evidence of spiritual vitality in Texas Baptist churches and in the Convention leadership.

However, change was in the air. Texas Baptists entered a "white water" stretch of the ongoing river, in which their Baptist ship was sorely tossed in the midst of swirling cross-currents and threatening rocks. The next chapter will describe some of the changes which have occurred in recent years.

CHAPTER 15

CHANGE AMIDST CONTINUITY,
1983–1998

IN 1996 ROBERT SLOAN, new president of Baylor University, ended the ban against dancing at the Baptist university on the Brazos. For 151 years, from Independence to Waco, dancing had been taboo on that campus, though students had sometimes engaged in "rhythmic foot functions," to which school officials had often turned a blind eye. President Sloan had the affirmative vote of the Board of Regents plus the recommendation of a committee of students, alumni and faculty to back up his own conviction that the ban on dancing was outmoded and needed to go. Sloan's announcement drew widespread media attention not only from Texas newspapers and television, but also from CNN, ABC News, CBS News and the Knight-Ridder news syndicate. Papers as far away as the *Los Angeles Times* and the *New York Times* headlined the new era of "Baylor Boogie."[1] The president promised that campus dances would be properly chaperoned, that no alcoholic beverages would be permitted, and that "we won't allow any obscene or provocative dancing."

The newly footloose Baylor students planned a huge street dance for April 18, 1996, which they promptly dubbed "Miracle on Fifth Street." With media trucks ringing the gala event, the tall president and his attractive wife Sue led off with a sedate waltz and then, to the enthusiastic cheers of the large crowd, broke into a lively jitterbug as student and faculty couples joined in the first official dance ever held on the Baylor campus.

Most Texas Baptists reacted to the new policy with more amusement than dismay, though some wondered out loud how President and Mrs. Sloan, such staunch Baptists, had learned to dance so well. A few elderly conservatives lifted eyebrows, but even their mild protests seemed half-hearted. In the long and heroic history of Texas Baptists, a school dance at Baylor cannot rank very high on the scale of important historical events. However, this event helped spotlight the spirit of change among Texas Baptists as the twentieth century was winding down. What was once unthinkable became thinkable. Baylor changed because Baptists had changed. In announcing its new policy, the university did not so much challenge Baptist morality as they skipped a step to catch up with where Texas Baptists had already moved. The unidentified Baylor student was right when she exclaimed, "It's a new day for Baylor!"

The 1990s also brought a new day for Baptists. As the new century and a new millennium approached, change was in the air both in the national SBC and among Texas Baptists. The 1990 SBC meeting in New Orleans marked the final victory of the fundamentalist faction and their control of the Convention was complete. Some of the outvoted moderates met in Atlanta in the summer of 1990 and formed the Cooperative Baptist Fellowship (CBF) as an alternate way of sponsoring Baptist missions and education. In the 1990s, the systematic purge of the SBC agencies continued as the victorious party installed their own people as heads of SBC agencies, seminaries, and mission boards. By 1997 the SBC in its "Covenant for a New Century" underwent its most extensive restructuring since the 1920s. Three of the four general boards of the SBC received new names and some of them were given enlarged assignments. Some of the SBC Commissions were abolished entirely, with their tasks dropped or parceled out to others. While all of the SBC seminaries took a rightward turn in theology, some of them resurrected ancient Baptist controversies by embracing strict Calvinism which held that only the predestined could be saved. New approaches to missions at home and overseas, new priorities in funding, and a new openness to cooperation with the larger evangelical community where appropriate marked the SBC in the last decade of the twentieth century.

Change also came to Texas Baptists. It seemed as if someone had flipped the "fast forward" switch as Texas Baptists hurtled from one major change to another. In 1990 Baylor University cut loose from BGCT control, and the shock of that event was compounded by the seismic upheaval over the firing of Russell H. Dilday as president of Southwestern Seminary in 1994. Responding to dramatic demographic shifts which had turned Texas into a major mission field, the BGCT adopted a new funding formula to provide more resources for starting new churches, and appointed committees to study ways to preserve historic Baptist teachings and provide Bible and mission study materials tailored to the needs of Texas churches. They also launched several new ministries to meet the new challenges that arose with the new times. The previous chapter traced elements of continuity despite change; it remains for this chapter to sketch out some of the changes in the midst of continuity.

CONTROVERSY IN TEXAS

It appears that Texas Baptists will end the twentieth century as they began it: embroiled in bitter controversy among themselves. They entered the century in conflict between the mainline "missionary" forces represented by leaders like George W. Truett and J. B. Gambrell, and the militant followers of ultra-conservative Samuel A. Hayden who later split off in the "BMA" faction. While many of the issues in the Baptist controversies of the 1890s and the 1990s are different, others are surprisingly similar and the contentious spirit of the "Haydenites" can be found among the current dissidents. There is also a remarkable geographical similarity, with the same regions of Texas first saturated with the "hardshell" views of Daniel Parker in the 1830s, with the divisive spirit of Samuel Hayden in the 1890s, and continued attacks upon the BGCT by ultraconservatives in the 1990s.

The story of the current SBC controversy has been told elsewhere and need not be repeated here except in briefest summary.[2] Throughout the twentieth century, controversy has flared up sporadically among Southern Baptists over the nature of biblical authority and how to interpret the Bible. In the 1920s, the fiery J. Frank Norris of Fort Worth led a series of attacks upon the Southern Baptist Convention and specifically against Baylor University in Waco and Southwestern Seminary in Fort Worth. The Norris movement attracted widespread attention and in 1934 a number of Texas churches pulled out of the BGCT to form their own rival group. In 1925 the SBC adopted its first formal confession of faith, The Baptist Faith and Message, largely in response to the Norris controversy.

In the early 1960s, Ralph H. Elliott, professor of Old Testament at the newly formed Midwestern Baptist Seminary in Kansas City provoked a firestorm with publication of his book, *The Message of Genesis*. The "Elliott Controversy" engulfed the entire SBC overnight. Texas Baptists were prominent in the response, including T. A. Patterson, executive secretary, E. S. James, editor of the *Baptist Standard,* and K. Owen White, pastor of FBC Houston, who wrote an influential condemnation of Elliott's views, the famous "Death in the Pot" article published in the *Baptist Standard*[3] and picked up by other Baptist papers. The Elliott controversy propelled White into the SBC presidency in 1962, beginning the trend for Convention presidents to be elected on the basis of their theology. The Baptist Sunday School Board in Nashville, which had published Elliott's book through its Broadman Press division, was drawn into the controversy and suspicion was cast upon their other materials, including the familiar Sunday School quarterlies. Elliott was dismissed from his teaching post at Midwestern Seminary and his book was withdrawn from publication. In 1963 the SBC adopted a revised version of the Baptist Faith and Message confession, but still the controversy would not subside.

In the 1960s the Sunday School Board launched its most ambitious publishing project, the ten-volume Broadman Bible Commentary. Volume I on Genesis-Exodus came out in 1969 and immediately stirred a new phase of the ongoing controversy. Many readers took strong exception to the commentary on Genesis, written by English Baptist scholar G. Henton Davies. The "Commentary Controversy" was widely discussed in Baptist papers and meetings and soon became the dominant issue in Southern Baptist thought. The controversy seemed to feed upon itself and fanned the embers of other forms of dissent. The 1970 SBC meeting in Denver, under the leadership of President W. A. Criswell, was marked by hostility—the messengers refused to hear the explanation of James L. Sullivan, head of the Sunday School Board, and they actually booed Herschel H. Hobbs, the respected elder statesman and former president of the SBC, when he urged restraint. The SBC voted to have Volume I withdrawn, and in 1973 a revised Volume I appeared, prepared by different writers. A motion to withdraw the entire commentary set was defeated, but later Broadman Press launched another commentary series, *The New American Commentary*, expected to run 40 volumes, to be prepared by writers who held more conservative views, specifically the Chicago Statement of Inerrancy. The Broadman commentary series will no longer be printed.

Two important developments emerged at the Houston Convention in 1979. First, Southern Baptists met a new word, *inerrancy*, applied to Scripture. For centuries Baptist confessions proclaimed their conviction that the Bible is God's true and inspired Word and that it is absolutely dependable. Since 1650 the adjective most often used by Baptists to describe their view of the Bible was *infallible*.[4] Meanwhile, conservative Calvinists in Europe had come to use another word, *inerrant*. While the two words mean much the same thing, in time *inerrant* came to be applied more to the condition of the text while *infallible* referred more to the message of the Bible. At any rate, *inerrant* was less familiar to Southern Baptists, and when it burst upon the SBC scene in 1979, it was linked with unlovely political associations and harsh attacks upon the SBC. However, the term became a code word and this phase of the ongoing conflict was known as the "inerrancy controversy." The conflict was further fueled by a few prominent Southern Baptists who did not want to use either word, infallible or inerrant, to describe the Bible.

The second development at Houston in 1979 was the appearance of a thoroughly organized political campaign, using precinct style politics, to capture control of the SBC. Houston Judge Paul Pressler and Dallas theologian Paige Patterson led this "take-over" effort, directing affairs from sky-boxes high above the arena where the SBC met, with political know-how and sophistication that would have done credit to either of America's national political conventions. In the early 1970s William Powell, then with the Home Mission Board, had developed a strategy which, he argued, would yield control of the SBC. The strategy was simple: elect the SBC president for ten consecutive years. Since the president appoints the committees that name other committees that nominate trustees for the institutions, including the seminaries, electing the president could in time put a different kind of trustees in charge of the institutions. Since trustees served five years and were eligible for reelection once, the process of change would take about ten years. Pressler and Patterson used Powell's strategy successfully, but they did not invent it as is sometimes asserted.[5] The 1979 Convention began what Jesse C. Fletcher called a ten-year "battle for the gavel."[6] The election of Adrian Rogers on the first ballot in 1979 started the process, and the extreme conservatives have controlled the election every year since. By 1990, all agreed, their victory was complete and during the 1990 convention in New Orleans, Pressler and Patterson staged an impromptu celebration at the Cafe de Monde where, they said, years before over coffee and beignets they planned the takeover.

By the late 1990s, inerrancy seemed less an issue, with the focus shifted to social issues and new forms of denominationalism. The ultraconservative churches that historically had given little through the Cooperative Program, preferring to channel their mission gifts through independent or non-denominational agencies, gained a new zeal for the CP once they were in control. They now praised the CP which they had previously criticized, and bitterly assailed any churches that dared to direct any of their giving outside that denominational pipeline.

Like a thick fog, "The Controversy" blanketed the Baptist landscape and it would not lift. Bill Pinson and others made a valiant effort to keep Texas Baptists focused on evangelism and missions, believing that Baptists busy with vital ministries have little time for distracting feuding. Some hoped that ignoring the controversy would make it go away, and the editor of the *Baptist Standard* was often criticized for telling Baptists what was going on in Baptist life. However, once their control of the national SBC was complete, the fundamentalist faction openly announced their intention to take over the state conventions, and by using the same strategy.[7] By the 1990s it was no longer possible to keep the controversy out of Texas. The struggle for the soul of Southern Baptists became also a struggle for the soul of Texas Baptists, and the controversy loomed on the horizon like some threatening storm. It affected almost every thing Texas Baptists did, and it shaped the environmment in which they ministered. Almost all of the changes described in this chapter were influenced directly by this super-charged atmostphere of controversy.

BAYLOR AND THE BAPTISTS

September 21, 1990, marked a defining moment in Texas Baptist history. On that day in Waco the Board of Trustees of Baylor University voted to adopt an amended charter which allowed the trustees to elect their own successors. This in effect cut the university loose from the Baptist General Convention of Texas which had elected the Baylor trustees since the merger of 1886. Application with the State of Texas for a charter change was made before the meeting, and the amended charter was filed with the Secretary of State the same day and went into effect immediately. The new charter was official and it was final before any public announcement was made. Baylor University was still a Texas Baptist school, but it was no longer under the control of the BGCT.

The shock waves from that action were immediate. As their oldest institution of any kind, and perhaps their most successful, Baylor University was near to the heart of Texas Baptists. Chartered under the Republic of Texas, Baylor was older than the state and predated the Southern Baptist Convention. Many Baylor alumni referred to the school as the "crown jewel" of Texas Baptists. For over a century, the BGCT had elected the trustees who controlled the university, and Texas Baptists who had poured untold millions into the school assumed that they owned it and had a right to determine its policies.

Part of the shock came from the way in which the action was taken. University leaders and trustee officers made no advance announcement of their intentions. In fact, many of the trustees learned of the proposal for a charter change only after their arrival for the meeting. When the trustees assembled, the first order of business was to set aside the previous agenda and move immediately to a vote on the charter change. Trustee chairman Winfred Moore, pastor of FBC, Amarillo, presided. Dewey Presley, trustee from Dallas, made the motion to amend the charter, and it passed by a vote of 30 to 7 with one abstention. By the time the news was announced, the change was a fact accomplished and Baylor's relationship to the BGCT was radically altered.

Neither Bill Pinson, head of the Executive Board, nor Jerry F. Dawson, coordinator of the Christian Education Coordinating Board, was informed of this intended action, though the BGCT constitution provides that any charter change must be approved by the CECB, the Executive Board, and finally by the Convention. Baylor's president, Herbert Reynolds, later explained that if he had informed leaders at the Baptist Building of their intention, it would have put them in a serious dilemma. Either they would have had to try to halt the action or later explain why they did not. He also feared that fundamentalists might obtain an injunction to prevent or delay the action. President Reynolds said the change was made to protect the university against a possible fundamentalist takeover. In some ways it was a reaction to developments in the SBC seminaries. Reynolds noted that the fundamentalists had said they would take over the SBC and they did it; they said they intended to take over the Texas convention and he saw no reason to doubt they meant it or that they might ultimately succeed.

Complaints against Baylor go back at least to the turn of the century when student J. Frank Norris criticized his teachers in Bible and especially in biology. However, the criticisms took on a more serious tone in the 1970s when influential pastor James T. Draper of Euless raised questions about the use of a textbook, *People of the Covenant,* in Bible classes. Houston layman Paul Pressler complained that some high school students whom he had taught in Sunday School found their faith challenged at the university. Paige Patterson, whose daughter considered attending Baylor before opting instead for Jerry Falwell's Liberty University in Virginia, joined the anti-Baylor protest, naming three professors in the religion department whose teachings he questioned.[8]

Soon these protests found organized expression. In 1988 a group of Baylor alumni formed an organization "United for a Better Baylor," and launched an effort to elect "conservative trustees" in order to bring about a "course correction" at Baylor.[9] An article in the May 1988 edition of the

Southern Baptist Advocate, a militant independent paper edited by a North Carolina pastor, urged Baylor alumni to make changes at Baylor, and asked, "Are you mad at the liberal bent of the Baylor Line?" Donny Cortimilia, a Baylor graduate and pastor of FBC Melissa, signed a six-page mailout in August, 1988, urging all Baylor exes to pay their alumni dues, attend the Baylor homecoming and alumni association and try to turn the school toward more conservative policies. "The problem at Baylor," the mailout said, "is not just liberal professors and administrators, but a board of trustees that set the policy and support the present situation at Baylor." The mailout said, "Baylor will never change until there is a board of trustees that will design and implement a new policy for a course correction at Baylor."[10] Reynolds and others at Baylor felt themselves under attack and felt they had reason for long-term concern. "The Fundamentalists have made it plain on many occasions," Reynolds wrote, "that Baylor University is one of the key institutions in this entire struggle."[11] He felt that fundamentalist control of Baylor would threaten both academic and financial stability of the school, make it more difficult to recruit top faculty and students, and would change the philosophy of the university from open inquiry to indoctrination of a strict party line. Reynolds even went so far as to say that given their typical mindset, he did "not consider it possible for the Fundamentalists to operate what we would properly call a university."[12]

The 1988 meeting of the BGCT at Austin had the theme of "Share Jesus Now" but all the talk was about the attacks against Baylor. The Convention president, Joel Gregory, divided his presidential message into two parts, one addressing the theme and the other on the "Baylor perplexities." Presnall Wood, editor, said "The Baptist Standard does not believe Texas Baptists want any perceived or real inquisition of Baylor or any of their institutions."[13] As the attacks increased, President Reynolds indicated that he would not sit idly by and see Baylor taken over by any extremist group. In a May 1988, article in the *Baylor Line,* newsletter of the Alumni Association, the president indicated that he might join other tenured faculty of Baylor in a class action lawsuit. Reynolds came away from the 1990 meeting of the SBC in New Orleans convinced that the fundamentalist victory was complete in the national body and that the state conventions might be next. He determined to act before the window of opportunity for Baylor closed.

Baylor's own law firm, plus an outside firm, made a detailed study of the Baylor charter. Baylor University was not established by any convention; indeed there was no Baptist convention in Texas in 1845, and as yet no Southern Baptist Convention. The school was established by a Baptist Educational Society which no longer exists. In the 1886 merger of Baylor University at Independence and Waco University to form Baylor University at Waco, the newly formed Baptist General Convention of Texas was given the privilege of electing trustees for the united school. However, the old provision from the charter of 1845 that trustees have the sole legal authority to amend the charter was never changed. The BGCT constitution provides that the state convention must approve charter changes for all its institutions, but Baylor argued that their 1845 charter antedated this provision and was not bound by it. In a series of questions/answers, the Baylor officials said: "Does the Board of Trustees of Baylor University have the power to amend the Charter without the approval of the Baptist General Convention of Texas? Yes. Baylor's Board of Trustees is vested with the sole authority to amend Baylor's Charter. There is no restriction or condition in Baylor's Charter or otherwise on the Board's authority. In such a case, Texas law provides that a majority of the Trustees in office have the sole authority to amend the Charter." The Trustees, they said, have always had this authority but have not hitherto exercised it. Another question was, "Doesn't the Convention's Constitution require Baylor's Board of Trustees to get approval from the Convention to change Baylor's Charter? No. The Convention's Constitution provides that the trustees of Baptist institutions shall be elected by the Convention, but this requirement is not binding on Baylor's Board of Trustees."[14]

When Pinson learned of the Baylor action, he immediately called for meetings of BGCT leaders to devise a response. On October 2 the Administrative Committee, George Gaston chair, called for a committee to study the matter. They set aside $30,000 from contingent funds to fund the committee's work, including travel and legal counsel.[15] They also voted to escrow money in the BGCT budget intended for Baylor, except the portion that went to ministerial tuition and faculty salary supplements. The Administrative Committee also made an eloquent statement about the importance of Baylor to Texas Baptists. They said,

> Baylor University is a highly esteemed, long-standing, valuable friend of Texas Baptists. The relationship of trust and cooperation which has existed between Baylor and the Baptist General Convention of Texas has been in place since 1886 and is worthy of preserving. Baylor has been the beneficiary of Texas Baptist prayer, the children of Baptist homes and churches, the cooperative gifts of Baptist stewardship, the wisdom and guidance of Baptist beliefs, the care of Baptist leadership, and the generosity of Baptist benefactors. Texas Baptists have received from Baylor a powerful influence for God's Kingdom in Texas and around the world. Christian leaders, trained and shaped by Baylor, fill the churches of Texas. Denominational leaders across the Southern Baptist Convention have been inspired to excellence through their Baylor heritage.[16]

At a called meeting on October 17, 1990, the Executive Board appointed a Committee on BGCT/Baylor Relationship, and named Robert E. Naylor, retired president of Southwestern Seminary, as chairman with Charles McIlveene as vice-chairman. Other members included Paul Armes, Betty Bell, Amelia Bishop, Al Burns, David Evans, A. E. Fogle, Rudy Gonzales, Jr., Mauriece Johnston, Edith Marie King, O. C. Madden, James R. Maples, J.K. Minton, John Morgan, Bill Peek, Julian Shaddix, Horner Shelton, Damon Shook, Bailey Stone, John Uxer, and Warner Wickes. Phil Lineberger, Robert Parker, George Gaston, and Sam Medina were ex officio members and of course Bill Pinson also worked closely with the committee.

Early on, the committee laid out four possible courses of action. They could acquiesce, litigate, separate from Baylor entirely, or negotiate a new relationship between the Convention and Baylor. Some wanted to litigate and felt the Convention could win in court, but that option was never seriously considered. Pinson, though he thought the BGCT might win a lawsuit, was convinced that in the long run all would be losers if they took this Baptist battle into the secular courts. The committee opted to negotiate, and said, "First, we committed ourselves to the concept that Baylor and the Baptist General Convention of Texas should maintain a close relationship. Second, we agreed that we should help provide the real or perceived security Baylor has stated it needs from a takeover by any extreme group."[17] The committee first asked Baylor to reconsider and reverse their decision, but of course they did not really expect that Baylor would do that and they were correct.

The new Baylor charter as first amended on September 21 provided a two-tier system of leadership. The *regents* would govern the university and 75% of them would be elected by the regents in a self-perpetuating system. There would also be 48 *trustees* who would serve as an advisory board but would have no governing power. These trustees would be elected by the BGCT, and the trustees in turn would directly elect 25% of the regents. Though the BGCT would not directly elect any regents, they would at least have an indirect voice in the governance of the school. The Naylor Committee objected to this two-tier system on two grounds: first, they felt this did not give the BGCT enough voice in the university and, second, they felt the use of the term *trustee* in this new sense would be confusing because throughout Texas Baptist life the term meant a member of a governing body.

The Committee on BGCT/Baylor Relationship and Baylor leaders engaged in intensive dialogue for months, with proposals and counter-proposals offered, considered, and mostly rejected. The Naylor group named a six-member "discussion group," led by Dick Maples, to meet with a similar small group at Baylor, headed by Thomas R. Powers. The small group met several times for candid discussions but could report no breakthrough solutions. The committee came up with a compromise proposal, known as the "Naylor Plan," which called for dropping the two-tier trustee system altogether. Instead, the Baylor regents would directly elect 25% of the governing body, and the BGCT would directly elect another 25%. The remaining 50% would be elected by the BGCT but only from a list of names submitted by the Baylor regents. The regents would submit two names for each vacancy with the BGCT choosing which to elect. Naylor felt this would give the university adequate protection against the encroachment of any extremist group and also preserve a meaningful voice for the Convention. The Naylor plan acknowledged that Baylor regents had authority unilaterally to amend their charter, but asked that they require a 90% vote or "super-majority" to change the Baptist identity of the school. The Committee said, "We believe that Baylor is protected from takeover by any extremist group by agreeing to these recommendations. The Committee believes that Baylor controls its destiny with the Regents determining 75% of the make-up of the Baylor Board."[18] Naylor felt this was the minimum that Texas Baptists could accept.

The Baylor people did not see it that way. They declined to make these changes because they felt it would give the BGCT control over 75% of the regents. In a May 3, 1991, letter to the committee, Reynolds said "The [Naylor] plan would have shifted to the Convention the right to elect seventy-five percent of Baylor's governing body. Such a move would not provide Baylor with the assurance it needs that it is in control of its own destiny and would create uncertainty about the University's future that would make it more difficult to attract quality faculty and students and substantial donors, and would adversely affect Baylor's standing in the academic community." However, Baylor did make some concessions. The regents adopted a resolution on May 3 in which they agreed to further amend the charter to eliminate the two-tier system and allow the BGCT to elect directly 25% of the Regents. However, they were adamant in rejecting other parts of the Naylor Plan. They said this plan "would undo the actions of September 21, 1990, and leave Baylor without adequate control of its own destiny and without adequate protection from attempts to gain control of the Baylor governing body by extremist groups through the battleground of Convention politics."

In a letter of May 28, 1991, to Bill Pinson, President Reynolds and Paul W. Powell, who had succeeded Winfred Moore as chairman of the Regents, explained further their unwillingness to weaken their earlier action. "Prior to September 21, 1990," they said, "Baylor University was subject to takeover by extremist groups through political processes because the entire governing board was elected by messengers attending the annual meeting of the Baptist General Convention of Texas. Baylor achieved protection from any threat of an extremist political group takeover by amending its Charter on September 21, 1990, so that its governing board is now elected 75 percent by the Regents themselves." As they saw it, "the Naylor Plan takes from Baylor and returns to the messengers the power to elect 75% of the Baylor Board of Regents, but there is no certainty that 50 percent of the Regents will be elected only from Baylor nominees." Under *Robert's Rules of Order,* the parliamentary guide used by the BGCT, messengers have a right to make substitute nominations from the floor and "there can be no assurance that the messengers will not nominate from the floor and, in fact, elect substitutes for those nominated by Baylor for election to the Baylor Board of Regents." The letter in effect concluded the negotiations, saying "there is nothing further for the Baylor Board to consider."

With negotiations stalled, an unofficial small group led by Phil Lineberger, BGCT president, met with a similar unofficial group from Baylor. They reached tentative agreements which were accepted by the full committee, despite the reluctance of some members including the chairman. These agreements were ratified by the Executive Board, and became the basis for final agreement between Baylor and the Convention. By these terms, Baylor agreed to change its amended charter to allow the BGCT to elect directly 25% of the Regents and they agreed that all the Regents would be Baptist and 75% of them Texas Baptists. They also agreed that in electing 75% of the governing body, the Regents would give due consideration to names suggested by the BGCT. The Baylor leaders also repeated their strong affirmations, which they had given from the first, that Baylor would continue to be a Baptist university, closely allied with the interests of Texas Baptists. Baylor's Baptist identity could be changed, they agreed, only by a vote of 80% of the regents. Since the BGCT elected 25% of the regents, such an event seemed unlikely. These were the most concessions Baylor would make, and they became the basis of the final agreement.

The Baylor issue dominated the 1991 Texas convention which was held, appropriately, at Waco. Robert Parker, chairman of the Executive Board, presented the negotiated agreement between Baylor and the Committee on BGCT/Baylor Relationship and recommended its adoption. Some messengers seemed to assume, mistakenly, that voting this agreement down would return Baylor to its former status. Ed Rogers, BGCT vice-president, responded to a messenger's point of order by pointing out that "The agreement does not sanction what Baylor did when it violated the Convention's Constitution. It simply contains the Convention's response to that violation. . . . The agreement is not a statement that Baylor's September 21 1990 action was lawful. It is simply an agreement for a new and different kind of relationship with Baylor."[19] Phil Lineberger spoke for the agreement, saying "I am convinced it is the closest relationship between the BGCT and Baylor which can be established at this time. It seems that the only alternatives of this agreement are to sue or separate from Baylor and I do not believe these would help us advance the Lord's Kingdom."[20]

Ed Young, pastor of 2nd, Houston, spoke against the agreement, describing it as an unacceptable compromise which set a dangerous precedent which other Texas Baptist institutions might follow. The agreement, if accepted, he said, would "constitute an acquiescence in and approval of a significant violation of the constitution of the BGCT and a betrayal of trust of those saints who have sacrificed to make Baylor a great Christian institution." In his substitute motion, Young asked the Baylor trustees to agree to binding arbitration led by a three-member arbitration team appointed by Billy Graham. If Baylor refused to enter into arbitration, or refused to abide by its decision, the substitute motion called on the BGCT to take legal action to overturn the Baylor decision.[21] Young's substitute motion was defeated, and the negotiated agreement was ratified by a vote of 5,745 to 3,992.[22] For the next two or three years there were sporadic efforts to find some way to force Baylor to undo its action, but in time most opponents came to agree with the old warrior, W. A. Criswell, who said,

"I've washed my hands of them. You are not going to get Baylor back . . . It's gone."[23]

Almost a decade after the change in relationship, it appeared that Baylor was just as much Baptist as before. If anything, the relationship between the University and the Convention was more cordial and cooperative than before. Most escrowed funds were long since released, except for $1 million diverted to a special scholarship fund to benefit young people from the Baptist children's homes. Baylor receives an annual appropriation from the budget of the BGCT, though considerably less than before the charter change. Most of funds Baylor receives are directed to ministerial tuition, scholarships, and to various religious projects on campus.

Some wondered if other schools might follow Baylor's example in casting off Convention control. A member of the Executive Board asked "what was being done to close the gap in the charter amendment situation that allows the withdrawal of institutions from the Baptist General Convention of Texas?" The Board attorney said he did not believe any such gap existed, but acknowledged that the Naylor Committee was studying the matter "to insure that they do not give any institution the ability to flee the control of the Baptist General Convention of Texas."[24] Such flight seemed unlikely since the charters of the various schools differed and most of them were more dependent upon BGCT money than Baylor was. Even so, leaders in the other universities were acutely aware of Baylor's action and the reasons given for it.

At the called meeting of the Executive Board on October 17, 1990, Bill Pinson put the Baylor issue in perspective. Minutes of that meeting record that, "Pinson spoke of the need for a response and the controversy surrounding this matter. He also admonished that the issue of Baylor's action is not of supreme importance. The supreme issue is the leading of the lost to the Lord Jesus Christ and seeing that Texas has a mission base to reach a lost world."[25]

EARTHQUAKE AT SOUTHWESTERN SEMINARY

As if one school crisis was not enough, Southwestern Seminary in Fort Worth experienced an upheaval on March 9, 1994, which sent shock waves throughout the state and beyond. Russell Hooper Dilday, Jr., president since 1978, was fired by the trustees on a vote of 26 to 7. Tensions between the administration and trustees had increased for several years as the board took on an ever more fundamentalist cast.

Dilday came from an old and honored Texas Baptist family. His father and namesake, R. H. Dilday, Sr., was longtime minister of education at FBC, Wichita Falls, and later headed the Church Ministries Department of the State Missions Commission of the BGCT. Young Dilday grew up in FBC, Wichita Falls, and later graduated from Baylor University. He participated in the youth revivalism of the time, and while a student at Southwestern Seminary he served as pastor of the Baptist church at Antelope in Jack County. Dilday received both Masters and Doctors degrees from Southwestern. During his graduate studies, Dilday pastored at FBC in Clifton and commuted to classes in Fort Worth. He was married to Betty Doyen, with the wedding ceremony performed by her pastor, Boyd Hunt, at FBC in Houston. After graduation from Seminary, Dilday served as pastor at Tallowood Baptist Church in Houston and at the prominent Ponce de Leon church in Atlanta. While in Atlanta, Dilday became more active in denominational leadership, serving as chairman of the board of trustees for the SBC Home Mission Board.

Upon the retirement of Robert E. Naylor, president of Southwestern since 1958, a trustee search committee chaired by James E. Carter recommended Russell Dilday as Naylor's successor. Dilday came to Southwestern as president-elect in 1977, and assumed the president's office January 1, 1978. He was not the only candidate for the job. Cal Guy, senior professor of missions at the Seminary, led an effort to elect Huber L. Drumwright, who was at the time dean of the School of Theology. Guy mistakenly thought he had enough trustee support to elect the popular Drumwright, but Dilday was nominated unanimously by the search committee and elected overwhelmingly by the trustees. Drumwright later left the Seminary to become Executive Secretary of the Baptist state convention in Arkansas. Ralph W. Pulley, a Dallas lawyer, was chairman of the Seminary trustees when Dilday was fired and, as chairman, was a key strategist in planning and accomplishing the firing.

Despite his outstanding credentials and mainline conservative theology, Dilday did not please the SBC ultraconservatives. He probably sealed his fate as far back as 1984 when he preached the annual sermon at the SBC in Kansas City. His topic was "Higher Ground," and he appealed to Southern Baptists to rise above the petty partisan political struggle between moderate conservative and ultraconservative wings of the denomination that even then was alienating brethren and diverting Baptist attention from ministry. He deplored the "shrewd brokers of power" who sought to control the Convention for their own purposes, and urged Baptists to leave the "misty flats of suspicion, rumor, criticism, innuendoes, guilt by association and the entire demonic family of forced uniformity."[26] Dilday's sermon was interrupted several times by applause but not everyone was cheering. The reaction of ultraconservatives to the sermon was angry. Perhaps many had assumed that the president of the largest SBC Seminary, the school with a reputation for conservatism, would join their conservative coalition.

Two Texas pastors, Cecil Sherman and Kenneth L.Chafin, organized an informal alliance to resist the fundamentalist takeover of the SBC. Both were doctoral graduates of Southwestern Seminary. Sherman grew up in the Polytechnic church in Fort Worth and was pastor of FBC in Ashville, North Carolina before returning to Fort Worth as pastor of the Broadway Baptist Church. Chafin was a former professor at both Southwestern and Southern seminaries and later served as pastor of the influential South Main Baptist Church in Houston. At a time when most Southern Baptists thought the fundamentalist upsurge would not amount to much, Sherman and Chafin raised a warning that if Southern Baptists did not resist while they could they would find their Convention taken over by a new and militant kind of Southern Baptist. Many SBC leaders felt the two Texans exaggerated the dangers and their warnings elicited little support, especially among the SBC agency heads. Dilday, while sympathetic with their desire to preserve the historic SBC, did not align himself or the Seminary with the Sherman/Chafin resistance. However, he did associate closely with a group of more "moderate moderates," including Keith R. Parks, head of the Foreign Mission Board; Roy L. Honeycutt, president of Southern Seminary; Lloyd Elder, head of the Sunday School Board, and Jesse C. Fletcher, president and later chancellor of Hardin-Simmons University in Abilene.

Because of what they called "inordinate publicity" about the firing of President Dilday, the trustees sent a letter to SBC pastors and DOMs explaining some of the reasons for their action. In that letter the trustees claimed that Dilday had created an impasse by refusing to cooperate with the trustees, that there were "irreconcilable differences" between the president and the board, that Dilday had criticized SBC leaders, and that the president was "dedicated to berate, misrepresent and assail those who hold the Bible to be God's inerrant, infallible and authoritative word."[27] In other releases they also complained that Dilday's nominees for addition to the faculty did not adequately represent their conservative views, that he would not require the School of Church Music to teach and practice a more popular and contemporary style of worship music, and that he did not bring enough conservative speakers to the daily chapel services. They also alleged that Dilday's own views of Scripture were "liberal," and that he suffered liberal professors to teach at Southwestern. However, when representatives from the SBC "Peace Committee" visited Southwestern Seminary, they raised no serious concerns about the Seminary, its president, or its faculty.

The trustees were also offended that Dilday had invited Keith Parks, longtime president of the Foreign Mission Board and later associated with the CBF, to speak in chapel, and they forced cancellation of the invitation. Some trustees accused Dilday of being confrontational, of "mismanagement" of the Seminary, of causing a decline in enrollment.[28] Dilday denied these charges, pointing out that enrollment had dropped at all six of the SBC seminaries. In response to the letter, Dilday said he was "appalled" at its "inaccuracies and distortions of truth."[29] However, even some of his friends felt that he could have cultivated a more cooperative relationship with the trustees; for example, he made little effort to conceal his disappointment with the qualifications of some of the new trustees coming on the board. Perhaps the main complaint was that Dilday was no part of the political faction that was in process of gaining control of the SBC.

Many were shocked not just that the president of Southwestern Seminary was fired, but by the way in which it was done. Just before he was fired, trustee leaders specifically assured Dilday that they had no intention of seeking his dismissal at that meeting. Later evidence showed that some trustee leaders had already made the decision to seek his dismissal and had already arranged to have the locks on his office door changed during the trustee session in order to prevent him from returning to his office. They also had the access code to Dilday's office computer changed. Trustee officers later defended the use of these tactics as necessary to carry out what they were convinced was God's will.[30] They feared that if Dilday or his supporters knew their plans they might be able to muster support which would have made the firing difficult or even impossible.

On the Baptist Richter Scale, the firing of Russell Dilday ranks as a major earthquake. On the morning of March 9, 1994, rumors spread like wildfire on campus that the trustees in closed meeting were even then in process of firing the president. Classes adjourned all over campus as professors, students, local pastors and some town people crowded into the Rotunda outside the Truett Conference Room where the meeting was held. This "come and go" crowd alternately prayed, sang hymns, or stood in stunned silence. Just before noon, Dilday emerged from the meeting and announced to the crowd, "The Seminary no longer has a president."

Dilday was offered certain benefits on condition that he would take immediate retirement and agree not to speak out against the Seminary or the trustees. Dilday later said the retirement package "was offered in a confrontational spirit, which I looked at long enough to realize while generous in total it was really a buyout, almost an effort to bribe me to leave, and no matter how generous I could not in good faith accept it."[31] When he refused, he was fired without any benefit package. However, the trustees later agreed to continue his salary and benefits to age sixty-five, still on conditions that Dilday felt would "muzzle" him. When he accepted appointment as special assistant to the president of Baylor University a few months later, the monthly salary payments ceased but the former president retained his freedom to speak his convictions. He was later named as distinguished professor in the new George W. Truett Seminary in connection with Baylor. The majority of Texas Baptists continued to hold Dilday in high respect as shown by his 1997 election as president of the BGCT.

Perhaps no single event in Texas Baptist history ever attracted so much attention as the Dilday firing, most of it unfavorable. The secular media reported the event nationwide, and the Baptist papers were filled with the news and reactions for months. Baptists overseas, especially in countries where Dilday had traveled and preached, shared in the shock and disbelief. The general concensus both in this country and abroad was that if Russell Dilday was not conservative enough for Southern Baptists, who possibly could be? Some wanted to request or require the trustees to reverse their action, and only clever political maneuvering prevented the issue from coming before the SBC in session in 1994 at Orlando, Florida. Many were distressed that at a time when Baptists were trying to cope with the epidemic of involuntary termination of pastors, the Seminary which provided most of the Texas pastors could find no other solution to their problems than a public firing. This seemed to provide a prototype and a legitimacy to churches which took the same solution.

Reactions to the Dilday firing were many. A few Southern Baptists, mostly in other states, applauded the trustees' action. However, in Texas the reaction was mostly negative. Many Texas Baptists were frightened, realizing that the bitter denominational fight with its angry purges had come to their doorstep. They were convinced that something must be done to protect the BGCT against the kind of takeover which had befallen the SBC. One Baptist wrote, "The firing of Russell Dilday . . . should serve as a wake-up call to any Texas Baptists who have yet to understand the seriousness of the fundamentalist threat to our state convention."[32] Some graduates returned their diplomas, and at least one Texas church, and perhaps more, withdrew from SBC affiliation. The fact that Texas Baptists were alerted to what could happen and motivated to resist was surely one factor in the failure of fundamentalists to take control of the BGCT. In the aftermath of what some called the "March Massacre," many Texas Baptists realized for the first time that Southwestern Seminary is not a Texas Baptist institution. In their heads they may have known that in 1925 the BGCT transferred title and control of Southwestern to the SBC, but in their hearts they still regarded the Fort Worth school as "their seminary." But the events of March, 1994, demonstrated in a shocking manner that Southwestern is not a Texas Baptist school and that Texas Baptists have little influence over its direction, though they continue to pour money into it through the Cooperative Program.

The Texas reaction to the firing of the popular president was intensified by the feeling that the SBC controversy had claimed another Texas victim. Dilday was only the most recent of a number of "Texas boys" who had been purged by the fundamentalist machine.

Bill Pinson was deluged with questions about what was going on at Southwestern Seminary. Despite the fact that the school was related structurally to the SBC and not the BGCT, Pinson wrote, "All the presidents have been at one time Texas Baptist pastors, including Dilday, an admired and respected native son. Texas Baptists have poured millions of dollars into the Seminary. Graduates serve in churches throughout the state. The Seminary profoundly affects us. Certainly we are concerned."[33] Many were asking why this drastic action was taken when Southwestern had received such high marks theologically and academically. Some Texas Baptists used this troubling incident to raise questions about the need for a new Texas seminary or a different relationship to the SBC. Acknowledging that the firing had brought deep pain to Texas Baptists, Pinson worried about the negative impact it might have on the churches. "What effect will the image of armed guards and changed locks have on lost people. Will the action be considered as an example of how to relate to church staff?" Always concerned primarily for winning the lost, Pinson said, "It seems that just as we begin to gather momentum in carrying out our Lord's commission another event disrupts and divides us."

Clearly the Dilday dismissal was a turning point not only for the Fort

Worth school, but for the Southern Baptist Convention and especially for Texas Baptists. The Southwestern upheaval convinced a number of leaders that Texas Baptists must provide for alternate forms of theological education under their own auspices. In time, such schools as the George W. Truett Theological Seminary in connection with Baylor and Logsdon School of Theology at Hardin-Simmons University in Abilene, gained more favor. The Executive Board of the BGCT also appointed a Theological Study Committee to make long-term plans for Texas-based ministry training. The firing of Dilday was also one factor in the rumble of unrest among Texas Baptists which led to appointment of the Effectiveness and Efficiency Committee in 1995. Editor Presnall H. Wood in a strong editorial in the *Baptist Standard,* entitled "Southwestern Seminary action spells big trouble for Baptists," said the reason for the firing was not theology. "The issue was not Dilday's belief in the Bible. Try as some might to stick the word liberal on Dilday to justify his firing, the charge will not stand. Then what was the issue? It was power. It was control. It was denominational politics."[34] Wood also said, prophetically as it turned out, that the Southwestern crisis would affect Texas Baptists for years to come. "It means," he said, "there is already a gap between the Baptist General Convention of Texas and the Southern Baptist Convention and this gap would be dangerously widened because of this action."

The Dilday firing provided the trigger for other events among Texas Baptists. The Texas Baptist Cooperative Program of 1994, the Theological Education Committee of 1994, the Effectiveness/Efficiency Committee of 1995, and the alleged distancing between the BGCT and the SBC all grew to a large extent out of the Southwestern Seminary upheaval. Perhaps all these would have taken place anyway in time, but the fact that they happened when they did and how they did cannot be separated from the action of the SWBTS trustees on March 9, 1994.

The seventh president of Southwestern Seminary, and Dilday's successor, was Kenneth S. Hemphill, who was elected in 1994. Hemphill graduated from Wake Forest University in North Carolina, and earned Master of Divinity and Doctor of Ministry degrees from the Southern Baptist Theological Seminary in Louisville. His PhD degree is from Cambridge University in England. Most observers agree that the new president is an outstanding preacher and communicator, and that he has shown grace and wisdom in a difficult post. Under his leadership, Southwestern has shown considerable advance in student enrollment and fund raising.

THEOLOGICAL EDUCATION IN TEXAS

At the first meeting of the Executive Board after Dilday was fired, Jerold McBride, pastor of FBC in San Angelo, made a motion to ask the Board to appoint "a committee of at least 15 to study the possible need for additional opportunities for theological education in Texas; that the committee evaluate the current theological education programs to determine their adequacies to meet the need of Baptist churches and other denominational entities in Texas."[35] McBride explained that the committee should consider whether current opportunities met the needs, and whether there is "a need for anything else regarding theological education in Texas." The motion passed, though with some opposition. This started a process that has not yet worked itself out in Texas. George Gaston of Abilene was named to chair the resulting Theological Education Study Committee.

This move to bring theological education closer to the churches was part of a larger trend. The earliest training for ministers among Baptists was church-based, usually with the pastor agreeing to take in two or three students to "read theology" and observe and sometimes participate in his daily pastoral work. In the early nineteenth century, such formal theological education as existed among Baptists in America was based in the colleges. One basic purpose for forming the string of Baptist colleges in the South before 1850 was to provide for ministerial education. There were no free-standing seminaries among Southern Baptists until 1859 when The Southern Baptist Theological Seminary originated out of the Bible department of Furman University in South Carolina. The first intention was to combine the seminary with the university, but in 1859 the seminary was separated from Furman in hopes that Baptists in other states would participate. After the Civil War the Southern Seminary was moved to Louisville, Kentucky.

Southern Baptists' next seminary grew out of the Bible department of Baylor University. The Baylor Theological Seminary was formed in 1905 and at first there was no thought of separating from the university. When it became obvious that the new school could not reach its full development in Waco the founder, B. H. Carroll, reluctantly decided to separate. The new seminary, already approved by the BGCT, moved from Waco to Fort Worth and was chartered as Southwestern Baptist Theological Seminary on March 14, 1908. These early schools reveal that Southern Baptists at first sought to develop universities that would combine both collegiate and theological studies, along with other professional studies like medicine, law, and others. The decision to separate collegiate and theological studies into separate schools was based on political and economic factors, not on educational philosophy. That division fit the needs of the 19th and 20th centuries, but may not fit the needs of the 21st as well. Many felt that a great Baptist university should offer the highest level studies in every relevant field, including theology.

Long before the present theological controversy, the trend among Southern Baptists seemed to be back toward university-based theological education. Advocates said this would bring ministerial studies closer to the churches and could reduce the number of years spent in preparation. There would be certain economies of including collegiate and theological studies on the same campus, with shared facilities and libraries. The median age of seminary students was rising, reported to be 32/33 in 1995.[36] Students with families, and many of them with pastorates, found it less feasible to cut local ties and move to one of the stand-alone seminaries. "A movement to bring ministry training closer to the places where students live and minister is rapidly emerging," said the committee.

Formation of the Theological Education Study Committee three months after the firing of President Dilday is one measure of Texas Baptist distress over that incident. Clearly there was a feeling that Texas Baptists should at least explore the possibility of providing a Texas-based training for Texas pastors. The committee made a progress report on September 13, 1994, and asked for more time to complete their work. They noted that Texas Baptists were already engaged in ministerial training through their eight universities and also through the Hispanic Theological Seminary in San Antonio. Even so, the committee concluded, "there are some gaps that exist in our training of leadership."[37]

As a part of their full year of study, the committee made a survey of the history and growth of SBC theological education. They found that an unofficial and unwritten tradition said that the SBC sponsored seminaries and the state conventions should sponsor colleges. However, that agreement had begun to break down as more seminaries put in college studies and even prepared to offer college degrees. By then a half-dozen or more Baptist universities, two of them in Texas, were offering theological degrees. They also found a number of ministerial students in universities who did not plan to attend any seminary, and whose graduate study if any would be the university masters degree which they could earn in one additional year beyond the baccalaureate. Other college students wanted a more "time-efficient" system in which they could have a pre-seminary major which could reduce their time toward a theological degree. The committee also noted some changes in the approach to training ministers in America, with "increased emphasis on mentoring and hands-on training" which, they said, could be better accomplished in smaller schools. The committee also noted the need for education for ministers without college degrees, and the vast and largely untouched need for more theological training for Texas Baptist lay people. Already some of these needs were being addressed through extension classes at Southwestern Seminary, the Hispanic Seminary, and the Ethnic Leadership Development.

The committee found a "resurgence of graduate theological education at BGCT related universities . . . [which] marks a return to an educational emphasis of earlier years. . . . Clearly, ministry training in Texas is once again in full-bloom among our BGCT related universities."[38] As more new churches are planted through the Texas 2000 efforts, even more ministers will be needed. Long before this committee was named, the Texas Baptist universities were expanding their ministry preparation programs. They also were addressing the needs for more theological studies for lay persons, and for the possibility of forming a Bible College.

On the basis of their study, the committee concluded that "the BGCT should strengthen its investment in the delivery of theological education for ministers." The recommendation was that after another year of transition, during which the same committee would continue to serve, the

BGCT should appoint a permanent Theological Education Committee (TEC). The work would be correlated through the CECB, but eventually the TEC would seek its own director. That director was named early in 1998 in the person of William M. Tillman, professor of Christian ethics at Southwestern Seminary.

Many of these trends were already underway, but clearly the SBC controversy hastened them along. "Not to be denied," said the study committee, "is the reality that theological controversy in Baptist life has given some impetus to ministry training within some of the state Baptist universities. They have felt the need to insure the availability of training which they perceive prepares ministers within the context of traditional Baptist principles and doctrines."[39] The interest of the universities was further stimulated when it appeared the BGCT might invest serious money in theological education.

This emphasis upon a Texas-based theological education was picked up in the report of the Effectiveness/Efficiency Committee which reported at the Austin convention in 1997. It appeared clear that Texas Baptists would offer their own program of theological training, from lay training institutes to graduate level studies. The Truett Seminary at Baylor and the Logsdon School of Theology at Hardin-Simmons were already in place. The BGCT also laid plans for an extensive network of training institutes available to lay persons, and launched an educational consortium among the several universities. The Hispanic Seminary in San Antonio modified its offerings to include more training for non-college students, and the Baptist Leadership Center provided refresher study for established ministers. Advocates insisted, unconvincingly, that these various efforts would not compete with Southwestern Seminary in Fort Worth.

PRESERVING BAPTIST DISTINCTIVES

The Baptists who controlled the SBC before 1979 and those who came to power later held divergent views on any number of beliefs and practices. The outvoted moderates claimed that historic Baptist doctrines were being subverted by new views, while the resurgents claimed they had recovered the true Baptist heritage. Clearly, many of the new SBC leaders held differing views on religious freedom, separation of church and state, the priesthood of the believer, pastoral leadership, the role of women in church, the place and function of Baptist conventions, and many other doctrines. Though they had lost control of the SBC, the moderates wanted to preserve what they regarded as the historic doctrines and practices of authentic Baptists.

At the Amarillo convention in 1994, John F. Baugh, an influential Houston layman, moved "that the president of the BGCT appoint a special committee to work hand in hand with the Office of Communications in preparing and making available materials for Texas Baptists on traditional Baptist distinctives and beliefs such as the authority of scripture, the autonomy of the local church, Baptist polity, and other distinctives, beliefs, doctrines and tenets expressed in the unaltered Baptist Faith and Message Statement of 1963."[40] The motion passed, and Brian Harbour, pastor of FBC in Richardson, was named to chair the nine member Baptist Distinctives Committee (BDC). This is an ongoing committee of the Convention whose assignment was defined as follows: "The Baptist Distinctives Committee shall have the responsibility of keeping Texas Baptists informed about important Baptist distinctives and heritage."

Soundings taken around the state confirmed that many Texas Baptists feared that some of their most precious doctrines were at risk from the new SBC leaders who either did not understand or did not value them. Former presidents of the SBC have sought to redefine religious liberty and have spoken out strongly against separation of church and state. Some concern was expressed when the SBC in San Antonio adopted a resolution which seemed to reject the historic concept of the priesthood of the believer. Many were startled to hear a prominent Texas pastor who was then running for election as BGCT president, say forcefully in the Southwestern Seminary chapel that "Separation of church and state is a lie!"[41] Even W. A. Criswell is on record as saying that "I believe this notion of the separation of church and state was the figment of some infidel's imagination."[42]

These revisionist views contrast sharply with the older historic view of Baptists, as expressed by the great George W. Truett, Criswell's predecessor in the Dallas pulpit. In his famous address from the East Steps of the Capitol in Washington, D.C., in 1920, Truett pointed out that Baptists have always stood for complete religious liberty for all. He then quoted Matthew 22:21, *"Render therefore unto Caesar the things which are Caesar's; and unto God the things that are God's."* (KJV) Truett concluded, "That utterance, once for all, marked the divorcement of church and state."[43]

Other doctrines also seemed at risk. The new dictatorial style of pastoral leadership favored by some ultraconservatives seemed to undercut the historic Baptist conviction about the priesthood of every believer, and dictatorial "CEO" pastors hardly practice the historic congregational role of the church. One leading fundamentalist pastor said, "the pastor of the church is the ruler" and should tolerate no opposition.[44]

The BDC issued a book of 24 sermons by Texas Baptist leaders on some distinctives, with Bill Pinson's leadoff sermon from Galatians 5:1 on "What Does it Mean to Be a Baptist Christian?" Pinson said, "Because Baptists believe in the priesthood of the believer, soul competency, and religious freedom there is no official statement of what it means to be a Baptist. Such a statement would fly in the face of basic Baptist convictions. However, most Baptists agree on certain basic beliefs." The executive director then set out some of these basic beliefs. Not all would agree with Pinson that there is no official listing of Baptist doctrines. Many of the more conservative folks want to define the Baptist Faith and Message Confession in a creedal sense. Already many denominational employees are required to sign it.

The committee engaged Darrel Baergen, chair of the Department of Communications at Hardin-Simmons University, to write three one-act plays suitable for presentation by local churches. Several HSU students presented these brief plays to good response in an alcove of the exhibits area during the BGCT meeting in Austin in 1997. In dramatic and colorful form, the students emphasized Baptist convictions on conversion, baptism by immersion, the authority of scripture, religious freedom, and missions.[45]

BGCT/HMB STUDY COMMITTEE

By the 1990s, Texas Baptists were sending about $10 million a year to the Home Mission Board of the SBC. In turn, the HMB would send about $1 million of that back each year for home mission projects like starting new churches in Texas. This was a far smaller percentage than most state conventions received back.[46] Not only did the HMB return only about 10% of the money it received from Texas, the agreement required that Texas spend all its share of the mission costs before the HMB would kick in at all. As population changes turned Texas into such a needy mission field, many Texas leaders felt the HMB should return more of the money for work in Texas. To look into the matter, Pinson appointed a BGCT/HMB Study Committee, chaired by Ed Schmeltekopf, the associate executive director. In their report on September 12, 1995, that committee acknowledged up front that "While Texas Baptists have a worldwide assignment, they understand that their unique responsibility is to reach the unchurched millions in Texas."[47] Their purpose was to explore ways in which Texas could fund the additional mission work needed within its borders.

With a detailed analysis of population changes in Texas, the committee amply demonstrated the pressing mission needs of the Lone Star State. They would need to start 3,600 new churches by A.D. 2000 just to stay even with the church to population ratio which had existed in 1955. Since the HMB had announced a major emphasis upon starting new churches, Pinson felt they would be open to helping in Texas. A series of conferences between the BGCT committee and the HMB yielded disappointing results. Not only would the HMB not agree to return more of the Texas money to Texas, but in 1995 the SBC voted that the HMB would return even less money to strong state conventions. Larry Lewis, head of the HMB, made the motion to "encourage these state conventions [the larger ones] to fund a greater portion of their internal mission strategies." In addition to their involvement in starting churches in their own state, Texas Baptists also had major home mission commitments in their partnership with the Minnesota-Wisconsin and Washington, D.C. conventions.

After their conferences with HMB leaders, "The conclusion reached by the Committee is that the Home Mission Board does not plan to increase significantly its funding for home mission work in Texas."[48] How-

ever, the needs were acute and the committee recommended that Texas
Baptists proceed with their plan to start at least 1,400 new churches by the
turn of the century. The money to purchase land, erect buildings, and
supplement the pastor's salary until the church could get on its feet would
have to come from somewhere. Another committee which reported in
Amarillo in 1994 offered a solution on a possible source of such funds.

TEXAS BAPTIST COOPERATIVE PROGRAM

The 1993 meeting of the BGCT authorized a committee "to study
how to enhance cooperative missions giving among all Texas Baptists."[49]
The resulting Cooperative Missions Giving Study Committee, chaired by
Cecil Ray, reported in 1994 at Amarillo. They reaffirmed the historic
Baptist conviction that all Baptist bodies are free and autonomous and
that they cooperate with others voluntarily and to the extent they wish to
do so. They noted that "Cooperative Program relationships between the
Southern Baptist Convention and state conventions always have been fra-
ternal and functional." The committee cited an important agreement
adopted by the SBC in 1928 that said, "All Baptist general bodies [con-
ventions] are voluntary organizations." Associations, state conventions and
the SBC may choose to cooperate for common ends, but they do not forfeit their own freedom and independence. "There is no relation of superiority and inferiority among Baptist general bodies. All are equal. All
make their appeal directly to individuals and churches. Each determines
its own objectives—financial or otherwise—and allocates its own funds to
the interests promoted by it."[50] Baptist bodies are autonomous but they
must not interfere with other autonomous Baptist bodies. To that end, the
1928 agreement said, "This Convention [SBC] disclaims all authority over
any state convention." The state conventions first receive funds from the
churches, and forward a portion on to Nashville. However, the SBC said
in 1928, "This arrangement . . . may be changed at any time."[51]

The Cooperative Giving Committee also noted that from the origin
of the Cooperative Program in 1925 up to 1978, both designated and undesignated gifts were counted as CP contributions. However, in 1978 the
SBC made a new definition that declared that henceforth only undesignated gifts counted. Even so, some states continued to count their designated gifts as part of their CP record. In 1991, the BGCT adopted a plan
whereby any church could omit up to five line items from the SBC or
BGCT budget and still have their gifts count in their CP total. Taking these
changes into account, a report to the 1994 BGCT said, "Consequently, a
wide spectrum of giving exists among our churches at present."[52]

The Amarillo plan established the "Texas Cooperative Program" by
which a church could direct its mission gifts to any number of Baptist causes and still have them count as CP contributions. The SBC leaders objected strenuously because under this plan a few churches directed some of
their mission gifts to the newly formed Cooperative Baptist Fellowship

(CBF). Just as the churches had a choice, so did individuals. Many churches allowed their members to have a say about the portion of their gifts that would go beyond the local church. They could designate their gifts to go to the SBC in Nashville as before, to the CBF, or only to Texas mission causes. They could choose to divide their gifts between the SBC and other Baptist groups on whatever percentage they chose. Most chose the traditional way, but those who made other choices created some bookkeeping challenges for churches and for the state convention treasurer.

Not all agreed with these recommendations, and a few members of the Cooperative Giving Committee brought a strong minority report. They feared the action would change the relationship between the SBC and BGCT, and would "promote division and conflict."[53] To them it seemed objectionable that the BGCT would now have "multiple alliances with various national organizations," and "The Southern Baptist Convention becomes just one of many options that a church may support or not." However, the majority report passed.

Another change at Amarillo was a reduction of the percentage of undesignated gifts from the churches that would be forwarded on to Nashville. The budget adopted at Amarillo for 1995 divided the undesignated receipts 35.50% to Nashville and 64.50% to remain in Texas.[54] That compares to 36.65% and 63.35% the year before.[55] The budget for 1996 further adjusted the percentages to 33% for outside causes, 67% for Texas ministries.[56] These were small percentage changes, but involved a considerable number of dollars. Several other states were making similar reductions and keeping more of their mission money in state. When the Lottie Moon and Annie Armstrong offerings are figured in, Texas Baptists still sent almost 50% of all receipts outside the state. Some Texas leaders recalled that in their negotiations with the HMB, it was the HMB representatives who first suggested that Texas might have to reduce its CP allocation in order to fund the new church starts needed in Texas. However, because Texas Baptists have a strong commitment to foreign missions, the budget changes carried an assurance that the percentage reduction of funds to the SBC would not result in a reduction of support for foreign missionaries.

The 1997 audit of total offerings reveals some amazing statistics. Total offerings through the BGCT were $97,918,242. Almost 48.6% ($47,553,664) went to world-wide causes while $50,364,578 went to Texas causes.

THE EFFECTIVENESS/EFFICIENCY COMMITTEE

At the San Antonio convention in 1995 Charles Davenport, pastor of FBC, Tulia, made a motion "that the President and Chairman of the Executive Board appoint a committee to consider the best ways to assure the maximum efficiency and effectiveness of BGCT cooperative efforts in missions, evangelism, education, ethics and human services, including management of legal concerns (including any revision of the Constitution,

By-laws, and Business and Finance Plan.)"[57] The motion passed without opposition, and the resulting committee took its name from the motion and became known as the Effectiveness/Efficiency Committee. It was composed of about 30 members chosen from different parts of the state and from all shades of theological views. Darold Morgan, highly respected retired head of the Annuity Board, was named chair. It now appears that this may prove to be one of the most influential committees in Texas Baptist history.

Several factors helped lead to this committee. The firing of President Dilday in 1994 was a major earthquake which shook up the Texas Baptist landscape. The failure in negotiations with the HMB to get a larger return for missions in Texas was another primary antecedent of the E/E Committee. The overwhelming reality that Texas had become a major mission field, with the need to start hundreds of new churches, was also a factor. About forty years had passed since the influential Booz, Allen and Hamilton study had reshaped Texas Baptist life in the 1950s, and thirty years had passed since the Committee of 100 had made some basic restructuring of the BGCT in the 1960s. Many felt it was time for another top to bottom look at the BGCT and its agencies with a view to finding better ways to do their work.

Perhaps no one could have predicted the directions the committee would take or how controversial it would become. Some said a far more radical motion was ready for presentation, and the two-year E/E study was created as an alternative to give time for spirits to calm. The E/E Committee was divided into seven sub-committees with chairs as follows: Administration and Communications, Jaclanel McFarland; Benevolence, Jerold McBride; Church Support, Ferris Akins; Constitution and Bylaws, John Uxer; Education, David Becker; Ethics, Ed Hogan; and Evangelism/ Missions, Leroy Fenton. Each subcommittee was assigned a staff liaison from the Baptist Building. The work of the E/E Committee was further spelled out in its mission statement. "The mission of the Effectiveness/ Efficiency Committee is to evaluate and recommend to the BGCT and other appropriate agencies changes in programs, procedures, relationships, funding and documents designed to maximize the effectiveness and efficiency of the BGCT."[58]

The committee met several times and each subcommittee had several meetings. There was free and open exchange of views, if not always agreement. Persons of differing theological perspectives openly shared their views. The full committee hammered together their final report by August 1997, before its presentation at the BGCT in Austin that November. The full report, "Toward a More Excellent Way," was published in the *Baptist Standard* of August 27, 1997. The report was also published in pamphlet form and widely distributed across the state and was widely read and discussed by Texas Baptists. The response showed some confusion and also pockets of opposition. When questions arose, Darold Morgan prepared a thirteen-page pamphlet on "Frequently Asked Questions about the Report of the Effectiveness/Efficiency Committee." The letters to the editor page of the *Baptist Standard* was open, as always, to Texas Baptists to express their opinions, support or reservations about the E/E Report. A few associations expressed questions or opposition but the report also met enthusiastic support.

The report strongly affirmed the present ministries of the BGCT. The committee cited a report showing that "Texas Baptist churches rank first nationally in church membership, total receipts, state mission offering giving, undesignated receipts, convention ministries budget, and allocations to Christian higher education."[59] They included a list of "administrative and convention initiatives" in recent years that strengthened the ministry of the BGCT and the churches. While calling for change and innovation, the E/E Committee found great value in the Convention's present work. They said, "The E/E Committee affirms the BGCT Executive Board staff and the leaders of Texas Baptist institutions for their commitment, creativity and continuing focus on missions, church planting, evangelism and ministry," while citing an American church growth specialist who called the BGCT "one of the most future-oriented and trend-setting regional judicatories in American Protestantism."[60] Even so, the committee felt, future challenges called for more innovation and new approaches.

The final report begins with a description of great spiritual need. "Baptists in Texas face enormous challenges. Texas is experiencing accelerating change at an unprecedented rate. In fact, it has become the fastest growing state in the nation. The mission base has become a mission field as it has experienced a huge influx of people from all over the United States and the world."[61] At least one half of the Texas population was unchurched, a number larger than the total population of 42 other states. While Texas Baptists are reaching more people, their efforts in evangelism and church starting are not keeping pace with the enormous population growth. The report also says that "Morally and spiritually, Texas is in crisis. Families struggle to stay intact. The Lone Star State is a national leader in many of the wrong things. Moral decay is pervasive, touching every level of society." There follows a litany of social crises, including crime, teen pregnancies, abortion, and child abuse. Texas has the third largest prison system in the world. In light of these overwhelming spiritual needs, the committee said, "Changes in culture and church life mandate careful scrutiny of how to do missions and where to spend mission dollars." Clearly, business as usual would not do. Texas Baptists needed to make a major new initiative to reach their state for Christ, and it would take some budget adjustments to do that.

The committee called for major changes, and faced upfront the reality that change is threatening to many people. But change is inevitable and, managed properly, can be constructive. While the gospel is unchanging and basic human spiritual needs for salvation abide, changes in society require the churches to be open to new ways to accomplish old tasks. "Churches and conventions must learn to embrace change and learn to adapt their methods to the changing culture." However, allegiance to basic biblical and Baptist principles must abide even amidst change. The committee expressed a concern that changes in the national SBC during their two years of restructuring "raised questions that Texas Baptists must address." They noted that "the Southern Baptist Convention has initiated and completed organizational changes that some view as centralizing authority." They also complain that the SBC budget instead of directing funds to missions and church starts, now directs more money to its "political action agency," an apparent reference to the SBC Christian Life Commission. In a sharp indictment, the report says "Baptist agencies, conference centers and publishing houses downplay their denominational identity. The impact is a trend away from the historic Baptist mission and ministry." Some said that in their effort to appeal to a broader evangelical market, the Sunday School Board had toned down the Baptist distinctives in their lesson materials, though SSB officials denied this.

When it was first published to the public, the E/E report attracted extensive comment, both for and against. Ronnie Yarber, administrative director of Southern Baptists of Texas, a group of militant ultraconservatives, said the report "will most likely prove to be the document that gives birth to a new state convention of Southern Baptist churches in Texas."[62] Yarber called the report "a treatise on the opposition to the work of Southern Baptists in Texas." Outsiders also got in their two cents' worth. Albert Mohler, president of the Southern Seminary in Louisville, called the report "wishful thinking" and implied that Texas Baptists have no legitimate complaints against the SBC. Richard Land, head of the Nashville CLC, called the report "inaccurate and inflammatory."[63] Jimmy Draper, head of the Nashville-based BSSB, objected strongly to the idea that Texas Baptists needed to provide their own Bible study literature.[64] Others spoke out as strongly for the report.

The E/E report affirmed that Texas Baptists are "conservative in doctrine and practice," but said "Southern Baptists in Texas cannot ignore the change created by the continuing crisis in denominational life. Efforts to control state conventions are obvious. Vital issues are at stake that must not fall prey to a mindset of control." The BGCT, said the committee, must continue to function as a servant of the churches and not fall into the current model of control.

Some key concepts surfaced during the study, and these guided the E/E Committee's conclusion. The committee agreed that starting new churches in Texas was a priority, and that Baptists must develop more effective strategies for evangelizing the lost. They called for intensification of the "church-first" strategy because "the local church is the key to reaching the lost." This "church-first" strategy may call for "a decentralization of denominational entities" in order to emphasize the crucial role of the local churches. The report called for enhancing missions education to make Texans aware of the vast mission field at their doorstep, and for flexible funding to provide for new initiatives in evangelism. The BGCT should enhance relationships with other state conventions and other Baptist bodies that share its ministry commitments, and continue to cultivate the closest cooperation with the 113 autonomous associations within the state for, they said, "The director of missions is close to the churches and is the first level of assistance for congregational leadership." In light of pressing needs, mission work in Texas must be expanded. "With the possibility of changes in funding through the North American Mission Board, it is more and more necessary for Texas Baptists to provide ways to reach Texas." This was a pointed reminder that if the NAMB (the old HMB) returned only 10 cents or less of each dollar Texas Baptists sent in, then Texas Baptists would have to keep more of their money at home. Texas Baptists were not asking others to do their home mission work. They were asking that the HMB use a little more of the Texas money for work in Texas.

Above all, Texas Baptists must stand firm upon the historic Baptist faith. As guiding principles of Baptists through the years, the committee identified the authority of scripture, believer's baptism, priesthood of the believer, soul freedom and separation of church and state. "Texas Baptists must continue to embrace the historic Baptist principles that honor local church decision-making and individual freedom." Clearly the committee felt that some of these principles were at risk in the new SBC.

The E/E Committee grouped its 16 recommendations into five general categories. Under *Ministry to Families,* they recommended that the CLC receive additional funding for its Hope for Home emphasis, and that the child care homes expand their services to minister to entire families. In *Multi-Cultural Ministries,* the committee recommended the creation of new ways to reach the various ethnic groups of Texas. It was said that Hispanics in Texas are increasing five times as rapidly as Anglos, and twice as fast as African-Americans. The report called upon the BGCT to accelerate its efforts to enlist, train and send "missionaries" for these and other people groups. The BGCT would also covenant to make its own staff more representative of the state's population diversity by hiring more ethnics. The committee also called for a Council for Multi-Cultural Academic Education to work with various ethnic groups and the Texas Baptist universities to elicit and cultivate future leaders and teachers from the ethnic populations.

Three levels of *Theological Education* in Texas are recommended. Schools like Truett Seminary at Waco and the Logsdon School of Theology at Abilene, and perhaps others, would receive support through the BGCT. In addition, a program of Theological Education for Laypersons would be established to address the vast interest perceived in the area of ongoing adult education. The committee had identified a large group of Texas lay persons who would participate in continuing theological education if given the opportunity. They also recommended that the Theological Education Committee should lead in forming a consortium of all the BGCT-related universities interested in participating with a goal of creating a Texas Baptist Theological College to provide a Bachelor of Applied Theology or an equivalent Bible College degree. This would bring together several elements of theological education which had been piecemeal before.

This would give Texas Baptists a comprehensive program of theological education from certificate to graduate degree levels. These proposals reflect a conviction that advanced academic degrees may not always provide the most relevant education for Texas Baptist ministers, particularly ministers among ethnic groups. The Bible College approach would be less academically intense but more practical and could reach a larger number of students. There was no thought that a separate school be formed, but that the existing Baptist universities could cooperate in offering classes and issue degrees in the name of a Texas Baptist Theological College.

There is no escaping the fact that these recommendations express some degree of dissatisfaction with the SBC seminaries, including the one in Texas. In addition to fear that extremist views would predominate, some committee members apparently felt that the typical three-year seminary degree coming on top of a four-year university degree may be, at least for some ministers, too heavy into academics and too light in the practical areas of actual ministry.

Under the category of *Partnership Missions,* the E/E Committee made far-reaching recommendations that would, in effect, establish the BGCT as a missionary sending body, but not in the traditional sense. They did not intend to compete with the IMB, but to explore innovation where needed while continuing to cooperate with the more traditional Baptist missionary groups both here and overseas. They called for Texas Baptists to expand their mission work to be ready to send volunteers to any task anywhere in the world. To correlate this great effort, they recommended that the BGCT employ one more fulltime staff member to work with Partnership Missions. They recommended that the BGCT consider affiliating with the Baptist World Alliance, a proposal that proved surprisingly controversial. This proposal came at a time when it appeared that the SBC might cut back or even drop its affiliation and funding of the BWA. No state convention had previously sought affiliation, but other states than Texas were interested. Texas Baptists felt that the BWA might soon need some extra funding if the SBC cut them off. This was another way for the BGCT to broaden its base of ministry. Another recommendation was that the BGCT work with other missionary sending groups to develop a system of "lay envoys" to be trained and sent out to preach, teach, and witness on international mission fields where they live and work. The SBC had a similar program a generation earlier.

One recommendation which one would think that Baptists would readily accept proved instead very controversial. Of the 16 recommendations, the 13th said "That the BGCT be affirmed as an autonomous body which will support mission causes in Texas and the world; and that the BGCT cooperate reciprocally with organizations and affiliations that complement its mission and its statement of purpose." For a Baptist group to claim to be autonomous is nothing new; all Baptist groups claim that. However, the BGCT appeared ready to practice their freedom. They would support mission causes not only in Texas, but throughout the world, and they would cooperate with any Baptist group that shared their commitment and goals. This is nothing more than Baptist groups had always claimed, but it sounded radical in a new day when the SBC exerted tighter control over its agencies. Texas Baptists would cooperate with the SBC but would not promise to confine their work only to that group.

Recommendation 14 dealt with *Biblically Based, Texas-Focused Literature*. In surveys made by the E/E Committee members, and in discussion that surfaced during their meetings, there appeared a surprisingly widespread dissatisfaction with the Sunday School literature from the Nashville Sunday School Board, though most Texas churches continued to buy at least some of it. Some felt the materials were increasingly fundamentalist in tone, while others found them shallow and pointless. Texas churches wanted "literature that is rooted in Scripture, that emphasizes missions and that honors Baptist distinctives and history," but they said "It is unrealistic to expect such materials from those who must provide for the entire nation and who increasingly focus on a non-Baptist market," an apparent reference to the Nashville BSSB.[65] Some adult classes, it was said, no longer cared for the concept of paperback throw away quarterlies. Some churches had already dropped the quarterlies in favor of materials from one of the several independent publishing houses, several of which put out attractive Bible-based study materials at competitive prices. There was also an expressed desire for literature that would publicize Texas mission needs and opportunities. Leaders of the Nashville SSB felt their materials already met these needs adequately.

In light of these perceived needs, the recommendation was "That literature and other resources for Sunday School, Discipleship Training, mission organizations and other Bible study groups be developed as either a supplement to existing materials or a substitute for existing materials for those who so choose. These materials will provide information on Baptist missions (with a special emphasis on Texas Baptist missions), Baptist distinctives, stewardship, ethics and other subjects." This was not a call for Texas to establish its own publishing house, but to provide selected materials as a supplement. As technology developed rapidly, there was some talk of putting Bible study lessons on the Internet for churches to access and use as they might choose. Clearly a new day was dawning and the concept of Sunday School was changing, and the old familiar "quarterly" looked like an endangered species.

The E/E Committee recommended one important change in the BGCT constitution in Article III on membership. The old constitution allows each cooperating church to have four messengers for the first 100 members and one additional messenger for each additional 100 members or major portion thereof, up to a maximum of 25. Under this plan, a large church can send 25 voting messengers without making any contribution whatever. The recommended change allows 2 messengers for the first 100 members or fractional part thereof (with or without any contribution at all), and 2 additional messengers for the first $250 dollars contributed to the BGCT budget during the previous year. A church could have one additional messenger for each additional 100 members or major portion thereof and each additional $1,000 dollars given during the previous year, up to a maximum of 25 messengers from any one church. Under this recommended change, a small church could have two messengers without making any contribution, and four with a modest mission contribution of $250 during the previous year. Under the new plan, no Texas Baptist church would be disenfranchised.

Constitutional changes must pass by at least a two-thirds majority at two successive conventions. This proposed change passed by 73% margin on the first reading in Austin, but must be voted on again in Houston in 1998.[66] Paul Pressler, the strategist generally credited with helping the fundamentalists take over the SBC, called the proposed change "an abomination" and promised to help turn out messengers in Houston in 1998 to defeat it. He was reported as calling the change "a poll tax on Texas Baptists."[67] Jerold McBride, pastor of FBC in San Angelo, pointed out that fundamentalists seem inconsistent in maintaining that churches must contribute in order to send voting messengers to the SBC, but that churches sending voting messengers to the BGCT need not contribute anything.[68]

This proposed change, if it passes the second reading, will bring the BGCT more into line with the SBC constitution. No church can send any voting messenger to the SBC unless the church is a "bona fide contributor" to SBC causes. Churches can send additional messengers for each additional 250 members or each additional $250 in contributions, up to a maximum of ten from any one church. The fundamentalists opposed this proposed constitutional change with surprising militance. In light of their desire to draw closer to the SBC, one might think they would welcome bringing the Texas constitution more into line with the SBC. The amendment, if passed, would restore provisions in the earlier constitution of the BGCT and its predecessor, the Baptist State Convention.

The E/E Committee concluded its report with a series of 53 "Affirmations and Referrals" to various boards and commissions of the BGCT. Most of these are more suggestions than mandates and it is left to the individual agencies whether or not they will follow up on these. No doubt all these suggestions will be considered, some will probably be adopted, some may be modified, and a few will perhaps be left to well-deserved oblivion. Some of the suggestions are: that in the interest of efficiency and economy the Baptist Building should upgrade its technology to communicate with Texas Baptists more by Internet and less by post office; that the BGCT enlist a contact person to relate to and encourage retired ministers in Texas; and that both the Mission Service Corps and Partnership Missions add staff members and expand opportunities for Texas volunteers to serve in Texas, the United States, and international missions. The Department of Student Ministries is asked to develop a strategy for reaching commuter students, and the CECB is asked to study ways to enhance scholarship aid to Texas ministerial students. The Report also suggests that the CECB be expanded to include a coordinator of theological education in Texas, and the CLC is asked to encourage the teaching of ethics in Texas Baptist schools, including greater emphasis on ministerial ethics. The Baptist hospitals are asked to consider linking together into one unified Texas Baptist Health Care System. Several of these proposals were already being implemented by early 1998.

One important "referral," likely to be acted upon, suggests "that name changes for Texas Baptist boards and commissions be considered to reflect more accurately their functions." This follows the pattern of the SBC which has recently renamed several of its boards. Some Texas Baptist agencies have already had name changes. Each Texas agency would study its own name and recommend any changes through the Administrative Committee and the Executive Board. In recent years, "welfare" has picked up negative political connotations, and the Human Welfare Coordinating Board may well seek a change. Even "Sunday School" may change its ancient name to reflect more accurately its major ministry of Bible study. When the Sunday School originated in the late 18th century, it was a "school" for poor children which met on Sunday, the only day of leisure for children in a culture with no child labor laws. Early Sunday Schools taught basic reading and writing, and in some schools children were given toothbrushes and combs and taught basic personal hygiene. However, over the years Sunday School changed. Among Southern Baptists, it includes not just children but all ages. Some adults are not attracted to the idea of returning to "school" and children who have been in school all week look for relief. Some Bible study groups meet at times other than Sunday and at places other than the church. Perhaps some name will be chosen that will reflect these changes.

When the E/E Report was presented at the Austin Convention in 1997, considerable opposition surfaced, though all the recommendations were ultimately accepted. Some feared the E/E Report would put distance between the state convention and the national SBC. Chairman Morgan repeatedly affirmed that was not the intent of the committee's work, though some committee members may not have shared that conviction. However, the report could increase the gap, depending on how it is implemented and what the SBC response may be. If there is distance between the BGCT and the SBC, Texas Baptists maintain that it was the SBC that moved. The report calls for Texas Baptists to sponsor their own theological education, their own mission work through Partnership Missions, and to provide at least some of their own Bible study literature. Some called the Report a declaration of Texas Baptist independence. In this Report, Texas Baptists not only affirm a cooperative independence, but also set out plans to practice it.

Clearly the E/E Report struck a responsive chord among Baptists not only in Texas but elsewhere as well. Baptist news writers named the Texas E/E Report as the leading Baptist story of 1997. While not so far along, other Baptist state conventions were moving in a similar direction.

BAYLOR HEALTH CARE SYSTEM

In 1997 the Baylor Health Care System did essentially what Baylor

University had done seven years earlier: it saved itself from a hostile takeover. For the Health Care System the threat was not fundamentalism, but the lure of big bucks if the Baylor Health Care System in Dallas and its affiliates could be sold off to a for-profit company. The combined market value of the several Baylor hospitals was said to exceed $1 billion dollars. Baylor Hospital had earned a national reputation as a premier healing institution. The Blue Cross insurance program as well as the American Association of Blood Banks originated there.

What is now known as the Baylor Health Care System had its beginnings in Dallas in 1903 under the name of Texas Baptist Memorial Sanitarium. With the vision of George W. Truett and R. C. Buckner, and the money of Colonel C. C. Slaughter, the hospital got off to a solid start. Over the years it grew rapidly as countless Baptists, and not a few non-Baptists, poured in hundreds of millions of dollars to create a medical facility without equal in the Southwest. In 1920 the BGCT authorized the hospital in Dallas (with its various "scientific schools") and Baylor University in Waco to operate under a single board of trustees. As a result, "Baylor in Dallas" was regarded as an integral part of "Baylor in Waco." The board of trustees had two executive committees, one to supervise the university and one to oversee the health care institutions in Dallas. This dual system worked well for many years, but rapid changes in health care required the hospitals to make prompt decisions, which was not always possible when they had to run every decision by the entire board of trustees of Baylor University. In 1981 the Baylor Health Care System was formed to serve as a holding company for all the health care institutions related to Baylor. Medical care was rapidly changing, with HMOs and government programs like Medicare, and some felt Baylor Health should make further changes.

The charter changes of 1990 not only removed Baylor University from BGCT control, but had a similar effect upon the Health Care System since it was still governed by the Baylor Regents, who were not elected by the BGCT. This caused no end of confusion. If Baylor University was no longer a Texas Baptist school, as some mistakenly said, what of the Health Care System? Who owned and controlled the billion dollar properties which had been accrued through the twentieth century?

Some folks in Waco took the approach that the Baylor Health Care System was an integral part of the university, and thus the university could sell it if it chose. The lure of what a *billion dollars* from the sale of surplus property could do for the school on the Brazos caused some to salivate. Some, at least, imagined they could sell the Dallas property (and the related Baylor health institutions in other cities) and use the money in Waco. One report said some Regents wanted "to sell the whole thing to an outsider and pocket the money for Baylor University."[69] A California-based syndicate, whose corporate history was not entirely unblemished, stepped forward to purchase the entire system and operate it on a for-profit basis.

However, it did not work out that way. Boone Powell, Jr. had run the Baylor Health system for 16 years, his father for 24 years before him. He strongly resisted the idea of any sale, and his Board chairman, former judge P. Oswin Chrisman, added his considerable political skills to block the deal. They were particularly shocked at the idea that the great Baylor System would become a money-making machine. The Health Care System made its own hasty and unannounced charter and bylaw changes to split up the various health care institutions so they could not be sold as a unit. It also turned out that under Texas laws regulating benevolences, most of the money from any sale of the Dallas hospital must remain in Dallas and could not be diverted to Waco. Powell and his associates mounted a powerful public relations blitzkrieg that turned the tide. Public opinion in Texas, both Baptist and non-Baptist, ran heavily against the idea of the sale. Bill Pinson also threw his considerable influence into the fray against the sale.

Powell said, "We were all agreed on two or three things. One of them was that the hospital system should not be sold. And that the hospital needed a different form of governance—that it needed to be free from the university."[70] The upshot was that in 1997 the Baylor Health Care System severed its ties to Baylor University, though they did not regard it as severance from the BGCT. The severance agreement provides for an all Baptist Board of Directors for the Baylor Health Care System and BHCS officials have indicated that the BGCT will have a voice in selecting future members of that board. Baylor University realized a little money out of the deal, but the BHCS came under its own separate board and was no longer subject to sale. Their relationship to the BGCT remained cordial as ever, but by early 1998 the exact details of that relationship had yet to be worked out.

In retrospect, many Texas Baptists find it incredible that any sale was contemplated. At the very least it appeared a violation of the trust of George W. Truett, Colonel Slaughter and countless others who made the hospital a reality. At the present time, the Baylor Health Care System is still intact, still Baptist, and still operating as a non-profit institution. There are no "For Sale" signs on the property.

TEXAS 2000

Bill Pinson and his ministry team at the Baptist Building and throughout the state have steadfastly refused to be sidetracked by controversy. Through stormy weather and calm, come what may, they have kept the focus squarely on evangelism, missions, and church growth. The "churches first" was more than a slogan; it expressed an unwavering commitment to winning people to faith in Christ, gathering them into New Testament churches, and discipling them through Bible study, prayer, and Christian fellowship. In fact, Pinson was once described as "a Johnny one-note" because of his unwavering emphasis upon evangelism and missions.[71] Universities might change their charters, hospitals might change their relation to the BGCT, dissidents might threaten to leave the BGCT and form a rival state convention, but through it all the work of evangelism, missions, and new church starts not only continued but picked up momentum.

D. L. Lowrie chaired the 74 member group from throughout the state that drew up plans for a great five-year program of ministry to close out the twentieth century. Named TEXAS 2000, this was an ambitious plan to strive for greater growth in every area of Texas Baptist life. The program was launched at the Evangelism Conference in Fort Worth in January, 1996, as more than 10,000 persons joined hands in prayer to share the gospel with every Texan by the year 2000. "The goal of Texas 2000 is humanly impossible," admitted Bill Pinson, but members of the Strategy Council "wept as they realized God could do what we could not do."[72] Texas 2000 was launched with a call for spiritual unity among Texas Baptists. Jack Graham of Prestonwood Church in Dallas and Dan Vestal of Tallowood Church in Houston, considered by many to symbolize the two general points of view, urged Texas Baptists to take steps of personal repentance and reconciliation so that nothing would interfere with the primary task of witnessing for Christ.

The Strategy Council determined at the outset not to get bogged down in setting numerical goals. Instead they set out a statement of purpose, affirmed certain priorities and values, and proclaimed a vision of sharing the gospel with every Texan by the year 2000. They urged each BGCT agency and institution, each association, and each church to catch the vision and set their own goals and plans to reach them.

"Why does the Baptist General Convention of Texas exist?" The Strategy Council began with that important question. Their answer: "The Baptist General Convention of Texas exists to encourage and assist churches, associations of churches, institutions and other Baptist entities in FULFILLING THE GREAT COMMISSION OF THE LORD JESUS CHRIST." [Emphasis theirs] The Convention exists for the churches, not the other way around. The Council identified five priorities: 1. *To share the gospel of Jesus Christ with the people of Texas, the nation, and the world* (Acts 1:6-8); 2. *To minister to human needs in the name of Jesus Christ* (Mt. 25:31-46); 3. *To equip God's people for ministry in the church and in the world* (Eph. 4:11-13); 4. *To develop Christian families* (Col. 3:16-21); 5. *To strengthen existing churches and start new congregations* (Mt. 16:18-19; Acts 15:36).

The bedrock Christian values which undergird these concepts and which these goals seek to express include: biblical authority; prayer and spiritual vitality; freedom and partnership of the churches; a renewed emphasis upon Baptist heritage, polity and doctrine; a reminder of the worth of all persons; the inclusion of all Texas Baptists; use of a diversity of methods to reach these goals; integrity and accountability in all things; and continued improvement toward excellence. The ultimate value, the Strategy Council concluded, was the advancement of God's kingdom on earth.

Texas Baptists were urged to embrace the vision and make it their own, and develop their own strategies for making it a reality. The vision statement is worthy of quotation in full. "To the Glory of God—Share Jesus with every person in Texas by the year 2000; Be a family of loving, joyful, obedient servants of Jesus Christ; Seek fresh new direction and power from the Holy Spirit through Scripture and prayer; and Develop Great Commission churches for all persons." Vision 2000, which operates alongside Texas 2000, is a similar plan developed by the Hispanic Baptist Task Force and adopted in 1993. Its goals include the starting of at least 600 new Hispanic Baptist Churches in Texas and baptizing at least 40,000 new Hispanic converts by 2000.

The BGCT adopted a goal as part of Texas 2000 to start at least 1400 new congregations by the turn of the century. As of the end of 1997, they were ahead of schedule.

When "Wildcat" Morrell started the first missionary Baptist church in Texas in 1837, he was convinced that *"the desert shall rejoice and blossom as the rose"* (Is.35:1). This pioneer preacher never lost his confidence that a great Baptist empire would arise in Texas. However, even the optimistic Morrell surely could not have imagined the growth which in 160 years from 1837 to 1997 would multiply missionary Baptist churches in Texas from 1 to 5693; from fewer than 25 Baptists to 2,696,169.

A NEW STATE CONVENTION?

On November 20, 1997, just after the Austin Convention, some of the thirty-member board of directors of the Southern Baptists of Texas voted in Dallas to pull out of the BGCT and start their own state convention. Their publication, the *Plumbline*, reported that "Southern Baptists of Texas, a conservative group disenchanted with recent actions by the Baptist General Convention of Texas, has begun the process of creating a new state convention."[73] No date was given for formation of such a convention, but a series of rallies around the state was announced, presumably to test the waters and elicit support for such a move.

The Southern Baptists of Texas (SBT) grew out of the Baylor Restoration Committee of 1991. The name was later changed to Conservative Baptist Fellowship of Texas, and in 1995 the present name was chosen. In 1996 SBT merged with another ultraconservative Texas group, Baptists With a Mission (BWAM), with SBT as the surviving name. The BWAM group published a quarterly paper, the *Texas Baptist,* which was merged into the *Plumbline,* published by SBT. Walt Carpenter, editor of the *Texas Baptist* became editor of the *Plumbline,* but was later succeeded by Skeet Workman of Lubbock. The present officers of SBT, who will serve as a transitional team, include Miles Seaborn of Fort Worth, president; Dee Slocum of Amarillo, vice-president; and Ronnie Yarber of Mesquite as executive director.

Tensions have increased between the ultraconservatives and the BGCT for many years, and talk of a rival convention in Texas is far from new. There are many issues of contention but perhaps the main one is that the SBT leaders want to follow the SBC in its new swing to the extreme right and apparently most Texas Baptists do not. In explaining their action, SBT leader Dave Parker said, "We have a desire to maintain a stronger relationship with the national Southern Baptist family."[74] In the same article Slocum said, "The Austin convention in and by itself is not the reason why our organization has mad [sic] this decision. It has been a collective process across the last four or five conventions. The triggering device was that it became apparent to everyone that this [the E/E Report] is an attempt by the leadership of BGCT to distance itself from the national SBC." Slocum, spokesman for the group, said "They [SBT] desire a stronger relationship with the SBC, not a weaker one. They want to move closer, not distance themselves . . . . [we] have to make a choice, to either be Texas Baptists or Southern Baptists."[75]

Another SBT writer said,"The Southern Baptists of Texas consider themselves the Texas arm of the Southern Baptist Convention."[76] Some mainline Texas Baptists found cause for concern in the idea that any state convention is "an arm of the SBC," regarding this as a new form of denominational polity which is foreign to Baptist theology and practice through the centuries. In historic Baptist polity, the state convention is no more an "arm" of the SBC than the SBC is an "arm" of the state convention. All Baptist organizations, from the local congregation to the Baptist World Alliance, are independent, autonomous, and free. They cooperate with one another to the extent each may choose, but no Baptist body is the "head" and none is an "arm." Some feared this "arm" concept would have a tendency to elevate the national convention to a kind of "headquarters" status for Southern Baptists, relegating state conventions to subordinate status.

Other issues which have troubled the ultraconservatives of Texas are the withdrawal of Baylor University from BGCT control, the new Texas Baptist Cooperative Program adopted at Amarillo in 1994, and the election of Russell H. Dilday as BGCT president in 1997. There have also been recurring charges that the BGCT has been supportive, or at least tolerant, of homosexuality among Baptists—charges which are not true. The conservatives have also expressed concern that there is a growing distance between the BGCT and the SBC, that there is too much bureaucracy in the BGCT, a lack of inclusiveness on Convention committees and boards, that the *Baptist Standard* is not under the firm control of the Convention and its coverage is biased against the ultra group, and that theological liberalism has made deep inroads among BGCT leaders. BGCT leaders have regularly and consistently pointed out that these concerns are unfounded.

Apparently the final straw was the overwhelming adoption of the E/E Committee report in Austin in 1997, which the ultraconservatives saw as virtual withdrawal from SBC cooperation. Slocum said that in Austin, "Texas declared itself as an independent Baptist convention." The SBT people opposed the report at every step with endless motions, substitute motions, points of order and parliamentary maneuvering. President Charles Wade presided with grace and patience, making sure that messengers had their say. He insisted that the recommendations be voted on one by one so that each could be explored fully, a process that took hours even though it was obvious from the first vote that the messengers would have approved the entire report in one vote. After hours of wrangling, when the vote finally came, each recommendation was adopted over-whelmingly.

One reason given by SBT leaders for their intended exit from the BGCT was based on an unfortunate misquotation from Charles Wade's presidential message. Dee Slocum was quoted as saying that "an addition-al factor" in their decision to leave the BGCT were remarks that outgoing president Charles Wade made in an interview with the Austin *American Statesman*.[77] Actually, Wade had no interview with the paper. What hap-pened is that a rookie reporter, who apparently knew nothing about Baptists and little more about legitimate journalism, paraphrased certain statements from a printed copy of Wade's presidential message. Since so much has been made about this statement, it is quoted here in full. What Wade actually said was,

> I have appealed to Southern Baptist leaders not to chide Texas Baptists for our determination to give our churches and their leaders freedom to make the decisions they believe are best for them in reaching out to do mission work in the world. Southern Baptist leaders will have our support if they will focus on missions and evangelism, but they will drive more and more Texas Baptists away if they focus on requiring conformity as a con-dition of cooperation.[78]

Here is how the reporter paraphrased Wade's remarks and made it appear he had said something entirely different.

> The outgoing Texas president, the Reverend Charles Wade of Arlington, said he's warned leaders of the Southern Baptist Convention "not to chide Texas Baptists for our determination to give our churches and their leaders freedom to make the decisions they believe are best for them in reaching out to do mission work in the world. Texas will support South-ern Baptist leaders if they focus on missions and evangelism *instead of try-ing to force all Baptists to believe the Bible is factual and scientifically true. If they don't back off from insisting on biblical inerrancy as a Baptist litmus test, then* "they will drive more and more Texas Baptists away."[79] [emphasis added]

The reporter never spoke with Wade personally, but said she thought this was an accurate paraphrase of what Wade said, and it was attributed to him as a direct quote. Wade later affirmed, "I did not say, never have said, and don't now believe that the Bible is not factual or scientifically true. The Bible is God's inspired and written word to us and is true and trustworthy." Members of FBC, Arlington, where Wade has been pastor for more than twenty years, were upset at the misrepresentation of their pastor. Jeff Williams, chair of the Deacon Council, wrote, "Charles Wade has always preached from the Bible. . . . He has left no doubt that he believes the Bible to be the inspired and authoritative Word of God."[80] In an impassioned response, Wade said that if SBT leaders intend to form a new convention because of remarks falsely attributed to him, then their "departure is based on a lie."[81]

Many ultraconservatives were present when Wade spoke, and they know what he said. If there is any doubt, both video and audio tapes confirm his exact words.

In early 1998 some SBT sympathizers prepared a leaflet accusing the BGCT and some of its leaders of gross errors in belief and behavior. They claimed that churches affiliated with the BGCT do not believe the Bible is the inspired Word of God, do not believe the virgin birth of Christ, accept homosexuality as a valid Christian lifestyle, advocate the ordination of women as deacons and ministers, and approve the ordination of homosexual deacons and ministers.[82] In a strong editorial entitled, "Time to stop telling lies, half-truths," Editor Toby Druin refutes these charges and reminds his readers of Proverbs 6:16 where "a lying tongue" is listed as one of six things the Lord hates.[83]

Even the gentle and irenic Pinson became irate at the distribution of what he called "untruths" about Texas Baptists.[84] Refuting these false charges, Pinson said "We cannot, we must not, we will not allow untruth to go unanswered." He said,

> It's contrary to the Bible to lie. . . . It's harmful to churches and pastors—causing division and leading churches to make decisions not based on fact. It spreads like poison on water, . . . And it's bad for evangelism. How many people will go to hell because we had to spend time answering these false charges rather than focusing on winning souls to the Lord Jesus Christ?[85]

Reaction to the announced exit of Texas ultraconservatives was decidedly mixed. Some expressed regret and promised to do all they could to bring reconciliation. Others showed little grief at the departure of a group they regarded as troublemakers. In a press release, Bill Pinson said "BGCT leaders have stated again and again that they do not want any group to break fellowship with the BGCT. . . . In my opinion, the reasons given in the press release for forming a new convention are not well founded and are not justification for such an act."

Pinson acknowledged that any Baptist group is free to do what it wills, but said "I pray that all Southern Baptists in Texas will find a way to continue to serve together in the power and direction of the Holy Spirit." Pinson pointed out that SBT sympathizers have not been excluded from leadership in Texas, but continue to serve on committees and commissions where their voices are heard. In a memo to SBC leaders, Pinson said, "the facts are not in keeping with the claim that the BGCT is leaving the SBC," and he pointed out several areas of cooperation between the state and national bodies. He also noted that Texas Baptists had sent more money to the SBC in the past year than any other state, and that "the leading increase in dollar amounts for CP came from Texas and the increase in the Texas percentage for the SBC was much greater than the CP increase for the SBC as a whole."[86] For the 1997 church year, Texas Baptist churches gave a total of $72.2 million, over 5% more than the previous year.[87] Roger Hall, treasurer, said this revealed the Texas Baptist family at its best. Bill Pinson said "This [record offering] shows that Texas Baptists are serious about supporting missions around the world, around the United States, around the great state of Texas and around the block."[88]

The claim of some militant conservatives that the BGCT has gone "liberal" simply will not stand the test of scrutiny. Pinson summed it up by saying,

> As a family of Baptists in Texas, we have endeavored to remain true to God's written Word, the Bible, and God's living Word, Jesus. While we may not agree on the interpretation of the Bible in every regard, we agree on essentials. We believe in God the Father, Son and Holy Spirit. We believe in Jesus the virgin born Son of God who lived a sinless life, died on the cross for our sins, rose from the grave, ascended to the right hand of the Father, and is coming again. We believe the Bible is truth and the sole authority for faith and practice. We believe in salvation by grace through faith; in believer's baptism; in the priesthood of the believer; in a regenerate church membership; in the governance of a church by members under the leadership of the Lord Jesus Christ; in autonomous churches which cooperate with one another voluntarily for missions, evangelism, education and ministry; in religious freedom and soul competency.[89]

Pinson also expressed regret that any group would choose to leave at a time when the Convention's ministries seemed to be receiving the Lord's blessings. It might seem that in these times, with the Lord's hand so clearly upon Texas Baptists for good, sincere Christians who valued missions and evangelism would want to join the BGCT, not leave it. In his report for 1997, Pinson noted that "The previous decade [the '80s] was the best in the history of our convention by every measurable statistic, and the decade of the '90s shows evidence of being even better."[90] The growth rate for Texas Baptists is greater than that of the SBC. Pinson attributed this progress to the fact that Texas Baptists had remained true to the Bible and kept the focus on ministry.

Wayne Allen, denominational stalwart and respected pastor of FBC in Carrolton, called for a committee of representatives from both sides to seek reconciliation. Not everyone favored that, however. Typical was Bill Turner, pastor at South Main Church in Houston, who did not favor any Texas version of the SBC "Peace Committee" of the 1980s. "Years ago," Turner wrote, "the work of an SBC 'Peace Committee' consumed months of work and thousands of dollars, leaving divisions clearer and deeper than ever. Texas Baptists have found a better answer—a tent wide enough for everybody. So no 'peace committees' please."[91]

Five representatives each from the BGCT and SBT met for a closed door conference in Dallas on January 28, 1998. Representing the BGCT were Bob Campbell of Houston, immediate past chairman of the Executive Board; Charles Davenport of Tulia, chairman of the Administrative Committee; Russell H. Dilday, BGCT president; and BGCT executive director, Bill Pinson; and for SBT, Randy McDonald of Garland; Miles Seaborn of Fort Worth, president of SBT; Dee Slocum of Amarillo, vice-president; Gerald Smith of Irving, secretary-treasurer; and administrative director Ronnie Yarber. After five hours of conversation, SBT leaders concluded that the differences "did not seem resolvable." In a joint statement released after the meeting, SBT leaders "indicated that they planned to proceed with the official formation of a new state convention."[92]

In his massive history of Texas Baptists, J. M. Carroll reflected upon problems caused by rival state conventions in Texas in the 19th century. He said, "the diffusion and duplication of denominational energies was especially hurtful. We could do no very great and worthy thing, and some things that we were doing were not done in the right spirit."[93] Only when a measure of unity returned to Texas Baptist life in the 1886 merger could Texas Baptists concentrate on their main task. The record shows they certainly did many great and worthy things. However, the unity was short-lived. In 1900, another group of disgruntled extremists, followers of Samuel Hayden, withdrew from the BGCT and formed the Baptist Missionary Association {the BMA}. Over the years they have remained a small group, always criticizing the work of the BGCT but doing little ministry of their own. Though all efforts at reconciliation have failed, over the years many of their more progressive churches and pastors have quietly returned to the BGCT. While history may or may not repeat itself, it is beyond doubt that the split of 1900 was good for the BGCT. With a harshly critical group removed, the Convention could and did get on with its work.

However, schism is probably more difficult now than in 1900. The fact that pastors of many of the churches that say they plan to line up with the new convention intend also to maintain some ties with the BGCT reveals how difficult it is to cut such historic ties. Leaders of the SBT announced that churches which line up with the new splinter convention need not sever all ties with the BGCT. Instead, they recommend dual affiliation in which the disaffected churches can maintain at least minimal ties with the old Convention. This seems inconsistent, for these are the same people who condemn other Texas Baptist churches who maintain ties with the BGCT while cooperating to some extent with the Cooperative Baptist Fellowship. Further, if, as they claim, they really believe that the BGCT is infected with liberalism and/or has withdrawn from cooperation with the SBC, one wonders why they are so anxious to maintain ties with such a suspect group by means of dual affiliation. Much is involved, including the eligibility of the ministers of such churches to have the state Convention continue to contribute a portion of their SBC Annuity Board retirement program, and continued eligibility to serve on BGCT boards and committees. Also, total withdrawal might promote precisely what they fear—further distancing between Texas Baptists and the SBC.

DECISIVE ACTION

On February 24, 1998, the Executive Board, acting for the BGCT, expelled the University Baptist Church of Austin from Convention affiliation, an action which attracted widespread media coverage. The Austin church not only received homosexuals into membership, but in 1994 ordained a homosexual man as deacon and defended certain homosexual behaviors as acceptable for Christians. The Austin Baptist Association expelled the church in 1995, and over the next four years efforts were made to disfellowship the church at the state convention as well. Some were concerned that it took the BGCT so long to take decisive action on the matter.

At the San Antonio convention of 1995 Don Workman of Lubbock moved to amend the BGCT constitution to exclude any church that accepted practicing homosexuals as deacons or ministers.[94] Because this called for a change in the constitution, it was referred to the Executive Board. The Board appointed a Messenger Study Committee, chaired by Hollie Atkinson, which recommended against a constitutional change on the grounds that the Convention already had adequate channels to exclude any church for sufficient reason. "We already possess," concluded the committee, "the foundation, the rationale, and the means to exclude messengers from churches. The Bible is the foundation, the Constitution is the rationale, and the Credentials Committee and the will of the body are the means."[95] They also doubted the wisdom of naming in the constitution only one sin that would merit exclusion. The report included a blunt and unequivocal condemnation of homosexual behavior, and confidently affirmed that "The Convention can and will deal with messenger seating issues as they arise with constitutional provisions already in place." The report passed despite intense opposition by some who felt that it implied toleration of homosexuality.[96]

At the 1996 convention in Fort Worth, Wideman moved that inasmuch as the Messenger Seating Committee had condemned homosexual practices, though refusing to change the constitution, "that this Convention go on record that the BGCT withdraw fellowship from University Baptist Church of Austin."[97] This motion was ruled out of order on the grounds that "No one from University Baptist Church has registered for this convention, therefore the motion is not applicable for this convention."[98] Historically, the primary way Baptists have disciplined or expelled churches is by refusing to seat their messengers. Leaders of the Austin church knew this and they simply sent no messengers, thus thwarting the will of those who wanted to make a statement against homosexual practices by excluding this church.

However, the problem escalated. A growing number of Texas Baptists of all theological flavors felt the Convention could and should take a definitive stand on this important moral issue, and some of the extreme conservatives claimed these maneuvers and delays showed that the BGCT approved, or at least tolerated, homosexual practices. To exacerbate matters further, UBC leaders not only accepted but defended some homosexual practices, and created a web page for the church that prominently proclaimed their BGCT affiliation. The implication was that Texas Baptists knew their practices and still retained them in affiliation. Leaders of the SBT gave the inability of the BGCT to distance itself from this church as one reason for their decision to form a separate convention.

Stung by the mounting criticism, and frustrated by their inability to deal with this problem in the traditional way through the Convention's credentials committee, the Executive Board finally acted. On January 30, 1998, the Administrative Committee, chaired by Charles Davenport of Tulia, voted unanimously to recommend to the Executive Board that the Austin church be expelled. In a letter to Larry Bethune, the pastor, Davenport said, "the open affirmation by the church of homosexual behavior, a practice which we believe to be in conflict with the teachings of the Bible and of the officially adopted position of the Convention, led us to the attached recommendation."[99]

At the February 24, 1998, meeting of the Board, Bethune made an impassioned defense of the church and urged that they not be expelled. Several board members also urged defeat of the motion to expel, or at least delay, pleading Christian charity, fear that such action impinged upon local church autonomy, or questioning whether there was precedent for the Board to take such action. However, the Board voted overwhelmingly to refuse all further contributions from UBC, or "any other church which openly endorses moral views in conflict with biblical teaching." Clyde Glazener, Executive Board chairman, interpreted the action as building "a wall between the church and convention, but it did not remove the church from the convention." He said that, "Only messengers to the convention's annual session can vote not to seat a church's messengers and thereby disassociate the convention from a church."[100] However, most Baptists will probably regard the Board's action as tantamount to expulsion and unless the church sends messengers to the Convention to test their standing, the matter will likely remain as it now stands.

Two things further should be noted. There was never at any time the slightest suggestion that the BGCT approved homosexual practices as an acceptable Christian lifestyle. The five year delay in dealing with the church grew mainly out of a desire to act within historic Baptist polity. Second, there is adequate precedent for the Convention to exclude churches for cause. In Texas, for example, some churches were ousted during the crises created by S. A. Hayden (1890s) and J. Frank Norris (1920s). According to Baptist polity, every Baptist body is autonomous *in its own sphere*. That means that church, association, state convention, and SBC have complete freedom to set their own membership standards. No one of these can tell the others what members they may or may not admit. The Austin church is perfectly free to admit whom it will as members and to ordain whom it will as officers. No Baptist association or convention has a right to tell that church or any other what to believe or practice, and the BGCT at no time tried to do that. The Austin church is just as free after February 24 as it was before to conduct its own internal life in complete liberty.

On the other hand, the association and state convention are also free to set their membership standards. Feeling that homosexual practices are sinful, Baptist associations and conventions have every right to determine that they will not accept into their fellowship messengers from churches that hold and defend such practices. To say the Convention lacks authority to expel messengers from churches whose practices and/or beliefs it feels are in violation of Scripture would compromise the Convention and deny historic Baptist polity.

What is new in this case is not that a church was challenged, but that it was done by vote of the Executive Board rather than the Convention, and that no specific messengers were involved. There is, however, SBC precedent for a similar action. In 1996, the Executive Committee of the SBC voted to expel two churches in North Carolina that had allegedly allowed homosexual practices and had blessed a same sex "marriage." The SBC in session later voted to approve the Committee's action. By constitution, in Texas the Executive Board acts for the Convention between sessions; in fact, legally, the Executive Board *is* the Convention between sessions. Whatever one might feel about the wisdom of the action, the Executive Board has a constitutional right to take the action it did. However, the authority of the Board is penultimate; they do not have the final word. The authority of the Convention in session is ultimate.

WHAT NEXT?

Bill Pinson often speaks of "white water management." Most people would prefer smooth sailing in calm water, but as Texas Baptists move to the 21st century it appears that they will continue to face "white water" turbulence.

Will the SBT folks really pull out of the BGCT and form their own rival state convention? If they do, how many churches will go along with them? The ultraconservatives of Virginia formed a splinter convention in 1996, but so far they have enlisted rather fewer churches than expected, many of which maintain ties both with the old convention and the new.

Will the great missionary-evangelism program, Texas 2000, stay on track in its effort to share the gospel with every Texan by the year 2000, or will divisive strife sap away its spiritual momentum?

Will the SBC acknowledge the historic freedom and autonomy of the state conventions, or will they continue to push a centralizing concept that reduces the state conventions to "arms" of the national body?

If the disaffected Southern Baptists of Texas do withdraw from the BGCT, will their departure cripple the parent Convention, or will their withdrawal free the BGCT for more effective ministry, as was the case in the BMA schism of 1900?

If there are two rival conventions in Texas, how will churches decide which one to affiliate with and support? Will churches be split over this decision, thus bringing a convention controversy directly into the churches?

Will the more conservative Southern Baptists, in Texas and elsewhere, be content to cooperate with others in the historic Baptist way, or will they demand complete control as the price of their cooperation?

If the militant conservatives withdraw completely, will their absence create a vacuum that might cause or allow the BGCT to drift leftward without the usual restraints?

No one knows for sure the answers to these questions. What we do know is that Texas Baptists have a glorious history, with heroes and heroines who have held their Baptist faith firmly, have witnessed consistently, have given sacrificially, have endured dangers and hardships aplenty, and have invested their lives in small rural and village as well as city churches. The desert really has blossomed as the rose, despite a few thorns, and Baptist churches and Baptist people are found throughout the Lone Star State.

Texas Baptists have survived many controversies, to emerge stronger than before, and one may be confident that they will survive the current one as well. The glorious past of Baptist Christians in the Lone Star State gives promise of an even more glorious future. Truly the desert has blossomed as a rose, but there are more blossoms yet to come.

Notes

AUTHOR'S PREFACE
1. Oral memoirs of James Henry Landes, Jr., Texas Baptist Oral History Project, Baylor University. 2 vols. 2,179.

CHAPTER 1
1. "Evidence of Coronado camp found in Texas Canyon," *Fort Worth Star-Telegram*, April 16, 1996, A, 18.
2. Some object that the term "Indian" to designate the pre-European population of America is a misnomer. However, "Native American" is too unwieldy and, besides, these people are no more "native" than others who came earlier or later. Lately, some historians use "Amerind" but that term has not yet caught on. The name "Indian" is, at least, clear.
3. T. R. Fehrenbach. *Lone Star: A History of Texas and the Texans.* New York: American Legacy Press, 1968, 73.
4. Harry Hansen, ed. *Texas: A Guide to the Lone Star State.* New York: Hastings House Publishers, 1969, 36.
5. Cited in Fehrenbach, 44.
6. Cited in David McComb, *Texas: A Modern History.* Austin: University of Texas, 1989, 1.
7. Fehrenbach, 25.
8. See J. M. Carroll, *A History of Texas Baptists.* Dallas: Baptist Standard Publishing Company, 1923, 9; Hansen, 39.
9. Cited in Carroll, 8.
10. Hansen, 106.
11. Cited in Robert A. Baker, *The Blossoming Desert: A Concise History of Texas Baptists.* Waco: Word Books, Publisher, 1970, 19.
12. Fehrenbach, 223.
13. Z. N. Morrell, *Flowers and Fruits in the Wilderness.* 3rd ed. St. Louis: Commercial Printing Company, 1882, 2.
14. Carroll, 55-56.
15. D. D. Tidwell, "Rev. Noah T. Byars," unpublished paper in the D. D. Tidwell Collection, File 319, Roberts Library, Southwestern Baptist Theological Seminary, Fort Worth, TX. I am indebted to Dr. Alan Lefever, Archivist of the Baptist Collection in Roberts Library, for a copy of Tidwell's detailed research. Tidwell draws some of his conclusions from T. R. Havins, "Noah T. Byars—A Study in Missionary Effort on the Frontier," PhD dissertation, University of Texas, Austin, 1941.
16. Carroll, 58-59.
17. Morrell, 82.
18. *Ibid.*
19. Fehrenbach, 351.
20. *Ibid.*, 356.
21. Morrell, 78-79.
22. Cited in Mrs. W. J. J. Smith, *A Centennial History of the Baptist Women of Texas 1830-1930.* Dallas: Woman's Missionary Union of Texas, 1935, 25.
23. *Ibid.*, 26.
24. From a notice by T. J. Pilgrim in *The Texas Gazette* (Brazoria, TX), September 25, 1829, 4.

CHAPTER 2

1. "Hardshell" is a nickname often applied to anti-missionary, Primitive or strict Calvinist Baptists.

2. Z. N. Morrell, *Flowers and Fruits in the Wilderness.* 3rd ed. St. Louis: Commercial Printing Company, 1872, 32-33.

3. J. M. Carroll, *A History of Texas Baptists.* Dallas: Baptist Standard Publishing Company, 1923, 167.

4. Some historians give a later date for Bays, but the best evidence favors the 1820 date.

5. Carroll, 20.

6. J. B. Link, *Texas Historical and Biographical Magazine.* 2 vols. Austin, 1891, I, 23.

7. Carroll, 24.

8. *Ibid.*, 26.

9. Morrell, 32.

10. Carroll, 28f.

11. Burleson, Mrs. Georgia C. *The Life and Writings of Rufus C. Burleson.* By the Author, 1901, 63.

12. Morrell, 13.

13. *Ibid.*, 15.

14. *Ibid.*, 17.

15. *Ibid.*, 18.

16. *Ibid.*, 19.

17. *Ibid.*, 48-49.

18. A "cane-brake" especially in Kentucky and Tennessee designates poor quality land infested with tall, but worthless, cane plants. A comparable Texas expression is "cedar-brakes." The poor land meant poor people and thus the expression came to mean hard times.

19. Morrell, 31.

20. *Ibid.*, 129-130.

21. For a sketch of Baylor's life and contributions, see J. B. Link, *Texas Historical and Biographical Magazine,* 2 vols. Austin, TX: 1891, I, 194f.

22. Link, I, 28.

23. See D. D. Tidwell, "Rev. Noah T. Byars," unpublished paper, D. D. Tidwell Collection, File 319, Roberts Library, Southwestern Baptist Theological Seminary, Fort Worth, TX.

24. Davis C. Woolley, ed., *Encyclopedia of Southern Baptists.* Nashville: Broadman Press, 1958, I, 216. See also Tidwell, "Rev. Noah T. Byars."

25. Tidwell, "Rev. Noah T. Byars."

26. Letter from R.E.B. Baylor to James Stribling, cited in Robert A. Baker, *The Blossoming Desert.* Waco: Word Books, 1970, 70.

27. *Ibid.*

28. Link, I, 31.

29. *Ibid.*, I, 26.

30. See Carroll, 61-75, for other brief biographies of other Baptists in early Texas.

31. Morrell, 35.

32. Link, I, 25.

33. Morrell, 55.

34. *Ibid.*, 80.

35. "Campbellite" is a name sometimes applied to those who hold the views of Alexander Campbell, who formed the Church of Christ movement in the 1830s.

36. Since both were received for baptism, reports that James Allcorn was a deacon are probably inaccurate.

37. Stephen F. Austin, "Family Register," Vol. 2, Handwritten Book, General Land Office, Austin, TX, 45-46.

38. *Austin Papers,* Vol. III, 21, as cited in L. R. Elliott, *Centennial History of Texas Baptists,* Dallas: Baptist Standard Publishing Company, 1936, 370n.

39. D. W. C. Baker, *A Texas Scrapbook.* New York: A. S. Barnes and Company, 1875, 75.

40. B. F. Fuller, *History of Texas Baptists*. Louisville: Baptist Book Concern, 1900, 81-82.

CHAPTER 3

1. J. M. Carroll, *A History of Texas Baptists*. Dallas: Baptist Standard Publishing Company, 1923, 166.

2. *Ibid.*

3. *Ibid.*,140. However, Robert A. Baker, always the careful historian-detective, raises questions about this and suggests that Mercer's gift was less and came later. See Baker's *The Blossoming Desert*. Waco: Word Books, 1970, 38.

4. Eugene Baker, *Nothing Better than This: The Biography of James Huckins*. Waco: Baylor University, 1985, 8.

5. J. B. Link, *Texas Historical and Biographical Magazine*. Austin, 1891, I, 184f.

6. Carroll, 146.

7. *Ibid*, 147.

8. *Ibid.*

9. Carroll, 153.

10. *Ibid.*, 157.

11. Eugene Baker, 26.

12. *Ibid.*, 41.

13. *Minutes*, Union Baptist Association, 1840,1,5.

14. *Ibid.*, 5,8-9.

15. *Ibid.*, 13.

16. *Ibid.*, 15-16.

17. *Ibid.*

18. *Ibid.*

19. Whether the Educational Society was *formed* in 1841 or merely *suggested* is not clear. Later *Minutes* seem to indicate that the Society was formed in 1843. The best evidence suggests that the idea for the Society was indeed approved in 1841, but disruptions from the Mexican invasion of 1842 delayed its implementation.

20. *Minutes*, Union Baptist Association, 1842, 11.

21. *Ibid.*, 1842, 14-15.

22. *Ibid.*, 1848, 9.

23. Eugene Baker, 46.

24. Cited in J.B. Link, I, 150.

25. Samuel B. Hesler, *A History of Independence Baptist Church 1839-1969*. Dallas: Executive Board of the Baptist General Convention of Texas, n.d., 23.

26. J.M. Carroll, 226.

27. J. B. Link, I, 160.

28. Z. N. Morrell, *Flowers and Fruits in the Wilderness*. 3rd ed. St Louis: Commercial Printing Company, 1882, 131.

29. Georgia J. Burleson, *The Life and Writings of Rufus C. Burleson*. For the Author, 1901, 249-250.

30. *Minutes*, Baptist State Convention, 1849, 9.

31. L. R. Elliott, ed. *Centennial History of Texas Baptists*. Dallas: Baptist General Convention of Texas, 1936, 49.

32. J. B. Link, I, 201.

33. *Ibid.*, 202.

34. J. M. Carroll, 245-246.

35. *Minutes*, Union Baptist Association, 1847, 4.

36. *Minutes*, Baptist State Convention, 3. Twenty-three churches appointed delegates, but those from the Providence Church in Burleson County did not attend. The church sent a letter instead.

37. *Ibid.*, 4-5.

38. *Ibid.*, 12.

39. *Ibid.*, 8.

40. *Ibid.*

CHAPTER 4

1. *Minutes*, BSC, 1854, 4. Whether the Convention as such observed the Lord's Supper, or the delegates merely observed with the host church, is not always clear.

2. *Ibid.*, BSC, 1849, 4,8.

3. *Ibid.*, 1848, 7.

4. *Ibid.*, 1848, 10-11.

5. *Ibid.*, 1849, 9.

6. *Ibid.*, 1856, 31.

7. J. M. Carroll, *A History of Texas Baptists*. Dallas: Baptist Standard Publishing Company, 1923, 244.

8. L. R. Elliott, *Centennial History of Texas Baptists*. Dallas: Baptist General Convention of Texas, 1936, 49. Many of these associations have been subdivided and bear different names today.

9. *Minutes*, BSC, 1868, 22-27.

10. *Ibid.*, 1849, 11.

11. Robert A. Baker, *The Blossoming Desert: A Concise History of Texas Baptists*. Waco: Word Books, 1970, 134.

12. J. B. Link, *Texas Baptist Historical and Biographical Magazine*. 2 vols. Austin, 1891, I, 361.

13. Georgia J. Burleson, ed. *The Life and Writings of Rufus C. Burleson*. No publication data listed, 1901, 166.

14. *Minutes*, BSC, 1857, 5, 7.

15. *Ibid.*, 1856, 11.

16. *Ibid.*, 1849, 10.

17. "The Black Rock Address," Black Rock, Md, September 28, 1832. Reprinted in H. Leon McBeth, ed. a Sourcebook for Baptist Heritage. Nashville: Broadman Press, 1990, pp.236-239.

18. J. M. Carroll, 436-437.

19. See Leon McBeth, *The First Baptist Church of Dallas: Centennial History (1868-1968)*. Grand Rapids: Zondervan Publishing House, 1968, 38.

20. *Minutes*, BSC, 1858, 7-8.

21. *Ibid.*, 1861, 9. The reference is to H. F. Buckner, who served as a missionary to the Indians.

22. *Ibid.*, 1856, 15.

23. Z. N. Morrell, *Flowers and Fruits in the Wilderness*. St. Louis, Commercial Printing Company, 3rd ed. revised, 1872, 128- 129.

24. Elliott, 47.

25. Cited in Tom Berger, *Baptist Journalism in Nineteenth-Century Texas*. Austin: University of Texas, no date given, 23-24.

26. *Minutes*, BSC, 1856., 16.

27. *Ibid.*, 1851, 14.

28. *Ibid.*, 1860, 5.

29. *Ibid.*, 1867, 22-23.

30. For an account of some of these plans, see *Albert Ray Niederer, Baptist Missionary Activity among the German People in Texas 1850-1950*. PhD diss., Baylor University, 1976.

31. The *Texas Baptist*, May 27, 1856, 2.

32. *Minutes*, BSC, 1859, 12.

33. From an unpublished paper on the Schmeltekopf family, copy in author's possession.

34. Joshua Grijalva, *A History of Mexican Baptists in Texas 1881-1981*, 9. Grijalva's book is the best source of information about Mexican Baptists in Texas.

35. *Minutes*, BSC, 1854, 16-17.

36. *Ibid.*, 1853, 12.

37. *Ibid.*, 1855, 16.

38. Carroll, 226.

39. *Minutes*, BSC, 1856, 12.

40. Carroll, 242.

41. *Ibid.,* 243.

42. *Minutes,* BSC, 1852, 19.

43. *Ibid.,* 1855, 11.

44. Berger, *Baptist Journalism,* 23.

45. *Minutes,* BSC, 1861, 4.

46. *Ibid.,* 1865, 7.

47. For a feature story on the camels, see "Texas Siftings" in the *Fort Worth Star Telegram,* May 3, 1998, E, 5.

48. *Minutes,* BSC., 1865, 15.

49. *Ibid.,* 1860, 11.

50. *Ibid.* 1866, 15.

51. *Ibid.,* 1852, 7.

52. B. F. Fuller, *History of Texas Baptists.* Louisville: Baptist Book Concern, 1900, 184.

CHAPTER 5

1. The *Texas Baptist Herald,* March 19, 1885, 2.

2. *Ibid.,* April 16, 1885, 2.

3. Not to be confused with a paper of the same name published 1855-1861. The Dallas paper began in 1874 as *The Religious Messenger* and was moved to Dallas in 1875 under the new name of *The Texas Baptist.*

4. Paul C. Petty, "The Organizational Development of the Baptist General Convention of Texas," Master of Theology diss., Southwestern Baptist Theological Seminary, Fort Worth, TX, 1960, 14-18.

5. *Minutes,* BGA, 1883, 27.

6. J. M. Carroll, *A History of Texas Baptists.* Dallas: Baptist Standard Publishing Company, 1923, 516.

7. For a comparison of these two styles of Baptist organization, with strengths and weaknesses of each, see H. Leon McBeth, *The Baptist Heritage: Four Centuries of Baptist Witness.* Nashville: Broadman Press, 1987, 347-350.

8. *Minutes,* BSC, 1873, 8.

9. *Ibid.,* 1885, 22.

10. *Ibid.,* 1878, 17.

11. *Ibid.,* 1872, 13f.

12. *Ibid.,* 1875, 7-8.

13. *Ibid.,* 1881, 6-8.

14. *Ibid.,* 1884, 12.

15. *Home Mission Monthly* (New York: American Baptist Home Mission Society), VII, 12-13. As cited in Baker, 144.

16. *Ibid.,* 1883, 42.

17. *Ibid.,* 1884, 15, 17.

18. B. F. Fuller, *History of Texas Baptists.* Louisville, KY: Baptist Book Concern, 1900, 169.

19. *Minutes,* BGA, 1868, 6-8.

20. *Ibid.,* 1869, 8.

21. *Ibid.,* 10.

22. *Ibid.,* 1881, 27.

23. *Ibid.,* 1872, 11.

24. Without much ethnic sensitivity, Baptists in those days distinguished between "wild Indians" and "civilized Indians." How to discern the difference between the two groups was not spelled out.

25. *Minutes,* BGA, 1879, 47. The quotation comes from the report of the Deacons Convention, but since their minutes are printed with the BGA minutes, they are not distinguished here.

26. Karen O'Dell Bullock, *Homeward Bound: The Heart and Heritage of Buckner.* Dallas: Buckner Baptist Benevolences, 1993, 47.

27. Robert A. Baker, *The Blossoming Desert: A Concise History of Texas Baptists.* Waco: Word Books, Publisher, 1970, 152.

28. For a discussion of the origin, teachings, and continuing impact of Landmarkism, see H. Leon McBeth, *The Baptist Heritage: Four Centuries of Baptist Witness*. Nashville: Broadman Press, 1987, 446-461.

29. For a discussion of this church split and the issues involved, see H. Leon McBeth, *The First Baptist Church of Dallas: Centennial History (1868-1968)*. Grand Rapids: Zondervan Publishing House, 1968, 73f.

30. See McBeth, *First Baptist Church of Dallas*, 75-80, for a more extensive discussion of this church split.

31. *Minutes*, BGA Called Meeting, February 24, 1880, 14.

32. *Minutes*, BGA, 1871, 20. Whether the objection was to the content of the literature, or the idea of producing literature for personal profit, is not clear.

33. *Ibid.*, 1881, 83.

34. Carroll, 431.

35. *Minutes*, BGA, 1868, 11.

36. *Ibid.*, 1877, 7.

37. Cited in Carroll, 558.

38. *Minutes*, Union Baptist Association, 1864, as cited in Carroll, 429.

39. Mrs. W. J. J. Smith, A Centennial History of the Baptist Women of Texas 1830-1930. Dallas: Woman's Missionary Union of Texas, 1933, 20.

40. *Ibid.*, 18, 19.

41. *Ibid.*, 27.

42. *Minutes*, BGA, 1869, 35.

43. *Minutes*, BSC, 1870, 10.

44. Frank Burkhalter, *A World-Visioned Church*. Nashville: Broadman Press, 1946, 100, 300.

45. For a popular account of Anne Luther Bagby, see Helen Bagby Harrison, *The Bagbys of Brazil*. Crawford, TX: Crawford Press, n.d.; for a more detailed analysis see Daniel Lancaster, "In the Land of the Southern Cross: The Life and Ministry of William Buck and Anne Luther Bagby," PhD diss., Southwestern Baptist Theological Seminary, Fort Worth, TX, 1995.

46. *Minutes*, BGA, 1884, 23.

47. Mrs. W. L. Williams, *Golden Years: An Autobiography*. Dallas: Baptist Standard Publishing Company, 1921, 96.

48. See Leon McBeth, *Women in Baptist Life*. Nashville: Broadman Press, 1979, 111-113.

49. *Minutes*, BSC, 1873, 8.

50. *Ibid.*, 1870, 13.

51. *Ibid.*, 1870, 17.

52. *Ibid.*, 1869, 39.

53. The *Texas Baptist Herald*, June 11, 1885, 2.

54. *Minutes*, BGA, 1868, 10.

55. *Ibid.*, 1880, 21.

56. *Minutes*, BSC, 1869. 17; 1870, 6.

57. The *Texas Baptist Herald*, August 6, 1883, 2.

58. *Ibid.*, 1883, 28.

59. *Minutes*, BGA, 1885, 28.

60. *Minutes*, BSC, 1885, 61.

61. Carroll, 649.

62. *Ibid.*, 651.

63. Technically, the *convention as such* did not vote. The convention was adjourned to a mass meeting, but nobody left their seats and the same crowd voted. See *Minutes*, Baptist General Convention of Texas, 1886, 23-24.

CHAPTER 6

1. J. B. Link launched the *Texas Baptist Herald* at Houston in 1865, moved it to Austin in 1883, and to Waco in 1886.

2. *Proceedings*, BGCT, 1887, 49-51.

3. *Ibid.,* 1887, 12.

4. *Ibid.,* 1886, 31.

5. The *Texas Baptist Herald,* August 5, 1886, 3.

6. *Ibid.,* August 12, 1886, 1.

7. *Proceedings,* BGCT, 1886, 47.

8. Cited in J. M. Carroll, *A History of Texas Baptists.* Dallas: Baptist Standard Publishing Company, 1923, 668-669.

9. *Proceedings,* BGCT, 1889, 37.

10. A. J. Holt, *Pioneering in the Southwest.* Nashville: Sunday School Board of the Southern Baptist Convention, 1922, 208.

11. Carroll, 689.

12. *Ibid.*

13. *Proceedings,* BGCT, 1894, 13.

14. *Ibid.,* 15.

15. B. F. Riley, *A History of Texas Baptists.* Louisville, KY: Baptist Book Concern, 1900, 319.

16. Eugene W. Baker, *To Light the Ways of Time: An Illustrated History of Baylor University, 1845-1986.* Waco: Baylor University Press, 1987, 53.

17. *Proceedings,* BGCT, 1886, 25.

18. *Ibid.*

19. Eugene Baker, 64.

20. *Ibid.,* 67.

21. *Ibid.,* 22-23.

22. For more details of this campaign, see Leon McBeth, *The First Baptist Church of Dallas: Centennial History (1868–1968).* Grand Rapids: Zondervan Publishing House, 1968, 120f.

23. *Ibid.,* 1894, 60-61.

24. John S. Tanner to B. H. Carroll, May 28, 1895, File 171, Carroll Papers, Roberts Library, Southwestern Baptist Theological Seminary, Fort Worth, TX.

25. Steward D. Smith, "The University of Mary Hardin-Baylor," in Jerry Dawson, ed., *Teaching Them . . . A Sesquicentennial Celebration of Texas Baptist Education, 1996.*

26. W. T. Walton, "Hardin Simmons University," The Encyclopedia of Southern Baptists. Nashville: Broadman Press, 1958, I, 593.

27. Xerox copy of the Decatur Baptist College charter of l898 and its renewal in 1948 in the author's possession.

28. Carroll, 422f.

29. *Proceedings,* BGCT, 1886, 30.

30. The *Texas Baptist and Herald,* August 12, 1886, 4.

31. *Ibid.*

32. *Ibid.*

33. *Proceedings,* BGCT, 1900, 142.

34. James Leo Garrett, Jr. *Living Stones: The Centennial History of Broadway Baptist Church, Fort Worth, Texas, 1882-1982,* 2 vols. Fort Worth: Broadway Baptist Church, 1984, I, 59.

35. *Ibid.,* 58f.

36. Cited in Garrett, 61.

37. *Ibid.,* 63-64.

38. Karen O'Dell Bullock, *Homeward Bound: The Heart and Heritage of Buckner.* Dallas: Buckner Baptist Benevolences, 1993, 70.

39. *Proceedings,* BGCT, 1900, 119-120.

40. *Ibid.,* 118.

41. *Ibid.,* 118.

42. Cited in Karen O'Dell Bullock, 71-72.

43. *Ibid.,* 59.

44. *Proceedings,* BGCT, 1887, 37.

45. Carroll, 610.

46. *Proceedings,* BGCT, 1900, 60.

47. *Ibid.*, 1887, 43. Emphasis theirs.

48. Presnall Wood and Floyd Thatcher. *Prophets with Pens*. Dallas: Baptist Standard Publishing Company, 1969, 13. This work is based upon Dr. Wood's doctoral dissertation at Southwestern Baptist Seminary, Fort Worth, TX.

49. *Ibid.*, 18.

50. B. F. Riley, *History of the Texas Baptists*. Dallas: For the author, 1907, 347.

51. Cited in Wood and Thatcher, 28.

52. A. J. Holt, Dallas, to B. H. Carroll, Waco, January 28, 1889, File 590, Carroll Collection, as cited in Lefever, 65.

53. Fuller, 388-89.

54. For a cogent account of Furtunism, see B. F. Fuller, *A History of Texas Baptists*. Louisville, KY: Baptist Book Concern, 1900, 398f. Fuller participated in the council of 1896 called by the minority to deal with Fortune's views.

55. The customary practice for Baptist churches in Texas at that time was to call the pastor for a period of one year, and at the end of that year ask church members to vote again on whether to renew the call. This "annual call" practice survived well past the World War II era, especially in rural churches, but is rare today.

56. *Minutes* of Ex Parte Council Held at the Call of the Minority of the First Baptist Church, Paris, Texas, February 11 & 12, 1896. Paris: P. H. Bennett, Printer, 1896, 12.

57. *Ibid.*, 14. Interestingly, no such charges were raised against B. H. Carroll, who divorced his first wife.

58. *Ibid.*, 402.

59. Jesse C. Fletcher, *The Southern Baptist Convention: A Sesquicentennial History*. Nashville: Broadman & Holman, 1994, 102.

60. T. P. Crawford, *Churches: To the Front!* China: No publication data, 1892. As cited in H. Leon McBeth, ed. *A Sourcebook for Baptist Heritage*. Nashville: Broadman Press, 1990, 328.

61. *Ibid.*, 328-330.

62. *Ibid.*, 331.

63. *Foreign Mission Journal*, September 1893, 37-41.

64. Rosalie Beck, "The Whitsitt Controversy: A Denomination in Crisis," PhD diss., Baylor University, Waco, TX, 1984.

65. William H. Whitsitt, *A Question in Baptist History*. Louisville: Charles T. Dearing, 1896.

66. Alan Lefever, *Fighting the Good Fight: The Life and Work of Benajah Harvey Carroll*. Austin: Eakin Press, 1994, 86.

67. The Southern Baptist Theological Seminary (Louisville, Kentucky), *Minutes* of Meeting of the Board of Trustees, May 6, 1897, Item 23, as cited in Robert A. Baker, *Tell the Generations Following*. Nashville: Broadman Press, 1983, 92-93.

68. Lefever, 90.

69. Cited in Beck, 97.

70. *Proceedings*, BGCT, 1897, 91.

71. *Ibid.*, 1896, 22-23.

72. *Ibid.*, 1897, 101.

73. *Ibid.*, 1895, 36.

74. Albert W. Wardin, ed., *Baptists Around the World: A Comprehensive Handbook*. Nashville: Broadman & Holman Publishers, 1995, 462.

CHAPTER 7

1. *Proceedings*, BGCT, 1901, 14.

2. *Ibid.*, 23.

3. *Ibid.*, 14.

4. J. Woodrow Fuller, "Texas, Baptist General Convention of," in *Encyclopedia of Southern Baptists*, Davis C. Woolley, ed. Nashville: Broadman Press, 1958, II, 1389.

5. B. F. Riley, *History of the Baptists of Texas*. Dallas: Published for the Author, 1907, 433.

6. One should not conclude from this that the Convention sponsored a hundred dif-

ferent forms of endeavor. In the typical pattern, a committee would report. A further committee would study that report and make recommendations. Yet another committee might be named to study the recommendations. This was time-consuming, but it was thorough. No proposal could make it through the Convention without careful analysis.

7. The letter is undated, but apparently written on Sunday, February 6, 1898. Copy in author's possession.

8. George W. Gray, "Out of the Mountains Came This Great Preacher of the Plains," *The American Magazine*, November 1925. In Truett Collection (TC), File 106, A. Webb Roberts Library, Southwestern Baptist Theological Seminary, Fort Worth, TX. This incident is described in greater detail in Leon McBeth, *The First Baptist Church of Dallas: Centennial History.* Grand Rapids: Zondervan Publishing House, 1968, 135-138.

9. The best biography of Scarborough is Glenn T. Carson, *Calling out the Called: The Life and Work of Lee Rutland Scarborough.* Austin: Eakin Press, 1996.

10. *Ibid.*, especially chapters 4 and 5.

11. Inez Boyle Hunt, *A Pilgrimage of Faith: Woman's Missionary Union of Texas 1880-1980.* Dallas: Woman's Missionary Union, 1979, 34.

12. Mrs. B. A. Copass, "The Women and Their Work," In L. R. Elliott, *Centennial Story of Texas Baptists.* Dallas: BGCT, 1936, 227.

13. J. M. Carroll, *A History of Texas Baptists.* Dallas: Baptist Standard Publishing Company, 1923, 880.

14. John W. Storey, *Texas Baptist Leadership and Social Christianity, 1900-1980.* College Station: Texas A&M University Press, 1986, 33.

15. Carroll, 862.

16. Mrs. B. A. Copass, "The Women and Their Work," Elliott, *Centennial Story,* 229.

17. *Proceedings,* BGCT, 1900, 16; 1914, 115.

18. *Ibid.*, 1901, 20.

19. *Ibid.*, 1905, 29.

20. *Ibid.*, 1901, 21.

21. *Ibid.*, 22.

22. From a letter written by Hollie Harper Townsend, published in Mrs. W. J. J. Smith, *A Centennial History of the Baptist Women of Texas 1830-1930.* Dallas: Woman's Missionary Union, 1933, 161-163.

23. *Ibid.*

24. *Proceedings,* BGCT, 1905, 30.

25. *Ibid.*, 1901, 25.

26. *Ibid.*, 1910, 87.

27. Presnall Wood, *Prophets with Pens: A History of the Baptist Standard.* Dallas: Baptist Standard Publishing Company, 1969, 31.

28. *Ibid.*, 75.

29. *Ibid.*, 77.

30. *Ibid.*, 75.

31. *Annual,* BGCT, 1913, 17-18.

32. *Ibid.*, 1910, 177.

33. *Ibid.*, 1910, 75.

34. *Ibid.*, 1907, 149.

35. *Ibid.*, 150.

36. *Ibid.*, 1914, 124.

37. *Ibid.*, 125.

38. See Karen Bullock, *Homeward Bound: The Heart and Heritage of Buckner.* Dallas: Buckner Baptist Benevolences, 1993, 90.

39. See Thomas R. Havins, "Baptist Benevolent Ministries," in Elliott, *Centennial Story,* 186n. The Missouri Baptist Sanitarium (St. Louis, 1884) and the Mayfield Sanitarium (St. Louis, 1896). Both were founded under the leadership of Dr. William H. Mayfield.

40. *Proceedings,* BGCT, 1910, 111.

41. *Ibid.*, 174.

42. The Margaret Home, founded in Greenville, SC, in 1904 provided a residence for the sons and daughters of foreign missionaries who came back to the States for education.

In 1914 the home was sold and the money put into a Margaret Fund to provide scholarship aid to such students. "Margaret" was the name of the grandmother of Mrs. Frank Chambers, an early donor.

43. Copass, in Elliott, *Centennial Story,* 226.

44. *Annual,* BGCT, 1914, 207.

45. Bullock, 89.

42. The Margaret Home, founded in Greenville, SC, in 1904 provided a residence for the sons and daughters of foreign missionaries who came back to the States for education. In 1914 the home was sold and the money put into a Margaret Fund to provide scholarship aid to such students. "Margaret" was the name of the grandmother of Mrs. Frank Chambers, an early donor.

43. Copass, in Elliott, *Centennial Story,* 226.

44. *Annual,* BGCT, 1914, 207.

45. Bullock, 89.

46. Inez Boyle Hunt, *A Pilgrimage of Faith: Woman's Missionary Union of Texas 1880-1980.* Dallas: Woman's Missionary Union, 1979, 30.

47. Jerry F. Dawson, ed. *Teaching Them . . . A Sesquicentennial Celebration of Texas Baptist Education.* Dallas: BGCT, 1996. See Thomas Storey, "Introduction," 2.

48. *Proceedings,* BGCT, 1909, 19-21, 64.

49. Cited in Dawson, 4.

50. *Ibid.,* 58.

51. *Ibid.,* 67.

52. Helen Bagby Harrison, *The Bagbys of Brazil* (Crawford, TX: Crawford Christian Press, n.d., 3, as cited in Alan Lefever, *Fighting the Good Fight: The Life and Work of Benajah Harvey Carroll.* Austin: Eakin Press, 1994, 81.

53. Lefever, 81.

54. *Ibid.,* 97.

55. Cited in Robert A. Baker, *Tell the Generations Following: A History of Southwestern Baptist Theological Seminary 1908-1983.* Nashville: Broadman Press, 1983, 121.

56. *Ibid.,* 120.

57. *Proceedings,* BGCT, 1906, 27.

58. *Ibid.,* 43.

59. *Baptist Standard,* September 14, 1905, as cited in Lefever, 100.

60. *Ibid.,* November 2, 1905.

61. *Ibid.*

62. *Proceedings,* BGCT, 1907, 51.

63. *Ibid.,* 51-52.

64. *Ibid.,* 54.

65. Rosalie Beck, "The Whitsitt Controversy: A Denomination in Crisis," PhD diss., Baylor University, 1984, 253.

66. Cited in Lefever, 93.

67. A. B. Miller to B. H. Carroll, June 12, 1896, File 208-1, Carroll Collection, Roberts Library, Southwestern Baptist Theological Seminary, Fort Worth, TX.

68. See Baker, 150-151. A street west of the campus bears the name of McCart, and other streets on Seminary Hill bear the names of Gambrell, Boyce and Broadus, but for some reason nothing at the Seminary or on adjoining streets carries the name of Winston.

69. Cited in Baker, 158.

70. *Proceedings,* BGCT, 1910, 80.

71. *Annual,* BGCT, 1914, 241.

72. *Ibid.* For discrepancy in the number of women students reported, see footnote 74.

73. W. W. Barnes, "Southwestern Baptist Theological Seminary," in *Encyclopedia of Southern Baptists,* ed. Davis C. Woolley. Nashville: Broadman Press, 1958, II, 1282.

74. There is a discrepancy in the number of women students reported in the fall of 1913. The Seminary report for 1913, though reported in the 1914 *Annual,* gives the figure at 75 (*Annual,* 1914, 15). The Baptist Women Mission Workers report (*Annual,* 1913, 289), gives only 60. Along with the universal tendency of schools to inflate their enrollment fig-

ures, one presumes there may have been women taking some classes who were not in formal degree programs.

75.Robert A. Baker, 164.

76. *Proceedings,* BGCT, 1912, 111-112.

77. *Ibid.,* 1913, 133f.

78. *Ibid.,* 1914, 76f.

79. Cited from copy of Constitution, *Annual,* BGCT, 1911, 10.

80. *Annual,* BGCT, 1914, 78.

81. *Ibid.,* 103.

82. *Ibid.,* 78.

83. *Baptist Courier,* May 4, 1916, as cited in William Wright Barnes, *The Southern Baptist Convention 1845-1953.* Nashville: Broadman Press, 1954, 174-175.

84. The Seventy-five Million Campaign was an effort to raise $75 million for SBC causes. For a discussion of the campaign and its impact, see H. Leon McBeth, *The Baptist Heritage.* Nashville: Broadman Press, 1987, 616f; and Jesse C. Fletcher, *The Southern Baptist Convention: A Sesquicentennial History.* Nashville: Broadman & Holman, 1994, 133-134.

CHAPTER 8

1. For a lucid discussion of Texas during the Depression, see T. R. Fehrenbach, *Lone Star: A History of Texas and Texans.* New York: American Legacy Press, 1983, 642f.

2. *Baptist Standard,* July 31, 1919, 5.

3. *Annual,* BGCT, 1915, 65.

4. *Ibid.,* 1927, 108, 119.

5. *Ibid.,* 103.

6. The title changed from time to time. After the mid-twenties, the top leader, the Corresponding Secretary, was often called the General Secretary, and the second highest office that had been Assistant Corresponding Secretary became Executive Secretary.

7. *Minutes,* Executive Board, BGCT, December 15, 1914, 7.

8. *Ibid.,* November 24, 1917, 2.

9. *Ibid.,* June 11, 1918, 1.

10. *Annual,* BGCT, 1915, 131.

11. Fehrenbach, 643.

12. *Annual,* BGCT, 1915, 178.

13. Fehrenback, 643-644.

14. *Annual,* BGCT, 1918, 77.

15. *Baptist Standard,* April 17, 1919, 23.

16. George W. Truett Diary, July 19, 1918, Truett File, Roberts Library, Southwestern Baptist Theological Seminary, Fort Worth, TX. Henceforth, Truett Diary.

17. *Ibid.,* January 10, 1919.

18. "Baptists Favor League of Nations," Nashville Tennessean, May 21, 1920, Truett File 37, Roberts Library, Southwestern Baptist Theological Seminary, Fort Worth, TX.

19. *Baptist Standard,* July 24, 1919, 7.

20. *Ibid.,* April 17, 1919, 6-7.

21. *Ibid.,* March 6, 1919, 7.

22. *Annual,* SBC, 1919, 19.

23. *Baptist Standard,* June 5, 1919, 5.

24. For an excellent sketch of the campaign, see Jesse C. Fletcher, *The Southern Baptist Convention: A Sesquicentennial History.* Nashville: Broadman & Holman, 1994, 133-134.

25. *Annual,* BGCT, 1920, 84.

26. *Ibid.,* September 18, 1919, 5.

27. *Ibid.,* December 18, 1919, 1.

28. *Annual,* SBC, 1920, 48-49.

29. Leon McBeth, *The First Baptist Church of Dallas: Centennial History (1868-1968).* Grand Rapids: Zondervan Publishing House, 1968, 145.

30. *Baptist Standard,* December 10, 1925, 7.

31. The Northern Baptist Convention, for example, collected only about $45 million of their $100 million goal.

32. William Wright Barnes, *The Southern Baptist Convention 1845-1953*. Nashville: Broadman Press, 1954, 224.

33. Ray E. Tatum, *Conquest or Failure? A Biography of J. Frank Norris*. Fort Worth: Manney Company, 1976. This is but one of several biographies of Norris.

34. *Ibid.,* 22. Warner Norris once beat his son until the boy was bloody and unconscious and, some say, might have beat him to death had not Mary his mother intervened.

35. E. P. Kirkland to F. S. Groner, handwritten letter in pencil on lined tablet paper, dated October 27, 1922, in Norris Files, Roberts Library, Southwestern Baptist Theological Seminary, Fort Worth, TX.

36. Baptist Missionary Association, the name given to Samuel A. Hayden's schismatic group after they split from the BGCT in 1900.

37. E. P. Kirkland to F. S. Groner, *op. cit.*

38. *Searchlight,* September 29, 1922, 1. This was an earlier name for the paper which became the *Fundamentalist*. A still earlier name was the *Fencepost*.

39. W. W. Barnes, unpublished Founders Day Address, 8, Barnes Files, Roberts Library, Southwestern Baptist Theological Seminary, Fort Worth, TX. This story is told in many places. See also William M. Shamburger, "A History of Tarrant County Baptist Association, 1886-1922," unpublished ThD diss., Southwestern Baptist Theological Seminary, Fort Worth, TX, 237.

40. *Annual,* BGCT, 1924, 16.

41. *Ibid.,* 1925, 18.

42. *Minutes,* Executive Board, BGCT, December 19, 1916, 11.

43. *Ibid.,* December 15, 1914, 19.

44. *Ibid.,* 1929, 103.

45. *Ibid.,* December 14, 1921, 13.

46. *Ibid.,* December 19, 1922, 61-62.

47. *Ibid.,* December 19, 1922, 60.

48. *Ibid.,* 1915, 63.

49. *Ibid.*

50. *Minutes,* Executive Board, BGCT, August 15, 1916, 5.

51. *Ibid.,* 7.

52. *Ibid.,* 7-8.

53. *Ibid.,* December 13, 1923.

54. *Ibid.,* July 8, 1924.

55. *Baptist Standard,* December 10, 1925, 7.

56. *Minutes,* Executive Board, BGCT, January 3, 1929.

57. *Baptist Standard,* January 3, 1929, 5.

58. *Ibid.,* September 4, 1919, 14.

59. *Ibid.,* December 26, 1929, 6.

60. *Minutes,* Executive Board, December 14, 1921.

61. *Baptist Standard,* November 19, 1925, 15.

62. *Ibid.,* March 13, 1919, 26.

63. *Annual,* BGCT, 1915, 65.

64. *Ibid.,* 1929, 116.

65. *Ibid.,* 1915, 65.

66. *Baptist Standard,* December 18, 1919, 1.

67. *Annual,* BGCT, 1918, 133.

68. *Ibid.,* 134.

69. *Annual,* BGCT, 1915, 32.

70. Lynn E. May, Jr. "The Baptist Student Union in Perspective," Part 1. The Baptist Student, October, 1961, 18.

71. Andrew Q. Allen, "A Brief History of the Baptist Student Missionary Movement and the Baptist Student Union in Texas," unpublished paper, dated January 1, 1929. Roberts Library, Southwestern Baptist Theological Seminary, Fort Worth, TX.

72. *Annual,* BGCT, 1919, 16.

73. *Ibid.*, 1920, 83. Boone says he began his work in December, 1919. See J. P. Boone, "The Early History and Development," *Quarterly Review,* October-December, 1948, 32.

74. J. P. Boone, "The Early History and Development," 30.

75. *Ibid.*, 1920, 83-84.

76. *Ibid.*, 1929, 67.

77. *Ibid.* The report says Howard Payne students conducted 52 revivals, with 879 conversions, 389 added to the churches by letter, 189 young people surrendered for Christian service, 1021 sermons preached, and two deacons ordained.

78. *Ibid.*, 1915, 59.

79. *Ibid.*, 57.

80. *Ibid.*, 58.

81. Simmons College in Abilene was in friendly cooperation with the BGCT but not under Convention control. Its trustees were elected by the Sweetwater Association.

82. *Ibid.*, 1915, 83.

83. The complete list is given in *Annual,* BGCT, 1928, 229, and in other places.

84. *Annual,* BGCT, 1928, 222-234. Much of the material in this section comes from this lengthy report, so each citation will not be footnoted separately.

85. *Ibid.*, 224.

86. Eugene W. Baker, *To Light the Ways of Time: An Illustrated History of Baylor University, 1845-1986.* Waco: Baylor University, 1987, 141-143.

87. *Ibid.*, 143.

88. *Ibid.*, 107.

89. Andrew Q. Allen, "A Brief History of the Baptist Student Missionary Movement and the Baptist Student Union in Texas," unpublished paper dated January 1, 1929. In Roberts Library, Southwestern Baptist Theological Seminary, Fort Worth, TX.

90. *Ibid.*, 15.

91. *Ibid.*, 1929, 83.

92. *Annual,* BGCT, 1915, 109, 117.

93. *Ibid.*, 111-112.

94. *Ibid.*, 111-112.

95. *Ibid.*, 116.

96. *Ibid.*, 109.

97. *Ibid.*, 233.

98. *Minutes,* Executive Board, BGCT, February 21, 1923.

99. For a detailed account of these years, see Karen O'Dell Bullock, *Homeward Bound: The Heart and Heritage of Buckner.* Dallas: Buckner Baptist Benevolences, 1993, 165f.

100. *Ibid.*, 166.

101. *Minutes,* Executive Board, BGCT, December 22, 1920.

102. Clinton S. Carnes, treasurer of the Home Mission Board of the SBC, in the 1920s embezzled almost $1 million dollars from the HMB. When this theft came to light in 1928, it threw the SBC into deeper debt and consternation.

103. *Baptist Standard,* April 9, 1925, 6.

104. *Ibid.*, April 30, 1925, 9.

105. *Annual,* BGCT, 1929, 102.

CHAPTER 9
1. EBM, April 25, 1932.

2. *Ibid.*, March 7, 1933.

3. 2 Cor. 4:8, KJV.

4. EBM, September 15, 1936.

5. *Ibid.*

6. By 1945 the name of the women's college had been changed to Mary Hardin-Baylor in honor of the generous gifts of John and Mary Hardin of Buckburnett.

7. Leslie R. Elliott, ed. *Centennial Story of Texas Baptists.* Dallas: Executive Board of the BGCT, 1936.

8. Record File of Pulpit Committee, 1944, First Baptist Church, Dallas. The other two finalists were Louie D. Newton and Duke K. McCall. W. A. Criswell was not among

those being considered until the latter stages of the search when he was recommended by John Hill of the Baptist Sunday School Board in Nashville.

9. *Annual,* BGCT, 1930, 20.

10. *Ibid.;* see also EBM, June 25, 1931.

11. *Annual,* BGCT, 1933, 93.

12. EBM, June 11, 1936.

13. For an excellent study of various dimensions of Williams's life and ministry, see H. C. Brown, Jr. and Charles P. Johnson, editors, *J. Howard Williams: Prophet of God and Friend of Man.* San Antonio: The Naylor Book Company, 1963.

14. W. M. Shamburger, "Campbell, Robert Clifford," Encyclopedia of Southern Baptists. Nashville: Broadman Press, 1958, II, 227.

15. EBM, March 4, 1941.

16. *Ibid.,* April 1, 1941.

17. *Annual,* BGCT, 1933, 113.

18. *Ibid.,* 1930, 93.

19. May 12, 1932, 5.

20. EBM, December 22, 1933.

21. *Ibid.,* March 7, 1933.

22. Robert A. Baker, *The Blossoming Desert: A Concise History of Texas Baptists.* Waco: Word Books, 1970, 213.

23. *Annual,* BGCT, 1931, 104.

24. *Ibid.,* 1939, 74.

25. EBM, September 15, 1936.

26. *Ibid.*

27. *Ibid.,* October 1, 1939.

28. *Ibid.,* April 6, 1943.

29. *Annual,* BGCT, 1930, 152.

30. *Ibid.*

31. J.Howard Williams to Walter N. Johnson, Mars Hill, North Carolina, September 24, 1930, J. Howard Williams Collection, Roberts Library, Southwestern Seminary, Box 2, No. 218.

32. *Ibid.*

33. Mrs. W. J. J. Smith, *A Centennial History of the Baptist Women of Texas 1830-1930.* Dallas: WMU of Texas, 1933, 56-57/

34. The story of Baptist women's contribution to missions has been told, but their pioneering efforts in Sunday School, their background role in the formation of the Baptist Sunday School Board in 1891, their role in the development of Baptist church stewardship, and their influence upon Baptist church worship patterns, especially in music, are yet to be told fully. For a brief discussion of these contributions, see Leon McBeth, Women in Baptist Life. Nashville: Broadman Press, 1979.

35. *Annual,* BGCT, 1933, 98.

36. *Ibid.,* 155.

37. *Ibid.,* 1941, 74.

38. The author well remembers being a very young pastor in West Texas when James Arnett was missionary for District Eight. In 1946 Brother Arnett gave the author his very first book, besides his Bible, in what would over the years become a sizable ministerial library (A. A. Davis, Lectures on Baptist History). At a time when this young pastor hardly realized there was such a thing as a state convention, Arnett was the connecting link between the local Baptist life in a remote section and the larger work of Baptists in Texas and beyond.

39. *Annual,* BGCT, 1933, 20.

40. EBM, December 4, 1934.

41. *Baptist Standard,* January 27, 1938, 1.

42. EBM, December 4, 1934.

43. *Ibid.,* August 22, 1944.

44. R. R. Cumbie, "The Rural Church Problem," *Baptist Standard,* May 26, 1932, 2.

45. *Annual,* BGCT, 1936, 20.

46. *Ibid.,* 25.

47. *Ibid.,* 21.

48. *Ibid.,* 24.

49. *Ibid.,* 21-22.

50. EBM, June 12, 1933.

51. *Annual,* BGCT, 1935, 17-18.

52. *Ibid.,* 1939, 21-22.

53. *Ibid.,* 1931, 104.

54. EBM, March 4, 1930.

55. *Baptist Standard,* May 5, 1932, 4.

56. *Minutes,* Executive Board, June 30, 1936.

57. *Annual,* BGCT, 1936, 96.

58. *Ibid,* 97-99.

59. *Ibid.,* 99.

60. *Ibid.,* 100.

61. EBM, March 4, 1930.

62. *Ibid.,* 92.

63. Joshua Grijalva, *A History of Mexican Baptists in Texas 1881-1981.* Dallas, 1982, 51.

64. *Annual,* BGCT, 1934, 92.

65. Grijalva, 68.

66. *Annual,* BGCT, 1933, 130.

67. *Ibid.*

68. *Ibid.,* 1934, 131.

69. *Baptist Standard,* May 3, 1945, 10.

70. *Annual,* BGCT, 1930, 103.

71. *Ibid.,* 114.

72. *Baptist Standard,* February 1, 1945, 10.

73. *Annual,* BGCT, 1934, 129; 1939, 105.

74. *Encyclopedia of Southern Baptists,* Nashville: Broadman Press, III, 1729.

75. *Annual,* 1930, 104.

76. *Ibid.,* 105.

77. *Ibid.,* 106.

78. *Ibid.,* 112.

79. *Ibid.,* 1931, 120.

80. EBM, December 4, 1934. The state BTS convention meeting a few weeks earlier in Lubbock had already taken similar action.

81. *Annual,* BGCT, 1933, 121.

82. *Baptist Standard,* February 1, 1945, 11.

83. Inez Boyle Hunt, *A Pilgrimage of Faith: Woman's Missionary Union of Texas 1880-1980.* n.p., Woman's Missionary Union, 1979, 43.

84. *Ibid.,* 120-123.

85. Jesse C. Fletcher, *The Southern Baptist Convention: A Sesquicentennial History.* Nashville: Broadman & Holman, 1994, 204, 233.

86. Hunt, 44-45.

87. *Ibid.,* 9.

88. *Baptist Standard,* February 10, 1938, 6.

89. *Annual,* BGCT, 1930, WMU report, 8.

90. Hunt, 47.

91. *Ibid.,* 45.

92. The WMU letter and the Board's reply are included in the *Minutes,* Executive Board, December 12, 1933.

93. EBM, March 13, 1945.

94. *Annual,* BGCT, 1930, 146. This apparently included not just colleges, but all the schools.

95. *Ibid.,* 1931, 140.

96. *Ibid.,* 146-147.

97. *Ibid.,* 1934, 137.

98. EBM, BGCT, March 3, 1942.

99. *Ibid.,* July 15, 1941.

100. *Ibid.,* June 2, 1942.

101. *Annual,* BGCT, 1933, 166.

102. *Ibid.,* 1931, 162.

103. *Ibid.,* 1938, 143-144.

104. *Ibid.,* 1939, 142-143.

105. *Ibid.,* 1934, 36.

106. EBM, December 6, 1938.

107. H. Leon McBeth, *Celebrating Heritage and Hope: Centennial History of the Baptist Sunday School Board,* unpublished manuscript, 174-177.

108. EBM, July 15, 1941.

109. For the story of Baptist colleges in Texas, see Jerry F. Dawson, ed., *Teaching Them . . . A Sesquicentennial Celebration of Texas Baptist Education.* Dallas: BGCT, 1996. Since extensive details are given in this book, less space will be given to colleges in this chapter.

110. *Annual,* BGCT, 1930, 92.

111. *Ibid.,* 1939, 30-31. This was college enrollment only, and did not include students in Texas Baptist academies, nursing schools, etc.

112. *Ibid.,* 31.

113. EBM, August 22, 1944.

114. *Baptist Standard,* April 28, 1932, 2.

115. Robert A. Baker tells portions of this story in his *Tell the Generations Following: A History of Southwestern Baptist Theological Seminary 1908-1983.* Nashville: Broadman Press, 1983, 257. Oral tradition at the Seminary adds other details.

116. *Ibid.,* 256.

117. *Baptist Standard,* January 18, 1945, 1.

118. *Annual,* BGCT, 1940, WMU report 47.

119. EBM, March 13, 1945.

120. Printed with EBM, March 13, 1945.

CHAPTER 10

1. *Baptist Standard,* January 17, 1946, 5.

2. *Ibid.*

3. *Annual,* BGCT, 1949, 56.

4. *Ibid.*

5. *Ibid.,* 62.

6. *Ibid.,* 63.

7. EBM, December 7, 1948.

8. *Ibid.,* December 16, 1947.

9. *Ibid.,* December 4, 1945.

10. *Ibid.,* June 3, 1952.

11. *Ibid.,* December 4, 1945.

12. *Ibid.,* December 2, 1952.

13. *Annual,* BGCT, 1946, 75.

14. Some of these were Betty Rexrode, daughter of Mr. and Mrs. M. D. Rexrode, associate in the Sunday School Department; Bill Howse III, son of Dr. and Mrs. W. L. Howse, Jr., professor at Southwestern Seminary; and Susan Ray, daughter of Pastor and Mrs. Cecil Ray of Lubbock. Though largely confined to an iron lung, Susan Ray later became a writer of note well-known among Southern Baptists.

15. EBM, December 5, 1950.

16. *Annual,* BGCT, 1948, 156; 1952, 75.

17. *Ibid.,* 1953, 153.

18. *Baptist Standard,* August 8, 1946, 10.

19. *Ibid.,* October 24, 1946, 1.

20. *Ibid.,* 1, 5.

21. EBM, December 5, 1950.

22. *Annual,* BGCT, 1946, 104.

23. *Ibid.,* 1953, 147.
24. *Ibid.,* 142.
25. *Baptist Standard,* April 14, 1949, 1.
26. *Annual,* BGCT, 1946, 97.
27. *Ibid.*
28. *Ibid.,* 98.
29. *Ibid.,* 104.
30. August 15, 1946, 4.
31. *Baptist Standard,* February 10, 1949, 11.
32. EBM, December 16, 1947.
33. *Annual,* BGCT, 1952, 140.
34. EBM, August 5, 1947.
35. *Baptist Standard,* September 12, 1946, 3.
36. EBM, June 3, 1946.
37. *Baptist Standard,* March 7, 1946, 12.
38. EBM, March 5, 1946.
39. *Ibid.,* December 10, 1946.
40. *Ibid.,* December 4, 1945.
41. *Ibid.,* March 5, 1946.
42. *Annual,* BGCT, 1953, 158.
43. *Ibid.,* 161.
44. *Baptist Standard,* January 31, 1946, 6.
45. Inez Boyle Hunt, *Century One, A Pilgrimage of Faith: Woman's Missionary Union 1880-1980.* Woman's Missionary Union, 1979, 52.
46. EBM, December 9, 1952.
47. *Baptist Standard,* May 16, 1946, 1.
48. Later reports listed the goal as $459,00. See *Baptist Standard,* July 4, 1946, 9.
49. *Baptist Standard,* November 28, 1946, 5.
50. *Annual,* BGCT, 1953, 13 of WMU Report.
51. *Ibid.,* 14.
52. *Ibid.,* 18.
53. *Baptist Standard,* January 3, 1946, 14.
54. *Ibid.,* May 2, 1946, 14.
55. *Annual,* BGCT, 1953, 201.
56. *Ibid.,* 203.
57. *Baptist Standard,* February 28, 1946, 14.
58. *Ibid.,* June 13, 1946, 7.
59. *Ibid.,* May 5, 1949, 15.
60. *Annual,* BGCT, 1946, 170.
61. EBM, March 4, 1946.
62. *Baptist Standard,* November 28, 1946, 1.
63. EBM, September 7, 1948.
64. *Baptist Standard,* February 21, 1946, 17.
65. EBM, April 19, 1946.
66. *Ibid.,* March 14, 1946, 1.
67. *Annual,* BGCT, 1946, 65.
68. EBM, December 5, 1950.
69. *Annual,* BGCT, 1946, 177-178.
70. EBM, June 3, 1946.
71. *Baptist Standard,* November 28, 1946, 1.
72. *Ibid.,* July 21, 1949, 5.
73. EBM, April 19, 1948.
74. *Ibid.,* July 12, 1949.
75. *Ibid.,* December 7, 1948.
76. *Ibid.,* September 4, 1951.
77. *Ibid.,* October 23, 1951.
78. *Ibid.,* December 9, 1952.

79. *Ibid.*, July 17, 1952.

80. *Ibid.*

81. *Ibid.*

82. *Annual*, BGCT, 1952, 135.

83. *Baptist Standard*, June 15, 1950, 3.

84. Oral Memoirs of Acker C. Miller, as cited in Billy David Stricklin, An Interpretive History of the Christian Life Commission of the Baptist General Convention of Texas, 1950-1977. PhD diss., Baylor University, Waco, Texas, 1981, 78-79.

85. *Annual*, BGCT, 1950, 181.

86. *Ibid.*, 188.

87. Stricklin, 2.

88. EBM, June 9, 1953.

89. Oral Memoirs of T. B. Maston, as cited by Stricklin, 74.

90. John W. Storey, *Texas Baptist Leadership and Social Christianity, 1900-1980.* College Station: Texas A&M University Press, 1986, 153. Koinonia Farm was an effort to create a Christian community similar to those of New Testament times, with a sharing of tasks and goods.

91. EBM, June 9, 1953.

92. Stricklin, 89.

93. *Annual*, BGCT, 1950, 200.

94. EBM, March 4, 1952.

95. *Ibid.*, December 9, 1952.

96. Carl R. Wrotenbery, "University of Corpus Christi: A Baptist College on Surplus Military Land," *Texas Baptist History*, Vol. X, 1990, 17. Wrotenbery served as director of libraries for the University of Corpus Christi.

97. *Ibid.*, 19.

* (Just as this book went to the printer, Eakin Press of Austin issued Carl R. Wrotenbery's new book, *Baptist Island College: An Interpretive History of the University of Corpus Christi, 1946–1973.*)

98. *Baptist Standard*, July 11, 1946, 5.

99. *Annual*, SBC, 1947, 46.

100. *Ibid.*, 1949, 45.

101. EBM, September 7, 1948.

102. Karen O'Dell Bullock, *Homeward Bound: The Heart and Heritage of Buckner.* Dallas: Buckner Baptist Benevolences, 1993, 232.

103. Cited from the Robert Cooke Buckner Papers by Bullock, 232.

104. *Ibid.*, 254.

105. *Baptist Standard*, September 5, 1946, 2.

106. *Annual*, BGCT, 1952, 118.

107. EBM, September 9, 1947.

108. *Ibid.*, June 6, 1950.

109. *Ibid.*, January 29, 1948.

110. *Ibid.*, March 8, 1949.

111. *Ibid.*, June 3, 1952.

112. Minutes, Finance Committee of Executive Board, May 30, 1947.

113. EBM, March 3, 1953.

CHAPTER 11

1. Plans and Policies Committee report to Executive Board, December 8, 1953.

2. Television was actually invented long before the 1950s, but it was in that decade that American homes first installed the "one-eyed monster" in large numbers.

3. EBM, July 10, 1953.

4. *Ibid.*, September 8, 1953.

5. *Ibid.*

6. James Leo Garrett, Jr., *Living Stones: The Centennial History of Broadway Baptist Church, Fort Worth, Texas, 1882-1982.* 2 vols. Fort Worth: Broadway Baptist Church, 1984. I, 373f. Feezor was pastor of the Broadway Church, 1943-1946.

7. *Ibid.*, 375.

8. EBM, December 8, 1953.

9. *Ibid.*, December 9, 1958.

10. EBM, December 8, 1953.

11. *Ibid.*

12. *Ibid.*

13. *Ibid.*

14. *Ibid.*, September 8, 1953.

15. *Ibid.*, June 9, 1953.

16. Taken from report of New Advance Committee, as presented to the Executive Board, EBM September 8, 1953.

17. EBM, May 31, 1955.

18. *Ibid.*

19. *Ibid.*

20. *Ibid.*, September 4, 1956.

21. *Ibid.*, March 3, 1959.

22. *Ibid.*

23. Booz, Allen, Hamilton Report, 1959, Vol. 3, introductory letter. Henceforth, "BAH Report."

24. *Ibid.*, Exhibit V, opposite page 89.

25. EBM, June 8, 1954.

26. BAH Report, 3, Exhibit VIII, opposite page 101.

27. EBM, June 5, 1956.

28. *Ibid.*

29. *Ibid.*

30. Jerry F. Dawson, ed. *Teaching Them . . . A Sesquicentennial Celebration of Texas Baptist Education.* Dallas: BGCT, 1996, 93.

31. *Ibid.*, 62-63.

32. BAH Report, 3, Exhibit XIII, opposite page 113.

33. Finance Committee Minutes, April 29, 1959.

34. BAH Report, 4, 25.

35. *Ibid.*, 110.

36. EBM, June 5, 1956.

37. *Ibid.*, June 3, 1958.

38. *Ibid.*

39. *Ibid.*, June 11, 1957.

40. *Ibid.*, November 6, 1956 and December 4, 1956.

41. *Ibid.*, June 11, 1957.

42. *Ibid.*

43. *Ibid.*, June 8, 1954.

44. BAH Report, 4, 74.

45. EBM, June 9, 1959.

46. *Baptist Standard,* August 26, 1959, 4.

47. *Ibid.*, September 16, 1959, 5.

48. *Ibid.*

49. *Ibid.*, September 16, 1959, 7-8.

50. *Annual,* BGCT, 1959, 22.

51. *Ibid.*, 23.

52. EBM, November 3, 1959.

53. *Annual,* BGCT, 1959, Survey Committee Report, 1.

54. *Ibid.*, September 10, 1957.

55. *Ibid.*, December 3, 1957.

56. *Ibid.*, October 1, 1959.

57. *Ibid.*

58. BAH Report, 1, 4.

59. *Ibid.*, 9-11.

60. *Baptist Standard,* October 21, 1959, 2.

61. *Annual,* BGCT, 1959, Survey Committee Report, 9.

62. EBM, June 3, 1958.

63. The Executive Board, for example, did not agree to close Decatur College out-right, move Wayland College to Lubbock or Amarillo, move Howard Payne College to Dallas, or accept government grants for their benevolent institutions, all of which were recommended by the BAH report.

64. *Annual,* BGCT, 1959, Survey Committee Report, 23.

65. *Ibid.,* 54.

66. *Ibid.,* 16.

67. *Ibid.,* 41.

68. BAH Report, 3, 7.

69. *Ibid.,* 3, 104.

70. *Ibid.,* 3, 72, 112.

71. *Ibid.,* 3, 118.

72. *Ibid.,* 3, 154-155.

73. *Ibid.,* 3, 184.

74. *Ibid.,* 79.

75. *Ibid.,* 89.

76. *Ibid.*

77. *Ibid.* 101.

78. *Ibid.,* 4, 1.

79. *Ibid.,* 4, 131.

80. *Ibid.* 4, 22.

81. *Ibid.,* 25.

82. *Ibid.,* 94-95.

83. *Ibid.,* 177-178.

84. *Ibid.,* 180.

85. EBM, December 8, 1959.

86. *Baptist Standard,* June 3, 1959, 2; and October 21, 1959, 2-3.

87. *Ibid.,* September 30, 1959, 4.

CHAPTER 12

1.Sydney E. Ahlstrom. *A Religious History of the American People.* New Haven: Yale University Press, 1972, 1079-1080.

2. *Ibid.,* 1081.

3. Mark A. Noll, *A History of Christianity in the United States and Canada.* Grand Rapids: William B. Eerdmans Publishing Company, 1992, 442.

4. *Annual,* BGCT, 1973, 65.

5. *Baptist Standard,* September 9, 1972, 6.

6. Oral Memoirs of Thomas Armour Patterson, A Series of Interviews Conducted August 1971—November 1976, Thomas L. Charlton, Interviewer. Texas Baptist Oral History Consortium, Printed Copy, 1978, in Roberts Library, Southwestern Baptist Theological Seminary, Fort Worth, Texas, 41. Cited henceforth as Patterson, Oral Memoirs. Much of the biographical information on Patterson is taken from these Oral Memoirs.

7. *Ibid.,* 197.

8. *Ibid.,* 227.

9. *Ibid.,* 245.

10. *Ibid.,* 238.

11. *Ibid.,* 340.

12. *Ibid.,* 201.

13. *Ibid.,* 205-206.

14. *Ibid.,* 341.

15. EBM, May 30, 1972.

16. *Ibid.*

17. *Ibid.,* emphasis theirs.

18. EBM, November 7, 1961.

19. *Annual,* BGCT, 1963, 160.

20. EBM, September 11, 1962.

21. *Annual,* BGCT, 1965, 54-56.

22. Ibid., 56.

23. EBM, June 16, 1967. Slightly different figures were reported on June 16, but were corrected at the Board meeting on September 12, 1967.

24. *Ibid.,* 1972, 84.

25. *Baptist Standard,* September 20, 1967, 7.

26. EBM, May 30, 1972.

27. *Annual,* BGCT, 1962, 100.

28. David Stricklin, An Interpretative History of the Christian Life Commission of the Baptist General Convention of Texas, 1950-1977. PhD diss., Baylor University, Waco, Texas, 1971, 92.

29. *Ibid.,* 1963, 201; 1965, 125.

30. *Baptist Standard,* October 18, 1972, 12-13.

31. "Texas, Baptist General Convention of," Encyclopedia of Southern Baptists, 4 vols. Nashville: Broadman Press, 1958, 1971, 1982. III, 2021 and IV, 2517. Hereafter, ESB.

32. EBM, March 8, 1966.

33. *Annual,* BGCT., 1968, 174.

34. *Ibid.,* 197.

35. *Ibid.,* 1968, 175.

36. *Ibid.,* 1972, 186.

37. *Ibid.,* 1965, 126.

38. *Ibid.,* 1965, 126; 1972, 186.

39. *Ibid.,* 1961, 150; 1972, 227.

40. EBM, September 13, 1966.

41. *Ibid.,* June 14, 1966.

42. *Annual,* BGCT., 1965, 128.

43. *Ibid.,* 129.

44. *Ibid.,* 1963, 212.

45. *Baptist Standard,* July 5, 1972, 7.

46. EBM, September 11, 1962.

47. Charles Lee Williamson to Harry Leon McBeth, October 16, 1996. Copy in author's possession.

48. EBM, September 12, 1962.

49. Williamson to McBeth.

50. William R. Carden, A Report to the Christian Education Commission of the Baptist General Convention of Texas, 1968, table following p.6. Hereafter, Carden Report.

51. *Annual,* BGCT, 1968, 84-86.

52. *Ibid.,* 1961, 96; 1972, 209.

53. EBM, September 13, 1960.

54. *Annual,* BGCT, 1961, 96.

55. EBM, March 7, 1961.

56. *Ibid.*

57. Patterson, *Memoirs,* 224.

58. EBM, November 11, 1963.

59. *Ibid.,* March 7, 1961.

60. *Ibid.,* December 5, 1969.

61. *Ibid.,* September 10, 1963.

62. *Ibid.*

63. The huge binder including the Carden Report is available in the archives of the BGCT, Dallas.

64. Carden Report, 46.

65. For a detailed analysis of this report, see *Baptist Standard,* August 7, 1968, 3.

66. *Baptist Standard,* July 31, 1968, 6.

67. *Ibid.,* August 7, 1968, 7.

68. *Annual,* BGCT, 1973, 151.

69. EBM, September 12, 1961.

70. *Annual,* BGCT, 1973, 190.

71. EBM, June 16, 1967.

72. *Annual,* BGCT, 1973, 191.

73. *Ibid.*

74. EBM, May 26, 1970.

75. *Ibid.,* May 25, 1971.

76. *Ibid.,* December 10, 1963.

77. *Annual,* BGCT, 1961, 67; 1973, 77.

78. EBM, November 7, 1961.

79. *Ibid.,* June 16, 1964.

80. *Ibid.,* June 4, 1963.

81. *Ibid.*

82. *Ibid.,* December 11, 1962.

83. Patterson, *Memoirs,* 222, 313.

84. Jesse C. Fletcher. *The Southern Baptist Convention: A Sesquicentennial History.* Nashville: Broadman & Holman, 1994, 222.

85. *Ibid.,* 222-223.

86. EBM, December 11, 1962.

87. *Ibid.,* December 10, 1963.

88. *Annual,* BGCT, 1964, 86.

89. *Ibid.,* 165.

90. EBM, June 6, 1961.

91. *Ibid.,* March 9, 1965.

92. *Ibid.,* September 13, 1966.

93. *Ibid.*

94. *Ibid.*

95. *Annual,* BGCT, 1966, 27.

96. *Baptist Standard,* March 8, 1967, 6.

97. EBM, September 9, 1969.

98. Patterson, Memoirs, 259.

99. Carl H. Moore, Serving Texas Baptists through a Ministry of Finance: Baptist Church Loan Corporation 1951-1983. No publication data given, 1983, 29.

100. *Baptist Standard,* January 25, 1967, 3.

101. Robert M. Foley, untitled and unpublished personal memoirs, 1996, 78-79, copy in author's possession.

102. *Baptist Standard,* November 15, 1967, 6.

103. *Ibid.,* March 22, 1967, 5.

104. The full report is carried in Annual, BGCT, 1967, 56-63.

105. Inez Boyle Hunt. *A Pilgrimage of Faith: Woman's Missionary Union of Texas 1880-1980.* Woman's Missionary Union, 1979, 70.

106. *Annual,* BGCT, 1967, 61.

107. *Baptist Standard,* November 15, 1967, 6.

108. *Ibid.,* January 19, 1972, 6.

109. *Ibid.*

110. *Ibid.*

111. *Annual,* BGCT, 1970, 27.

112. For a report of this survey, see *Annual,* BGCT, 1971, 42-44.

113. *Baptist Standard,* August 16, 1972, 12-13.

114. *Ibid.*

115. Patterson, *Memoirs,* 217.

116. EBM, October 26, 1970.

117. Nashville: Broadman Press, 1961. For a brief description of this controversy, and other phases of SBC controversies of the time, see H. Leon McBeth, *The Baptist Heritage.* Nashville: Broadman Press, 1987, 679f.

118. *Baptist Standard,* January 10, 1962, 7. Portions of this article are reprinted in H. Leon McBeth, ed. a Sourcebook for Baptist Heritage. Nashville: Broadman Press, 1990, 500-501.

119. EBM, March 6, 1962.
120. Patterson, *Memoirs,* 277.
121. *Ibid.,* 276.

CHAPTER 13
1. Oral Memoirs of James Henry Landes, Jr., Texas Baptist Oral History Project, Baylor University. 2 vols. 2, 62. Cited hereafter as Landes *Memoirs.*
2. *Ibid.,* 2, 249.
3. *Ibid.,* 2, 38. Most of the biographical data on Landes is taken from his oral memoirs.
4. *Ibid.,* 1, 54.
5. *Ibid.,* 2, 252.
6. *Ibid.,* 2, 243.
7. *Ibid.,* 1, 222.
8. *Ibid.,* 1, 183-184.
9. *Ibid.,* 1, 201-202.
10. *Ibid.,* 2, 213f.
11. *Ibid.,* 213.
12. Landmarkism was the name given to the rigid ultraconservative movement of J. R. Graves in the 19th century which emphasized the local church and diminished the role and importance of denominational agencies.
13. Landes *Memoirs,* 2, 2, 67.
14. *Ibid.,* 1, 184, 188.
15. Executive Board Minutes, March 14, 1972. Cited hereafter as EBM.
16. *Ibid.*
17. The final report is carried in full in the convention Annual, 1974, 29-60.
18. *Annual,* BGCT, 1974, 30.
19. There had been some debate in Texas, especially among Independent Baptists, about whether church homes were obliged to meet standards of care and operation set by the government.
20. *Annual,* BGCT, 58-59.
21. *Ibid.,* 60.
22. *Ibid.,* 40.
23. *Ibid.,* 42.
24. Landes Memoirs, 2, 213.
25. *Ibid.,* 1, 217.
26. Landes Memoirs, 2, 218.
27. EBM, May 28, 1974.
28. *Ibid.,* September 13, 1977.
29. *Ibid.*
30. EBM, March 11, 1975.
31. *Ibid.*
32. *Ibid.,* September 10, 1974.
33. Oral Memoirs of Elmin Kimboll Howell, Jr. Texas Baptist Oral History Consortium, Institute for Oral History, Baylor University, 1980-1981, 125. Cited hereafter as Howell Memoirs.
34. *Ibid.,* 225.
35. EBM, December 6, 1977.
36. William J. Damon, unpublished Report To Texas Baptists, 9. Copy in author's possession.
37. *Ibid.,* 14.
38. *Ibid.,* 16.
39. *Annual,* BGCT, 1982, 150.
40. Damon, 20.
41. *Ibid.,* 18.
42. *Ibid.,* 43.
43. *Ibid.,* 60. See pp. 59-68, for a report on this extensive survey.

44. *Baptist Standard,* June 15, 1977, 3.

45. EBM, September 13, 1977.

46. *Annual,* BGCT, 1982, 151.

47. *Ibid.*

48. EBM, March 9, 1982.

49. *Ibid.*

50. *Annual,* BGCT, 1982, 150.

51. EBM, December 9, 1980.

52. *Ibid.,* December 7, 1976.

53. Landes Memoirs, 1, 205-206.

54. *Ibid.,* 230.

55. *Baptist Standard,* January 26, 1977, 5.

56. *Ibid.,* March 30, 1977, 4.

57. *Ibid.,* March 23, 1977, 12-13.

58. *Ibid.,* April 13, 1977, 5.

59. Landes Memoirs, 1, 232. "Bold Mission Thrust," sometimes written "BMT," was the name of an SBC convention-wide evangelism and mission emphasis in which the states were expected to cooperate.

60. *Baptist Standard,* June 15, 1977, 5.

61. *Annual,* BGCT, 1977, 203.

62. EBM, September 14, 1976.

63. Landes Memoirs, 1, 198-199.

64. *Ibid.,* 1, 199.

65. EBM;, June 1, 1976.

66. *Ibid.,* September 12, 1978.

67. *Annual,* BGCT, 1978, 71.

68. EBM, September 12, 1978.

69. *Ibid.,* December 4, 1979.

70. *Ibid.,* December 9, 1980.

71. *Ibid.,* June 3, 1980.

72. Landes Memoirs, 2, 187.

73. *Ibid.,* 1, 224-225.

74. *Ibid.,* 2, 179.

75. *Ibid.,* 2, 76.

76. *Ibid.,* 2, 112.

77. *Ibid.*

78. EBM, December 7, 1982.

79. Association Records of Particular Baptist Churches in England, Wales and Ireland to 1660. In three parts. Edited by B. R. White. London: Baptist Historical Society, 1971. Part 1, p.10.

80. *Ibid.,* Part 3, p.163.

81. *Annual,* BGCT, 1975, 26.

82. *Ibid.,* 1976, 60.

83. *Ibid.,* 67.

84. The author served on that committee and was one of those who advocated that charismatic practices per se not be listed as the grounds for exclusion.

85. Landes Memoirs, 2, 71.

86. EBM, June 8, 1982.

87. *Ibid.*

88. *Ibid.*

89. *Ibid.*

90. Landes Memoirs, 1, 202.

91. *Ibid.,* 2, 12.

92. *Ibid.,* 2, 51.

93. Landmarkism was an extremist movement led by J. R. Graves; Samuel Hayden gave his name to a movement which is sometimes abbreviated as the BMA; and J. Frank Norris of Fort Worth led a sizeable fundamentalist exodus from the BGCT.

94. Bill J. Leonard, *God's Last & Only Hope: The Fragmentation of the Southern Baptist Convention* (Grand Rapids: Wm. B. Eerdmans, 1990; Ellen M. Rosenberg, *The Southern Baptists: A Subculture in Transition* (University of Tennessee Press, 1989).

95. James C. Hefley, *The Truth in Crisis: The Controversy in the Southern Baptist Convention* (Dallas: Criterion Publications, 1986).

96. Mark A. Noll, *A History of Christianity in the United States and Canada* (Grand Rapids: Wm. B. Eerdmans, 1992).

97. Landes Memoirs, 2, 97.

98. *Ibid.*, 98.

99. *Ibid.*, 2, 219.

100. *Ibid.*, 2, 232.

CHAPTER 14

1. Executive Board Minutes, May 18, 1982. Cited hereafter as EBM.

2. *Ibid.*

3. Oral Memoirs of James Henry Landes, II, 246f. Cited hereafter as Landes Memoirs.

4. EBM, April 28, 1982.

5. J. M. Carroll. *A History of Texas Baptists.* Dallas: Baptist Standard Publishing Company, 1923, 630. Some reports say Pinson gave the land, while others say he sold the land to Buckner. Both reports are, in a measure, true. The land was appraised for $1,216, but Pinson let Buckner have it for only $500.

6. The present First Baptist Church of Dallas was formed in 1868. It is the fourth church in Dallas to bear that name. Of the other three, two died and one moved away to Pleasant View. At that time, Pleasant View was a rural area a few miles northeast of Dallas. Today it is in the center of the city of Dallas.

7. Leon McBeth. *The First Baptist Church of Dallas: A Centennial History, 1868-1968.* Grand Rapids: Zondervan Publishing House, 1968, 23-24.

8. Carroll, 993.

9. *Annual,* BGCT, 1996, 75.

10. *Ibid.*, 1994, 73.

11. *Ibid.*, 82.

12. EBM, March 6, 1984.

13. EBM, June 7, 1988.

14. *Ibid.*, March 10, 1987.

15. *Baptist Standard*, January 29, 1986, 3.

16. *Ibid.*

17. *Ibid.*, September 10, 1986, 9.

18. EBM, March 12, 1991, includes charts reporting the results of the five year effort. Information here is cited from that report.

19. *Ibid.*, December 8, 1981; March 15, 1983, September 9, 1983.

20. *Baptist Standard*, November 30, 1988, 6.

21. Wilma Reed, Ken Camp, and Elmin Howell, Jr. *With These Hands: Celebrating 25 Years of River Ministry.* Vol. II. Dallas: River Ministry Department of State Missions Commission, 1992, 8. Cited hereafter as Hands II.

22. *Annual,* BGCT, 1995, 119.

23. *Hands II,* 110.

24. *Ibid.*, 1996, 115.

25. EBM, March 15, 1983.

26. *Ibid.*, March 8, 1988.

27. *Baptist Standard*, February 21, 1990, 7.

28. Book of Reports, BGCT, 1997, 14.

29. Samuel P. Pearis, IV, "Outline History of Mission Service Corps," unpublished paper dated January 22, 1997, 5. In author's possession. Cited hereafter as Pearis, Outline. Much of the data given here on MSC comes from Pearis's notes.

30. *Annual,* BGCT, 1996, 76.

31. Pearis, Outline, 14, 40.

32. *Annual,* BGCT, 1996, 76.

33. Book of Reports, BGCT, 1997, 14.

34. *Baptist Message,* November 20, 1997, 12.

35. *Baptist Standard,* November 26, 1997, 4.

36. *Ibid.*

37. EBM, September 10, 1985.

38. *Ibid.,* December 4, 1984.

39. *Annual,* BGCT, 1983, 164.

40. *Baptist Standard,* October 22, 1997, 3.

41. EBM, December 8, 1987.

42. *Baptist Standard,* October 22, 1997, 3.

43. Personal interview with Jerry F. Dawson, Baptist Building, Dallas, November 19, 1997.

44. *Ibid.*

45. EBM, December 5, 1989.

46. *Annual,* BGCT, 1996, 83-84.

47. *Ibid.,* 84.

48. *Baptist Standard,* January 22, 1986, 4.

49. *Annual,* BGCT, 1994, 85; 1996, 84.

50. *Ibid.,* 96.

51. *Ibid.,* 1996, 93-94.

52. *Ibid.,* 94.

53. EBM, March 8, 1988; June 7, 1988.

54. Jesse C. Fletcher. *The Southern Baptist Convention: A Sesquicentennial History.* Nashville: Broadman & Holman Publishers, 1994, 300; see also David Beale, Southern Baptist Convention: House of Sand? Greenville, S.C.: Unusual Publications, 1985, 33; and Billy P. Keith, W. A. Criswell: *The Authorized Biography.* Old Tappan, N.J.: Fleming Revell, 1973, 123.

55. *Baptist Standard,* September 28, 1988, 4.

56. *Ibid.*

57. *Ibid.,* November 12, 1986, 6.

58. *Annual,* BGCT, 1996, 111-117.

59. EBM, September 10, 1985.

60. *Ibid.*

61. *Ibid.,* December 10, 1985.

62. *Ibid.,* 169.

63. *Annual,* BGCT, 1996, 122.

64. *Baptist Standard,* September 10, 1986, 9.

65. Gene White, editor, *New Church News,* Published quarterly by Texas Baptist Missions Foundation of BGCT, Summer, 1997, 5.

66. *Ibid.,* Fall, 1997, 1.

67. New Church Starts by Ethnicity, Church Extension Department, September 30, 1997.

68. Informs, October-December, 1997, 4.

69. *Baptist Standard,* February 28, 1990, 10.

70. Informs, October-December, 1997, 1.

71. Criminal Justice Ministry, undated pamphlet issued by Texas Baptist men.

72. *Annual,* BGCT, 1996, 116.

73. *Ibid.,* 62-63.

74. Book of Reports, BGCT, 1997, 92-93.

75. Baptist Church Loan Corporation, Annual Report, 1996, 6. See also Book of Reports, BGCT, 1997, 22.

76. Kenneth Smart. *A Sacred Trust: The Story of the Baptist Foundation of Texas.* 2nd ed. Dallas, 1980, 186.

77. *Ibid.,* 186f.

78. *Baptist Standard,* August 20, 1986, 5.

79. Women of Purpose Network, undated pamphlet, Woman's Missionary Union of Texas.

80. EBM, March 4, 1986.

81. *Ibid.*, December 9, 1986.

82. *Baptist Standard,* January 28, 1998, 2.

83. *Ibid.*, October 8, 1997, 1.

84. EBM, September 10, 1996.

85. *Ibid.*

86. *Ibid.*, June 5, 1984.

87. *Baptist Standard,* January 15, 1986, 5.

88. *Ibid.*, June 4, 1986.

89. William M. Pinson, Jr. *Partnership: Associations and State Conventions.* Unpublished address, June 15, 1997, available from Pinson's office at the Baptist Building in Dallas.

90. *Ibid.*, 2.

91. *Ibid.*, 7.

92. *Annual,* BGCT, 1990, 209.

93. EBM, December 5, 1989.

94. *Ibid.*, March 6, 1990.

95. *Annual,* BGCT, 1989, 77.

96. *Ibid.*, June 5, 1990.

97. Book of Reports, BGCT, 1997, 20.

98. EBM, September 14, 1993.

99. *Ibid.*

100. *Baptist Standard,* November 6, 1996, 6.

101. *Ibid.*, March 28, 1990.

102. *Ibid.*, November 26, 1997, 1.

103. EBM, December 9, 1986.

104. *Ibid.*

105. Some of the information in this section comes from a personal interview with Presnall H. Wood on May 6, 1998. Some of the material is not yet available in print.

106. Presnall H. Wood. "The Right to Know—The Baptist Way," in Dick Allen Rader, ed. Fibers of our Faith: The Herschel H. And Frances J. Hobbs Lectureship in Baptist Faith and Heritage at Oklahoma Baptist University. Franklin, TN: Providence House Publishers, 96.

107. *Annual,* BGCT, 1996, 82.

108. *Ibid.*

CHAPTER 15

1. The Baylor Line, Spring 1996, 11.

2. A considerable literature has grown up around the SBC controversy. Two of the better and less inflammatory books are James C. Hefley, *The Conservative Resurgence in the Southern Baptist Convention.* Hannibal, MO.: Hannibal Books, 1991 (Fundamentalist perspective); and David T. Morgan, *New Crusades, New Holy Land: Conflict in the Southern Baptist Convention, 1969-1991.*The University of Alabama Press, 1996 (Moderate perspective).

3. *Baptist Standard,* January 10, 1962, 7.

4. William Kiffin and others, *Heart Bleedings for Professors Abominations,* London: 1650, gives the first example of Baptists using the term "infallible" to describe the Bible. For a summary of *Heart Bleedings,* see H. Leon McBeth, ed., *A Sourcebook for Baptist Heritage.* Nashville: Broadman Press, 1990, 70.

5. David T. Morgan. *New Crusades, New Holy Land: Conflict in the Southern Baptist Convention, 1969-1991.* Tuscalussa: University of Alabama Press, 1996, 35-37.

6. Jesse C. Fletcher, *The Southern Baptist Convention: A Sesquicentennial History.* Nashville: Broadman and Holman, 1994, 259.

7. Morgan, 188-189.

8. *Baptist Standard,* November 2, 1988, 9.

9. *Ibid.*, October 5, 1988, 9.

10. *Ibid.*

11. The Baylor Line, March 1988, 18.

12. *Ibid.*

13. *Baptist Standard*, November 2, 1988, 6.

14. Baylor University Department of University Communications, News Release, September 21, 1990.

15. Summary of Minutes, Administrative Committee, October 2, 1990. Included with EBM.

16. *Ibid.*

17. Report of Committee on BGCT/Baylor Relations, printed with EBM, June 11, 1991,

18. EBM, June 11, 1991.

19. *Ibid.*, 53

20. *Annual,* BGCT, 1991, 50.

21. *Ibid.*

22. *Ibid.*, 54.

23. *Western Recorder* (KY), March 25, 1992, 7.

24. *Ibid.*, March 12, 1991.

25. *Ibid.*, October 17, 1990.

26. *Baptist Message,* (LA), June 21, 1984, 5.

27. *Baptist Standard*, April 6, 1994, 4.

28. *Alabama Baptist,* March 24, 1994, 1, 7, 8.

29. *Ibid.*

30. *Baptist Standard*, April 27, 1994, 5.

31. *Ibid.*, April 6, 1994, 4.

32. *Ibid.*, March 23, 1994, 2.

33. *Ibid.*, 7.

34. *Ibid.*, March 16, 1994, 2.

35. EBM, June 7, 1994.

36. *Ibid.*

37. *Ibid.*, September 13, 1994.

38. *Ibid.*, September 12, 1995.

39. *Ibid.*

40. *Annual,* BGCT, 1984, 55.

41. Richard Scarborough, November 14, 1996, TC 18094.

42. Robert L. Maddox, "Dr. Criswell Spoke Too Quickly," *Church and State,* 37:23, October 1984.

43. George W. Truett, "Baptists and Religious Liberty," May 16, 1920, reprinted in H. Leon McBeth, ed. A Sourcebook for Baptist Heritage. Nashville: Broadman Press, 1990, 471.

44. "Criswell explains how to be a good pastor," *Baptist Standard,* January 12, 1994, 11.

45. Darrel Baergen, Three One Act Plays. Dallas: BGCT, The Baptist Way, 1997.

46. EBM, September 12, 1995.

47. *Ibid.*

48. *Ibid.*

49. *Annual,* BGCT, 1993, 54.

50. *Annual,* SBC, 1928, 32-33.

51. *Ibid.*

52. *Annual,* BGCT, 1994, 148.

53. *Ibid.*, 150.

54. *Ibid.*, 66.

55. *Ibid.*, 1993, 63.

56. *Ibid.*, 1995, 69.

57. *Ibid.*, 1995, 56.

58. Book of Reports, BGCT, 1997, 79.

59. *Ibid.*, 80.

60. *Ibid.* The quote is taken from Lyle Schaller, *The New Reformation.* Nashville: Abingdon Press, 1995, 24.

61. Book of Reports, BGCT, 1997, 80.

62. Baptist Press Release, August 29, 1997.

63. *Ibid.*

64. Associated Baptist Press Release, August 27, 1997.

65. *Ibid.*

66. Texas Baptists Committed, December 1997, 1.

67. *Ibid.*, 5.

68. *Ibid.*

69. Carol Marie Cropper, *D*, August, 1997, 56.

70. *Ibid.*, 58.

71. *Baptist Standard,* November 26, 1997, 4.

72. *Ibid.*, January 24, 1996, 3.

73. Plumbline, December 1997, 1.

74. *Ibid.*, 8.

75. *Ibid.*

76. *Ibid.*, 10.

77. *Baptist Standard,* December 3, 1997, 6.

78. *Ibid.* Reprinted from Wade's presidential message.

79. Charles Wade, Memo to Toby Druin, November 25, 1997.

80. *Baptist Standard,* January 7, 1998, 9.

81. *Ibid.*, December 3, 1997, 6.

82. *Ibid.*, February 25, 1998, 4.

83. *Ibid.* It was later revealed that a Mineral Wells pastor had prepared the ballot for his own church and, when questioned about it, softened his charges considerably. See *Baptist Standard,* April 1, 1998, 4.

84. *Ibid.*, March 4, 1998, 6.

85. *Ibid.*

86. Memo, November 25, 1997, from Bill Pinson to Morris Chapman, Jimmy Draper, Kenneth Hemphill, Dellana O'Brien, Jerry Rankin, and Bob Reccord.

87. *Baptist Standard,* January 7, 1998, 1.

88. *Ibid.*

89. Statement from William M. Pinson, Jr., undated, issued by Thomas J. Brannon, Director of Communications for the BGCT, Dallas.

90. *Baptist Standard,* December 3, 1997, 5.

91. *Ibid.*, January 7, 1998, 4.

92. *Ibid.*, February 4, 1998, 1.

93. J. M. Carroll. *A History of Texas Baptists.* Dallas: Baptist Standard Publishing Company, 1923, 640.

94. *Annual,* BGCT, 1995, 56.

95. EBM, June 4, 1996.

96. The full report is also printed in *Annual,* BGCT, 1996, 69.

97. *Annual,* BGCT, 1996, 52.

98. *Ibid.*, 54.

99. Charles Davenport to Larry Bethune, January 30, 1998. Copy attached to EBM, February 24, 1998.

100. *Baptist Standard,* March 4, 1998, 1.

Bibliographic Essay

The available sources to reconstruct a history of Baptists in Texas are extensive. There are a few gaps, of course, especially for the early years, but after the arrival of Z. N. Morrell in 1835 we have more records. Any history of Texas Baptists must begin with Z. N. "Wildcat" Morrell who first crossed the Sabine into Texas in 1835. For more than forty years this intrepid pioneer crisscrossed the state, forming churches, shaping Baptist belief and behavior, and imprinting early Texas Baptists with missionary zeal. His book, *Flowers and Fruits in the Wilderness* (first published in St. Louis in 1872 and republished several times since), is the first written account of Baptists in Texas. *Flowers and Fruits* is neither a history nor a journal, but a mixture of both, and it may be regarded as a primary source. It is rich in historical detail, in biography, and in conveying the spirit of early Baptists in Texas.

Other pioneers, especially James Huckins, William Tryon and R. E. B. Baylor left correspondence and papers which are invaluable for reconstructing the early history of Texas Baptists. These papers are available at Baylor University. The first organization of Texas Baptists, beyond a few local churches, was the Union Baptist Association. Its formation in 1840 is amply documented and its annual reports are full of primary information about Baptist people and churches, and its "circular letters" offer a valuable commentary on issues then current on the Texas frontier. These minutes are available in the Texas Baptist Historical Collection at Southwestern Seminary in Fort Worth.

The Baptist State Convention, the first Baptist convention in the state, was formed in 1848 and records of its formation and its annual reports are available. Unfortunately, the minutes of the Board of Directors of the BSC apparently have been lost. A diligent search has turned up no copies of them. The minutes of the rival state convention, the Baptist General Association, are also available, as are some minutes from three other rival conventions in Texas. The various Texas conventions merged in 1886, forming the Baptist General Convention of Texas. We have a complete run of the annual reports of the BGCT from 1886 to the present, and they form a goldmine of indispensable information about the programs and progress of Texas Baptists.

In 1914 the BGCT underwent an extensive restructuring which changed the way the state convention functioned. An Executive Board was formed in 1914 which assumed many of the functions previously reserved to the convention. That Board has been enlarged and its functions expanded several times, and we have complete minutes of its sessions since 1914. These Executive Board Minutes

(EBM) include not only the detailed deliberations of the Board, but also reports of its various standing committees, and complete reports of several important study groups and task forces. These Board minutes provide perhaps the single most important primary resource for a study of the work of the BGCT since 1914. These minutes are available in paper copies, microfilm and, as of 1997, a digitized CD-ROM which allows the researcher to access the minutes by computer.

Another valuable source of information is the two-volume *Texas Baptist Historical and Biographical Magazine* (Austin, 1891) by J. B. Link, early Texas Baptist newspaper editor. The subtitle tells Link's purpose: "Designed to give a Complete History of the Baptists of Texas from their First Entrance into the State, and other Historical Matters of Interest to the Denomination." Link's two volumes were recently reprinted in four volumes (Baptist Standard Bearer, Inc., Paris, Arkansas, 1997).The relevant portions of this work are so valuable that one can overlook several chapters whose relevance is questionable.

For many years the Sunday School and Training Union had their own separate state bodies before the work was fully integrated into the BGCT, and of course these early bodies kept records which prove very useful. In late 1997 Ronald C. Ellison's new book, *Texas and Baptist Sunday Schools, 1829-1996* (Austin: Eakin Press, 1997), came from the press. This will be a valuable addition to the growing literature on Texas cultural and religious history but, to my regret, it came too late to be consulted extensively for the present work..The Woman's Missionary Union (or women's groups of similar name) related to the BSC, the BGA and, after 1886, the BGCT, kept extensive records, all of which are available today. Later the Baptist men's organization (of various names) had a separate annual meeting, with extensive records. The records of these groups were later printed with the BGCT Annuals.

Several Texas Baptist pioneers have left extensive correspondence and other papers which provide valuable information, much of it not available elsewhere. Particularly helpful are the papers of B. H. Carroll and his brother J. M. Carroll, George W. Truett (including his personal diaries), L. R. Scarborough, J. Frank Norris, J. B. Gambrell, J. B. Cranfill, and others.

Early Baptist newspapers form an extremely valuable source of information, beginning with *The Texas Baptist* (1855), *The Texas Baptist Herald* (1865), *The Religious Messenger* (1874 in Paris, moved to Dallas in 1875, renamed *The Texas Baptist,* edited by R. C. Buckner), *The Baptist News* (1888, moved from Honey Grove to Dallas, renamed *The Western Baptist,* and under new ownership renamed the *Baptist Standard,* published in Waco for a time and then moved to Dallas). We do not have complete runs of all these papers, but the more important ones are extant.

By far the most valuable newspaper source is the *Baptist Standard*, published in Dallas since 1892 and the property of the BGCT since 1910. This "people's paper" has long since become "the Baptist paper of record" in the Lone Star State. For over a century, week after week, the *Baptist Standard* has recorded, without fear or favor, the story of what Texas Baptists were saying, doing, and threatening to do. It has become the most widely circulated Baptist paper in the world, with influence far beyond Texas. It would not be possible to compile a valid history of Texas Baptists without extensive reference to the *Standard,* and fortunately a complete run of its issues is available. In addition to the papers themselves, one finds valuable interpretative data in *Baptist Journalism in Nineteenth-Century Texas,* by Tom Berger (Austin: University of Texas, 1969). More recent Baptist papers like *Baptists Committed* (Moderate) and *The Plumbline* (Fundamentalist) give valuable information and insight into the current climate of Texas Baptists.

The BGCT has preserved in its archives an extensive collection of important study commissions, task force reports, and other special occasion records. They have complete files on the Booz, Allen and Hamilton (BAH) report of 1959, plus the five bound volumes of that report, which led to extensive restructuring of the Convention, along with files on the Committee of 100, the elaborate Carden Report, several church-state studies, and of course the more recent study groups like the Effectiveness/Efficiency Committee report of 1997.

Oral History Memoirs, a fairly recent form of historical data, also provide a valuable source of information on Texas Baptists. Particularly helpful are memoirs of BGCT executive secretaries (later directors) such as Forrest C. Feezor, T. A. Patterson, and James H. Landes. Other helpful memoirs include those of Elmin K. Howell, Jimmy R. Allen, T. B. Maston, Foy D. Valentine, James M. Dunn, H. B. Ramsour, J. M. Dawson, Harold A. Haswell, E. N. Jones, James E. Basden, C. Wade Freeman, W. R. White, Levi Davis Wood, and others.

Some secondary books contain such eye-witness accounts that they may be regarded as primary sources. Among these are *The Life and Writings of Rufus C. Burleson*, by his wife Georgia J. Burleson (published by the author, 1901); *Pioneering in the Southwest*, by A. J. Holt (Nashville: Sunday School Board of SBC, 1923); *Ten Years in Texas*, by J. B. Gambrell (Dallas: Baptist Standard, 1910); *Dr. J. B. Cranfill's Chronicle: A Story of a Life in Texas* (New York: Fleming H. Revell, 1916); and *The Life and Labors of Major W.E. Penn, the Texas Evangelist* (published by Mrs. W. E. Penn, 1896).

There have been a number of general histories of Texas Baptists, such as *A History of Texas Baptists*, by B. F. Fuller (Louisville, KY: Baptist Book Concern, 1900); *A History of the Baptists of Texas*, by B. F. Riley (Dallas, 1907); *Centennial Story of Texas Baptists*, L. R. Elliott general editor (Dallas, BGCT, 1936); *A Century With Texas Baptists*, by J. M. Dawson (Nashville: Broadman Press, 1947); *Frontiersmen of the Faith: A History of Baptist Pioneer Work in Texas, 1865-1885*, by Zane Allen Mason (San Antonio: The Naylor Company, 1970); and *The Blossoming Desert: A Concise History of Texas Baptists*, by Robert A. Baker (Waco: Word Books, 1970). However, by far the most valuable early history of Texas Baptists is *A History of Texas Baptists*, by J. M. Carroll (Dallas: Baptist Standard Publishing Company, 1923). Carroll's massive 1030 page masterpiece has been twice reprinted, and continues to be an indispensable source of Texas Baptist data. Carroll wrote as an eye witness and participant of much of the history he records, and in addition to cogent narrative and interpretation, his book includes reams of primary source materials incorporated into the book in extensive block quotes. Also helpful is J. M. Carroll's 1895 collection, *Texas Baptist Statistics* (no publisher indicated). Some of this information was incorporated into his 1923 volume.

Among journals, nothing has been so relevant and helpful as *Texas Baptist History: The Journal of the Texas Baptist Historical Society* (published since 1981). This journal includes extremely valuable articles and research notes on Texas Baptist persons, places, and events. The *Journal* also from time to time reprints valuable source documents not readily available elsewhere.

The Woman's Missionary Union of Texas is well accounted for, not only by their extensive records, but also by a number of helpful histories. Among these are *A Centennial History of the Baptist Women of Texas, 1830-1930*, by Ada Williams Smith (Mrs. W. J. J.), 1933; *Candle by Night: A History of Woman's Missionary Union, Auxiliary to the Baptist General Convention of Texas, 1800-1955*, by Roberta Turner

Patterson (Mrs. T. A.), 1955; and *Century One: Pilgrimage of Faith, 1880-1980,* by Inez Boyle Hunt (WMU, 1979, n.p.) Amelia Bishop, former state president, is reportedly preparing a new history of the WMU in Texas.

Some helpful regional and associational histories include *A Baptist Century Around the Alamo, 1858-1958,* by Ramsey Yelvington and others (San Antonio, 1958); *A History of the Waco Baptist Association of Texas,* by J. L. Walker and C. P. Lumpkin (Waco, 1897); *The Spiritual Conquest of the Southwest,* by J. M. Dawson (Nashville: Sunday School Board of SBC, 1927); *The Story of the Union Baptist Association 1840-1976,* by R. G. Commander (Houston, 1977); *Southern Baptists of Southeast Texas: A Centennial History, 1888-1988,* by John W. Storey and Ronald C. Ellison (Beaumont, 1988); *O Zion, Haste: The Story of Dallas Baptist Association,* by Carr M. Suter, Jr. (Dallas: DBA, 1978); and *Cowboys, Cowtown and Crosses: A Centennial History of Tarrant Baptist Association,* by James E. Carter (Fort Worth: TBA, 1986). A one-of-a-kind publication is *Texas Baptist Family Album, 1885-1995,* compiled by Jerilyn Armstrong (Dallas: BGCT, 1995). This book includes hundreds of photographs along with many brief biographical vignettes. Another engaging one-of-a-kind work is *With These Hands,* by Wilma Reed, Ken Camp, and Elmin K. Howell (Dallas: State Missions Commission of BGCT, n.d.). This is a two-volume history of the Rio Grande River Ministry in Texas including information not available elsewhere.

There are scores of histories of local Baptist churches in Texas and some of them tell not only the story of one congregation but also illustrate something of the life of Baptists of the entire era and area. Among these are *Seventy-Five Years in Nacogdoches: A History of the First Baptist Church, 1884-1959,* by William T. Parmer (Dallas, 1959); *The First Baptist Church of Dallas: Centennial History, 1868-1968,* by Leon McBeth (Grand Rapids: Zondervan Publishing House, 1968); *And God Gave the Increase: Centennial History of First Baptist Church, Beaumont, Texas,* by William R. Estep (Beaumont, 1972); and *Living Stones: The Centennial History of Broadway Baptist Church, Fort Worth, Texas, 1892-1992,* by James Leo Garrett, Jr. (Fort Worth, 1994). *A History of Independence Baptist Church, 1839-1969, and Related Organizations,* by Samuel B. Hesler (Dallas: BGCT, n.d.), is especially helpful.

Biographies of Texas Baptist leaders have been extremely helpful. One thinks of older works such as *George W. Truett: A Biography,* by Powhatan W. James (Nashville: Broadman Press, 1945); *The Life and Legend of J. Frank Norris, the Fighting Parson,* by Homer G. Ritchie (published by the author, 1991). James was a son-in-law of Dr. Truett and Ritchie was a protégé and successor of Dr. Norris, so these are more eulogies than critical biographies. *God's Rascal: J. Frank Norris & the Beginnings of Southern Fundamentalism,* by Barry Hankins (Lexington: University Press of Kentucky, 1996) fills a gap by providing an excellent study of one of the more colorful and influential Texas Baptist personalities. Other recent, and excellent, biographies include *Fighting the Good Fight: The Life and Work of Benajah Harvey Carroll,* by Alan J. Lefever (Austin: Eakin Press, 1994); *Calling Out the Called: The Life and Work of Lee Rutland Scarborough,* by Glenn T. Carson (Austin: Eakin Press, 1996); and Karen O'Dell Bullock, *Homeward Bound: The Heart and Heritage of Buckner* (Dallas: Buckner Benevolences, 1993). All three of these excellent volumes began as doctoral dissertations at Southwestern Seminary. Eugene W. Baker has written excellent biographies of two Texas Baptist pioneers, *Nothing Better than This; The Biography of James Huckins, First Baptist Missionary to Texas,* and *A Noble Example: A Pen Picture of William M. Tryon, Pioneer Texas Baptist Preacher and Co-Founder of Baylor University.* Both of these were published by Baylor University Press in 1985, and form volumes 1 and 2 of the Baylor University Founders Series. Surprisingly, there is as yet no adequate biography of George W. Truett.

Doctoral and Masters dissertations form another excellent source of information on Texas Baptists; and their bibliographies provide good leads to other primary and secondary sources. More doctoral dissertations on Texas Baptists have been written at Southwestern Seminary than anywhere else, though a few have been written at other schools. Especially helpful are: *A History of Tarrant County Baptist Association, 1886-1922,* by William M. Shamburger (ThD diss., SWBTS, Fort Worth, 1953); *The Ethics of George Washington Truett,* by Thurmon E. Bryant (ThD diss., SWBTS, Fort Worth, 1959); *History of the Texas Baptist Standard 1888-1959,* by Presnall H. Wood (ThD diss., BGCT, 1964, later published as *Prophets with Pens* in 1969); *The Organizational Development of the Baptist General Convention of Texas,* by Paul Carson Petty (ThM diss., SWBTS, Fort Worth, 1960); *The Negro Excision from Baptist Churches in Texas, 1861-1870,* by Paul W. Stripling (ThD diss., SWBTS, Fort Worth, 1967); *W. F. Howard and Baptist Student Union Work in Texas, 1943-74: An Historical Study,* by Charles Wayne Ashby (EdD diss., SWBTS, Fort Worth, 1977); *Baptist Missionary Activity among the German People in Texas, 1850-1950,* by Albert Ray Niederer (PhD diss., Baylor University, Waco, 1976); *Interpretative History of the Christian Life Commission of the Baptist General Convention of Texas, 1950-1977,* by Billy David Stricklin (PhD diss., Baylor University, Waco, 1981); *An Historical Study of the Life and Times of R.E.B. Baylor: His Contributions to Texas and Texas Baptists,* by Gary L. Snowden (PhD diss., SWBTS, Fort Worth, 1996); *A Comparison of the Leadership of George W. Truett and J. Frank Norris in Church, Denominational, Interdenominational and Political Affairs,* by Kelly D. Piggott (PhD diss., SWBTS, Fort Worth, 1993); *Striving for a Greater Yield: The Life and Ministry of Baptist Denominational Leader John Howard Williams,* by Thomas O. High (PhD diss. SWBTS, Fort Worth, 1997); *The Life and Ministry of Eldred Douglas Head: Leadership in the Midst of Transition,* by Joe Franklin Morrow (PhD diss., SWBTS, Fort Worth, 1995); *The Life and Work of J. M. Carroll,* by William G. Storrs (PhD diss., SWBTS, Fort Worth, 1995); *Texas Baptist Political Attitudes Under Four National Governments, 1835-1865,* by David Marshall (MA diss., Texas Tech University, Lubbock, 1986); *He Changed Things: The Life and Thought of J. Frank Norris,* by Clovis Gwin Morris (PhD diss., Texas Tech University, 1973); and *Men and Movements Influenced by J. Frank Norris,* by Royce Measures (PhD diss., SWBTS, 1976).

Some of the Baptist universities in Texas have their own histories, few of them so extensive as *Baylor at Independence,* by Lois Smith Murray (Baylor University Press, Waco, 1972), or *To Light the Ways of Time: An Illustrated History of Baylor University, 1845-1986,* by Eugene W. Baker (Baylor University Press, Waco, 1987). An extremely helpful recent book is *Teaching Them: A Sesquicentennial Celebration of Texas Baptist Education,* Jerry F. Dawson and John W. Storey, editors (Dallas: BGCT, 1996). John W. Story has also written the well-researched *Texas Baptist Leadership and Social Christianity, 1900-1980* (College Station: Texas A&M University Press, 1986).

Two helpful books on specialized subjects are *A History of Mexican Baptists in Texas,* by Joshua Grijalva (Dallas: BGCT, 1982) and *Ethnic Baptist History,* by Joshua Grijalva (Impresso en Colombia, 1992). There is at present no adequate history of Black Baptists in the Lone Star State.

A very helpful book which has been updated several times is *A Sacred Trust: The Story of the Baptist Foundation of Texas,* by Kenneth Smart (Dallas: Baptist Foundation of Texas, 1970, 1980). Other BGCT agencies are reportedly preparing their own histories.

One of the most unusual, but valuable, sources on the famous S. A. Hayden-J. B. Cranfill controversy in Texas is *The Hayden-Cranfill Conspiracy Trial, Stenographically Reported*, by E. E. Gibson, Herbert Morris, and Charles I. Evans (Dallas: Texas Baptist Publishing House, 1899). This contains the actual trial testimonies and arguments by counsel on both sides, including not only the conspiracy trial of Hayden against Cranfill but also the libel prosecution of Hayden by Cranfill.

And, finally, Jesse C. Fletcher's valuable volume, *The Southern Baptist Convention: A Sesquicentennial History* (Nashville: Broadman & Holman, 1994), has a great deal of material on and insights concerning Baptists in Texas, as does *Tell the Generations Following: A History of Southwestern Baptist Theological Seminary, 1908-1983*, by Robert A. Baker (Nashville: Broadman Press, 1983).

A Statistical Epilogue

Historical Tables of Texas General Bodies

Baptist State Convention—1848-1873

Time	Place	President	Secretary	Cor. Secretary	Con. Sermon by
1848	Anderson	H.L. Graves	J. G. Thomas	R. C. Burleson	Z. N. Morrell
1849	Houston	J.W.D. Creath	R. S. Blunt	R. C. Burleson	R.H. Taliaferro
1850	Huntsville	H. L.	Graves	G. W. Baines, Sr.	R. C. Burleson
1851	Independence	R. E. B. Baylor	G. W. Baines, Sr.	R. C. Burleson	J. W. D. Creath
1852	Marshall	H. L. Graves	G. W. Baines, Sr.	R. C. Burleson	Jas. Huckins
1853	Huntsville	H. L. Graves	J. B. Stiteler	R. C. Burleson	G. Tucker
1854	Palestine	Jas. Huckins	G. W. Baines, Sr.	R. C. Burleson	G.W. Baines, Sr.
1855	Independence	Jas. Huckins	J. M. Maxey	J. B. Stiteler	H. Garrett
1856	Anderson	Jas. Huckins	H. Clark	A. Daniel	H. L. Graves
1857	Huntsville	H. L. Graves	H. Clark	W. Montgomery	J. P. Pritchard
1858	Independence	R. C. Burleson	H. Clark	W. Montgomery	P. B. Chandler
1859	Waco	R. C. Burleson	O. H. P. Garrett	M. Ross	J. W. D. Creath
1860	Independence	H. Garrett	O. H. P. Garrett	D. R. Wallace	H. Clark
1861	Huntsville	H. L. Graves	O. H. P. Garrett	H. Clark	Z. N. Morrell
1862	Waco	H. L. Graves	W. E. Oakes	N. W. Crane	N. W. Crane
1863	Independence	H. L. Graves	B. S. Fitzgerald	W. Montgomery	S. G. O'Bryan
1864	Huntsville	H. L. Graves	Geo. W. Graves	H. Clark	J. H. Stribling
1865	Anderson	H. L. Graves	Geo. W. Graves	B. S. Fitzgerald	J. W. D. Creath
1866	Independence	H. L. Graves	Geo. W. Graves	B. S. Fitzgerald	J. J. Sledge
1867	Gonzales	H. L. Graves	H. Clark	O. H. P. Garrett	H. F. Buckner
1868	Independence	H. L. Graves	H. F. Buckner	H. Clark	S. C. Orchard
1869	Galveston	H. L. Graves	O. H. P. Garrett	H. Clark	S. B. McJunkin
1870	Brenham	H. L. Graves	O. H. P. Garrett	H. Clark	
1871	Bryan	W. C. Crane	O. H. P. Garrett	G. W. Graves	
1872	Independence	W. C. Crane	O. H. P. Garrett	W. Fontaine	
1873	Austin	W. C. Crane	O. H. P. Garrett	W. Fontaine	G. W. Prickett
1874	Galveston	W. C. Crane	O. H. P. Tarrett	W. Fontaine	F. M. Law
1875	Calvert	W. C. Crane	O. H. P. Garrett	H. Clark	H. W. Dodge
1876	Independence	W. C. Crane	O. H. P. Garrett	F. Keifer	H. L. Graves
1877	Bryan	W. C. Crane	O. H. P. Garrett	F. Keifer	G.W. Baines, Jr.
1878	LaGrange	W. C. Crane	O. H. P. Garrett	P. Hawkins	R. Andrews, Jr.
1879	Independence	W. C. Crane	O. H. P. Garrett	P. Hawkins	
1880	Austin	C. C. Chaplin	O. H. P. Garrett	P. Hawkins	J. B. Hardwick
1881	Galveston	C. C. Chaplin	O. H. P. Garrett	P. Hawkins	Wm. Howard
1882	Belton	C. C. Chaplin	O. H. P. Garrett	O. C. Pope	C. C. Chaplin
1883	San Antonio	C. C. Chaplin	O. H. P. Garrett	O. C. Pope	C. C. Chaplin
1884	Waxahachie	C. C. Chaplin	O. H. P. Garrett	O. C. Pope	R. A. Massey
1885	Lampasas	F. M. Law	O. H. P. Garrett	W. R. Maxwell	P. Harris

Texas Baptist General Association 1853-1854

Time	Place	President	Secretary	Cor. Secretary	Con. Sermon by
1853	Larrissa	I. H. Lane	Wm. Davenport	G. C. Baggerly	M. Lepard
1854	Tyler	Geo. Tucker	Wm. Davenport	Rev. Isaacs	

Baptist Convention of Eastern Texas—1855-1867

Time	Place	President	Secretary	Cor. Secretary	Con. Sermon by
1855	Tyler	W. H. Stokes	Wm. Davenport		
1856	Marshall	Jesse Witt	W. H. Stokes	J. M. Griffin	
1857	Larrissa	G. S. Bledsoe	S. P. Hollingsworth	Jesse Witt	
1858	Gilmer	W. H. Stokes	S. P. Hollingsworth	J. F. Kelly	W. H. Stokes
1859	Bonham	A. E. Clemons	S. J. Wright	J. F. Kelly	D. B. Morrill
1860	Tyler	J. S. Bledsoe	J. R. Malone	J. F. Kelly	J. S. Bledsoe
1861	Quitman	J. M. Griffin	J. R. Malone	J. F. Kelly	W.B. Featherstone
1862					
1863	Tyler				
1864					
1865					
1866	Harris Creek	D. B. Morrill	J. T. Hand	Bro. Manning	
1867	Ladonia	D. B. Morrill	J. T. Hand	N. P. Moore	

Baptist General Association—1868-1885

Time	Place	President	Secretary	Cor. Secretary	Con. Sermon by
1868	Chatfield	J. E. Harrison	J. T. Hand	R. C. Burleson	W. J. Brown
1869	Tyler	A. E. Clemons	J. T. Hand	R. C. Burleson	Josiah Leake
1870	Paris	A. E. Clemons	J. T. Hand	R. C. Burleson	J. F. Johnson
1871	Fairfield	J. W. Speight	J. T. Hand	R. C. Burleson	R. C. Burleson
1872	Rowlett Creek	J. W. Speight	J. T. Hand	R. C. Burleson	B. H. Carroll
1873	Jefferson	R. C. Burleson	J. T. Hand	A. Weaver	R. C. Burleson
1874	Dallas	R. C. Burleson	J. T. Hand	A. Weaver	R. C. Buckner
1875	Sherman	R. C. Burleson	J. T. Hand	A. Weaver	J. M. Lewis
1876	Waco	R. C. Burleson	J. T. Hand	A. Weaver	G. T. Wilburn
1877	Paris	R. C. Burleson	S. J. Anderson	R. C. Buckner	B. H. Carroll
1878	Fort Worth	R. C. Burleson	S. J. Anderson	R. C. Buckner	W. O. Bailey
1879	Pittsburg	R. C. Burleson	S. J. Anderson	R. C. Buckner	S. A. Hayden
1880	Dallas	(called)	S. J. Anderson	I. B. Kimbrough	
1880	Ennis	R. C. Buckner	S. J. Anderson	W. H. Parks	W. A. Jarrel
1881	Waco	R. C. Buckner	S. J. Anderson	W. H. Parks	D. L. Smythe
1882	Sulphur Springs	R. C. Buckner	S. J. Anderson	G. W. Pickett	G. W. Pickett
1883	Cleburne	R. C. Buckner	S. J. Anderson	A. J. Holt	G. W. Pickett
1884	Paris	R. C. Buckner	S. J. Anderson	A. J. Holt	S. J. Anderson
1885	Ennis	L. L. Foster	S. J. Anderson	A. J. Holt	J. E. Eoff

East Texas Baptist Convention—1877-1885

Time	Place	President	Secretary	Cor. Secretary	Con. Sermon by
1877	Overton	A. E. Clemons	Geo. Yarbrough	W. O. Bailey	
1878	Henderson	A. E. Clemons	Geo. Yarbrough	F. L. Whaley	W. G. Caperton
1879	Longview	J. A. Kimball	Geo. Yarbrough	F. L. Whaley	H. E. Calahan
1880	Tyler	J. H. Stribling	Geo. Yarbrough	F. L. Whaley	W. H. Carroll
1881	Tyler	W. R. Maxwell	Geo. Yarbrough	F. L. Whaley	J. A. Kimball
1882	Buena Vista	W. R. Maxwell	Geo. Yarbrough	Doc Pegues	R. Andrews
1883	Longview	W. R. Maxwell	Geo. Yarbrough	Doc Pegues	A. E. Clemons
1884	Tyler	J. A. Kimball	Geo. Yarbrough	Tully Choice	
1885	Center	W. H. Hendrix	Geo. Yarbrough	J. A. Kimball	A. J. Peddy

North Texas Baptist Convention—1879-1883

Time	Place	President	Secretary	Cor. Secretary	Con. Sermon by
1879	Allen	W. L. Williams	J. C. Jones		
1880	Dallas	J. K. Bumpas	J. C. Jones	J. J. Sledge	
1881	Fort Worth	I. B. Kimbrough	S. H. Dixon	J. H. Curry	
1882	Weatherford	W. E. Penn	W. H. Gough	I. B. Kimbrough	
1883	Bells	J. K. Bumpas	J. N. Haney	H. M. Burroughs	

Central Texas Baptist Convention—1880-1885

Time	Place	President	Secretary	Cor. Secretary	Con. Sermon by
1880	Dublin	P. B. Chandler	J. G. O'Brian	J. T. Harris	
1881	Mt. Zion Church	A. C. Graves	J. G. O'Brian	G. W. Clark	R. D. Ross
1882	Turnersville	P. B. Chandler	J. G. O'Brian	C. L. Graves	W. D. Powell
1883	Carlton	G. W. Roberts	J. W. Staton	J. G. O'Brian	J. T. Harris
1884	Abilene	P. B. Chandler	J. G. O'Brian	F. B. Chandler	
1885	Hico	W. J. Shaw	B. C. Williams	J.C.R. Lockhart	

Baptist General Convention

(The Consolidated Body—1886-1998)

Time	Place	President	Secretary	Cor. Secretary	Con. Sermon by
1886	Waco	A. T. Spalding	O.H.P. Garrett	A. J. Holt	
			S. J. Anderson	W. R. Maxwell	
1887	Dallas	A. T. Spalding	M. P. Matheney		
			S. J. Anderson	A. J. Holt	F. H. Kerfoot
1888	Belton	A. T. Spalding	J. B. Cranfill		
			J. M. Carroll	A. J. Holt	R. T. Hanks
1889	Houston	A. T. Spalding	T. S. Potts		
			A. E. Baten	J. B. Cranfill	A. J. Fawcett
1890	Waxahachie	L. L. Foster	T. S. Potts		
			A. E. Baten	J. B. Cranfill	A. T. Farrar
1891	Waco	L. L. Foster	T. S. Potts		
			A. E. Baten	J. B. Cranfill	R. B. Garrett
1892	Belton	R. C. Burleson	T. S. Potts		
			A. E. Baten	J. M. Carroll	B. H. Carroll
1893	Gainesville	R. C. Burleson	A. E. Baten		
			J. H. Truett	J. B. Cranfill	C. L. Seashols
1894	Marshall	R. C. Buckner	A. E. Baten		
			J. H. Truett	J. M. Carroll	J. A. Ivey
1895	Belton	R. C. Buckner	A. E. Baten		
			J. H. Truett	M. D. Early	T. B. Pittman
1896	Houston	R. C. Buckner	A. E. Baten		
			J. H. Truett	M. D. Early	A. H. Mitchell
1897	San Antonio	R. C. Buckner	A. E. Baten		
			J. H. Truett	J. B. Gambrell	W. L. Skinner
1898	Waco	R. C. Buckner	A. E. Baten		
			J. H. Truett	J. B. Gambrell	W. M. Harris
1899	Dallas	R. C. Buckner	A. E. Baten		
			J. H. Truett	J. B. Gambrell	J. S. Tanner
1900	Waco	R. C. Buckner	A. E. Baten		
			F. M. McConnell	J. B. Gambrell	D. I. Smythe
1901	Fort Worth	R. C. Buckner	A. E. Baten		
			F. M. McConnell	J. B. Gambrell	O. L. Hailey
1902	Waco	R. C. Buckner	A. E. Baten		
			F. M. McConnell	J. B. Gambrell	Jeff D. Ray
1903	Dallas	R. C. Buckner	A. E. Baten		
			F. M. McConnell	J. B. Gambrell	G. W. McCall

Year	City				
1904	Waco	R. C. Buckner	A. E. Baten		
			F. M. McConnell	J. B. Gambrell	Forrest Smith
1905	Dallas	R. C. Buckner	A. E. Baten		
			F. M. McConnell	J. B. Gambrell	W. A. Hamlett
1906	Waco	R. C. Buckner	A. E. Baten		
			F. M. McConnell	J. B. Gambrell	J. F. Norris
1907	San Antonio	R. C. Buckner	A. E. Baten		
			F. M. McConnell	J. B. Gambrell	W. S. Splawn
1908	Fort Worth	R. C. Buckner	A. E. Baten		
			F. M. McConnell	J. B. Gambrell	George W. Baines
1909	Dallas	R. C. Buckner	A. E. Baten		
			F. M. McConnell	J. B. Gambrell	B. H. Carroll
1910	Houston	R. C. Buckner	A. E. Baten		
			D. R. Peveto	F. M. McConnell	E. F. Lyon
1911	Waco	R. C. Buckner	D. R. Peveto		
			G. O. Key	F. M. McConnell	S. M. Provence
1912	Fort Worth	R. C. Buckner	D. R. Peveto		
			G. O. Key	F. M. McConnell	B. A. Copass
1913	Dallas	R. C. Buckner	D. R. Peveto		
			G. O. Key	F. M. McConnell	R. L. Gillon
1914	Abilene	S. P. Brooks	D. R. Peveto		
			G. O. Key	J. B. Gambrell	R. F. Jenkins
1915	Austin	S. P. Brooks	D. R. Peveto		
			G. O. Key	1914-1918	M. E. Weaver
1916	Waco	S. P. Brooks	D. R. Peveto		
			G. O. Key	1914-1918	George W. Truett
1917	Dallas	M. H. Wolfe	D. R. Peveto		
			J. L. Truett	1914-1918	J. B. Tidwell
1918	Dallas	M. H. Wolfe	J. L. Truett		
			I. J. White	F. S. Groner	D. B. Clapp
1919	Houston	M. H. Wolfe	J. L. Truett		
			I. J. White	1918-1928	M. T. Andrews
1920	El Paso	J. D. Sandefer	J. L. Truett		
			I. J. White	1918-1928	Wallace Bassett
1921	Dallas	J. D. Sandefer	J. L. Truett		
			I. J. White	1918-1928	T. Y. Adams
1922	Waco	J. D. Sandefer	J. L. Truett		
			I. J. White	1918-1928	O. L. Power
1923	Galveston	O. S. Lattimore	J. L. Truett		
			I. J. White	1918-1928	M. E. Hudson
1924	Dallas	O. S. Lattimore	J. L. Truett		
			I. J. White	1918-1928	W. W. Melton
1925	Mineral Wells	O. S. Lattimore	J. L. Truett		
			I. J. White	1918-1928	W. W. Melton
1926	San Antonio	Pat M. Neff	J. L. Truett		
			I. J. White	1918-1928	E. P. West
1927	Wichita Falls	Pat M. Neff	J. L. Truett		
			D. B. South	1918-1928	W. R. White
1928	Mineral Wells	Pat M. Neff	J. L. Truett		
			D. B. South	T. L. Holcomb	J. A. Held
1929	Beaumont	L. R. Scarborough	J. L. Truett		
			D. B. South	W. R. White	Marshall Craig
1930	Amarillo	L. R. Scarborough	J. L. Truett		
			D. B. South	1929-1931	M. A Jenkins
1931	Waco	L. R. Scarborough	J. L. Truett		
			D. B. South	J. H. Williams	W. M. M. Wolf
1932	Abilene	J. C. Hardy	J. L. Truett		
			D. B. South	1931-1936	H. J. Matthews
1933	Fort Worth	J. C. Hardy	J. L. Truett		
			D. B. South	1931-1936	W. W. Chancellor
1934	San Antonio	J. C. Hardy	J. L. Truett		
			D. B. South	1931-1936	E. T. Miller
1935	Houston	J. B. Tidwell	J. L. Truett		
			D. B. South	R. C. Campbell	G. L. Yates

Year	City	President			
1936	Mineral Wells	J. B. Tidwell	J. L. Truett		
			D. B. South	1936-1941	W. H. McKenzie
1937	El Paso	J. B. Tidwell	J. L. Truett		
			D. B. South	1936-1941	E. D. Head
1938	Dallas	J. H. Williams	J. L. Truett		
			D. B. South	1936-1941	J. H. Williams
1939	San Antonio	J. H. Williams	J. L. Truett		
			D. B. South	1936-1941	J. Ralph Grant
1940	Houston	A. D. Foreman, Sr.	J. L. Truett		
			D. B. South	W. W. Melton	A. J. Holt
1941	Abilene	A. D. Foreman, Sr.	J. L. Truett		
			D. B. South	1941-1945	E. S. James
1942	Fort Worth	A. D. Foreman, Sr.	Roy L. Johnson		
			D. B. South	1941-1945	George W. Truett
1943	Dallas	W. R. White	Roy L. Johnson		
			D. B. South	1941-1945	J. M. Dawson
1944	San Antonio	E. D. Head	Roy L. Johnson		
			D. B. South	1941-1945	E. F. Cole
1945	Fort Worth	E. D. Head	Roy L. Johnson		
			D. B. South	1941-1945	Porter M. Bailes
1946	Mineral Wells	E. D. Head	Roy L. Johnson	J. Howard	
			D. B. South	Williams	C. E. Hereford
1947	Amarillo	Wallace Bassett	Roy L. Johnson	J. Howard	
			D. B. South	Williams	A. D. Foreman, Jr.
1948	Houston	Wallace Bassett	Roy L. Johnson	J. Howard	
			D. B. South	Williams	Forrest Feezor
1949	El Paso	Wallace Bassett	Roy L. Johnson	J. Howard	
			D. B. South	Williams	J. H. Landes
1950	Fort Worth	William Fleming	Roy L. Johnson	J. Howard	
			D. B. South	Williams	R. H. Cagle
1951	Houston	William Fleming	Roy L. Johnson	J. Howard	
			D. B. South	Williams	A. B. Rutledge
1952	Fort Worth	F. C Feezor	Roy L. Johnson	J. Howard	
			D. B. South	Williams	Perry F. Webb
1953	San Antonio	James N. Morgan	Roy L. Johnson	Forrest C.	
			D. B. South	Feezor	Woodson Armes
1954	Fort Worth	James N. Morgan	Roy L. Johnson	Forrest C.	
			D. B. South	Feezor	Carl Bates
1955	Houston	Ralph Grant	Roy L. Johnson	Forrest C.	
			D. B. South	Feezor	W. Herschel Ford
1956	Corpus Christi	J. Ralph Grant	Roy L. Johnson	Forrest C.	
			D. B. South	Feezor	Grady W. Metcalf
1957	Fort Worth	E. H. Westmoreland	Roy L. Johnson	Forrest C.	
			D. B. South	Feezor	Sterling Price
1958	San Antonio	E. H. Westmoreland	Roy L. Johnson	Forrest C.	
			D. B. South	Feezor	H. Guy Moore
1959	Corpus Christi	M. B. Carroll	Cecil G. Goff	Forrest C.	
			D. B. South	Feezor	James Leavell
1960	Lubbock	M. B. Carroll	Cecil G. Goff	Forrest C.	
			D. B. South	Feezor	Gordon Clinard
1961	Austin	James H. Landes	Cecil G. Goff		
			D. B. South	T. A. Patterson	John Rasco
1962	Fort Worth	James H. Landes	Cecil G. Goff		
			D. B. South	T. A. Patterson	Vernon Elmore
1963	San Antonio	K. Owen White	Cecil G. Goff		
			D. B. South	T. A. Patterson	W.M. Shamburger
1964	Corpus Christi	Abner V. McCall	Cecil G. Goff		
			D. B. South	T. A. Patterson	Woodson Armes
1965	Houston	Abner V. McCall	Cecil G. Goff		
			D. B. South	T. A. Patterson	Herbert Howard
1966	Dallas	J. C. Chadwick	Cecil G. Goff		
			D. B. South	T. A. Patterson	James Coggin
1967	Lubbock	J. C. Chadwick	Cecil G. Goff		
			D. B. South	T. A. Patterson	W. Fred Swank

Year	City				
1968	Fort Worth	Gordon Clinard	Cecil G. Goff D. B. South	T. A. Patterson	B. J. Martin
1969	San Antonio	Gordon Clinard	Cecil G. Goff D. B. South	T. A. Patterson	Ralph Langley
1970	Austin	Jimmy R. Allen	Cecil G. Goff D. B. South	T. A. Patterson	Winfred Moore
1971	Houston	Jimmy R. Allen	Cecil G. Goff Irby Cox	T. A. Patterson	Ralph M. Smith
1972	Abilene	L. P. Leavell	Jay L. Skaggs Irby Cox	T. A. Patterson	James Flamming
1973	Corpus Christi	L. P. Leavell	Jay L. Skaggs Irby Cox	T. A. Patterson	Buckner Fanning
1974	Amarillo	Ralph M. Smith	Jay L. Skaggs Irby Cox	James H. Landes	W. C. Everett
1975	Dallas	Ralph M. Smith	Jay L. Skaggs Irby Cox	James H. Landes	Robert E. Naylor
1976	San Antonio	James G. Harris	Jay L. Skaggs Irby Cox	James H. Landes	Ed Brooks Bowles
1977	Fort Worth	M. E. Cunningham	W. E. Normon Irby Cox	James H. Landes	Browning Ware
1978	Austin	M. E. Cunningham	W. E. Normon Irby Cox	James H. Landes	Jimmy R. Allen
1979	Lubbock	M. E. Cunningham	W. E. Normon Irby Cox	James H. Landes	Russell H. Dilday
1980	Houston	Carlos McLeod	W. E. Normon Irby Cox	James H. Landes	Ray Summers
1981	Waco	Carlos McLeod	W. E. Normon Irby Cox	James H. Landes	John Bisagno
1982	Corpus Christi	D. L. Lowrie	W. E. Normon Irby Cox	James H. Landes	William B. Tolar
1983	Amarillo	D. L. Lowrie	W. E. Normon Irby Cox	W.M. Pinson, Jr.	Paul Powell
1984	Dallas	Winfred Moore	W. E. Normon Irby Cox	W.M. Pinson, Jr.	Jack Ridlehoover
1985	San Antonio	Winfred Moore	W. E. Normon Irby Cox	W.M. Pinson, Jr.	James Semple
1986	El Paso	Paul Powell	Roger Hall Irby Cox	W.M. Pinson, Jr.	Omar Pachecano
1987	Fort Worth	Paul Powell	Roger Hall Irby Cox	W.M. Pinson, Jr.	Roy Fish
1988	Austin	Joel Gregory	Roger Hall Irby Cox	W.M. Pinson, Jr.	Donald C. Brown
1989	Lubbock	Joel Gregory	Roger Hall Irby Cox	W.M. Pinson, Jr.	B. O. Baker
1990	Houston	Phil Lineberger	Roger Hall Irby Cox	W.M. Pinson, Jr.	Lester Collins
1991	Waco	Phil Lineberger	Roger Hall Irby Cox	W.M. Pinson, Jr.	Robert Sloan
1992	Corpus Christi	J. Richard Maples	Roger Hall Irby Cox	W.M. Pinson, Jr.	Laney Johnson
1993	Dallas	J. Richard Maples	Roger Hall Irby Cox	W.M. Pinson, Jr.	D. L. Lowrie
1994	Amarillo	Jerold R. McBride	Roger Hall Irby Cox	W.M. Pinson, Jr.	Rudy Sanchez
1995	San Antonio	Jerold R. McBride	Roger Hall Irby Cox	W.M. Pinson, Jr.	Don Newbury
1996	Fort Worth	Charles Wade	Roger Hall Irby Cox	W.M. Pinson, Jr.	Joe Ratliff
1997	Austin	Charles Wade	Roger Hall Irby Cox	W.M. Pinson, Jr.	Levi Price, Jr.
1998	Houston	R. H. Dilday, Jr.	Roger Hall Irby Cox	W.M. Pinson, Jr.	

TEXAS BAPTIST STATISTICAL SUMMARY BY ASSOCIATIONS–1997

INFORMATION BASED ON DATA RECEIVED FROM ANNUAL CHURCH PROFILES AS REPORTED THROUGH
ASSOCIATIONS MISSION DATA HAS BEEN ADDED TO CHURCH DATA TO GENERATE ASSOCIATIONAL TOTALS

Chs.	Ms. Associations	Bap-tisms	Membership Res.	Membership Total	Sun. Sch. Enr.	Av. At.	Disc. Train.	Music Enr.	WMU Enr.	Bro. Enr./Par.	Total Rec.	Undesign. Gifts	Coop. Prog.	Gifts to Asn. Miss.	Tot Miss. Expend
39	7 Abilene	793	19,075	33,886	17,943	7,542	5,405	2,954	1,182	788	12,963,673	8,969,400	589,337	168,666	1,568,848
62	11 Amarillo	1,292	32,067	53,685	25,777	11,856	8,684	4,365	1,974	1,443	20,522,098	15,407,805	1,399,231	316,990	2,587,847
98	21 Austin	1,593	43,030	65,207	39,385	16,904	10,207	6,100	2,211	1,070	38,605,125	24,441,064	1,370,589	319,443	5,394,713
57	8 Bell	1,156	21,397	37,149	19,519	7,757	6,027	3,683	1,601	1,389	13,703,470	9,237,485	995,204	178,617	1,744,825
22	0 Bi-Stone	159	5,336	7,875	3,878	1,982	697	840	387	153	2,806,527	2,408,736	261,511	37,548	508,770
15	3 Big Bend	59	1,038	2,696	1,180	562	378	87	142	70	772,440	633,276	51,956	17,960	152,945
29	1 Big Spring	173	5,527	10,646	4,466	1,876	590	869	320	232	3,083,809	2,712,949	264,964	72,415	465,770
57	5 Blanco	324	7,604	13,074	6,164	2,892	1,528	926	577	488	4,021,212	3,185,244	330,648	85,325	638,019
59	10 Bluebonnet	1,170	16,737	22,945	13,623	6,653	3,784	2,294	856	564	11,032,114	8,388,688	578,362	167,844	1,193,582
22	0 Bosque	132	3,028	5,529	2,518	1,182	391	569	254	42	1,594,968	1,270,103	120,274	29,135	220,160
47	4 Bowie	524	16,857	24,270	13,156	5,552	3,133	2,731	1,102	713	10,312,763	7,521,468	724,582	168,675	1,242,691
14	4 Brady	43	1,716	2,968	1,294	519	142	254	130	80	751,770	595,401	54,019	12,479	101,632
40	5 Brown Co.	344	9,736	15,132	7,812	3,489	2,407	1,417	673	382	5,019,263	4,000,230	410,747	79,747	744,428
20	3 Burnet-Llano	251	7,235	10,001	5,685	2,399	768	1,048	597	555	4,151,819	2,924,312	315,234	64,745	764,860
8	0 Callahan	59	2,190	3,403	1,322	645	390	228	144	84	810,873	664,976	81,133	10,461	161,269
13	2 Canadian	139	3,091	5,718	1,998	1,107	673	602	387	280	1,990,730	1,689,315	239,731	37,417	446,758
18	3 Caprock	84	3,497	6,048	2,212	1,109	546	619	415	217	1,465,355	1,211,664	134,523	34,780	265,155
14	1 Castle Gap	136	2,184	5,047	1,773	836	609	449	317	85	1,515,465	1,156,357	121,239	13,644	182,896
21	7 Cherokee	213	4,753	7,585	3,857	1,936	452	711	338	174	2,925,791	2,342,390	277,877	43,717	553,790
37	10 Cisco	297	7,055	11,347	5,268	2,580	1,868	813	616	377	3,234,936	2,612,490	244,798	72,718	521,462
36	5 Coastal Bend	258	5,792	10,536	4,235	2,247	1,310	506	459	291	4,115,783	2,575,635	219,532	62,839	437,511
18	0 Coleman Co.	47	1,399	2,557	1,064	520	200	133	196	75	594,075	497,503	57,529	15,571	106,674
61	10 Collin	1,064	28,202	38,098	26,555	11,534	5,534	5,615	3,118	1,126	23,883,573	16,684,083	1,214,984	281,758	3,056,085
39	9 Colorado	297	7,701	13,639	6,554	2,756	1,513	1,144	861	451	4,195,185	3,336,137	292,630	83,855	552,358
20	4 Comanche	123	3,207	4,896	2,521	1,196	385	601	350	167	1,456,273	1,134,999	119,692	28,567	233,573
39	9 Concho Valley	587	14,460	23,613	11,631	5,448	3,143	2,131	984	549	10,272,874	7,052,998	755,692	193,116	1,403,618
24	1 Cooke County	167	5,196	7,277	3,638	1,994	1,062	987	462	351	2,719,898	2,070,101	254,186	38,236	428,375

54	10	Corpus Christi	846	21,275	36,035	17,542	6,788	6,126	3,251	1,190	828	16,119,661	10,235,092	661,424	192,821	1,481,793
23	3	Corsicana	214	6,428	9,960	5,660	2,645	926	1,068	459	206	3,917,615	2,955,384	345,353	50,308	598,626
23	3	Coryell	119	4,521	7,807	3,367	1,399	1,851	591	269	408	1,931,249	1,659,946	151,129	35,987	289,757
51	7	Creath Brazos	487	14,525	24,985	12,484	6,103	1,500	1,912	695	365	9,796,064	7,599,624	778,298	115,647	1,469,027
282	184	Dallas	8,734	177,660	283,371	171,824	67,722	41,858	25,599	10,676	7,175	151,525,494	98,374,204	6,386,367	1,455,247	13,673,655
32	3	Del Rio-Uvalde	190	4,178	8,324	3,517	1,784	1,264	681	688	335	2,707,973	2,097,221	228,169	62,723	483,939
67	13	Denton	469	24,836	57,441	24,213	10,612	5,907	4,850	1,498	807	20,201,549	14,367,293	1,041,377	367,258	2,076,383
51	8	El Paso		10,951	20,650	8,896	4,458	3,330	1,742	1,006	600	8,063,598	5,799,639	406,168	106,691	873,142
24	8	Ellis	420	10,344	12,803	9,025	3,960	2,550	1,394	240	179	7,051,682	4,994,463	331,782	73,277	671,886
32	3	Emmanuel	337	10,269	14,217	7,392	2,763	1,318	1,141	641	236	5,062,634	4,149,329	445,656	111,314	764,364
46	4	Enon	214	7,953	12,039	6,031	3,033	1,060	1,445	414	247	3,961,374	3,363,930	300,577	104,368	574,152
23	2	Erath	257	6,478	9,435	4,754	2,187	2,063	775	749	392	3,413,216	2,522,416	175,740	47,833	517,221
17	1	Falls	66	2,340	3,483	1,424	784	211	208	177	53	946,686	758,836	115,104	49,049	222,282
34	1	Fannin	275	7,624	11,328	5,513	2,625	1,089	987	400	177	2,860,724	2,375,280	191,007	73,306	401,714
48	16	Frio River	244	7,015	11,924	5,843	2,800	1,194	869	717	339	4,127,352	3,218,502	215,117	73,961	502,609
40	13	Galveston	522	16,381	27,703	12,227	5,144	3,821	1,908	1,152	695	8,735,730	7,103,718	605,964	185,755	1,237,024
25	4	Gambrell	172	3,013	4,757	2,453	1,381	624	558	540	187	1,899,707	1,347,037	158,285	39,174	274,960
90	9	Golden Tri.	1,136	41,603	70,885	32,612	12,693	6,716	6,053	2,530	1,404	25,726,305	20,795,771	2,062,271	313,114	3,457,814
21	4	Gonzales	109	3,256	5,463	2,819	1,256	626	608	359	241	2,130,675	1,504,918	218,775	46,207	669,039
56	5	Grayson	693	18,511	29,940	14,797	7,125	3,874	2,829	1,270	746	9,858,987	8,000,762	750,411	182,636	1,397,177
38	18	Gregg	834	27,650	37,370	21,319	9,571	5,061	3,611	1,457	839	17,839,725	13,126,615	1,271,684	157,811	2,212,931
46	5	Guadalupe	471	11,553	18,443	9,992	4,020	5,238	1,854	1,056	573	7,383,627	5,812,891	572,916	129,030	1,060,696
51	9	Gulf Coast	905	22,268	35,163	19,443	7,465	3,264	2,884	1,379	728	13,066,328	10,198,700	986,746	231,884	1,983,606
14	4	Hamilton	51	1,477	2,536	1,091	580	113	345	95	55	737,252	610,524	68,990	15,796	128,404
64	7	Harmony Pittsburg	561	16,129	23,537	12,442	5,887	4,191	2,399	1,153	736	9,753,132	7,780,277	918,402	177,837	1,672,120
17	2	Haskell Knox	77	2,558	5,338	1,979	997	256	352	303	204	1,318,477	1,100,169	106,994	24,642	264,474
30	10	Henderson	667	10,116	13,651	7,444	3,744	1,356	1,747	553	288	6,391,666	5,107,358	400,065	987,815	737,213
21	1	Hill	88	3,195	5,502	2,847	1,432	680	585	323	235	1,928,873	1,574,095	162,635	22,307	321,719
55	7	Hunt	544	15,082	22,909	11,636	5,349	2,327	2,037	947	441	8,678,058	6,006,443	525,484	104,311	1,051,616
26	4	Independence	188	4,916	7,331	4,072	1,974	649	729	382	238	3,600,260	2,826,045	227,052	51,364	482,621
13	0	Jack	35	1,971	2,879	1,677	628	194	276	130	44	983,855	729,768	55,459	8,054	125,924
46	12	Johnson	574	17,329	25,244	13,944	6,000	2,724	2,590	1,298	677	9,372,196	7,007,204	654,366	114,672	1,322,971
21	4	Kaufman	354	9,041	13,075	6,850	3,282	1,106	1,073	796	446	5,394,947	4,044,523	410,592	91,709	666,686
14	0	Lamesa	71	3,133	5,339	2,483	1,032	455	535	361	209	1,843,709	1,431,347	209,089	28,440	349,855
17	4	Lampasas	223	4,293	9,722	3,240	1,588	1,024	452	282	233	2,097,379	1,596,166	149,931	35,399	89,752
10	1	Leon	94	2,125	3,104	1,478	749	572	276	194	112	1,072,940	829,640	103,959	23,457	184,317
30	3	Llanos Altos	117	5,080	10,334	4,026	1,936	1,253	841	562	293	2,852,091	2,306,668	226,106	48,462	434,461
74	14	Lubbock	1,012	30,186	46,504	23,864	10,137	6,648	4,585	2,978	1,937	21,141,688	14,367,630	1,441,168	308,951	2,392,410

		Association															
29	8	Medina River	265	7,874	11,930	6,927	3,064	1,854	1,429	575	485	6,577,167	4,474,715	520,231	125,534	956,703
23	6	Midland	372	11,976	20,820	11,912	4,896	2,110	2,151	1,296	586	11,690,184	7,652,128	969,525	123,825	2,182,791
19	0	Milam	93	2,676	4,618	1,925	896	349	500	255	109	1,359,712	1,100,606	98,871	28,976	200,567
19	0	Mitchell-Scurry	164	4,167	7,850	4,249	1,871	445	859	483	242	2,593,880	2,090,293	282,6193	4,011	462,478
15	2	Montague	104	3,304	5,490	2,950	1,230	392	566	207	216	1,600,331	1,349,412	145,486	32,468	239,426
38	1	Neches River	217	6,126	8,796	4,076	2,278	785	838	398	125	3,325,564	2,438,842	232,782	39,111	399,139
32	2	New Bethel	222	5,123	8,360	3,914	1,911	1,362	689	658	365	2,675,731	2,179,094	238,757	47,662	437,617
31	3	Odessa	543	13,746	22,627	9,436	4,537	2,774	2,090	636	419	9,150,401	5,845,000	396,255	65,561	766,397
21	2	Palo Duro	371	10,674	21,817	9,330	3,683	1,981	1,814	661	408	5,484,957	4,382,993	535,068	97,997	1,051,433
24	3	Palo Pinto	252	4,265	7,596	3,344	1,645	780	727	585	191	2,156,729	1,709,879	189,385	47,045	336,010
21	2	Paluxy	271	6,470	9,212	5,495	2,462	1,698	1,175	408	197	4,572,195	3,468,109	336,600	76,765	537,305
21	2	Panfork	137	3,819	6,431	2,879	1,363	1,964	684	383	151	1,968,194	1,662,752	187,081	44,721	345,846
46	6	Parker	658	14,284	20,259	9,798	4,895	3,070	2,081	748	532	9,219,076	5,526,544	467,421	141,101	849,876
23	3	Pecos Valley	186	4,786	9,592	3,402	1,521	904	666	238	66	2,683,526	1,845,816	166,231	17,672	281,888
21	0	Permian	158	5,100	10,123	4,509	1,773	1,089	867	630	311	3,447,831	2,708,060	283,633	30,604	525,152
22	4	Red Fork	257	6,141	11,610	4,800	2,052	911	903	676	299	3,114,042	2,334,153	232,324	56,456	417,039
47	7	Red River	315	11,351	17,573	8,924	4,236	1,383	1,491	549	300	6,092,784	4,696,302	519,221	81,894	898,265
46	7	Rehoboth	401	9,477	13,507	7,435	3,730	891	1,683	778	331	4,769,380	3,817,071	461,867	95,098	747,375
91	50	Rio Grande	969	16,215	26,110	16,346	8,761	4,467	2,577	1,792	1,006	10,950,630	7,245,157	614,689	160,144	1,190,743
14	1	Robertson	50	2,132	3,447	1,344	723	226	272	185	88	1,043,842	869,371	77,039	23,550	182,172
17	1	Runnels	109	2,542	4,603	1,789	811	212	316	170	126	989,151	838,858	120,589	26,779	218,340
37	1	Rusk Panola	290	9,937	13,812	7,577	3,586	1,707	1,641	995	436	6,586,134	4,952,859	541,371	85,921	970,732
30	2	Sabine Valley	267	7,031	10,851	5,443	2,634	1,234	1,212	585	315	4,425,797	3,556,426	379,905	103,534	642,867
26	3	Saline	301	7,348	10,748	5,793	2,597	1,836	1,192	530	289	4,579,249	3,379,825	339,481	60,167	579,720
23	3	Salt Fork	196	5,141	9,627	3,984	1,811	791	754	455	264	3,155,643	2,289,510	232,554	33,187	437,192
152	42	San Antonio	1,968	54,803	94,643	38,412	17,368	12,936	6,656	3,244	1,891	35,326,751	26,792,580	1,264,139	331,455	2,706,036
34	13	San Felipe	564	10,648	16,224	10,286	5,096	3,517	2,067	691	441	9,242,080	7,114,126	483,939	135,652	957,045
35	5	San Jacinto	655	18,448	29,149	13,264	5,372	2,574	2,112	998	672	10,329,432	8,014,283	703,736	162,061	1,301,532
7	1	San Saba	34	1,214	2,078	807	445	84	116	21	15	523,765	402,427	75,690	14,396	129,570
43	4	Shelby Doches	384	10,591	16,010	8,404	4,299	2,466	1,980	799	545	7,472,861	5,188,767	518,543	100,004	1,186,592
69	15	Smith	1,104	37,936	47,982	28,052	14,245	5,716	6,055	2,493	1,997	29,575,014	18,930,269	1,842,402	226,600	2,996,554
33	2	Soda Lake	285	11,251	16,244	7,364	3,465	2,383	1,421	632	339	5,637,429	4,445,687	542,712	100,872	886,340
24	4	South Plains	188	6,468	11,349	4,138	1,934	1,088	1,010	575	361	3,419,694	2,737,395	286,379	42,221	659,959
29	5	Staked Plains	303	8,518	15,945	7,232	3,411	1,431	1,476	721	547	4,770,575	3,764,565	423,846	61,666	781,615
13	0	Sweetwater	97	2,943	6,119	2,180	950	268	463	221	89	1,368,790	1,169,780	116,912	22,328	197,889
203	91	Tarrant	3,820	123,700	185,711	111,337	47,927	39,472	20,679	6,579	4,073	103,318,455	72,217,360	5,123,824	997,977	10,194,704
12	4	Trans Canadian	141	4,4277	,158	4,085	1,837	972	1,180	419	301	2,833,621	2,536,802	319,450	29,194	588,896
40	5	Trinity River	358	9,168	14,510	7,001	2,933	1,671	938	809	472	4,568,340	3,353,308	300,539	170,666	612,550

89	25 Tryon Evergreen	1,577	42,933	61,563	34,877	14,231	7,142	6,173	1,739	1,037	26,859,431	19,717,894	1,394,473	368,231	2,702,819
330	152 Union	9,872	239,873	314,561	160,791	73,165	43,502	21,261	9,709	10,683	167,807,815	102,432,621	4,475,233	1,281,368	11,955,171
49	5 Unity	649	17,348	24,588	13,006	5,412	2,664	2,204	1,239	519	8,567,390	6,971,369	643,328	131,908	1,139,649
25	4 Van Zandt	439	7,828	10,912	6,153	2,970	1,056	1,239	636	344	3,965,316	3,266,692	336,270	56,722	580,651
83	19 Waco	949	31,635	54,805	24,637	11,907	12,872	4,559	2,387	1,053	24,579,777	15,047,420	1,099,497	235,578	2,332,555
31	4 West Central	146	5,316	9,777	3,668	1,896	859	856	270	163	2,490,687	1,952,156	161,484	42,224	338,128
60	3 Wichita Archer Clay	845	24,415	41,662	19,008	8,472	5,482	4,108	1,732	1,336	13,197,333	10,819,284	1,044,892	178,380	1,749,388
32	7 Williamson	648	13,863	18,052	13,564	5,340	3,642	2,045	819	438	8,869,061	6,202,893	525,822	154,525	982,019
32	7 Wise	267	6,039	9,051	4,505	2,178	881	779	543	321	3,345,782	2,471,071	213,492	32,551	391,042
68	4 Non-Aligned	146	3,501	3,830	3,017	1,651	178	360	170	257	2,257,119	2,079,286	53,333	2,212	140,019
4,784	1,083 State Total	67,574	1,740,944	2,704,690	1,410,617	624,176	374,916	247,230	112,894	71,855	1,188,484,988	834,446,047	66,060,330	14,543,459	134,364,750

TRENDS IN THE BAPTIST GENERAL CONVENTION OF TEXAS, 1960 TO 1997

	1960	1970	1980	1990	1997
Churches	3,848	3,835	3,945	4,335[b]	4,767
Missions	489	493	468	918[b]	1,100
Total Members	1,622,529	1,896,811	2,217,940	2,539,117	2,704,690
Resident Members	1,170,158	1,281,514	1,449,567	1,577,152	1,740,944
Baptisms	60,010	57,756	66,360	64,763	67,574
Other Additions	128,375[a]	104,915[a]	109,772[a]	104,161[b]	98,698
Sunday School Enrollment[c]	1,155,499	1,105,445	1,152,892	1,346,482	1,410,617
SS Average Attendance	588,975	512,994	538,049	600,639	624,176
Music Enrollment[c]	96,481	165,724	205,257	260,171	247,230
WMU Enrollment[c]	195,329	124,710	127,749	145,088	112,894
Brotherhood Enrollment[c]	93,489	60,187	62,638	76,737	71,855
Discipleship Training Enrol.[c]	477,212	380,166	225,895	295,341	374,916
Total Receipts	88,650,697	146,570,636	442,659,143	847,532,250[b]	1,188,484,988
Total Mission Expenditures	16,311,930[a]	25,063,072[a]	76,398,476	120,683,678	134,364,750
Cooperative Program Giving	9,407,983[a]	13,793,393[a]	36,229,291	59,912,833	66,060,330
State Missions Giving	263,776[a]	1,305,679[a]	2,858,971[a]	4,356,374[b]	5,159,146
Associational Missions Giving	NA	2,177,910	6,478,489	11,182,316	14,543,459

Source: Baptist General Convention of Texas Annuals, except where noted; Research & Information Services, BGCT.
Data for Minnesota-Wisconsin have been omitted from 1960, 1970 and 1980.

a SBC Handbooks   b Annual Church Profile computer files   c Definitions changed over time.

Index

Sewell, Donald E., 371, 373
sexual revolution, 284
Shaddix, Julian, 380, 427
Shady Grove Baptist Church (Grand Prairie), 351
Shamburger, W. M., 273, 330, 347, 348
Shannon Prairie, Texas, 37
"Share Jesus Now," 365
Share the Food Program, 235-236
Shearin, George, 258, 282
Shelton, Horner, 427
Sherman, Cecil, 292, 432-433
Sherman, Texas, 72, 251
Shipman, Moses, 14, 25
Shook, Damon, 427
Simmons (College) University, 100-101, 103, 127, 141, 214, 218, 219
Simmons, James B., 100
Simms, A. M., 91, 92
Sims, Richard, 293
Singing Men of Texas, 339
Singletary, D. J., 395
  Don S., 316
Singleton, Gordon G., 219
"Sister Cities," program, 339
Sister Grove Association, 48
Skaggs, Jay, 291, 355, 362, 363
Skiles, Elwin, 273, 315
Slack, Bennie, 410, 415
Slater, Norvelle, 241
Slaughter, C. C., 103, 104, 113, 121, 124, 131, 138, 158, 452, 453
  Minnie, 81, 104
slavery, 10, 14, 29, 31, 32, 43, 45, 51, 53-54
Sledge, R. J., 85
Sloan, Robert B., Jr., 377, 420
  Sue, 420
Slocum, Dee, 455, 456, 457, 459
Slover, David, 346, 380
Smaller Membership Church Task Force, 405-406
Smalley, Freeman, 14
Smith, Abner, 13, 23, 24, 33
  Al, 186
  Blake, 327
  Catlow, 166
  Connie, 343
  Deaf, 8
  Gerald, 459
  M. V., 77, 85, 112, 124
  Mrs. W. J. J., 78
  Ralph, 353-355, 365
  William L., 295-296
  Winifred L., 229
Smyth, Earl B., 181, 201, 216
  Mrs. Earl B. (Rosalind), 235

Soda Lake Association, 41, 48
South Africa, 387
South Carolina Baptist State Convention, 42
South Main Baptist Church (Houston), 208, 432, 459
South Texas Baptist College, 102
South Texas Children's Home, 266, 306
South Texas Educational Conference, 102
Southeastern Texas Baptist Hospital (Beaumont), 251
Southern Baptist Advocate, 426
Southern Baptist Convention (SBC), 26, 78, 118, 120, 126, 168, 193, 211, 235, 236, 266, 274, 275, 352, 356-357, 396, 400, 451
  Annuity Board of, 110, 153, 159, 186, 250, 252, 335, 348-349, 366-367, 375, 409, 414
  Christian Life Commission (CLC), 245, 271, 446
  Confession of Faith adopted by, 187
  constitution of, 81
  controls SWBTS, 185, 431-436
  controversy concerning, 323-324, 421-441, 446
  Executive Committee of, 89, 129, 152-153, 355, 463
  Foreign Missions Board (FMB), 50, 67, 94, 116-117, 123, 130, 153, 177, 206, 211, 215, 233, 236, 322, 325, 327, 337-342, 374, 376, 433, 448
  formation of, 32, 39, 69
  fundamentalism in, 421-441, 448-449
  Home Missions Board (HMB), 20, 45, 49, 65, 67, 68, 69, 70, 76, 153, 177, 200, 206, 221, 243, 263, 298, 299, 322, 355, 371, 374, 389, 390, 394, 423, 432, 441, 443, 444, 447
  IMB, 376, 448
  naming of, 37
  Peace Committee of, 459
  proposes new convention, 455-460, 463
  Radio/TV Commission of, 235
  relation to state conventions, 355

Relief and Annuity Board of, 125, 159, 186, 335
$75 Million Campaign, 127, 153, 155, 168, 170, 171, 195, 227
75th anniversary, 163-164
Social Service Commission of, 244
and theological education, 431-441, 447-448, 451
30,000 Movement of, 296
Southern Baptist Publication Society, 52, 76
Southern Baptist Seminary (Cochrane, Alberta), 401
Southern Baptist Sunday School Union, 52, 76
Southern Baptist Theological Seminary, 67, 83, 90, 99, 103, 118, 127, 144, 145-147, 159, 166, 437
Southern Baptists of Texas (SBT), 446, 455-460
Southern Seminary, 256, 433, 446
Southwest Texas State University, 377
Southwestern Baptist Theological Seminary (SWBTS), 99, 103, 126, 127, 128, 143-150, 155, 157, 158, 166-167, 171, 183-185, 193, 202, 203, 219-221, 224, 230, 252, 286, 330, 346, 418-419, 421, 422, 431-436, 437
Southwestern Baptist Theological Seminary Alumni Association, 220
Southwestern Publishing Company, 76
Southwestern Seminary, 96, 140, 152, 359, 361
Spalding, A. T., 87
Speakers' Tournaments, 294
speaking in "unknown tongues," 351
Speight, J. W., 96-97
Spilman, B. W., 176
Spooner, Bernard M., 389
Spraggins, Thomas, 25
Spring Break, 381
Springer, R. A., 196, 216, 227, 236, 255, 257, 273, 286, 289, 291, 317, 363
Spurgeon, Charles Haddon, 148
Staked Plains Baptist Association, 143
Stallworth, Ann Hasselstine, 211
Stamford, 157
Stanton, C. A., 80